IS THAT BIEDERMEIER?

Amerling, Waldmüller, and More

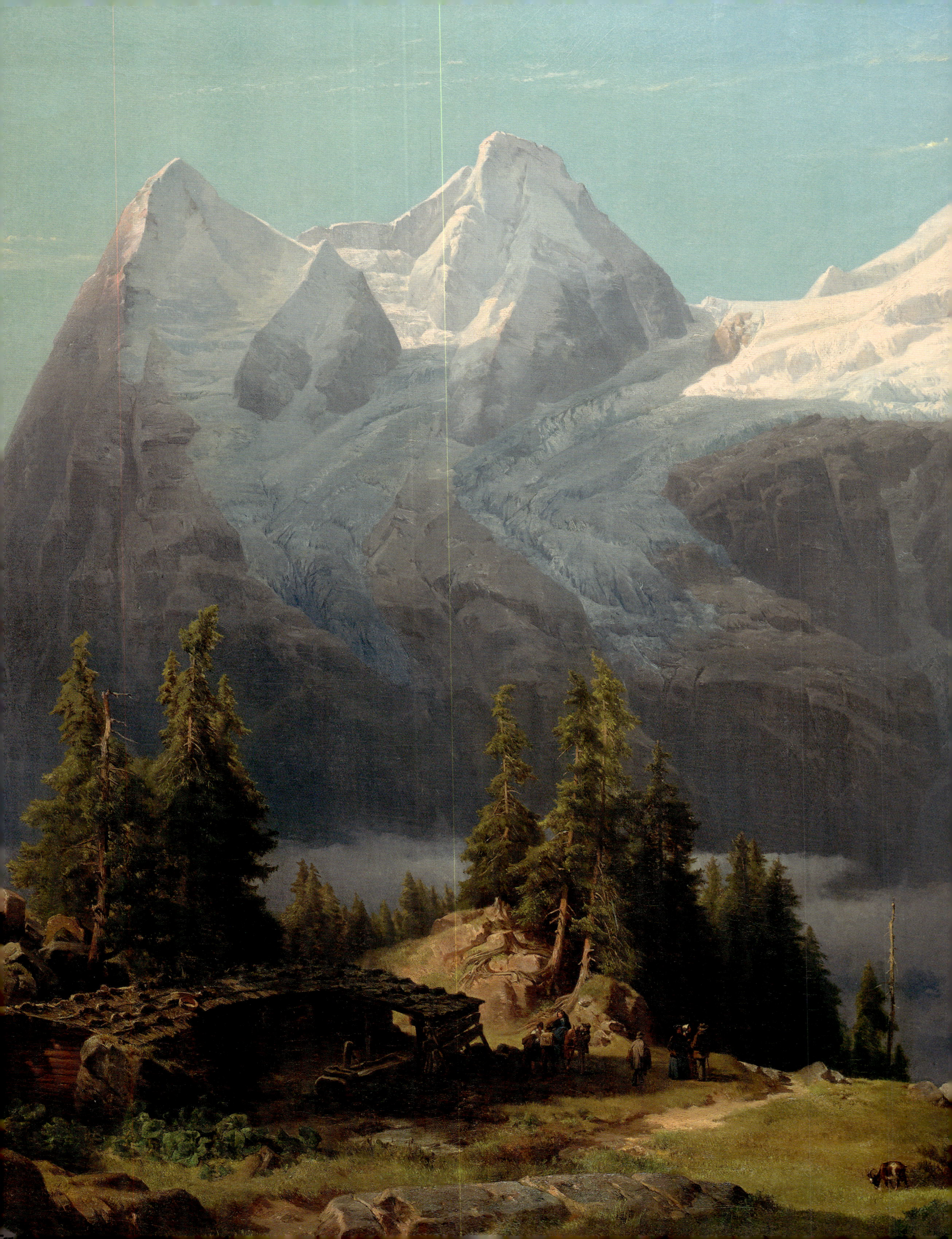

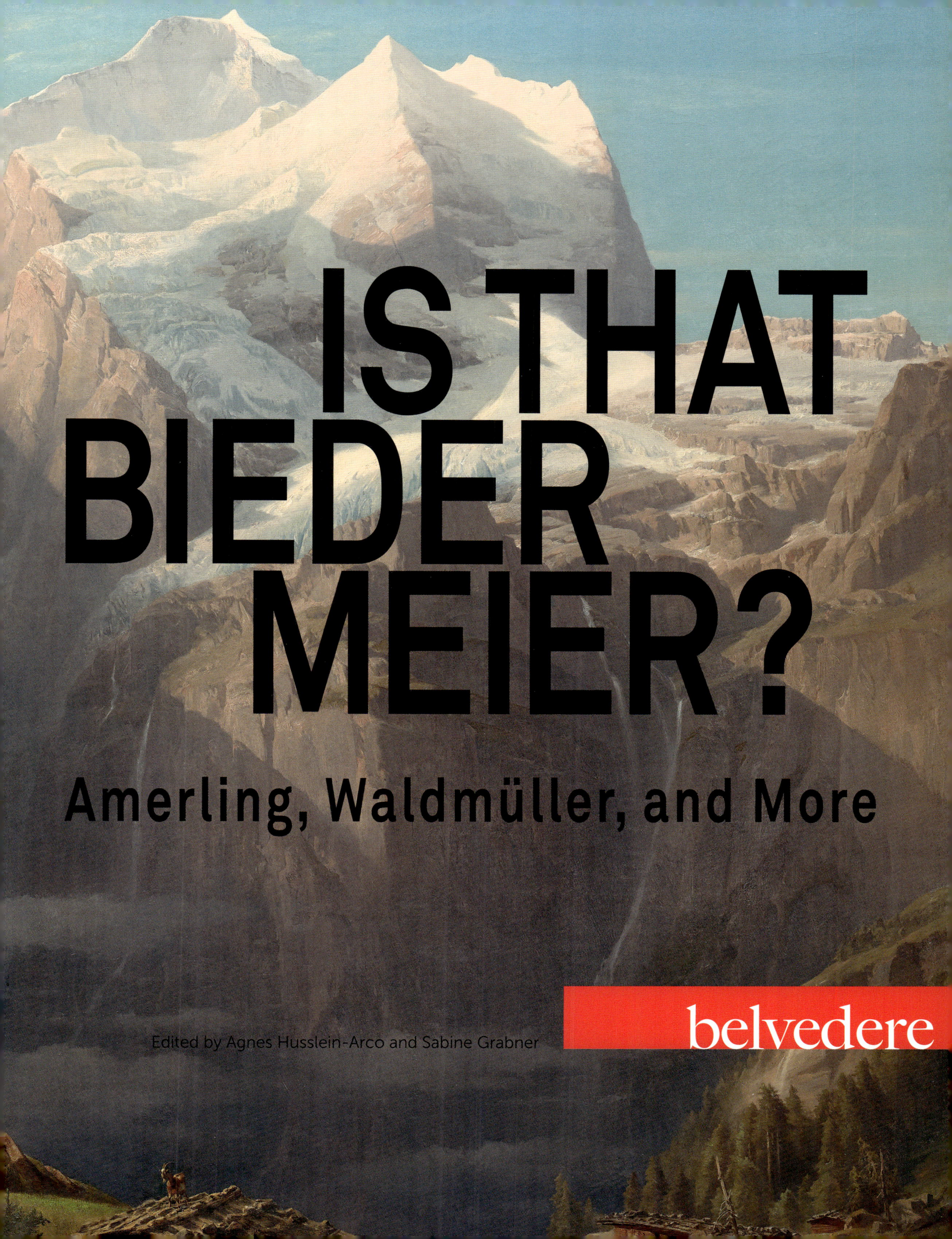

IS THAT BIEDER MEIER?

Amerling, Waldmüller, and More

Edited by Agnes Husslein-Arco and Sabine Grabner

belvedere

Agnes Husslein-Arco

Sabine Grabner

Sabine Grabner

Radim Vondráček

Eszter Békefi

Fernando Mazzocca

Christian Witt-Dörring

Werner Busch

Stéphane Paccoud

Arnika Schmidt

Kasper Monrad

Udo Felbinger

Elke Doppler

CONTENT

6 What is Biedermeier?

10 Biedermeier or Nestroy Era

14 Art for the Bourgeoisie in Imperial Vienna

26 The Idealized Image and Reality: Biedermeier in Bohemia after 1830

36 Biedermeier in Hungary

48 Painting in the Kingdom of Lombardy-Venetia 1820–1860: The Long Period of Romanticism

60 Viennese Furniture 1820–1860: Compositional Aspects as an Expression of Changing Tastes

68 Waldmüller's Anti-Academism and its Tradition

76 Plates

254 Near and Far: French painting and Biedermeier

264 Art in Great Britain at the time of the Biedermeier: Parallels and Influences

274 The Copenhagen School of Painters 1830–1860

284 "And in feeling art completes itself." Painting in Germany 1820–1860

292 The "Schwarz Artists": Observations on the Revival of "Old Viennese" Genre Painting

306 The Artists

309 Authors

311 Picture Credits

312 Colophon

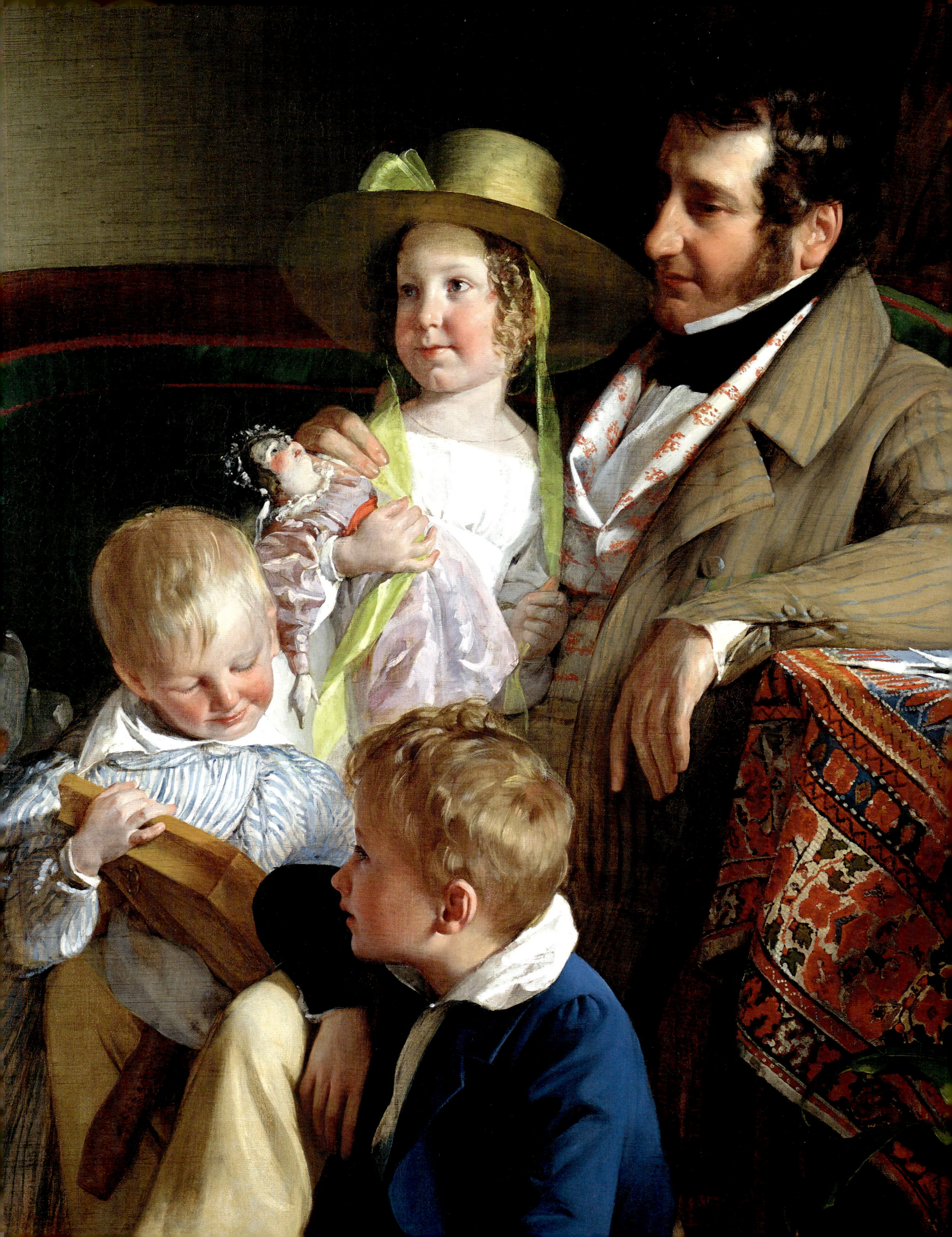

WHAT IS BIEDERMEIER?

Agnes Husslein-Arco

The fictional character Weiland Gottlieb Biedermaier rose to fame in the mid-nineteenth century. A school teacher with a leaning toward domesticity, this upstanding citizen became the symbol of an entire epoch, which, from the twentieth century onward, would be known simply as "Biedermeier." It refers to that turbulent period of European history characterized by political power changes, revolutions, and repressive state control. As public life felt increasingly unpleasant, the bourgeoisie withdrew more and more to the safety of their own four walls. These rather worrying developments in the pre-1848 period—which, as history shows, did not end well—have been viewed by posterity through rose-tinted glasses and tinged with romantic notions. For many today, "Biedermeier" conjures up Waldmüller's cheerful scenes of children, Nestroy's plays, elegant interiors, or the impish genre paintings by the German artist Carl Spitzweg.

Would it not be justified, though, to argue that Biedermeier was first and foremost a sociological phenomenon? Undeniably, this prevailing mood in society will also have had an influence on the visual arts. Yet, whereas the Revolution of 1848 marked a caesura in political developments and caused lasting changes to people's lives, artists such as Ferdinand Georg Waldmüller and Friedrich von Amerling continued painting beyond this date, and their work should therefore be reconsidered as a whole. This is why the Belvedere's current exhibition focuses on painting from 1830 through 1860 in the countries formerly in the Habsburg Empire. *Is that Biedermeier? Waldmüller, Amerling, and More* set out to reevaluate the evidence, and the results shed a completely new light on painting in those decades.

The Belvedere houses a wide-ranging collection of Austrian art from all eras. Within this, the collection of nineteenth-century art is one of the museum's largest and comprises an abundance of exquisite masterpieces. Over the past years in particular, many projects have been launched that aim to take a closer look at these holdings. One of the priorities of the Belvedere's research is to place a focus on lesser-known artists, in addition to art history's greats, and to introduce them through exhibitions. Following up on this extensive research into individual artists, it also makes sense to revisit certain historical periods in painting because, as always in scholarship, theories continue to be valid until evidence is presented to refute them. This leaves us questioning whether, in fact, a distinctive Biedermeier style of painting ever existed at all. Over recent years, this hypothesis has been thoroughly researched at the Belvedere, yielding some fascinating results.

As previously suggested, mid-nineteenth century paintings in Austria have long been seen in a clichéd light. Granted, this may apply mainly to portraiture and genre scenes, of which there exists a wealth of outstanding examples. It has, however, emerged that it is insufficient to simply label these en masse as "Biedermeier." For in these images the viewer is presented with far more than the mere depiction of domestic bliss. Waldmüller's oeuvre is an excellent example and, in many respects, reveals some striking developments. Indeed, Waldmüller is of stellar importance in Austria. In keeping with the vogue of the time, he did not portray his aristocratic or bourgeois families in their homes but against landscape backdrops. However, he added a brilliant innovation to this trend by skillfully presenting his figures in the same light as the surrounding scenery. The resulting impression was revolutionary, as the figures really appear to be standing in the midst of nature.

Friedrich von Amerling, *Rudolf von Arthaber with his Children Rudolf, Emilie, and Gustav, Looking at the Portrait of their Deceased Mother*, (detail), 1837
Belvedere, Vienna

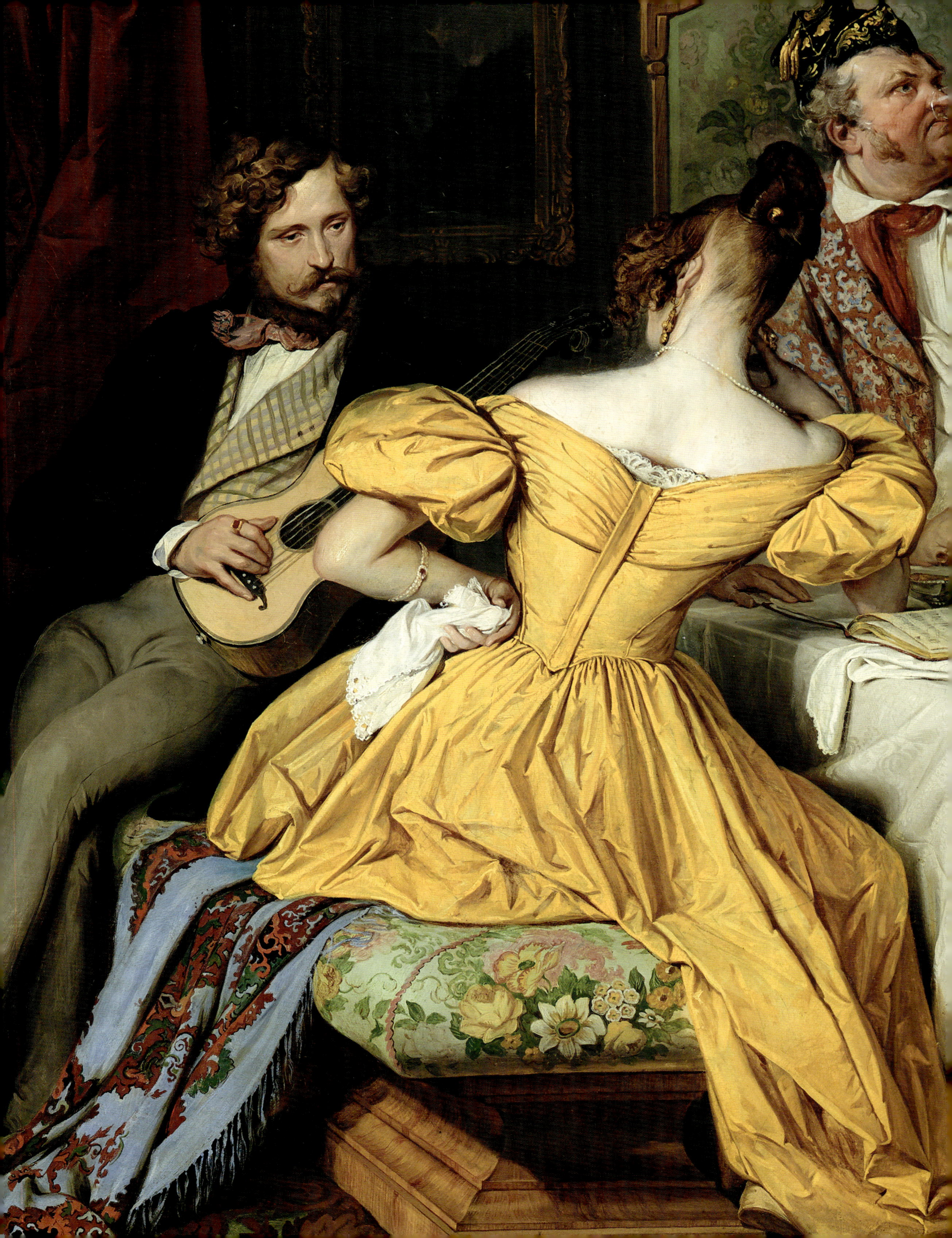

This distinctive lighting was to become a characteristic of his paintings and drew flocks of admirers from the very start of his career. These light effects added a special appeal to his everyday scenes of rural and peasant life, and their fascination endures to this day.

And yet, these depictions are a far cry from the stereotypical Biedermeier style, especially considering that they were created after 1848, and essentially contradict key Biedermeier concepts. Waldmüller's paintings presented the bourgeoisie with a complete contrast to the realities that had forced them into their "domestic prison" and helped them break out of this confinement in their thoughts. This example clearly demonstrates the inadequacy of any reference to "Biedermeier painting." Waldmüller and his colleagues were dependent on their patrons and were serving a market that called for Biedermeier-style scenes, but the scope of these artists' oeuvres, the range of their subject matter, always went much further. As the concept of this exhibition does not see the 1848 Revolution as a cut-off point, a vast spectrum of painting from this period comes to light, far exceeding all that "Biedermeier" was hitherto seen to encompass. For, in actual fact, we are dealing with a realm of images that should at long last be recognized for its innovation and diversity.

I should particularly like to thank the curator of the exhibition, Sabine Grabner, who has devoted years of dedicated research to this subject. The show successfully introduces visitors to a new perspective on painting between 1830 and 1860. Furthermore, the exhibition does not concentrate on Austria alone, since, especially during this period, we can assume that there were reciprocal influences between Austrian painting and that of the Monarchy's crown lands. The exhibition therefore features artists from Bohemia, Hungary, and the former Kingdom of Lombardy-Venetia. I am also thrilled that this project has presented an opportunity to show important works that were slumbering in the stores and have rarely been on public display in the past. Thanks to the outstanding work of our conservation department, they have been restored to their original splendor, as demonstrated by the example of Albert Zimmermann's *Sunset on Lake Hintersee in Berchtesgaden*.

My thanks are, of course, also due to our many lenders who have entrusted us with their precious works and thus contributed to the exhibition's success. Without the generous support of museums and private individuals, this project could never have been realized.

Finally, I am delighted that this exhibition catalogue has now also become an important art-historical compendium. Our new art-historical approach has resulted in a reinterpretation of art from the period around 1850. But, even more than that, it has produced a handbook that directly compares art from Austria and the countries of the Habsburg Empire with painting from France, Britain, Germany, and Northern Europe. In so doing, both the specific characteristics and the reciprocal influences have come to the fore.

Is that Biedermeier? Waldmüller, Amerling, and More invites you on an exciting journey of discovery that will illustrate why, in art history, the term "Biedermeier" should henceforth be used with a little more deliberation...

Josef Danhauser, *The Rich Glutton* (detail), 1836
Belvedere, Vienna

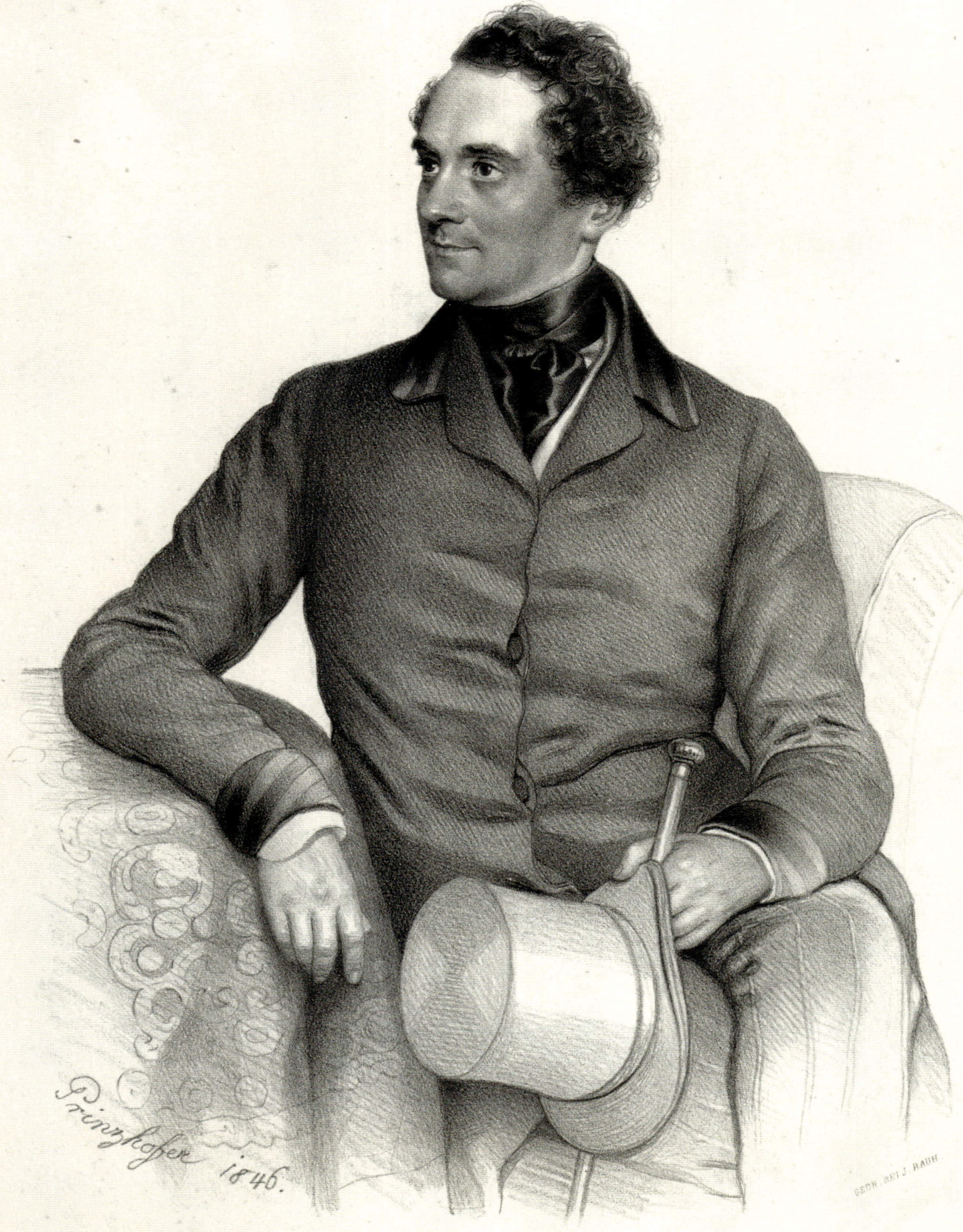

Den größten Meister im Treffen man jenen nennt,
Wo man die Getroffenen allsogleich erkennt;
Den größten Pfuscher im Treffen kann man daher das Schicksal nennen,
Denn die es trifft mit seiner schweren Hand, sind selten wieder zu erkennen

J. Nestroy

BIEDERMEIER OR NESTROY ERA

Sabine Grabner

"Biedermeier" designates the period from 1815 to 1848/49, between the Congress of Vienna and the revolution that shook the Austrian Empire and large parts of central Europe. It started with the reorganization of Europe and ended with the populist revolt against restrictions and in favor of freedom of speech, a free press, and for the removal of censorship and the restrictive provisions of the Carlsbad Decrees, which had been agreed in summer 1819 and were applicable from then onward in all German Confederation states. In Austria this did indeed bring about an end to the repressions for a short time in Austria, and the departure of the feared Chancellor Metternich was also seen as a victory. But the success was of short duration and was soon overturned by the neo-absolutist rule of Emperor Franz Joseph I, who imposed new restrictions on the population (New Year's Eve Patent). Nor did the revolution put an end to pauperism, the creeping impoverishment of the working population, the powerlessness of farm workers, smallholders, and day laborers, which increased beyond the mid-century in parallel to the progress of the Industrial Revolution and led to the rise of the working proletariat.

From a historical point of view, however, Biedermeier is firmly established as the era of the bourgeoisie. After the Napoleonic Wars had ended, the middle classes were finally able to claim the achievements of the French Revolution for themselves and developed a powerful self-awareness, reflected, especially in Vienna, in an increase in business activity and economic prosperity. By 1830 at the latest, with the foundation of the Society for the Promotion of Fine Arts (Verein zur Beförderung der bildenden Künste), the Vienna bourgeoisie also began to take a leading role in cultural affairs. The wealthy middle classes became the most important customers for artists; they defined tastes, determined pictorial subject matter, and flocked to art exhibitions. Overall, society appeared to have become filled with a carefree lust for life. Newspapers, illustrated magazines, and paintings depicted social gatherings, country outings, and other entertainments. The musical compositions of the time—typified by Johann Strauss the Elder or Josef Lanner—conveyed a similar feeling. Over the years, people seemed to have come to terms with the situation and got used to keeping liberal opinions to themselves and refraining from any criticism of the Metternich system. Johann Nestroy (1801–1862) described the mood: "We even had freedom of opinion, as long as we kept those opinions to ourselves. It was a bit like the rules for dogs: You were allowed to have one, as long as you kept it on a leash! If you let it run free, it would be put down. In other words, we had plenty of liberties, but not a trace of freedom."[1] Nestroy was one of the few writers at the time to comment with polished words on the nature of this volatile period and to record it for posterity. He managed to outsmart the censors with his humor, pointed wit, and clever insinuations, winning the hearts of Vienna's theater-going public into the bargain.

A critical frame of mind prompted two amateur writers in southern Germany to publish poems, albeit with less wit and finesse, under the pseudonym Weiland Gottlieb Biedermaier. They made him a schoolmaster from Swabia, whose "little house, tiny garden, unsightly spot of earth, and the meager existence of a despised village schoolmaster were enough to grant him earthly bliss."[2] The name stuck. The authors—a doctor Adolf Kussmaul (1822–1902) and the lawyer Ludwig Eichrodt (1827–1892)—began in 1855 (!) to publish these poems in the Munich magazine *Fliegende Blätter*, mocking the blinkered and narrow-minded attitudes of their contemporaries. In

August Prinzhofer, *Johann Nestroy*, 1846
Österreichische Nationalbibliothek, Vienna

spite of their modest literary pretensions, these poems became highly popular in southern Germany, and it was not long before the term "Biedermaier" (the "a" was replaced by the more common "e" later in the century) became synonymous with artless or ignorant people.[3]

The designation caught on, not only in the region where it originated, but also in Austria, and—although the inhabitants of the imperial capital did not quite think like the Swabian village schoolteacher Weiland Gottlieb Biedermaier, either at the beginning or the end of the nineteenth century—the term "Biedermeier" became established to describe the Metternich era in particular. Around the turn of the twentieth century, it also began to be used to refer to a particular style, initially in furniture design—in fact, Hevesi went as far as claiming it as a genuine Viennese style.[4] A radical change was in fact taking place in attitudes to applied arts, and the new historical term gave a fresh quality to what had until then been described as a "Krähwinkel" monstrosity[5]. This upgrading might also have been fostered by the major Congress of Vienna exhibition in 1896 at the Vienna Museum of Art and Industry (now MAK),[6] where not only Empire furniture but also items from the 1820s and 1830s were on display—for the first time in a museum context—drawing public attention to the craftsmanship and tasteful design typical of the early nineteenth century. "The Congress exhibition made the Viennese public realize that their Biedermeier was after all something rather splendid, homegrown, and worthwhile," said Hevesi in his review of this first encounter by inhabitants of Secessionist Vienna with the furnishing style of their grandparents.[7]

By 1900 the term "Biedermeier" had established itself firmly in cultural history. It was applied soon afterwards to literature, music, and painting as well, despite the fact that this tended to blur its actual meaning: Biedermeier might have been appropriate to describe a historical period, but not a style. Thus, unlike Baroque, there is no such thing as "Biedermeier style" or "Biedermeier painting," because the term is not directly associated with a form of artistic expression—such as painting technique, formal design, or pictorial content. Strictly speaking, a "Biedermeier picture" can refer only to an evocation of Biedermeier characteristics, in other words, a depiction of "the bourgeois citizen and his habitat, documenting the ingress of the bourgeois lifestyle and philosophy into the higher social classes and viewing and interpreting the life of the lower classes from a bourgeois perspective," as Willi Geismeier put it in his definitive publication on Biedermeier art and culture.[8] In that regard, the term "Biedermeier," like "Realism," can be applied to different eras, since motifs meeting this definition can be found whenever the prevailing taste is dictated by the bourgeoisie, as was the case until far into the twentieth century.

Beyond the domestic idyll or the tranquility of country life, there are many works of quite disparate content and execution that were completed during the so-called Biedermeier era. This exhibition highlights this diversity in the choice of subject and form of artistic expression. Incidentally, the discussion on the correct use of the term Biedermeier is as old as the term itself. Contrary to present-day practice, around 1900 it was used with great circumspection in an art context and was avoided altogether for a long time in connection with painting, until 1922, when Paul Ferdinand Schmidt published a book entitled *Biedermeier-Malerei*[9] and thus established the term in art literature.[10]

The exhibition concentrates on portrait, landscape, and genre paintings completed between 1830 and 1860, a period of continuous development in painting. It also looks beyond present-day Austria to the former boundaries of the Habsburg Empire, with paintings from Hungary, Czech Republic, Slovenia, and northern Italy. The selection of artists is based on their year of birth, between 1790 and 1820, so as to be able to provide a comparison of artists who were exposed to a similar historical background and educational context. Paintings from the 1850s are of particular interest in this regard, as they tend to be included, if necessary, in the Biedermeier period (especially the famous genre paintings by Ferdinand Georg Waldmüller), but more often remain in the archives because they don't quite fit into any historical theme. And yet, it is evident that, from the late 1820s onwards, painting was in a state of continuous evolution in terms of technique, style, composition, and subject matter, reaching a peak precisely around the middle of the century. The high quality of the paintings from this time are like a last surge at the threshold of new forms of expression, before Historicism or Impressionism opened up the gateway to fresh styles. Alongside the paintings, a selection of furniture demonstrates the great variety of forms at this time. Together with the seats and armchairs shown in the paintings, they reflect the aesthetic tastes of the haute bourgeoisie and aristocracy in the mid-nineteenth century.

The connections between the development of painting in the different countries, the impact of the political situation, and the influence of the academies, are discussed, not only in the essay about the situation in Vienna but also in the contributions by Eszter Békefi, Fernando Mazzocca, and Radim Vondráček. Elke Doppler looks at the development of genre painting until the end of the nineteenth century and its late resurgence at that time. Stéphane Paccoud, Arnika Schmidt, Udo Felbinger, and Kasper Monrad examine artistic developments in France, Britain, Germany, and Scandinavia to round off the picture of European painting in the mid-nineteenth century. Werner Busch deals with Ferdinand Georg Waldmüller's special significance as a teacher and painter. And finally, Christian Witt-Dörring, whose advice on the selection of seating furniture was also invaluable, writes about the developments in furniture design between 1820 and 1860.

The question "Is that Biedermeier?" can be asked again and again in this context and gives food for thought at every turn. Perhaps this era would be more readily accepted, particularly by the younger generation, if it had a different name. In any event, the social and artistic climate in imperial Vienna is more aptly personified by a figure quite different from the Swabian schoolmaster: During this same period, Johann Nepomuk Nestroy offered a wealth of pithy commentaries reflecting the thoughts and attitudes of his fellow citizens, leaving us with a most vivid picture of the time.

1 Johann Nestroy, *Freiheit in Krähwinkel, Posse mit Gesang in zwei Abteilungen und drei Akten*, Act 1, Scene 7 (premiere 1848).

2 This description introduced the figure of Weiland Gottfried Biedermaier in the issue of *Fliegende Blätter* in which the poems under this pseudonym were published for the first time; *Fliegende Blätter*, no. 492 (1855), p. 102.

3 Others frequently cite the origins of the term "Biedermeier" as the poems *Biedermanns Abendgemütlichkeit* and *Bummelmeiers Klage* (printed in *Fliegende Blätter*, no. 147 [1848], p. 24) by Josef Victor Scheffel (1826–1886), also the poem *Herr Biedermeier: Mitglied der besitzenden und gebildeten Klasse* by the journalist Ludwig Pfau from Heilbronn; see also Willi Geismeier, *Biedermeier: Das Bild vom Biedermeier, Zeit und Kultur des Biedermeier, Kunst und Kunstleben des Biedermeier* (Leipzig, 1979), pp. 9–13.

4 Ludwig Hevesi, "Biedermeier und Komp.," in *Altkunst – Neukunst: Wien 1894–1908* (Vienna, 1909), pp. 188–92; Hartwig Fischel, "Das Wiener Interieur von einst und jetzt," in *Das Interieur*, 1st yr. (1900), pp. 97–112.

5 Ludwig Hevesi, *Oesterreichische Kunst im 19. Jahrhundert. Erster Teil: 1800-1848* (= Geschichte der modernen Kunst II) (Leipzig, 1903), p. 105.

6 Hevesi 1903 (see note 5), p. 106; see also ibid., "Die Winterausstellung im Österreichischen Museum," in *Kunst und Kunsthandwerk*, 2nd yr. (1899), p. 2.

7 Hevesi, 1909 (see note 4), p. 189.

8 Geismeier, 1979 (see note 3), p. 94.

9 Paul Ferdinand Schmidt, *Biedermeier-Malerei. Zur Geschichte und Geistigkeit der deutschen Malerei in der ersten Hälfte des 19. Jahrhunderts* (Munich, 1922).

10 For the origins of the term "Biedermeier" and its establishment in the language, see Geismeier 1979 (see note 3); also *Bürgersinn und Aufbegehren. Biedermeier und Vormärz in Wien*, exh. cat., Historisches Museum der Stadt Wien (Vienna, 1987); Gerbert Frodl, *Wiener Malerei der Biedermeierzeit* (Rosenheim, 1987); ibid., ed., *19. Jahrhundert* (= Geschichte der bildenden Kunst in Österreich 5) (Munich et al., 2002); Hans Ottomeyer/Klaus Albrecht Schröder/Laurie Winters, *Biedermeier: Die Erfindung der Einfachheit*, exh. cat., Albertina Vienna et al. (Vienna, 2007).

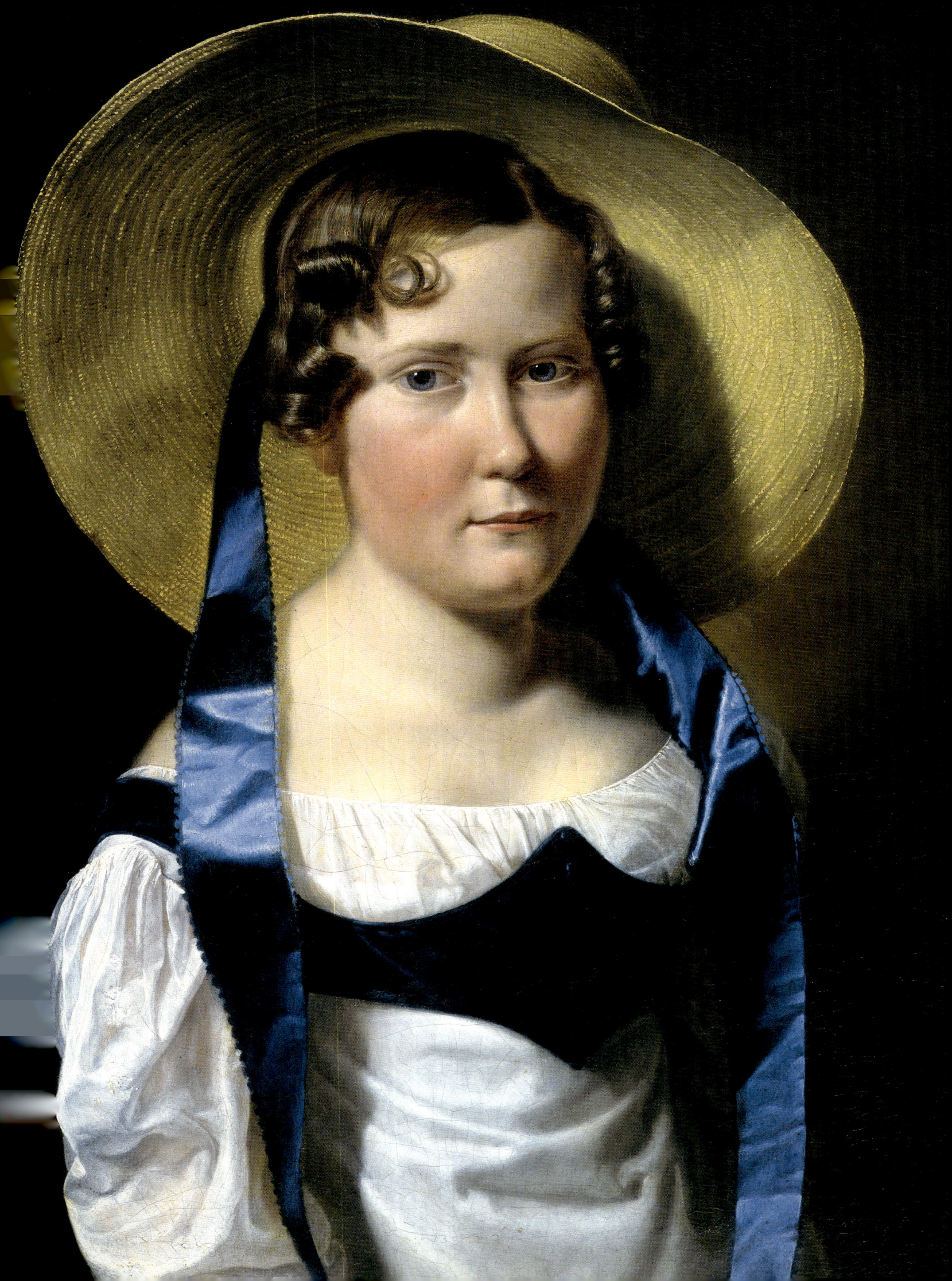

ART FOR THE BOURGEOISIE IN IMPERIAL VIENNA

Sabine Grabner

"Bourgeois and romantic—actually, romantic and bourgeois; and also historical in between, and all a little muddled up." This is how Ludwig Hevesi described painting in the early nineteenth century in Austria.[1] This era is indeed notable for the different styles appearing in parallel. In general, Baroque Classicism continued to exert its influence into the new century, especially in the work of Friedrich Heinrich Füger (1751–1818) and Johann Baptist Lampi the Elder (1751–1830). Romanticism developed at the same time and, although it failed to enjoy the popularity it experienced during this time in France or Italy, for example, it was clearly reflected in religious painting, where it found its expression especially in the strict formal language of the Nazarenes. Most Viennese and Austrian painters in the first half of the century, however, sought to reproduce a picture that was true to nature, often with realistic traits as well, hence the term "Biedermeier Realism" to describe the artistic development of this period. Hevesi called this conglomeration of styles "bourgeois" in reference to the mood of the time. The years in question were shaped by a self-assured bourgeoisie actively involved in artistic life. The promotion of art was no longer in the benelovent hands of the imperial household, the aristocracy, or the church, but was also actively and financially supported by the wealthy bourgeoisie, in other words, owners of property and businesses, restaurant and hotel operators, and proprietors of large manufacturing companies. Art had become public property.

Fig. 1: **Ferdinand Georg Waldmüller**, *Philippine Böhmer, later Hofrätin Lötsch (Girl with a Straw Hat)*, c. 1817
Belvedere, Vienna, on loan from a private collection

Art associations and the Akademische Kunsthandlung

The start of the new era was marked by the establishment of the first art association in Vienna in 1830. The Society for the Promotion of Fine Arts (Verein zur Beförderung der bildenden Künste) was the first initiative in Austria driven by the private sector to enliven the domestic art scene.[2] Neither the board nor the members were artists, but rather art lovers whose aim was "to encourage contemporary Austrian artists through the purchase of good-quality works by them and to promote the fine arts to a wider public," as was announced in June 1830 in the newspaper *Der Wanderer*.[3] Like similar societies in Germany and Switzerland, the Viennese society used the income from members' subscriptions to purchase works of art that were later distributed to members via a lottery system. It also undertook "to make a copper engraving or lithograph of at least one of the acquired artworks per year and to offer a print for each share."[4] In doing so, the organization helped revitalize the art scene in the imperial capital. Quite clearly, the prospect of potentially obtaining an oil painting through the payment of a small membership subscription was a great incentive, and within a short time the group had a large number of shareholders.[5]

The new art association did not merely awaken an appreciation of art among the population, it also triggered a response from the Imperial Academy of Fine Arts, the leading institution for all art matters in the Habsburg monarchy. Until then, the Academy had been responsible for the training of young artists and for their development through scholarships, exhibitions, and recommendations for official commissions by the court or church. However, the precarious economic situation after the Napoleonic Wars and the Congress of Vienna led to a dearth of financial resources for the arts and a stagnation in the number of public commissions. The Academy's exhibitions were also few and far between: After the 1816 exhibition, the next show was not organized until 1822. The shortage of work for artists had to be addressed, and new possibilities were therefore sought to stimulate public interest. This was the reason for the establishment in 1820 of the Akademische Kunsthandlung, an art store in the former Academy building on Annagasse.[6] It was formally approved by Prince Klemens Wenzel von Metternich, curator of the Academy,[7] but managed not by the Academy but by a private art and book dealer. The establishment itself, with its entrance right on Annagasse, took up two floors, the lower floor for art supplies and the upper floor for the sale of artworks. Artists could submit works for sale on commission, but the techniques used had to be those taught at the Academy. It ran successfully for ten years before being replaced by the art association mentioned earlier, with its flexible combination of exhibitions and art purchases, and finally closed in 1834.

The art association also motivated the Academy to reduce the interval between its exhibitions, so that from 1834 onwards exhibitions were held annually.[8] By this time, art and exhibitions had captured the interest of many people in the imperial capital and it was "the done thing to visit [exhibitions] and to be able to talk about and discuss them," as Joseph Preleuthner wrote in his report on the tenth anniversary of the art association.[9] He went on: "To the degree that members of the public became interested in art, they also joined the Society, since the ownership of works of art was increasingly seen as something valuable and desirable. As the Society thus aroused the interest in art of large sections of the educated middle class, its influence also spread widely and continues to do so."[10]

Local newspapers also picked up this interest, with descriptions of exhibitions and critiques of pictures running over several pages. They also reported on art exhibitions in northern Italy, particularly the activities of the academies in Venice and Milan, as these institutions were directly answerable to the Imperial Academy in Vienna, at least as long as the Kingdom of Lombardy-Venetia existed. There were few reports during the Metternich era, i.e. until 1848, about art from other European countries, however, apart from the works by the Milanese Giuseppe Molteni, who, as an "Austrian," presented *A Shepherdess from Brianza* at the 1839 Academy exhibition,[11] where the painting was purchased by the art association.[12]

The situation at the Vienna Academy did not change fundamentally after the Revolution of 1848, and exhibition activities continued to concentrate extensively on domestic artists, as is evident from the catalogues. This stagnation, which was also rooted in a fear of comparing domestic art production with that of the international market, led in 1850 to the founding of yet another organization, the Austrian Art Association (Österreichischer Kunstverein), which presented the Austrian public with an innovative program. Like the Society for the Promotion of Fine Art, which remained active, the new association also promoted contemporary art. To that end it organized exhibitions at its premises in the center of Vienna with works by national and international artists, purchasing works for an annual lottery with the proviso—and this was the novelty—that a third of these should be works by foreign artists.[13]

The initiator, co-founder, and long-time president of the Austrian Art Association was Rudolf von Arthaber,[14] an industrialist from Vienna and manufacturer of the "Viennese shawl," who had discovered European art while on his business travels and himself owned an impressive collection of international contemporary art. His appreciation of art had attracted attention in the 1830s, as even then he already owned major works, which are now in public collections in Vienna, Schweinfurt, and Dresden, including Josef Danhauser's *The Rich Glutton* (plate p. 135, top). It is said that the idea of transferring the Biblical story of *The Monastery Soup* (plate p. 135, bottom) to Biedermeier Vienna came from him. We know what Arthaber looked like from a large family portrait by Friedrich von Amerling showing the collector and his children in an opulent setting (plate p. 109).

Over thirty years of Austrian painting

The 1830s marked an early highpoint in the development of Austrian painting in the first half of the nineteenth century. During that decade, all segments of secular bourgeois painting—portrait, landscape, and genre—reached a new quality in terms of technique, composition, and narrative power. Portraiture had the longest tradition in Austrian painting and, even in the eighteenth century, sitters no longer disappeared behind the insignia marking their social position but were shown with a realistic interpretation of their appearance and personality.[15] Apart from the main portraitists of the early nineteenth century, notably the skillful miniaturist Moritz Michael Daffinger (1790–1849), the technically gifted Franz Eybl, and the imaginative

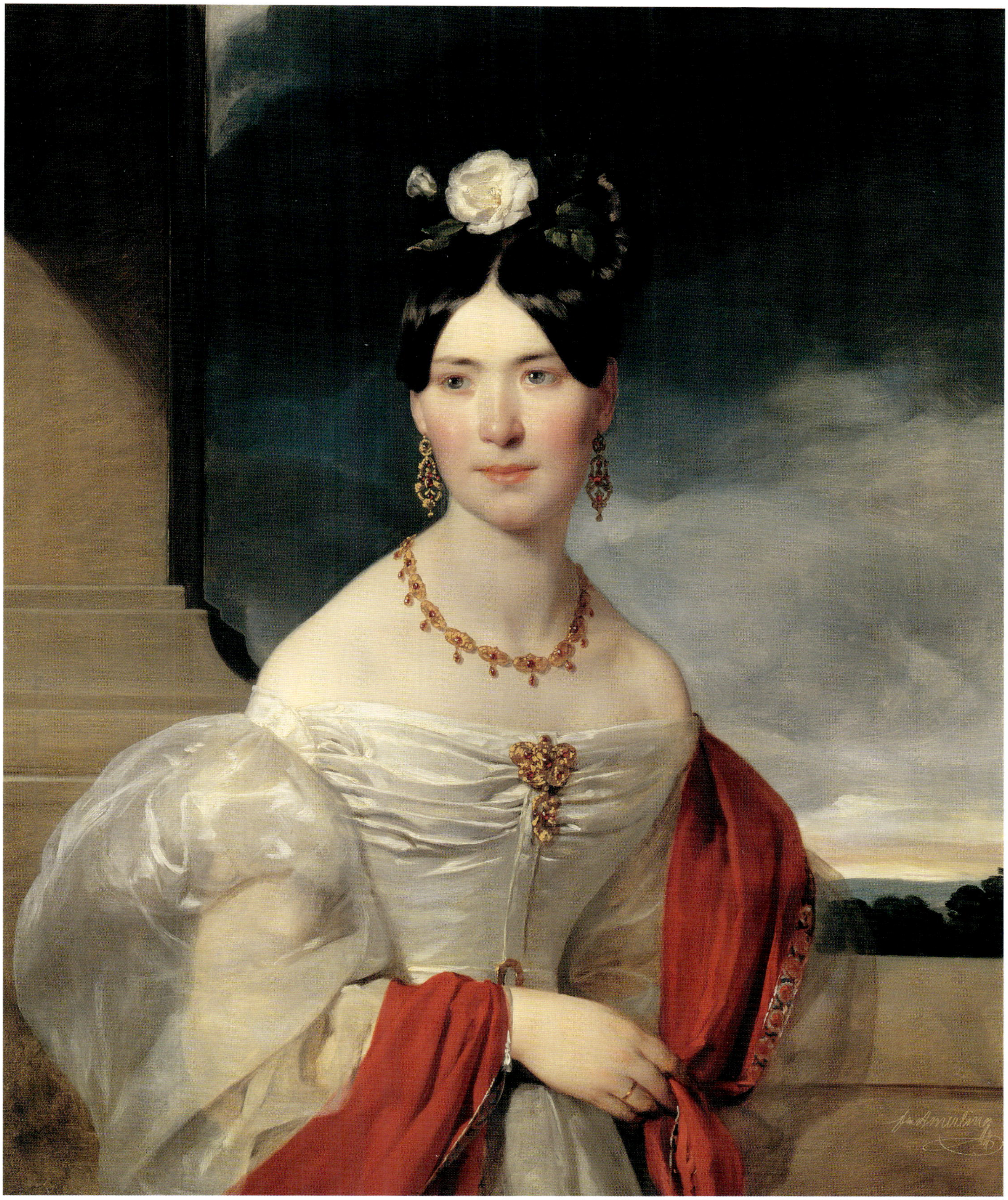

Fig. 2: **Friedrich von Amerling**, *Marie Freiin Vesque von Püttlingen*, 1832
Belvedere, Vienna

Johann Baptist Reiter, Friedrich von Amerling and Ferdinand Georg Waldmüller were particularly notable, even if their approaches were diametrically opposed.

Waldmüller's particular approach to art originated from a commission to paint the portrait of an older woman "as she is" (*Henriette von Stierle-Holzmeister*, 1817, Alte Nationalgalerie, Berlin). This instruction must have seemed daunting to him at first but ultimately led to a highly realistic portrayal. "The only right way, the eternal, inexhaustible source of all art—contemplation, perception, and understanding of nature—revealed itself to me," he explained.[16] From then on, the study of nature formed the basis for all of his artistic creation, in portrait and landscape, genre painting and still life (fig. 1).

Waldmüller's almost photographic depiction of the human face, the detailed portrayal of what he saw in the moment, can be contrasted with the portraits by Amerling, the second grand master of this discipline in Vienna. Amerling's conception of portraiture was based on observation. He studied his subjects in their entirety, registering their expressions and gestures to produce a rounded picture of their personality. As can be seen in the portrait *Marie Freiin Vesque von Püttlingen* (fig. 2), he was not interested in making his subject appear more beautiful, because he considered her attractiveness to be only superficial: On closer inspection it becomes apparent that what is depicted here is a young girl with a slightly too soft chin and not yet fully formed facial features. Amerling arrived at this "obliquely truthful" form of depiction through British portrait painting and the works of Thomas Lawrence (1769–1830) and Joshua Reynolds (1723–1792), which he had studied during a prolonged visit to London in 1827–1828. He also drew on the portrait style of Johann Baptist Lampi the Elder, who around 1800 was much revered in central and eastern Europe. Born in South Tyrol, Lampi had spent a long period at the royal court in Warsaw and the Czar's court in St. Petersburg, before working as a professor of history painting (there was no official chair for portrait painting) from 1797 to 1822 at the Imperial Academy in Vienna. It is possible that Amerling had already discovered Lampi's portraits while studying there and recognized how tastefully and softly he modeled his subjects' faces, emphasizing their individuality and mediating between the public and private figure. Amerling's work clearly reflects the late Baroque origins of the Viennese portrait tradition and contributed to its continued development well into the nineteenth century. The Hungarian artist József Borsos and the Slovenian Mihael Stroj, both of whom studied at the Vienna Academy, and Franz Schrotzberg from Vienna may also be mentioned in this context.

In genre and landscape painting, two teachers at the Imperial Academy had a particular influence. Both of them could look to incisive experience acquired abroad. Johann Peter Krafft (1780–1856) had come as a young man from Hanau, Germany, to study history painting in Vienna and had then rounded out his knowledge in Napoleonic Paris. The other teacher, the Viennese landscape painter Josef Rebell (1787–1828), had developed his distinctive depictions of nature during a stay of several years in Rome, Naples, and Campania. His style had fascinated Emperor Francis I to such an extent that he appointed him director of the Imperial Painting Gallery and head of the landscape painting class at the Academy. Rebell's key achievement was to bring sunlight into painting. He was able to brighten the palette of his depictions of nature so far that they give the viewer the impression of looking through a window out into the open.

Apart from the challenge of the studio light, a naturalistic composition was the other major preoccupation of landscape painters at the time. They were at pains to eliminate the Neoclassicist foreground props, as in Franz Steinfeld's 1824 painting *View of Hallstatt* (fig. 3). The regular summer excursions to the Salzkammergut and Berchtesgaden by Friedrich Gauermann, Waldmüller, Josef Feid (1806–1870), Friedrich Loos, and others reflect the artists' endeavors to paint realistic landscapes. During this gradual painterly conquest of nature, extensive references to Dutch landscape painting can still be discerned for some time, for example, the solitary forest moods of Jacob van Ruisdael (1628–1682), the ruggedly romantic nature scenes of Allart van Everdingen (1621–1675), and particularly Meindert Hobbema (1638–1709), whose treetops are lit from behind to make the leaves appear flooded with sunlight—a technique that Waldmüller in particular was inspired to imitate. This combination of painting natural phenomena and real-life observation resulted in a number of Alpine landscapes in which the realistic depiction, the main aim of landscape painters of the time, also brimmed over into dramatic exaggeration, as in *Sunset on Lake Hintersee in Berchtesgaden* by Albert Zimmermann (plate p. 235).

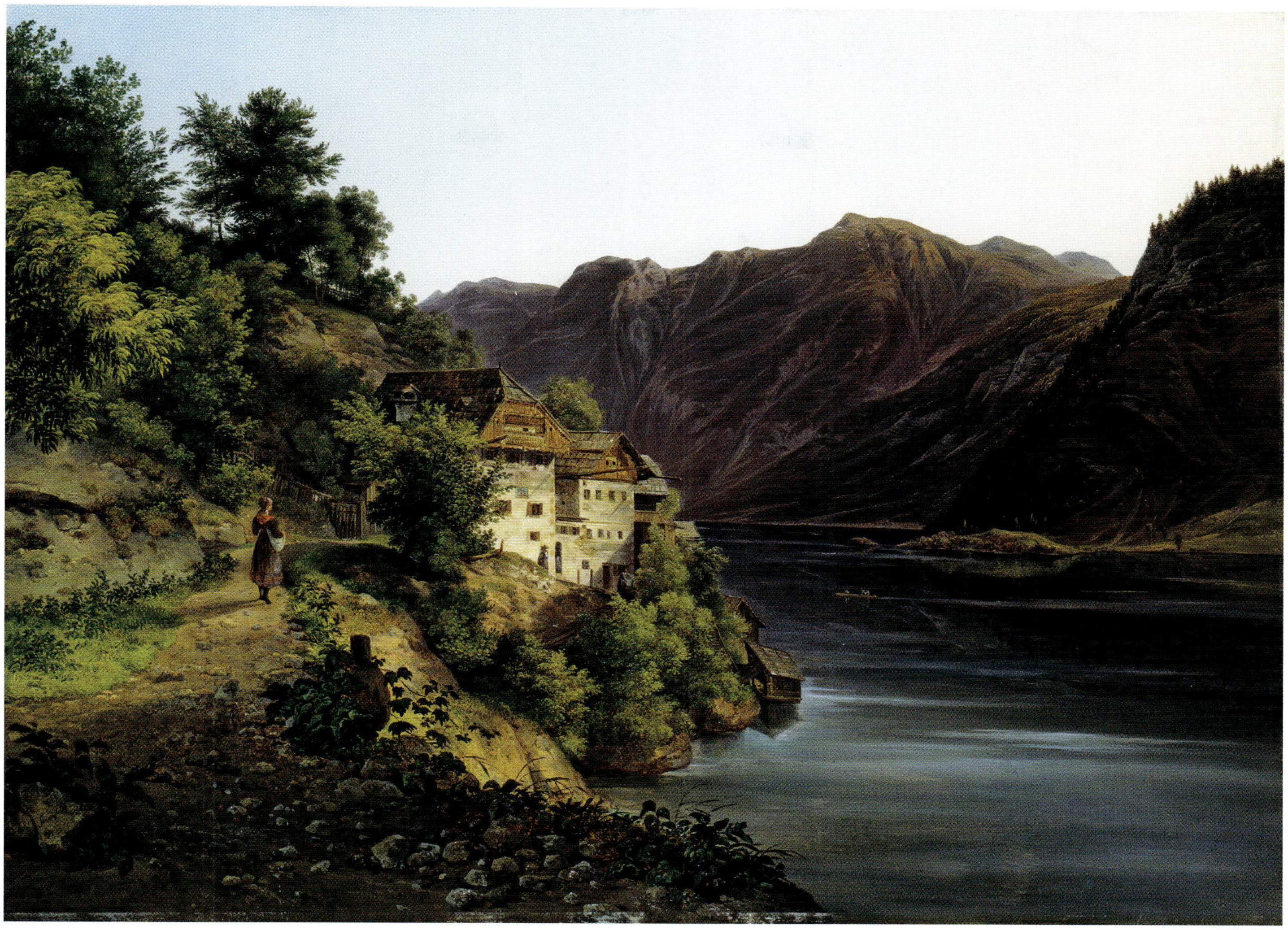

Fig. 3: **Franz Steinfeld**, *View of Hallstatt*, 1824
Niederösterreichische Landesmuseen, St. Pölten

At the same time, Waldmüller sought to depict a general idea of nature. The classic "postcard motif" he had chosen initially to tackle his compositional problems gradually became less important to him. The slice of nature became the *pars pro toto*, and humans and animals became components of a larger whole. In this way, Waldmüller paved the way for landscape painting in the second half of the century, taken up in the poetic realism or "atmospheric Impressionism" of artists like Emil Jakob Schindler (1842–1892) or Eugen Jettel (1845–1901).[17]

Johann Peter Krafft, the other influential teacher at the Vienna Academy, had studied the modern approach to history painting in Paris, where the depictions of current political events had proved extremely popular. Taking inspiration from this, he painted the large-format *The Militiaman's Departure* (Belvedere, Vienna) in 1813, the year of the Battle of Leipzig, a propaganda picture whose depiction of a domestic scene as the soldier sets off to fight was designed to highlight the values being defended in the war against Napoleon. Art historians are still divided today whether this picture is a genre-like history painting or the first Viennese genre painting. At all events, it gave rise to the development of a style oscillating between history and genre that exploited the instruments of Romanticism while translating the Neoclassicist ideas into a realistic form.

From 1823, as corrector of history painting at the Imperial Academy, Krafft taught his students the different varieties of this discipline, the illustration of historical and literary events and their transposition into a contemporary context. He also encouraged depictions of personal experience. As a result, prospective

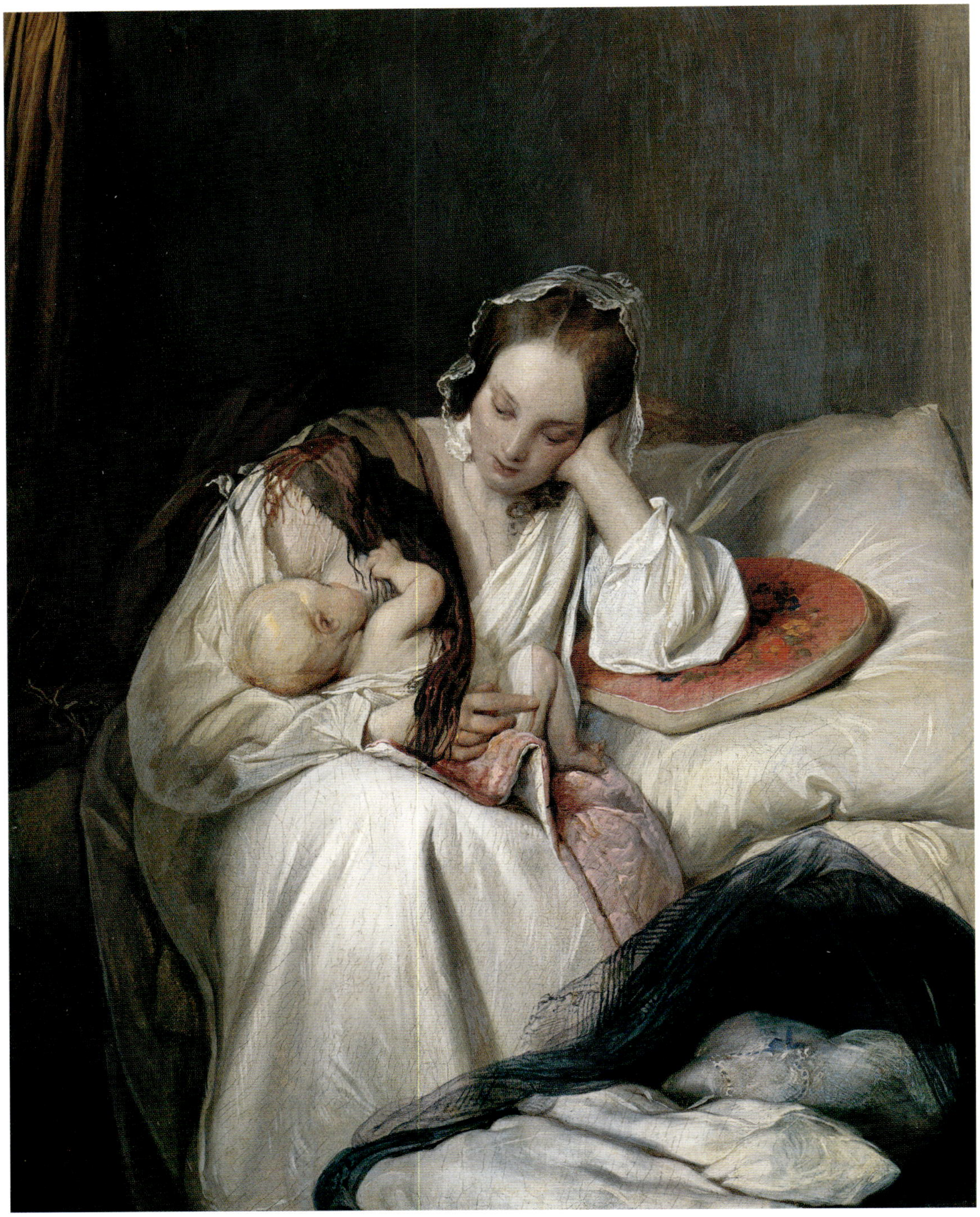

Fig. 4: **Josef Danhauser**, *A Mother's Love (the Artist's Wife and Child)*, 1839
Belvedere, Vienna

history painters finally began to lose their reluctance to paint subjects that, although highly popular as lithographs—for example, the scenes with craftsmen or market women by Josef Lanzedelli the Elder (1772–1831)—had hitherto been regarded as "unacademic" by the art world. And it was not long before life in all its facets became a favorite subject for paintings—intimate family scenes (fig. 4), everyday life in the town or countryside (fig. 5), military life, religious celebrations, and other festivities—themes that Bruno Grimschitz described as the "history of everyday life."[18] The young artists took inspiration from the Dutch genre painting of the seventeenth century, which they were able to study in various public collections, although they omitted the symbolic references often found in them, which were not compatible with the here-and-now thinking of the Viennese. By contrast, the genre pictures of the late 1820s and 1830s retained the Neoclassicist thinking, with the heroes' exemplary deeds being transferred to ordinary people, thus sending a moralizing message to the public. The emotive depictions of beggars or weeping children, so popular at

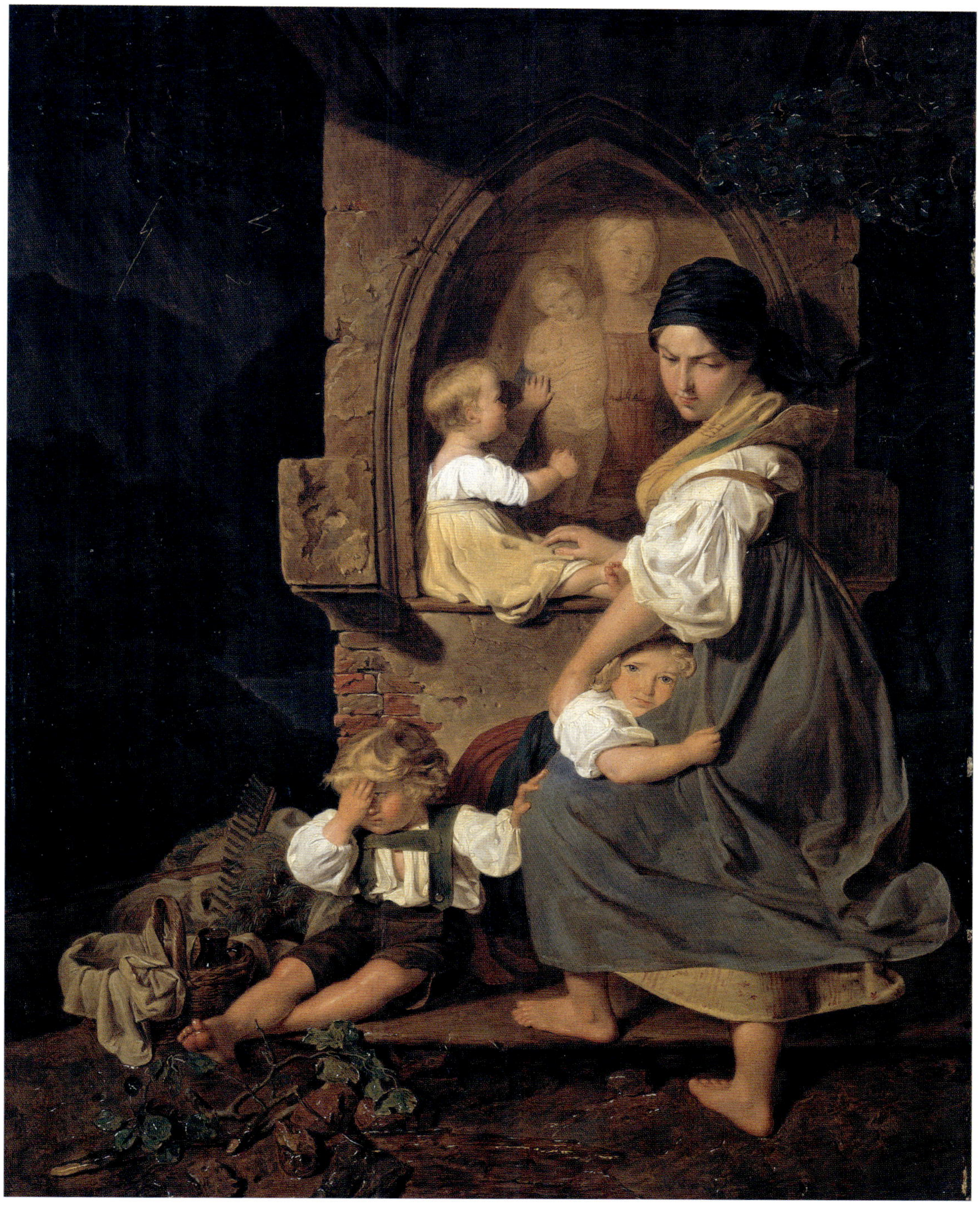

Fig. 5: **Ferdinand Georg Waldmüller**, *Shelter from the Approaching Thunderstorm*, 1832
Neue Galerie am Universalmuseum Joanneum, Graz

the time, were merely a fashionable offshoot of this trend.

Josef Danhauser was also one of Krafft's students, and the teacher must have recognized his intellect and encouraged his *vis comica* and inclination toward the flexible combination and pictorial development of narratives. Danhauser was the artist who perfected the art of Viennese genre painting. Eduard Ritter's figurative paintings have a similar narrative richness, but in his case the mere enjoyment of painting prevails over the deeper underlying meaning. Artists of the time covered a wide range of different themes, in many cases with a complete narrative within one picture, but often simply capturing a particular moment, as in the work of Peter Fendi.

Friedrich von Amerling has a special place in this context. Although his works are without a doubt connected with Vienna and the Biedermeier era, they are outsiders, running contrary to the prevailing tenor. Amerling did not wish to tell stories with his "genre pictures," but rather concentrated on the portrayal of beautiful women, full- or half-length, and in various

Fig. 6: **Friedrich von Amerling**, *Young Eastern Woman*, 1838
The Cleveland Museum of Art, Cleveland, Mr. and Mrs. William H. Marlott Fund

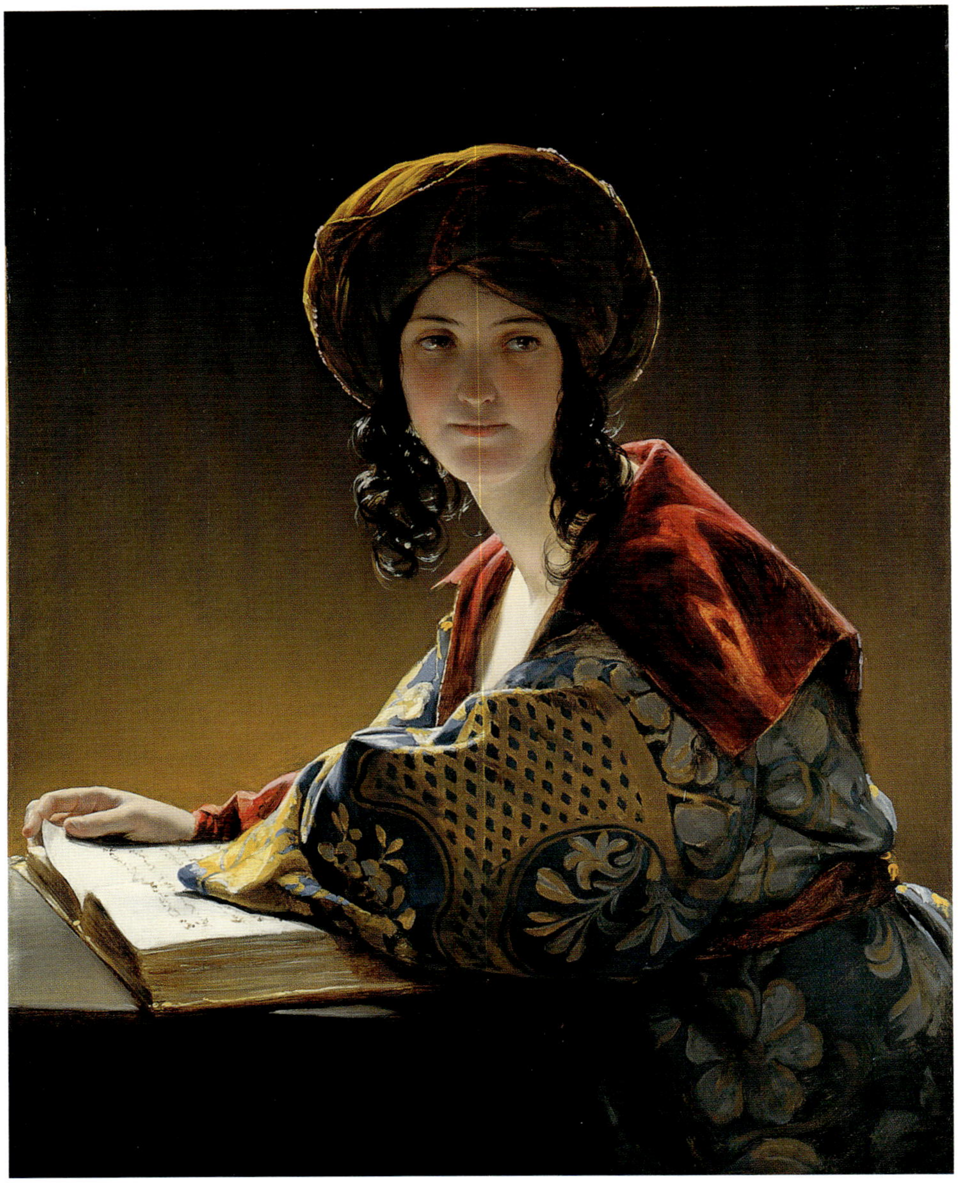

Fig. 7: **Friedrich von Amerling**, *The Souvenir* (*L'assopita*), 1838
Galleria degli Uffizi, Florence

positions, sometimes in Oriental clothing as in *Young Eastern Woman* (fig. 6) or dressed in mourning as in *The Widow* (plate p. 119). In this he used all his skill to enhance the attractiveness of his subject. The origins of this genre type are diverse: British theatrical portraiture, Titian and Venetian painting of the Cinquecento, and, later, Natale Schiavone and contemporary Lombard painting. Amerling was in regular contact with Giuseppe Molteni and also painted a portrait of Francesco Hayez while visiting Milan in 1838. It is possible that Amerling had the idea for paintings like *Girl with Doves* (plate p. 157) or *The Souvenir* (*L'assopita*; fig. 7) after studying the work of his northern Italian colleagues.

Artists like Amerling, Waldmüller, Danhauser, and Johann Baptist Reiter stand out among the painters of this time. Their work was not in line with the traditions of the Academy, which from 1829, under Johann Nepomuk Ender, Leopold Kupelwieser (1796–1862), and Joseph Führich (1800–1876), adopted the ideas of the Nazarenes (Josef Rebell died in December 1828 and Johann Peter Krafft became director of the Imperial Painting Gallery in early 1829). Reiter's frank depictions of girls (fig. 8) or the portrayal of the artist and his wife as farm laborers (1848, Szépművészeti Múzeum, Budapest) are to be understood as a statement about artistic freedom. Peter Fendi and Waldmüller were also among the first artists in Vienna to address the pauperization of their fellow citizens in paintings of a more socially critical nature (plate p. 221). Waldmüller's pictures of repossession, eviction, or child labor are far removed from the depictions of cute beg-

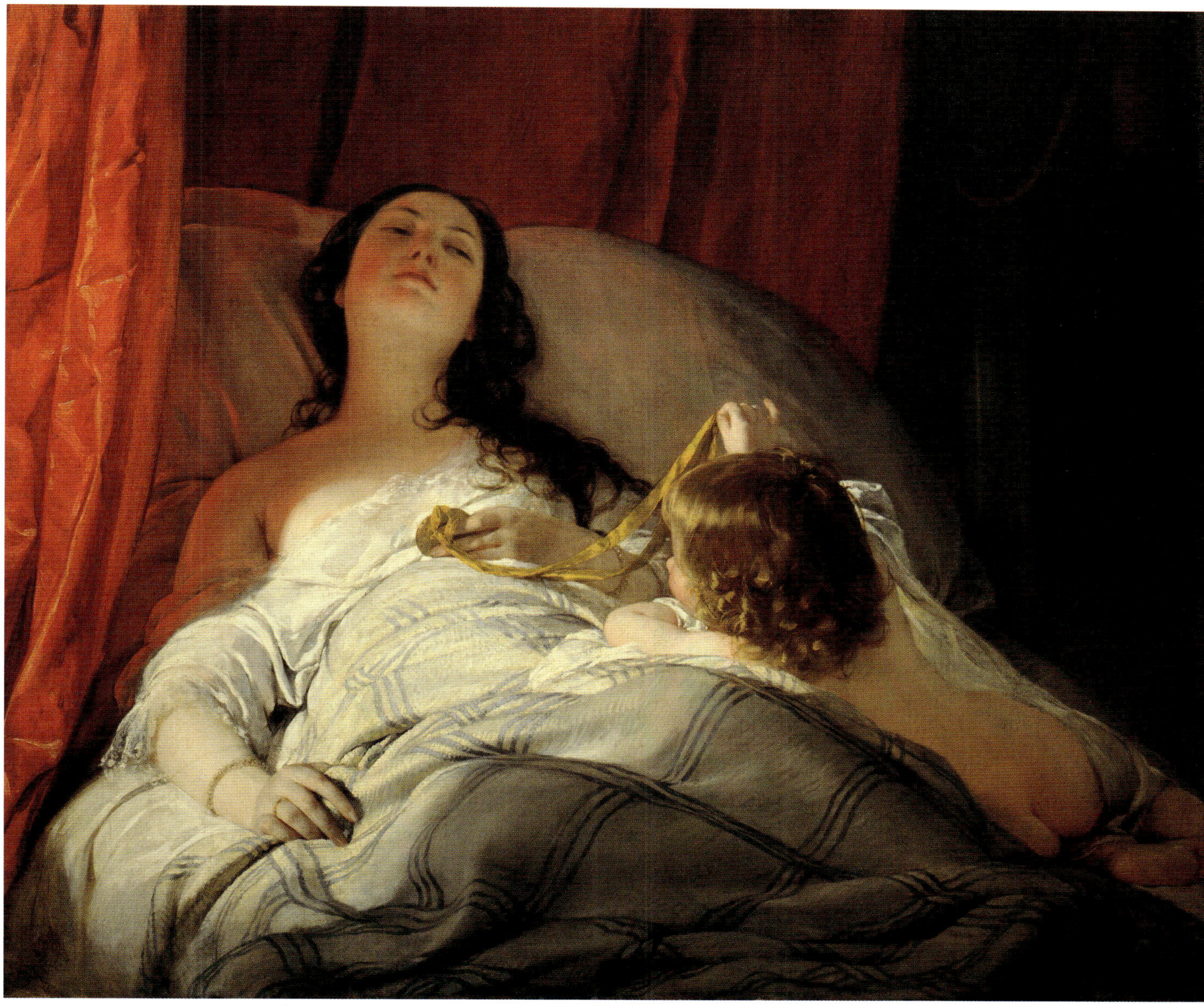

ging children so popular at the time, but are indicative of the artist's confrontation with reality. Waldmüller painted *Repossession* (Wien Museum) in 1847, at a time when criticism of the system was still forbidden. He also continued in his endeavors to capture nature as realistically as possible. This is evident in his exceptional genre scenes from the 1850s, such as *On Corpus Christi Morning* (plate p. 225), *Time of Roses* (fig. 9), or *Early Spring in the Vienna Woods (The Violet Pickers)* (plate p. 229), which show people in harmony with nature. These pictures helped to establish the outstanding reputation of Viennese painting at home and abroad, especially after the rediscovery of Waldmüller by the Secessionists around 1900.

1 Ludwig Hevesi, *Österreichische Kunst 1800–1848* (= Geschichte der modernen Kunst 2) (Leipzig, 1903), p. 45.

2 For the Society of Fine Arts of 1830, see Sabine Grabner, "Die 'Moderne Schule' in der kaiserlichen Gemäldegalerie und andere Bestrebungen zur Förderung der zeitgenössischen Kunst im 19. Jahrhundert," in Gerbert Frodl/Hadwig Kräutler, eds., *Das Museum: Spiegel und Motor kulturpolitischer Visionen/The Museum: Mirror and Motivator of Cultural-political Visions. 1903–2003 – 100 Jahre Österreichische Galerie Belvedere; Konferenzband zum gleichnamigen Symposium anlässlich des 100-jährigen Bestandes des Museums 2003* (Vienna, 2004), pp. 99–104.

3 *Der Wanderer* (1830), no. 176, June 25, 1830.

4 Wienbibliothek im Rathaus, Handschriftensammlung, ZWH 656 (Gesellschaftsprotokolle), no no./KV 1832, March 8, 1832.

5 Joseph Preleuthner, "Ueber das Wirken des Wiener Kunstvereines nach seinem zehnjährigen Bestande im Jahre 1841," in *Wiener Zeitschrift für Kunst, Literatur, Theater und Mode* (1841), no. 102, June 28, 1841, pp. 809–13, and no. 103, June 29, 1841, pp. 817–22.

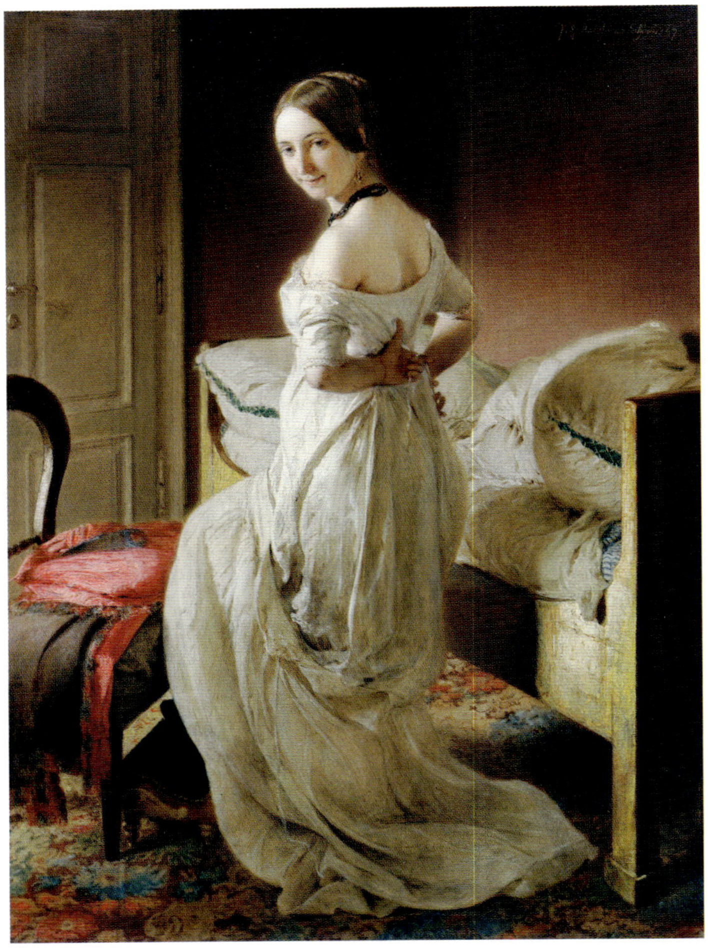

Fig. 8: **Johann Baptist Reiter**, *Lady in a Negligée*, 1847
Belvedere, Vienna, loan from Verein der Freunde der Österreichischen Galerie Belvedere

6 For the Akademische Kunsthandlung, see Grabner 2004 (see note 2), pp. 95–99.
7 UAAbKW (Universitätsarchiv der Akademie der bildenden Künste Wien), VA 1818, fol. 225–26.
8 The art association's intention was to encourage competition between artists (Franz Pietznigg, ed., *Mitteilungen aus Wien. Monathsschrift*, vol. 5 [1835], pp. 121–22). In view of the growing list of members, it also had a greater need for works of art. As its statutes stated that only works from current Academy exhibitions could be included, the board was caught on the horns of a dilemma. The situation was not resolved until 1836, when the statutes were modified to include works from the artists' studios (Wienbibliothek im Rathaus, Handschriftensammlung, ZWH 656 [Gesellschaftsprotokolle], no. 136/KV 1836).
9 Preleuthner, 1841 (see note 5), no. 102, p. 810.
10 Ibid.
11 *Kunstwerke, öffentlich ausgestellt im Gebäude der Österreichisch-kaiserlichen Akademie der vereinigten bildenden Künste bei St. Anna Im Jahre 1839* (Vienna, 1839), no. 436.
12 Philotechnos, "Molteni's 'Schäferin aus der Brianza' (436) ist ein Bild von Kraft und Wirkung, und daher auch vom Kunstverein angekauft," in *Der Humorist*, 3rd yr., no. 91, May 8, 1839, p. 363. The picture was won in the art association auction of July 25, 1839, by Field Marshal Lieutenant Baron Joseph von Bonomo (*Wiener Zeitung* [1839], no. 172, July 29, 1839, p. 1067).
13 The art association's program is summarized in *Bericht des leitenden Comité des Oesterreichischen Kunst-Vereines in Wien über die vier Verwaltungsjahre 1852/53 bis 1855/56* (Vienna, 1857); see also *Statuten und Geschäfts-Ordnung des österreichischen Kunst-Vereines* (Vienna, 1859).
14 For Arthaber's diverse activities, see Sabine Grabner, "Rudolf von Arthaber. Kaufmann und Mäzen," in *Parnass: Das Kunstmagazin*, 22nd yr., no. 4 (2002), pp. 86–93.
15 Michael Krapf, "Das Porträt 1700–1840: Die Konzentration auf das Antlitz als 'Spiegel der Seele,'" in ibid./Sabine Grabner, eds., *Aufgeklärt bürgerlich. Porträts von Gainsborough bis Waldmüller 1750–1840*, exh. cat., Österreichische Galerie Belvedere, Vienna (Munich, 2006), pp. 8–25.
16 Ferdinand Georg Waldmüller, *Das Bedürfnis eines zweckmässigeren Unterrichts in der Malerei und plastischen Kunst. Angedeutet nach eigenen Erfahrungen*, 2nd reprint (Vienna, 1847), quoted in Rupert Feuchtmüller, *Ferdinand Georg Waldmüller – 1793–1865: Leben, Schriften, Werke* (Vienna/Munich, 1996), p. 339.
17 Walter Krause, "Waldmüller und die Landschaftsmalerei," in Agnes Husslein-Arco/Sabine Grabner, eds., *Ferdinand Georg Waldmüller 1793–1865*, exh. cat., Belvedere, Vienna/Musée du Louvre, Paris (Vienna, 2009), pp. 79–85.
18 Bruno Grimschitz, *Maler der Ostmark* (Vienna, 1940), p. 14.

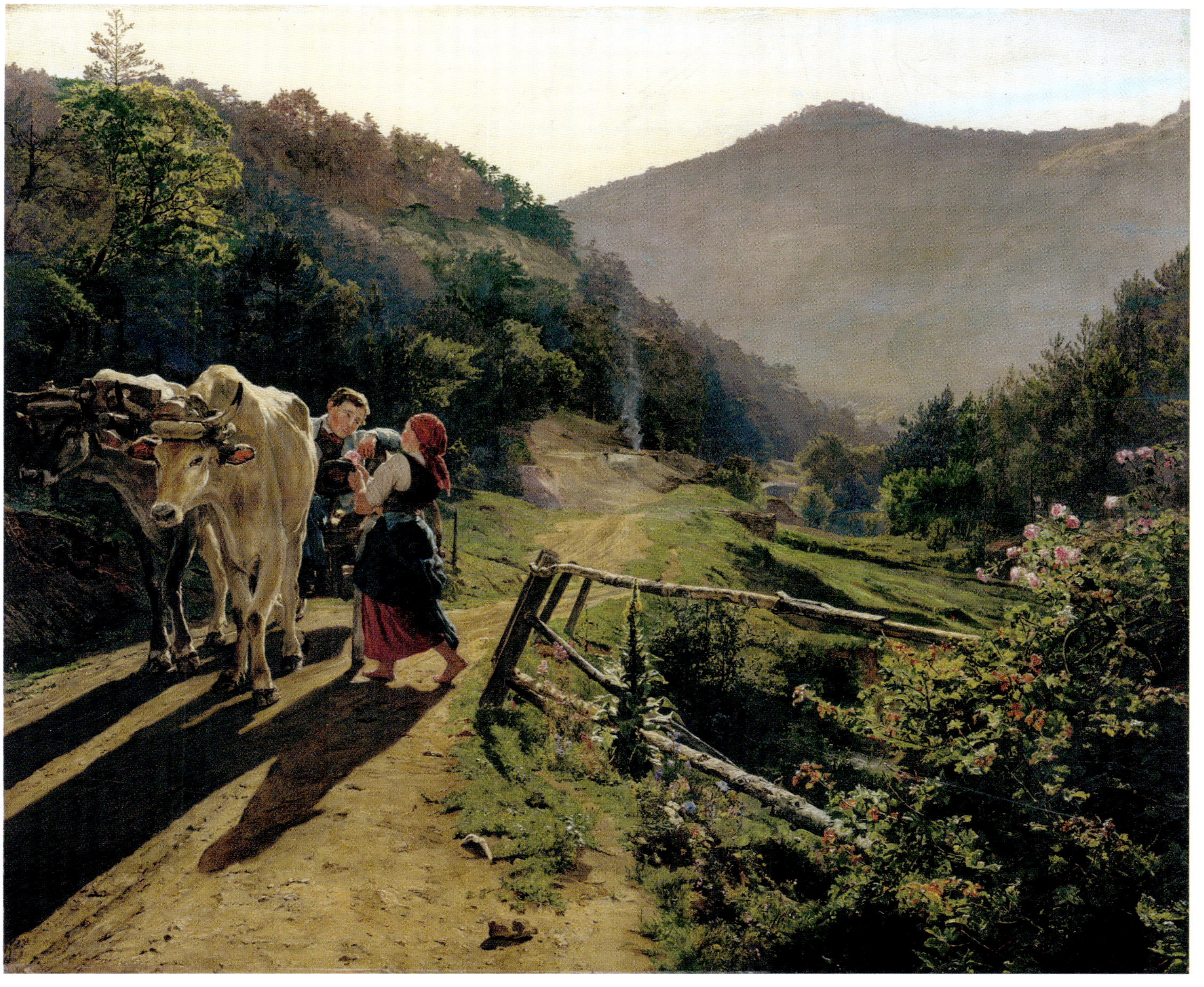

Fig. 9: **Ferdinand Georg Waldmüller**, *Time of Roses*, c. 1864
Wien Museum

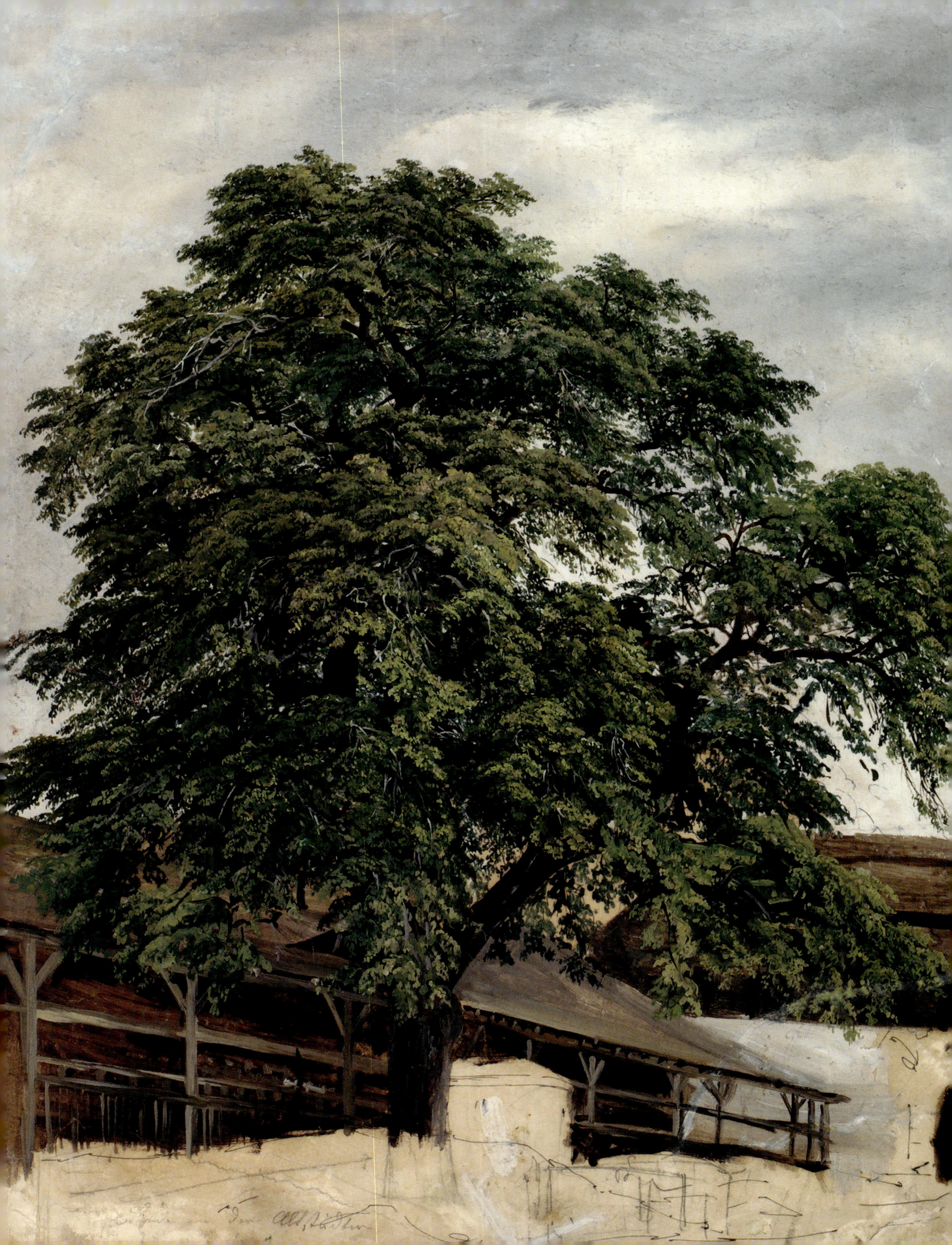

THE IDEALIZED IMAGE AND REALITY: BIEDERMEIER IN BOHEMIA AFTER 1830

Radim Vondráček

Like in some older German-language works, Biedermeier was seen in Czech art history as an unproblematic synonym for a comfortable bourgeois life, for a restrained, politically conservative basic outlook, combined with a perceived escape into domesticity. Biedermeier often referred to a period that brought together features of an entire era, mostly equated in Czech literature with the time preceding the 1848 revolution, known in German as the *Vormärz*. Overall, Biedermeier generated little interest in Bohemia, possibly also on account of the German origin of the term, and, until recently, essays on it in the Czech-speaking realm tended to reflect traditional, misleading clichés.[1] For decades, an open discussion of the true nature of the phenomenon was lacking, which, moreover, was reduced to the less contentious area of the applied arts. Individual attempts at a broader interpretation were weighed down by ideological judgements. This was particularly noticeable in the fine arts, in which the term Biedermeier was associated with artistic naivety and an ideological vacuum; at best with an unexciting, highly descriptive clarity. In Czech art, Biedermeier was mostly referred to dismissively, in relation to its artistic shallowness, stolidity, or naïve solemnity.[2] For this reason, second-rate works were often categorized as Biedermeier, while outstanding creations by Czech painters of that time were interpreted as an expression of other styles—of Neoclassicist "Objectivity," Sentimentalism, Romanticism, or early Realism.[3] Most popular of all was the revolutionary-tinted "patriotic Romanticism,"[4] which occupied a privileged position in Czech art history all throughout the twentieth century, no matter whether it was preferred for national reasons or through the lens of the ideological concept of "progressive art." As a result, Biedermeier was pushed into the background, and opportunities for its deeper interpretation were limited.

Nonetheless, as early as the 1930s, it was also realized in Czech intellectual circles that the established terms of Neoclassicism, Romanticism, and Realism were inadequate to describe the essence of artistic development in the period following the Congress of Vienna. These turned out to be insufficient both for the visual arts and for literature.[5] Especially in literature and German studies, promising approaches were made around that time toward understanding this particular artistic direction, which endeavored to achieve a balance between idealized image and reality, bringing them together in a harmonious and life-affirming manner.[6] Czech Germanists made an important contribution here toward a new interpretation of the works of Adalbert Stifter and Karel Jaromir Erben, using them as examples to refute the idea of seeing Biedermeier as carefree or naïvely good-natured.[7] Vojtěch Jirát and many other literary scholars saw in the Biedermeier way of life a means of overcoming existentially threatening passions and dark powers, a kind of compensation for the profound doubt of human beings teetering on the brink of the modern age.

These intellectual impulses still form fertile ground to this day for an understanding of the relationship between ideal and reality, with which the dominant ideas and artistic trends of that time made their mark. In the Bohemian lands, a pronounced Romanticism did not become the defining feeling of life, nor the preferred form of artistic expression. Any exalted subjectivism, individualism, or value skepticism was offset by a quest for balance, by the norms of a collective understanding of a patriotic society, or through respect for a higher order. The concept of a sensible "healthy middle way" reinforced the need for restraint and self-control. Deliberations about the "healthy medium" as a category excluding all ex-

Fig. 1: **Antonín Mánes**, *Lime Tree in the Brick Hut in Prague's Old Town*, 1828/29
Národní galerie v Praze/ The National Gallery in Prague

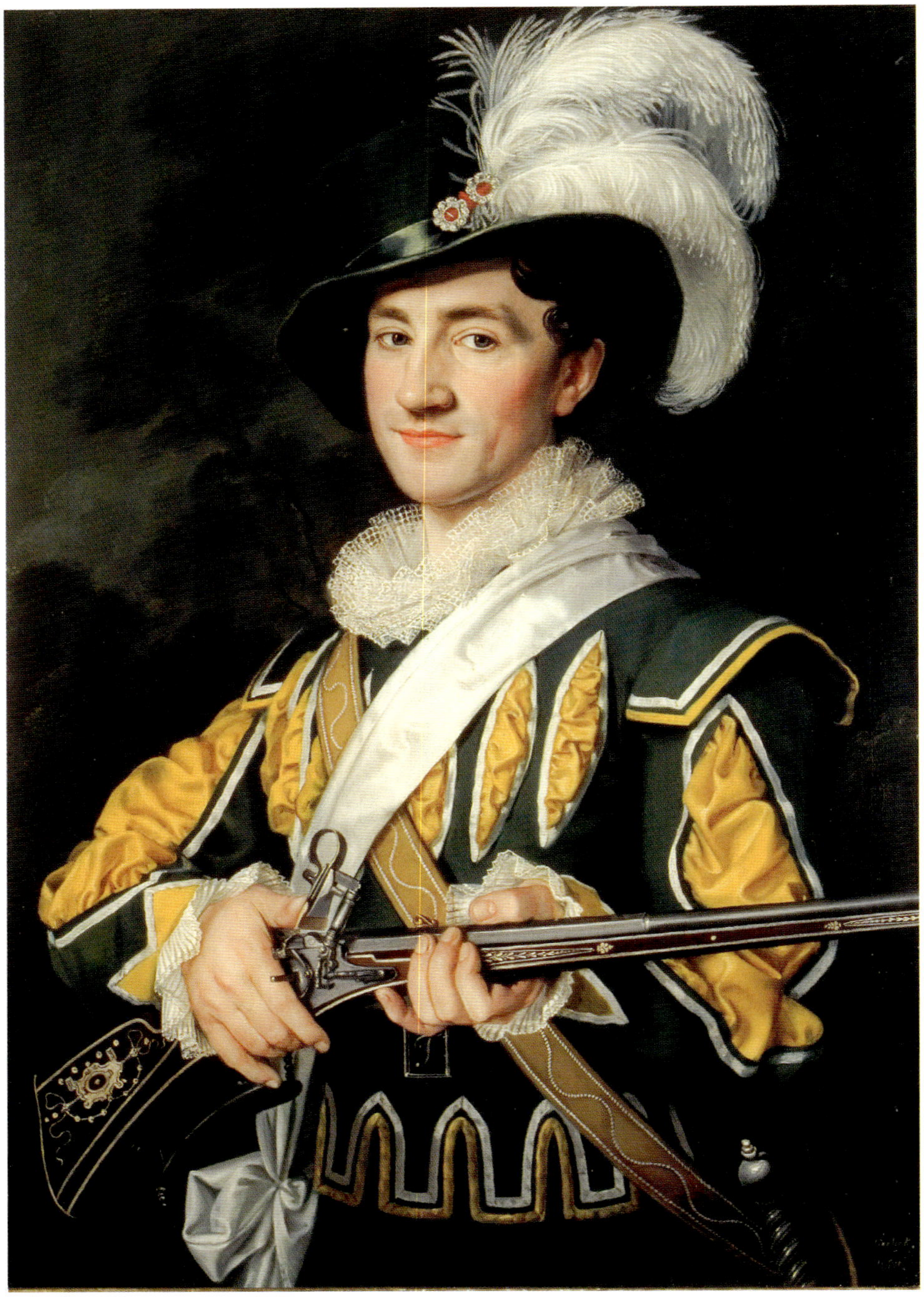

Fig. 2: **Antonín Machek**, *Portrait of Alois Jelen in the Role of Max from "Der Freischütz,"* 1826
Národní galerie v Praze/ The National Gallery in Prague

tremes played an important role in Czech thinking during the nineteenth century, and this was not restricted to the realm of ethics alone.[8] Herder's notion of the "middle order" very much came into play here. In the understanding of the Czech national renaissance, it also included a positive assessment of Bohemia's geographical situation as a hub between western and eastern Europe. This central location established stability, it enabled the smoothing-out of extremes in politics as in life, a connecting and harmonizing of differences.[9]

In line with literary research, the newly constituted relationship between reality and the ideal can also be seen as the key moment for understanding the visual art of Biedermeier in Bohemia. From the beginning of the nineteenth century, initially in the graphic arts and then gradually also in painting, an ever closer relationship toward reality and greater attention toward everyday life can be observed. These tendencies are characteristic of the drawings and graphic works of Joseph Bergler, the first director of the Academy of Fine Arts in Prague, which was founded in 1799 by the Society of Patriotic Friends of the Arts. Bergler's satirical drawings, caricatures, and morality plays, which drew their themes from urban life, can be seen as the direct predecessors of Bie-

Fig. 3: **Antonín Machek**, *Portrait of Terezie Palacká with her Children*, 1837
Private collection

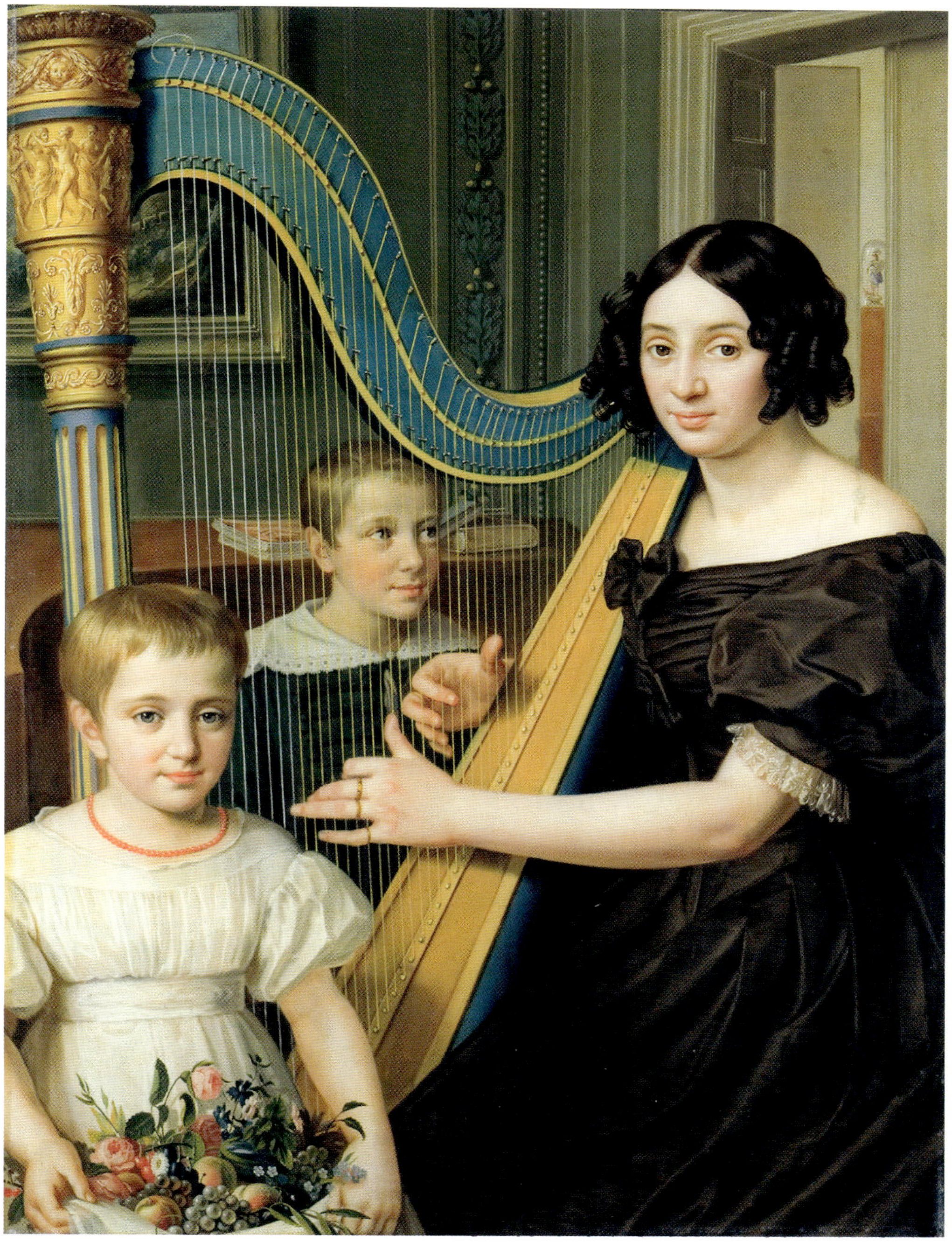

dermeier genre painting.[10] Daily life in the streets and in the family was similarly reflected in the works of Bergler's students at the Prague Academy, for example, Joseph Karl Burde or Leopold Krones.[11] A delicate relationship with the reality of nature developed at the School of Landscape Painting at the Prague Academy, founded in 1806 and run by Karel Postl. Instead of Neoclassicist, ideally composed landscapes, Postl's students soon created precisely illustrated *vedute*, such as those of Anton Pucherna, for example, or detailed outdoor studies, as created by Antonín Manes, for instance, whose sensitive oil sketches from the 1820s set in the surroundings of Prague or North Bohemia (fig. 1) effectively heralded the birth of modern Czech landscape painting.[12]

Highly important influences for further artistic development emerged in the period after the Congress of Vienna in areas that were not established academically in Prague, above all in portraiture. Up until then, this had enjoyed no relevant artistic status in Prague, attracting only few talented artists. The clearest break with the previous Neoclassicist portrait tradition came with the works of Antonín Machek, who, after a short period of study at the Vienna Academy (1799–1800) and subsequent work in Linz and Graz, settled in Prague around 1814. Machek

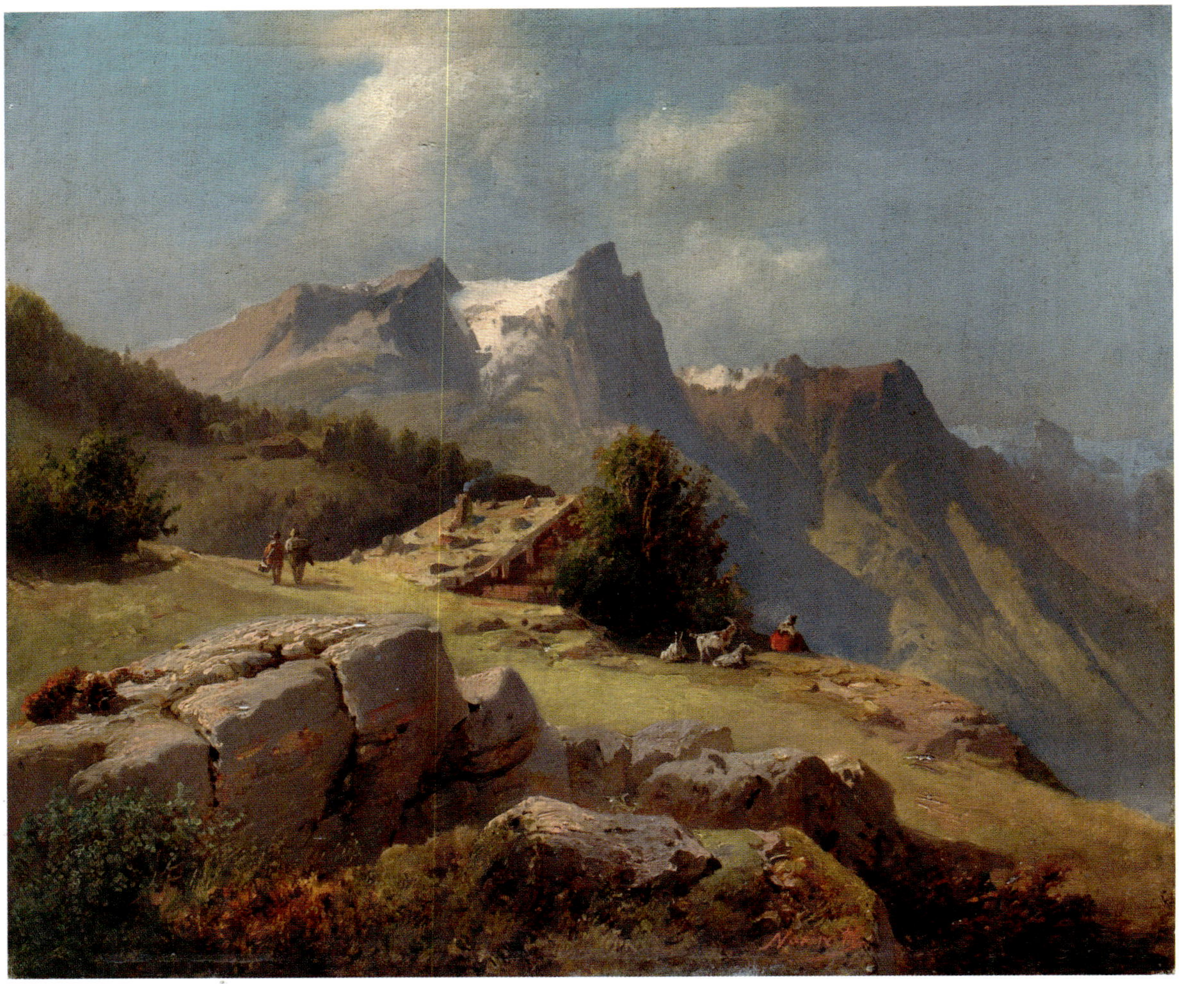

Fig. 4: **Josef Navrátil**, *Mettenberg in the Swiss Alps*, 1843
Národní galerie v Praze/
The National Gallery in Prague

Fig. 5: **August Piepenhagen**, *Alpine Lake with Boat*, 1840s
Národní galerie v Praze/ The National Gallery in Prague

retained in his portraits the clear and plastic forms characteristic of Neoclassicism, yet successively brightened his color palette, increasingly turning his attention to objective, empirical observation and the depiction of details of faces, clothing, and accessories or accompanying attributes (fig. 2). His best works radiate verve, immediacy, and intimacy, awakening a feeling of emotional closeness.[13]

Nevertheless, the ongoing painterly "discovery of reality" did not signify a shift toward a strictly realistic depiction. The landscape or portrayed subject remained highly idealized. What emerged was a transformation of the ideal world, which now assumed a different form to the Neoclassicist dreams of Arcadia, coming closer to life. Man no longer aspired to the far-off or the eternal, yearning instead for the nearby and attainable. Heaven comes down to earth, the bucolic landscape acquires a more real shape, becoming the landscape of one's homeland. Biedermeier created the ideal of a "beautiful life," in which happiness is found through one's own efforts, through responsibility and restraint, through joy in the small things of everyday life. The mood in Machek's portraits catches that of the period, the lifestyle of Biedermeier with its conviviality, moderation, and serenity, as also advocated by contemporary handbooks on "dietetics" and "kalobiotics," which were espousing the principles of a healthy and long life. As the Bohemian spa physician and promoter of natural healing methods Karl Heidler writes: "Nothing destroys human health more, and faster, than sad emotions and passions."[14]

The contemporary playing of the "beautiful life" called for a new type of idyll in the "here and now." In the conservative environment of the Prague Academy, artists could only find this idyll by circuitous routes, however. The ideal of high art with its religious and historical themes left only limited space for the creation of a Biedermeier idyll, although, from the 1820s onwards, genre motifs also made inroads into the aforementioned traditional academic fields. One example of this are the sentimental, sweetly intimate features of the works of František Tkadlík, one of Joseph Bergler's most talented pupils.[15] This applies primarily to those works created

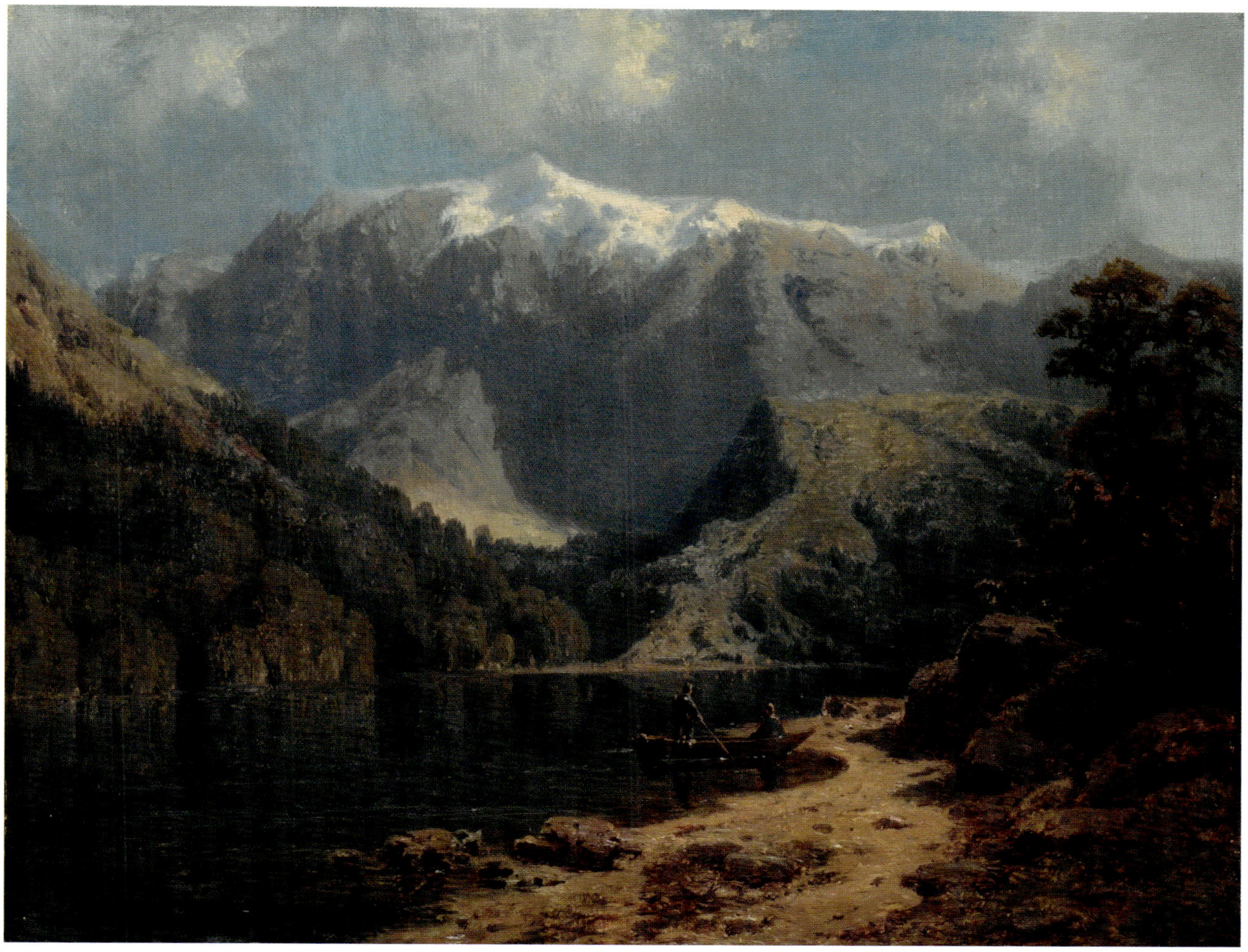

during Tkadlík's stay in Vienna during the first half of the 1820s, such as the *Madonna with Distaff* (around 1822), which was originally conceived for the altar of the parish church in Warnsdorf in North Bohemia.

A similar increase in idealizing tendencies can be observed in Antonín Machek's portrait works of the 1830s. The call for a faithful representation of reality is increasingly accompanied here by a proliferation in decorative elements, above all in details of clothing such as bonnets, shawls, lace etc. The painter had a penchant for Verist depictions of materials and textiles, their brilliance, and folds. The objective, restrained ethos of the earlier portraits was forgotten; the ensemble creates the impression of festivity and splendid ornamentation. The illusion of a festive family idyll was created in his more elaborate group portraits, such as that of Terezie Palacká with her children (fig. 3), which shows the family of the famous Czech historiographer František Palacký, or in the stiff, almost photographic arrangement of the Wehle manufacturing family, which, incidentally, also illustrates the rise of the Jewish bourgeoisie in the city of Prague.

In Machek's or Tkadlík's work, the period around the late 1830s and early 1840s already signified an end phase, which was accompanied by a certain decline in their creative power. In Bohemian landscape painting, by contrast, this was a period of renewal. During the 1830s, the painterly depiction of landscape not only became the focal point of interest for the Prague public, especially the middle classes, it also increasingly established a foothold among critics and in academic teaching. In 1836, reforms took place at the School of Landscape Painting of the Prague Academy, and Antonín Mánes was appointed as its director. His work combined a sensitive interest in a realistic depiction of nature—as we already know from his earlier studies—with ideally composed landscapes, to which he returned around this time. It is conceivable that Mánes wanted to accommodate the call on the part of the school's conservative founder, as well as the contemporary aesthetic sensitivities in Prague, which criticized the "slavish imitation of nature," and demanded that landscape painting should express the "existence of the spiritual principle" in nature.[16] The

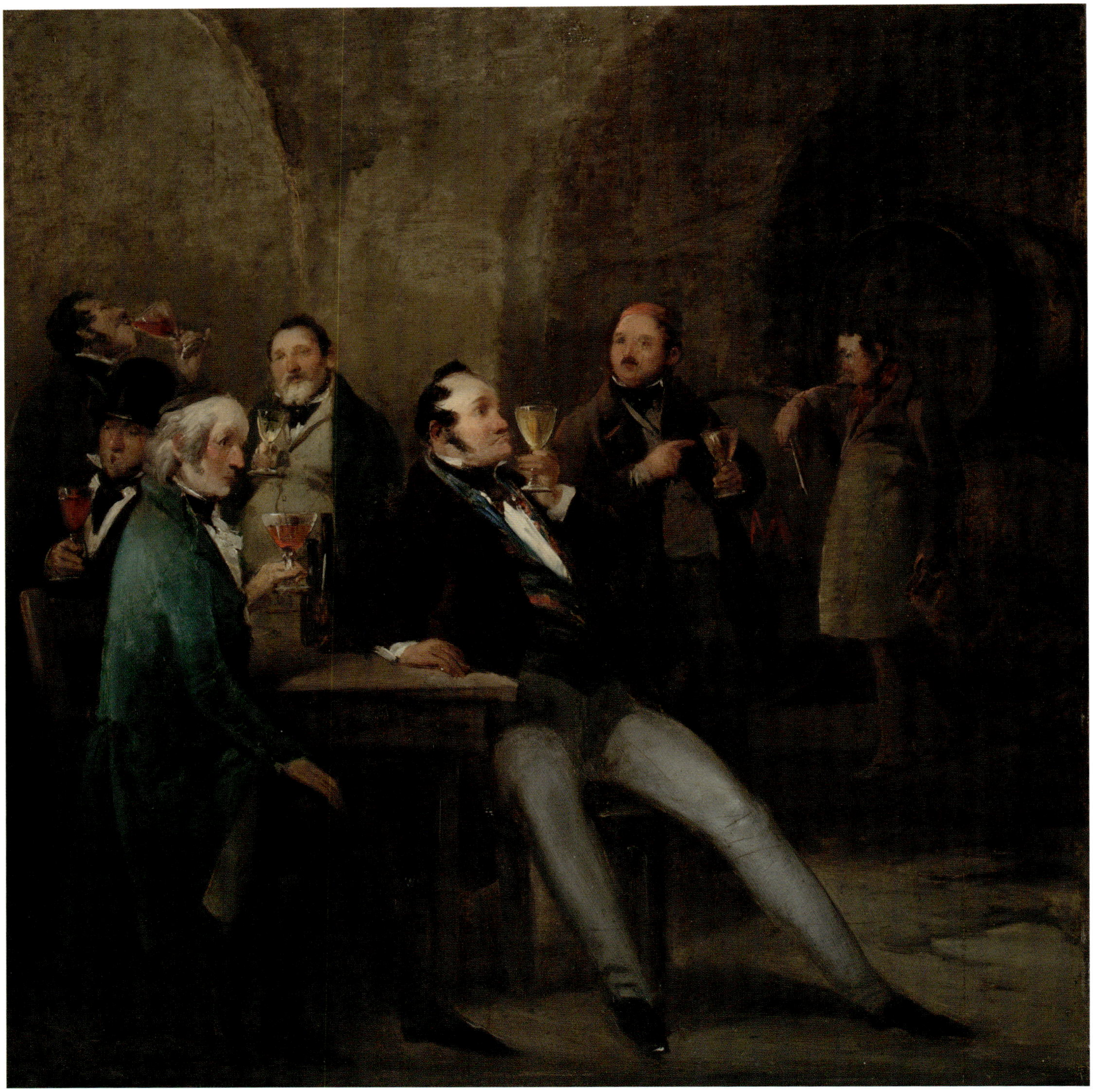

depiction of the real Bohemian landscape (although sometimes glorified and decidedly idyllic) remained his artistic program, however, which he also urged his students to adopt. One of these was Friedrich Havránek, the most gifted of Mánes's younger students, who, after the latter's death, continued his studies at the School of Landscape Painting under Maximilian Haushofer, drawing inspiration from the Munich school. The capturing of the landscape's atmospheric and painterly aspects—in the spirit of the works of Haushofer, Christian Morgenstern, or Carl Rottmann, among others—was accompanied in Havránek's work by a growing passion for natural details.[17] His landscape paintings from the Sázava valley (plate p. 192) or the area around the Salm dominion at Rájec nad Svitavou (plate p. 193) are characterized by the remarkably meticulous reproduction of every detail—crumbling plaster, roof textures, vegetation, and rock formations. Of all the Bohemian painters, Havránek probably fulfilled most of

Fig. 6: **Josef Navrátil**, *In Chlumecký´s Cellar*, 1850s
Národní galerie v Praze/ The National Gallery in Prague

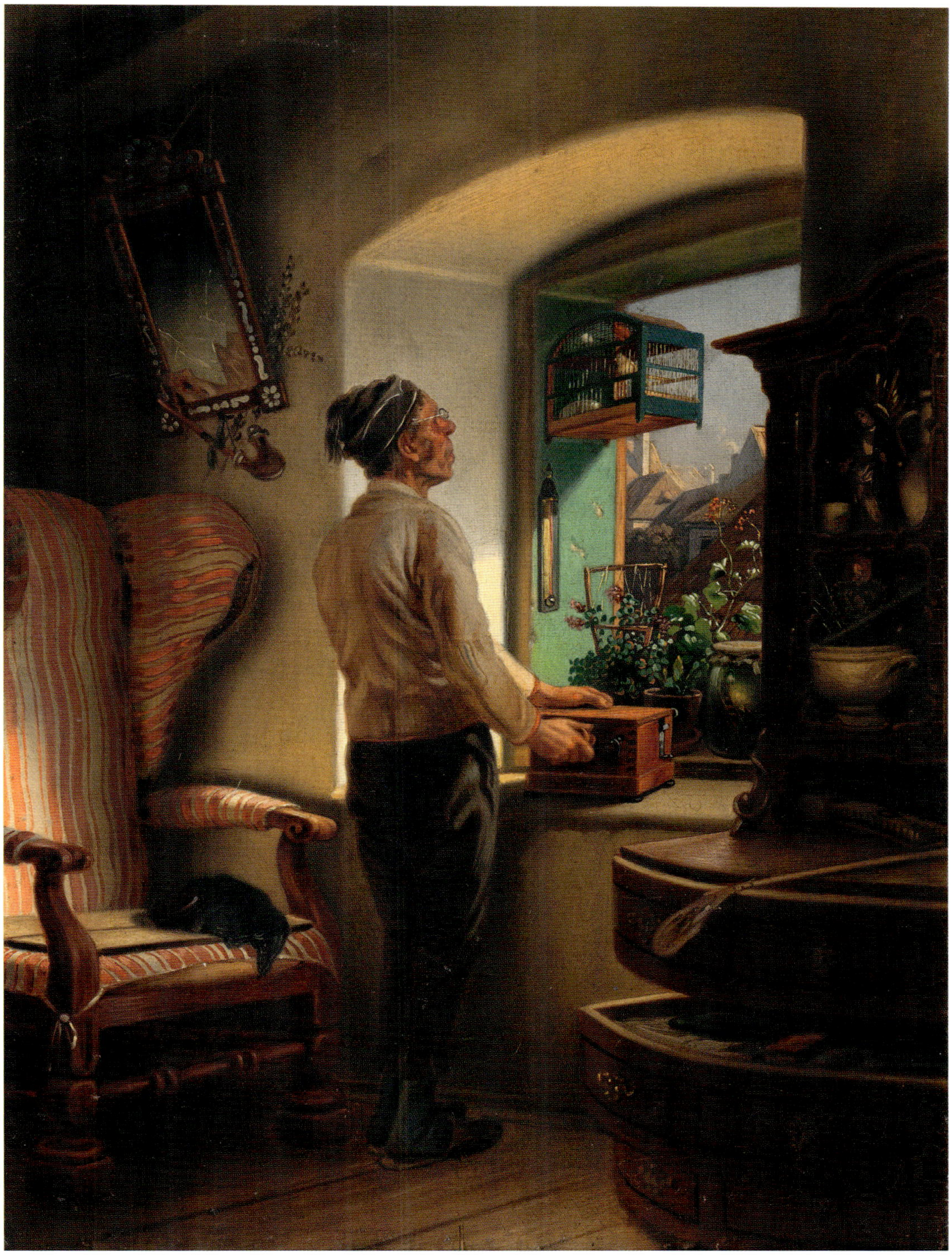

Fig. 7: **Quido Mánes**, *Old Bachelor (Singing Lesson)*, c. 1863
Národní galerie v Praze/ The National Gallery in Prague

all the Biedermeier ideal of an attentive, highly detailed description of natural reality, a maximal objectivization of the perceived, which would give the viewer a sense of existential security and enable him to overcome his subjective skepticism.

By the 1840s, striving for a detailed depiction of things was no longer seen as being in contradiction to the higher mission of art. In fact, the empirical, objective description, enabling the capturing of a higher order concealed within the object, became an essential requirement. The love of objects and of detail in landscape painting, as in the literary essays of writers like Adalbert Stifter, was no trivial Naturalism, but had an ideal dimension—it expressed awe before the eternal metaphysical order of the world, admiration for the "gentle law" of reality and of life.[18] The description of the objective world in painting and literature led to a synthesis of material and idea, of visible reality and hidden meaning.

This balance between real and ideal components that typifies Biedermeier can similarly be observed in the works of other Bohemian landscape painters of the period. The widely talented Josef Navrátil, who had originally trained as a house painter, enjoyed success at the time with his small gouache paintings featuring idyllic Alpine scenes. These were irresistibly attractive due to their lightness of execution and color, as well as their echoes of the Second Rococo style (fig. 4). Equally popular were August Piepenhagen's small-format landscape pictures (fig. 5), also much praised by Adalbert Stifter. Piepenhagen's atmospheric landscapes, depicted at different times of the day and in different moods, pointed to a higher connection between the cycles of man and of nature, their harmony and an order beyond the human existence. According to Stifter, these masterpieces understood how to depict the "sun-vibrancy and shadow-calm" of our mountains and lakes "with the most trueness to nature and greatest transparency," while treating the subject "with the most profound love and deepest warmth."[19] In his landscape pictures, which recall seventeenth century Dutch painting, Piepenhagen, like Jacob van Ruisdael, often chose the simplest material, which allowed him, using very few means, "to reveal, in a kind of eternity, the abundance of his own rich interior."[20] As Stifter wrote in an exhibition review in the early 1860s, a misty, moonlit landscape by Piepenhagen (plate p. 170) "lets us feel the mystery of the night, which neither conceals all, nor reveals all. And therein lies the poetry of the night, which we feel so drawn to and fascinated by."[21] It was this "denseness of poetry" that Stifter most admired in Piepenhagen's pictures.

In the 1830s, yet another approach to the painterly depiction of an idyllic world emerged in the Prague art scene: genre painting. At the Academy, this illustration of daily life remained excluded for a long time, longer even than portrait or landscape painting. We therefore first come across it in graphic works and drawings. It comes as no surprise that the first painted genre scenes depicting contemporary Prague were presented publicly in an exhibition organized by Alois Klar in 1832 in protest to the official Academy exhibitions.[22] These works are now missing, however, and so the oldest existing genre work is an 1840 depiction of the Prague Old town Christmas market by Josef Koruna. In his private oil sketches, Josef Navrátil also painted contemporary life on the streets (fig. 6), and Anton Gareis the Elder created highly imaginative graphic works on this theme. In painting, it was Antonín Mánes' sons who were most active in genre subjects: the doyen of nineteenth century Bohemian painting, Josef Mánes (creator of the famous *Seamstress* in the early 1850s), as well as Josef's younger brother Quido. The latter subsequently specialized in genre painting, finding his niche in nineteenth-century Bohemian art in this prosaic counterpart to serious and "sublime" historical or religious painting. In Bohemian art, the depiction of small, everyday occurrences (and mishaps) in the lives of kitchen boys, innkeepers, and seamstresses—often with moralizing undertones—crowns the Biedermeier image of an idyllic world. Regardless of any trifling worries, it presents a "sunny world," almost without shadow. Jan Loriš once described 1850s genre painting, in connection with the works of Quido Mánes (such as *Old Bachelor*, around 1863, for example, fig. 7), as conjuring up the feeling that "there is no humdrum everyday life, only the quiet and calm of a Sunday seemingly swathing everything in a holiday mood."[23] The celebratory, therapeutic dimension of Biedermeier cheer and serenity is convincingly cast in pictorial form here.

Genre depictions of daily life did not reach their apogee in Bohemian art until the 1850s and 1860s, so later than in neighboring countries. This late ebbing away of Biedermeier, almost like an Indian summer, was connected with particular aspects of the arts world in Prague, such as the conservative environment of the Academy, with the development trajectories of the different art disciplines in Bohemia, but also with the preferences of the patriotic Czech society during the era of national renaissance, bearing in mind that history painting, unlike the genre painting of the time, played a significant role in supporting the argument. Nevertheless, this delayed development in the visual arts also converges with the development of central European Biedermeier literature, including the work of Adalbert Stifter, whose highly popular novel *Indian Summer* was also not published until 1857.

A similar evolution played out in Czech-language literature, too. The greatest celebration of idyllic country life was Božena Němcová's *Babička (The Grandmother)* of 1855. The notion that everything that mattered in Biedermeier took place in the 1820s and early 1830s is mainly an intellectual construct for textbooks, to provide a comprehensible sequence of trends and artistic styles. In fact, we also encounter similar patterns, that do not give consideration to different local conditions, partial anachronisms, and individual preferences in taste, in the applied arts. Efforts to allocate the majority of Biedermeier works to the period before the arrival of Historicism, above all the Second Rococo period, must be confronted with archive sources that often bear witness to surprising temporal shifts. This was the case, for example, with a Lyra bureau from the collections of the Museum of Decorative Arts in Prague, which corresponded in style with designs from the period around 1830 and was thus exhibited for decades with this descriptor. Until restoration work uncovered a previously hidden dating, wich revealed that we were in fact dealing with the work of a carpenter from the northern Moravian region of Bruntál and, counter to all "art-historical" expectations, the bureau was from 1842.

1 For more detail on this, see Radim Vondráček, "The History and Reception of Biedermeier," in ibid., ed., *Biedermeier: Art and Culture in the Bohemian Lands 1814–1848* (Prague, 2010), pp. 10–33.
2 Cf. for example Luděk Novák, *Antonín Machek* (Prague, 1962), pp. 100, 119 and passim.
3 Such as in the works of Eva Petrová, Luděk Novák, Eva Reitharová, or Naděžda Blažíčková.
4 The works of Antonín Machek, František Tkadlík, Antonín Mánes, among others were characterized in this way.
5 Paul Kluckhohn was the first to point out the need for a new term: Paul Kluckhohn, "Biedermeier als literarische Epochenbezeichnung," in *Deutsche Vierteljahrsschrift für Literaturwissenschaft und Geistesgeschichte*, 8th vol. (1935), pp. 41–43.
6 See Wilhelm Bietak, *Das Lebensgefühl des "Biedermeier" in der österreichischen Dichtung* (Vienna/Leipzig, 1931).
7 Stanislav Sahánek, *Literární biedermeier v německém písemnictví* (Bratislava, 1938); Vojtěch Jirát, *Erben čili Majestát zákona* (Prague, 1944). Also, earlier, Wilhelm Kosch, *Adalbert Stifter und die Romantik* (Prague, 1905).
8 See Radim Vondráček, "Biedermeier as a Current of Values and Ideas," in Vondráček 2010 (see note 1), pp. 57–59.
9 For more on this, see Vladimír Macura, *Znamení zrodu. České národní obrození jako kulturní typ* (Prague, 1995), pp. 170–177.
10 See as a summary of Bergler's graphic work, Roman Prahl, *Grafika v Praze 1800–1830 a Josef Bergler* (Prague, 2007). An essential work on Bohemian art around 1800 and on Bergler's school is ibid., ed., *Prague 1780–1830. Kunst und Kultur zwischen den Epochen und Völkern* (Prague, 2000).
11 On his graphic works, see Prahl 2007 (see note 10). Recently on Burdes's works, Petr Šámal/Kristýna Brožová, *Umění inspektora: Josef Karel Burde (1779–1848)* (Prague, 2015).
12 See Eva Reitharová, *Antonín Mánes* (Prague, 1967).
13 The only complete monograph is Luděk Novák, *Antonín Machek* (Prague, 1962).
14 Carl J. Heidler, *Allgemeine Regeln für den Gebrauch der Gesundbrunnen und Heilbäder*, 2nd ed. (Prague, 1847), p. 18.
15 For an overview, see the complete monograph by Eva Petrová, *František Tkadlík* (Prague, 1960). New research on Tkadlik's work is due to be published by the end of 2016.
16 See exhibition reviews by Anton Müller in the Prague newspaper *Bohemia*, quoted from Reitharová 1967 (see note 12), p. 77.
17 Naděžda Blažíčková, *Bedřich Havránek 1821–1899*, exh. cat. National Gallery, Prague (Prague, 1985), p. 15 and passim.
18 On Stifter's concept of objectivity and understanding of things in his work, see Knut E. Pfeiffer, *Kunsttheorie und Kunstkritik im neunzehnten Jahrhundert: Das Beispiel Adalbert Stifter* (= Bochumer Studien zur Publizistik- und Kommunikationswissenschaft) (Bochum, 1977), especially pp. 57–59.
19 Quoted from Fritz Novotny, "Stifter und Piepenhagen," in *Adalbert Stifter, der Maler*, exh. cat. Stadtmuseum Linz-Nordico (Vienna, 1978), p. 49. For more detail on Piepenhagen's work, see Naděžda Blažíčková, ed., *August Bedřich, Charlotta a Louisa Piepenhagenovi*, exh. cat. National Gallery, Prague (Prague, 2009).
20 Quoted from Novotny 1978 (see note 19), p. 50.
21 Quoted from Novotny 1978 (see note 19), p. 50.
22 See *Ausstellung von Kunst-Werken zu Prag. Im Monate März 1832. Veranstaltet vom Professor Aloys Klar* (Prague, 1832) (no. 25: Anton Gareis, *Zwei Scenen beim Eintritt ins Theater*).
23 an Loriš, *Quido Mánes* (Prague, 1937), p. 56.

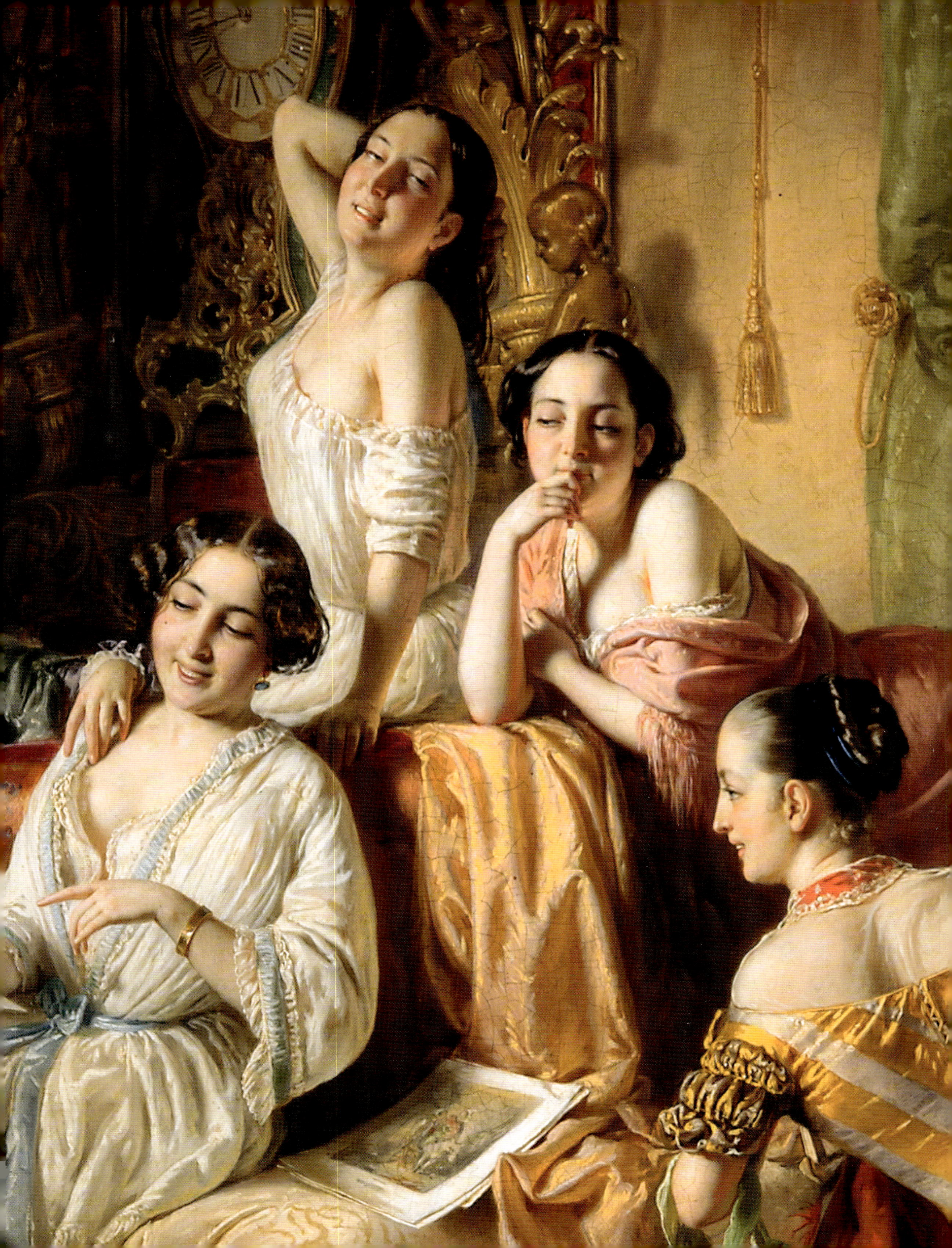

BIEDERMEIER IN HUNGARY

Eszter Békefi

This article aims to describe the Hungarian Biedermeier era as an art-historical period and to consider its interpretation in later times. The study of exhibitions and museum guidebooks from the twentieth and twenty-first centuries that present works from the mid-nineteenth century allows us to portray both the period under examination as well as changes in Hungarian iconography.

The term "Reform Era" is commonly used in Hungarian art historiography to identify the early nineteenth century. This era came to a close with the Hungarian Revolution and War of Independence in 1848–49. The ideology and institutional system of the Hungarian nation state began to take shape around that time. The bourgeois reforms also involved an important cultural shift. The Hungarian language reform (also known as the "neologist movement"), which had begun in the second half of the eighteenth century and was already showing clear results by the early nineteenth century, became a driving force in the awakening of a national consciousness. At the start of the era, language and literature, naturally suitable for expressing national sentiment, were practically the only bearers of national culture. Hungarian painting around 1840 was oriented more on the international—mainly Austrian—school. The desire to establish a national character, already met by literature, was not fulfilled by the visual arts until the final third of the century, mainly through the work of the painter Mihály Munkácsy (1844–1900) and his contemporaries and, later on, by the Hungarian Secession, which integrated traditional "folk art" motifs, and through the advent of Modern art. At the same time, Hungarian art history writing, in its efforts to respond to prevailing literary and historic trends, was reluctant to adopt the German term "Biedermeier" and its other foreign equivalents. As I will describe in the following, the term also had to overcome numerous historiographical hurdles in Hungary, while even in international academic literature its definition was frequently changed and reevaluated.

József Borsos, *Lányok bál után* (*Girls after the Ball;* detail), 1850
Museum of Fine Arts – Hungarian National Gallery, Budapest

Recognition phase: 1900–1919

Taking place in this first phase was the initial documentation of a new style, which was also only just being discovered abroad, as well as the identification of Hungarian artists that could be grouped under this new category.

In the early twentieth century, the Hungarian Biedermeier became a topic of discussion in Hungarian academic literature and—almost simultaneously—in international academic discourse.[1] In 1913, an exhibition entitled *Magyar biedermeier művészet* (*Hungarian Biedermeier Art*) was organized at the private museum of Lajos Ernst, whose objective was to showcase Hungary's artistic tradition by presenting artists who, although modern, still worked figuratively. One year after this show, in 1914, Zoltán Farkas's book *A biedermeier* was published, in which the author made use of findings and concepts from German Biedermeier research.[2] Farkas considered the Biedermeier a passing trend and lifestyle, and argued that there had never been such a thing as a "Hungarian Biedermeier," as the lack of a bourgeoisie and of a certain emotional reserve had prevented a true reception of the style in Hungary. What was generally considered as Biedermeier, he argued, was merely a fashion. These views were quite unusual at the time, but later became increasingly popular.

A characteristic element of Hungarian art history publications of the time was the list of masters. The aim was to establish which painters could be counted as Hungarian artists.[3] With regard to the period discussed here, three categories emerged: The first included foreign-born artists who worked for Hungarian clients (such as Josef Kreutzinger [1757–1829], and, later, Johann Peter Krafft [1780–1856] and Johann Nepomuk Ender). Some of these artists lived permanently in Hungary, for example, Friedrich Johann Gottlieb Lieder (1780–1859) or travelled there, such as Thomas Ender

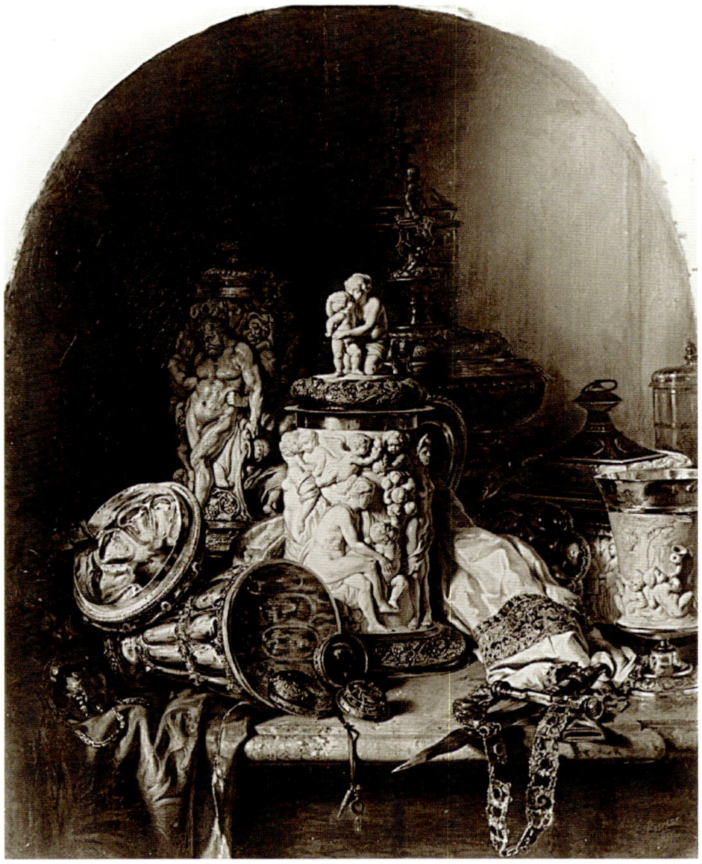

Fig. 1: **József Borsos**, *Díszedény-csendélet* (*Still Life with Decorative Vessels*), 1850
Museum of Fine Arts – Hungarian National Gallery, photo archive

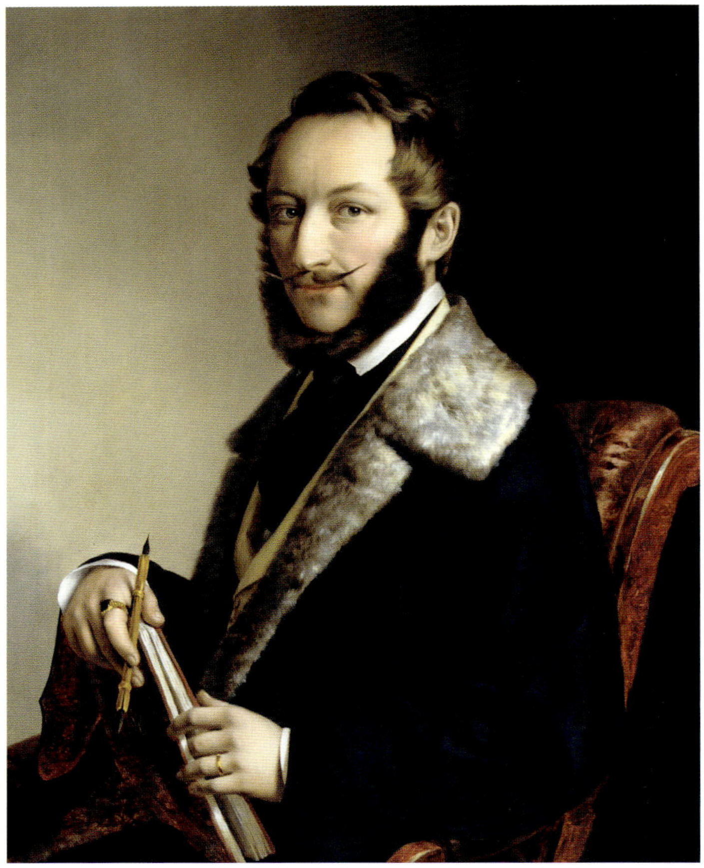

Fig. 2: **Miklós Barabás**, Önarckép / *Self-Portrait*, 1841
Museum of Fine Arts – Hungarian National Gallery, Budapest

(1793–1875). Indeed, some had settled in Hungary to the extent of being active participants in the country's cultural life, such as Johann Donat (1744–1830) and Jacopo Marastoni (1804–1850) from Venice. The second category included artists who were of Hungarian origin, but worked primarily abroad: Károly Markó the Elder, Károly Brocky (1808–1866), and József Borsos. Finally, the third category comprised Hungarian artists who worked in Hungary: Miklós Barabás, Henrik Weber (1818–1866), Károly Sterio (1822–1862), and Alajos Györgyi Giergl (1821–1863). While this categorization does, of course, still remain valid today, detailed analysis has raised numerous questions, since the art world of the time did not orient itself along the borders of the subsequent nation states. A painter could therefore be active in several locations at once. A good example of this is Borsos, mentioned above, who was born in the western Hungarian town of Veszprém and then lived and studied in Vienna. After returning home in 1861, he worked as a photographer and later as an innkeeper. He regularly sent paintings to the exhibitions of the Pesti Műegylet (Pest Art Society) while living in Vienna, where one of his works (*Still Life with Decorative Vessels*) was purchased by Emperor Franz Joseph I at the Vienna Kunstverein in 1850 (fig. 1). Following the demise of the Austro-Hungarian Monarchy, this work arrived back in Hungary under the 1932 Austro-Hungarian agreement.[4] Another painting, which had also been purchased by the Emperor, still remains in the possession of the Austrian state: *View from Venice (Palazzo Grassi)* a work created in 1846 by August Theodor Schoefft, a Hungarian painter who was less popular with Hungarian critics in the early twentieth century.[5]

Identification phase: 1920–1945

In the second phase, the objective was to identify Hungarian characteristics on the basis of general trends.

The trauma after the Treaty of Trianon, which allocated two-thirds of the territory of Hungary to surrounding states in 1920, led to increased nationalism, which also became noticeable in scholarly works.[6] Most academic contributions defined Biedermeier as the period up to the end of the Hungarian Revolution of 1848–49 or until the Austro-Hungarian Compromise of 1867, and presented it as a time in which the population, exhausted by the Napoleonic Wars, turned toward the material aspects of life. For the average Hungarian, who was increasingly leaning toward right-wing ideologies and resisting modern, progressive trends, it was easy to identify with the Biedermeier's yearning for peace and domesticity. The Biedermeier experienced a renaissance in the form of a "neo-Biedermeier"—namely, in the paintings displayed at the Budapest Hall of Art, the exhibition space favored by mainstream artists. It was no coincidence that it was in this very institution that the highly successful second Biedermeier exhibition took place in 1937.[7] The number of academic works on Biedermeier also increased around that time. In his book about Hungarian Biedermeier painting, Jenő Kopp identified as the specifically Hungarian characteristics, on the one hand, the Neoclassicist tradition of rural portrait painters with little formal training and, on the other hand, the highly educated artists who had emigrated and did not fit in with the backward conditions in Hungary, but also had no place in Italian, English, or Viennese art historiography. According to Kopp, Hungarian painting, which was seen as the painterly equivalent to the language reform, was more or less rooted between these two poles. Its foundations were laid by Miklós Barabás (fig. 2).[8]

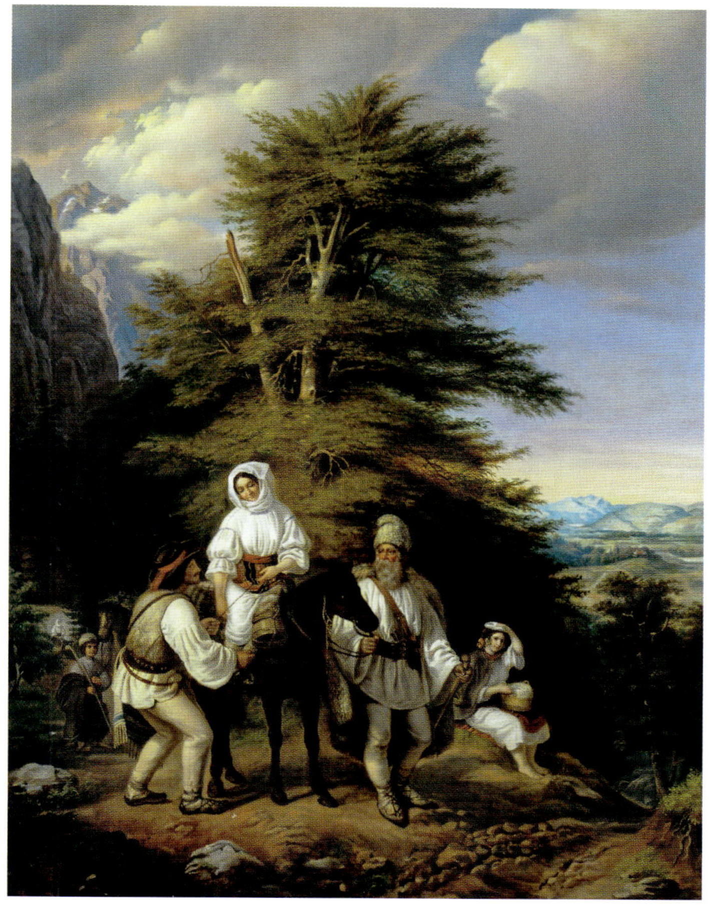

Fig. 3: **Miklós Barabás**, *Vásárra menő roman család (Romanian Family Going to the Fair)*, 1843/44
Museum of Fine Arts – Hungarian National Gallery, Budapest

In the interwar period, numerous studies were carried out and many artists' biographies published. For most authors it was important to accentuate that elusive "Hungarian character." Jenő Kopp's objective in his essay on József Borsos was "to discover in him the threads that, with the immutable strength of a racial bond, make his art truly Hungarian."[9] Along these lines, the traits of a national character in Borsos's work, in comparison to the work of Viennese artists, were his temperament and his strong use of color. Likewise, in 1937, Károly Sterio was described as a true Hungarian artist although he was born into an immigrated Greek family and had studied abroad.[10]

A more precise analyst of national character was the art historian Károly Lyka, who, between 1922 and 1956, published a series on Hungarian art, based on Hungarian sources.[11] The period in question is addressed in the publication *A táblabíró világ művészete (Art of the High Court Judges)*.[12] Lyka used this oft-quoted, though never really widely used term instead of "Biedermeier," which was commonly used in the media. For Hungarians, the latter term had negative connotations and sounded strange and foreign: "[The word] casts a disrespectful shadow on an era that for us is not so much seen as representing a time of petty bourgeois in cotton night-caps, but also a time made glorious by great personalities such as Kőrösi Csoma, Széchenyi, Kossuth, Petőfi, Bolyai, and Semmelweis."[13] Nevertheless, the term "táblabíró" had almost entirely disappeared from the Hungarian language by the end of the twentieth century.[14]

Yet the process during which the expression "Biedermeier" was erased from Hungarian academic literature over the course of the second half of the century, did not begin with Lyka. In fact, it was the impact of Elek Petrovics, who was active as director of Budapest's Szépművészeti Múzeum (Museum of Fine Arts) between 1914 and 1935.[15] In his inaugural speech at the Hungarian Academy of Sciences in 1933, Petrovics referred to Biedermeier as "Viennese School" and "Bourgeois Realism."[16] Therein lies the root of the later development,

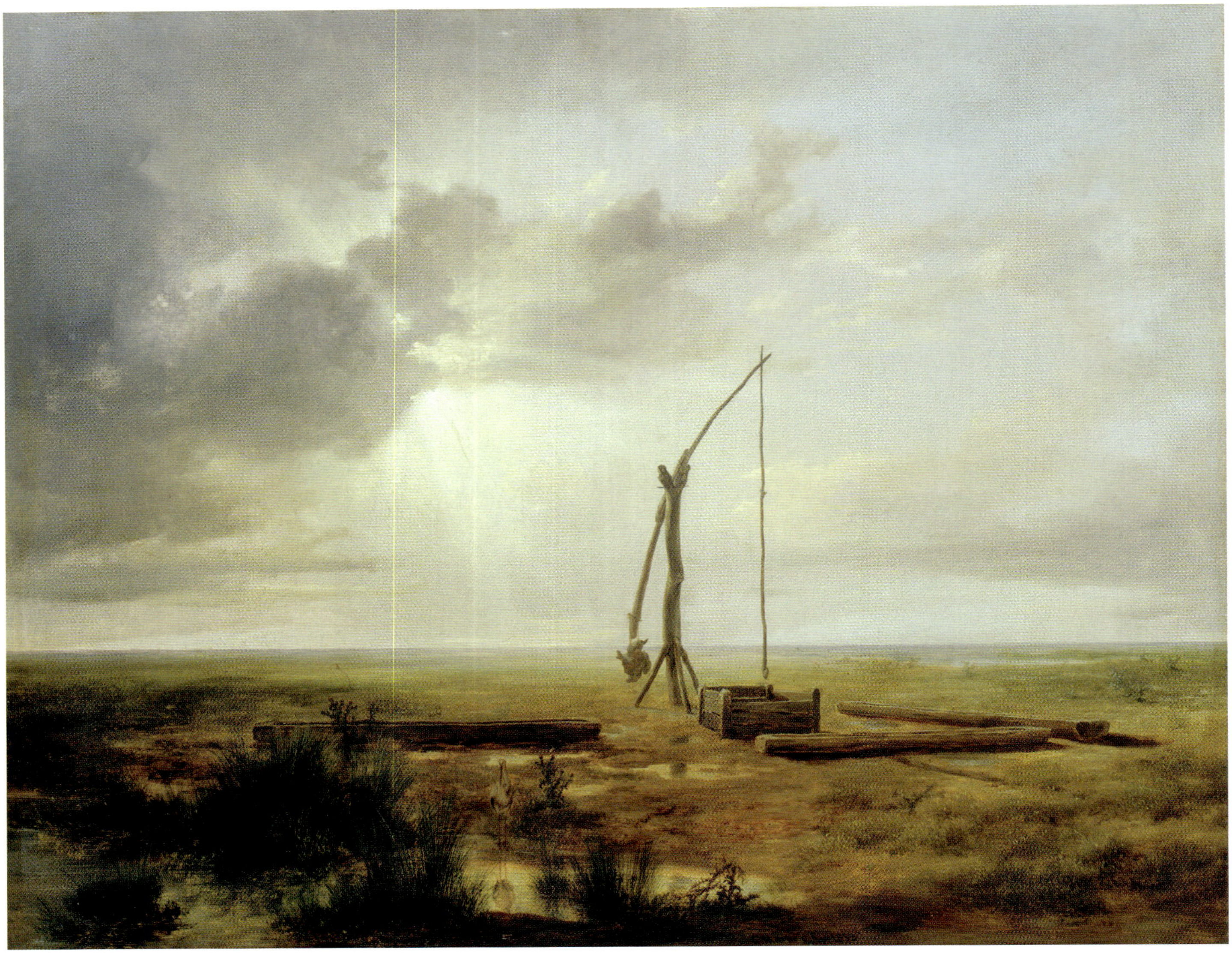

Fig. 4: **Károly Markó the Elder**, *Puszta*, 1853
Museum of Fine Arts – Hungarian National Gallery, Budapest

whereby the word Biedermeier was banished for quite some time from academic discourse and confined to the jargon of art dealers and critics. Petrovics defined the period as a distinctly transitional phase, in which something was only just emerging from a void. This point of view also remained firmly anchored later on. It is no coincidence that his successors, who organized the previously mentioned Biedermeier exhibition of 1937, were lacking in personal and professional integrity.[17]

Selection phase: 1945–1960

In the third phase, depending on the prevailing ideological and conceptual trends, only specific elements of Biedermeier were emphasized.

Hungary's post-war art-historical narrative neglected the Biedermeier. It was seen as a transitional period in which, although there were several high-quality painters working in Hungary, these were not actively involved in Hungarian art life. The term Biedermeier was henceforth long absent from academic literature. The attempt to distance oneself from the style favored by the state of the previous political era obviously played a role here, as did the Socialist ideology's antipathy toward the "bourgeois" style. In the 1950s, the themes of art history research were determined by the principles of a "progressive tradition" and Stalinist aesthetics. This is clearly evident in art historian Dénes Radocsay's foreword to Edit Hoffmann's posthumously published Barabás monograph,[18] in which the author either criticizes the

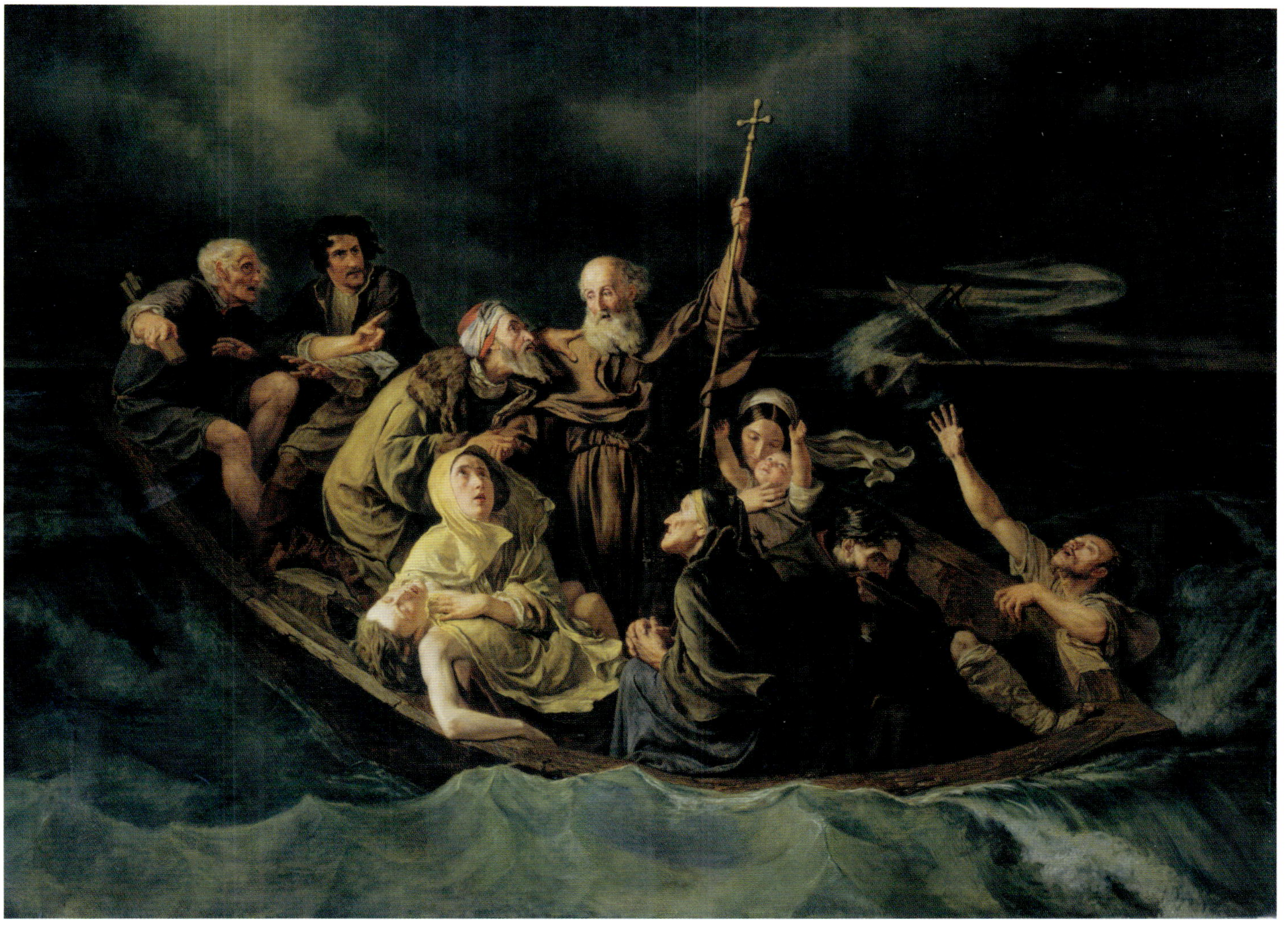

Fig. 5: **Mihály Zichy**, *Mentőcsónak* (*Lifeboat*), 1847
Museum of Fine Arts – Hungarian National Gallery, Budapest

book's content or attempts to justify why an essay written in the previous era should even be published at this time.

During the Stalinist era, the folkloristic elements of the Biedermeier provoked fascination and were widely accepted, as they were also in line with the aesthetics of the period. For this reason, special attention was paid to folk genre paintings, which were seen as early attempts at "Realism." An example of this is Miklós Barabás's painting *Vásárra menő roman család* (*Romanian Family Going to the Fair,* fig. 3).[19] Another theme that fitted well with the communist era's ideological trends was the struggle for independence. This included not just depictions of a contemporary event—these were created, too, yet rarely yielded truly original works[20]—but also symbolic paintings, often in the form of historical allegories, referring to the failure of the War of Independence. These many-figured folk or history paintings, romantic compositions on the tragic fate of the people, were already indicative of the next period in art. Yet, since art history after 1945 deemed this next period as the more important one, the art of the era preceding it was seen as a transitional phase, as the first stage in an evolutionary development, whose painters were considered precursors to the great artists that followed, such as Bertalan Székely and Viktor Madarász, among others.

Parallel to this, an important paradigm shift in Hungarian art historiography also had an impact. In his inaugural lecture of 1950, the art historian Lajos Fülep attempted to draw a distinct line between the concepts of "art in Hungary" and "Hungarian art."[21] After a critical examination of the art-historical works of the previous period, he distanced himself from the nationalist-chauvin-

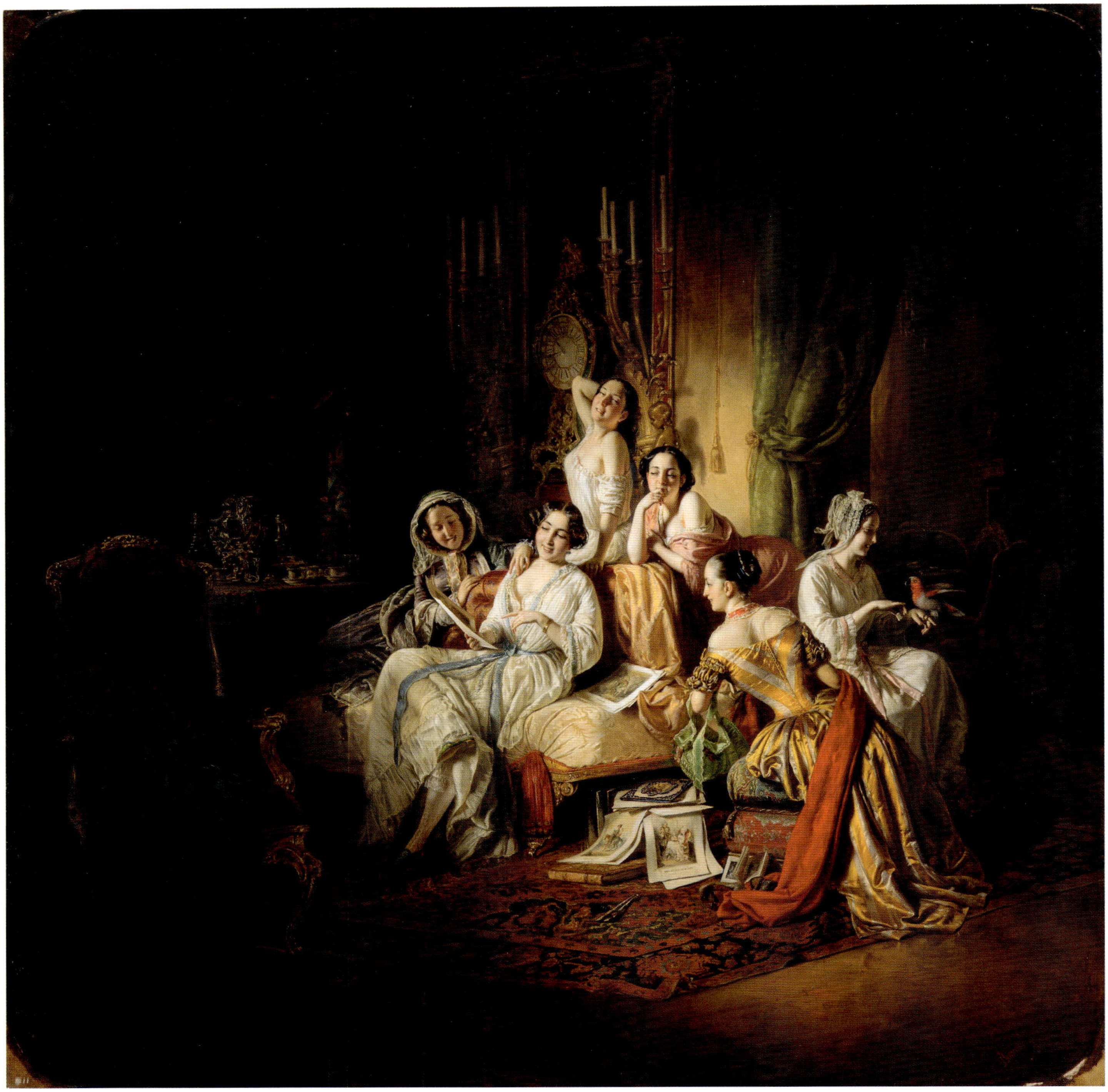

Fig. 6: **József Borsos**, *Lányok bál után* (*Girls after the Ball*), 1850
Museum of Fine Arts – Hungarian National Gallery, Budapest

istic interpretation of the contemporary concept of nation and defined future areas of research. His ideas became a guiding principle in later considerations about the classification of art-historical periods. Henceforth, the time before 1800 was generally referred to as "art in Hungary," the time after 1800 as "Hungarian art." This made it easier for Hungarian artists to join the central European art-history discourse. It must be made clear, however, that regarding the period under consideration the objective was still to identify the specifically Hungarian elements, rather than to examine developments that may have occurred in parallel with international trends. It is therefore hardly surprising that their investigation remained secondary.

Categorization phase: 1960–1990

In the fourth phase, as the system of art institutions in Hungary gained in strength, more in-depth research became possible.

From the 1960s onwards, an increasing number of academic publications appeared, partly due to the stabilization of the cultural institutions in Hungary. The Hungarian Academy of Sciences launched an eight-volume series of reference books on the arts. Unfortunately, the volume on the nineteenth century remains as yet unpublished. Nonetheless, illustrious authors produced several smaller summary works on the development of Hungarian art from its beginnings through to the present. In these works, reservations against the term "Biedermeier" remained predominant; new terms were introduced to describe the period: classicizing or bourgeois Romanticism; bourgeois, folkloristic, or romantic Realism. The ambiguity of these alternative terms is also reflected in the fact that the *Lexicon of Hungarian Art*, published around that time, provided a precise description of the relevant period and its artists under the term "Biedermeier," without even mentioning any of these other terms.[22] Naturally, there were always art historians who used the term quite happily, such as the author Endre Csatkai[23] in his work on the painter Sándor Kozina (plate p. 203). By contrast, in her work about the European art of the time, the art historian Anna Zádor simply classified the Austrian (and other central European) painters as Romantic artists.[24] This approach had already been championed in earlier times. For example, in 1911, Barabás was described as "the most renowned portraitist of the Romantic era," and Borsos as "a representative of the Viennese form of Romantic genre painting, the so-called Biedermeier genre."[25] This phenomenon, which is still evident today, can be regarded as a delayed effect of the art-historical debate of the pre-war era.

In the writings of the art historian Lajos Németh,[26] the term "Biedermeier" is used and defined as "a typically bourgeois or petit-bourgeois style composed of a blend of Neoclassicism and Romanticism." Németh nonetheless describes Barabás's paintings as a meeting of "tamed Neoclassicism, Romanticism, and bourgeois Sentimentalism" and counts Markós's landscape paintings among the artworks of "late Neoclassicism" or, in the case of those with Hungarian themes, even describes them as "striving toward a folkloristic Realism." A comparison of the painting *Puszta* by Károly Markó the Elder (fig. 4) and the stylistically and thematically related poem *Az alföld* (*The Plains*) written in 1844 by Sándor Petőfi, one of Hungary's most famous poets, makes it clear why a combination of the categories of "tamed Romanticism" and "Biedermeier" is more suitable for describing the two works in question. Both works understand the landscape of the great Hungarian plain as a symbol of national identity, the spatial embodiment of a longed-for idyll. Stylistically, however, they are no different from Biedermeier works of the neighboring countries.

In 1981, an exhibition entitled *Art in Hungary 1830–1870* opened at the Magyar Nemzeti Galéria (Hungarian National Gallery) in Budapest, in which the Biedermeier was no longer considered an introductory or transitional phase.[27] In the descriptions of the works, the term Biedermeier was used as a stylistic descriptor, without interpreting it further or extending its meaning to cover the entire period. The authors simply used the term as it was established in the art market. At any rate, the exhibition's focus was clearly not on stylistic issues. It was a major thematic show, offering a detailed overview of examples from abroad that enabled an important revision of earlier theories. On this occasion, Borsos's work *Az özvegy* (*The Widow*, plate p. 209) was compared to Austrian genre paintings, such as Peter Fendi's *The Sad Message* (1838, Wien Museum).

From the 1980s onward, a new horizon for research opened up in Central and Eastern Europe. Authors at home and abroad began to look beyond national borders. In the context of our discussion here, this first became apparent in a contribution by Katalin Sinkó,[28] who analyzed, among other works, the early masterpiece *Mentőcsónak* (*Lifeboat*, fig. 5) by Mihály Zichy (1827–1906), Ferdinand Georg Waldmüller's most famous Hungarian disciple. At first glance, the composition recalls Romantic shipwreck motifs from France. However, in contrast to the monumental French coverage of contemporary tragedies, this painting is a continuation of the traditional *Navicella* depictions with added psychological realism, as required of a Biedermeier genre painting. That is, the painting is only seemingly Romantic, but in fact is guided by the spirit of Austrian painting.[29]

Integration phase: from 1990

Finally, the fifth phase (which began with the regime change and is still ongoing) is characterized by the endeavor to place Hungarian art within a central European context.

Recognizable in Hungary since the 1990s is a gradual paradigm shift in the art-historical discourse. In place

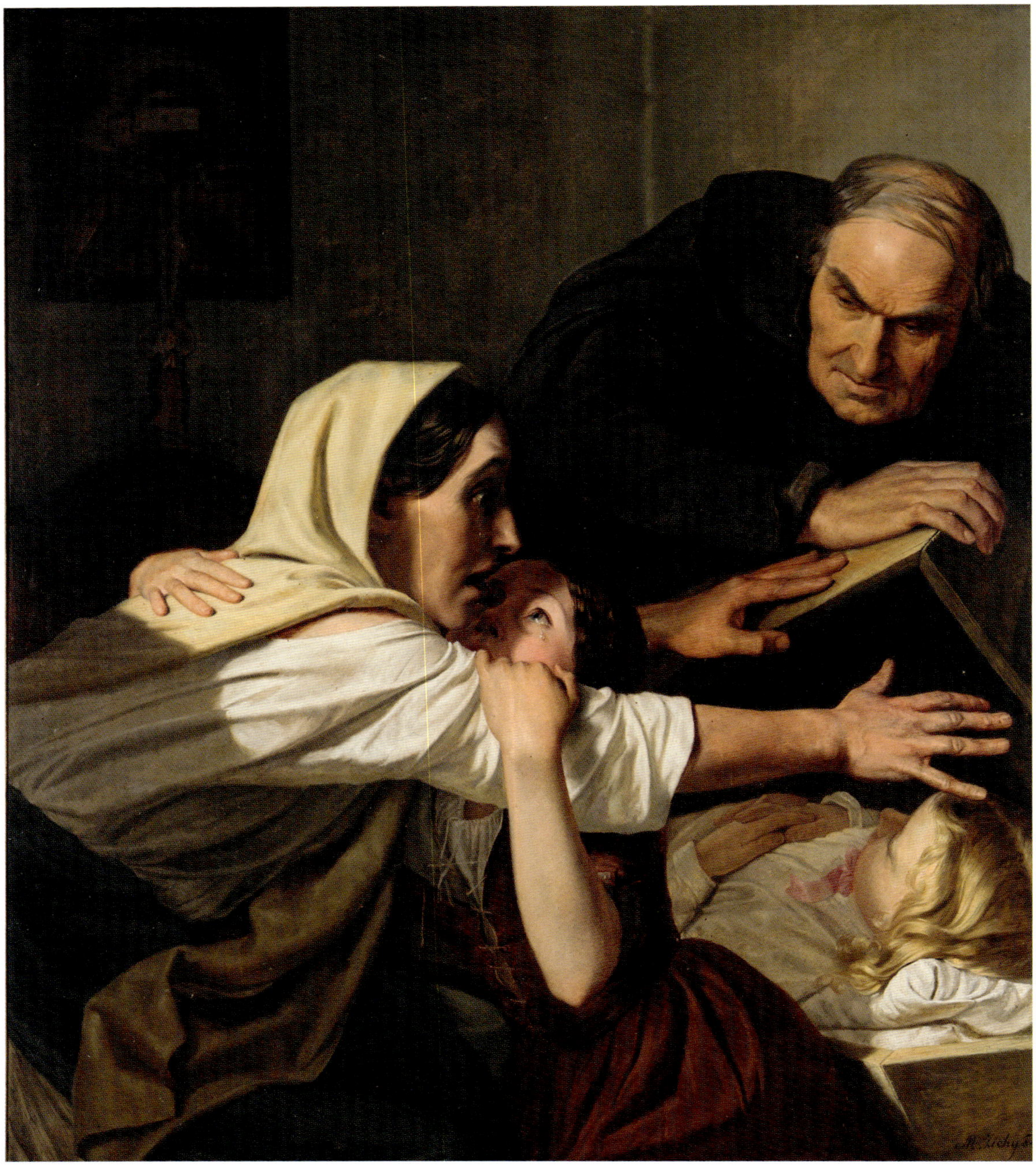

Fig. 7: **Mihály Zichy**, *A koporsólezárás* (*Sealing the Coffin*), 1846
Museum of Fine Arts – Hungarian National Gallery, Budapest

of the "Hungarian," an integrated central European art historiography began to emerge, above all with regard to the evaluation of medieval and contemporary art history, but also that of the nineteenth century. The Biedermeier era in an intellectual-history context was analyzed in depth in the volume *A biedermeier kora nálunk és Európában* (*The Biedermeier period at home and in Europe*), published by Helikon in 1991. Represented therein are the ideas of several foreign authors, as well as reviews from contemporary European art literature. The desire to treat the neighboring countries as a regional unit is highly evident in this publication.[30] The term "Biedermeier" surfaces here for the first time in an academic context relating to painting—in an article by Gabriella D. Szvoboda.

The same author wrote a monograph on the history of the Pest Art Society.[31] This institution, the first public exhibition space in Hungary, stood at the very beginning of the involvement of the general public in Hungarian fine arts, in the education of artists and audiences, and in the shaping of art criticism and aesthetic terminology. Although founded with the intention to support Hungarian art, the organization also caused an upsurge in the international art market in Pest. As a result of this double role, it was almost constantly subjected to vehement attacks and was not only accused of being

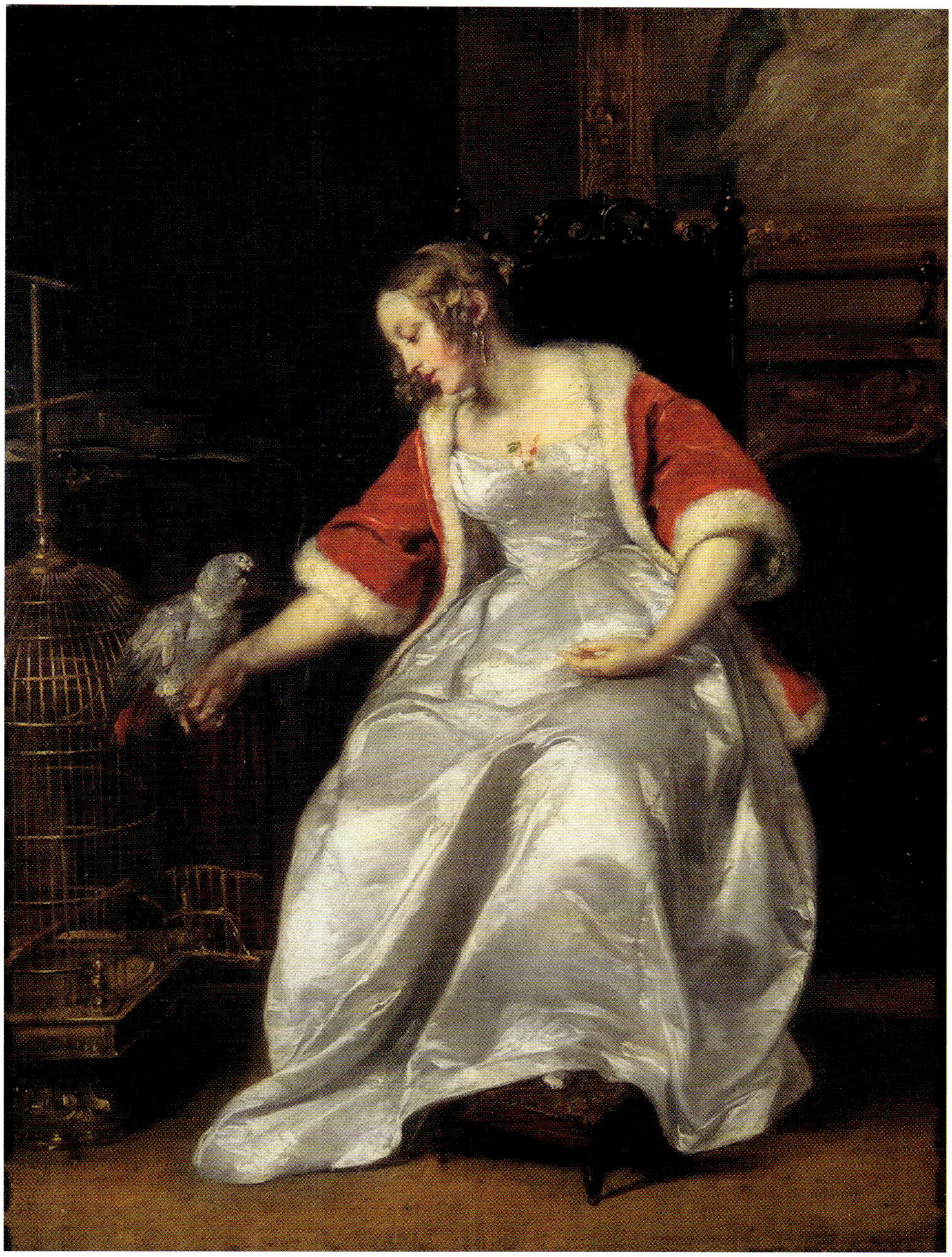

Fig. 8: **Károly Brocky**, *Szeret engem (Does He Love Me?)*, after 1847
Museum of Fine Arts – Hungarian National Gallery, Budapest

"anti-national" by contemporary art critics, but also neglected by later art-historical research.[32]

An interesting episode from the most recent Hungarian art history research was an exhibition in 2009 on the life and work of the Hungarian painter and photographer József Borsos,[33] who has already been mentioned several times. Compiling Borsos's relatively small oeuvre raised numerous style-related questions. The painter, who worked in Vienna and had always been classified as a Biedermeier artist, combined in his works a "tamed Romanticism" as well as Orientalism (see *Libanoni emír* [*Emir of Lebanon*, plate p. 163]), Second Rococo, and "Hollandism." This realization determined the framework of further research. *Lányok bál után* (*Girls after the Ball* fig. 6), possibly Borsos's most well-known painting, became the starting point for Nóra Veszprémi's essay in which she describes the Second Rococo characteristics of Biedermeier, based on contemporary sources, reviews, and recollections.[34] The same author also examined the relationship between Romanticism and Biedermeier.[35] With regard to the overarching themes and topics, outstanding dramatic works, such as Mihály Zichy's *A koporsólezárás* (*Sealing the Coffin*, fig. 7), demonstrate that Romanticism was a decisive element in the prevailing tastes of the time. The relationship to Dutch painting could also be examined in this context.

Here, starting points would be—along with parallels in society—dominant genres, the three-dimensional painting style, precise observation, or the use of color. Similarities between Brocky's *Szeret engem* (*Does He Love Me?*, fig. 8) and Gerard Ter Borch's paintings already attracted attention in 1938. However, a deeper examination of the phenomenon has not yet taken place.[36]

In my personal opinion, the broader interpretation of the term Biedermeier better suits Hungarian painting, as it includes the differences in quality from the 1830s until the end of the 1850s, and shows a uniformity of style that also characterizes central European works. It therefore seems justified to use the same uniform stylistic designation for all, i.e., the term Biedermeier, which places the international context more at the forefront.

Present concepts attempt to address these questions. The latest Hungarian publication on the topic already interprets the period in the "extended" meaning of the term Biedermeier, including the 1850s.[37] The aim of current research is to free the era of previously dominant prejudices and present a new perspective on Biedermeier, seeing it as a characterful international style, widely adopted throughout central Europe and with its center in Vienna. A style that, from 1840, the year of the first exhibition by the Pesti Műegylet, until the founding of the National Society of Hungarian Fine Arts in 1861, also exerted a strong influence on the Hungarian art world.

1 Richard Hamann, *Die deutsche Malerei im 19. Jahrhundert* (Leipzig, 1913).

2 Zoltán Farkas, *A biedermeier* (Budapest, 1914); Zoltán Farkas (1880–1969) was a far-sighted Hungarian publicist and supporter of the progressive arts in the first half of the twentieth century.

3 This was especially important as a definition of the "Hungarian school" became ever more pressing later on. See also Erzsébet Király/Enikő Róka/Nóra Veszprémi, eds., *XIX. Nemzet* és *művészet. Kép* és *Önkép*, exh. cat. Magyar Nemzeti Galéria, Budapest (Budapest, 2010), pp. 201–225; as contemporary source, see also Zsigmond Ormós, *Adatok a művészet történetéhez* (Pest, 1859), pp. 22–29.

4 György Szücs/Nóra Veszprémi, eds., *Borsos József festő* és *fotográfus (1821–1883)*, exh. cat. Magyar Nemzeti Galéria (Budapest, 2009), pp. 164–165, cat. no. 118.

5 Belvedere, Vienna, inv. no. 7783.

6 "Now that the present situation of Hungary forces us to list our national values, we turn to the past of Hungarian art with a keen attention and dedicate ourselves fully to detecting as many forgotten reminiscences as possible." Margit B. Baktay, *A biedermeier kor elfeledett festője Györgyi (Giergl) Alajos* (Budapest, 1938), p. 1.

7 *Magyar biedermeier kiállítás*, Műcsarnok, Budapest 1937/38, organized by Dénes Csánky, László Balázs Piri, and János Héjjas. (See note 17.)

8 Jenő Kopp, *A magyar biedermeier festészet* (Budapest, 1943); Jenő Kopp (1900–1977) was a staff member and later director of Fővárosi Képtár (Municipal Gallery, Budapest). Under his leadership, Fővárosi Képtár evolved into the largest collection of Hungarian artworks. In 1957 this was integrated into the collection of the Magyar Nemzeti Galéria (Hungarian National Gallery). During the communist era, Kopp's career stalled due to political reasons.

9 Jenő Kopp, *Borsos József* (Budapest, 1933), p. 3.

10 István Gothard, "Sterio Károly akadémiai festőművész élete és művei," in *Vasi Szemle*, February 1, 1937, p. 67, 71.

11 From 1906 to 1947, Károly Lyka (1869–1965) wrote the entries about Hungary in Thieme–Becker's *Allgemeines Lexikon der Bildenden Künstler (General Dictionary of Artists from Antiquity to the Present)*. The journalist and art historian Lyka, who initially wanted to become a painter, became acquainted with the circle around the Hungarian painter Simon Hollósy in Munich in 1887. He later became involved in the artists' colony and school in Nagybánya (today's Baia Mare in Romania), the cradle of modern Hungarian painting.

12 The judges of the royal high court were elected by the counties of Hungary in reward for their commitment to community affairs.

13 Károly Lyka, *A táblabíró világ művészete* (Budapest, 1922), p. 7.

14 With the exception of a few authors who still use the term out of respect for Lyka.

15 Elek Petrovics (1873–1945) was the director of Budapest's Szépművészeti Múzeum and, as such, was held in high esteem. Thanks to his far-sightedness and his close ties with modern artists and wealthy art collectors, the museum' collection was much expanded under his leadership.

16 Elek Petrovics, *Jegyzetek művészetünk történetéhez a XIX. század első felében* (Budapest, 1933).

17 Dénes Csánky (1885–1972) succeeded Petrovics as director of the Szépművészeti Múzeum in 1935, after his predecessor was forced into early retirement, despite the outrage of artists and the public. In 1944, as government commissioner, Csánky appropriated artworks from Jewish owners. After the war he lived in Brazil. László Balázs Piri (1908–1993) was a right-wing radical who published in Nazi magazines. After the war he lived in Peru. János Héjjas (1906–2001), graphic artist and art historian, participated in the war as a Hussar officer and then emigrated to the West.

18 Dénes Radocsay, "Bevezetés," in Edit Hoffmann, *Barabás Miklós* (Budapest, 1950), pp. 5–9; Edit Hoffmann (1888–1945) was an art historian and museologist specializing in prints, illuminated codices, and nineteenth-century Hungarian art. At the start of his career, Dénes Radocsay (1918–1974) focused on nineteenth-century art and contemporary critique, and later wrote notable works on the art of the Late Middle Ages.

19 The painting was exhibited at the Kunstverein in 1844 and also in Pest in 1845. Contemporary audiences there found it easy to identify with the depiction, even though the subjects portrayed were not dressed in Hungarian national costumes—as reported by local newspapers—but depict a "Romanian family." The painting was later donated to the National Museum's Painting Gallery by a marksmen's club.

20 See Lajos Vayer, "A magyar művészet 1848/49-ben," in *Szabad Művészet*, 2nd ed., no. 3 (1948), pp. 65–69.

21 Lajos Fülep, *A magyar művészettörténet feladata*, 1950, inaugural lecture at the Academy of Sciences (Budapest, 1951) (English translation: https://arthistoriography.files.wordpress.com/2014/11/veszprc3a9mi-trans-fulep.pdf [accessed on August 20, 2016]).

22 István Genthon/Anna Zádor (eds.), *Művészeti lexikon*, 4 vols. (Budapest, 1965–1968).

23 Endre Csatkai, "Kozina Sándor, elfeledett magyar, biedermeier festő (1808–1873)," in *Művészettörténeti* Értesítő, 19th ed., no. 1 (1970), pp. 24–40. The art historian Endre Csatkai (1896–1970) studied the monuments, music, and cultural life of the city of Sopron and its surroundings in northwestern Hungary. Before World War II, he was researching the estate—unfortunately later destroyed—of the forgotten painter Sándor Kozina from Felsőpulya (today Oberpullendorf, Austria).

24 Anna Zádor, *Klasszicizmus* és *romantika* (Budapest, 1976), p. 273–281. The influential art historian Anna Zádor (1904–1995) taught art history at Budapest University and focused above all on the history of (Neoclassicist) architecture.

25 Simon Meller, "A magyar művészet kialakulása a XIX. század első felében," in *Művészet*, 10th ed., no. 4 (1911), pp. 174–186.

26 Lajos Németh, "Magyar képzőművészet a 19. század derekán," in Nóra Aradi (ed.), *A művészet története Magyarországon a Honfoglalástól napjainkig* (Budapest, 1983), p. 336. The art historian Lajos Németh (1929–1991) was known above all as a scholar of art theory and of the Hungarian masters of the twentieth century (e.g., Tivadar Csontváry Kosztka, Béla Kondor, and János Nagy Balogh).

27 A designation of the period was simply avoided. The exhibition, which was accompanied by a book, was preceded by endless periodization debates, starting as far back as the 1960.

28 Katalin Sinkó (1941–2013) was the first authority in Hungary, still uncontested today, whose academic interest was devoted from the outset to the art of the nineteenth century. In her comprehensive work, she examined cultural phenomena in close relation to each other, keeping an open mind and adopting a multidisciplinary approach.

29 Katalin Sinkó, "Ideálkép, portré, életkép," in *Ars Hungarica,* 15th ed., no. 1 (1987), pp. 53–54; on the same painting, see also Petrovics 1933 (see note 16), p. 22.

30 The literary historian Béla Zolnai had also attempted this in his writings. His volume about the Hungarian Biedermeier (*A magyar biedermeier*) was published in 1940, but was subsequently banned and reissued in 1993.

31 Gabriella Szvoboda Dománszky, *A Pesti Műegylet története. A képzőművészeti nyilvánosság kezdetei a XIX. században Pest-Budán*, Miskolc (2007).

32 The Műegylet was subject to frequent attacks from the national-liberal newspaper *Pesti Hírlap* (founded by Hungary's great political reformer Lajos Kossuth). But the organization was also not acknowledged in the later art-historical canon. It does not even feature in the list of Hungarian art institutions in the appendix of Ernő Marosi's comprehensive work. Cf. "A magyar művészettörténet történetének kronológiai vázlata. Művek és intézmények," in Ernő Marosi, ed., *A magyar művészettörténet-írás programjai* (Budapest, 1999), pp. 381–386.

33 Szücs/Veszprémi 2009 (see note 4).

34 Nóra Veszprémi, "The Emptiness behind the Mask: The Second Rococo in Painting in Austria and Hungary," in *The Art Bulletin*, 96th ed., no. 4 (2014), pp. 441–462.

35 Nóra Veszprémi, *Fölfújt pipere* és *költői mámor. Romantika* és *művészeti közízlés a reformkori Magyarországon* (Budapest, 2015).

36 János Héjjas, "A magyar biedermeier-kor művészete," in *Magyar Művészet*, 14th ed., no. 1 (1938), p. 22.

37 Gabriella Szvoboda Dománszky, *Magyar Biedermeier* (Budapest, 2014).

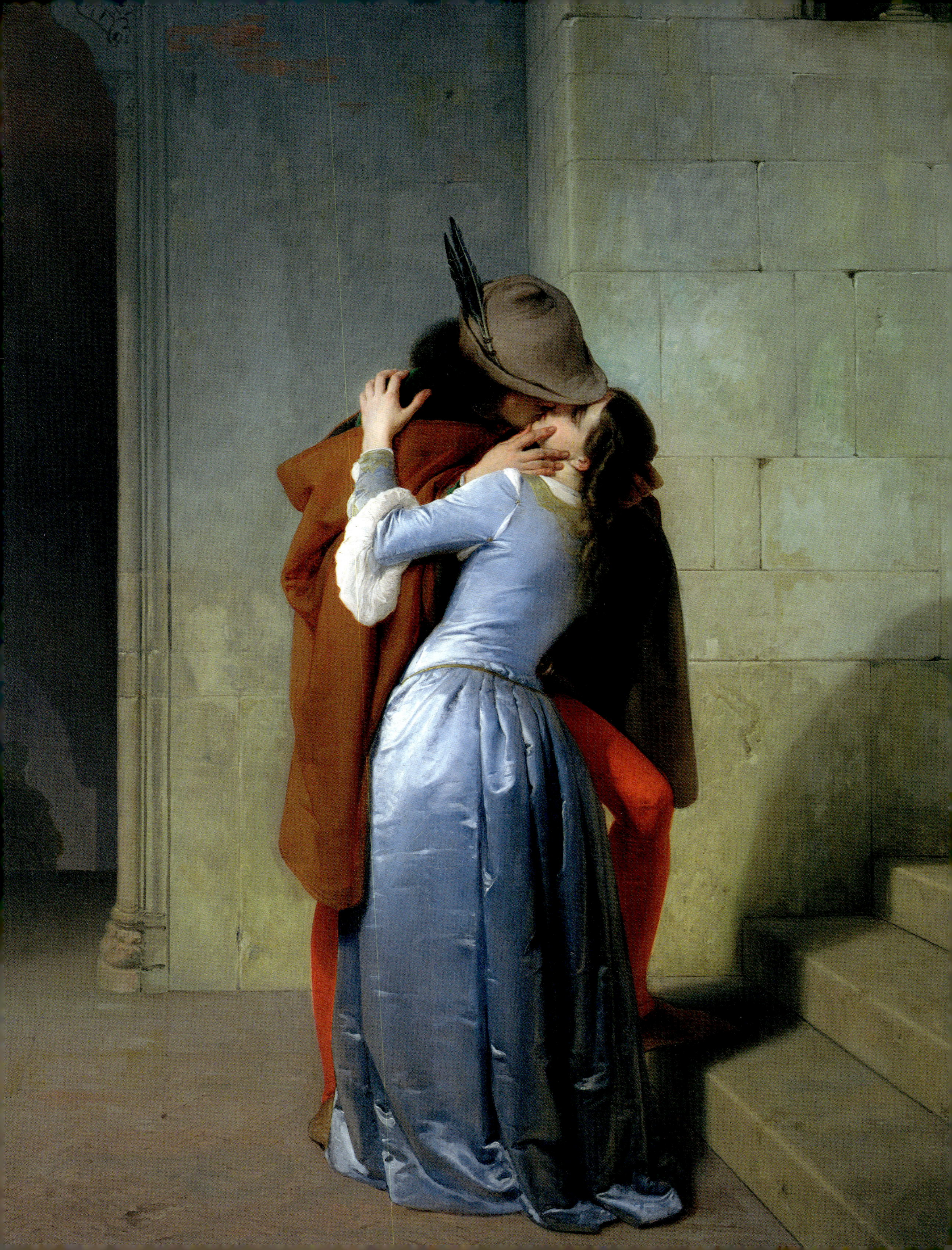

PAINTING IN THE KINGDOM OF LOMBARDY-VENETIA 1820–1860 THE LONG PERIOD OF ROMANTICISM

Fernando Mazzocca

Francesco Hayez[1] was the undisputed leading light in Italy's Romantic movement. He greatly influenced the development of painting during the period of restoration in northeastern Italy, specifically in the regions of Lombardy and Venetia, which at that time were one kingdom under Austrian rule. Two of his most famous paintings marked the beginning and end of this long era in art history. The first was *Pietro Rossi prigioniero degli Scaligeri* (Pinacoteca di Brera, Milan),[2] which in 1820 was sent from Venice to Milan, where it was exhibited with great success at the Accademia di Belle Arti di Brera. The last was *Il bacio* (fig. 1), which was presented at a special exhibition organized in Milan in 1859 to mark the victorious arrival of the troops of Victor Emmanuel II and Napoleon III. This momentous event marked Italy's liberation from foreign rule and its birth as an independent nation, which was officially proclaimed in 1861. Politically and culturally, the period from 1820 to 1860 thus coincides with the emergence of a national consciousness and identity. Art, and in particular the highly revered genre of history painting, made a major contribution to this process known as "Risorgimento."

The success of the painting *Pietro Rossi* marks a turning point, the conclusion of the glorious Neoclassical era when, especially during the Napoleonic period, Milan had achieved supremacy as an art center, placing it on a par with Rome.[3] This relatively small history painting alludes to the situation in modern Italy, rather than classical antiquity and mythology or allegories, which were the key subjects of Italy's two leading Neoclassical artists: Andrea Appiani (1754–1817), who created the decorations to glorify Napoleon at the Palazzo Reale,[4] and Giuseppe Bossi (1777–1815), a painter of monumental works inspired by the Greek tragedies and the great classics of Italian literature by Dante, Petrarch, and Ariosto. Hayez, by now the quintessential independent artist and proud of it, became the focus of a heated debate between Neoclassicists and Romantics that raged in the Milanese journal *Il Conciliatore*, coming to a head between 1818 and 1820 (while Hayez was painting *Pietro Rossi*). The debate was spearheaded by the Lombard Giuseppe Carpani, an official in the service of the Viennese court, and the intellectual Andrea Majer from Venice: the one defending the eternally valid "beautiful ideal" of Neoclassicism, the other championing a new beauty, inspired by more recent history and the cult of sensibility.[5]

Hayez had initiated a new style of history painting that was to apply to Romanticism as a whole. The content—inspired by recent history and therefore "national"—and the emotions of the characters, intimately observed and individualized, no longer emulated classical models but looked to the early Renaissance paintings by Giovanni Bellini, Carpaccio, and Giorgione, as well as Renaissance masters such as Titian, Jacopo Bassano, and Lorenzo Lotto. Following recent successes at the Brera exhibitions—where Hayez had presented two, now missing, paintings in 1821 and 1824[6]—the artist was finally to be confirmed as the leader of Italy's Romantic school. The pictures were inspired by *Il conte di Carmagnola*, the famous tragedy by Alessandro Manzoni (1785–1873), considered to mark the beginning of Romanticism in literature. They were also admired by Stendhal (the pen name of Marie-Henri Beyle, 1783–1842), who on various occasions—even in a text as important as *Salon de 1824*—described Hayez as "the foremost living painter," particularly because his "expression of the characters is vivid and profound: One senses this painter has a deep soul," and, moreover, declared that Hayez "teaches me something new about the passions he paints." Hayez had established himself as a painter of passion and love, that great Romantic subject, addressing a modern myth in his monumental painting *L'ultimo bacio di Giulietta e Romeo* (1823, Villa Carlotta, Tremezzo). This work was exhibited in 1823, the year Hayez finally moved from Venice to Milan. He left his home city at a time of grave

Fig. 1: Francesco Hayez, *Il bacio*, 1859
Pinacoteca di Brera, Milan

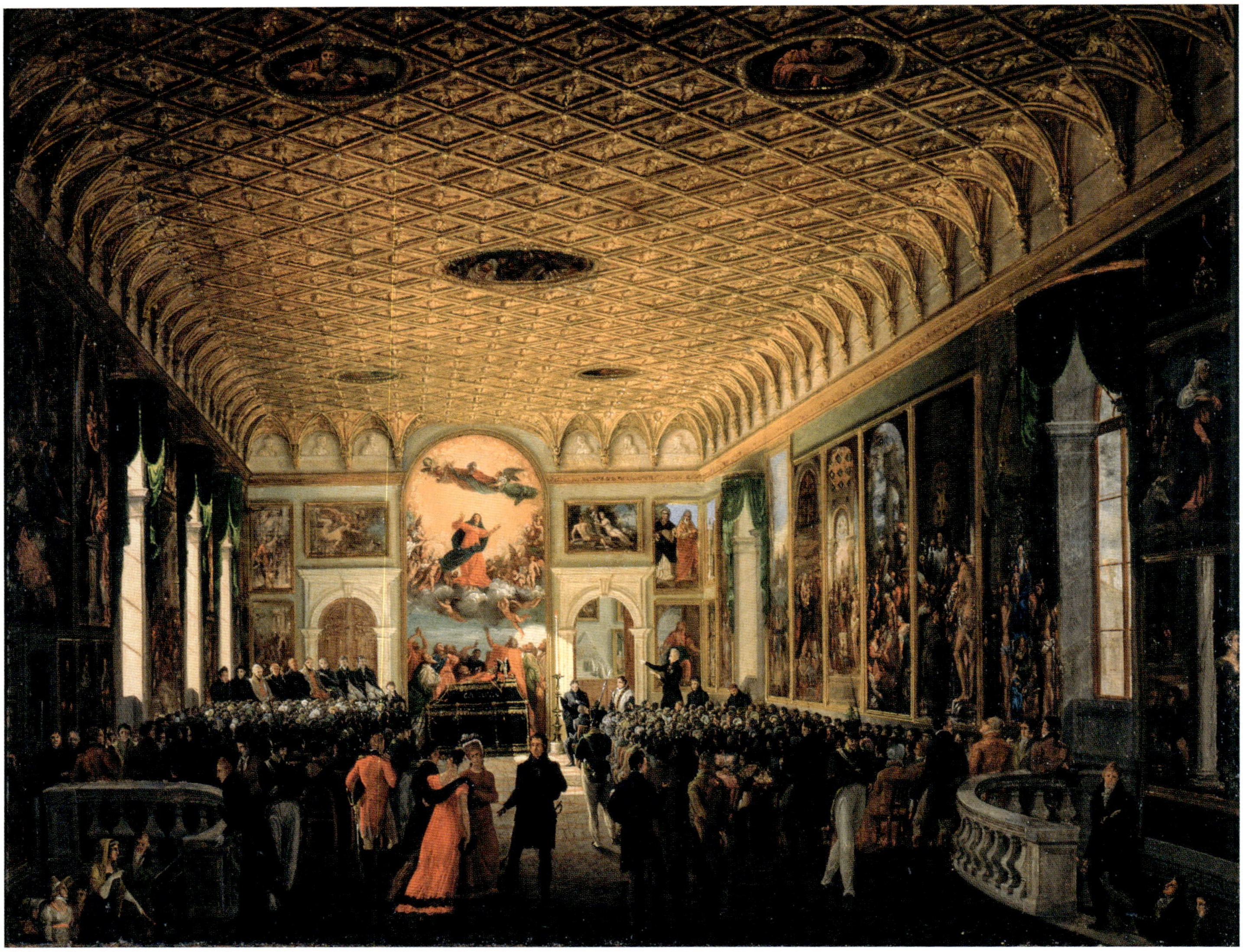

Fig. 2: **Giuseppe Borsato**, *Leopoldo Cicognara recita l'orazione funebre davanti alla salma di Canova all'Accademia di Venezia*, 1824
Museo d'Arte Moderna di Ca'Pesaro, Venice

economic and cultural decline, when it had already lost its supremacy as an art center and was living on past glories (celebrating Titian in particular, whose altarpiece *Santa Maria Assunta* had been transferred from the Frari Church to the Accademia) and the memory of Antonio Canova, who had died in 1822. This is demonstrated in a painting by Giuseppe Borsato (1771–1849) that commemorates the funeral ceremony in honor of the great sculptor (fig. 2). Borsato and Hayez were the first among a series of painters to work on murals in public buildings such as the Palazzo Reale and the palaces of the aristocracy located between Venice and Padua.[7]

Milan was entirely focused on modernity, not just in the arts, but also culturally and economically, and was in the process of becoming Italy's greatest center for contemporary art. It gradually secured a supremacy in the art world that would last an entire century.[8] The annual exhibitions staged by the Accademia di Belle Arti di Brera became a key and exclusive date, their importance continuously growing throughout the century.[9] Newspapers and specialist journals reported on the shows, informing an ever-growing, highly interested public about the artworks. These people were also avid readers of the new, popular Romantic literature and regular theatergoers, with the Scala undisputedly at the heart of this cultural world, albeit not only showing operas but also staging grand costume balls.

The Milan exhibitions also attracted great interest from abroad, including influential personalities such as

Ludwig Schorn who, from 1822, wrote annual reports in the Stuttgart-based journal *Kunst-Blatt*, or the previously mentioned Stendhal who was often in Milan. The press was involved in the fierce debates that divided the public into Neoclassical traditionalists and supporters of the new Romantic ideals. With their abundant and varied works, these exhibitions were the first port of call for collectors not just from Milan and Lombardy but also from other parts of Italy, as well as for frequent visitors from abroad.

The interest of the public, critics, and collectors was focused primarily on history painting.[10] Another important contender in this field, besides Hayez, was the older Bolognese painter Pelagio Palagi (1775–1860). Palagi had moved from Rome to Milan back in 1815[11] and was a great rival of the Venetian painter throughout the 1820s, before being called to the court of King Karl Albert in Turin in 1832.[12] Palagi reconstructed history, even more recent history, in the Neoclassical style using a cool, objective, and philological approach, whereas Hayez's painting was far less academic, a style that appeared more free, original, and captivating, especially as he moved away from paintings with a single hero to give ordinary people center stage. These include works such as *Pietro l'Eremita che predica la prima Crociata* (1827–1829, private collection) and *Gli abitanti di Parga che abbandonano la loro patria* (1826–1831, Musei Civici, Brescia), for which the critic Defendente Sacchi, the greatest supporter of the Romantic movement, coined the term *pittura civile* ("civil" painting). Thanks to Hayez and his supporters, history painting thus gained a political value and the past was depicted to serve as an example for the present. This was not only for the sake of patriots conspiring against the Austrian government, but also for a wider public receptive to the idea of a national identity, who regarded themselves as Italian rather than subjects of a foreign power. The exiled patriot Giuseppe Mazzini recognized the importance of history painting in general and Hayez in particular for the Risorgimento. He described the artist in a long essay about the "pittura moderna italiana," published in London in 1841, as a "democratic genius," the "great idealistic Italian painter of the nineteenth century," and "master of the school of history painting so essential for the concept of Italy as a nation."[13]

Gathering works from every region in the Kingdom of Lombardy-Venetia, the Brera exhibitions not only reflected the renewal and primacy of history painting

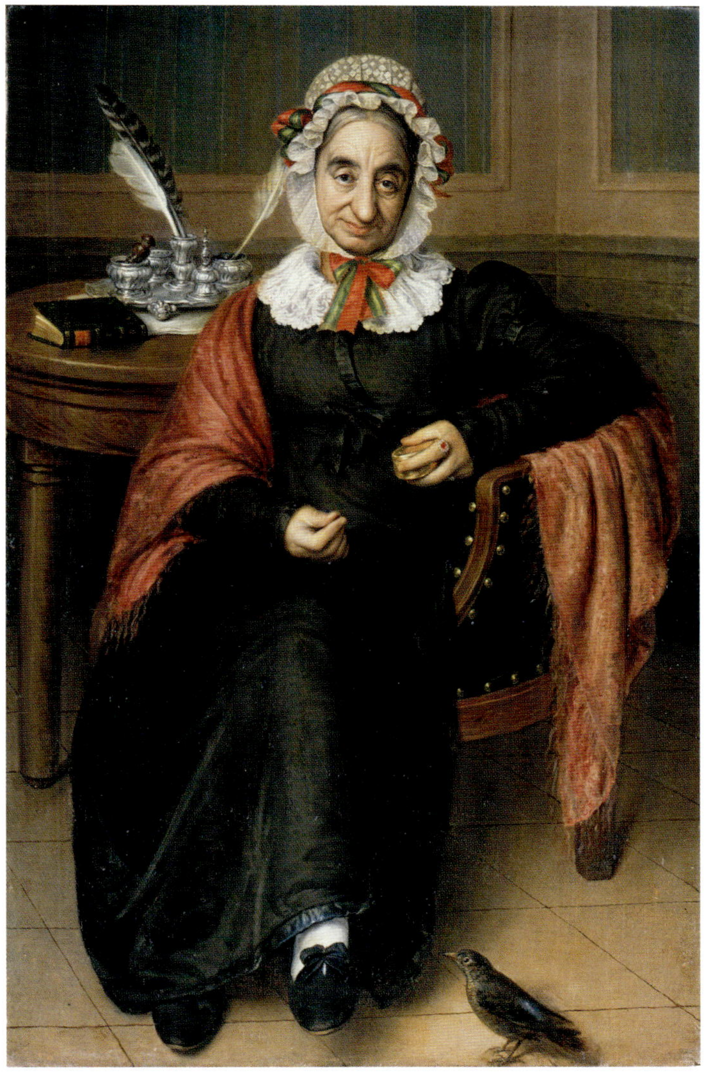

Fig. 3: **Giovanni Carnovali ("Il Piccio")**, *Contessa Anastasia Spini*, c. 1840
Accademia Carrara—Museo, Bergamo

but also a fundamental change in other genres, starting with portraiture. Collectors vied for the great history painters such as Hayez and Palagi but other specialists also held their own, including Giuseppe Molteni[14] and Eliseo Sala[15] from Milan and Placido Fabris (1802–1859),[16] Michelangelo Grigoletti,[17] and Giuseppe Tominz[18] from the region between Venice and Trieste.[19] We can see how the "casually private" portrait came to the fore, showing sitters in their typical surroundings to highlight character, social role, and family background. By contrast, for people of high social standing, the psychological study predominated, which tended to extol the noble spirit, sensibility, and intelligence of the sitter. Perhaps the most original portraits in this genre, characterized by a disconcerting honesty and experi-

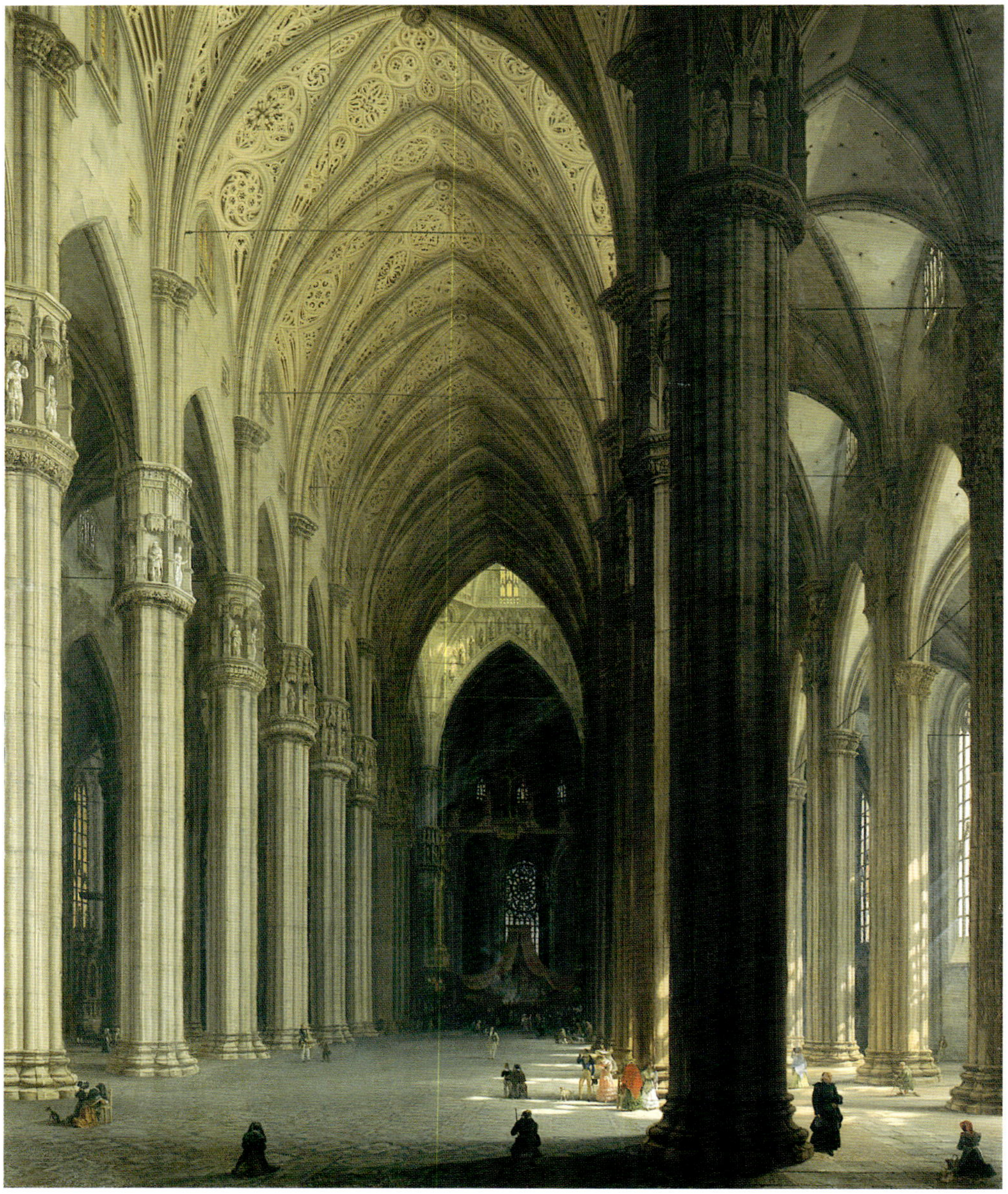

Fig. 4: **Giovanni Migliara**, *Interno del Duomo di Milano*, 1826
Fondazione Cariplo, Iniziative Patrimoniali S. p. A., Milan

Fig. 5: **Angelo Inganni**, *Veduta della piazza del Duomo di Milano dal Coperto dei Figini*, 1842
Private collection

mental style, were the depictions of nobility and intellectuals from the region between Cremona and Bergamo, painted by the brilliant and eccentric Giovanni Carnovali, known as "Il Piccio" (1804–1873, fig. 3).[20]

A true innovation was the emergence and development of the so-called "perspective painting," practiced by artists who had trained together with the set designers at the Accademia di Brera's acclaimed Scuola di Prospettiva.[21] With an optical precision on a par with Dutch seventeenth-century painting, they depicted the exteriors and especially the interiors of historic buildings that were the pride of Italian culture. Key examples include Milan Cathedral, Certosa di Pavia, and the Basilica di Sant'Ambrogio, but also buildings outside Lombardy, such as Orsanmichele in Florence, the Venetian churches Santa Maria Gloriosa dei Frari and Santi Giovanni e Paolo or, beyond Italy's borders, the impressive Gothic church of Brou in Bourg-en-Bresse and the Neo-Gothic Hautecombe Abbey with the tombs of the counts and dukes of Savoy. This style was the specialism of artists such as Giovanni Migliara[22] (1785–1837; fig. 4), Luigi Bisi (1814–1886), Angelo Inganni[23] (1807–1880; fig. 5), and Federico Moja (1802–1885), the latter also teaching it at the Accademia di Belle Arti in Venice, where he was professor of perspective from 1845. Their fascinating images of Italy's beautiful landmarks were sought-after by collectors from Italy and abroad. Bisi, professor of perspective at the Brera from 1851 to 1886 and contributor to exhibi-

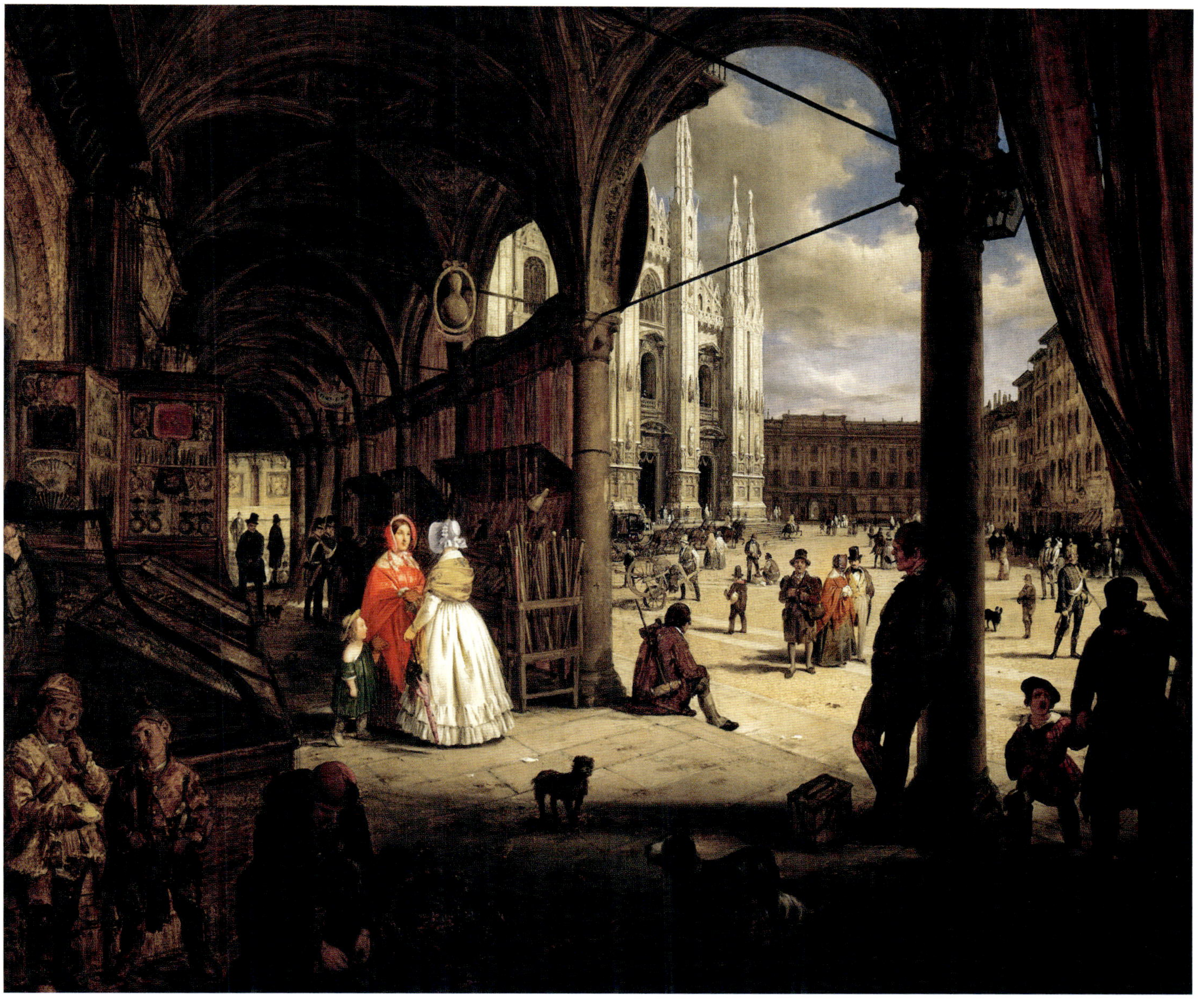

tions in Milan between 1831 and 1859, proved particularly ingenious here. A striking example is the vast interior of Milan Cathedral (fig. 6), commissioned by Emperor Ferdinand I of Austria as a reminder of the place where he had been crowned King of Lombardy-Venetia in 1838.

A further successful innovation was the "narrative landscape," providing a setting for real historical events, such as the duel of Barletta or the battle of Legnano, or literary subjects inspired by Ariosto and Shakespeare, as presented at the Brera exhibitions between 1831 and 1838 by the Turin-born aristocrat Massimo d'Azeglio.[24] Furthermore, in the 1830s and 1840s, a number of versatile artists—such as Giovanni Migliara, Giuseppe Canella (1788–1847), and especially Angelo Inganni from Brescia—created so-called "urban" paintings. These vividly captured the everyday life of the wealthier classes on the elegant streets in Milan's city center, but also showed the people on the banks of the canals, one of the city's characteristic features at the time, which was lost when the canals were covered over in the twentieth century. Locations such as these allowed painters to experiment with atmospheric effects, which they then included in their landscapes. Canella from Verona is a case in point, an artist who had lived for a long time in Spain, Holland, and Paris (1822–1831) before enjoying a successful career in Milan up until his death in 1847.[25] In contrast to landscapists such as Marco Gozzi (1759–1839) and Pietro Ronzoni (1781–1862) from Bergamo and Luigi Basiletti (1780–1860)

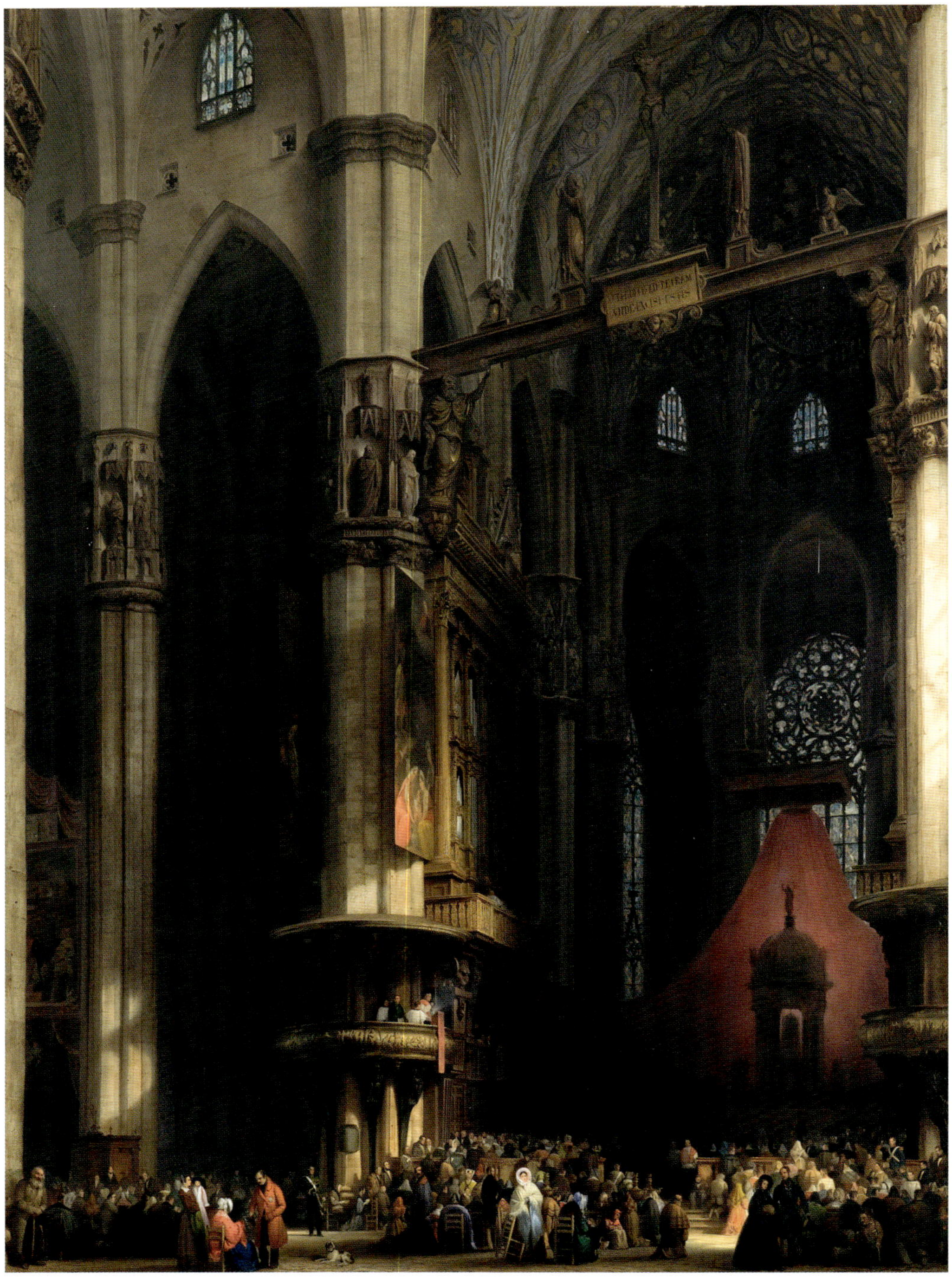

Fig. 6: **Luigi Bisi**, *Interno del Duomo di Milano*, 1840 Fondazione Cariplo, Iniziative Patrimoniali S. p. A., Milan

Fig. 7: **Lodovico Lipparini**, *La morte di Marco Botzaris*, 1841 Civico Museo Sartorio, Trieste

from Brescia, who still adhered to a rational and idealized approach, Canella was the greatest exponent of landscape as an expression of emotional states, a device also evident in the novel *I promessi sposi* (*The Betrothed*) by Manzoni. The influence of this book was crucial for the success of genre painting, which began with Giuseppe Molteni's famous *Spazzacamino assiderato dal freddo* (*Chimney Sweep*, 1837) for the Austrian Minister of the Interior, Count Franz Anton von Kolowrat-Liebsteinsky. Subsequently, artists painted evocative scenes from daily life, celebrating the family as a pillar of society, subjects that gradually guided public interest away from history painting. In the 1840s and 1850s, the greatest exponents of genre painting were Molteni, Inganni, and especially the brothers Domenico and Gerolamo (1825–1890) Induno. Inspired by the seventeenth- and eighteenth-century Lombard tradition, their works, with their emphasis on sensibility and emotion, reflected a softened Realism and expressive pathos.

The new appreciation also changed history painting. Some artists followed in Hayez's footsteps, for ex-

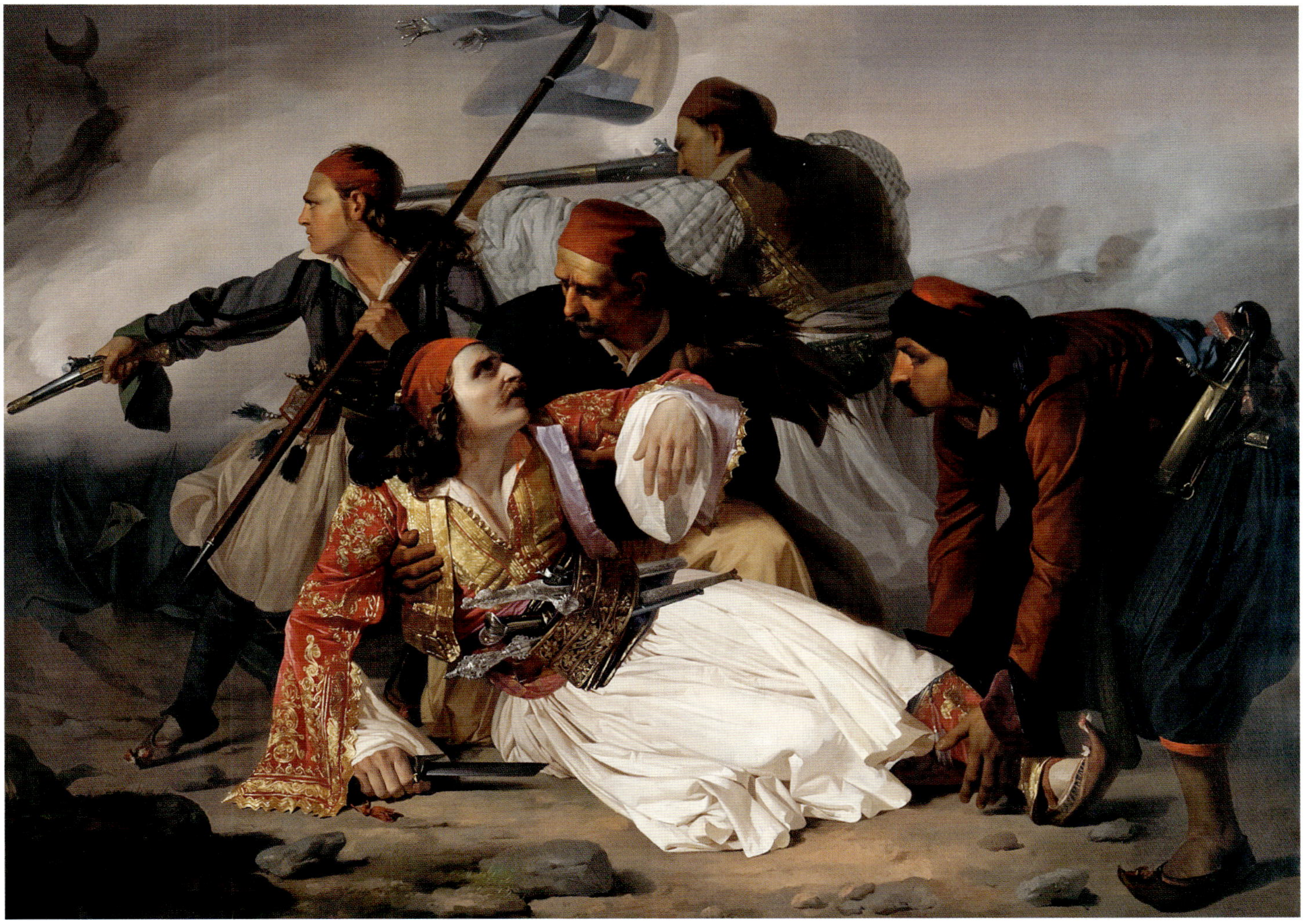

ample the Venetian painter Ludovico Lipparini (1802–1856), who throughout the 1840s concentrated on contemporary history and had great success depicting the Greek War of Independence (fig. 7). Other artists, especially younger painters, were enthralled by the painting *The Last Day of Pompeii* by the Russian artist Karl Pavlovich Bryullov (1830–1833, Russian Museum, St. Petersburg), exhibited in 1833 in Milan and probably one of the most famous paintings of the century. Cherubino Cornienti (1816–1860), Pasquale Massacra (1819–1849), and Federico Faruffini (1831–1869) from Pavia, Carlo Arienti (1801–1873) from Milan, and Pompeo Marino Molmenti from Venice all represented the new avant-garde in history painting and, in contrast to Hayez, experimented with different subject matter and a new formal language. Their paintings are characterized by a degree of Realism with an emphasis on expressing emotions, captured in rapid, more cursory brushwork.

Another innovative approach can be found in the landscapes and vedute by the Venetian artist Ippolito Caffi (1809–1866), who was also involved in the Risorgimento. The painter looked for new subject matter in episodes from history, for example the revolts in Rome and Venice in 1849, showing the cities under fire. He was a highly original artist who explored photography very early on and created vedute and panoramas with striking effects. He also displayed a predilection for atmospheric situations, especially nocturnal scenes that juxtaposed moonlight and artificial light, for example from the recently introduced gas lighting.

The sojourns of Molteni in Vienna (1836) and Hayez in Vienna and Munich (1837) provided an opportunity for comparison with Austrian painting, above all with Friedrich von Amerling who was so admired in Milan. The work of both artists developed significantly as a result of this experience. Molteni was influenced by the charms of Biedermeier (fig. 8), while Hayez tackled new subjects with an increasing formalism and eventu-

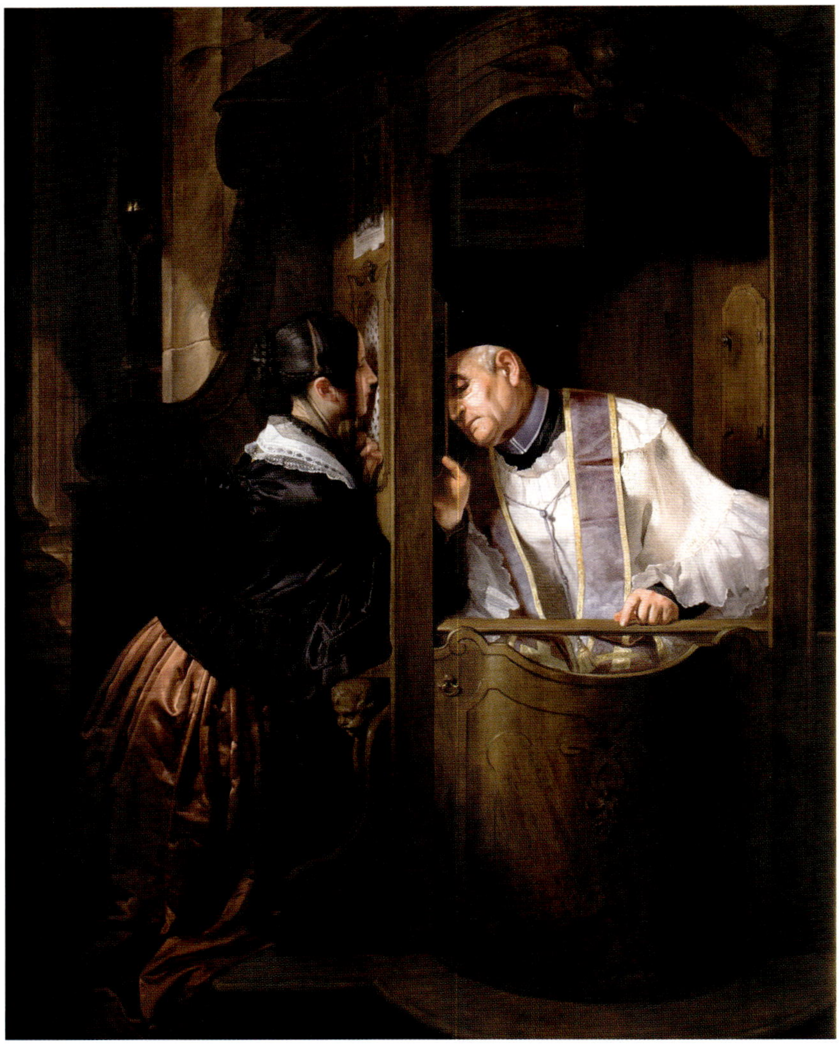

Fig. 8: **Giuseppe Molteni**, *La confessione*, 1838
Fondazione Cariplo, Iniziative Patrimoniali S. p. A., Milan

Fig. 9: **Francesco Hayez**, *I due Foscari* (*L'ultimo abboccamento di Jacopo Foscari con la propria famiglia*), 1838–1840
Fondazione Cariplo, Iniziative Patrimoniali S. p. A., Milan

ally, between the 1840s and 1850s, adopted novel approaches to history painting. He favored Venetian subjects, ranging from the outstanding work *I due Foscari* (*L'ultimo abboccamento di Jacopo Foscari con la propria famiglia*, painted in 1840 for Emperor Ferdinand I and much-admired in Vienna; fig. 9), to the unsettling depiction *Il consiglio alla vendetta* (1851, Liechtenstein. The Princely Collections, Vienna–Vaduz). This painting dates from the same time as *La meditazione* (fig. 10), a reflection of his outstanding ability to capture the female nude as well as an expression of his personal disappointment about contemporary politics after the Revolution of 1848/49.

In 1855, Hayez featured prominently at the Austrian Pavilion of the Paris World's Fair with four key history paintings and three portraits. Another significant contributor was Domenico Induno (fig. 11), who exhibited seven genre pictures. By contrast, Viennese artists were only represented with six paintings by the famous Ferdinand Georg Waldmüller. In fact, when compared with the Austrian painters such as Rudolf von Alt, Josef Führich (1800–1876), Leopold Kupelwieser (1796–1862), Heinrich Stohl (1826–1889), and Remy van Haanen (1812–1894), Italian artists were clearly in the majority. There was a large contingent from Lombardy in particular, uniting respected artists from the old and young generations: Luigi and Michele Bisi, Giuseppe Sogni, Molteni, Eliseo Sala, Inganni, Andrea Appiani jun., Arienti, Gerolamo Induno, Cornienti, Luigi Scrosati, and Eleuterio Pagliano. Venetia sent the work of far fewer artists but these included both the old Natale Schiavoni and the young Caffi.[26]

The contribution of Giuseppe Bertini (1825–1898) was also important. He added a new slant to history painting by emphasizing the patriotic importance of Dante. In 1845, his painting *L'Incontro di Dante con frate Ilario* won the major competition at the Accademia di Brera. Further glory followed in 1851, when he exhibited the monumental stained-glass window showing the *Triumph of Dante* (*Trionfo di Dante*) at the Great

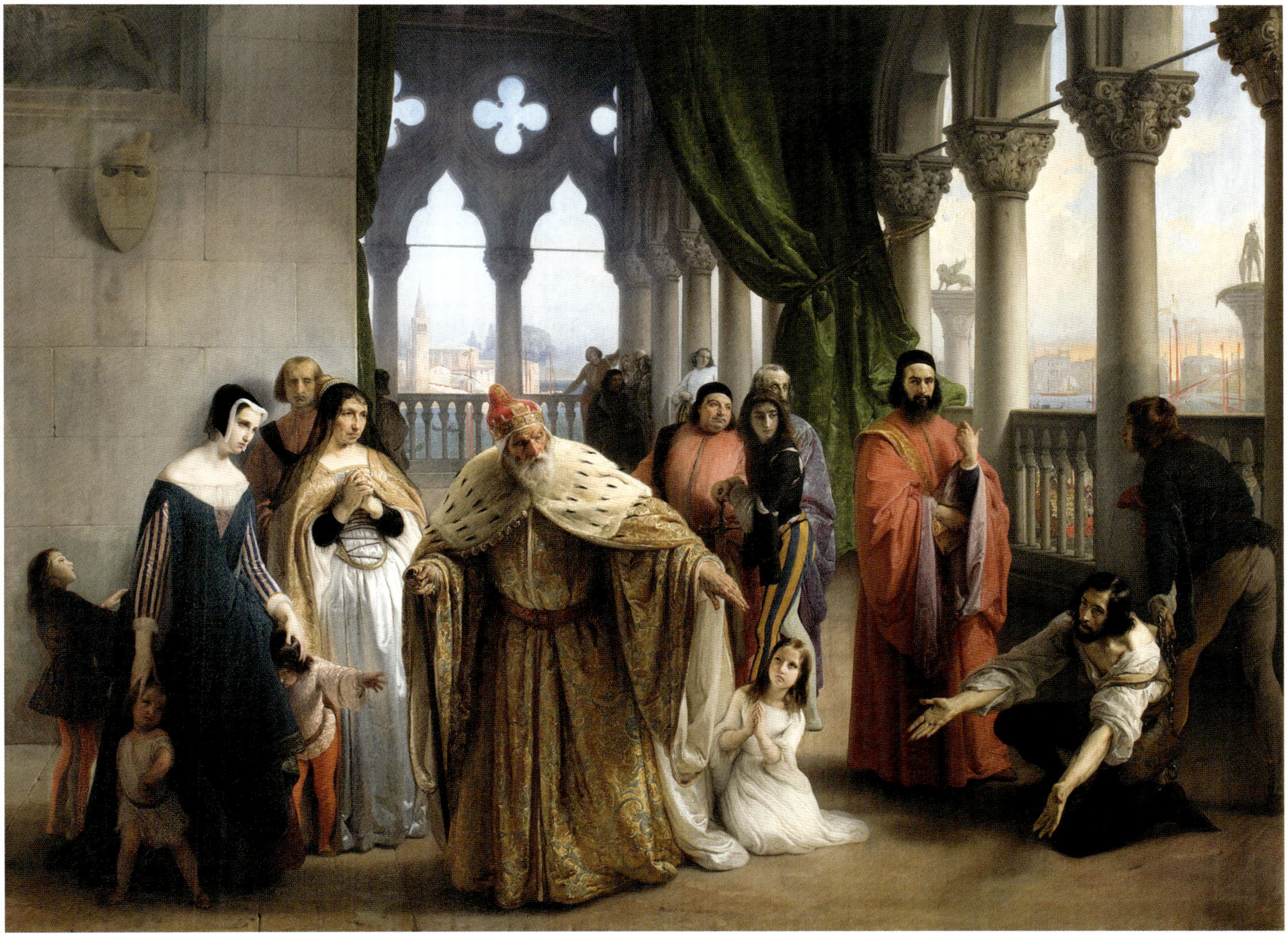

Exhibition in London. This was then housed at the Pinacoteca Ambrosiana and a smaller version was acquired for the studio of the great collector Gian Giacomo Poldi Pezzoli.[27] The main new trend in the 1850s, however, was the depiction of current events, such as the tragic destruction of the young Roman Republic by the French army in 1849 and the famous Crimean War (1853–1856). Both of these historical events were depicted by Gerolamo Induno, who was a volunteer in Rome and a war reporter for the Piedmontese army in the Crimea. He documented these episodes in exceptional paintings, for instance the moving depiction *Trasteverina uccisa da una bomba* (1850, Galleria Nazionale d'Arte Moderna, Rome) as well as many paintings of the Crimean War, including the imposing *Battaglia della Cernaja* of 1857 (Gallerie d'Italia, Milan). These works anticipate the battle paintings celebrating the victorious Second War of Independence and were star attractions at the Brera exhibitions from 1859. It was here that Hayez encapsulated the spirit of Romanticism in his important painting *Il bacio* and thus bolstered the hopes of this nascent nation.

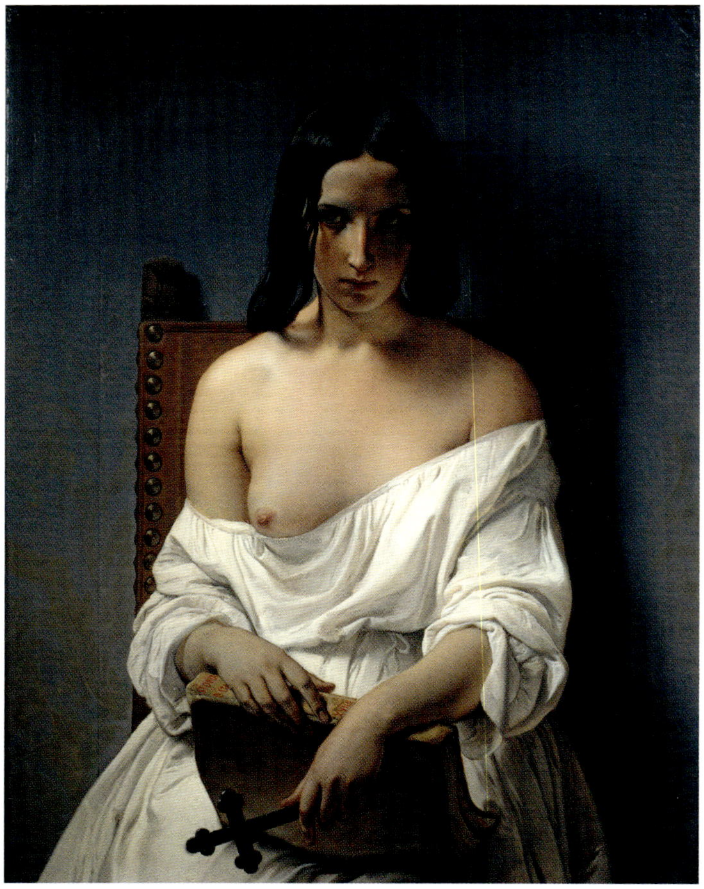

Fig. 10: **Francesco Hayez**, *La meditazione* (*L'Italia nel 1848*), 1851
Civica Galleria d'Arte Moderna, Verona

1 Maria Cristina Gozzoli/Fernando Mazzocca, eds., *Hayez*, exh. cat. Palazzo Reale and Palazzo di Brera, Milan (Milan, 1983); Fernando Mazzocca, *Francesco Hayez: Catalogo ragionato* (Milan, 1994); Fernando Mazzocca, ed., *Francesco Hayez*, exh. cat. Gallerie d'Italia, Milan (Cinisello Balsamo, 2015).

2 The long original title, intended to explain this little-known episode from the Renaissance to the audience can be rendered as follows: *Pietro Rossi, lord of Parma, stripped of his lands by the Scaligeri, lords of Verona, is asked, at the Castle of Pontremoli, which he was defending, to assume command of the Venetian army that is about to move against his enemies, and is tearfully beseeched by his wife and two daughters not to accept the mission.*

3 Enrico Colle/Fernando Mazzocca/Alessandro Morandotti, *Milano Neoclassica* (Milan, 2001); Carlo Capra/Franco Della Peruta/Fernando Mazzocca, eds., *Napoleone e la Repubblica Italiana*, exh. cat. Rotonda della Besana, Milan (Milan, 2002).

4 Francesco Leone, *Andrea Appiani, pittore di Napoleone: Vita, opere, documenti (1754–1817)* (Milan, 2015).

5 Fernando Mazzocca, ed., *Scritti d'arte del primo Ottocento* (Milan/Naples, 1998), pp. 74–77, 90–113.

6 The first version was acquired by the Milanese Count Francesco Arese, the second by Margrave Bethmann from Frankfurt.

7 Concerning the history of painting in Venetia during the period of restoration, see Sergio Marinelli/Giuseppe Mazzariol/Fernando Mazzocca, eds., *Il Veneto e l'Austria: Vita e cultura artistica nelle città venete 1814–1866*, exh. cat. Palazzo della Gran Guardia, Verona (Milan, 1989); Giuseppe Pavanello, ed., *La pittura nel Veneto: L'Ottocento* (Milan, 2002), 2 vols.

8 For a summary see Eleonora Bairati/Marco Rosci, eds., *Mostra dei Maestri di Brera (1776–1859)*, exh. cat. Palazzo della Permanente, Milan (Milan, 1975); Fernando Mazzocca, "La pittura dell'Ottocento in Lombardia," in *La pittura in Italia: L'Ottocento*, ed., Enrico Castelnuovo (Milan, 1991), vol. I, pp. 87–155; Fernando Mazzocca, "Il Romanticismo 1815–1848" and "Dal realismo alla Scapigliatura," in *Ottocento lombardo. Arti e decorazione* (Milan, 2006), pp. 133–79, 247–83; Fernando Mazzocca, "1800–1860: Da Napoleone all'Unità," in *Ottocento: Da Canova al Quarto Stato*, eds. Fernando Mazzocca/Maria Vittoria Marini Clarelli/Carlo Sisi, exh. cat. Scuderie del Quirinale, Rome (Milan, 2008), pp. 27–45.

9 Maria Cristina Gozzoli, "Contributi alle Esposizioni di Brera (1805–1859)," in *Istituzioni e strutture espositive in Italia: Secolo XIX. Milano, Torino* (= Quaderni del Seminario di Storia della critica d'arte, Scuola Normale Superiore, Pisa 1), (Pisa, 1981), pp. 3–60; Roberto Ferrari, ed., *"Vado a Brera." Artisti, opere, generi, acquirenti nelle Esposizioni dell'800 dell'Accademia di Brera* (Brescia, 2008).

10 An important work on the history and success of this genre is still: Sandra Pinto, ed., *Romanticismo storico*, exh. cat. Palazzo Pitti, Florence (Florence, 1973); Fernando Mazzocca, "Il modello accademico e la pittura di storia," in Castelnuovo 1991 (see note 8), vol. II, pp. 602–28.

11 Renzo Grandi/Cristiana Morigi Govi, eds., *Pelagio Palagi, artista e collezionista*, exh. cat. Museo Civico, Bologna (Bologna, 1976); Claudio Poppi, ed., *Pelagio Palagi, pittore*, exh. cat. Museo Civico, Bologna (Milan, 1996).

12 Fernando Mazzocca, "Palagi a Milano: gli anni del compromesso romantic," in *L'ombra di Core: Disegni dal fondo Palagi delle biblioteca dell'Archiginnasio*, ed. Claudio Poppi, exh. cat. Galleria d'Arte Moderna, Bologna (Bologna, 1989), pp. 27–45.

13 Quoted from Fernando Mazzocca, ed., *Romantici e Macchiaioli: Giuseppe Mazzini e la grande pittura europea*, exh. cat. Palazzo Ducale, Genoa (Milan, 2005).

14 Fernando Mazzocca, ed., *Giuseppe Molteni 1800–1867 e il ritratto nella Milano romantica*, exh. cat. Museo Poldi Pezzoli, Milan (Milan, 2000).

15 Sergio Rebora, ed., *Eliseo Sala: Un ritrattista e la sua committenza nell'Italia romantica 1813–1879*, exh. cat. Museo Civico, Treviglio (Cinisello Balsamo, 2001).

16 Paolo Conte/Emanuela Rollandini, *Placido Fabris, pittore 1802–1859* (Belluno, 2004).

17 Gilberto Ganzer/Vania Gransinigh, *Michelangelo Grigoletti* (Milan, 2007).

18 Alessandro Quinzi, *Giuseppe Tominz* (Trieste, 2011).

19 For a wider discussion of the changes in portraiture see Francesco Leone/Maria Vittoria Marini Clarelli/Fernando Mazzocca/Carlo Sisi, eds., *Da Canova a Modigliani: Il volto dell'Ottocento*, exh. cat. Palazzo Zabarella, Padua (Venice, 2011).

20 Fernando Mazzocca/Giovanni Valagussa, eds., *Piccio, l'ultimo romantico*, exh. cat. Santa Maria della Pietà, Cremona (Cinisello Balsamo, 2007); Renzo Mangili, *Piccio: Tutta la pittura e un'antologia grafica* (Bergamo, 2014).

21 Francesca Valli, ed., *Due secoli di progetto scenico: Prospettive d'invenzione 1802–1861*, exh. cat. Accademia di Brera, Milan (Milan, 1998).

22 Arturo Mensi, *Giovanni Migliara (1785–1837)* (Bergamo, 1937); Maria Cristina Gozzoli/Marco Rosci, *L'opera grafica di Giovanni Migliara in Alessandria* (Alessandria, 1977).

23 Fernando Mazzocca, ed., *Angelo Inganni 1807–1880: Un pittore bresciano nella Milano romantica*, exh. cat. Palazzo Bonoris, Brescia (Milan, 1998).

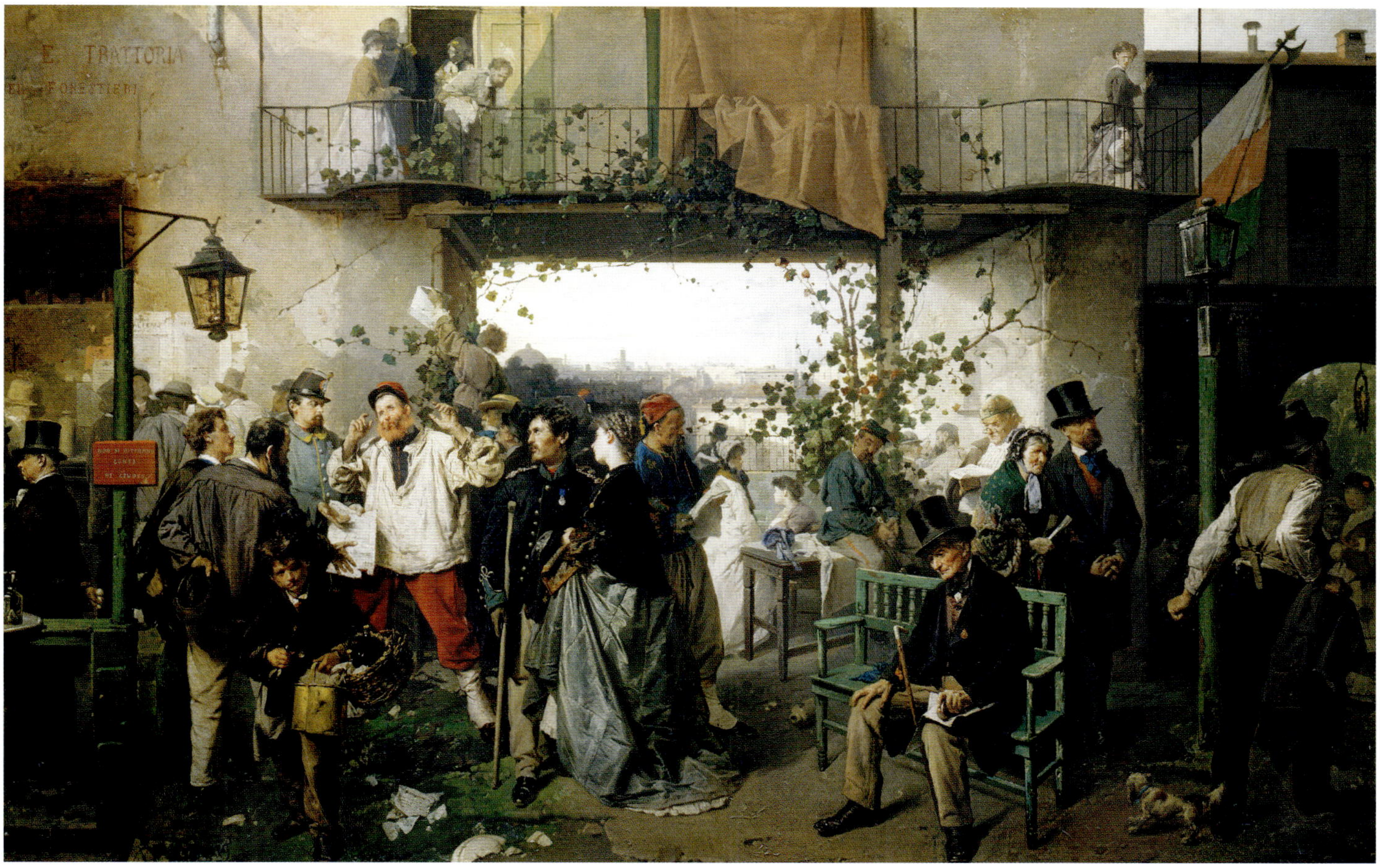

Fig. 11: **Domenico Induno**, *Il bollettino del giorno 14 luglio 1859 che annunziava la pace di Villafranca*, 1862
Galleria Nazionale d'Arte Moderna, Rome

24 Virginia Bertone, ed., *Massimo d'Azeglio e l'invenzione del paesaggio istoriato*, exh. cat. Galleria Civica d'Arte Moderna e Contemporanea, Turin (Turin, 2002).

25 A general overview of the landscapists and vedutisti is provided in the still relevant standard work by Maria Cristina Gozzoli and Marco Rosci, *Il volto della Lombardia da Carlo Porta a Carlo Cattaneo: Paesaggi e vedute 1800–1859* (Milan, 1975). For further information about Canella see Maurizio Mondini, ed., *Giuseppe Canella 1788–1847: Paesaggi e vedute nei Civici Musei di Brescia*, exh. cat. Galleria aab, Brescia (Brescia, 1994); Marina Botteri Ottaviani/Giorgio Marini/Fernando Mazzocca, eds., *Corot e Canella: La nostalgia del lago*, exh. cat. Museo Civico, Riva del Garda (Riva del Garda, 2008).

26 *Exposition Universelle de 1855: Explication des ouvrages* [...] *des artistes vivants étrangers et français exposés au Palais des Beaux-Arts* (Paris, 1855), pp. 1–6, 593–601.

27 Lavinia M. Galli Michero, *Lo studiolo del collezionista restaurato: Il gabinetto dantesco del Museo Poldi Pezzoli* (Milan, 2002).

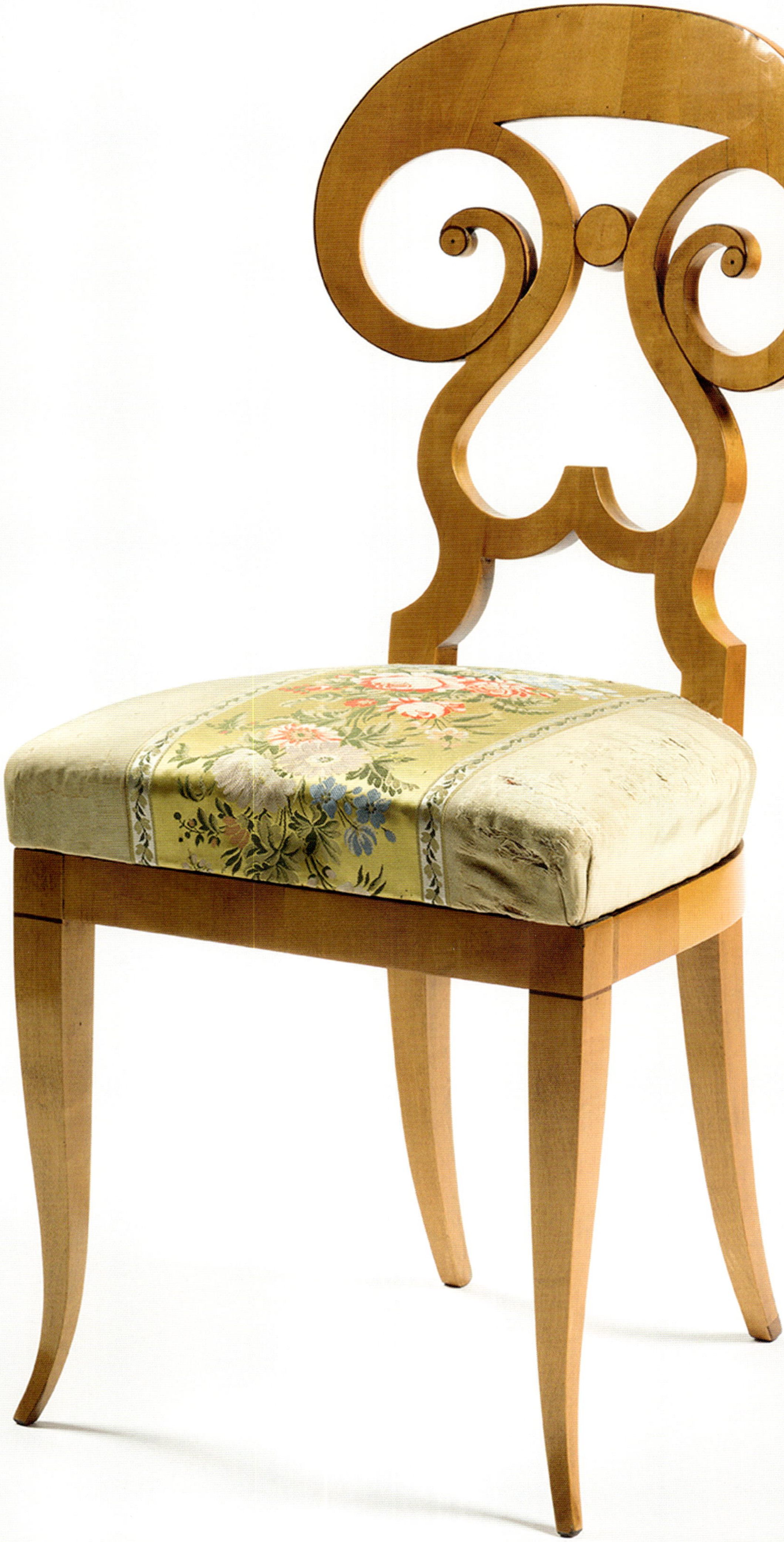

VIENNESE FURNITURE 1820–1860 COMPOSITIONAL ASPECTS AS AN EXPRESSION OF CHANGING TASTES

Christian Witt-Dörring

Displaying and discussing furniture within the context of an exhibition on central European painting from 1820 to 1860 can be considered a special challenge. Linking two such different expressive media as painting and furniture can yield entirely new criteria in terms of approach. Other than the predetermined framework of time and location, nothing connects the two a priori that would assist in their shared display. Hence the need arises to search for commonalities beyond the purely chronological classification. Both painting and furniture are means of expression, be it on the part of the creator or that of the consumer. Produced under the same sociopolitical conditions, they thus come to reflect them. It is therefore possible to start from the premise of a shared mood that finds its specific, formal-aesthetic expression. Yet what are the common features that allow us to clearly categorize paintings and items of furniture from the years 1820 to 1860 as belonging to a particular style? Are there any common formal-aesthetic approaches that were simultaneously adapted to changing tastes in both media? What follows is an attempt to answer these questions.

Fundamentally, an item of furniture possesses a spatial expansion, whereas painting represents a three-dimensional object projected onto a two-dimensional surface. Both media are able to choose between a closed or open form, an emphasis on the surface or the play of light and shadow, a surface with or without texturing, the primacy of contour or of volume, a more graphic or more painterly expression, the emphasis or negation of "tectonics," and content that is either temporally homogenous or non-homogenous. The interactions between these pairs of opposites will be used in the following as criteria for analysis to explain the formal changes in furniture design between 1820 and 1860, thereby enabling a temporal categorization.

Fig. 1: Chair, Vienna, c. 1820
MAK – Austrian Museum of Applied Arts / Contemporary Art, Vienna

In principle, furniture production for the first thirty years of the nineteenth century followed the form canon of Neoclassicism. From the 1830s, this canon began to blend with décor and structural elements of historical styles, creating hybrid forms. These were then abandoned, initially with a few exceptions around 1850, and eventually on a broader basis, as a result of the exploration of styles that set in with the applied arts reform of the 1860s. From then on, historical styles were used in their pure, "archeologically correct" forms. This chronological classification is only valid, however, for centers of art that responded swiftly to new trends and influences. For locations at a distance from these centers, or for artisans and designers less open to innovation, the old, outdated forms of expression endured for much longer. Furthermore, when classifying a piece of furniture in terms of time and location it also needs to be judged as a design unit comprising function, form, material, production technique, and décor, to reach a valid conclusion. If one of the listed criteria deviates from the ideal, it can provide important clues from which to draw certain conclusions. In this essay, we refer to the specific developments in Vienna. As the political, cultural, and social center of the Austrian Empire, Vienna was the starting and reference point for the predominant tastes from which the crown lands took their bearings.

For Viennese furniture, the year 1820 did not mark any particular caesura in terms of taste. Neoclassicist characteristics from the late eighteenth century were still being continued in the construction, proportions, and exterior design of furniture. If you take away the contemporary décor as dictated by fashionable tastes of the time,[1] you are left with furniture that in its basic features could originate from the late eighteenth century. The overall impression is not monumental, but light and delicate. Contributing to this are a number of decisions that are coherent in terms of taste. The furniture is not designed purely for a frontal perspective, but attention is also paid to the sides. The dimensions of individual constructive elements, such as legs and

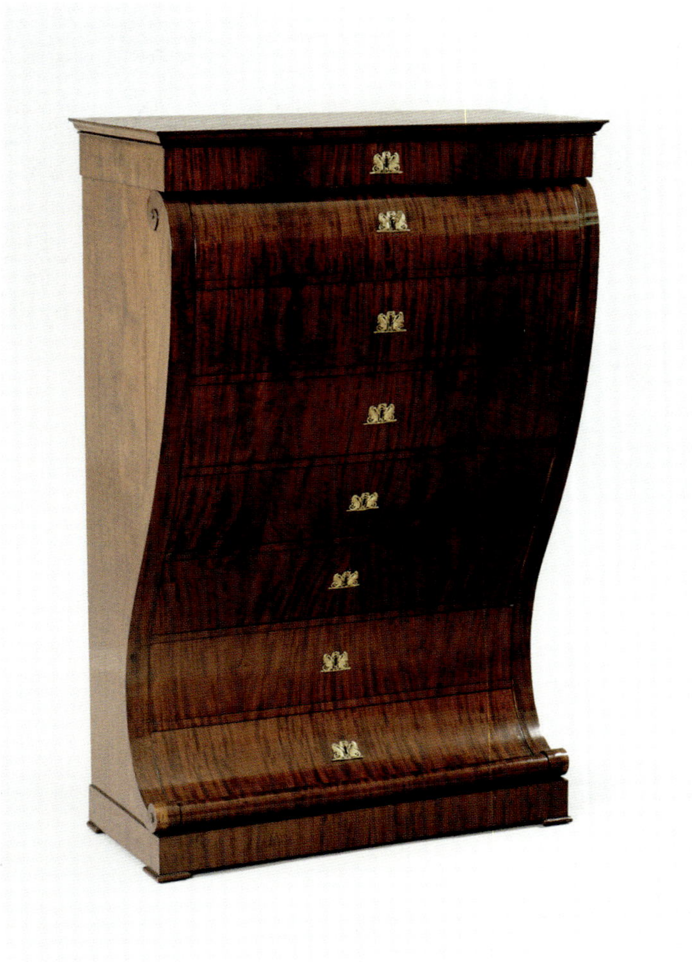

Fig. 2: Danhauser furniture factory; chiffonier table no. 17, Vienna, c. 1820–25
Bayerisches Nationalmuseum, Munich

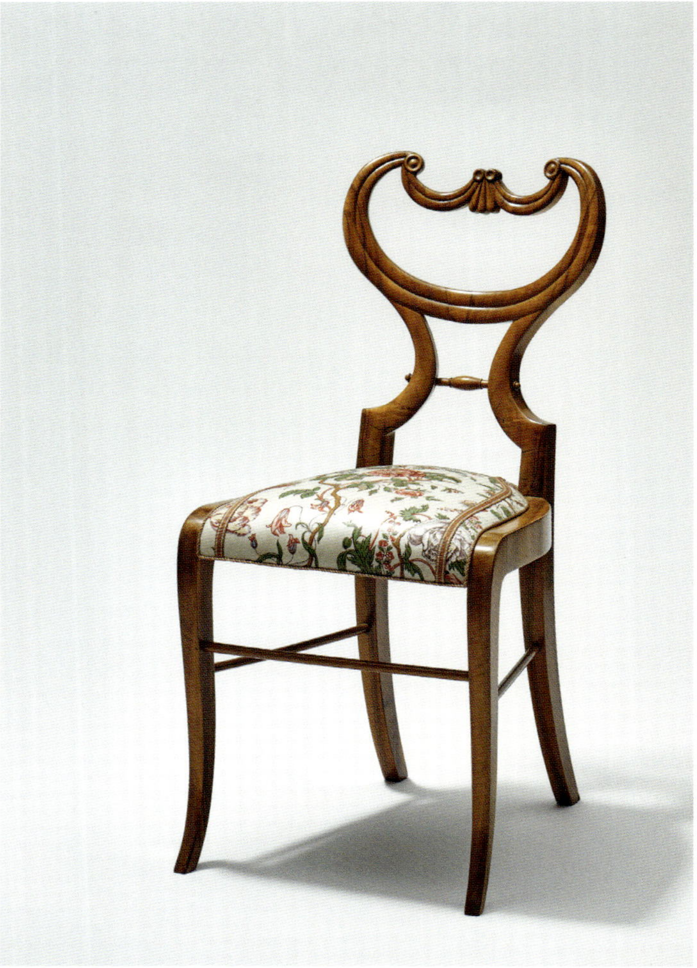

Fig. 3: Chair, Vienna, c. 1830–35
MAK – Austrian Museum of Applied Arts / Contemporary Art, Vienna

profiles, are deliberately small, allowing a transparency that also suggests mobility. The furniture piece attains its visual stability through a clear emphasis on tectonics and construction. To achieve this, the joints between individual constructive elements are accentuated rather than smoothed, thus making each component legible as a distinctly separate part of the whole. The furniture seems graphic in its overall appearance, evoked by sharp contours that define both its outer boundary and its interior structure. The latter arises as a result of the clearly discernible separation of frame and panels, often emphasized by using different colors for the different parts. A light surface is given a darker frame or vice versa. This frame may be three-dimensional, in the form of mouldings, or flush, as a veneer band (fig. 1). Light and dark surfaces are clearly separated from each other. Even the ephemeral play of light and shadow is given clear boundaries and is not allowed to flow freely across a uniformly smooth surface. The surface, simultaneously the bearer of structure and décor, is composed of a complex pattern of diverse materials (including wood, paste, brass, copper, mother-of-pearl, and ivory) and techniques (such as marquetry, penwork, carving, and cast metal). In seating furniture, the upholstery is accorded a role equal to that of the cabinetry. Although more short-lived due to faster deterioration of the materials and is such also subject to changing fashions, seat panel and covering are conceived as integral components of an overall design. Accordingly, the one cannot fulfill its original design intentions without the other. They correspond, in essence, to the principles discussed above, in that the upholstery likewise exhibits a clearly defined, angular contour. Light colors are framed by dark gimps or cords and vice versa. They serve to explain the tectonics: The trims are not merely there to mask the upholstering nails, but also, for

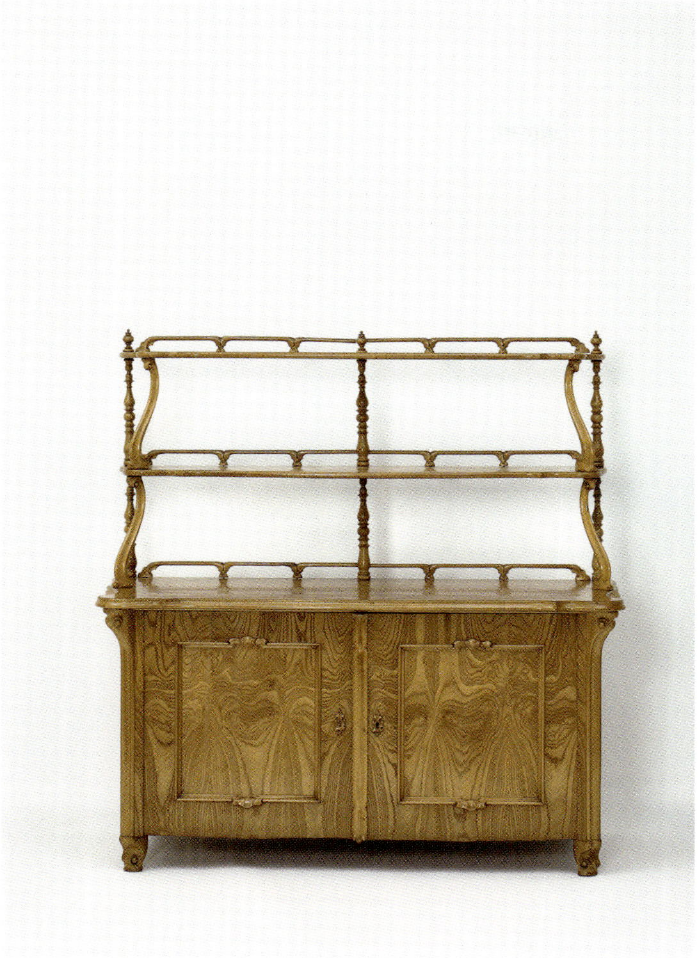

Fig. 4 : Sideboard, Vienna, c. 1840
MAK – Austrian Museum of Applied Arts / Contemporary Art, Vienna

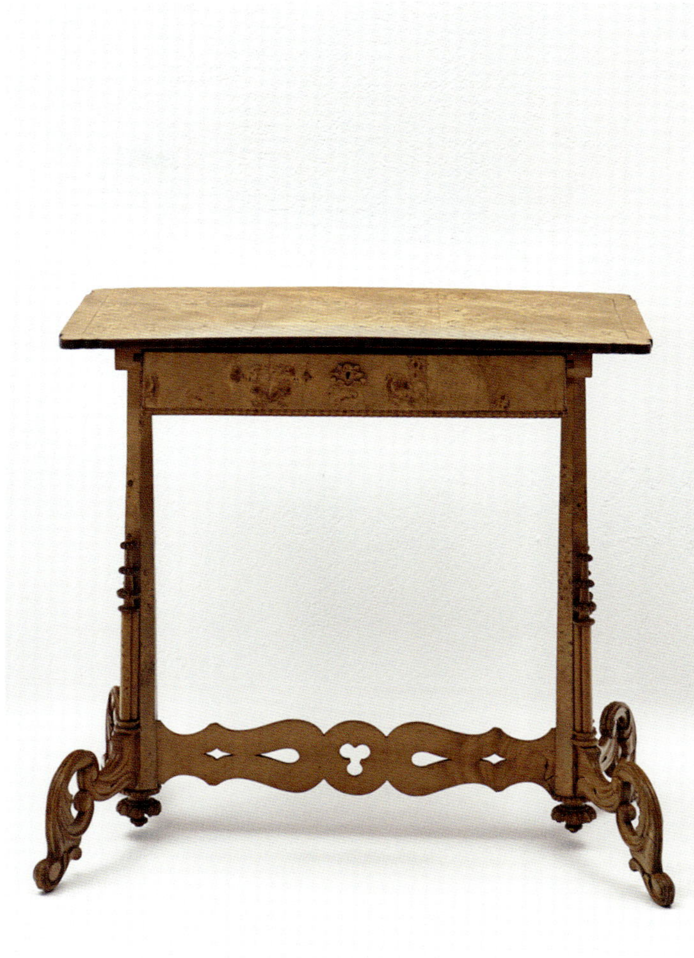

Fig. 5: Small table, Vienna, c. 1835–40
MAK – Austrian Museum of Applied Arts / Contemporary Art, Vienna

example, to emphasize the defining structural elements of the seat's edge. To prevent the visual impression of the seat "leaking" off its front edge, it needs a horizontal boundary in the form of a trim.

It is not often that we are so precisely informed about the date of a change in taste in Viennese applied arts. In 1825, Wenzel Carl Blumenbach published a contemporary overview of the Viennese industrial arts production with illustrated examples:[2] "For many years, we sought to enhance the appearance of furniture through gilded and bronzed carving, by applying quantities of mounts and ornamentation of pressed and varnished tombac, or genuine gilded bronze metal; however, since 1823 and 1824, this form of ornament has become less common, and at last Viennese taste has largely proscribed it, demanding in its place a purer form of cabinet-making. As a result, Viennese furniture has now become heavier and more solid, replacing the previous showy décor with truer and nobler forms, with smooth and fluted columns, beautiful socles and capitals, cornices, trims, etc., but [it] also requires more knowledge of draftsmanship and more diligent and skillful craftsmen."[3] In fact, a radical reorientation in Viennese tastes occurred at this time. The Empire style, hitherto adopted from France only as superficial embellishment and applied to English furniture forms of the late eighteenth century, was now absorbed in its more substantial form. This meant, as Blumenbach also remarked, that furniture forms were now infused with a monumental radiance, as had been prevailing in France since 1800. This development may have been a consequence of the ultimate dethroning of Napoleon, resulting in France no longer being seen as the enemy. At least it now also occurred in those countries that had not been under direct or indirect French rule, which, besides Austria, included England and Russia. As had

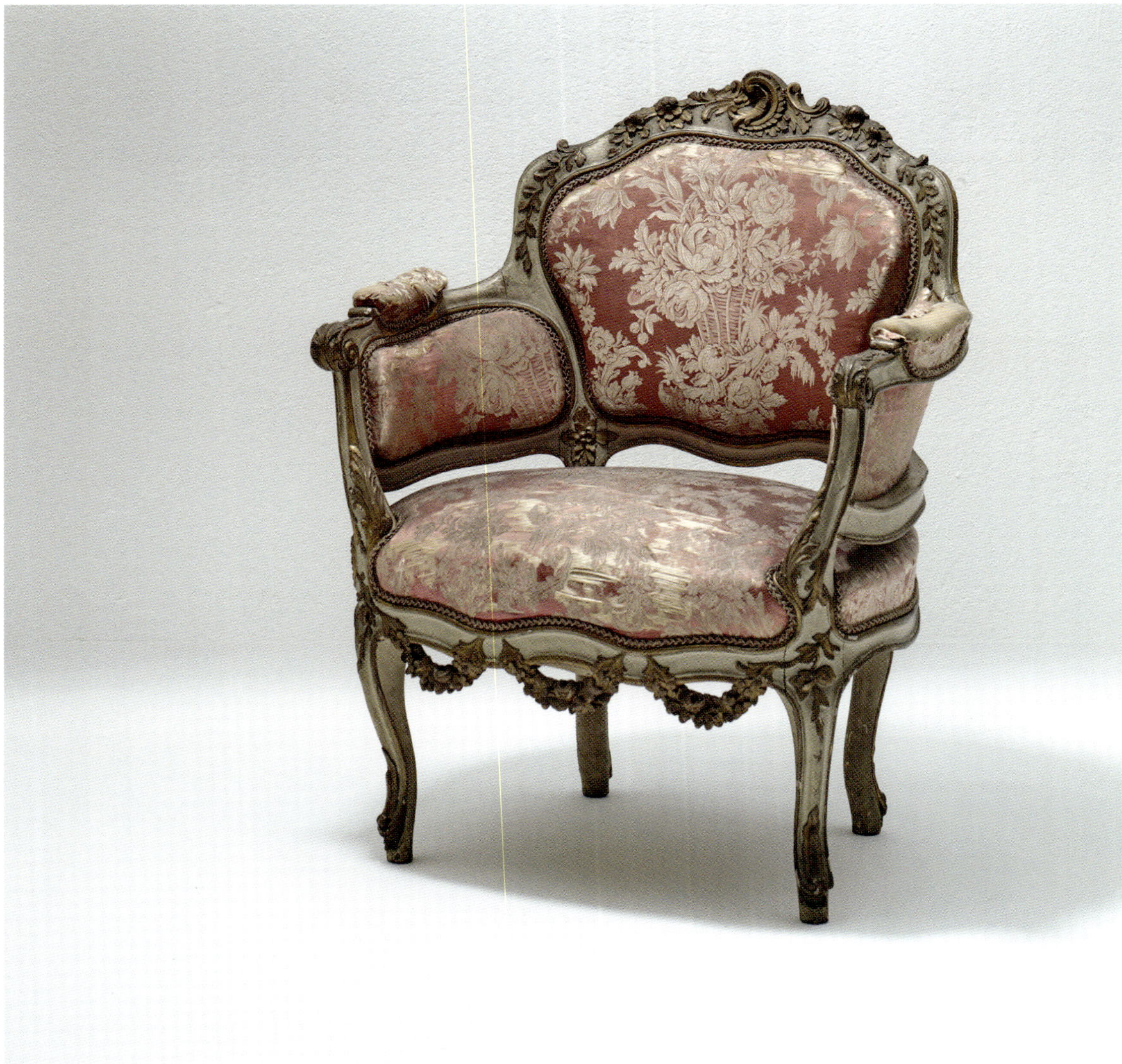

Fig. 6 Armchair, Vienna, c. 1850–55 MAK – Austrian Museum of Applied Arts / Contemporary Art, Vienna

Fig. 7 Sideboard, Vienna, c. 1855 MAK – Austrian Museum of Applied Arts / Contemporary Art, Vienna

already been the case in the beginning of the nineteenth century, more expensive furniture decorated in the Empire style and less expensive versions without applied decoration were available.

The new monumentality of the furniture required a radical departure from the characteristics identified so far. Since monumentality almost always involves a frontal orientation that emphasizes the presentation aspect, the entire design process now focused on this. In its placement within the room, the furniture was thus arranged against the walls, leaving the center of the room free. The piece of furniture no longer presented itself as the sum of its individual constructive parts, but rather as a total volume deserving of our undivided attention. Its volume was no longer defined by individually framed, separate elements, but by one free-flowing surface. The eye was no longer distracted from the total volume by different types of wood in various colors, but the entire piece was covered by one and the same wood veneer. Although the tectonic qualities of structural components were taken into account, they were no longer prominent as individual design elements. The continuous veneer, covering the entire piece and negating its horizontal and vertical components, made sure of that. The texture and definition of the wood grain, chosen according to financial resources, now replaced the previous diversity of decorative elements and different crafts techniques. All of this created the impression of a closed form, in contrast to the open, delicate, and more permeable furniture from the beginning of the century. Until the end of the 1820s, more rounded forms increasingly replaced the former angular appearance of furniture, which further supported this closed form. It also yielded new scope for the interplay of light and shadow. Light could now glide unhindered across the uniform surface of the glossy French polish (fig. 2). The same aesthetic principles were also applied to the upholstery of the seats. Instead of using fabrics with small,

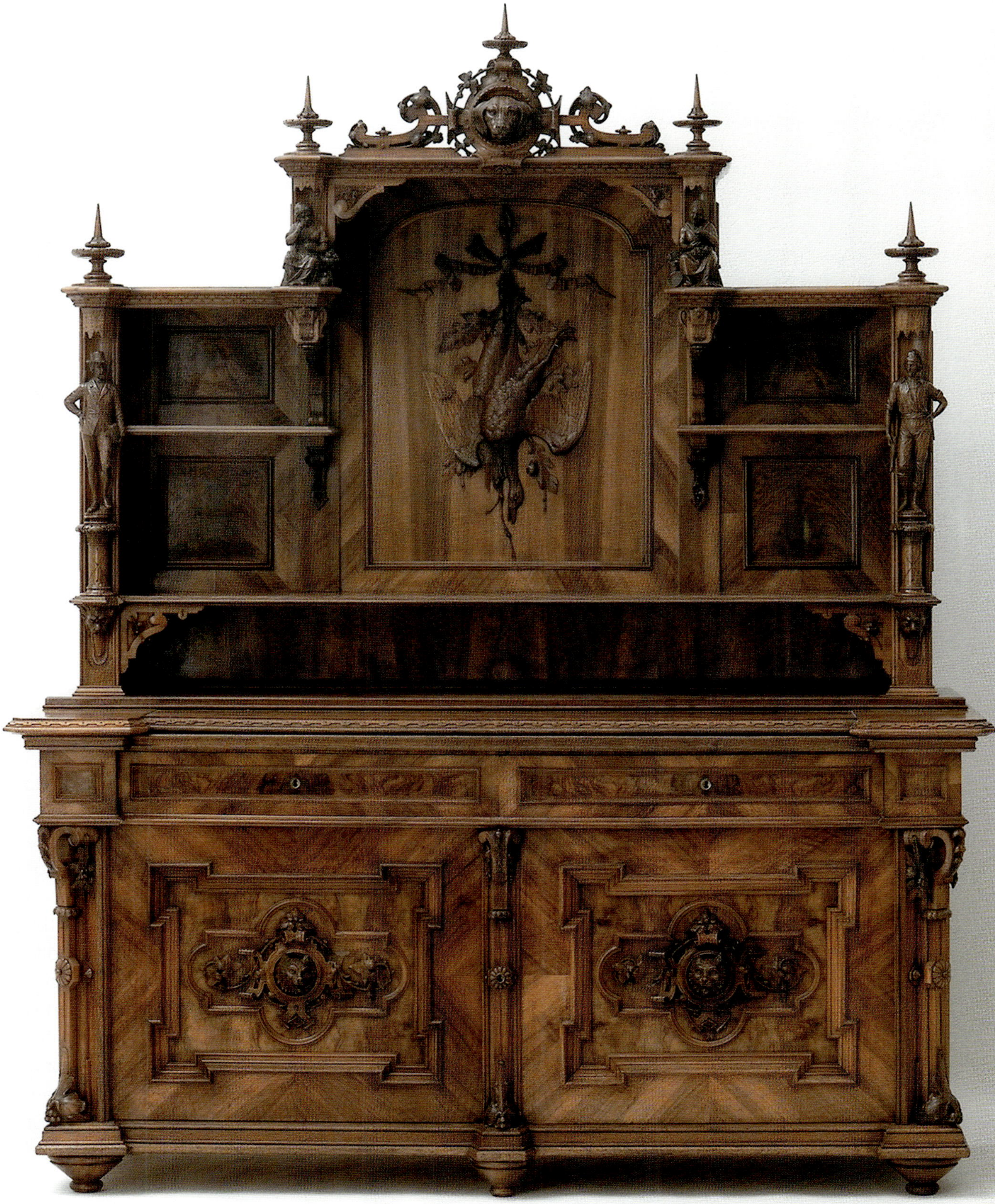

intricate patterns, which tend to generate a more closed visual image, printed and glazed calico, known as chintz, became fashionable, and seats were covered in floral, increasingly proliferate patterns. In the same way that the continuous wood grain negated the horizontal and vertical constructive elements, the floral pattern would flow from the horizontal seat surface onto the vertical plane of the cushion (plate p. 244).

After 1830, the arrangement of furniture within the room changed. The wall was no longer its main point of reference. Furniture slowly began to conquer the center of the room. This entailed a departure from its original monumentality and frontal orientation. It now spoke more through its contours than its volume. The open form, permeable vis-à-vis the space, was given preference over the closed form. Furniture once again became the sum of its individual constructive components. At this time flat boards still dominated, but now appeared increasingly in combination with three-dimensional components, often in the form of scrolls and acanthus leaves (plate p. 238). The seats, now more flexible and mobile in their arrangement in the room, were of lighter construction, the upholstery no longer angular in shape, but with a curved edge and flatter padding. The upholstery edge was also no longer defined by a trim, but would give the impression of flowing into the space in front (fig. 3). In storage furniture, carcass and inlays were kept flat but visible and once again structured the appearance of the furniture. The previously free-flowing veneer defining the volume of the furniture was now given a thin frame by means of color-contrasted veining defining individual constructive elements. Rather than marking out the edges of the sheet of veneer, this traced its contours nearer the center of the decorated or veneered surface. The veneer figure thereby remained open toward the outer edges. The graphic contours, limited to clearly defined areas, now appeared together with pictorial elements. In the second half of the 1830s, a rivalry arose from this that had no clear winner. Thus the dominance of Neoclassicism was broken and, with the resumption of historical styles and long-neglected crafts techniques, a reorientation in tastes began (fig. 4).

Furniture design at the end of the 1830s was no longer subject to the canon of Neoclassicist forms but still continued its proportions in essence, while abandoning the monumentality. Régence, Rococo, and Gothic forms were back in vogue and defined the appearance of furniture (fig. 5). These forms provided inspiration, yet were not fully understood. Thus external features such as contours and ornamentation were adopted without considering their structural unity with the furniture body. As a result, contexts determined by the cultural-historical evolution of their design were suspended. Historically diverging contents were combined and re-assembled, like random building blocks, into something new. An example of this is the treatment of the historic forms of Régence and Rococo (figs. 4, 6, 7). Initially these were evident only in details, such as the leaf and strapwork of the rocaille and in the furniture's curved contours. The furniture body itself did not project into the space, it still retained its Neoclassicist frontal orientation. The three-dimensional curves of the Rococo were frozen in the two-dimensional plane. They were sawn out of the board or glued on in rocaille shapes. The ornament was not carved and therefore not an organic part of the wood. The same held true for the old crafts techniques, such as carving, marquetry, or bridlework, which were taken up again at this point. Their material-specific qualities were corrupted in the form of surrogates. The congruence of materials and colors specific to a particular time and style was lost. Dark contents were rendered light, and vice versa. Ultimately, this aesthetic approach manifested itself in a negation of the hitherto valid sense of proportions and materiality. Tectonic components were processed non-tectonically. Traditional proportions that clearly related to a monumental message became mere decorative details. A picture emerges that consists of strung-together details and no longer produces a clear overall concept—as though a painting was held together only by its frame, or like a canvas that only shows staffage. In the end, the painterly and the graphic element appear together, yet without clearly identifying themselves as such. They are present, but cannot merge to form a harmonious whole.

The characteristics of Viennese furniture outlined above remained prevalent until around 1850. After that, the treatment of historical information began to change as a result of the emergence of art history and the inclusion of architects in the design process. In the course of art-historical research, more and more information on characteristics specific to a style became available. A cataloguing and categorizing process took place, encompassing not only the old styles, but also old crafts techniques. Old contexts were reunited and the old styles were once again applied according to their intrinsic qualities. Their semantic content enabled period furniture to stand on an equal footing with a genuine antique. For furniture forms, this development signified a clarification of their aesthetic mood. It meant that the furniture had to communicate a clear message. Depending on the chosen style, this requires an unambiguous choice between painterly or graphic expression, open or closed form, emphasis of contour or volume, and a predomincance of surface or of the play of light and shadow (fig. 7). Gothic, Renaissance, and Rococo as carriers of specific historical information all have equal markets according to the functional context that society has assigned them. With their help, the interior space becomes an atmospheric painting in a uniformly self-contained, colorful mood.

1 Contemporary tastes demanded decorative elements in the French Empire style.

2 Wenzel Carl Blumenbach, *Wiener Kunst- und Gewerbsfreund oder der neueste Wiener Geschmack: in Gold-, Silber-, Bronze-, Eisen-, Stahl- u. a. Metall-Arbeiten, in Equipagen und Riemzeug, in Meubeln, Tapezierer-, Drechsler- und Töpfer-Arbeiten, Gläsern u.s.w.* (Vienna, 1825).

3 Blumenbach 1825 (see note 2), vol. 1, p. 3.

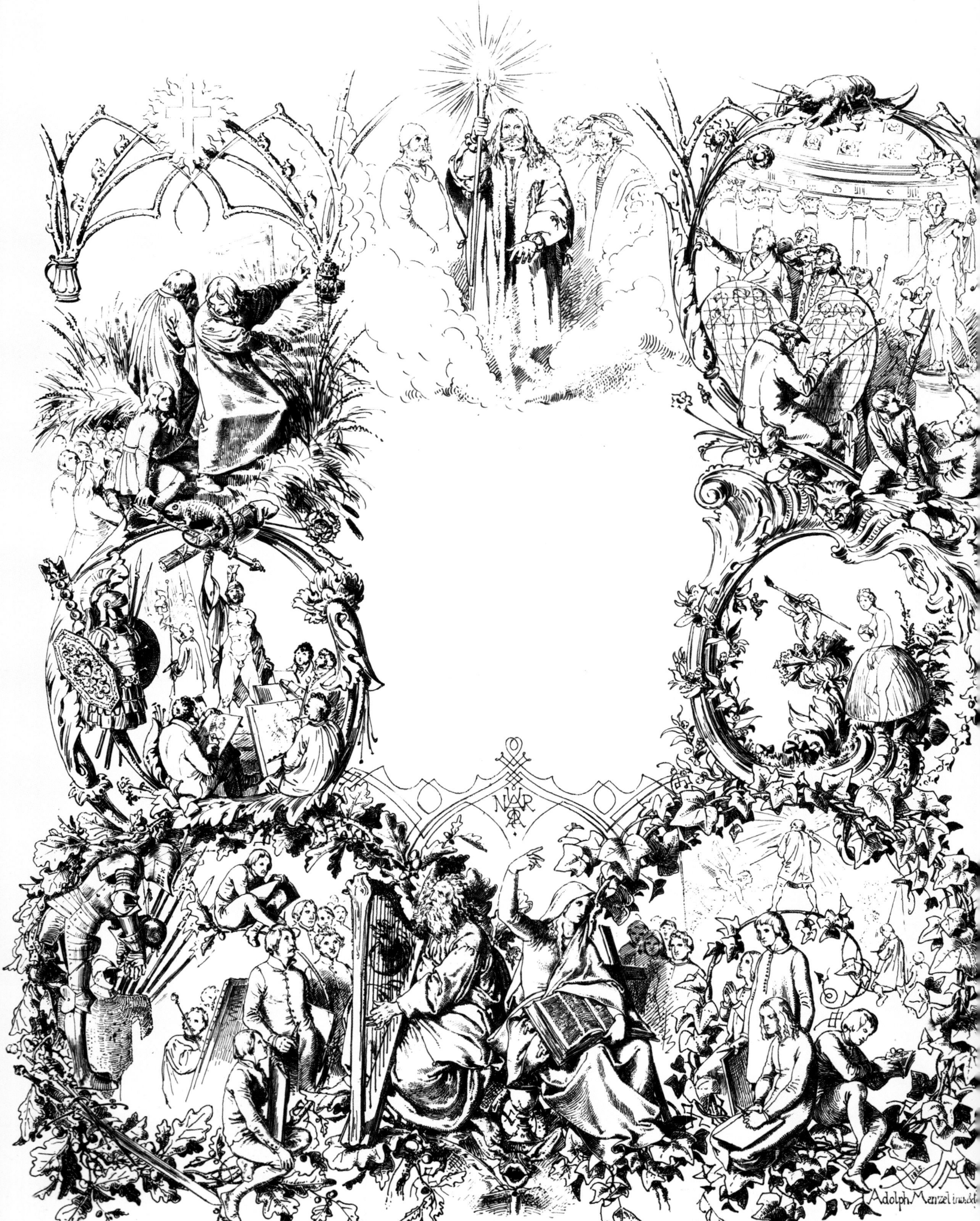
Adolph Menzel inv: &

WALDMÜLLER'S ANTI-ACADEMISM AND ITS TRADITION

Werner Busch

Ferdinand Georg Waldmüller's fundamental questioning of the academy's right to exist as an educational institution for artists did not arise without prior conditions. His attack on the academy, of which he was a member, served to develop and justify his understanding of realism. Anti-academic leanings have existed for as long as there have been academies. From the outset, art academies have propagated a concept that, on the one hand, was to provide an idealistic superstructure for art and comprehends art as the result of intellectual production, while, on the other hand, declared that art could be taught and learned. The crucial element in this is the sketch, the *disegno*, which, in order to perform its function, is doubly connoted. *Disegno* is an intellectual sketch, which finds its manifestation in the outline. The line, as the abstraction of form, is deemed closest to the intellect, very much in contrast to color, which merely accomplishes a materialization of form and is therefore subordinate. What can be taught and learned are, on the one hand, the high ideal of art as intellectual production and, on the other hand, the transformation to a fixed form of the *prima idea* laid out in the design—through model studies and studies of exemplary works. Instruction in model studies can assist in this. This kind of concept of theoretical superstructure and practical substructure demands the formation of a theory connecting the two. Countless art theoretical treatises have refined and carried forth these basic ideas.

Contrasting that, an entirely different approach asserted itself from the very outset. Because this approach had its roots in painting practice, academic quarters invariably accused it of propagating blatant imitation of nature, of being trivial handiwork. This approach is not derived from any lofty idea, largely omits the sketch design stage and even perspective and anatomical studies, which in academic tradition form the basis of all execution, and instead simply applies brush to canvas to arrive at a colorful form. Since there is no binding sketch at its base, corrections are made throughout the painting process, as forms respond to and mutually modify each other as they emerge.

This is not a process that can be theorized, but certainly one that requires historical legitimation, so as not to succumb to the omnipresent accusation that it simply reproduces what the artist sees before him and is entirely void of intellectual work.[1] Representatives of this concept felt legitimated through reference to classical artists. And, of course, the sculpture of antiquity was widely known, even if only from Roman copies, and could also serve as a model for the academic artists. Ancient painting, by contrast, was not readily available. Nonetheless, we know the names of classical artists and their high social status, mainly from Pliny the Elder's *Natural History*, where certain works are also exemplarily described.[2] This takes on the literary form of the "artist anecdote."[3] At the core of most artist anecdotes is the artist's ability to depict reality in the most astonishingly realistic way. When Pliny the Elder speaks of Lysippus, he has him say (and thereby designates an argument that can be understood as entirely anti-academic) "that it was Nature herself, and no artist, that he proposed to imitate." ("naturam ipsam imitandam esse, non artificem.")[4] The idea is the conquest of nature through art. And this conquest is expressed in various forms in his anecdotes: Grapes painted by Zeuxis being pecked at by passing birds; a stallion attempting to mount a mare painted by Apelles; the painting of a snake silencing birds; real quails trying to join a quail painted by Protogenes; passersby paying reverence to a portrait placed in a window; etc.[5] This last anecdote, however, is not from Pliny, but from Vasari's biography of Titian, and the person depicted in the portrait was said to have been Pope Paul III.[6]

Anecdotes tend to be memetic, and thus a variation of the Titian anecdote also exists relating to Rembrandt.[7] Titian and Rembrandt were equally connected to a tradition of painting that refrained largely from

Fig. 1: **Adolph Menzel**, cover page for Athanasius Graf Raczynski's *Geschichte der neueren deutschen Kunst*, vol. 3 (Berlin, 1841) Kupferstichkabinett, Staatliche Museen zu Berlin

compositional sketches and instead created their images through a process of exploration directly on the canvas. Accordingly, hardly any preliminary drawings by Titian exist, although hundreds of drawings by Rembrandt have been preserved. Nonetheless, on examining these more closely, one perplexingly realizes that barely twenty of these are directly connected to a work. And on investigating those more closely, they turn out to be for the most part intermediary drawings, that is, they arose when the artist became stuck in his working process on the canvas and corrections in the painting itself bore no results, so he tried to arrive at a solution to the problem by drawing a few quick sketches on paper—whereby it was not about correctness of perspective or anatomy, but solely about the creation of a convincing depiction. Incidentally, the same applies to the few existing drawings by Titian: They, too, arose during the painting process.[8]

Thus, at this point we can establish that there are two types of art production that stand in contrast to each other; an academic and a non-academic, a line-based and a color-based, one that places intellectual invention above all else, and one that understands inspiration as arising in the material process. The one wants to arrive at an ideal nature, the other considers itself obliged solely to the substance of nature.

In the late eighteenth century, the attack on the academy's dominance was carried out from yet another vantage point, because artists felt stymied by the academy and hampered in their free development. The prerequisites for this were, briefly put, *Sturm und Drang* with its concept of genius and, shortly thereafter, the philosophical debate on artistic autonomy. The idea that absolute obligation to nature and the notion of genius, i.e., autonomy, could come together in one concept is difficult to comprehend, but fundamental for understanding Waldmüller's position. Mainly, however—and Waldmüller's writings will also show this—it brings the intellect into play again, through the back door of an anti-academic concept. For the freedom of independent decision can easily be interpreted as the result of mental processes.

Asmus Jakob Carstens undoubtedly delivered the most relevant blend of anti-academism and the concept of autonomy in his justly famous letter of February 20, 1796 to the curator of the Berlin Academy of Arts, Minister Friedrich Anton von Heinitz, who, after all, had granted Carstens a Rome fellowship.[9] Carstens had already been quite frank when confronting his patron von Heinitz, who had also appointed him professor at the Royal Academy in Berlin. During the preparations for an exhibition of his work in Rome, he wrote in an invective against the Academy: "The usefulness of this institution stands on shaky ground anyway,"[10] adding that it was the duty of a king to support a genius when nature had produced one. And: "For a monarch, supporting a genius brings the same honor for posterity as having won a battle and captured provinces."[11] That was strong stuff, which was to be eclipsed the following year, when von Heinitz demanded that Carstens return his paintings from the exhibition in Rome as they belonged to the Berlin Academy: "I wish to tell your Excellency that I do not belong to the Berlin Academy but to mankind. It never entered my mind nor have I ever pledged myself to become the slave of an academy for the rest of my life in return for a pension that was granted to me for a few years in order to further my talent. [...] My faculties have been entrusted to me by God; I must be a conscientious steward to them, so that when the day comes and I am told: render account of your stewardship, I need not say: Lord, the talent that Thou hadst entrusted me I buried in Berlin."[12]

The source of these extremely self-confident thoughts is not so difficult to establish. In Rome, Carstens lived together with Carl Ludwig Fernow, an artist who had become an art theorist and gave lectures in Kantian philosophy for the German artists in Rome, having studied in Jena under the Kant disciple Carl Leonhard Reinhold. He most likely helped Carstens in composing his letter, concerning both the application of the concept of autonomy and Carstens's claims under private law with respect to a state institution such as the Academy. Fernow himself had stated that artists were "penned up together in the ghetto of an academy [...] where they are forced to mechanically turn the wheels of the state machine."[13] This, so Fernow, resulted in artistic deformation. On the concept of autonomy he wrote: "Freed art, discharged of the support—but also the dictate—of religion must henceforth rely upon itself [...]."[14] In fact, Carstens had already been prepared for these thoughts while still in Berlin, in the form of the autonomy ideas as expressed by Karl Philipp Moritz—who, like Carstens, taught at the Berlin Academy. As early as 1785, i.e., before Kant's *Critique of Judgment*, written in 1790, Moritz had penned an essay entitled "Über den Begriff des in sich selbst Vollendeten" ("On the Concept of the Complete in Itself"),[15] and in 1788 he remarked in his text "Über die bildende Nachahmung des Schönen" ("On the Formative Imitation of Beauty"): "Beauty merely wants to be viewed and experienced—and created—for its own sake."[16] Furthermore, in Berlin, Carstens belonged to the circle around architect Hans Christian Genelli, a member of the Academy Council, as well as of a commission tasked with making proposals for its reform. This resulted in an extensive text by Genelli, whose influence on Carstens remained unnoticed, as the paper was not published until 1800.[17] However, the commission had been set up soon after Friedrich Wilhelm II's accession to power in 1786 and was associated with the Academy reform carried out by von Heinitz.[18]

It seems highly likely that Waldmüller was aware of this text in his proposals for Academy reform, which culminated in the suggestion of total dissolution. The correspondences are extensive. Right at the start of his script, Genelli asserts: "It has occurred to me, and to several others, that the epoch of the foundation of academies has always accompanied that of a decline in the arts, in every land where these had otherwise thrived."[19] "This circumstance seems to offer strong supposition that said academies themselves have, at the very least, contributed to the acceleration of the decay."[20] He goes on to say that an artist could not be tied to a single style and that the academic curriculum taught things that "according to their nature, cannot be taught, but must clearly be left to their own cultivation."[21] He considered the strict separation of genres detrimental, "since the different branches go hand in hand and, in fact, comprise only one single art."[22] Waldmüller would later express this practically verbatim, stating that the relationship between student and master ought to be a personal one. Genelli thus already demanded what would become Waldmüller's credo: masterclasses in the form of an intimate studio community.[23] Furthermore, he proposed that, on completing their studies, artists should be awarded contracts by the state so as to ensure their livelihood.[24] This idea, too, can be found in Waldmüller's text, which makes it surprising that the influence of Genelli's writing on Waldmüller has hitherto gone unnoticed. The parallels could be further pursued into minute details. For Genelli, too, who argued against all academic norms, dissolved the academy from the inside with his proposals—which was also Waldmüller's aim.

Before finally turning to Waldmüller, we will explore a further position that is highly consistent with Waldmüller's understanding of nature and reality: that of Adolph Menzel, which, in turn, is based on the deliberations of Gottfried Schadow and Aloys Hirt. Since Menzel himself did not engage in theoretical reflection, we shall examine one drawing which is indicative of his philosophy: his title page from 1835 for Athanasius Graf Raczynski's third volume of *Geschichte der neueren deutschen Kunst*.[25] The date is of importance, as in 1835 Raczynski had not even written his text for the third volume, which was to be devoted primarily to the Berlin arts since Carstens. Menzel thus offered his view of the recent—not just—German art, which, as could be demonstrated, entirely contradicted Raczynski's version on many points. Nonetheless, Menzel's drawing was still used as the cover picture for the third volume when it was published in 1841 (fig. 1). Interestingly, Raczynski's work was first published in French. Menzel's cover follows the principles of arabesque as developed by Philipp Otto Runge: axial symmetry, with the source of the arabesque located at the bottom of the axis, from where it grows outward to either side, re converging at the center on the top of the page. As with Runge, the whole is to be conceived as a dialectical triad: thesis, antithesis, synthesis, or: genesis in the underworld, flowering in the world, and culmination in the otherworldly; or at least this is the interpretation by Philipp Otto Runge and Eugen Napoleon Neureuther.[26] Menzel and, incidentally, also E. T. A. Hoffmann with the covers he designed himself, made use of this dialectic in a more ironic way. For both, the romantic longing for the otherworldly did not seem very convincing against the backdrop of current conditions—their focus is on mocking the existing.

Thus, in Menzel's arabesque, the root at the bottom of the axis of symmetry, the source of all that follows, is far from positively connoted. In the case of Runge's *Times of Day* cycle, in *Day,* the source and nurturer of the unfurling growth is represented by a fish mouth spouting spring water. Menzel, on the other hand, in a clearly ironic paraphrase of Runge's life-giving source, shows a blinkered donkey, its mouth wide open, wielding a quill and writing in a book entitled "Recensio." This stands for the donkey-brained critic responsible for art's current misery. The arabesque grows from here outward to either side, separating six fields, each devoted to a different current in art—and all are subjected to Menzel's verdict.

The starting points above the donkey's head are a bard on the left and the embodiment of religion on the right. They refer to profane and Christian historical painting, which in the fields alongside are represented to the left by Wilhelm von Kaulbach and his followers, and to the right by Peter von Cornelius and his entourage, antipodes within the Munich art scene. Kaulbach standing and provocative, Cornelius with a halo working on *The Last Judgment* in the Ludwigskirche, which was to cause his Waterloo in Munich. Appearing first in the left strand above Kaulbach is the School of David, with the master shown working on the completion of his *Intervention of the Sabine Women*. Above it, we see a group of Nazarenes in long robes.

On the right-hand strand, above Cornelius, set within a rocaille cartouche, Rococo is criticized as distorting nature. The flower from which the hand of the artist grows turns out to be a lace cuff; the Venus standing next to it wears a crinoline—a motif invented by William Hogarth who used it to poke fun at the tastes of high culture.[27] A satyr in the crest of the cartouche mocks this puzzle picture. Above it is a dignified gathering in the Pantheon, yet the Apollo Belvedere is just being issued with a fig leaf; so, here too, despite all Classicism, we see nature being distorted. The two uppermost fields both point toward the center, where, in the tradition of Runge, the arabesque is to find its synthesis, its culmination in the transcendental—only Menzel does not believe in this. So, in the top center of his arabesque, Dürer strides toward us like a divine apparition, illuminating the world with a large torch, yet the cloud at his feet emanates from an incense cauldron; behind him we see Peter Vischer, creator of the Shrine of St. Sebaldus in Nuremberg, Lucas Cranach the Elder, and Hans Holbein the Younger. The old German as the original source is to become the model for the art of the present. This had been propagated by the Nazarenes and also by Goethe with his recommendation to follow Dürer's illustrations for the Prayer Book of Emperor Maximilian I in Johann Nepomuk Strixner's lithographs.[28] And so it is Goethe who leads the flock of Pantheon visitors and points toward Dürer. But his advice to embark upon the path back to Dürer is a retrogression, as implied by the lobster in the crest of the arabesque field. And in the field with the Nazarenes on the left, the path to Dürer-style salvation is offset by a sign pointing in the opposite direction.

So why do none of the art positions Menzel presents lead anywhere? Because the whole lot of them has betrayed nature, as Menzel points out in an anagram that is easily deciphered as "Natura" with a question mark. This is found on the axis of symmetry, above the bard and the figure of religion. Nature should have been the starting point for the latest developments in art, instead, the current path leads astray. Only one character in the entire arabesque is excluded from this fallacy: Gottfried Schadow, who sits in the top right arabesque field in front of Goethe, facing the opposite direction, easily recognizable by his fur coat, worn in summer as in winter, and by the eyeshade. Their juxtaposition is a reference to the battle fought out over the Berlin arts in 1800/01.[29] Goethe had accused the arts of blunt naturalism, of a prosaic zeitgeist that was killing their poetry. In part he blamed a nationalism that came at the expense of a responsibility to humanity as such. Schadow responded in an astonishingly direct way to Germany's hitherto uncontested intellectual hero, dismissing his idealism as mere affectation and defending a "characteristic" concept of reality. His use of the term "characteristic" reveals that he was in fact acting as a mouthpiece for Aloys Hirt, whom Goethe and Schiller had asked in 1797 to submit a contribution on "the characteristic" for Schiller's literary journal *Die Horen*. They were none too pleased with the result, an essay entitled "Versuch über das Kunstschöne." For Hirt, there was no fundamental difference between beauty in art and in nature. He saw nature as the general, which was expressed individually by art. According to Hirt, the individual becomes a characteristic determination of the general of its own accord, and also becomes typical of its own accord. Goethe was dismayed by this amalgamation. For him, in the wake of Kant, only art could do justice to beauty as the highest intellectual principle. While Goethe held on to the ideal, Hirt and Schadow aimed to legitimate the commitment to absolute, faithful representation of nature, or *Naturrichtigkeit*, for example by taking measurements of the human body at different stages of its development. In doing so, they followed Enlightenment traditions, such as the genetic model by Georges-Louis Leclerc de Buffon in his *Histoire naturelle*, which no doubt also had an influence on the arts, for example when Pigalle turned the classical putti into chubby babies with large heads and infant bodies.[30]

Menzel was entirely committed to the concept of reality as propagated by Hirt and Schadow: the truth of nature rather than idealized natural beauty. Waldmüller took up this very same juxtaposition. Waldmüller also continually upheld Menzel's attack of art critique as responsible for art's misdevelopment. Those who drank from this well had swallowed contaminated water, drawn from idealistic theory, academicism, and classical art models, renouncing nature as the true source of art. Waldmüller disseminated his anti-academicism in three main papers: The first, *Das Bedürfnis eines zweckmässigen Unterrichts in der Malerei und plastischen Kunst angedeutet nach eigenen Erfahrungen*, was published in Vienna in 1846 and in 1847 in a second extended edition with a longer introduction. This then resulted in the second publication, *Vorschläge zur Reform der österreichisch-kaiserlichen Akademie der bildenden Künste* in 1849. The third comprehensive text bore the seemingly humble title *Andeutungen zur Belebung der vaterländischen bildenden Kunst* (Vienna, 1857). Whereas the first two publications could still just about be understood as proposals for a reform of the Academy as an institution, the later text was an undisguised, direct attack on the Academy's right to exist. This could only result in Waldmüller's suspension. The arguments in the three successive works remained the same, but were becoming ever more urgent. At their base was an absolute commitment to nature. Yet Waldmüller understood early on, like Hirt, Schadow, and also Menzel, that the call for complete adherence to nature would almost inevitably lead to the accusation of pure, crude naturalism without any intellectual content. Insofar, right at the beginning of his "Justification" in 1847, he felt compelled to emphasize the role the intellect played in his technique for creating art. Tying art to preconceived norms would lead it to falsehood, he claimed. Nature alone was an unadulterated mirror of reality, to which the artist was obliged. "It is true that in the artwork the spirit, which enlivens the form, lends the same its imprint; but spirit and form must both be equally true, otherwise the effect will always be incomplete. The truth that is in spirit will, anyway, never befriend the affectation in the form, and even the most consummate beauty of form will never be able to reconcile us with the spiritual affectation in its conception."[31] Waldmüller's concept of spirit never becomes entirely clear, neither here nor in later formulations. Perhaps we may conceive of his ideas as follows: The artist views the reality of human activities; his feelings convince him of the truth of what he sees. By depicting it, he unveils the moral dimension that lies at the root of what has been seen. Apparently this happens automatically, as with Hirt and Schadow. Thus, art production per se is a perception process and this precisely is its intellectual part. Thus, the artist has the ability to distinguish the truthful from the untruthful.

This concept is based in Enlightenment traditions, as betrayed by Waldmüller's use of the term "affectation." In Julius Bernhard von Rohr's *Einleitung zur Ceremoniel-Wissenschaft der Privat-Personen*, written in 1728, appropriate behavior is legitimated solely through moral philosophy. As we know, Rohr was a student of Christian Wolff, and so he states: "The highest and most perfect qualities lose their value when combined with affectation; everyone then sees them merely as a contrived duty, rather than as a free and natural effect of true virtue."[32] Daniel Chodowiecki's print series *Natürliche und affectirte Handlungen des Lebens* from 1778/79, which was published in the *Göttinger Taschen-Calender* almanac,[33] stands in direct succession to this tradition. Internalized behavior is set against externalized behavior, and intellect is confirmed as the inner motivation for internalized behavior. Thus, according to Waldmüller, intellect strives not for an ideal abstract, but for concrete inner feeling.

But this can be expressed even more precisely, since, consciously or not, Waldmüller's concept of the spirit is clearly based on Neoplatonic ideology. And this connects not only Hirt, Schadow, and Waldmüller, but also, despite all apparent differences, binds these naturalists to Goethe and the entire Neoplatonic tradition. To explore this briefly: Dürer, who had been introduced to Marsilio Ficino's Neoplatonism by his Humanist peers in Nuremberg, believed that art was a gift of God, which filled the artist with an awareness of the true beauty of the human body. "God alone knows this, those to whom he reveals it, they know it too."[34] And this artistic inspiration, according to Dürer, will come from "infusions from above."[35] In this way, the artist has "within himself a host of figures."[36] This tradition may explain why Waldmüller focused solely on the study of the human figure.

In *Maxims and Reflections*, Goethe aptly formulates the process of inspiration. "True symbolism is where the particular represents the general, not as a dream or a shadow, but as a living, momentary revelation of the Inscrutable."[37] Hirt and Schadow, and Waldmüller too, could have easily subscribed to this. Schadow later yielded slightly by modifying his concept of naturalism, which he had deliberately overplayed in his confrontation with Goethe, insofar as he stipulated a dimension of grace, quasi as the artistic addition to merely conceiving what is seen in nature.[38] Both Goethe and Schiller had defined grace as beauty in movement. So, when Schadow attests to grace in his sculptural work he elevates the argument to include the process of artistic animation. Not only the artist is inspired but, ultimately, also the work. In the artwork's effect, this inspiration appears as animation—and this marks the guiding principle of all realistic art, and especially that of Waldmüller.

The question is whether, above and beyond the concept of spirit, Waldmüller's art represents a good equivalent for this animation of the work itself. This is indeed the case, and is embodied in Waldmüller's concept of the role of light.[39] The depiction of his figures in a low morning or evening light, particularly distinct in his later work, with long, strong shadows that intensify the contrast of light and dark, can be thought of as a way of imbuing the figures with power, a process of animation through a divine ray of light. I don't want to dwell on the fact that such an intensification of the actuality of appearances also has an inherent tendency toward torpidity, as though the figures were frozen at the moment of extremely fervid movement. All hyperrealism is subject to this. What matters here is that, against the backdrop of Waldmüller's concept of spirit, inspiration, and animation, we can also reach an appreciation of the core of Waldmüller's criticism of the academy and his proposal to replace the entire academic curriculum with a masterclass system. He was able to study this system at the School of David in Paris and was most likely also inspired by Genelli's promotion of masterclasses. Likewise, undoubtedly serving him as example was Wilhelm Schadow's reform of the Düsseldorf Academy, as set down in his 1828 treatise *Meine Gedanken über eine folgerichtige Ausbildung des Malers*, which also culminated in the suggestion of masterclasses[40] and may still have served Joseph Beuys in his criticisms of the Düsseldorf Academy centuries later.

Its more profound meaning may be seen in the sense that the master was to be considered an "inspired" being who, through his example, imbues his students with spirit, so that each of them in their own way—an aspect that was particularly important to Waldmüller—would become inspired, too. The objective was not to imitate the style of the master—a concept Waldmüller vehemently opposed—but his mere existence as an artist should serve as inspiration and model. Insofar, he calls for the "intellectual freedom of art," is opposed to all "stylization," like Carstens, he considers the state obliged to subsidize the chosen artist, he rejects the "division of art into different subjects," and propagates the autonomy of art and artists: "The foundation of all art is complete in and of itself."[41]

Thus, Waldmüller's attack on the academy is not to be interpreted primarily as the claim of a disgruntled artist lacking in public recognition, but as what it actually is: a blueprint for an alternative vision for art and artists, cloaked—perplexingly—in a labored realism.

1 On *disegno* see Karen-Edis Barzman, *The Florentine Academy and the Early Modern State: The Discipline of Disegno* (Cambridge, 2000); Giorgio Vasari, *The Lives of the Artists*, trans. Julia Conway Bondanella and Peter Bondanella (Oxford, 2008), pp. 2ff.; Hein-Th. Schulze Altcappenberg/Michael Thimann, eds., *Disegno: Der Zeichner im Bild der Frühen Neuzeit*, exh. cat. Kupferstichkabinett Staatliche Museen zu Berlin (Berlin, 2007). On the opposition of drawing/color see Thomas Puttfarken, "The Dispute about 'Disegno' and 'Colorito' in Venice," in Peter Ganz/Martin Gosebruch, eds., *Kunst und Kunsttheorie 1400–1900* (Wiesbaden, 1991), pp. 75–99; Werner Busch, *Das unklassische Bild: Von Tizian bis Constable und Turner* (Munich, 2009), pp. 74–90.

2 Pliny the Elder, *The Natural History* John Bostock/H.T.Riley, ed., http://www.perseus.tufts.edu/hopper/text?doc=Perseus%3Atext%3A1999.02.0137%3Abook%3D34%3Achapter%3D19 (accessed on August 24, 2016).

3 Ernst Kris/Otto Kurz, *Die Legende vom Künstler: Ein geschichtlicher Versuch*, with a foreword by Ernst Hans Gombrich (Frankfurt a. M., 1974) [Vienna, 1934].

4 Quoted from Pliny the Elder (see note 2), book 34, chapter 19

5 Kris/Kurz 1974 (see note. 3), pp. 90–91.

6 Giorgio Vasari, *Vite de' più eccellenti pittori, scultori, ed architetti*, 9 vols., ed. Gaetano Milanesi, Florence 1878–1885, vol. 8 (Florence, 1882), p. 294.

7 Roger de Piles tells the anecdote with reference to a woman's portrait by Rembrandt, which he had purchased, *Abrégé de la vie des peintres*, 2nd ed. (Paris, 1715), p. 432.

8 See on this, in detail, Busch 2009 (see note 1), pp. 76–82, 140–158; ibid., "Unklassische Werkprozesse: Zeichnung und Sinnstiftung," in Joachim Jacoby/Martin Sonnabend, eds., *Raffael als Zeichner. Die Beiträge des Frankfurter Kolloquiums* (Petersberg, 2015), esp. pp. 20–26.

9 Werner Busch, "Akademie und Autonomie: Asmus Jakob Carstens' Auseinandersetzung mit der Berliner Akademie," in *Berlin zwischen 1789 und 1848: Facetten einer Epoche*, exh. cat. Berlin Academy of the Arts (Berlin, 1981), pp. 81–92.

10 Quoted from Busch 1981 (see note 9), p. 81.

11 Quoted from Busch 1981 (see note 9), p. 81.

12 Quoted from Busch 1981 (see note 9), pp. 82–83.

13 Quoted from Busch 1981 (see note 9), p. 84.

14 Carl Ludwig Fernow, *Leben des Künstlers Asmus Jakob Carstens: Ein Beitrag zur Kunstgeschichte des achtzehnten Jahrhunderts* (Leipzig, 1806), pp. 249–251.

15 Karl Philipp Moritz, "Über den Begriff des in sich selbst Vollendeten," in ibid., *Werke*, ed. Horst Günther, 3 vols. (Frankfurt a. M., 1981), vol. 2, pp. 543–548.

16 Karl Philipp Moritz, "Über die bildende Nachahmung des Schönen," in ibid. 1981 (see note 15), p. 571.

17 Hans Christian Genelli, *Idee einer Akademie der Bildenden Künste* (Braunschweig, 1800).

18 On Heinitz's reform, see Hans Müller, *Die Königliche Akademie der Künste zu Berlin, 1696 bis 1896. I. Teil* (Berlin, 1896), esp. chapters 11–14, pp. 137–198; see also J. C. Frisch, "Fragment über die Idee, eine Akademie der Künste in Berlin in Bezug auf Fabriken und Gewerke gemeinnütziger zu machen," in *Monatsschrift der Akademie der Künste und mechanischen Wissenschaften zu Berlin*, vol. 1, 2nd section, 1788, pp. 67–75.

19 Genelli 1800 (see note 17), p. 2.

20 Genelli 1800 (see note 17), p. 3.

21 Genelli 1800 (see note 17), p. 6.

22 Genelli 1800 (see note 17), p. 71.

23 Genelli 1800 (see note 17), p. 73.

24 Genelli 1800 (see note 17), pp. 33–34.

25 Werner Busch, *Die notwendige Arabeske: Wirklichkeitsaneignung und Stilisierung in der deutschen Kunst des 19. Jahrhunderts* (Berlin, 1985), pp. 75–89; ibid., "Die Arabeske – Ornament als Bedeutungsträger: Eine Einführung," in Busch/Petra Maisak, eds., *Verwandlung der Welt. Die romantische Arabeske*, exh. cat. Freies Deutsches Hochstift – Frankfurter Goethe-Museum, Kunsthalle Hamburg (Petersberg, 2013), esp. pp. 26–27 and cat. no. 170, pp. 325–327.

26 On the principles of the arabesque, see Werner Busch, "Goethe und Neureuther – Die Arabeske: Ornament oder Reflexionsmedium?" in Jochen Golz/Albert Meier/Edith Zehm, eds., *Goethe-Jahrbuch*, vol. 128 (Göttingen, 2011), pp. 127–158.

27 Ronald Paulson does not include Hogarth's pictorial invention *Taste in High Life* in his catalogue of graphic works, as it is a reproduction by someone else based on Hogarth's corresponding painting; see *William Hogarth 1697–1764*, exh. cat. Neue Gesellschaft für Bildende Kunst e. V., Staatliche Kunsthalle Berlin (Gießen, 1980), cat. no. 81, pp. 122–125.

28 Jutta Reinisch, "Dürers Randzeichnungen zum Gebetbuch Kaiser Maximilians I. und Johann Nepomuk Strixners lithographische Wiedergabe von 1808," in Busch/Maisak 2013 (see note 25), pp. 72–73 and cat. nos. 33–35, pp. 75–77.

29 On the annotated sources and subsequent debates, see Wolfgang Beyrodt/Werner Busch, eds., *Kunsttheorie und Kunstgeschichte des 19. Jahrhunderts in Deutschland*, vol. 1, *Kunsttheorie und Malerei: Kunstwissenschaft. Texte und Dokumente* (Stuttgart, 1982), pp. 91–100; Hilmar Frank, "Goethe, Schadow und das Formgesetz der Plastik," in Bernhard Maaz, ed., *Johann Gottfried Schadow und die Kunst seiner Zeit*, exh. cat. Kunsthalle Düsseldorf; Germanisches Nationalmuseum Nürnberg; Nationalgalerie Berlin (Cologne, 1994), pp. 141–147; Harald Tausch, "Das vermessene Charakteristische: Zu Aloys Hirts römischer Ästhetik," in Claudia Sedlarz, ed. *Aloys Hirt. Archäologe, Historiker, Kunstkenner* (= Berliner Klassik: Eine Großstadtkultur um 1800, vol. 1) (Hannover-Laatzen, 2004), pp. 69–103.

30 Julia Kloss-Weber, *Individualisiertes Ideal und nobilitierte Alltäglichkeit. Das Genre in der französischen Skulptur der zweiten Hälfte des 18. Jahrhunderts* (= Kunstwissenschaftliche Studien, vol. 174) (Berlin/Munich, 2014), pp. 249–289.

31 Ferdinand Georg Waldmüller, "Das Bedürfnis eines zweckmäßigen Unterrichts in der Malerei und plastischen Kunst angedeutet nach eigenen Erfahrungen" (1846, 2nd ed. 1847), in Rupert Feuchtmüller, *Ferdinand Georg Waldmüller (1793–1865): Leben, Schriften, Werke* (Vienna, 1996), p. 329.

32 Johann Bernhard von Rohr, *Einleitung zur Ceremoniel-Wissenschaft der Privat-Personen*, reprint of the 1728 Berlin edition, edited and annotated by Gotthardt Frühsorge (Leipzig, 1989), p. 77; see also Werner Busch, *Das sentimentalische Bild: Die Krise der Kunst im 18. Jahrhundert und die Geburt der Moderne* (Munich, 1993), pp. 312–317.

33 Jens-Heiner Bauer, *Daniel Nikolaus Chodowiecki: Das druckgaphische Werk* (Hannover, 1982), nos. 553–576 (= E.256 II and E.319 II).

34 Quoted from Franz Fuhse/Konrad von Lange, eds., *Dürers schriftlicher Nachlaß* (Halle a. d. S., 1893), pp. 221–222.

35 Quoted from Fuhse/Lange 1893 (see note 34), p. 297.

36 Quoted from Fuhse/Lange 1893 (see note 34), p. 298.

37 Johann Wolfgang von Goethe, "Maximen und Reflexionen," in ibid., *Werke* (= Hamburg edition), vol. 12, *Kunst und Literatur*, 10th ed. (Munich, 1982), p. 471 (no. 752). English: http://www.gutenberg.org/files/33670/33670-h/33670-h.htm (accessed on August 8, 2016).

38 Johann Gottfried Schadow, "Die Werkstätte des Bildhauers," in *Eunomia*, 2nd vol., no. 10, 1802, pp. 346–363.

39 Feuchtmüller 1996 (see note 31), pp. 39, 66, 268–269, 272 [in Waldmüller's *Schriften*: pp. 358–359, 391].

40 Primary source excerpts and commentaries in Beyrodt/Busch 1982 (see note 29), pp. 162–168; the essay was first published as Wilhelm Schadow, "Meine Gedanken über eine folgerichtige Ausbildung des M," in *Berliner Kunst-Blatt*, no. 9, September 1828, pp. 265–272.

41 Feuchtmüller 1996 (see note 31), pp. 330, 335, 353, 356, 358, 361, 368.

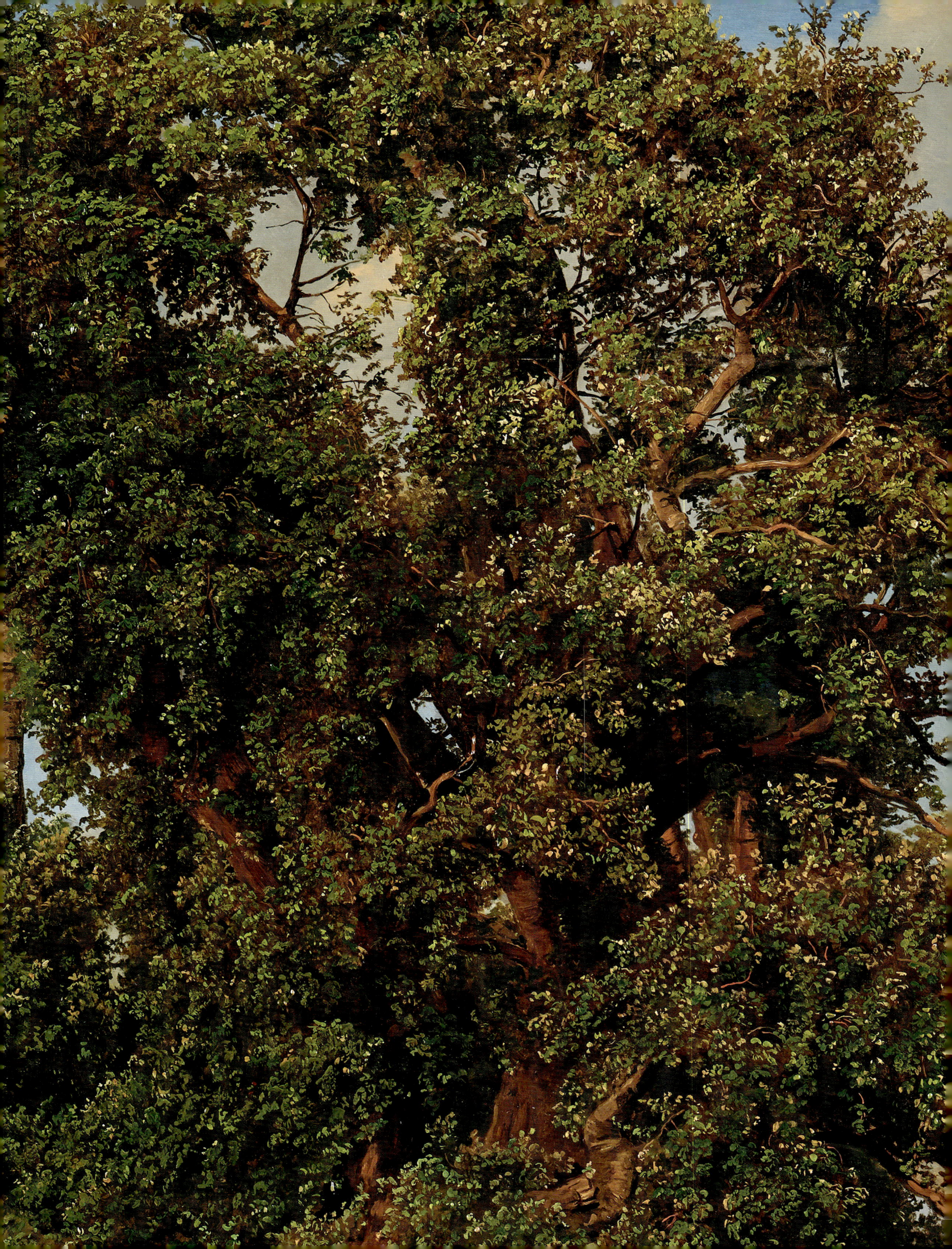

Plates

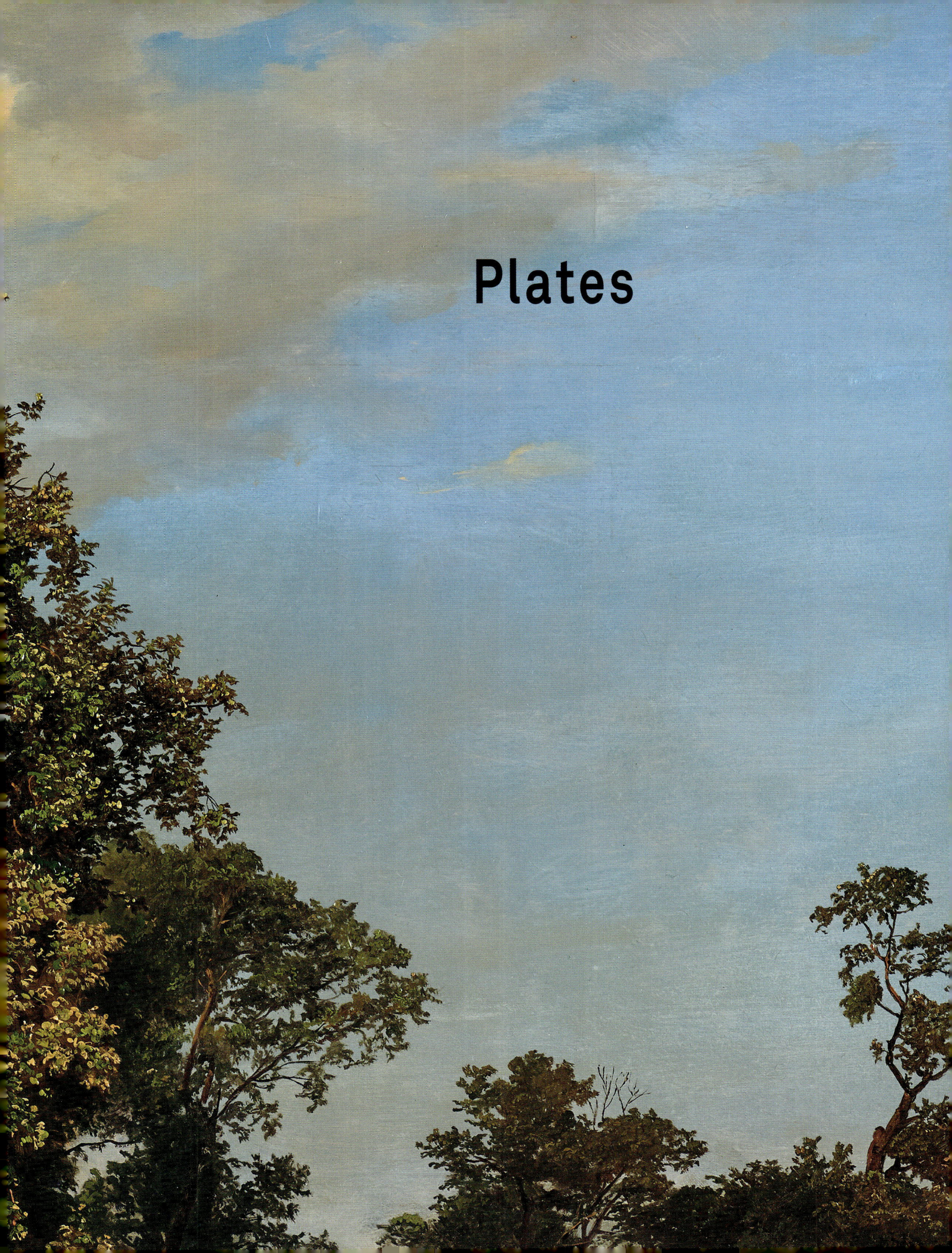

Francesco Hayez
Venus Playing with Two Doves (Portrait of the Ballerina Carlotta Chabert), 1830
Oil on canvas, 183 × 137 cm
Signed (lower left): F. HAYEZ / 1830
MART—Museo d'Arte Moderna e Contemporanea di Trento e Rovereto Deposito Fondazione Cassa di Risparmio di Trento e Rovereto, inv. no. MART 1198

This life-sized portrait of a naked woman caused a scandal in Milan in 1830. Hayez presented the painting at an exhibition at the Brera immediately upon completion, prompting a chorus of outrage that filled the newspapers for days. The sitter, Carlotta Chabert, was a celebrated ballerina, known to all the cultured Milanese from the stage. It was also common knowledge that she was the lover of Count Gerolamo Malfatti from Trento. Even greater outrage was felt about comparing a person from the theater with the Roman goddess Venus, especially as elevating a mere mortal to the echelons of the gods had previously been reserved for high-ranking individuals or sovereigns, as Fernando Mazzocca notes.[1] Yet this allusion, widely felt to be an arrogant presumption, was exactly what the patron Malfatti had intended. At the same time, the scandal only enhanced the fame of the Venice-born artist, who had been teaching history painting at the Brera Academy for about seven years. The similarity of the portrayal to Jean-Auguste-Dominique Ingres's *Valpinçon Bather* (1808, Louvre, Paris) cannot be missed, and reflects Hayez's veneration of the French master, whom he had been able to meet as a budding artist on a study trip to Rome. With the woman's pose, Hayez may also have been alluding to French Neoclassical portraiture, for example, the work of François Gérard. Mazzocca also references the Neapolitan *Venus Callipyge* as a source of inspiration (Museo Archeologico, Naples).[2] Hayez has skillfully captured the balance between the figure's soft body and its marble-statuesque qualities, without this image of a nude woman ever straying into eroticism.

Fernando Mazzocca, ed., *Hayez dal mito al bacio*, exh. cat. Palazzo Zabarella, Padua (Venice, 1998), pp. 142–43; Alessandra Tiddia, ed., *Nuovi ospiti a Palazzo delle Albere: Donazioni e depositi del XIX secolo 2004–2008*, exh. cat. MART—Museo d'Arte Moderna e Contemporanea di Trento e Rovereto (Trento, 2008), pp. 88–89, with further literature; Maria Vittoria Marini Clarelli/Fernando Mazzocca/Carlo Sisi, eds., *Ottocento: Da Canova al Quarto Stato*, exh. cat. Scuderie del Quirinale, Rome (Milan, 2008), p. 166; Fernando Mazzocca, ed., *Francesco Hayez* (Milan, 2015), pp. 168–71 (Cecilia Ghibaudi).

SG

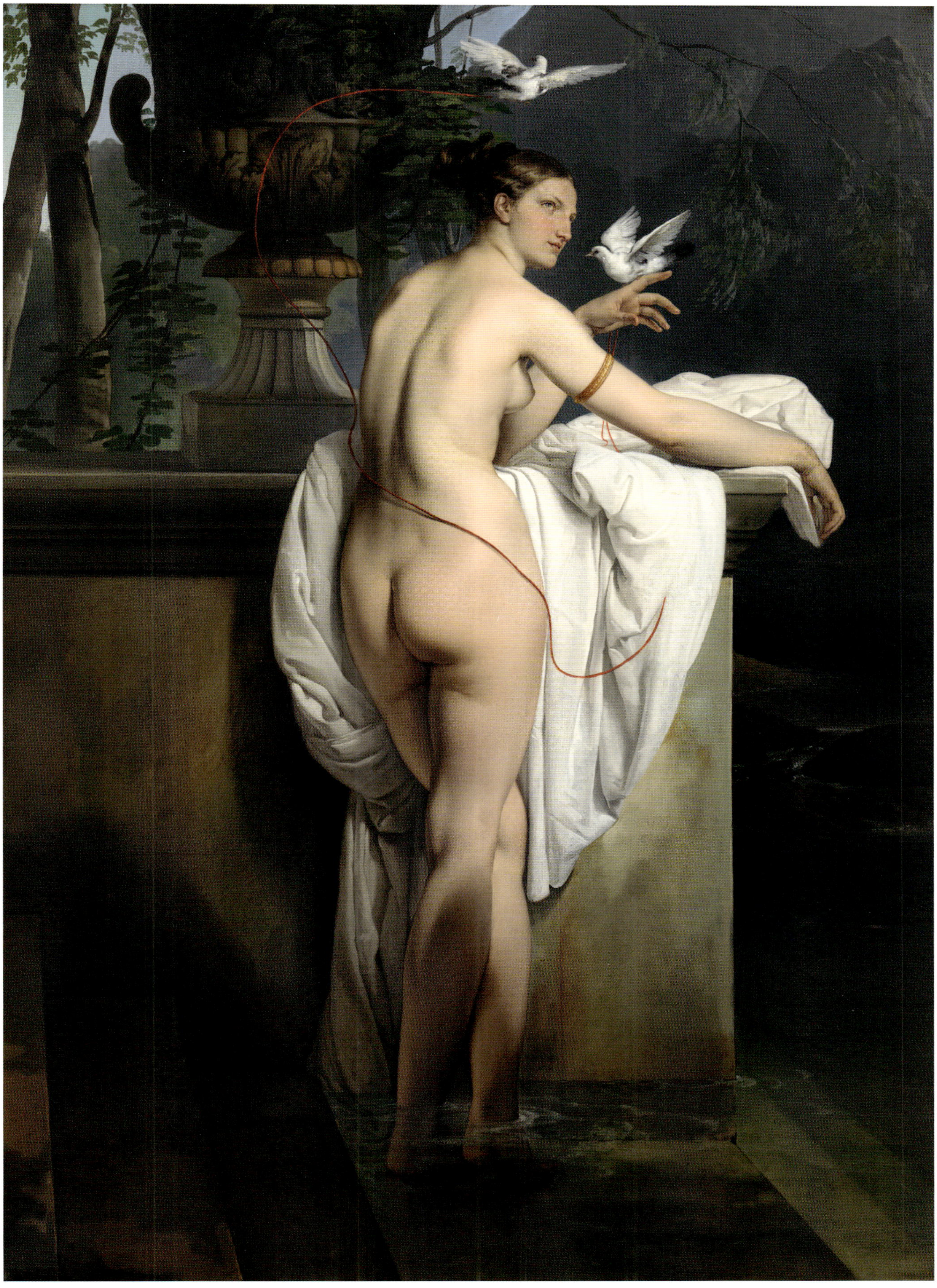

Giuseppe Tominz
Drago Popovich, 1832–1835
Oil on canvas, 123 × 87.5 cm
Unsigned
Museo Civico Revoltella, Trieste - Galleria d'arte moderna, inv. no. 684

Giuseppe Tominz
Giovanni Milost, known as Zuan delle Rose, before 1830
Oil on canvas, 53 × 47.5 cm
Unsigned
Polo museale del Friuli Venezia Giulia, Galleria Nazionale d'Arte Antica, Trieste, inv. no. 80

When Tominz settled in Trieste in 1830, he already had a reputation as an innovative portraitist. As a result, his studio in Casa Allodi on Via San Lazzaro soon became a popular gathering point for members of the haute bourgeoisie. Tominz's ability to capture the essence of a person and also to complete his pictures quickly stimulated demand throughout the entire Austrian Littoral region and explains the large number of portraits painted by him during this time.

While working in Gorizia, where he lived from around 1818, he had already developed a style with well-defined three-dimensional figures. The form and clear colors were true to the Neoclassicist ideal, but he went beyond this with his extremely realistic depiction of the natural surroundings. He also sought out the distinctive features of his sitters and emphasized them to bring their personality to the fore. Thus he put a trademark rose in the buttonhole of *Giovanni Milost* (plate p. 82), who was never seen without one and was known in Gorizia as a result as "Zuan delle Rose." Tominz's skill is even more evident, however, in the subject's mischievous smile, expressing his knowing complicity in this clever artistic device.

For the portrait of *Drago Popovich* (plate p. 81), painted a short while later in Trieste, Tominz made reference to a heroic deed performed by his subject. Born in 1799, Popovich, an inhabitant of Trieste with Serbian roots, owned a large shipping company, which he had expanded in the 1830s as far as the Black Sea. For that reason, Tominz shows a maritime scene behind the figure. However, this is not just an ordinary view of the sea designed to illustrate the subject's profession, but it shows the very shipwreck Popovich suffered with his brig *Aristide* off the coast of Marseille in 1832, and which he as the ship's captain had been able to master most auspiciously.[3] In front of this backdrop, the man presents himself confidently and aloof, immaculately dressed with tasteful accessories. The portrait is undated but must have been painted shortly after the shipwreck, as it was shown in 1835 at the painter's first solo exhibition in Sala del Ridotto in the Teatro Grande in Trieste.[4]

Jožef Tominc (1790–1866), exh. cat. National Gallery, Ljubljana (Ljubljana, 1967); *Jožef Tominc: Fiziognomija slike*, exh. cat. National Gallery, Ljubljana (Ljubljana, 2002), cat. no. 20; Alessandro Quinzi, *Giuseppe Tominz* (Collana d'Arte della Fondazione CR Trieste, vol. 13) (Trieste, 2011), cat. nos. 32 and 64 (with further reading).

SG

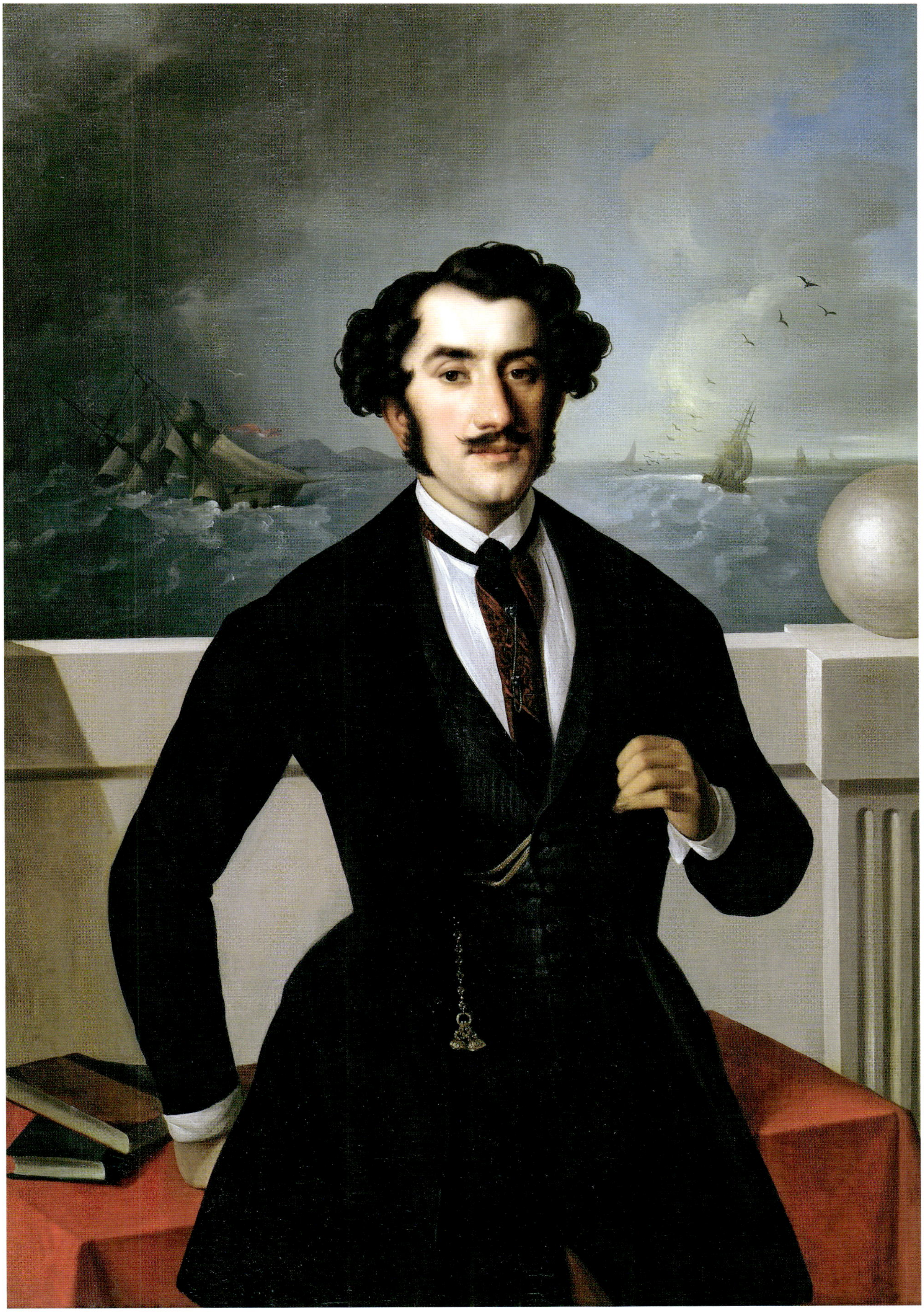

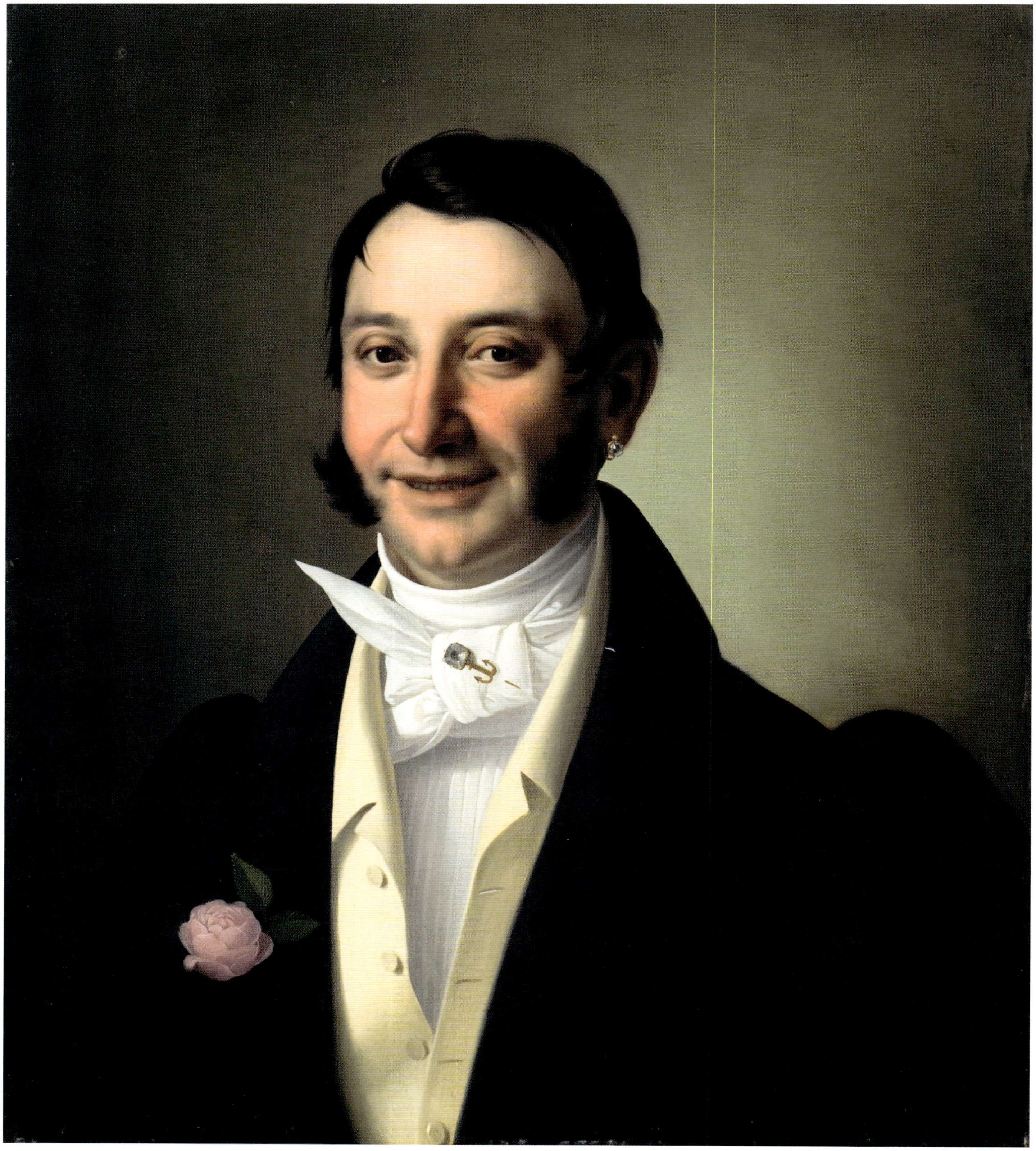

Giuseppe Tominz
Giovanni Milost, known as Zuan delle Rose, before 1830

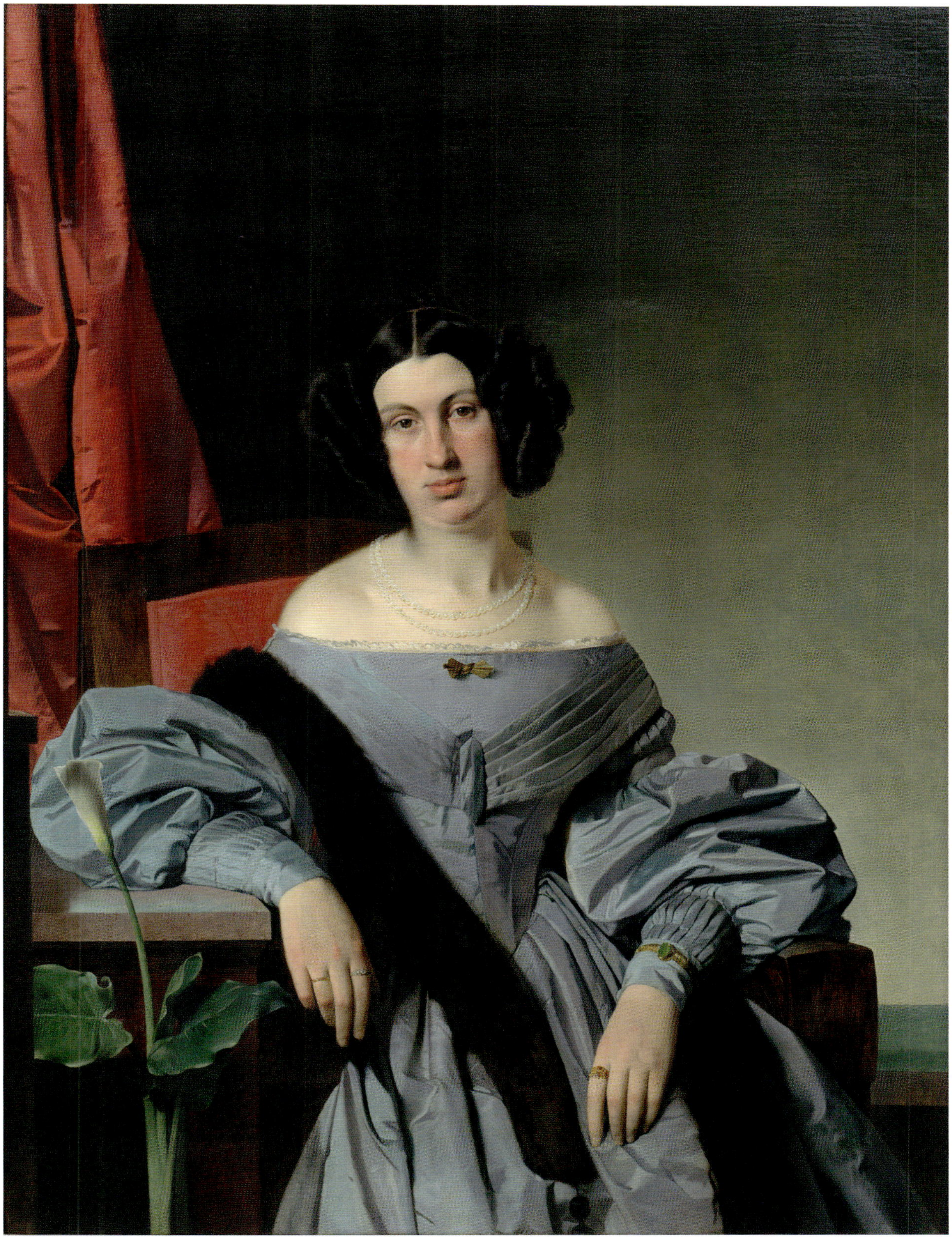

Franz Eybl
Franziska Schweighofer, Wife of the Piano Manufacturer Johann Michael Schweighofer, 1839
Oil on canvas, 122.7 × 97.2 cm
Signed (lower left): F. Eybl 839
Wien Museum, inv. no. 104.414

Ferdinand Georg Waldmüller
Self-Portrait as a Young Man, 1828
Oil on canvas, 95 × 75 cm
Signed (lower left): Waldmüller / 1828 / Aet. 35
Belvedere, Vienna, inv. no. 2121

Although this painting is a self-portrait, props such as brushes, palette, easel, or studio surroundings are missing. Waldmüller evidently had no intention of emphasizing his profession or building a narrative around his existence as an artist, nor did he want to question himself, as was the case with self-portraits by his contemporaries like Friedrich von Amerling or Johann Baptist Reiter. Instead he presents himself as an elegantly dressed, fashion-conscious young man with tastefully color-coordinated cravat, gloves, and top hat. It is possible that he wished to point to his versatility as an artist, because the painterly technique is outstanding. He has observed his face and all the details of his clothing with great precision, summoning all his skill to present them on canvas accordingly. At the same time, the portrait may also be seen as a demonstration of his compositional talent, his gift for skillful arrangement so as to place the subject to best advantage. Finally, the intention of the inscription at the bottom right, "1828 [in] Aet[atis]. 35"—indicating that he painted this at the age of thirty-five, probably in June to judge by the peony—is to emphasize a Humanist sensitivity and his skill at painting flowers.

In other words, it is a picture in which Waldmüller shows off all his talents. Its particular status in Austrian art, however, is due to its convincing effect as an outdoor portrait. For once, the natural setting does not look like a stage backdrop, but rather gives the impression that the subject is indeed sitting on a bench in the middle of the Vienna Woods. Waldmüller had understood that the only way to achieve visual harmony between a figure and the natural surroundings was through the light and that only by showing both subjects in the same sunlight could a unified picture be created. This realization is typical of his exceptional powers of observation and his constant searching as a result. Waldmüller kept this picture with him throughout his life. It was not until the death of his second wife in 1878 that it ended up in the Imperial Picture Gallery and from there in the Belvedere collection.

Klaus Albrecht Schröder, *Ferdinand Georg Waldmüller*, exh. cat. Kunstforum Länderbank, Vienna (Munich, 1990), pp. 72–73; Rupert Feuchtmüller, *Ferdinand Georg Waldmüller, 1793–1865: Leben, Schriften, Werke* (Vienna/Munich, 1996), pp. 50–51, cat. rais. no. 234; Gerbert Frodl, ed., *19. Jahrhundert* (= Geschichte der bildenden Kunst in Österreich 5) (Munich et al., 2002), p. 281; Sabine Grabner/Michael Krapf, eds., *Aufgeklärt bürgerlich: Porträts von Gainsborough bis Waldmüller 1750–1840*, exh. cat. Österreichische Galerie Belvedere, Vienna (Munich, 2006), pp. 280–81 (Sabine Grabner).

SG

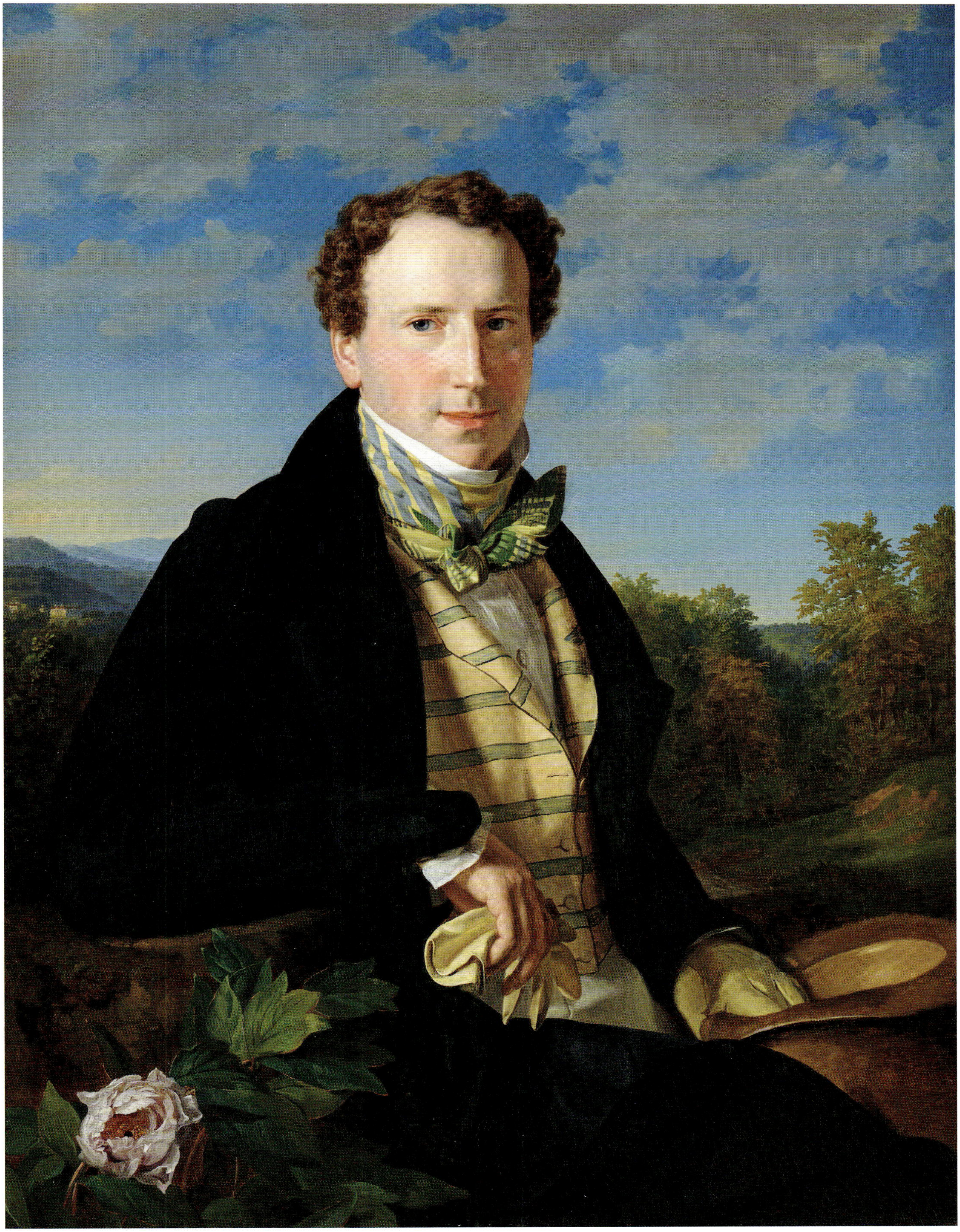

Johann Mathias Ranftl
Carl, Mathias, and Katharina Wisgrill, 1832
Oil on canvas, 140 × 109 cm
Signed (lower right): Ranftl 1832.
Wien Museum, inv. no. 146.670

Ranftl painted this children's portrait shortly after his return from Russia. He had spent almost two years there, mostly in Moscow and also a few months in St. Petersburg.[5] He earned his living by painting portraits, and the length of his stay would indicate that he had plenty of commissions. He had previously studied history painting at the Academy in Vienna with Johann Peter Krafft (1780–1856), but his skill at characterizing the human physiognomy was acquired afterwards. He developed an excellent technique and also used high-quality materials, as this portrait from 1832 demonstrates.

The subjects, Carl Wisgrill (born 1827) in the center, flanked by his siblings Katharina (born 1828) and Mathias (born 1829), were the children of the master carpenter Mathias Wisgrill (1794–1863) and his wife Elisabeth (1804–1856).[6] The family, which had been working in this trade for several generations, lived on the Danube Canal on the corner of Franzensbrückenstrasse and Schüttelstrasse. They spent the summer months in Baden and later in Grinzing, where the family had a country house on a large estate between Himmelstrasse and Strassergasse. The Grinzing church and Kahlenberg hill in the background of the picture would suggest that Ranftl painted the children there. Even though he arranged the figures in the form of an equilateral triangle, the composition does not appear static, as the group is dominated by the striding boys, with only Katharina resting on the floor. The smaller boy's pose with his arm raised recalls one of the figures in *The Hülsenbeck Children* by Philipp Otto Runge (1805/06, Kunsthalle Hamburg), which Ranftl no doubt knew from a reproduction. It may also have been inspired him to use the motif of the striding children, although Ranftl justifies the pose by including the bunny rabbit held on a leash by Mathias. The movement also recalls the British conversation piece style, in which the rigid poses of children (and adults) give way to casual movement.

L. A. Frankl, "Mathias Johann Ranftl: Biographische Skizze," in *Neue Freie Presse*, morning edition, no. 1758, July 21, 1869, n.p.; Leo Grünstein, "Johann Matthias Ranftl," in *Neue Freie Presse*, evening edition, no. 14547, February 21, 1905, pp. 3–4; Susanne Walter, "Die Familien Wisgrill, Lang und von Förster: Ein genealogischer und kulturhistorischer Streifzug durch das Wiener Patriziat," in *Wiener Geschichtsblätter*, 57th yr., no. 2, 2002, pp. 126–53, especially pp. 136–42.

SG

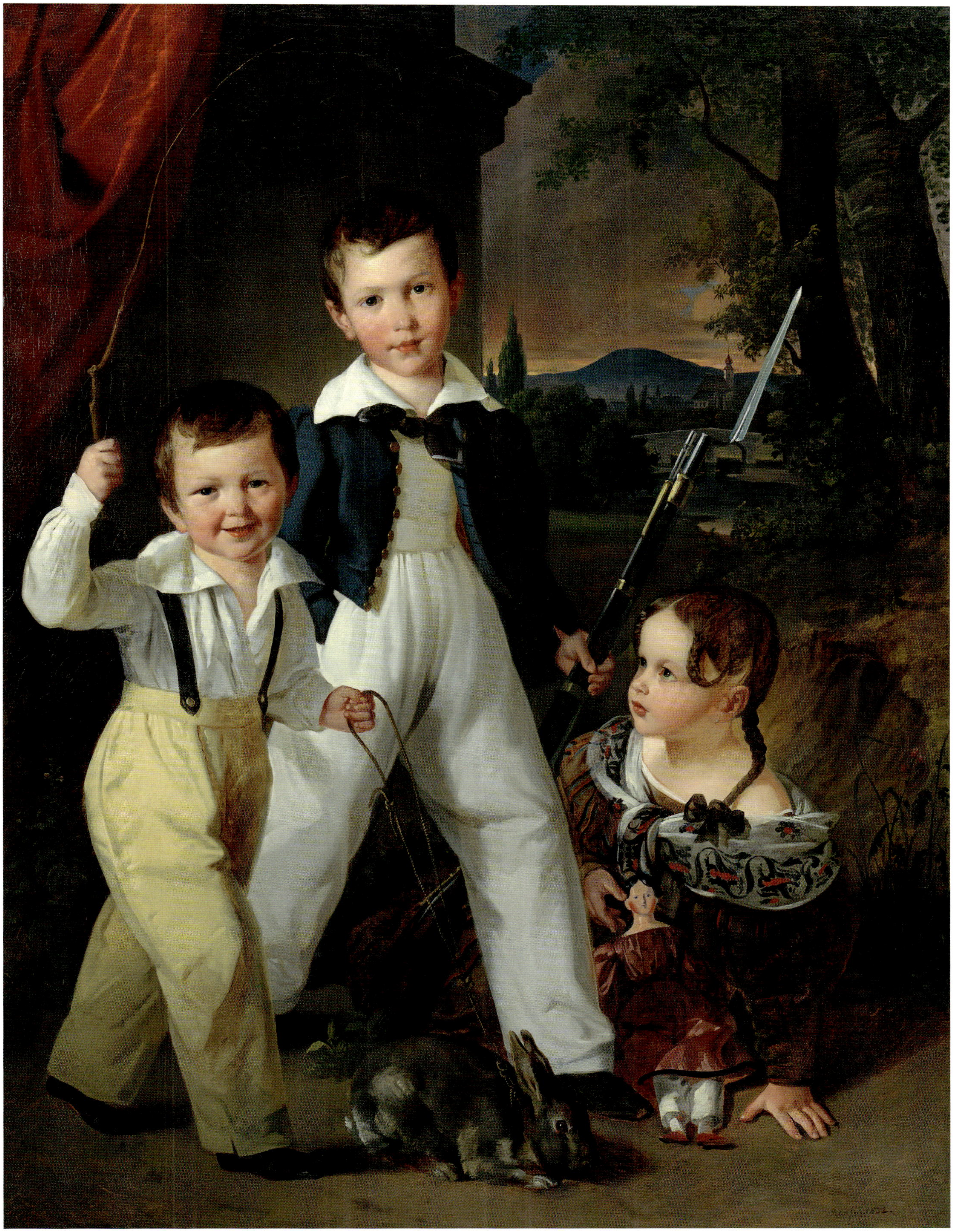

Michelangelo Grigoletti
Portrait of the Artist's Parents, 1829
Oil on canvas, 49 × 65 cm
Inscription on the reverse: Coll'industre sua man e bei colori / Michelangelo dipinse le due immagini, / che rappresentan li suoi genitori / anno 1829
Musei Civici, Pordenone, inv. no. 127

In this portrait, Grigoletti, who was from Rorai Grande, a suburb of Pordenone, has created a memorial to his parents. It unmistakably reflects their son's gratitude as, although not wealthy, his parents had supported his training as an artist. Teresa Di Michieli and Osvaldo Grigoletti are facing each other while also looking out of the picture, a stance typical of late Roman portraits of married couples.[7] Their faces have been captured with great detail and realism and their eyes seem to express their emotional bond with their son. In his choice of colors the young artist showed particular skill and taste in that he enlivened the otherwise dark attire with his mother's red cloak. He also included curls of hair straying onto his mother's forehead in the Neoclassical style.

Grigoletti only painted a few portraits as he was mainly a history painter. He had studied the subject at the Academy in Venice under Teodoro Matteini (1753–1831) and Odorico Politi (1785–1846), where the latter soon recognized and nurtured the young man's artistic talent. Besides numerous works for churches in Friuli-Venezia Giulia, Grigoletti painted altarpieces for Hungarian churches, specifically for the Basilica of Erlau (Eger) and for the large cathedral of Gran (Esztergom), commissioned by Ladislaus Pyrker, who was the patriarch of Venice until 1827 and then Archbishop of Erlau (Eger). While in Venice in 1838, Emperor Ferdinand I also commissioned a painting about Venetian history from Grigoletti, with the artist choosing as his subject the last meeting of Doge Francesco Foscari with his son Giacomo (*Doge Francesco Foscari Banishes his Son Giacomo* or *I due Foscari*, c. 1838, Belvedere, Vienna).[8] This large-scale narrative painting, ceremoniously presented in 1843 to a select circle of art connoisseurs in the Rittersaal of the Hofburg, was subsequently included in the Academy exhibition where it enjoyed great popularity among the Viennese public.[9]

Gilberto Ganzer, ed., *Michelangelo Grigoletti*, exh. cat. Museo Civico d'Arte, Pordenone (Pordenone, 2002), pp. 114–15; Giuseppe Bergamini, ed., *Tra Venezia e Vienna: Le arti a Udine nell'Ottocento*, exh. cat. Chiesa di San Francesco, Udine (Milan, 2004), pp. 398–99 (Vania Gransinigh); Gilberto Ganzer/Vania Gransinigh, *Michelangelo Grigoletti* (Milan, 2007), with catalogue raisonné and further literature.

SG

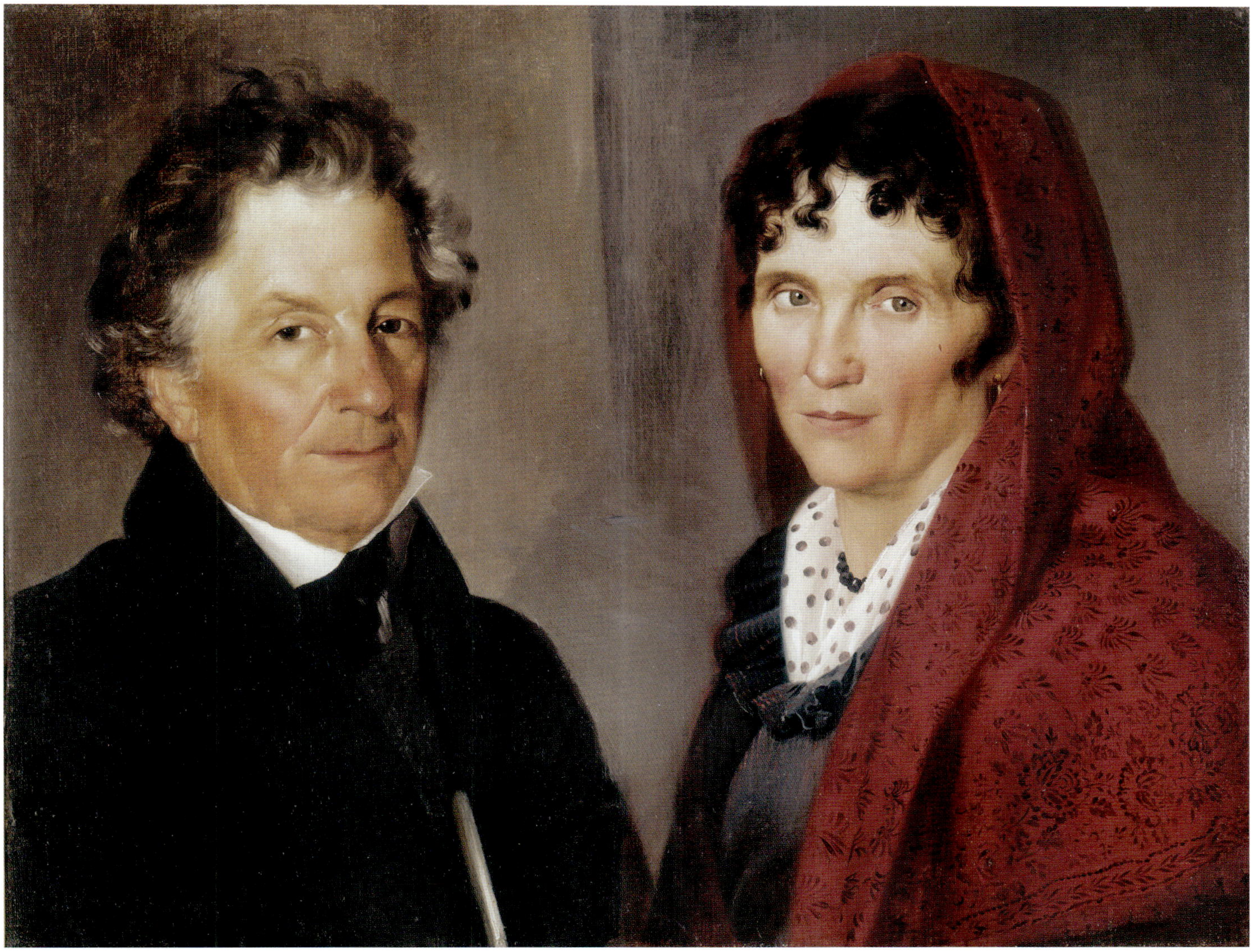

Giuseppe Tominz
David Buchler with His Wife Euphorine, née Maffei and his Six Sons, 1829
Oil on canvas, 159 × 194 cm
Unsigned
Buchler Family

The large portrait of the Buchler family challenged Tominz's capabilities and was thus of particular significance to him. He had only recently completed his first three-figure group portrait (*Three Women from the Moscon Family*, 1829, National Gallery, Ljubljana). The new commission required him to combine eleven figures in one painting. There was also a lot at stake for the artist as this was one of his first commissions in Trieste and he was therefore at pains to make a good impression and not to commit any blunders. To avoid any stiffness in the arrangement, he gave each of the figures a particular pose or activity designed to create a sense of interaction between the sitters. The composition of the group is interesting in this regard, because Tominz abandoned the classic triangular arrangement, opting for a wide format instead and placing the figures practically in a row in the lower half of the picture. The empty space above, which takes up half of the canvas, is filled with props, architectural elements and a bunched curtain exposing a view of the landscape. In this way he drew attention to the bronze statue of Mercury standing tall above the heads of the family. It is possible that the client David Buchler (1779–1839) had specifically asked for this statue to be given prominence in the picture so as to draw attention to his profession. He was a merchant from Munich who had settled in Trieste in 1808 to establish a business trading in spices and coffee. With his wife Euphrosine, née Maffei (1798–1887), he had eleven children, of whom the six sons can be seen in the group portrait. According to Coronini, the picture was painted to mark Buchler's election as president of the Trieste chamber of commerce in 1829.[10] It was shown two years later at the third exhibition of the Società Minerva in Trieste.

Jožef Tominc (1790–1866), exh. cat. National Gallery, Ljubljana (Ljubljana, 1967); Barbara Jaki, *Meščanska slika: Slikarstvo prve polovice 19. stoletja iz zbirk Narodne galerije*, exh. cat. National Gallery, Ljubljana (Ljubljana, 2000), pp. 264–65; Alessandro Quinzi, *Giuseppe Tominz* (Collana d'Arte della Fondazione CR Trieste, vol. 13) (Trieste, 2011), cat. no. 37 (with further reading).

SG

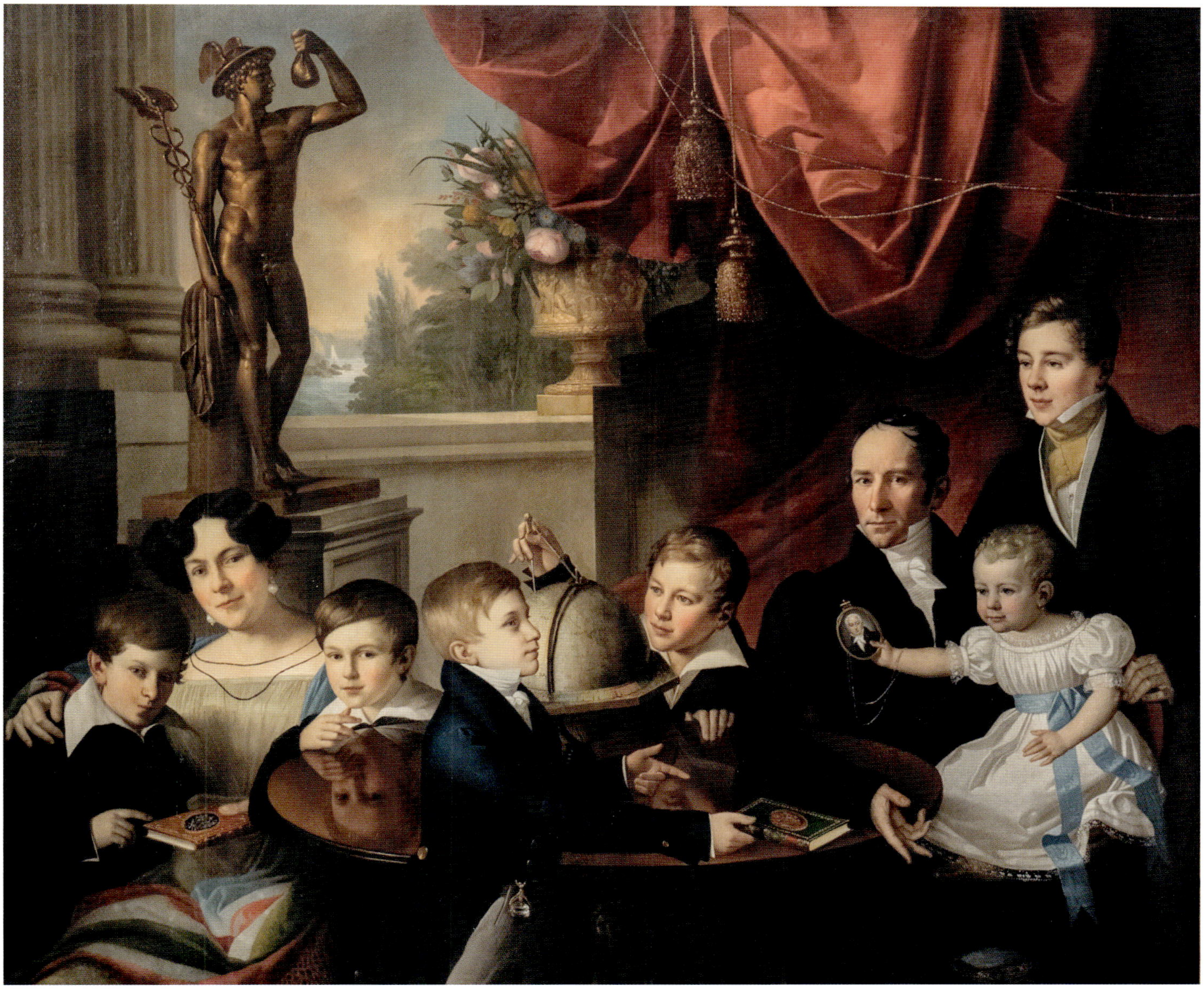

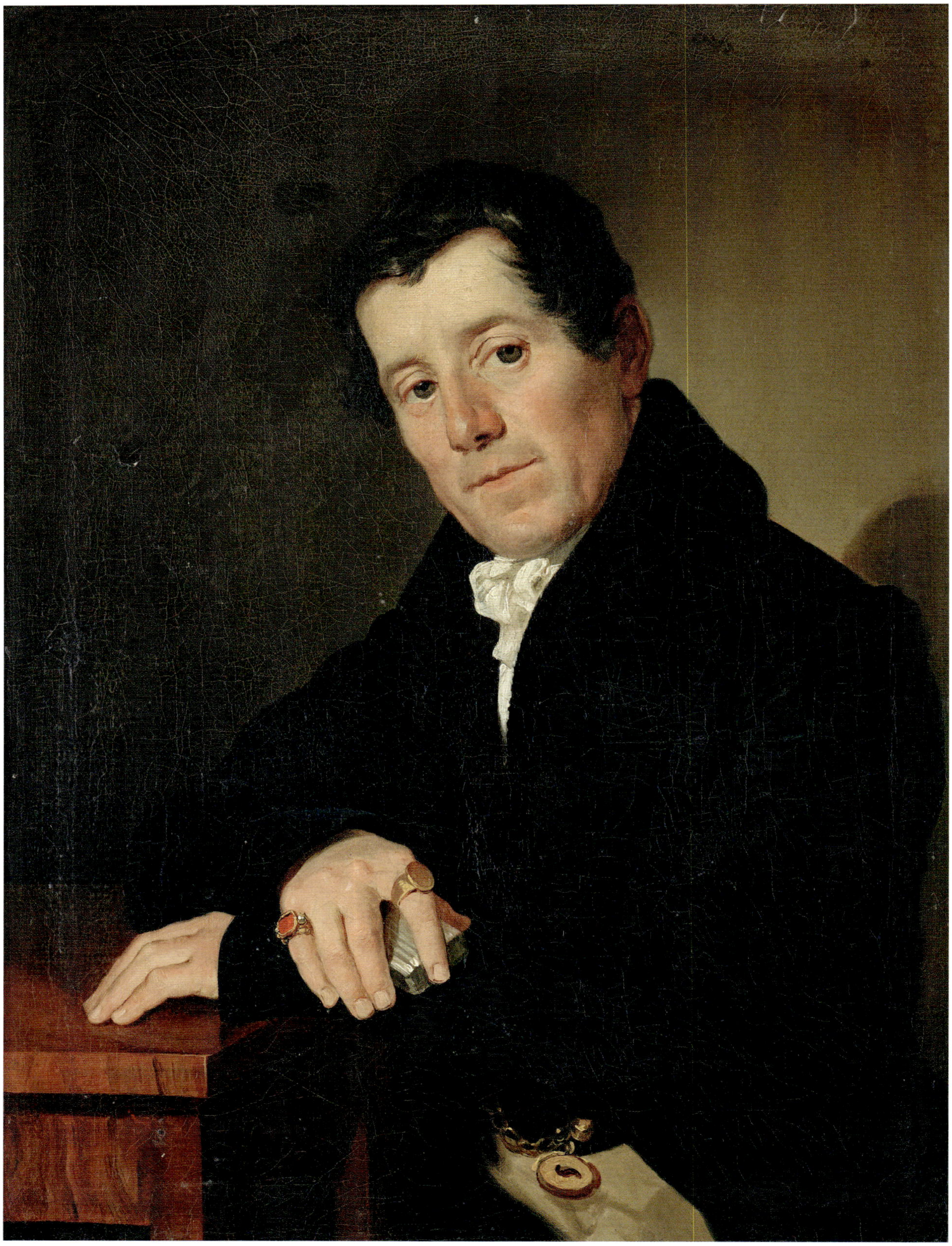

Eduard Ritter
Portrait of a Man, 1830s
Oil on canvas, 37.2 × 29.4 cm
Unsigned
Dr. Rudolf Schuster

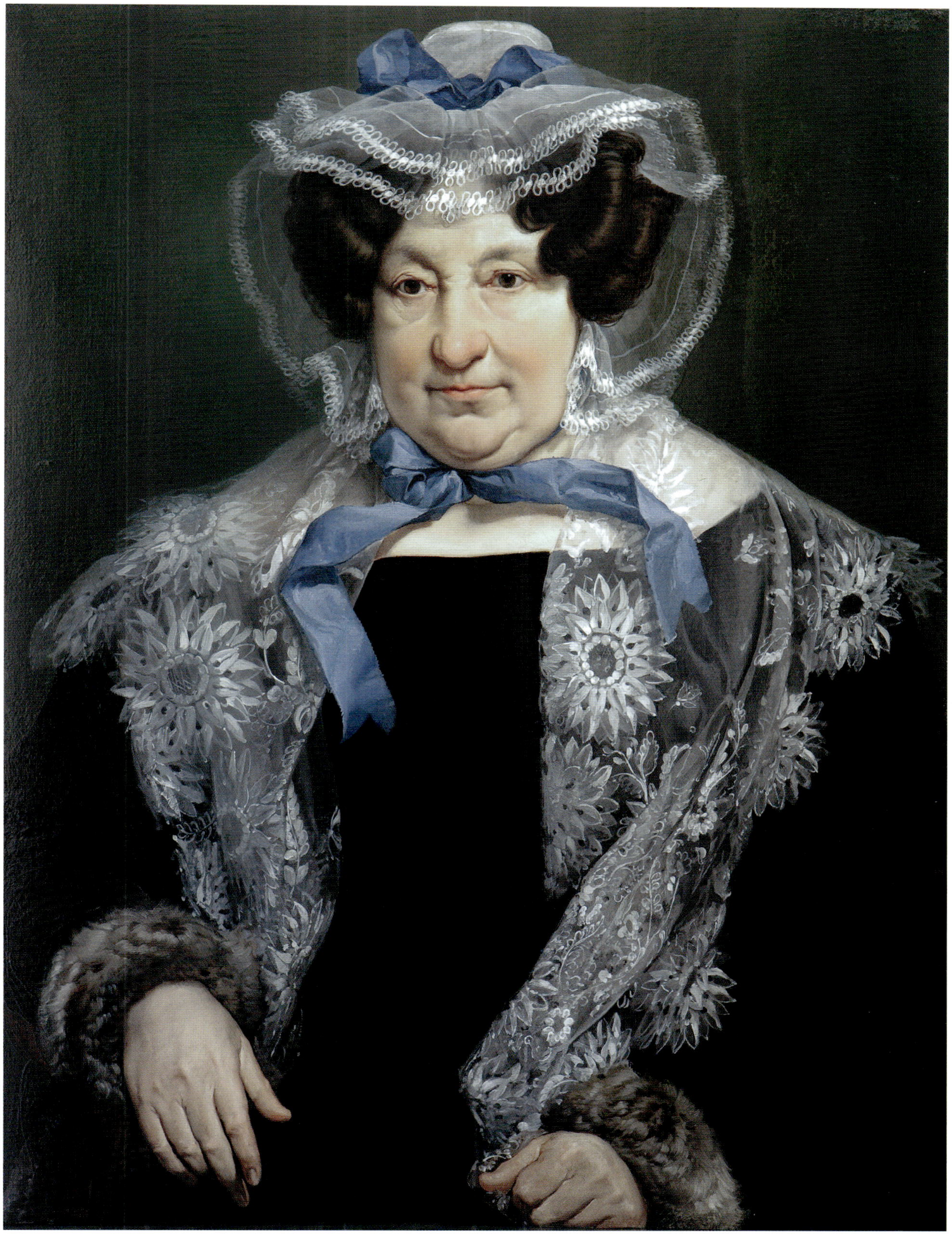

Francesco Hayez
Portrait of Federica Cristina Mylius Schnauss, 1828
Oil on wood, 74 × 58 cm
Unsigned
Associazione Villa Vigoni—Centro Italo-Tedesco, Loveno di Menaggio (CO)

Josef Danhauser
Anna von Hell, 1833
Oil on canvas, 134 × 96 cm
Signed (lower left): Danhauser / 1833
Private collection, Vienna

Besides painting genre scenes, Danhauser was also a portraitist. Regarding the latter, a group of drawings from the 1830s, showing several of his artist colleagues and friends in half-length portraits, deserves a mention. Some of these were reproduced by various engravers and lithographers.[11] It was more unusual for Danhauser to paint portraits in oils, so this recently discovered picture is particularly interesting. The portrait shows a standing woman and is signed on the lower left and dated 1833. According to the painter's list of pictures, that year he did indeed work on a large-scale, three-quarter-length portrait that he describes as "Frau v. Hell."[12] There are no further details, however. The woman in the painting, possibly also the patron, must have been wealthy, because these three-quarter-length portraits were one of the most expensive types of portraiture as the composition of both figure and space placed high demands on the artist. Her clothing also reveals her affluence: Her elegant lilac dress, with sumptuous lace trimmings and large leg o'mutton sleeves, was the height of fashion, as was the hat that tastefully completes her outfit. Other expensive details include the gold jewelry embellished with pearls and gemstones and the exquisite cashmere shawl she is holding with one leather glove. The figure faces slightly to one side in the composition, a device often encountered in Danhauser's work, for example in the portrait of *Anna Streit*, the artist's mother-in-law, from the same year (Oberösterreichisches Landesmuseum, Linz).

But who was this "Frau v. Hell"? According to the list of paintings, she gave Danhauser a further commission that same year, as there is a record of an "Altarpiece, Magdalene and Christ, for Frau v. Hell."[13] This refers to *Noli me Tangere*, a picture now in a private collection. When this painting was sold at the Dorotheum in 1907 "from an old Viennese private collection,"[14] the foreword in the auction catalogue stated: "This missing artwork has all of a sudden reappeared in all its vibrant colors [...] after, for decades, most beautifully adorning a small private chapel for the Viennese bourgeois family Gsiller in the former Held property in the district of Neubau, and being used only occasionally in public as an altar painting in the Corpus Christi procession."[15] The first edition of Lehmann's Vienna address book records that in 1859 an "imperial-royal official's widow" called Anna Gsiller lived in the Viennese suburb of "Neubau, Hauptstrasse 228."[16] If you trace the occupants of this address back in time, in 1833 a certain Anna Hell—the woman depicted here—appears as the owner of the house.[17] This name does not feature in the property records of subsequent years, but instead Anna Grolig (also Grollig or Krolig) is cited as living at this address, so presumably Anna Hell married a Herr Grolig after this was painted.[18] Not much later, the property was transferred to the aforementioned Gsiller family. The same applies to the portrait of *Anna von Hell*, given to the new owners as a gift following the death of a lady with this name.

Arthur Roessler, *Josef Danhauser* (Vienna/Leipzig, n.d. [1911]); Arthur Roessler, *Josef Danhauser* (Vienna, 1946); Veronika Birke, comp., *Josef Danhauser (1805–1845): Gemälde und Zeichnungen*, exh. cat. Albertina, Vienna (Vienna, 1983), p. 37; Sabine Grabner, *Der Maler Josef Danhauser: Biedermeierzeit im Bild. Monografie und Werkverzeichnis* (= Belvedere catalogues raisonnés 1), (Vienna/Cologne/Weimar, 2011).

SG

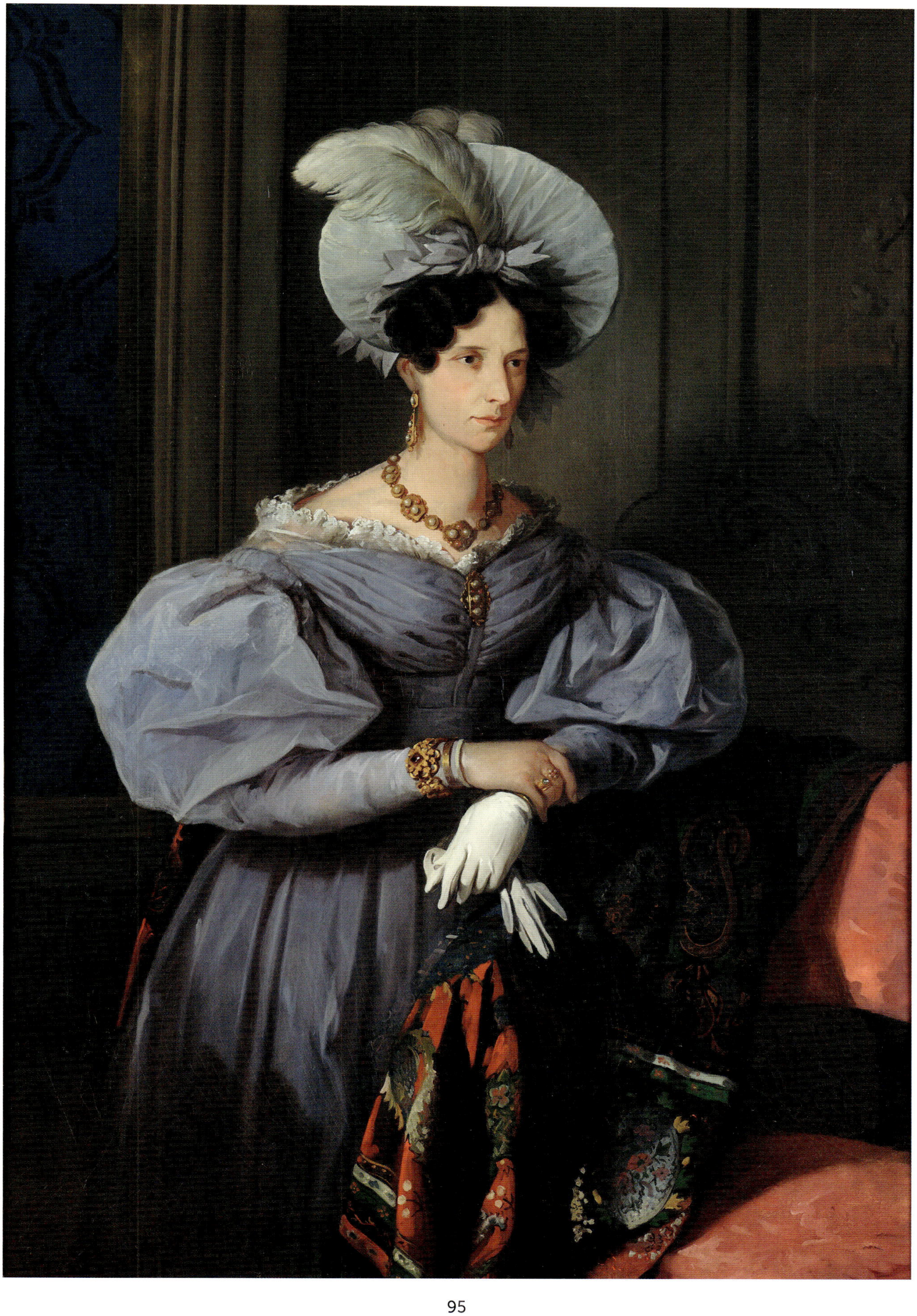

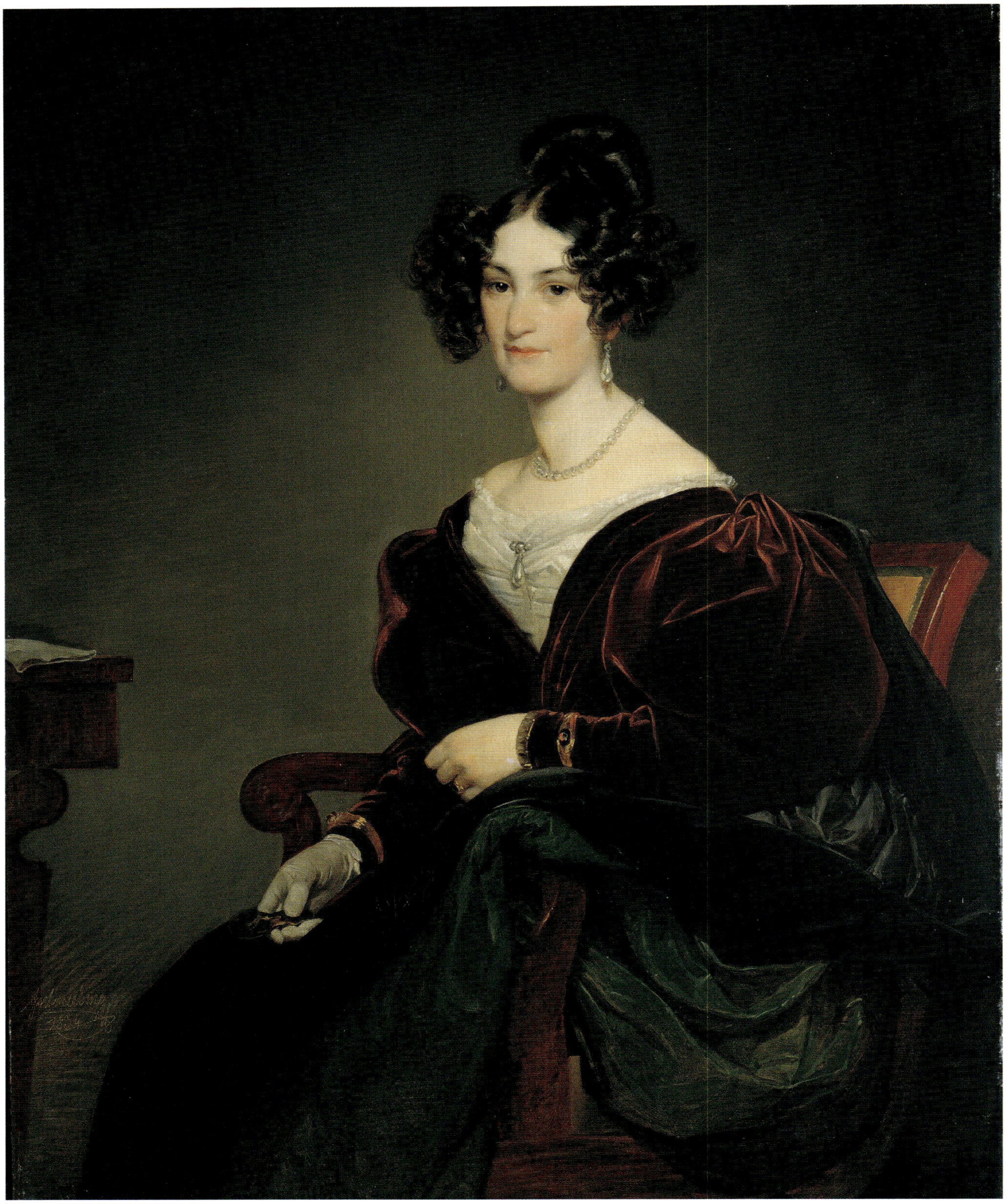

Friedrich von Amerling
Amalie Klein, née von Henikstein, 1834
Oil on canvas, 127 × 103.5 cm
Signed (left at the side): Fr Amerling 1834
Belvedere, Vienna, inv. no. 3832

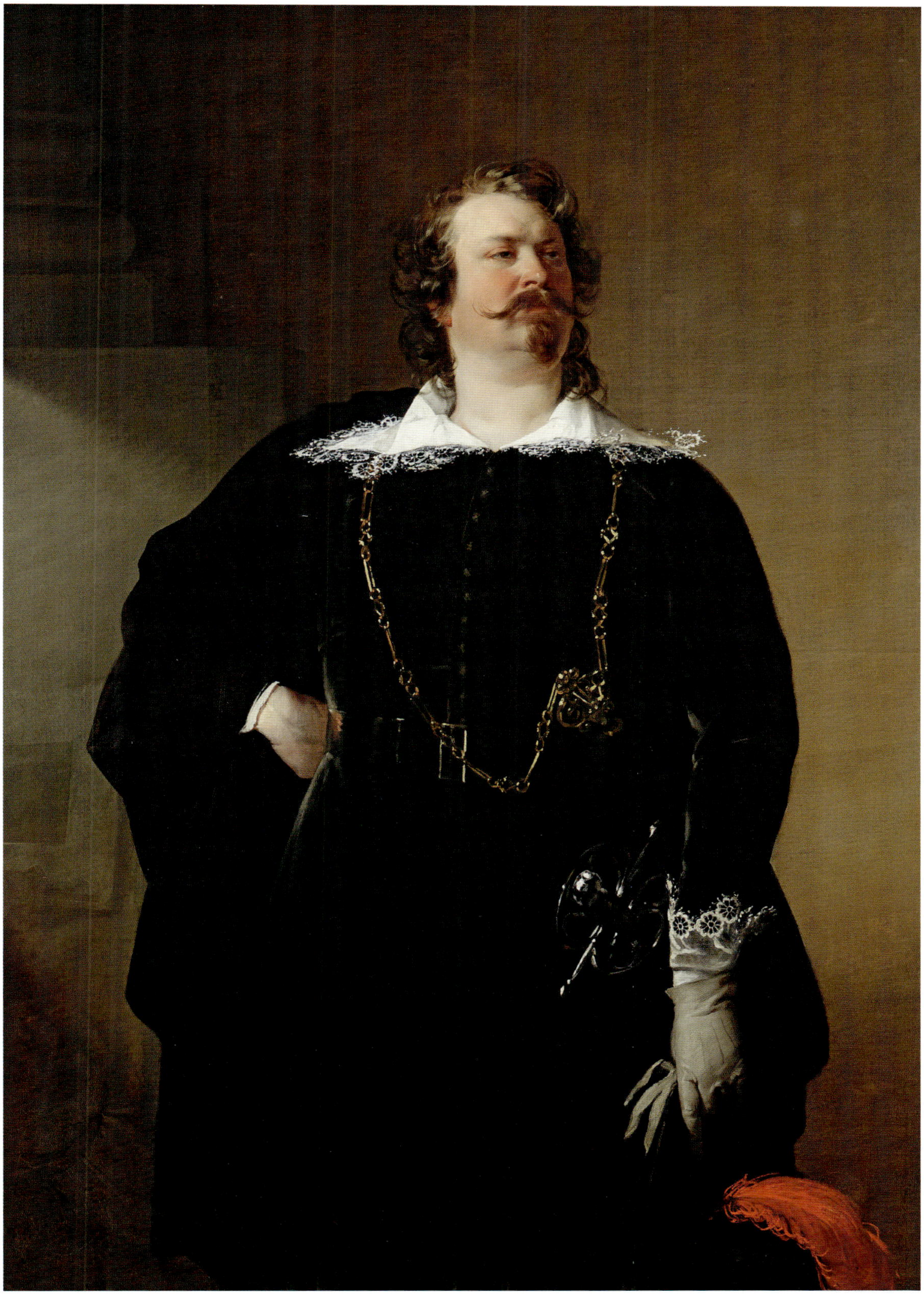

Friedrich von Amerling
Flemish Mayor (*Baron Pfuel?*), 1836
Oil on canvas, 141.5 × 104 cm
Signed (lower left): Fr. Amerling / 1836
Belvedere, Vienna, inv. no. 2683

Massimo d'Azeglio
Vendetta, c. 1835
Signed (lower right): Azeglio
Pinacoteca di Brera, Milan, inv. no. Reg. Cron. 790

It is obvious that only moments earlier a brutal fight has taken place here, which cost one of the combatants his life. He is lying in a pool of his own blood, mourned only by a dog, while his horse trots away unperturbed. At the top right, we can see the silhouette of a rider with two figures running toward him—possibly the victors in the fight.

The scene is in a remote area; the wild thistles in the foreground seem to suggest that it is somewhere in the south. Then again, the gnarled, weathered tree recalls Dutch seventeenth-century landscapes, for example by Jacob van Ruisdael (1628–1682) or Philips Wouwerman (1619–1668), a comparison also called to mind by the low-angle perspective and the dramatic cloud formations gathering at the top of the path. In Rome, where d'Azeglio lived with his family from 1818, he had studied the work of the northern landscapists, and there are also accounts of him sketching from nature on long walks. It is uncertain to what extent his father, a minister to the Holy See, supported his son's artistic ambitions, as he had expected him to train as an officer. Soon after his father died, in 1831, Massimo d'Azeglio moved to Milan where he became highly successful as a painter. That same year, in May, he married Giulia, the daughter of the poet and novelist Alessandro Manzoni (1785–1873). Manzoni encouraged the literary ambitions of d'Azeglio, who then started writing novels alongside painting. In addition, he wrote about political issues, supporting the notion of an independent Italy, although he did not share Republican interests and instead aspired to a kingdom that encompassed northern and central Italy.

Vendetta was painted at a tumultuous time in the artist's personal life. Shortly before, in 1834, his first wife had died giving birth to their daughter. In August 1835, he married again. His second wife, Luisa Maumary, was a distant relative of his first wife. We do not know what inspired this painting. It is interesting to note how the artist has embellished this scene from nature with a subject from historical literature, a complete contrast to contemporary landscape painting from other countries, for instance the work of Friedrich Gauermann. The presentation of the painting in 1835 at the Brera Academy exhibition in Milan brought the artist great acclaim and resulted in his appointment as an honorary member of this institution.

Silvestra Bietoletti/Michele Dantini, *L'Ottocento italiano: la storia, gli artisti, le opera* (Florence, 2002), p. 52; Virginia Bertone, *Massimo d'Azeglio e l'invenzione del paesaggio istoriato*, exh. cat. GAM—Galleria Civica d'Arte Moderna e Contemporanea Torino (Turin, 2002).

SG

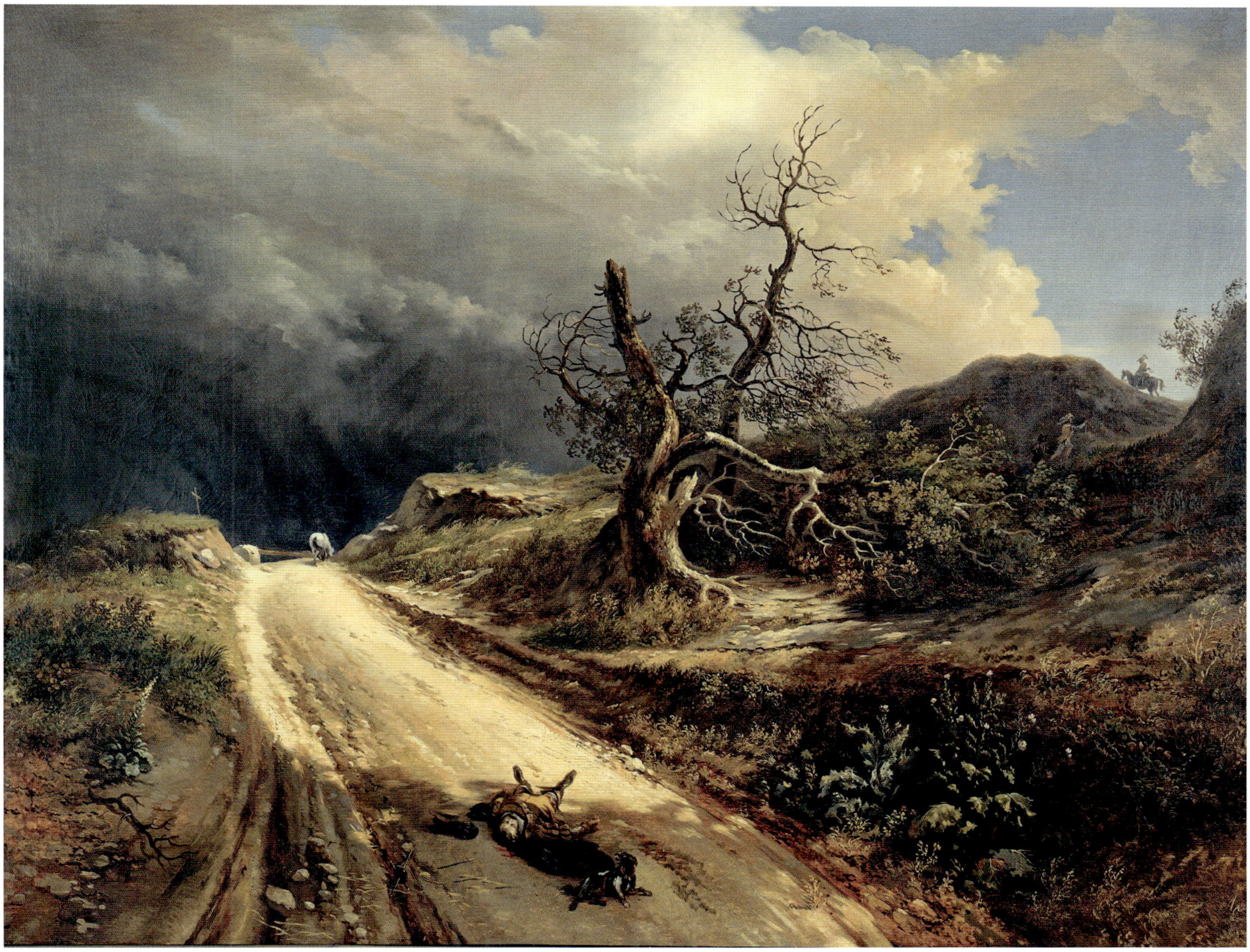

Friedrich Gauermann
A Vulture on a Dead Stag, 1832
Oil on canvas, 147 × 115 cm
Signed (lower right): F. Gauermann. / 1832.
Belvedere, Vienna, inv. no. 3012

Friedrich Gauermann
An Alpine Farm at Untersberg in Salzburg, 1835
Oil on canvas, 74 × 91.5 cm
Signed (lower middle): F. Gauermann. / 1835.
Private collection

Friedrich Gauermann
Cowshed in the Evening, 1846
Oil on wood, 66 × 85 cm
Signed (lower right): F. Gauermann
Private collection

From his early youth, Gauermann had drawn from nature at his home in the small hamlet of Scheuchenstein at the foot of the Schneeberg mountain. His father Jacob Gauermann (1773–1843), who ran a farm there and was also a court painter for Archduke Johann, gave him support and tuition. While studying at Vienna's Imperial Academy from 1824 to 1827 he was influenced by the realistic representation of nature by Josef Rebell (1787–1828). Gauermann further honed his skills by copying seventeenth-century Dutch landscapes at various public galleries, especially the Imperial Picture Gallery at the Upper Belvedere. Based on this, he developed his personal style focusing mainly on rural life, with people and animals integrated as a natural part of the scenery. It is rare to find peaceful landscapes bathed in sunshine in Gauermann's work. Instead he preferred a dramatic atmosphere, such as the hectic bustle of farmers as a thunderstorm gathers, forests and lakes lashed by gales, or gruesome animal fights, as demonstrated, for example, in the dramatic scene *A Vulture on a Dead Stag* (plate p. 101). These landscapes as well as his many depictions of resting cows and goats make him a direct successor to the Dutch artists he emulated, Jacob van Ruysdael (1628–1682) and Paulus Potter (1625–1654). Gauermann loved to create rural idylls and combine these with a slice of real nature, for example in the *Alpine Farm at Untersberg in Salzburg* (plate p. 102). By contrast, *Cowshed in the Evening* (plate p. 103) is one of the rare examples that explores light, the rays of the setting sun piercing the stable's gloom. More striking than his finished oil paintings, however, are the artist's preliminary studies, all of which were painted from nature and are characterized by the spontaneous rendering of details (examples can be found in particular at the Niederösterreichisches Landesmuseum, St. Pölten, and the Academy of Fine Arts, Vienna, collection of prints and drawings). These studies shed light on the painter's working methods, revealing them to be fundamentally different from other artists such as, for example, Waldmüller. Unlike Waldmüller, who tackled the existing scene as a whole, Gauermann did not take a holistic view, but completed several detail studies, which he then combined to create a striking painting. His own open-air studies thus blend with parts of the picture copied from the Old Masters, yet still present a vivid example of nature as experienced by the artist in his home region, as well as in the Salzkammergut or in the area around Berchtesgaden, where all through his life he enjoyed walking in search of new motifs.

Rupert Feuchtmüller, *Friedrich Gauermann 1807–1862* (Rosenheim, 1987), with catalogue raisonné; Wolfgang Krug, *Friedrich Gauermann 1807–1862*, exh. cat. Niederösterreichisches Landesmuseum, St. Pölten (Vienna/Munich, 2001).

SG

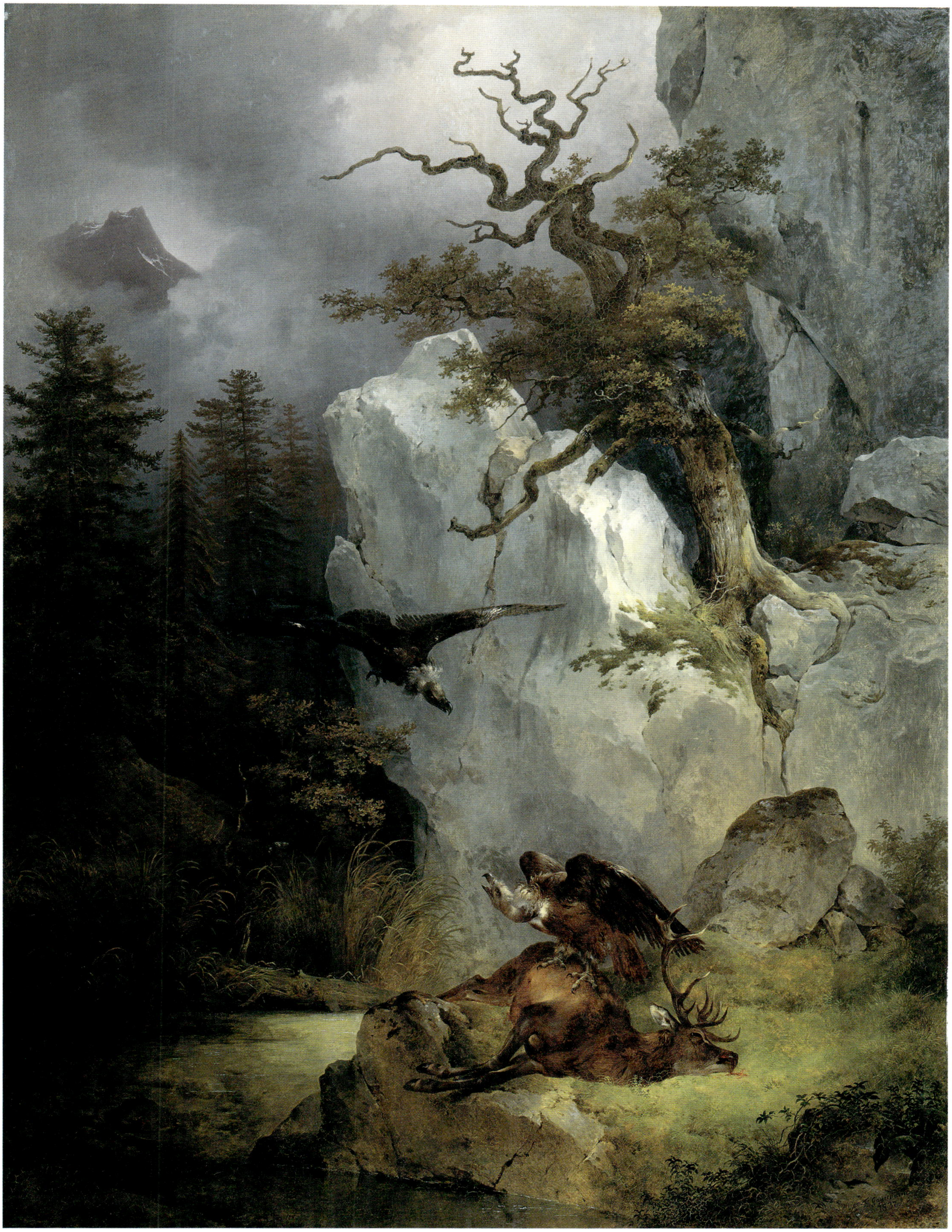

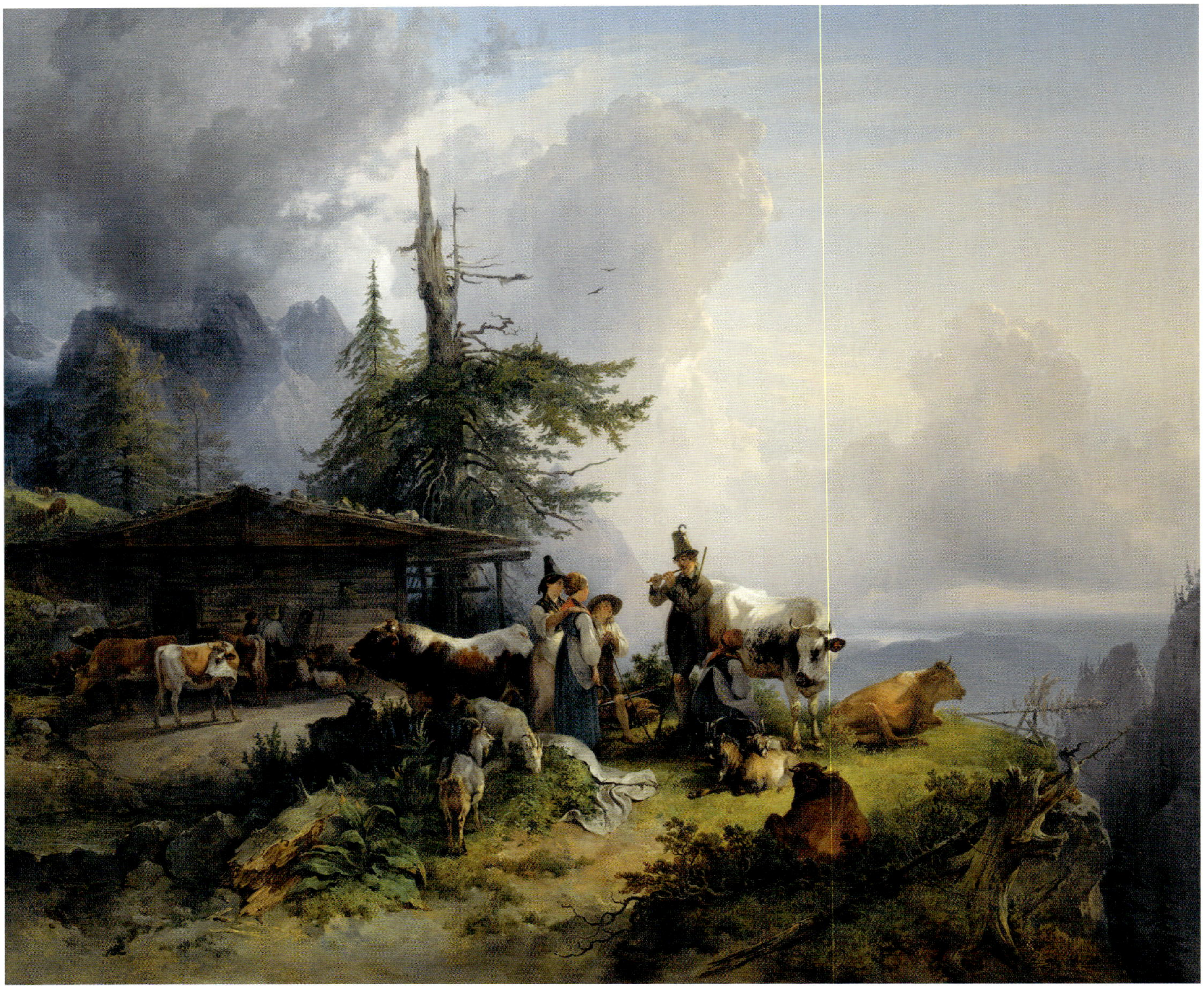

Friedrich Gauermann
An Alpine Farm at Untersberg in Salzburg, 1835

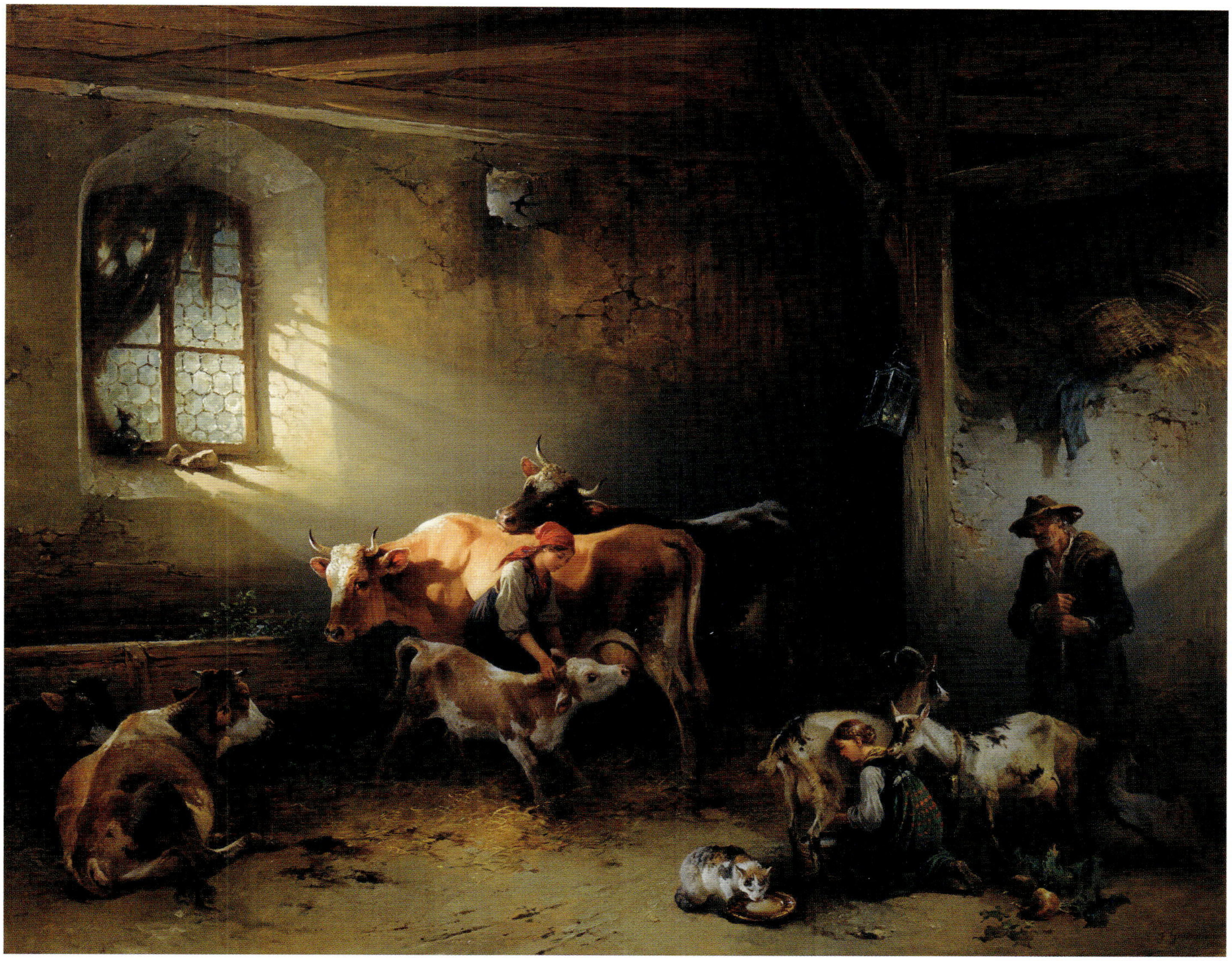

Friedrich Gauermann
Cowshed in the Evening, 1846

Peter Fendi
Scene from the Flood of 1830, 1830
Oil on canvas, 95 × 110 cm
Signed (lower right): P. Fendi f. 1830
Wien Museum, inv. no. 24.433

This picture refers to the great disaster that, at the end of February 1830, held the whole of Vienna in suspense. A sudden thaw had set in, causing such a tremendous ice dam on the Danube on the evening of 27 February that "until the following day in the afternoon [...] eleven of the great Tabor bridge's piles were torn away by the force of the ice."[19] The newspaper *Der Wanderer* continues: "Although the water has drained away from the streets of the inner city (Vienna), the suburbs affected by the flood are still under water, which is why there are still no exact casualty numbers. Tragically, over thirty bodies have been found so far and they include a number of children."[20] The affected districts of Leopoldstadt and Roßau, the lower-lying suburbs of Vienna, were essentially cut off until the flood waters abated. Peter Fendi based his painting on this event and captured the horrendous circumstances of the population living along the unregulated Danube. This work is both a documentation and a genre picture and may therefore be termed a "contemporary history painting." Based on the stories of individual victims, the painter captured the catastrophe, showing people saving themselves, assisting others, crying for help, or drowning in the deluge. To impose some control on the composition of this turbulent scene, he compressed the events into a triangle, adding further drama by placing a lamp shining down at its apex. In the background, almost disappearing from view, is the striking tower of St. Leopold's parish church.

Peter Fendi is most famed for his outstanding watercolors with their exceptional airy lightness and whimsical precision. His patrons and clientele came from the imperial family and the aristocracy as well as the haute bourgeoisie. Applying paint in glazes, a technique he had refined in his watercolors, was also an approach he used in his oil paintings, conveying a special painterly appeal. His genre paintings are usually of domestic scenes, in which he would often highlight social wrongs and the plight of his fellow people. Fendi actually painted for his own pleasure, as his main profession was as a draftsman and engraver at the Imperial and Royal Cabinet of Coins and Antiquities. The *Scene from the Flood of 1830* clearly reveals the artist's fundamental knowledge of history painting acquired at the Imperial Academy. Nevertheless, this work is a great exception in his oeuvre.

Gerbert Frodl, *Wiener Malerei der Biedermeierzeit* (Rosenheim, 1987), p. 25; Michael Krapf, "Das moralisierende Element im Wiener Sittenbild," *Bürgersinn und Aufbegehren. Biedermeier und Vormärz in Wien 1815–1848*, exh. cat. Historisches Museum der Stadt Wien (Vienna, 1988), pp. 148–56, especially p. 153; Walter Koschatzky, *Peter Fendi (1796–1842): Künstler, Lehrer und Leitbild* (= Veröffentlichungen der Albertina, no. 38), (Salzburg/Vienna, 1995).

SG

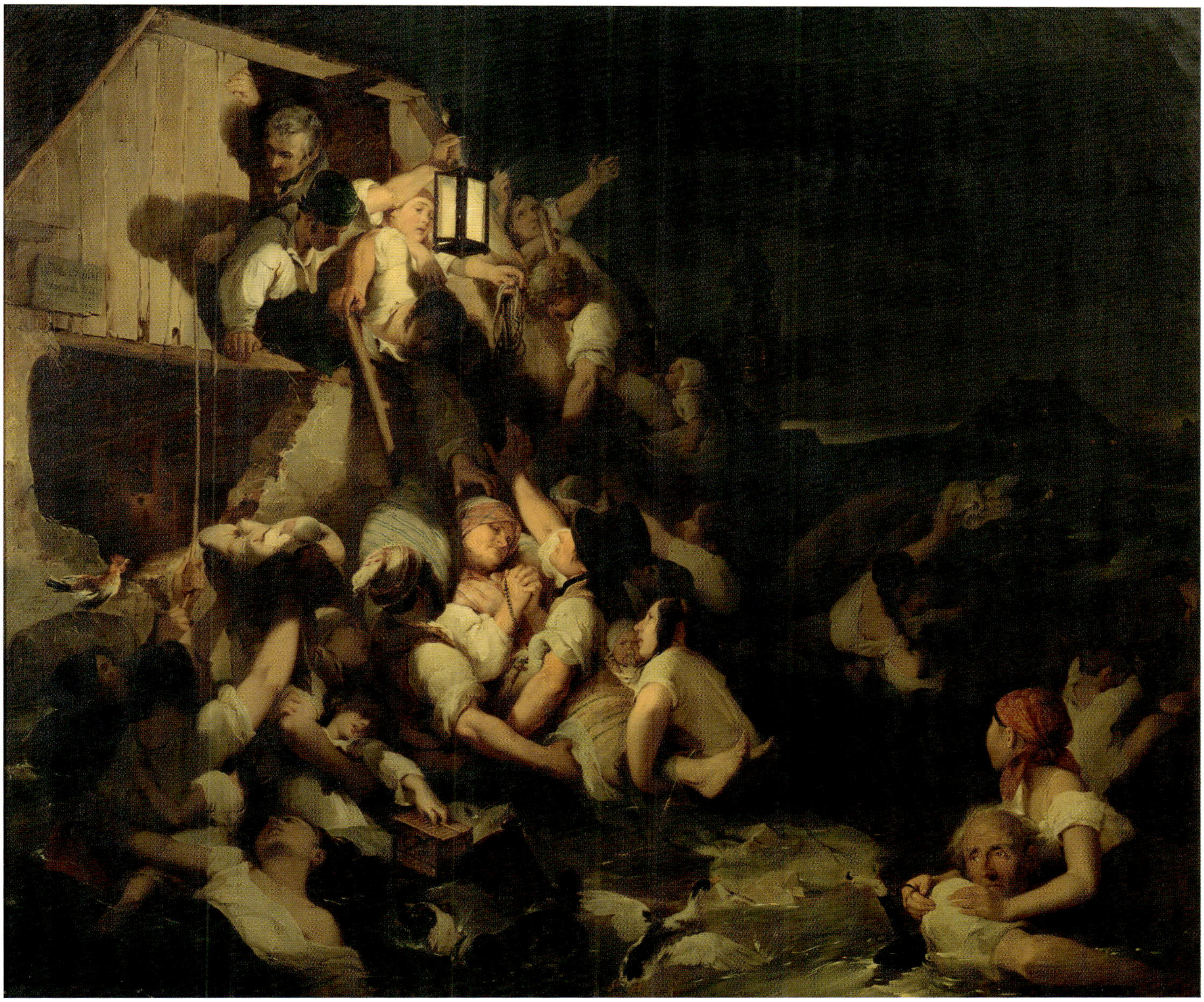

Odorico Politi
The Model of the Painter, 1837/38
Oil on canvas, 63.5 × 49 cm
Unsigned
Udine Civic Museums and Gallery of History and Art, inv. no. 283 Ancient Art Gallery Collection

Politi was one of the most important history painters in Friuli and the Julian March in the first half of the nineteenth century. He came from a wealthy family in Udine, which enabled him to study at the Accademia di Belle Arti in Venice. He was influenced in particular by Teodoro Matteini (1753–1831). After studying, Politi went to Rome to further develop his skills. Together with Francesco Hayez, a fellow student from Venice and winner of the Rome prize awarded by the Venetian Accademia, he moved in the circle around Antonio Canova (1757–1822). His study of sixteenth- and seventeenth-century art was also of great significance for his development as an artist, and he was able to integrate this skillfully in his Classicist-influenced formal style. Shortly after his return to Udine, he decorated his family's palazzo with frescos in this manner. In 1816 he moved to Venice and began to concentrate on religious themes. He was appointed professor of history painting at the Venetian Accademia in 1831. Numerous works of art, altarpieces, and murals by him can be found in churches throughout Friuli and the Julian March. In 1835 he collaborated with Michelangelo Grigoletti and Ludovico Lipparini (1802–1856) on the decoration of Sant'Antonio Taumaturgo (also Sant'Antonio Nuovo), a church in Trieste built between 1823 and 1849 by Pietro Nobile (1774–1854). Apart from this task, which brought him great acclaim, in 1837 he started painting the ballroom of the Palazzo Reale in Venice (today Museo Correr), a secular commission of equal significance.

It was around the same time that he painted this unconventional portrait of his model, probably his most well-known oil painting. The picture is notable for its unadorned nature and the delicate pink and beige skin tones contrasting tastefully with the dark hair and eyes. The girl's nakedness and sidelong glance give the picture a great sensuality. Antonio Garlatti noted the similarity in the portrayal with the work of Jean-Auguste-Dominique Ingres (1780–1867), a contemporary French artist whom Politi admired for his combination of realism and idealism.[21]

Sergio Marinelli/Giuseppe Mazzario/Fernando Mazzocca, eds., *Il Veneto e l'Austria: Vita e cultura artistica nelle città venete 1814–1866*, exh. cat. Palazzo della Gran Guardia, Verona (Milan, 1989), p. 145; Antonio Garlatti, "Odorico Politi: La vita e le opere," in Giuseppe Bergamini, ed., *Tra Venezia e Vienna: Le arti a Udine nell'Ottocento* (Milan, 2004), pp. 141–53; Alessandra Tiddia, *La coscienza del vero: Capolavori dell'Ottocento da Courbet a Segantini* (Milan, 2015), p. 183 (Ilaria Cimonetti).

SG

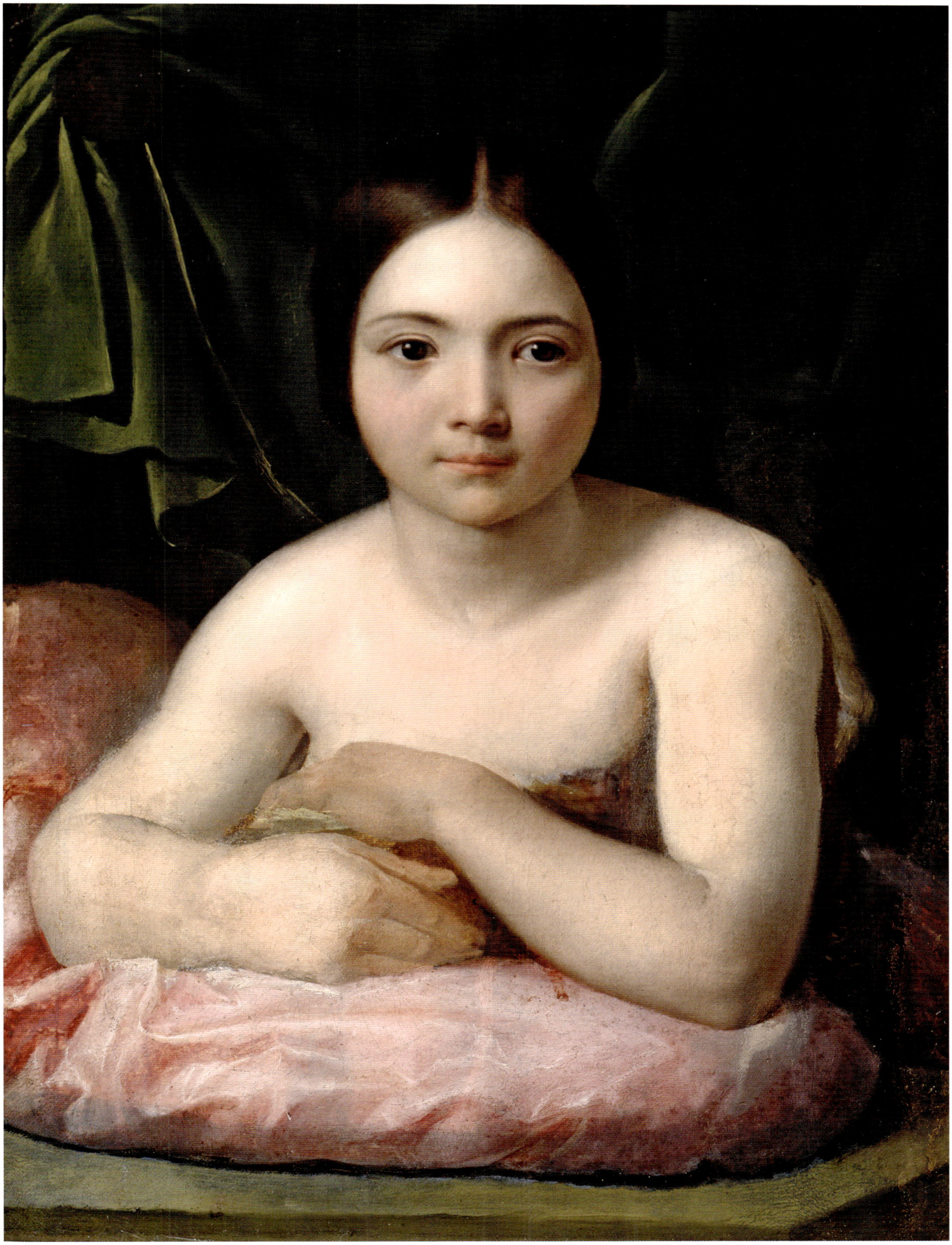

Friedrich von Amerling
Rudolf von Arthaber with his Children Rudolf, Emilie, and Gustav, Looking at the Portrait of their Deceased Mother, 1837
Oil on canvas, 221 × 155 cm
Signed (lower right): FrAmerling / 1837
Belvedere, Vienna, inv. no. 2245

Rudolf Arthaber (1795–1867, from 1841 Rudolf von Arthaber) was one of the most well-known personalities in Vienna in the mid-nineteenth century, a man who was behind some major achievements both as an industrialist and art patron.[22] His name is inextricably linked with the Viennese shawl, that exquisitely worked, vibrant fashion accessory, a must in any self-respecting lady's wardrobe following the Congress of Vienna. Arthaber was also highly acclaimed for his work for social causes and his support of artists. In 1850 he founded the Österreichischer Kunstverein (Austrian Art Association) and was its president for many years; he also owned an important collection of Austrian and international art that was housed at his villa at Hohe Warte to the north of Vienna.[23]

Amerling's portrait, showing the man in the bosom of his family, does not reveal the slightest hint of his public work. It is a private group portrait depicting the family grieving their wife and mother, Johanna Georgine Caroline, née von Scheidlin (1805–1833), who had died four years earlier. Their sadness has been reawakened by the small picture that Gustav, the youngest son,[24] is showing his father and siblings, in all likelihood a portrait of his mother. The shared memories of their past family life forges an emotional bond between the figures. And even though they are all looking in different directions, the compositional framework, combining the figures in a parallelogram, creates a physically compact group. In addition to the unifying effect of a shared emotion, the painter has introduced the deceased mother on a second occasion by including her large portrait on the background wall.[25] In this way, Amerling created probably his greatest group portrait. There is no record of whether it was painted in the Arthaber family home or in the artist's studio. The painter was certainly highly gifted at representing a homely atmosphere and has created a classic example of the elegant interiors in Vienna at the time, seen to epitomize a bourgeois lifestyle and family values.

Gerbert Frodl/Klaus Albrecht Schröder, eds., *Wiener Biedermeier: Malerei zwischen Wiener Kongreß und Revolution*, exh. cat. Kunstforum der Bank Austria, Vienna/Österreichische Galerie Belvedere, Vienna (Munich, 1992), cat. no. 65 (Ingried Brugger); Sabine Grabner, "Friedrich von Amerling: Porträtist des Hofes, der Aristokratie und des gehobenen Bürgertums," in *Cashmere: Der Shawl in der Malerei des Biedermeier*, ed. Erika Mayr-Oehring (Salzburg, 2000), pp. 55–60; Gerbert Frodl, ed., *19. Jahrhundert* (= Geschichte der bildenden Kunst in Österreich 5), (Munich etc., 2002), pp. 351–52; Sabine Grabner, ed., *Friedrich von Amerling: 1803–1887*, exh. cat. Österreichische Galerie Belvedere, Vienna (Leipzig, 2003), pp. 157–59; Sabine Grabner, *Mehr als Biedermeier: Klassizismus, Romantik und Realismus in der Österreichischen Galerie Belvedere* (Munich, 2006), pp. 90–91.

SG

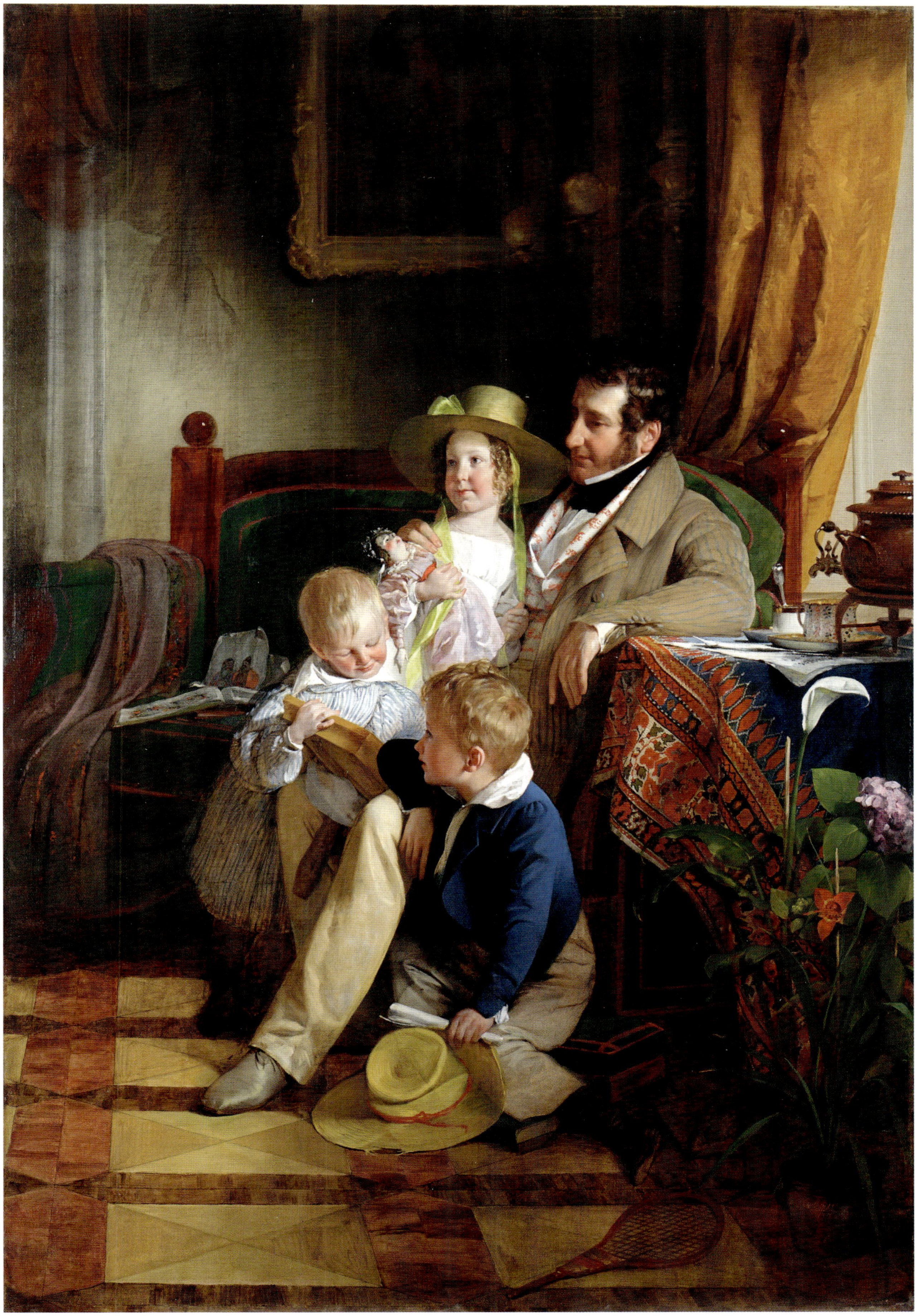

Mihael Stroj
Alojzija Pesjak, 1835
Oil on canvas, 63 × 50 cm
Signed (lower left): Stroj pin 835.
National Gallery of Slovenia, Ljubljana, inv. no. NG S371

Mihael Stroj
Dr. Blaž Crobath, after 1840
Oil on canvas, 90 × 76 cm
Unsigned
National Gallery of Slovenia, Ljubljana, inv. no. 377

Mihael Stroj
Ivana Debevec, 1840s
Oil on canvas, 99 × 74.5 cm
Unsigned
National Gallery of Slovenia, Ljubljana, inv. no. 369

Stroj was one of the most famous nineteenth-century painters in Slovenia and Croatia. Most of his work was completed in Zagreb and Ljubljana, where he was in great demand as a portrait painter. In Croatia in particular he also painted churches and pictures with religious content. He studied from 1821 at the Imperial Academy in Vienna and trained as a history painter with Franz Caucig (1755–1828), Anton Petter (1781–1858), and Johann Peter Krafft (1780–1856). In 1826 he contributed two portraits, one a self-portrait, to the Academy exhibition.[26] It is not known when he left Vienna. From 1830 he worked mostly in Zagreb, but by 1842 was living permanently in Ljubljana, where he soon received numerous commissions, particularly from the bourgeoisie and aristocracy. His work was appreciated for its outstanding characterization and pleasant settings. He focused on his sitters, extensively doing without decorative accessories. It was the figure itself, perhaps a characteristic pose or gesture, that gave the depiction its particular charm.

The young girl *Alojzija Pesjak* (plate p. 111), for example, is shown playing coyly with cherries, the dark red of the fruit setting off her pale skin color and white dress. The deep blue in the background behind the casually seated child is particularly effective, possibly representing a cloth draped over the seat. By contrast, the frontal postures of *Ivana Debevec* (plate p.113) and *Dr. Blaž Crobath* (plate p. 112) are quite formal. Both portraits are fascinating on account of the magnificent arrangement, demonstrating Stroj's mastery of black pigment. He was highly skillful at reproducing subtle nuances, from shiny silk to matt cloth, endowing his portraits with a stately elegance. Furthermore, in the portrait of the woman, the braids and pearls in the coiffure, recalling Venetian Renaissance portraits,[27] divert attention from the somewhat plain face. The success of Stroj's work is derived from this interaction between emphasis and deflection, a skill reminiscent of the Viennese painter Friedrich von Amerling. Whether these two painters ever met is not known.

Barbara Jaki, *Meščanska slika: Slikarstvo prve polovice 19. stoletja iz zbirk Narodne galerije*, exh. cat. National Gallery, Ljubljana (Ljubljana, 2000), pp. 210–49.

SG

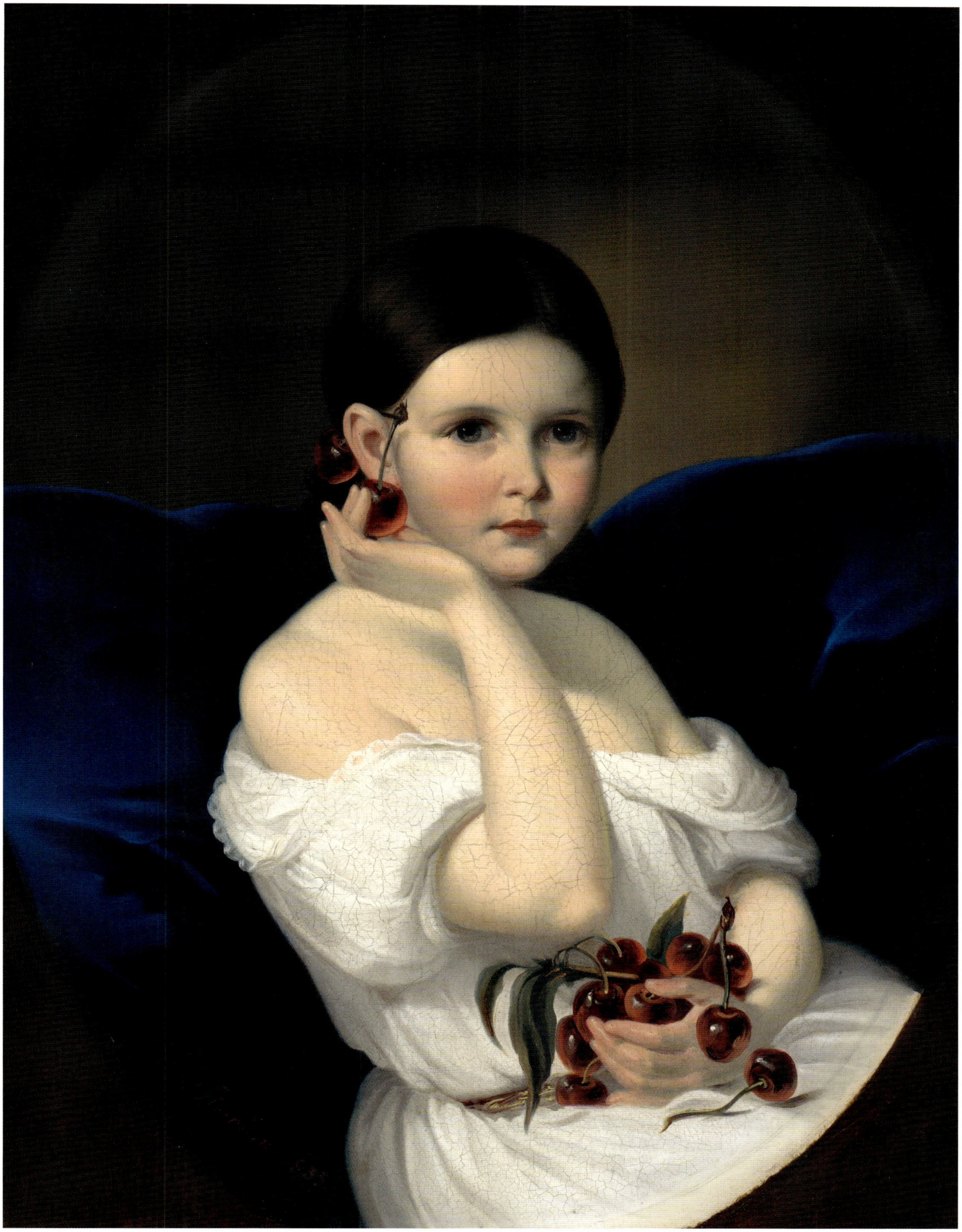

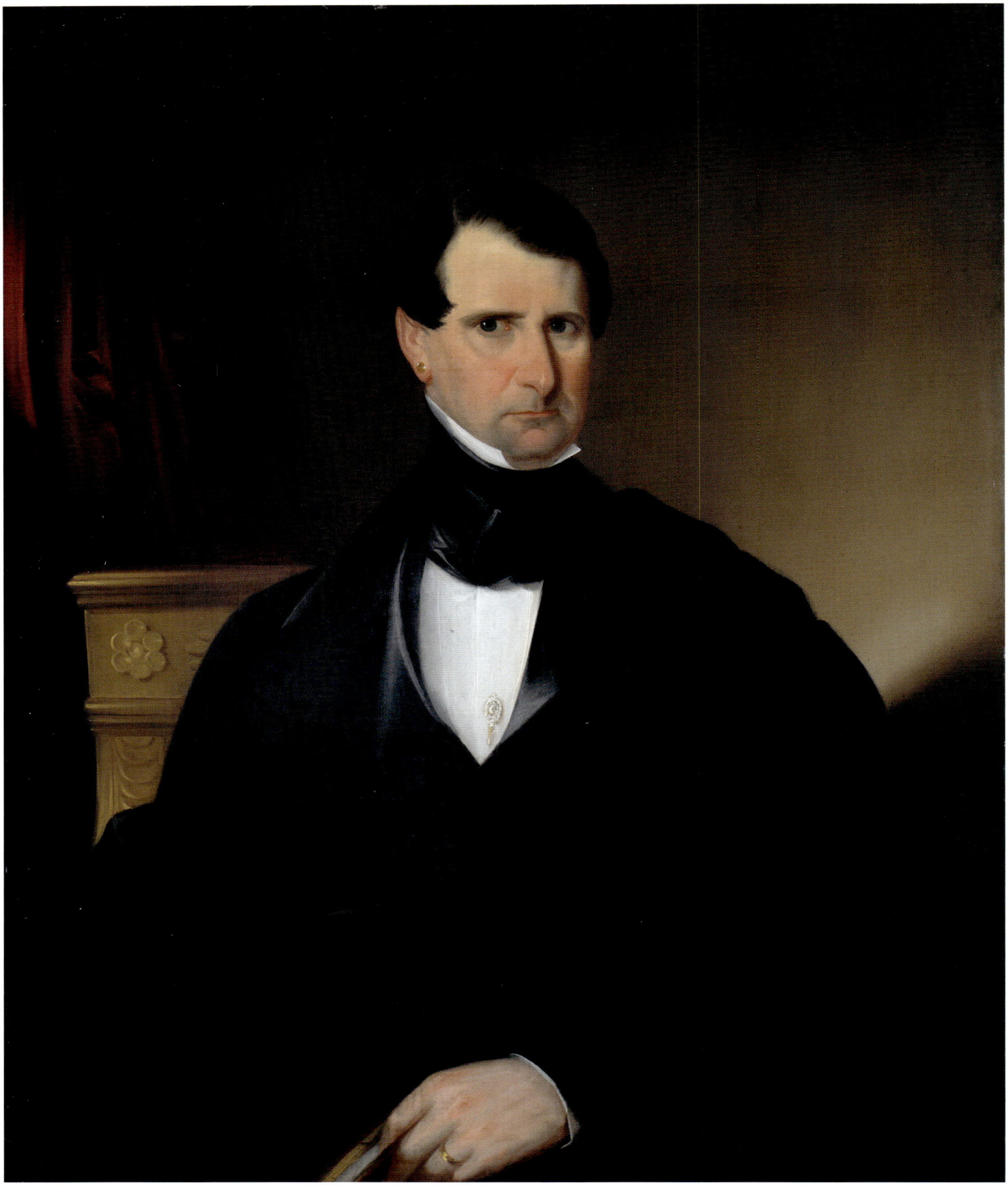

Mihael Stroj
Dr. Blaž Crobath, after 1840

Mihael Stroj
Ivana Debevec, 1840s

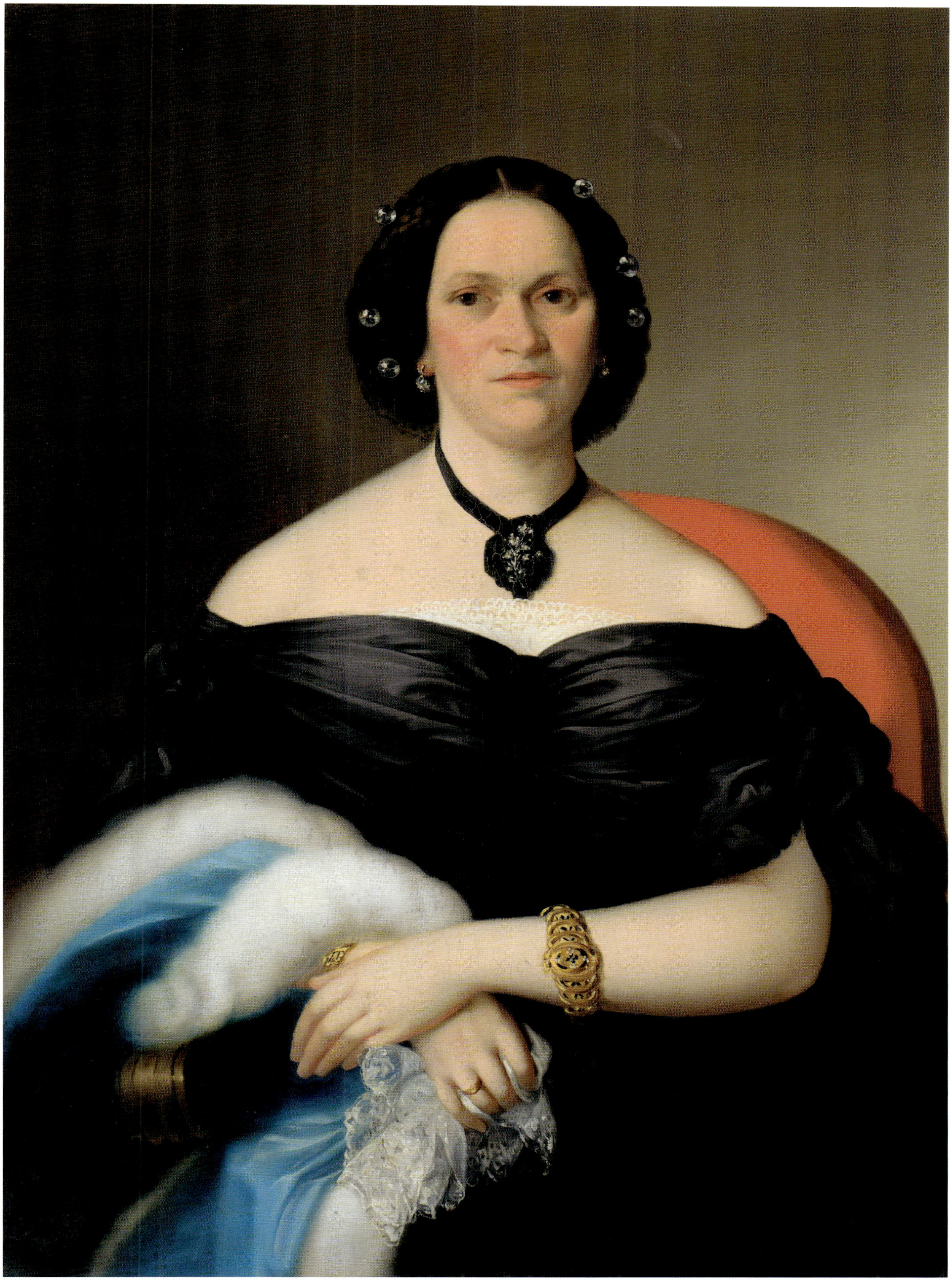

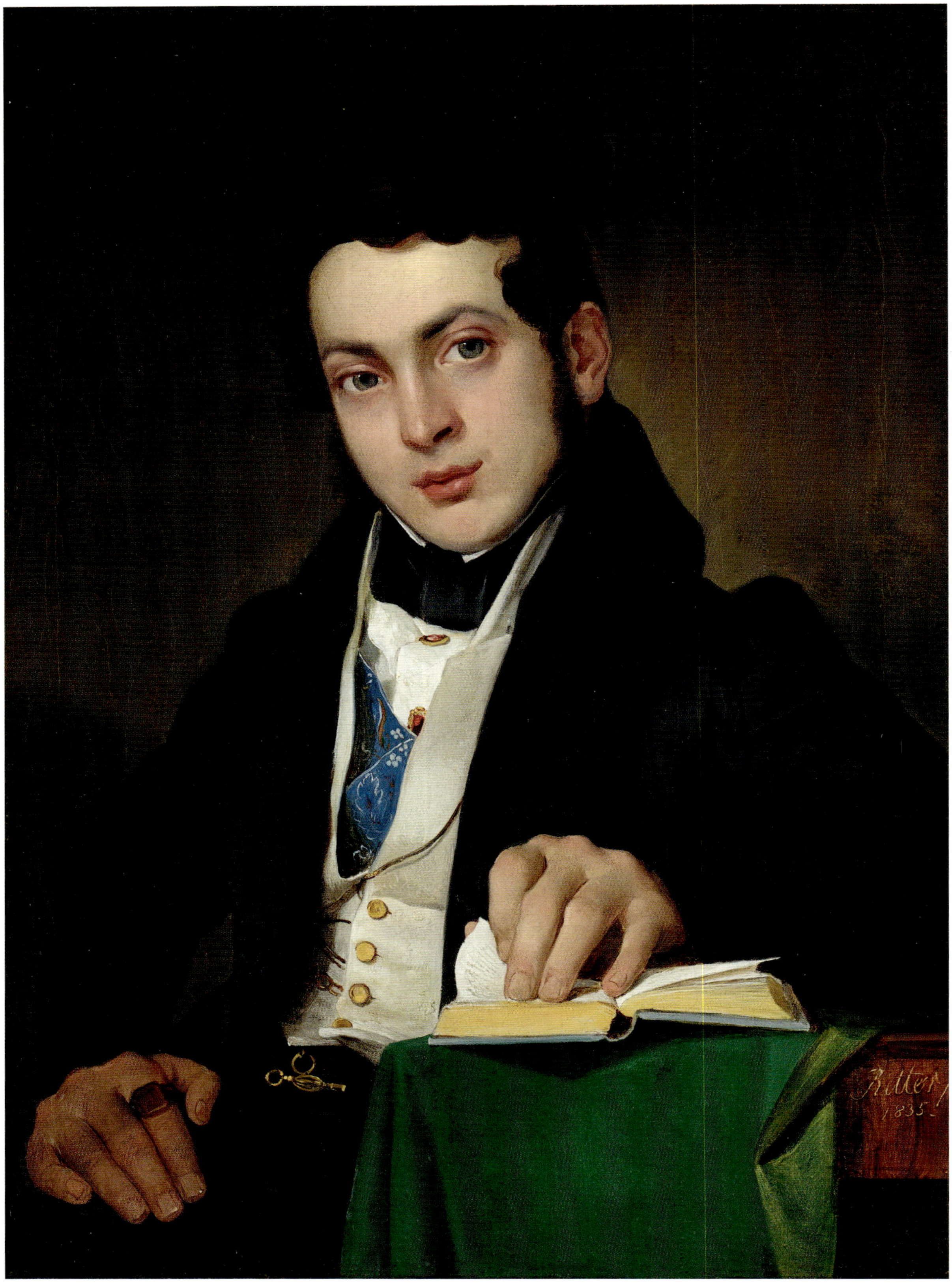

Eduard Ritter
Seated Young Man in a Black Frock-Coat, 1835
Oil on canvas, 38.5 × 30 cm
Signed (lower right): Ritter p. / 1835.
Belvedere, Vienna, inv. no. 5028

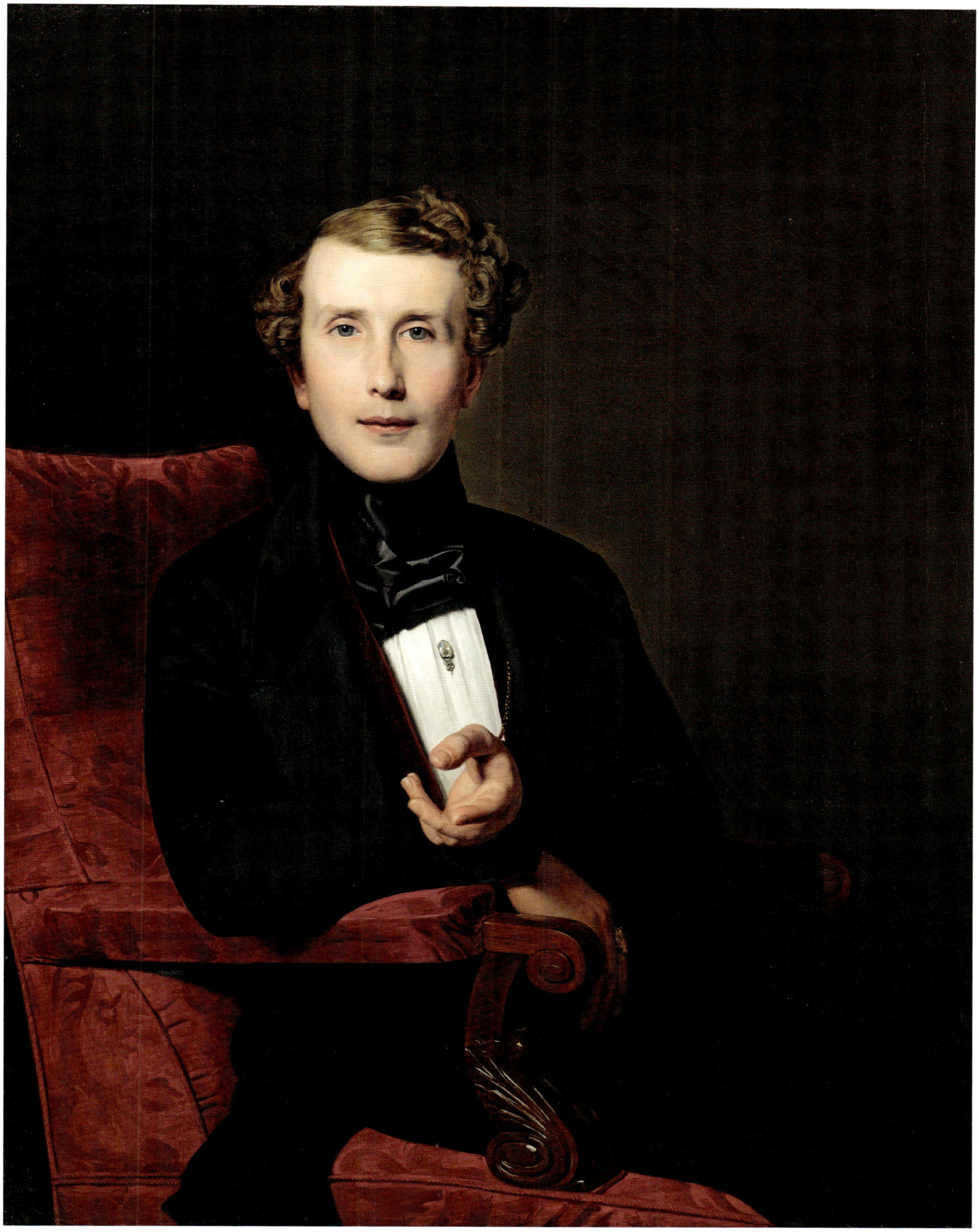

Ferdinand Georg Waldmüller
Young Man in a Black Suit Sitting on a Red Armchair, 1842
Oil on canvas, 100 × 81.5 cm
Signed (lower right): Waldmüller 1842
Belvedere, Vienna, on loan from the Society of Friends of the Österreichische Galerie Belvedere, inv. no. Lg 1091

Friedrich von Amerling
Young Girl with a Book, 1839
Oil on canvas, 59 × 49 cm
Signed (on the spine of the book): Friedr. Amerling 839
Private collection

Friedrich von Amerling
The Lute Player, 1838
Oil on canvas, 99 × 82 cm
Signed (left at the side): FrAmerling / 1838
Belvedere, Vienna, on loan from the Academy of Fine Arts Vienna, inv. no. Lg 40

Friedrich von Amerling
The Widow (*Elise Kreuzberger*), 1836
Oil on canvas, 84.5 × 67 cm
Signed (lower right): FrAmerling / 1836
Wien Museum, inv. no. 140.535

A comparison of Amerling's depictions with genre paintings by his contemporaries naturally sheds light on the artist's aims. He was not interested in narrative and certainly not in pointing the moral finger, nor was his aim to convey literary or historical content, but instead his sole concern was the aesthetic arrangement. Whether the girl was shown glancing up from her book or playing the lute was immaterial, because her attractive face was all that mattered to the painter. He aimed to show this to its best possible advantage and employed a tasteful selection of colors and a brilliant painting technique to add to his subjects' charms. A touch of melodrama, as demonstrated by *The Widow*'s imploring upward gaze, was an exception. Incidentally, the woman is Elise Kreuzberger, one of Amerling's favorite models.

This very distinctive type of Viennese genre painting could draw on a wide range of examples from the history of art. Sources of inspiration could have been Titian (1476/77 or 1489/90–1576) and possibly Bartolomé Esteban Murillo (1618–1682) as well as the fancy-dress portrait so popular in British painting since the eighteenth century. Amerling would have had ample opportunity to see the latter during his time in London in 1827/28. A delight in dressing up, as expressed in this style of portraiture, reflected a penchant shared by artist and model alike. Furthermore, this form of representation fitted wonderfully with Amerling's love of portrait painting and his outstanding ability to capture the human face. Based on this, he developed his pictorial concept, which had a great impact in the nineteenth century, not only in Austrian painting. The face and upper body of an attractive young woman dominated the center—filling the picture and viewed slightly from below—and any potential subject matter arose almost exclusively from her expressions, gestures, and props. But, above all, the sophisticated lighting contributes to the picture's elegance and explains the appeal of these single-figure genre paintings.

Günther Probszt, *Friedrich von Amerling: Der Altmeister der Wiener Porträtmalerei* (Zurich/Leipzig/Vienna, 1927), cat. rais. nos. 368, 431, and 1145; Gerbert Frodl/Klaus Albrecht Schröder, eds., *Wiener Biedermeier: Malerei zwischen Wiener Kongreß und Revolution*, exh. cat. Kunstforum der Bank Austria, Vienna/Österreichische Galerie Belvedere, Vienna (Munich, 1992), cat. no. 63 (Sabine Grabner); Sabine Grabner, ed., *Friedrich von Amerling: 1803–1887*, exh. cat. Österreichische Galerie Belvedere, Vienna (Leipzig, 2003), pp. 214–18.

SG

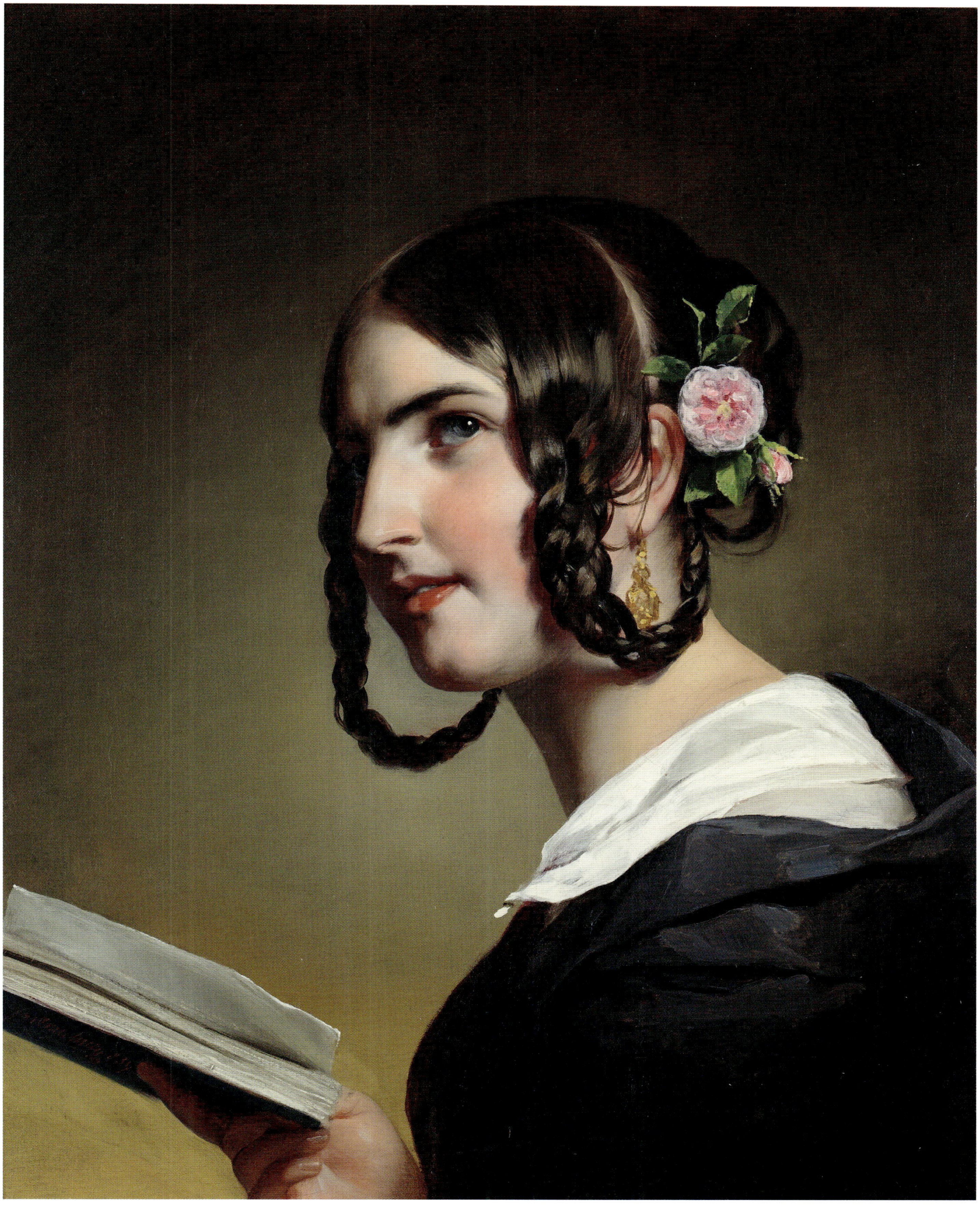

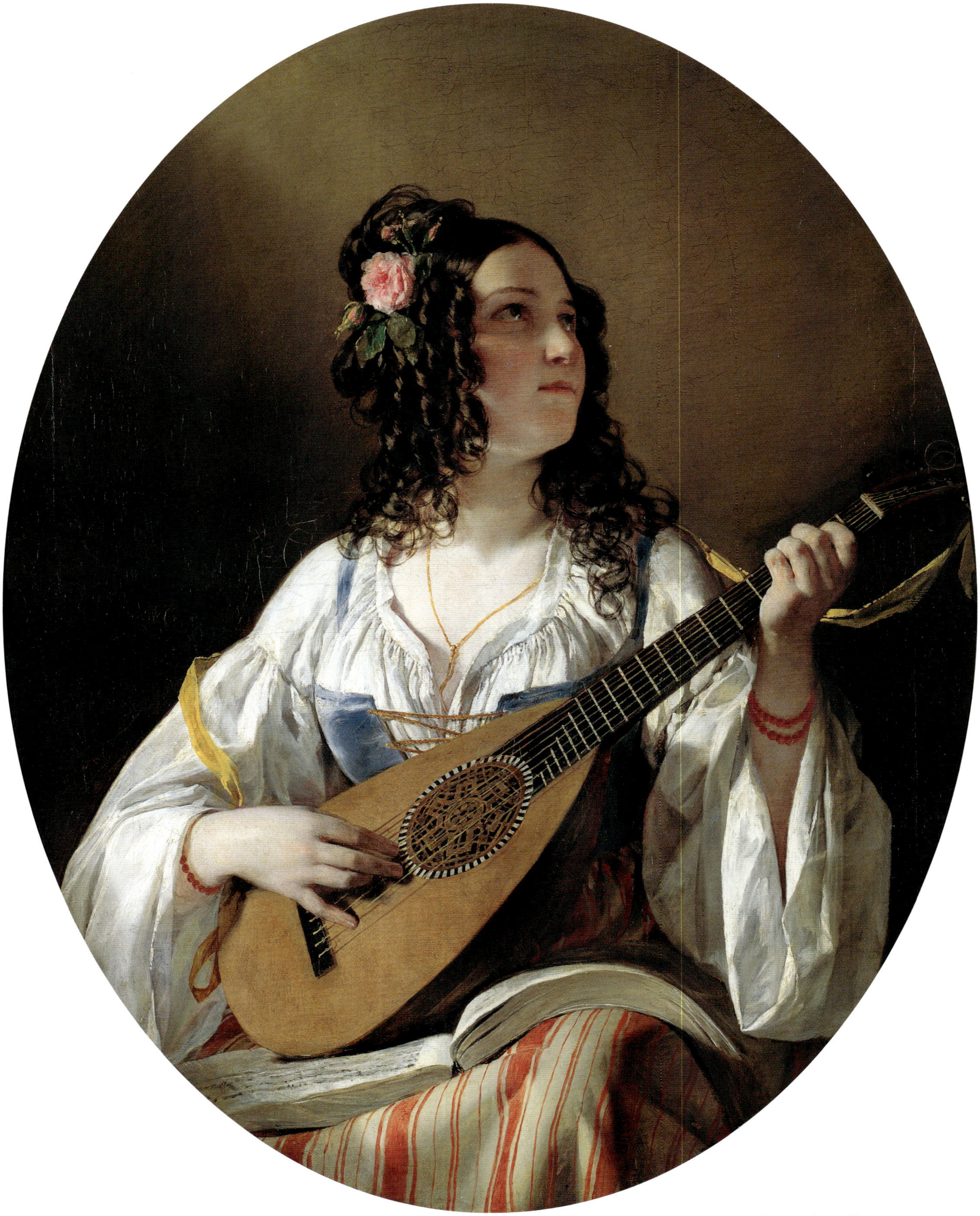

Friedrich von Amerling
The Lute Player, 1838

Friedrich von Amerling
The Widow (*Elise Kreuzberger*), 1836

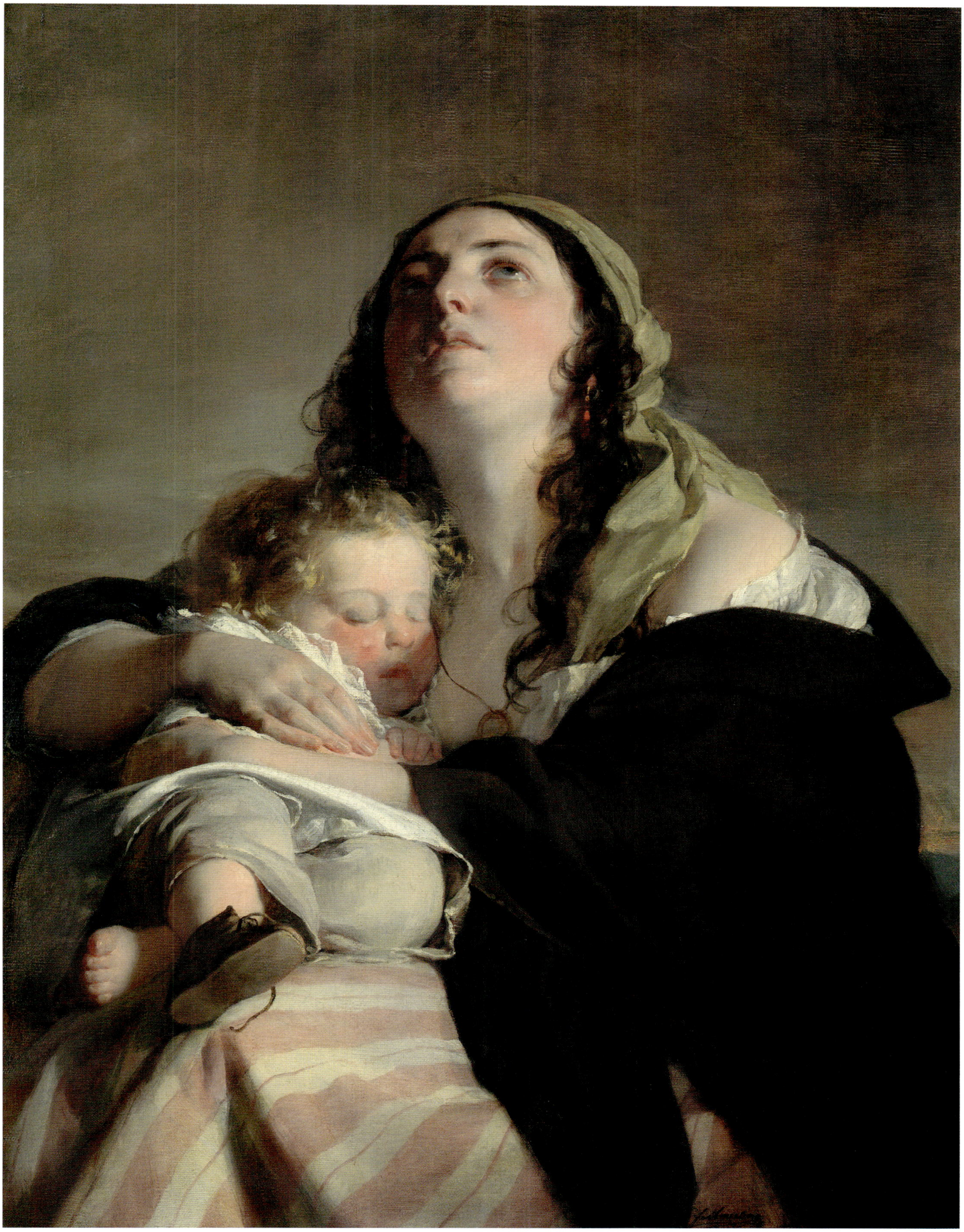

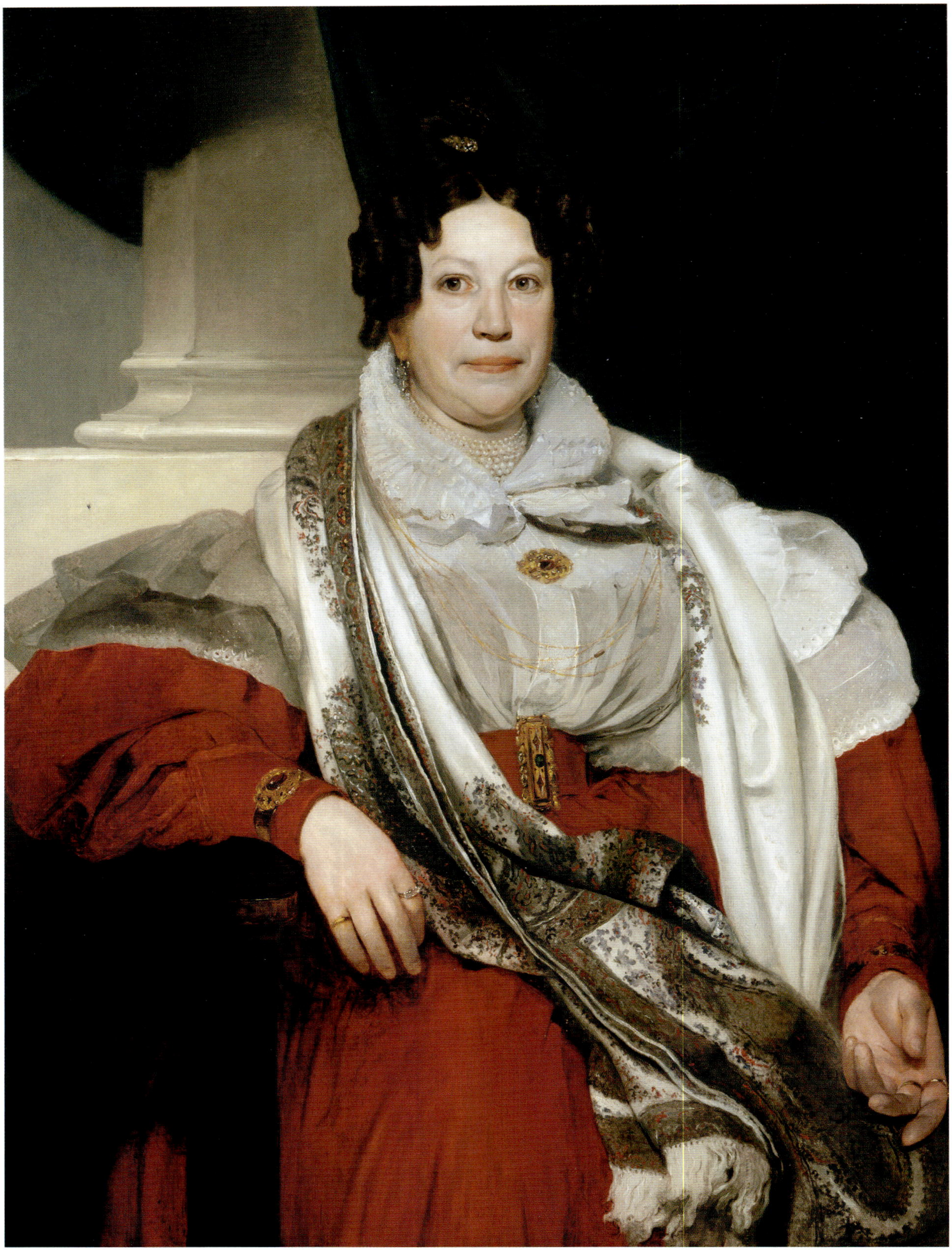

Johann Baptist Reiter
The Innkeeper Barbara Meyer, 1836
Oil on canvas, 109 × 85 cm
Inscription on the reverse: Barbara Meyer bürg=Gastgeberin: geborne Bauer / im Jahre 1787. / Zimmermeisterstochter von Laxenburg. / gemalt von Joh. Reiter 836. Belvedere, Vienna, inv. no. 3658

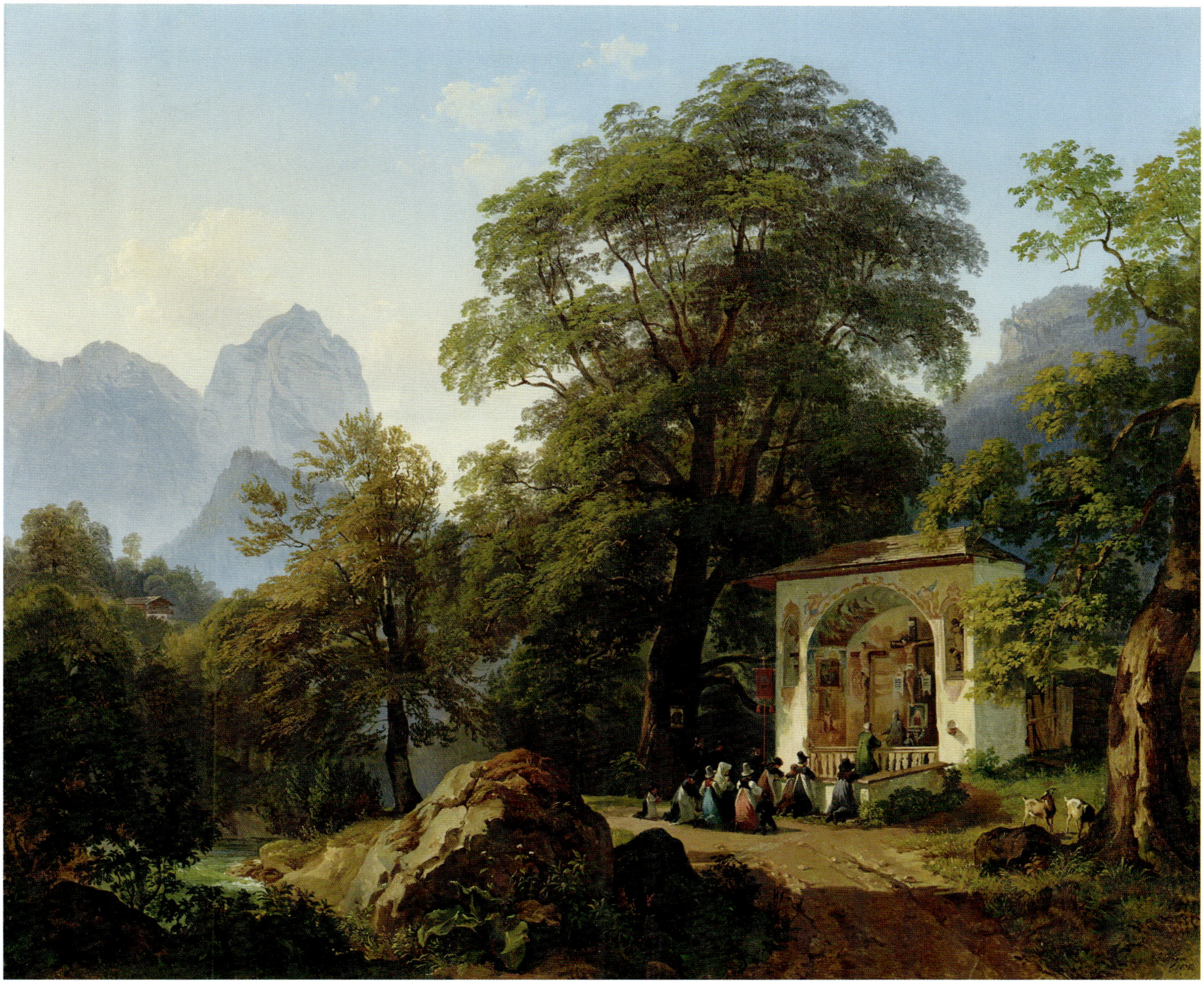

Josef Höger
Forest Chapel, 1835
Oil on canvas, 76.5 × 95.5 cm
Signed (lower right): J. Höger / 1835.
Belvedere, Vienna, inv. no. 8044

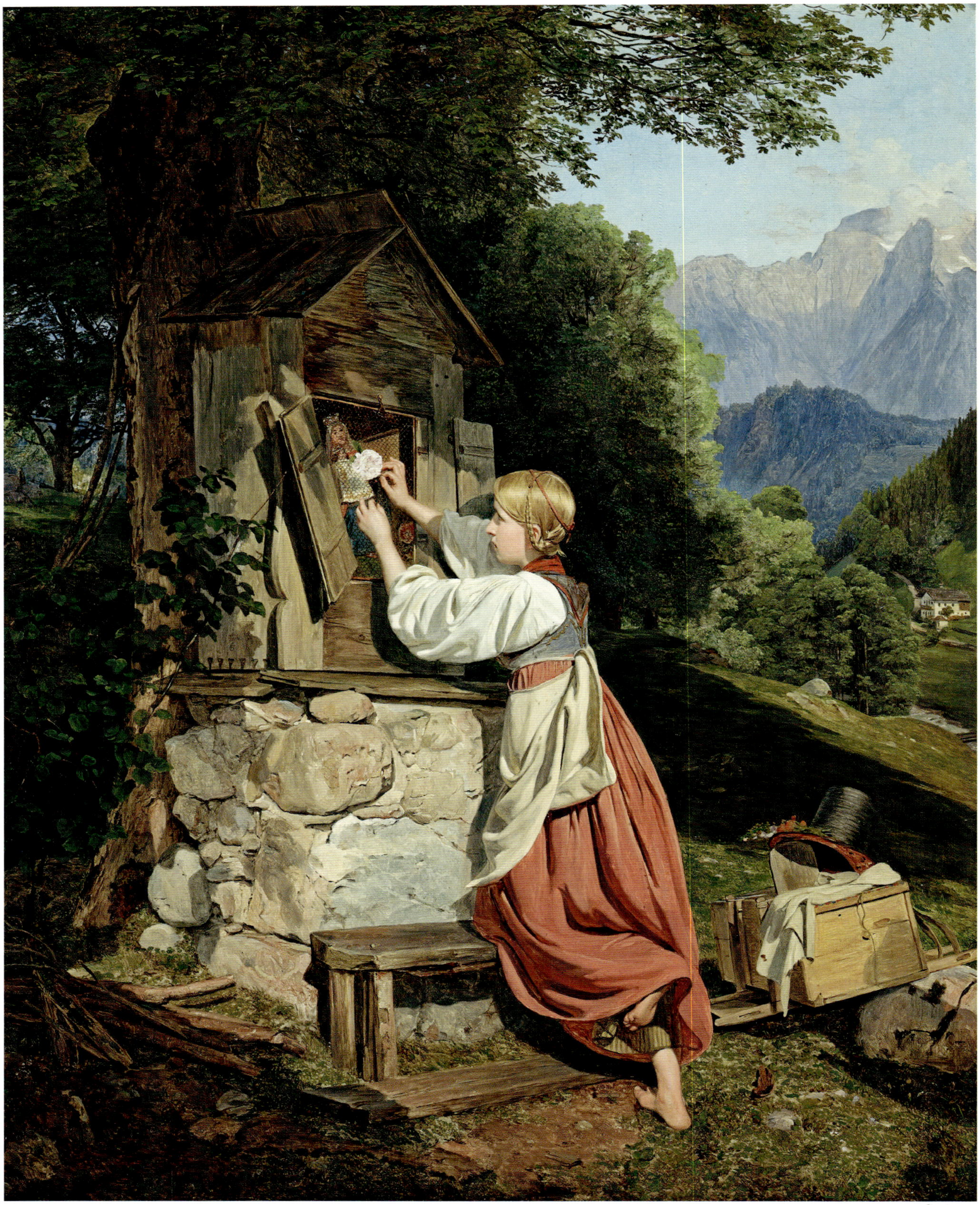

Ferdinand Georg Waldmüller
A Girl Decorates the Virgin Mary with a Rose, 1836
Oil on wood, 55.5 × 44.5 cm
Signed (lower center, under the bench): Waldmüller 1836
Belvedere, Vienna, inv. no. 5603

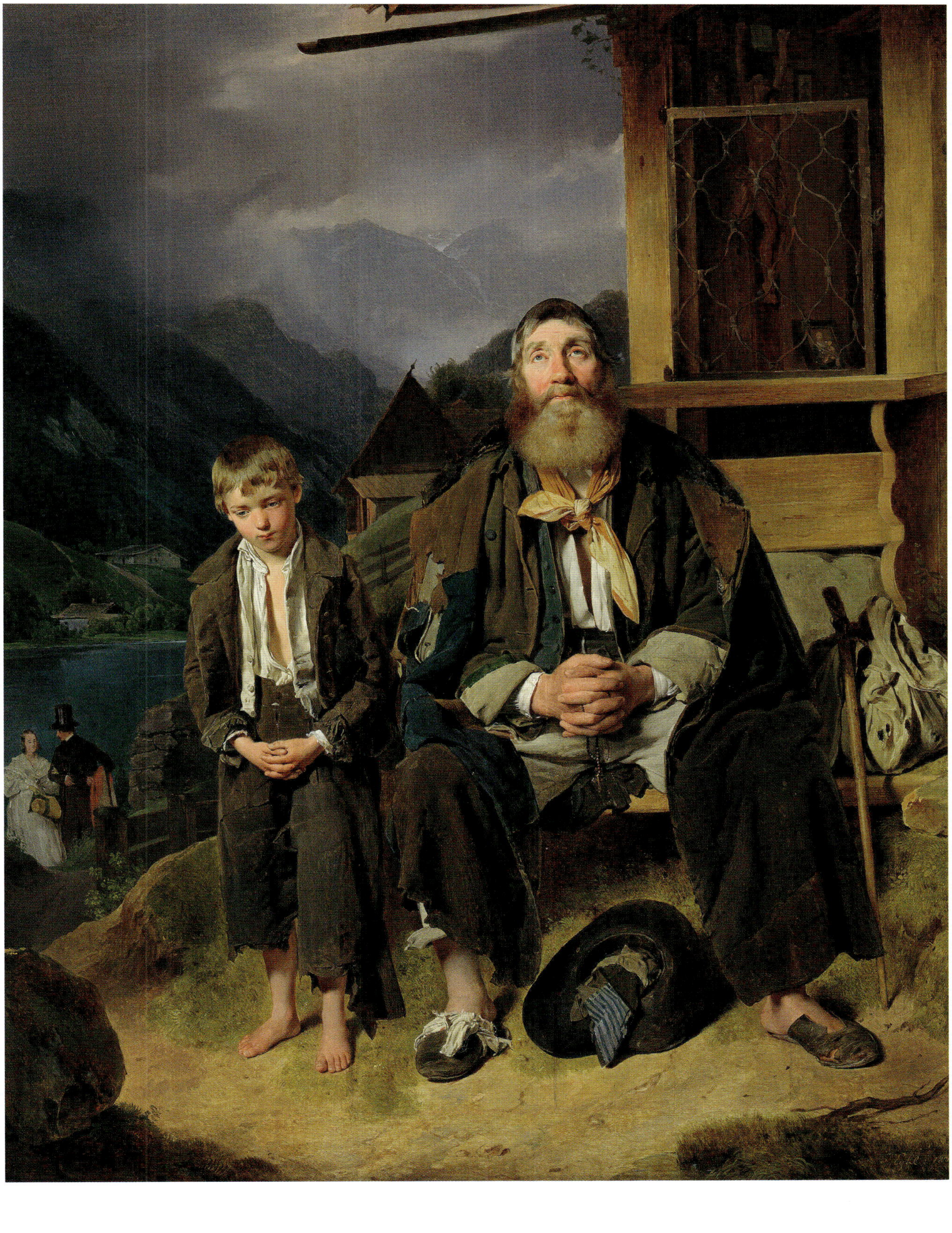

Franz Eybl
The Beggar, 1837
Oil on wood, 58.8 × 48 cm
Signed (lower right): Eybl. 1837
Wien Museum, inv. no. 10141

Friedrich Loos
View of the Fortress Hohensalzburg from Mönchsberg Hill in Salzburg, 1826–35
Oil on cardboard, 30 × 40.5 cm
Unsigned
Belvedere, Vienna, inv. no. 3181

This painting, dominated by the sheer cliff face of the Mönchsberg in Salzburg, with a distant glimpse of the Hohensalzburg Fortress, is one of the most unusual and also fascinating works by Friedrich Loos. The direct juxtaposition of foreground and distance heightens the contrast between the natural and man-made scene. The sun serves to unite the two, casting its rays with equal intensity on both and structuring the vista with well-placed zones of light and shadow. This is complemented by dense vegetation, its verdant green bathed in light, providing a striking contrast against the summery sky.

There is no record of what motivated Loos to paint this scene. It is known, however, that in 1826 he moved from Leipzig to Salzburg to work on the panorama of his fellow academician Johann Michael Sattler (1786–1847). Heinrich Schwarz has speculated that, while out seeking subjects for this commission, Loos may have stumbled upon the very spot from which Johann Christoph Erhard (1795–1822) had drawn a view of the Mönchsberg some years before him (1818, Kunsthalle, Hamburg).[28] Loos may have had this painting in mind, and the graphic clarity of the rock formations suggests that he must also have been thinking of the words of his esteemed teacher, the landscapist Johann Nepomuk Schödlberger (1779–1853)[29]: "The emerging artist assiduously consults the history of nature and takes what he can use from this. In the same way as everything in nature has its individual character, so each mountain, rock, and stone has its own physiognomy [...]."[30] There is no record of the date when the painting was finished. Loos was in Salzburg until completing the panorama in 1835. Then, following some longer spells in Vienna and Rome, he moved to northern Germany and spent the last years of his life in Kiel.

Andreas Andresen/Joseph Erhard Wessely, eds., *Die deutschen Maler-Radirer (Peintres-Graveurs) des neunzehnten Jahrhunderts nach ihren Leben und Werken*, vol. 2 (Leipzig, 1867), pp. 198–209; Ulrich Christoffel, *Friedrich Loos 1797/1890: Ein unbekannter Maler aus dem Salzkammergut* (= Drucke der Münchner Meisterschule 7) (Munich, 1937); Heinrich Schwarz, *Salzburg und das Salzkammergut*, 3rd ed. (Vienna/Munich, 1958); Elfriede Baum, "Salzburger Landschaften von Friedrich Loos," *Mitteilungen der Österreichischen Galerie*, yr. 12, no. 56 (1968), pp. 47–70; Sabine Grabner, *Romantik Klassizismus Biedermeier in der Österreichischen Galerie Belvedere*, 2nd ed. (Vienna, 1997), pp. 94–95; Agnes Husslein-Arco/Rolf H. Johannsen, eds., *Friedrich Loos: Ein Künstlerleben zwischen Wien, Rom und dem Norden*, exh. cat. Belvedere, Vienna (Vienna, 2015).

SG

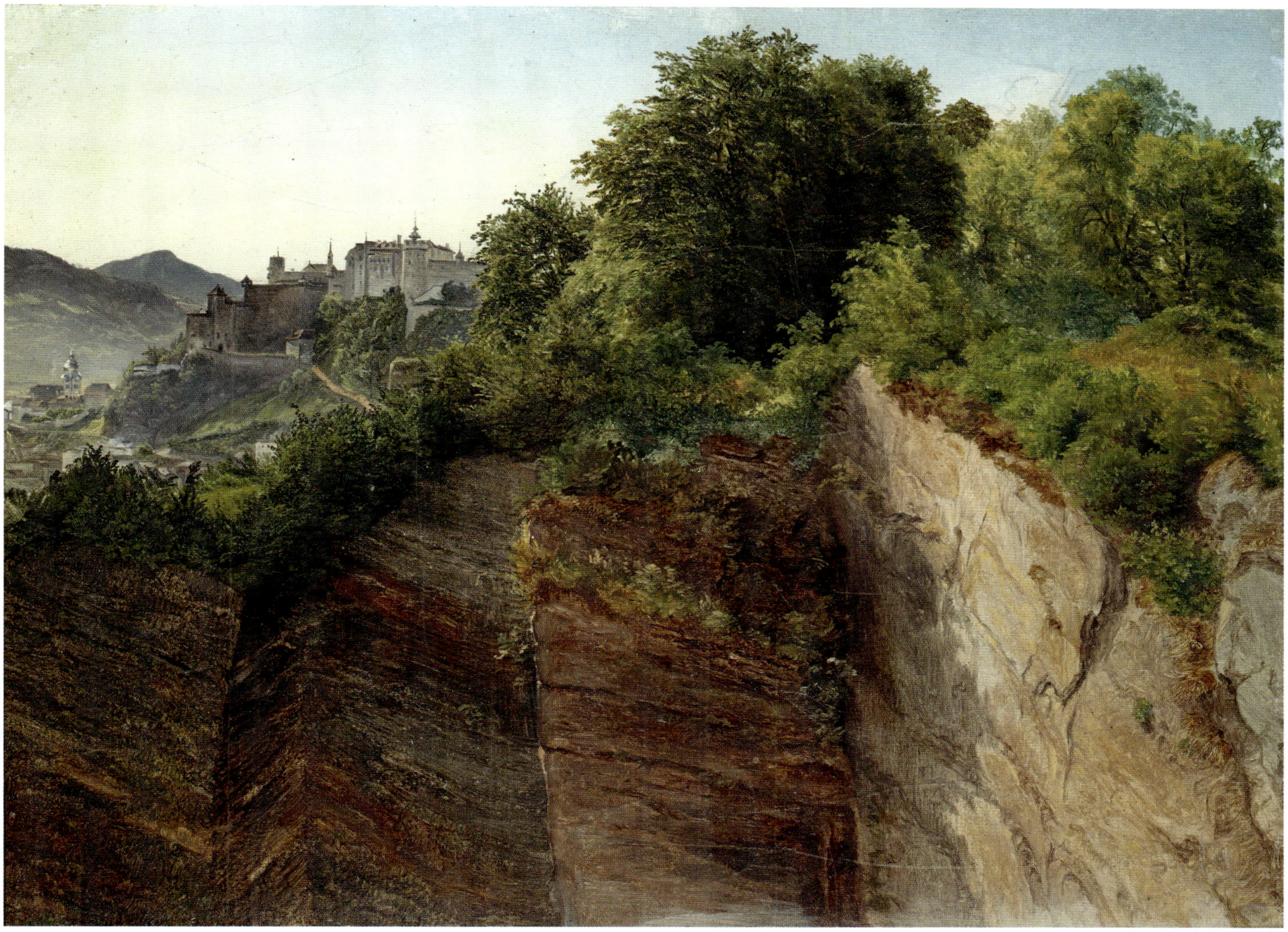

Thomas Ender
The Grossglockner with the Pasterze Glacier, 1832
Oil on canvas, 39 × 54 cm
Signed and inscribed (lower right): Thom. Ender. Nach der Natur 1832.
Belvedere, Vienna, inv. no. 6068

Thomas Ender's importance for Austrian art stems mainly from his watercolors. Early on in his career, the artist found his own personal style of representing nature, never lingering on details, but always seeking a balanced combination of close-up and distant views. The foundations for his work as a painter were laid by studying landscape drawing at the Imperial Academy in Vienna from 1806 to 1813 under Laurenz Janscha (1749–1812) and Christoph Albert Dies (1755–1822). He then honed his skills under the hot sun of Brazil, where he spent several months in 1817/18. The views he painted later, on his many travels through Austria, the crown lands, Italy, and the Levant, are of striking perfection in their sparkling colors and characterization of the landscape.

Although the artist rarely achieved a comparable quality in oils, *The Grossglockner with the Pasterze Glacier* is one of the most significant works in Austrian art, as it was one of the very first depictions of the high mountains in Austrian painting. It was Archduke Johann who had recognized Thomas Ender's artistic and documenting talents and appointed him in 1829 as one of his court painters. Ender was tasked with documenting the Alps in Styria, Carinthia, Salzburg, and North and South Tyrol for the archduke's collection. In summer 1832, he and the archduke set out to cross the Pasterze glacier. The tour led them from Heiligenblut on the Carinthian side[31] across the Pasterze and, passing the Grossglockner to the south, on to the Kalser Tauern, with Archduke Johann noting his geological and botanical observations in his diary.[32] In addition to these entries, Ender did several drawings,[33] which he later used as resources for his oil paintings. Probably the most striking representation of the Pasterze is captured in the Belvedere's painting, since it does without staffage figures as well as being the most objective depiction of the scene. At the center we can see the wide, fissured glacier, with the Grossglockner rising up on the opposite side, and the foothills of the Johannisberg in the background on the right. Ender did his drawings from the platform dubbed "Johanneshöhe" after Archduke Johann's visit and renamed "Franz-Josephs-Höhe" in 1856.

It should also be mentioned that the Pasterze glacier has shrunk by more than half in the 180 years since Thomas Ender captured this landscape and the painting is therefore very important for glacier research.

Alexander Wied, "Österreich," *Die Alpen in der Malerei* (Rosenheim, 1982), pp. 177–240, especially p. 184; *Biedermeier: Gemälde aus der Österreichischen Galerie Belvedere*, exh. cat. Österreichische Galerie Belvedere im Minoritenkloster Tulln (Vienna, 2005), p. 64; Sabine Grabner, *Mehr als Biedermeier: Klassizismus, Romantik und Realismus in der Österreichischen Galerie Belvedere* (Munich, 2006), pp. 98–99.

SG

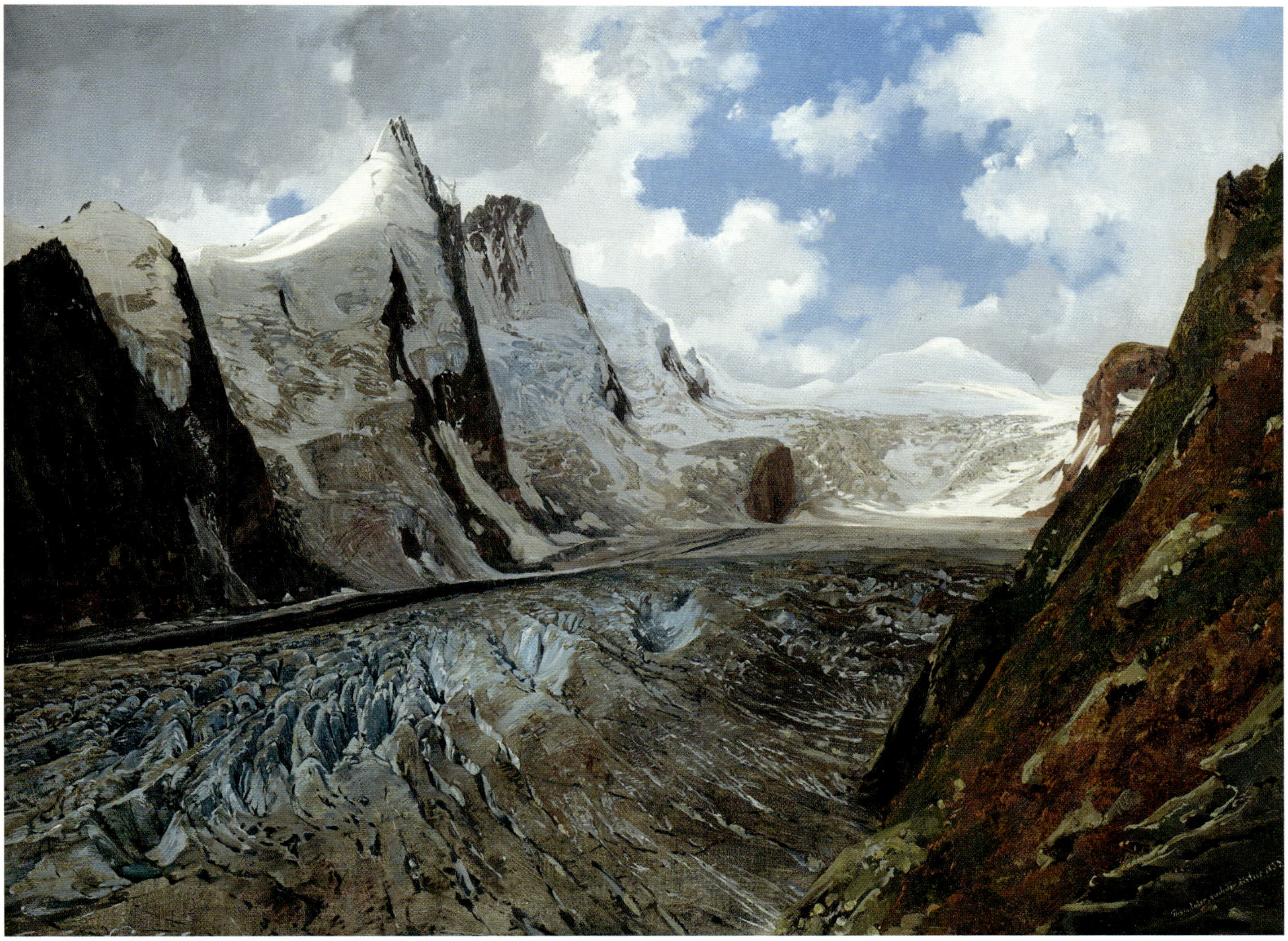

Franz Steinfeld
Lake Hallstatt, 1834
Oil on wood, 57 × 48 cm
Signed (lower right): Steinfeld / 1834.
Belvedere, Vienna, inv. no. 5023

Steinfeld is considered one of the great names in Austrian landscape painting. Like Ferdinand Georg Waldmüller, he was an enthusiastic supporter of plein air painting, advocating it as the basis for credible depictions of nature. In fact, Steinfeld held this opinion long before Waldmüller turned to landscape painting and was already spending his summer months painting nature studies in the late 1810s. His favorite locations for this were the Salzkammergut and the Berchtesgadener Land, regions that had recently been discovered for the arts by the brothers Ferdinand (1785–1841) and Friedrich Olivier (1791–1859). Unlike them, however, Steinfeld tended less toward a romantic view of nature, seeking to find his personal expression through the precise observation of natural phenomena. It was not long before he met other like-minded artists on his travels in those regions, in particular Friedrich Gauermann and Friedrich Loos, and later also Waldmüller. His first picture, *View of Hallstatt* (fig. p. 19), painted in 1824, shows the region realistically and without any foreground props. Peter Pötschner described the picture as marking the birth of Viennese Biedermeier landscape painting,[34] and it became the prototype for a style that was to remain valid until well beyond the mid-century.

This picture of Lake Hallstatt painted ten years later uses a similar formal language. The smooth surface of the lake fills the canvas, gently curving into the background and vying for the viewer's attention with the Dachstein motif lying in the shadow of the bright summer sky above.

Given Steinfeld's outstanding achievements in landscape painting, it is surprising that he was not appointed as a corrector until 1837. He finally became professor of landscape painting at the Imperial Academy in Vienna in 1845, a post he held until 1859.

Constant von Wurzbach, *Biographisches Lexikon des Kaisertums Österreich*, vol. 37 (Vienna, 1878), pp. 81–87; Peter Pötschner, *Franz Steinfeld und die Überwindung des Barocken in der Wiener Landschaftsmalerei*, unpublished diss., Vienna, 1951; ibid., "Franz Steinfelds 'Hallstätter See' von 1834," in *Mitteilungen der Österreichischen Galerie*, 6th yr., no. 50 (1962), pp. 29–32; ibid., *Genesis der Wiener Biedermeierlandschaft* (= Wiener Schriftenheft 19) (Vienna, 1964); Gerbert Frodl, *Wiener Malerei der Biedermeierzeit* (Rosenheim, 1987).

SG

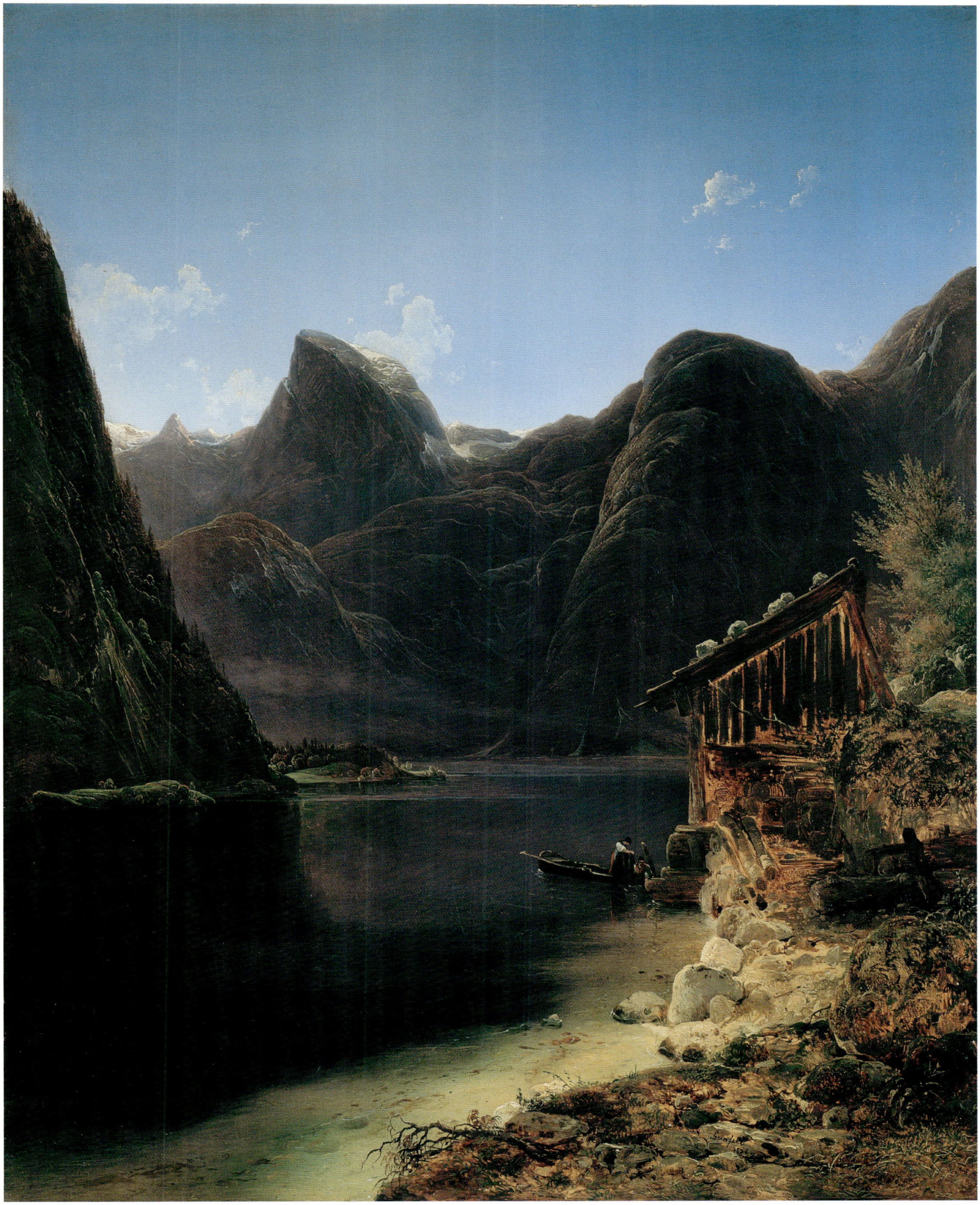

Adalbert Stifter
View of Viennese Suburban Houses (*Beatrixgasse*), 1839
Oil on wood, 34 × 41 cm
Signed (lower right): Stifter / 1839
Belvedere, Vienna, inv. no. 1284

Adalbert Stifter is known above all as a writer. Stories like *Indian Summer* or *Witiko* emulate Goethe's concept of art and education. It is less well known that Stifter was a landscape painter for a long time before he turned to writing. Born in Oberplan in the Bohemian Forest (today Horní Planá, Czech Republic) in 1805, he attended the monastery school at the Kremsmünster Benedictine abbey. It was there that he received his only painting tuition from the school's art teacher; other than that he remained entirely self-taught. He started studying law in Vienna in 1826 but abandoned his studies without graduating, shortly before taking his final exam. In 1848 he moved to Linz, where he was appointed regional school inspector for Upper Austrian elementary schools. Soon afterwards he started writing exhibition reports and reviews for the Upper Austrian Art Association founded in 1851. Seriously ill and suffering from depression, he died in 1868 as a result of a suicide attempt.

In his early works from the 1830s, Stifter remained true to realistic depictions of nature, but as he matured as a painter his style became increasingly free. In his later work, he attempted to depict emotions and feelings in what might be regarded as "symbolic landscapes." The atmospheric portrayals of nature in his poems find an echo in his paintings.

View of Viennese Suburban Houses is surprising at first glance, since the plain firewalls and rooftops were an unusual motif in the 1830s. At the same time, the choice of a narrow view and the emphasis on mood are in keeping with the Biedermeier taste of the time. The picture probably shows the view from Stifter's apartment on Beatrixgasse (now in Vienna's 3rd district). Between 1826 and 1839 Stifter lived at different addresses in Beatrixgasse. It was here that he wrote his short story *Feldblumen*, in which he describes a similar view from a window: "[...] the height of the room, above other apartments, allows me to see an ample piece of sky, but also chimneys galore and several roofs and suburban spires."[35] The view opens out between tall firewalls and across several rooftops into the distance. In the background we can make out the hazy silhouette of other parts of the city: a slightly clumsy St. Stephen's Cathedral and the Kahlenberg hill behind it. The warm sunlight, the delicately colored sky, and the quiet courtyard in the foreground convey an idyllic and familiar impression. The colors are subordinate to the light and refract to create a uniform tone that contributes essentially to the atmospheric depiction.

Fritz Novotny, "Stifter und Piepenhagen," in ibid., *Über das Elementare in der Kunstgeschichte und andere Aufsätze* (Vienna, 1968); ibid., *Adalbert Stifter als Maler*, revised ed. (Vienna, 1979); Brigitte Hauptner, *Adalbert Stifter und die zeitgenössische Landschaftsmalerei*, unpublished thesis, Vienna, 1995; ibid., "'... unvergleichlich an Stimmung ...': Die künstlerischen Beziehungen zwischen Adalbert Stifter, August Piepenhagen und Carl Blumauer," in *Kunstjahrbuch der Stadt Linz 1996/97* (Vienna, 1998), pp. 54–86; ibid., *Adalbert Stifter: Der Schriftsteller als Maler* (Vienna, 2000).

BH

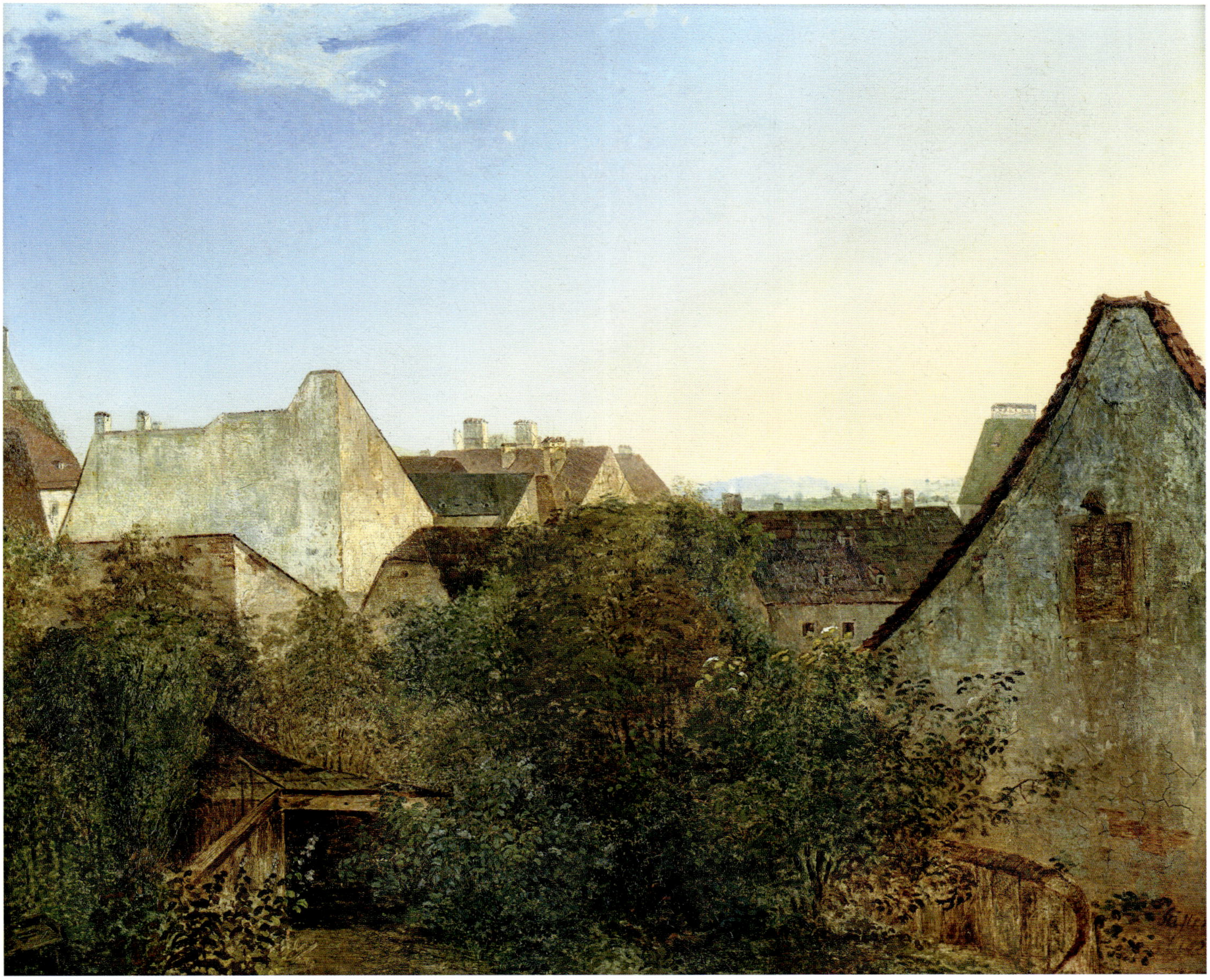

Rudolf von Alt
Stephansdom (*St. Stephen's Cathedral*), 1832
Oil on canvas, 46 × 57.5 cm
Signed (lower left): Rudolph Alt 1832
Belvedere, Vienna, inv. no. 2081

Rudolf von Alt was born into a family of artists: Both his father Jakob (1789–1872) and brother Franz (1821–1914) were draftsmen and painters. The two sons were taught at home and Rudolf's talent soon outshone that of his brother. The final polish was added by his studies at the Academy from 1825 to 1831, first with Karl Gsellhofer (1779–1858), then under Josef Rebell (1787–1828) and Josef Mössmer (1780–1845). After this time, Rudolf and his father Jakob went on many walking tours through the countries of the Habsburg Empire and beyond, capturing the most important and picturesque regions in watercolor. Father and son divided their work, with Rudolf completing the drawings and Jakob transforming these into lithographs.

Their collaboration started with the series *Vienna's Sights and Surroundings Drawn from Nature*, comprising twelve lithograph views, which was published in 1832. The main sheet in this collection was a depiction of St. Stephen's Cathedral seen from Stock-im-Eisen-Platz. This became one of Rudolf von Alt's most famous views and St. Stephen's his most frequently depicted motif. The artist himself stated that he had drawn or painted the cathedral about one hundred times during the course of his long life.[36] The source for this painting was the same watercolor of 1831 on which the above-mentioned lithograph was based (Bundesmobilienverwaltung, Imperial Furniture Collection, Vienna). The perspective is particularly interesting in this view, as Rudolf von Alt has altered it to open up the constricted space of the square in front of the Gothic cathedral. St. Stephen's is depicted from a worm's-eye perspective, set only against the sky, which has the effect of emphasizing it as a solitary symbol, Vienna's main landmark at the very heart of the city. By using this device, the young artist surpassed Carl Schütz's hitherto prevailing view of the cathedral for his Vienna series, published by Artaria.[37] Shortly afterward, Alt captured this view in an oil painting, bringing the cathedral closer to the pictorial boundaries and thereby heightening its presence. The so-called Lanzansky Haus on the right and the building with the awning on the left stabilize the composition, while the vivid staffage figures enliven the scene and illustrate the urban bustle around the cathedral.

This view of St. Stephen's Cathedral is Rudolf von Alt's first architectural picture in oils. It is also the very first oil painting to show the redesigned Stephansplatz after being altered in 1792 on the instructions of Emperor Francis II (I).

Rudolf von Alt presented this painting at the Academy exhibition in 1832,[38] where it was acquired for the Imperial Picture Gallery.

Ludwig von Hevesi, *Rudolf Alt: Sein Leben und sein Werk* (Vienna, 1911); Walter Koschatzky, *Rudolf von Alt: 1812–1905* (Salzburg, 1975), p. 44; Klaus Albrecht Schröder/Marie Luise Sternath, eds., *Rudolf von Alt. 1812–1905*, exh. cat. Albertina, Vienna (Vienna, 2005), p. 95; Sabine Grabner, *Mehr als Biedermeier: Klassizismus, Romantik und Realismus in der Österreichischen Galerie Belvedere* (Munich, 2006), pp. 74–75; Marianne Hussl-Hörmann, ed., *Rudolf von Alt: Die Ölgemälde* (= im Kinsky Editionen 1), (Vienna, 2011), pp. 37–38 and cat. rais. no. 4.

SG

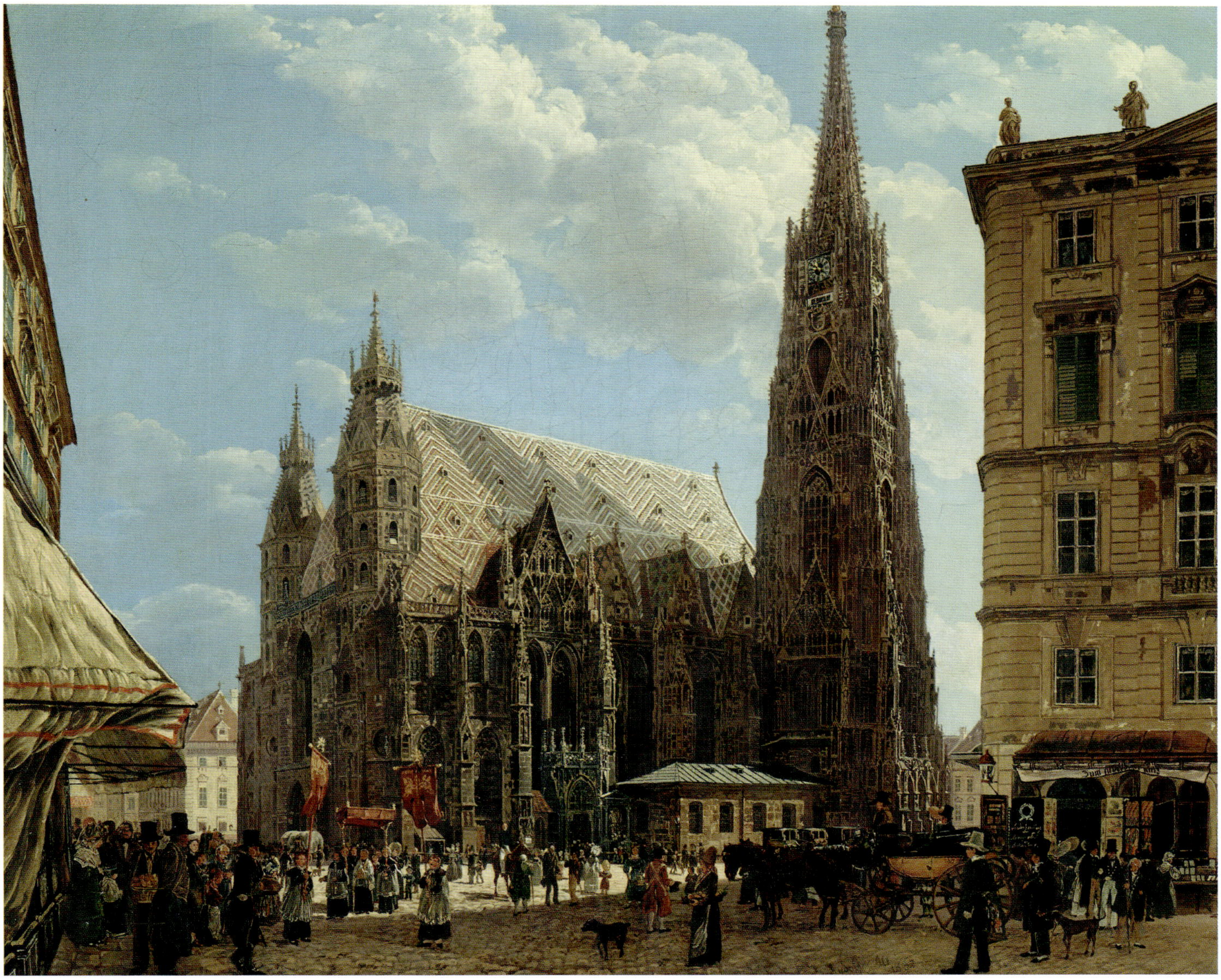

Josef Danhauser
The Rich Glutton, 1836
Oil on canvas, 84 × 131 cm
Signed (lower right, on the doorjamb): Danhauser Wien 1836
Belvedere, Vienna, inv. no. 2087

Josef Danhauser
The Monastery Soup, 1838
Oil on wood, 85.5 × 130 cm
Signed on the edge of the table: PEPI DANHAUSER px 18..
Belvedere, Vienna, inv. no. 2088

Danhauser, who had been trained as a history painter at the Imperial Academy in Vienna, soon realized that subjects from religious sources or about the history of the fatherland were of interest to only a small group of buyers. As a result, he tried to endow history painting with new meaning. For his depiction *The Rich Glutton*, he chose the first part of the Biblical parable of the rich man and poor Lazarus (Luke 16, 19–21), transporting the event into the present and gathering a group of figures in contemporary dress over a meal. This was essentially nothing new, as this religious subject had been given a contemporary slant on many occasions in the history of art. Yet Danhauser's version resulted in a reinterpretation of the story, as the beggar did not remain passive, as in the Biblical narrative, but became actively involved in events by alerting this sophisticated gathering to his dire situation. This direct confrontation with penury triggers various reactions, all vividly portrayed by the artist. In this way, he could transform the religious history painting into a contemporary genre scene and thus a character study.

Originally devised as an independent work, two years later the artist painted a sequel to the picture. *The Monastery Soup* shows the same cast of characters from the previous painting at the moment when they recognize each other again. They are no longer in their host's tastefully decorated garden pavilion but in a room where monks give soup to the poor. All that is left of the former glutton's wealth is his dog and a brightly colored piece of material. Suddenly he recognizes the man sitting opposite him as the beggar from bygone times who, full of forgiveness, offers to share his bread, purging the former glutton of his past vices. Even when these works were first finished, they were compared to William Hogarth's series, such as *The Rake's Progress* (1733) or *Industry and Idleness* (1747), which had been widely disseminated as prints. However, whereas in Hogarth's work the story went on a merciless downward spiral, the positive turn in Danhauser's paintings reflects the mentality of the Viennese Biedermeier period. Incidentally, the similarity between the story of the glutton and the main character in Ferdinand Raimund's magic play *The Spendthrift* (*Der Verschwender*), which premiered in 1834, was also recognized at that time.

Veronika Birke, comp., *Josef Danhauser (1805–1845): Gemälde und Zeichnungen*, exh. cat. Albertina, Vienna (Vienna, 1983), nos. 28 and 31; Sabine Grabner, *Mehr als Biedermeier: Klassizismus, Romantik und Realismus in der Österreichischen Galerie Belvedere* (Munich, 2006), pp. 80–81; Sabine Grabner, *Der Maler Josef Danhauser: Biedermeierzeit im Bild. Monografie und Werkverzeichnis* (= Belvedere catalogues raisonnés 1) (Vienna/Cologne/Weimar, 2011), pp. 62–70, cat. rais. nos. 208 and 226, with further literature.

SG

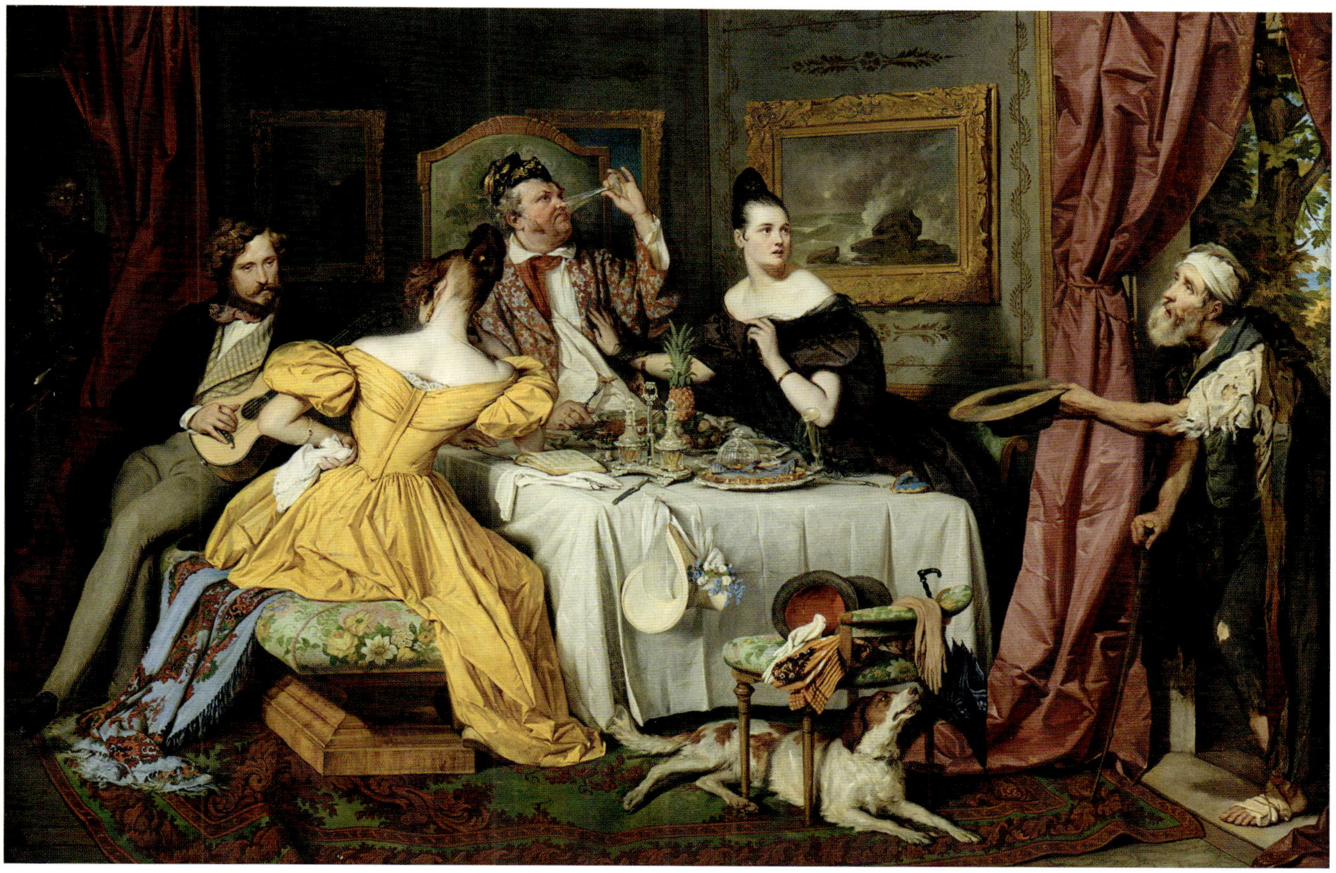

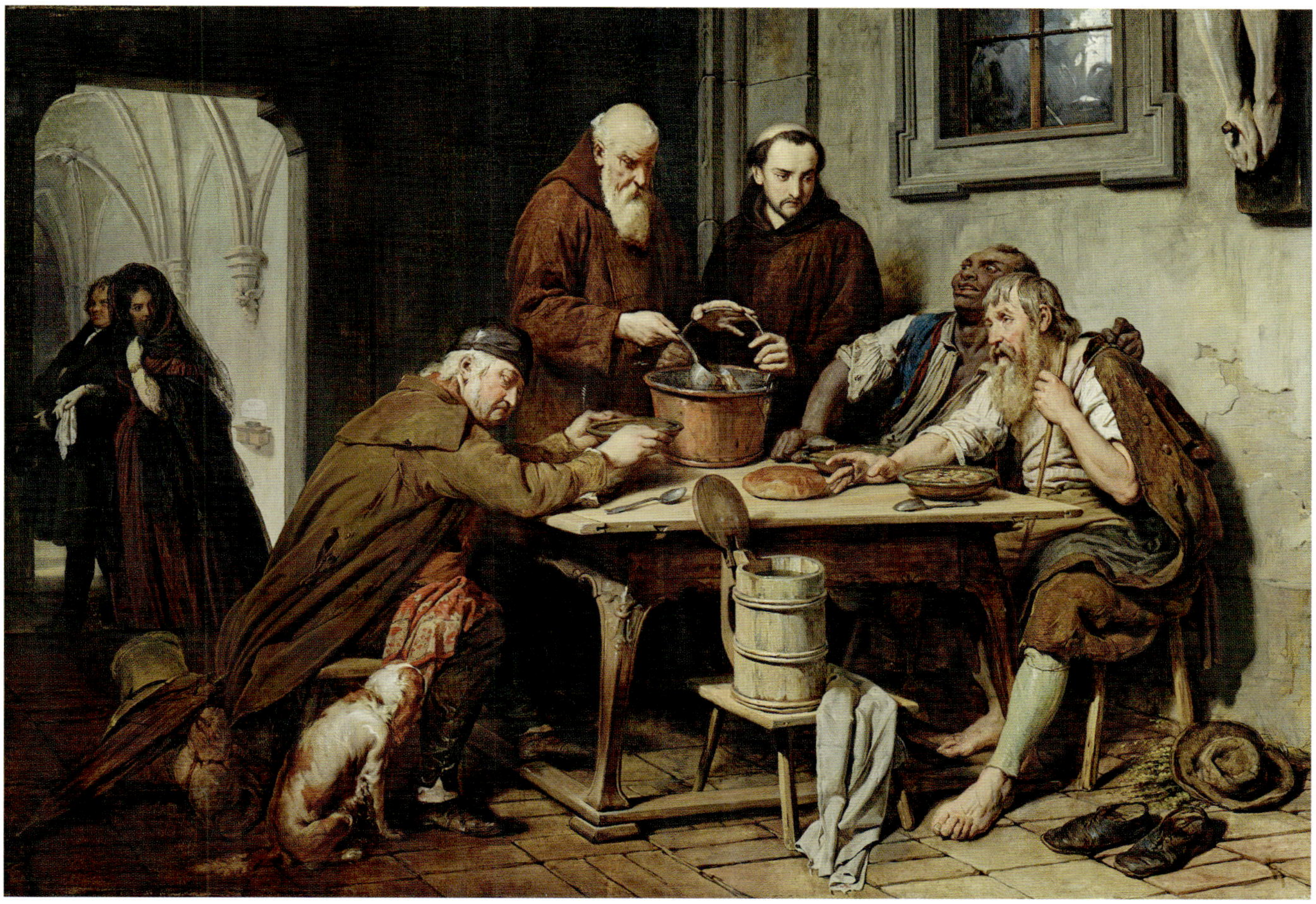

Eduard Ritter
The Declaimer, 1840
Oil on wood, 58 × 73.5 cm
Signed (lower left): Eduard Ritter 1840
Dr. Rudolf Schuster

Eduard Ritter
The Sick Musician, 1847
Oil on wood, 48.5 × 60 cm
Signed (lower right): E. Ritter 1847
Belvedere, Vienna, inv. no. 3632

Ritter's genre pictures are of high narrative value. They are mostly depictions of trivial events from daily life in and around Vienna. Ritter took inspiration from observing of his fellow men. In this he was not so much interested in offering social or moralizing messages, but first and foremost in entertaining his audience.

According to his biographical notes, which have been preserved by his descendants, Ritter attended the Imperial Academy in Vienna from 1829 to 1834, where he received tuition primarily in drawing. This was typical of the traditional academic curriculum, in which drawing was the basic requirement, whereas painting was regarded not as an artistic activity but a craft to be acquired by the would-be artist on his own. Ritter wrote on this subject: "As I never received any training in painting, I often visited competent artists and watched them paint, acquiring technical skills in this way."[39] One of these painters might well have been Josef Danhauser, only a few years his senior, who had himself been a student at the Vienna Academy and had discovered narrative genre painting through the corrector and history painter Johann Peter Krafft (1780–1856). Ritter's group listening to the words of the "declaimer" recall Danhauser's humorous narrative pictures. The audience's reactions to the orator and the subplots in the picture illustrate the artist's sophisticated talent for observation. The picture may have been inspired by Danhauser's *Reading the Will* (plate p. 143), which also shows different human responses, something Ritter depicted with outstanding skill. The composition of this many-figured group and their expressive gestures are equally convincingly portrayed.

The close connection Ritter felt with the slightly older Danhauser is evident in *The Sick Musician*. In this painting he directly quotes his recently deceased colleague in the picture above the bed showing a figure sitting at the piano, which is taken from Danhauser's *Liszt at the Piano* from 1840, now at the Alte Nationalgalerie in Berlin.

SG

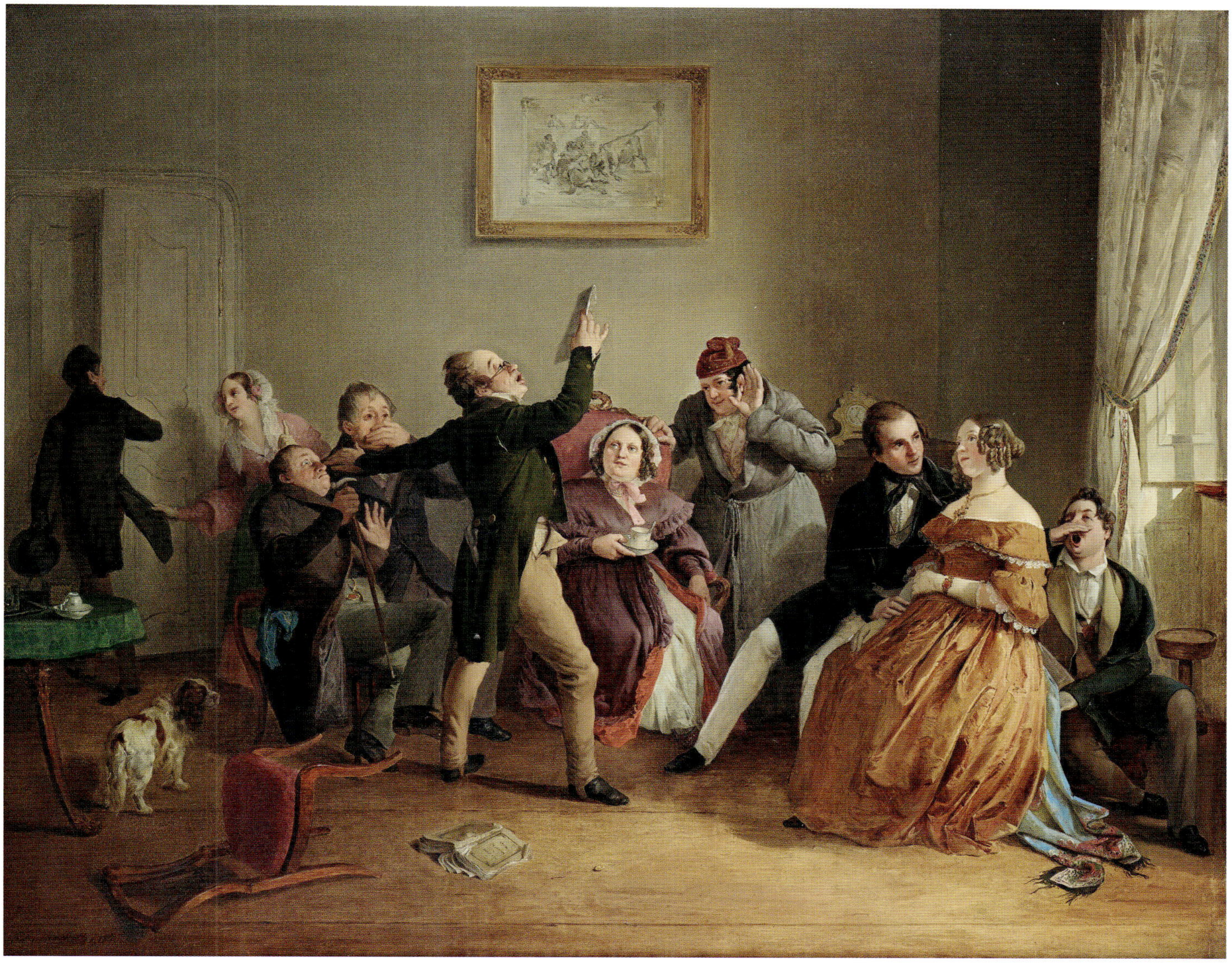

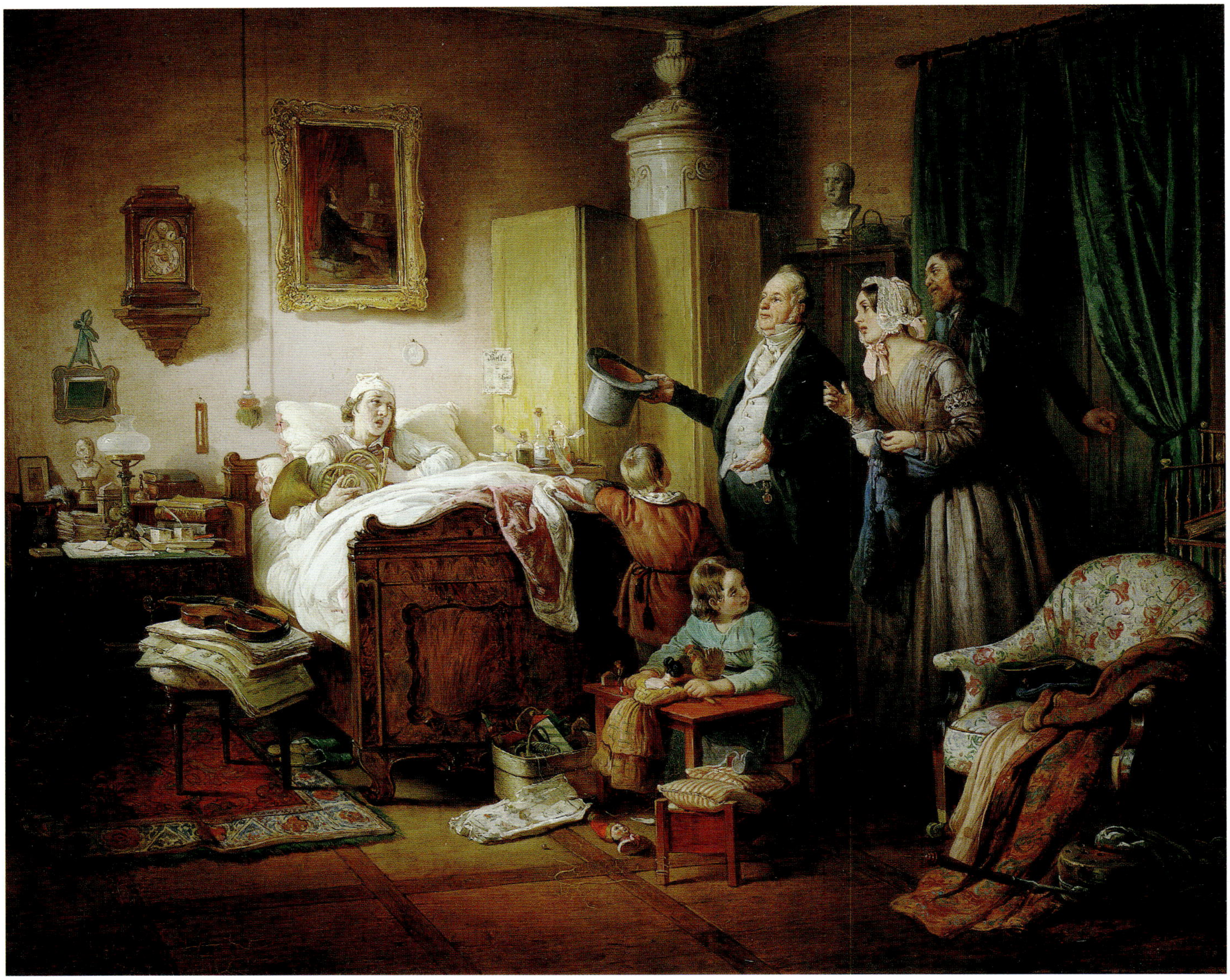

Eduard Ritter
The Sick Musician, 1847

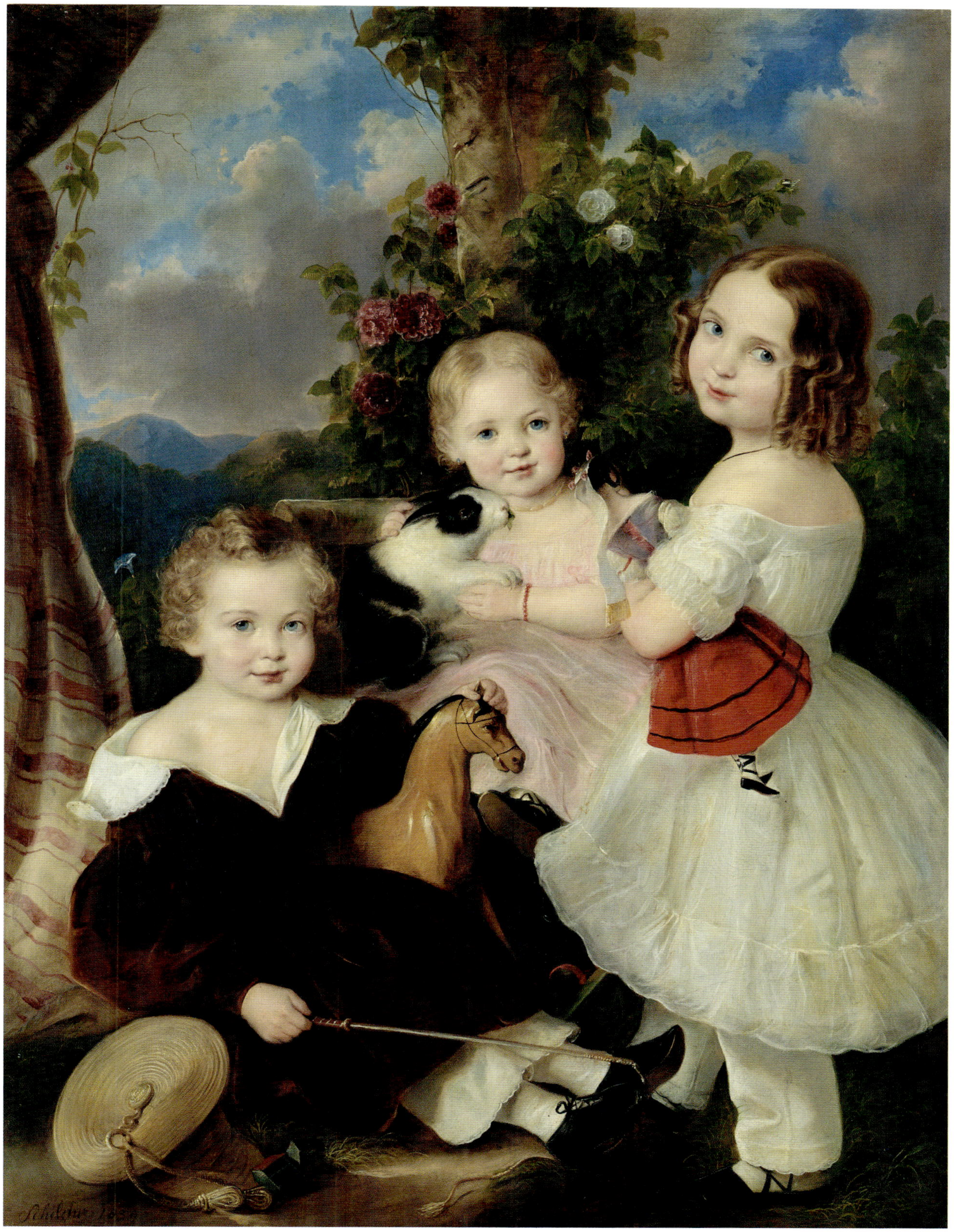

Friedrich Schilcher
Franziska, Georg, and Anna Püringer, Children of Lorenz and Anna Püringer, the Owners of the Hotel "Schwarzer Adler" on Taborstrasse in Vienna, 1839
Oil on canvas, 111 × 88,5 cm
Signed (lower left): Schilcher 1839
Private collection

Josef Danhauser
The Game of Chess, 1839
Oil on canvas, 135 × 175 cm
Signed (lower center): Jos Danhauser 1839
Belvedere, Vienna, on loan from the Goal Arts Foundation, Freeport, Bahamas, inv. no. Lg 1108

In this composition, Danhauser was inspired by a literary source, as was so often the case in his work. However, the original idea—the game of chess between Adelheid von Walldorf and the Bishop of Bamberg at the beginning of the second act in Goethe's *Götz von Berlichingen*—is only hinted at here. Several drawings, today at the Wien Museum and the Albertina in Vienna, trace the development of the composition and show how the protagonists' friendly accord turns into a fierce battle for fame and existence. In the end, only the essential subject, a woman beating a man at chess, remains. The fact that a female chess piece, the queen, has the greatest power in the game enhances the depiction's ambiguity. It is also no coincidence that the stone sculpture on the right shows Hercules with Omphale, and thus alludes to the enslavement of the Greek hero by the Queen of Lydia.

Danhauser was not only a painter but also the artistic director of the furniture factory founded by his prematurely deceased father Josef Ulrich Danhauser (1780–1829), with modern designs leading to an outstanding reputation in Austria and further afield. In this painting, the artist has placed his figures in a setting of his own creation. Entitled *Part of a Salon in Blondel Style*, this interior design was already known to the Viennese public, as Danhauser had used it to advertise his family's furniture factory in the *Wiener Zeitschrift* in September 1838, one year before this painting was completed.[40] It should also be noted that this is one of the first pictures in European painting that vividly depicts a salon gathering.

Veronika Birke, comp., *Josef Danhauser (1805–1845): Gemälde und Zeichnungen*, exh. cat. Albertina, Vienna (Vienna, 1983), pp. 69–75; George Encil, ed., *Experience and Adventures of a Collector* (Paris, 1989), pp. 303–4; Sabine Grabner, *Mehr als Biedermeier: Klassizismus, Romantik und Realismus in der Österreichischen Galerie Belvedere* (Munich, 2006), pp. 86–87; Sabine Grabner, *Der Maler Josef Danhauser: Biedermeierzeit im Bild. Monografie und Werkverzeichnis* (= Belvedere catalogues raisonnés 1), (Vienna/Cologne/Weimar, 2011), pp. 96–100, cat. rais. 244.

SG

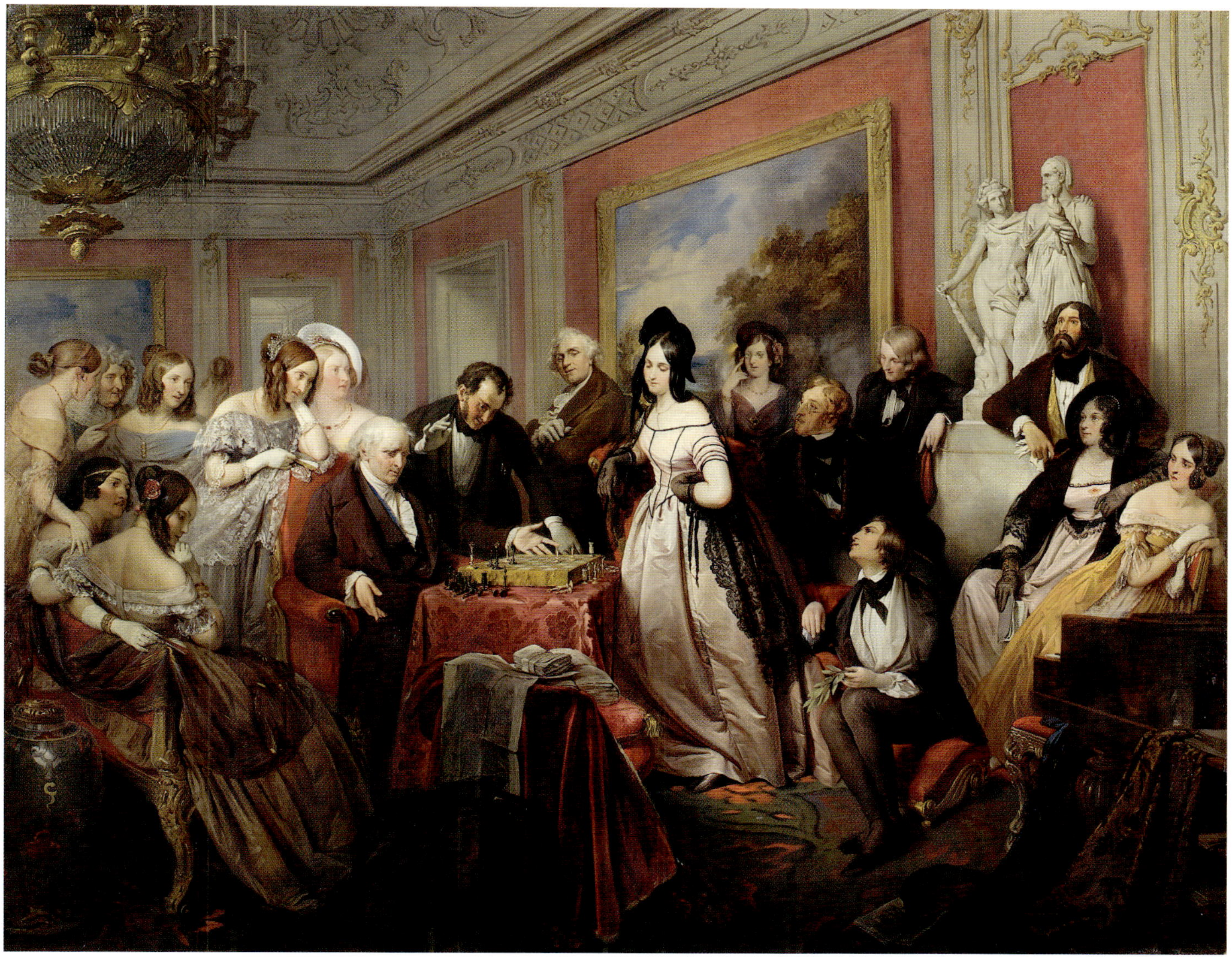

Josef Danhauser
Reading the Will, 1839
Oil on wood, 95 × 114 cm
Signed (lower center): J. D. /1839
Belvedere, Vienna, inv. no. 2086

While studying to be a history painter at the Vienna Academy, Danhauser had been trained to tell stories through images. This approach required both drawing skills and a special insight, as the quality of the history painting hinged on the artist's ability to capture the essence of the text and choose the appropriate moment that also implies both prelude and sequel to the depicted scene. It was precisely for this reason that history painting in the early nineteenth century was regarded as the jewel in art's crown. Danhauser, however, was not fulfilled by the classic subjects of this genre—medieval history or the Old and New Testaments—and sought further sources of inspiration in contemporary literature. It was against this background that he painted the large-scale depictions *The Game of Chess* (plate p. 141) and *Reading the Will*. The latter was in all likelihood inspired by Sir Walter Scott's novel *Guy Mannering, or The Astrologer*, which was extremely popular in Vienna at the time. Danhauser concentrates on the reading of the will, its unexpected content causing a fateful turn in the story. His painting shows the different reactions to the reading, with the behavior of the characters transforming the depiction into a genre painting and a snapshot of society. Danhauser's contemporaries already compared his *Reading the Will* to the work of the same name by the Scottish painter David Wilkie (1785–1841, fig. p.272), which had been commissioned in 1820 by King Max Joseph I of Bavaria (now at the Neue Pinakothek in Munich). Yet they also recognized the differences in approach, because, although both paintings show the reading of a will in the home of the testator, Wilkie shows the people, while Danhauser shows their reactions.

A few years later, in 1844, Danhauser tackled this subject again (*Reading the Will II*, Liechtenstein, The Princely Collections, Vaduz–Vienna). This time the figures are slightly different and the scene recedes further into the picture space with the effect that it seems less immediate.

Veronika Birke, comp., *Josef Danhauser (1805–1845): Gemälde und Zeichnungen*, exh. cat. Albertina, Vienna (Vienna, 1983), no. 37; Gerbert Frodl, ed., *19. Jahrhundert* (= Geschichte der bildenden Kunst in Österreich 5) (Munich etc., 2002), pp. 349–50 (Sabine Grabner); Sabine Grabner, *Der Maler Josef Danhauser: Biedermeierzeit im Bild. Monografie und Werkverzeichnis* (= Belvedere catalogues raisonnés 1) (Vienna/Cologne/Weimar, 2011), pp. 96–100, cat. rais. 245, with further literature.

SG

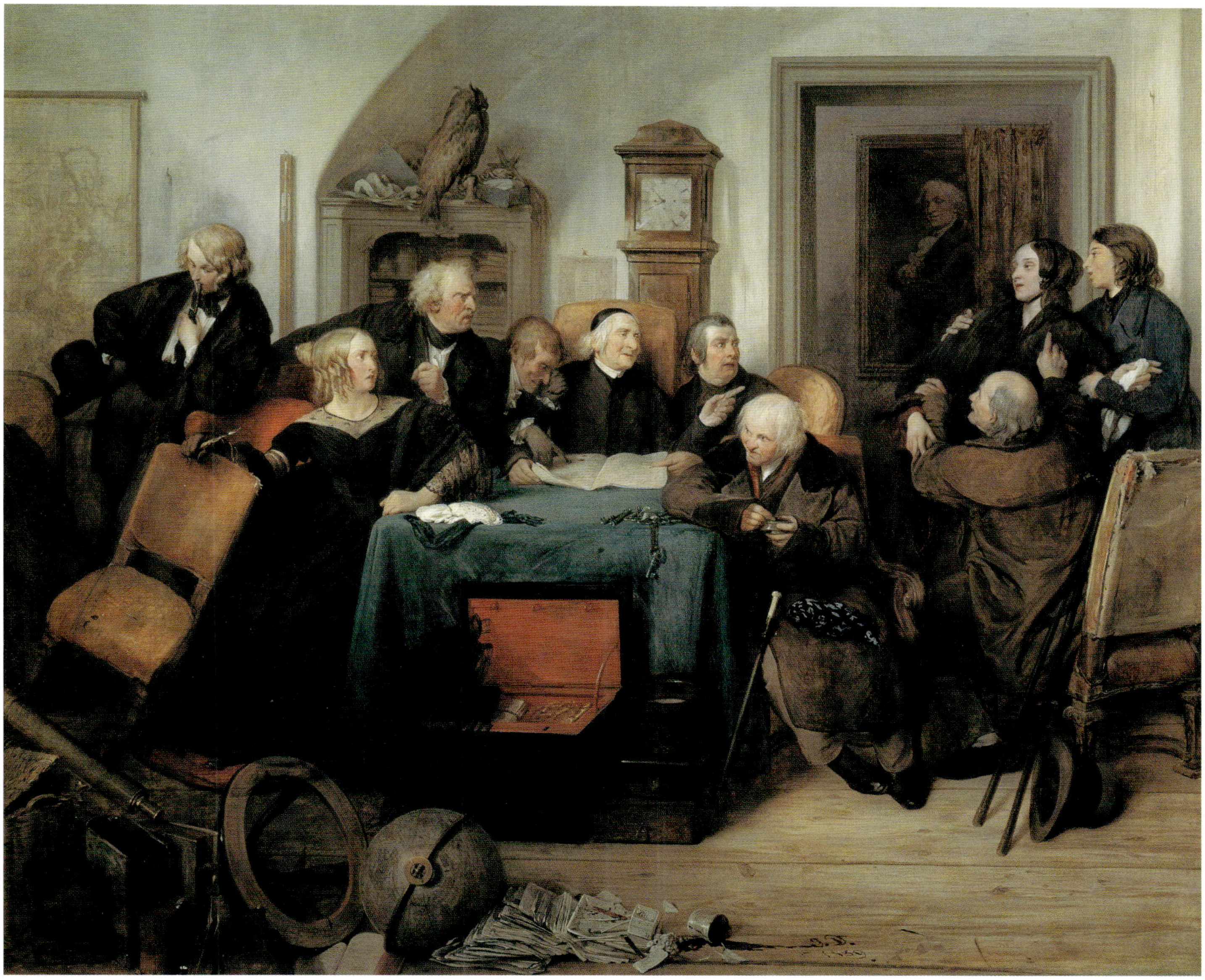

Ernst Christian Moser
Return of the Prize-Winning Alpine Singers, 1845
Oil on canvas, 44.7 × 55.2 cm
Signed (left on tree stump): 6.4.1845 E. Moser
KR Hubert Steinleitner

Ernst Christian Moser
The Reconciliation, 1847
Oil on wood, 62.6 × 78.2 cm
Signed (lower right): E. Ch. Moser 1847
Neue Galerie am Universalmuseum Joanneum, Graz, inv. no. I/915

Moser was one of the most important nineteenth-century portrait and genre painters in Styria. His drawing talent was recognized early on, and although his family was poor he was able to pursue an artistic career. He moved to Vienna in 1828 to study history painting at the Imperial Academy. He arrived at an extremely interesting time for the arts with the new significance assumed by history painting under the corrector Johann Peter Krafft (1780–1856). During the 1820s, Krafft encouraged his students to make their pictorial narratives as lifelike as possible and to choose contemporary themes. It was not long before Moser developed an outstanding virtuosity, above all in figurative painting, but also in picture composition, which inspired him to take on more complicated challenges such as the *Return of the Prize-Winning Alpine Singers*. He depicts the various figures admirably, the natural movements conveying the impression of a harmonious, convivial gathering. He also cleverly divided the narrative into a main and secondary theme, neither of which takes on a dominant role. Thus, the group admiring the prize, a chain of silver coins, does not stand out more than the other group around the second singer. Only the setting is perhaps a little incongruous, since the wooden structure and the shape of the tree recall seventeenth-century Dutch painting, while the view of the lake and mountains of the Salzkammergut on the right are more modern. When Moser presented this picture at the Academy exhibition in Vienna,[41] he had already been teaching at the drawing academy in Graz for five years. In addition to his teaching position, he also took on portrait commissions, which were very popular on account of his sensitive interpretation of figures. A further characteristic feature of his paintings is the use of bright but delicately nuanced colors imbued with glowing radiance. A fine example of his outstanding technical skill is *The Reconciliation*, one of the few Austrian paintings of the time to show a bourgeois household. The room is furnished with great taste and attention to detail, and the occupants are fashionably and elegantly dressed. The interaction within the group is also very natural, although, despite the meaningful glances and gestures, the narrative is largely open to interpretation.

E. Sperl-Moser, *Ernst Christian Moser, ein Maler der Grazer Biedermeierzeit*, unpublished diss., Graz 1933; Wilfried Skreiner, comp., *Ernst Christian Moser, 1815–1867*, exh. cat. Neue Galerie am Landesmuseum Joanneum im Künstlerhaus, Graz (Graz, 1968); Gudrun Danzer, "Ernst Christian Moser, *Die Versöhnung*," in ibid./Peter Peer/Christa Steinle, eds., *Zur Natur des Menschen: Genremalerei des 19. und frühen 20. Jahrhunderts aus der Sammlung der neuen Galerie* (Weitra, 2006), pp. 54–55.

SG

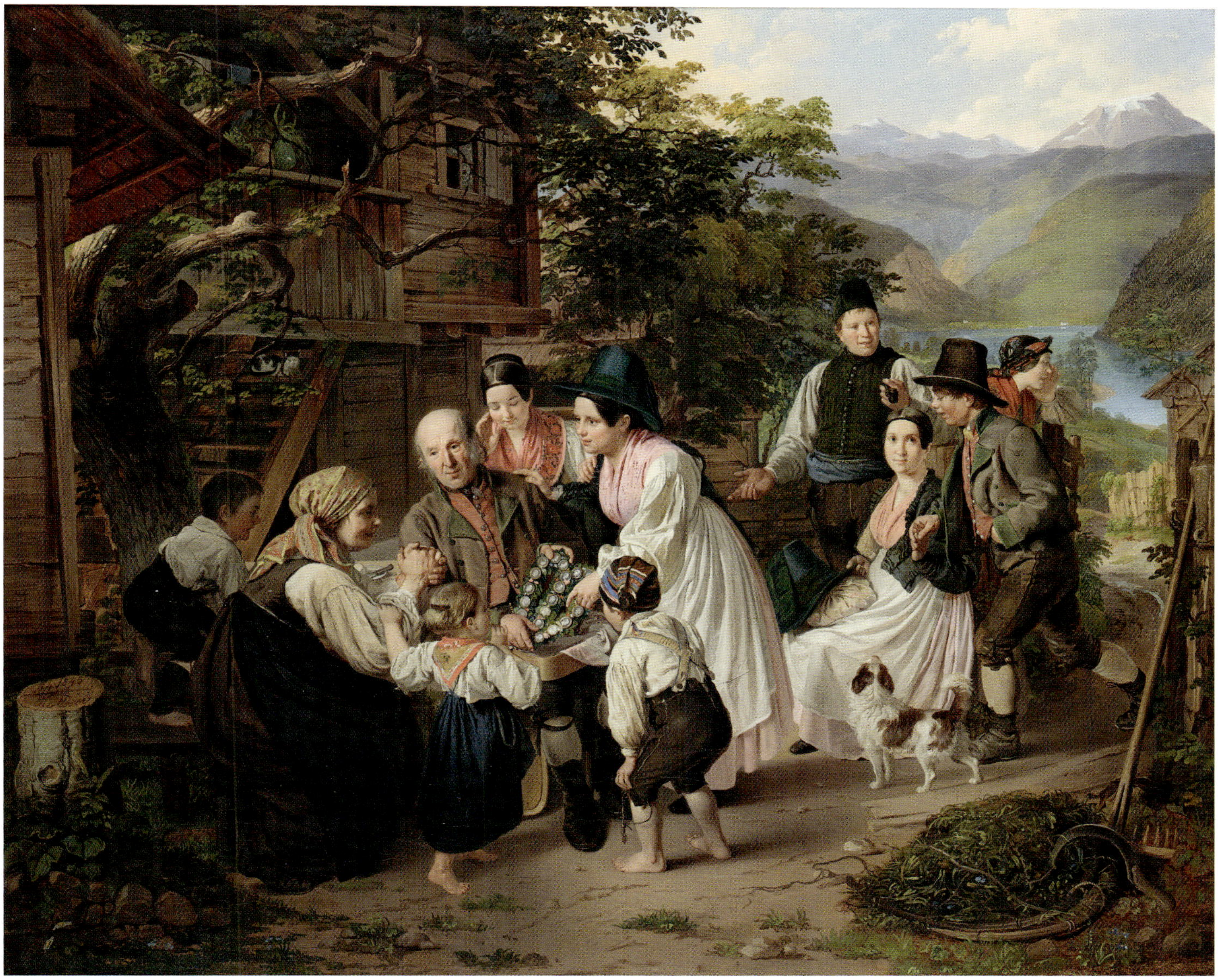

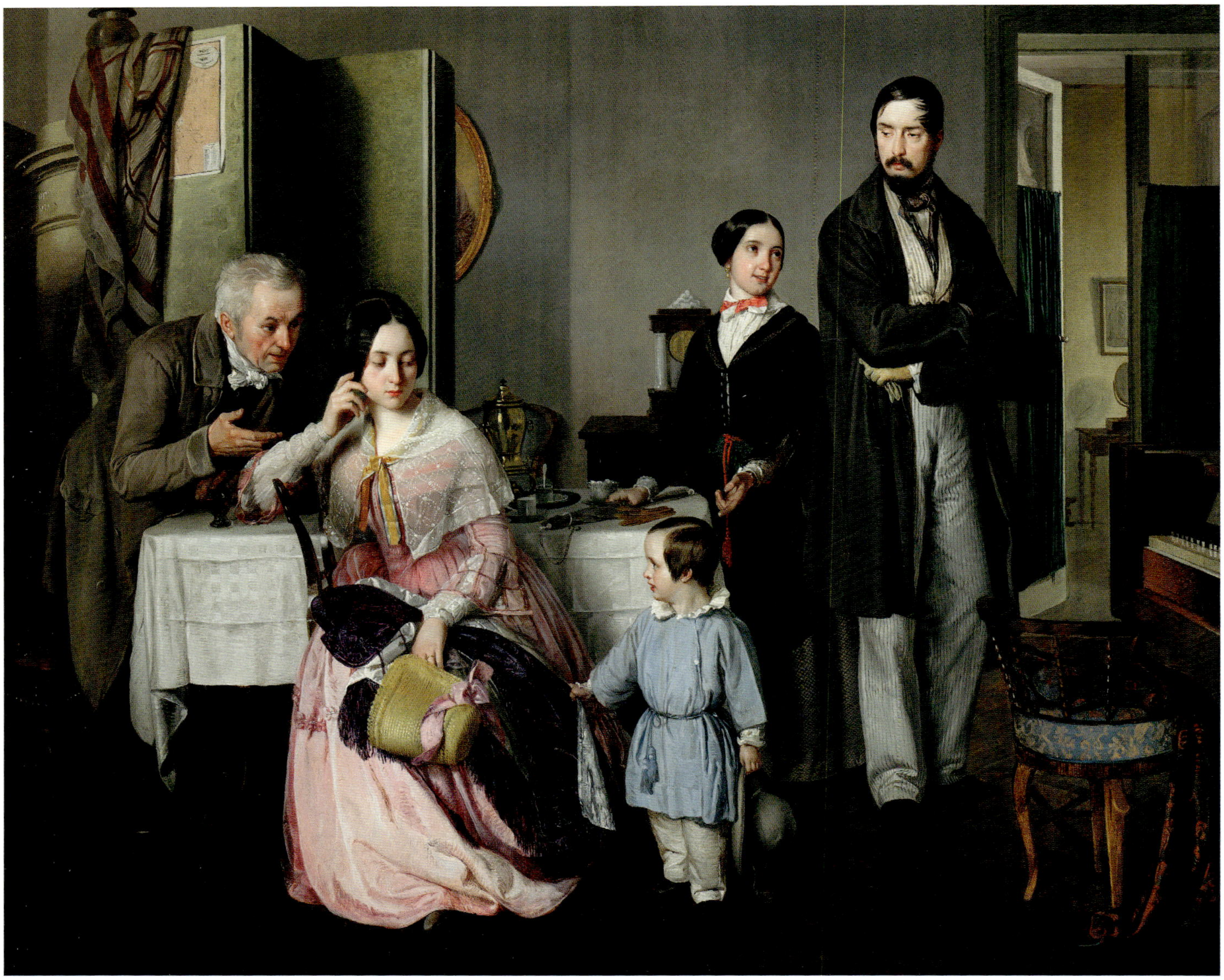

Ernst Christian Moser
The Reconciliation, 1847

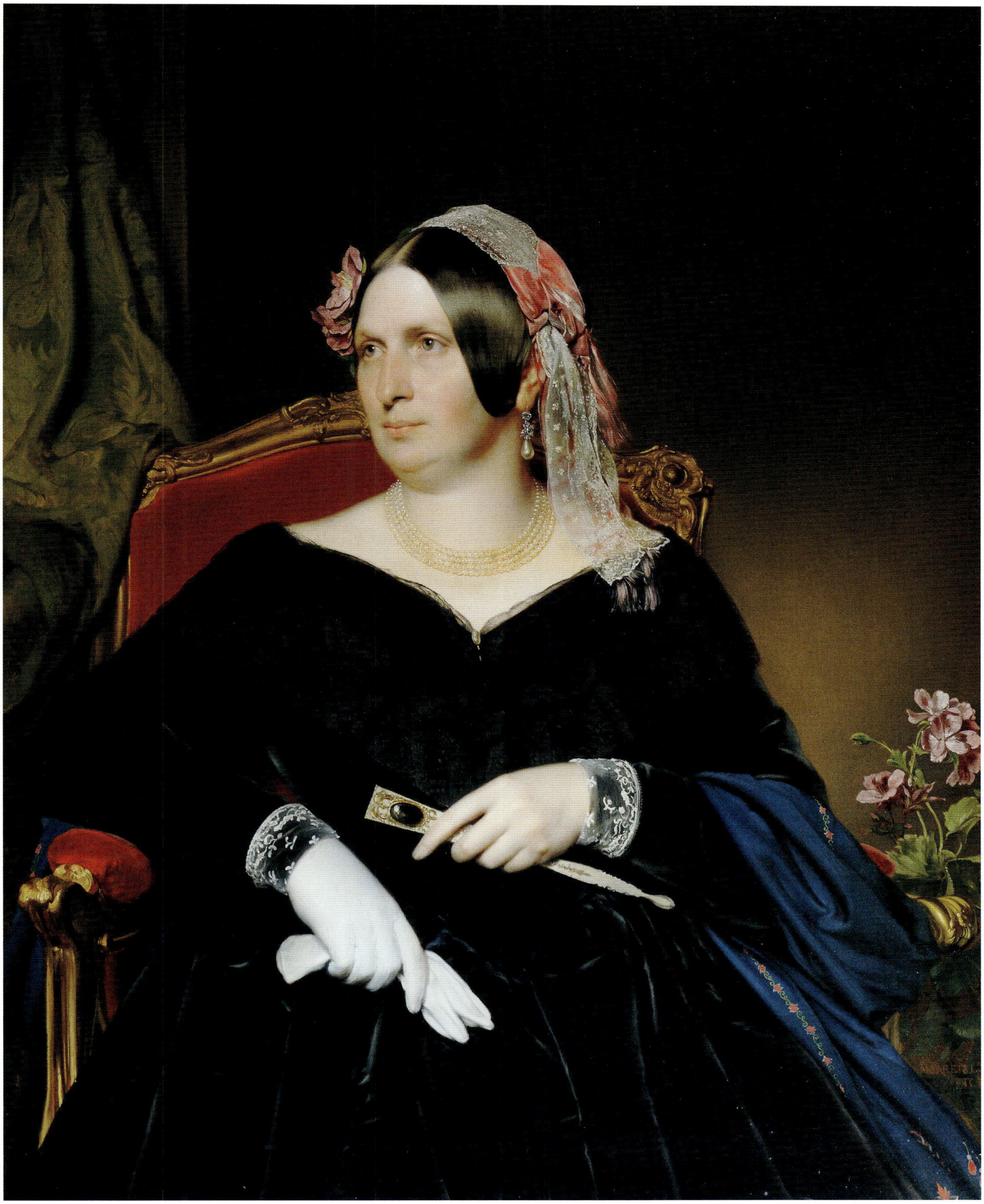

Franz Eybl
Lady on an Armchair, 1846
Oil on canvas, 111 x 91 cm
Signed (lower right): F. EIBL. / 846.
Belvedere, Vienna, inv. No. 2367

Antonín Machek
The Family of the Industrialist I. J. Wehle, c. 1840
Oil on canvas, 117 × 94 cm
Unsigned
The City of Prague Museum, inv. no. 33.167

Machek, born in 1775 in a small village in eastern Bohemia, is the oldest artist to feature in this exhibition. His versatility as an artist enabled him to adapt developments in art to serve his own purpose and be innovative at the same time (figs. pp. 28, 29). His career was very varied. After drawing tuition in Prague, he spent a brief spell at the Vienna Academy (1799/1800), a period that was, nevertheless, decisive for his future. For it was in Vienna that he learned the new technique of lithography that would provide him with a lifelong income. In 1813 he founded the first lithographic printing office in Bohemia. He followed the contemporary fashion of focusing on patriotic historical subjects, bringing numerous series onto the market. Besides working as a painter of decorative schemes and depicting religious scenes for altarpieces, he was most acclaimed as a portraitist. His first successes were in Linz, where he lived for several years before 1813. Machek specialized in a realistic portrayal of people's faces, an aspiration few artists shared at the beginning of the century. At the same time, he valued the detailed rendering of materials and aimed to capture textural qualities. Only a few group portraits are known by this artist, which is why this image of seven figures from the family of the industrialist Wehle is of particular interest. The artist refrained from painting a conversation piece, a genre suited to the depiction of multiple figures, but instead grouped the standing children around their seated parents. All the characters gaze out of the picture, with the exception of the youngest daughter, and Machek also added a glimpse of Prague's Castle District in the background. Although the girl's gesture, offering a garland of flowers to her parents, recalls the Neoclassical portrait tradition, the painting is strikingly honest in its rendering of the physiognomies and the sense of three-dimensional space that gives the figures a physical presence.

Biedermeier: Art and Culture in Central Europe 1815–1848, exh. cat. Palazzo della Ragione, Padua (Milan, 2001), pp. 170–71 (Radim Vondráček); Radim Vondráček, ed., *Biedermeier: Art and Culture in the Bohemian Lands 1814–1848*, exh. cat. Museum of Decorative Arts in Prague and Gallery (Prague, 2010); Šárka Leubnerová, ed., *19th-Century Art: From Neoclassicism to Romanticism. Guide to the Exhibition of the Collection of 19th-Century Art,* National Gallery in Prague, Salm Palace (Prague, 2015), p. 103; *Saur/De Gruyter Allgemeines Künstlerlexikon: Die bildenden Künstler aller Zeiten und Völker*, vol. 86 (Munich etc., 2015), pp. 161–62 (A. Wagner-Wilke).

SG

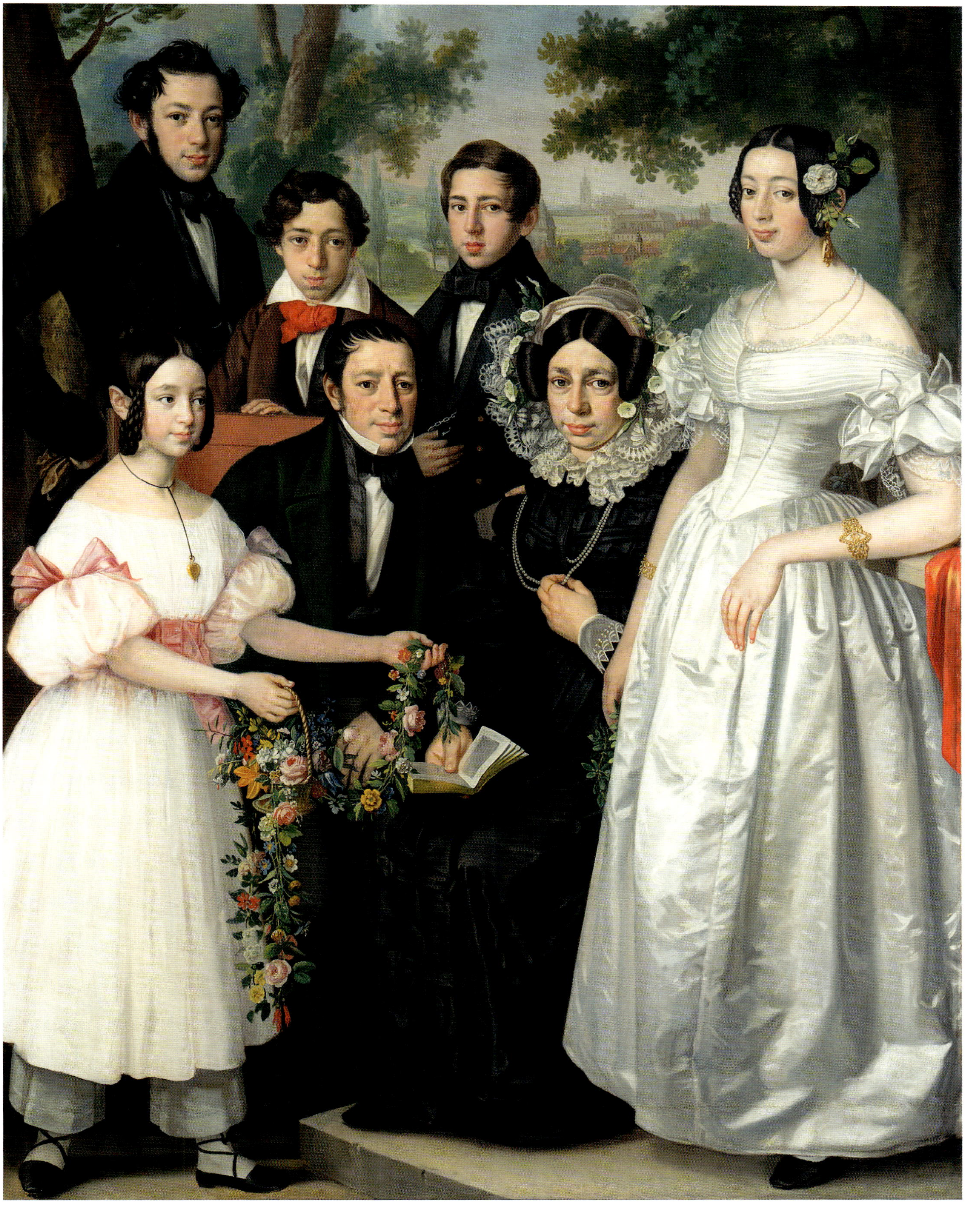

Ludwig Ferdinand Schnorr von Carolsfeld
The Large Pine next to the Brühl near Mödling, 1838
Oil on canvas, 67 × 114 cm
Signed (lower left): 18 LS [lig.] 38.
Belvedere, Vienna, inv. no. 3167

Schnorr von Carolsfeld arrived in Vienna from Königsberg at the age of sixteen to study with Friedrich Heinrich Füger (1751–1818) at the Imperial Academy. He was soon adopted by the circle of German Romantic artists surrounding Friedrich Overbeck (1789–1869) but did not participate in the protest by the Brotherhood of St. Luke (Nazarenes) against the artistic ideals of the Vienna Academy, nor did he follow them to Rome. He worked thereafter for Archduke John and designed the windows in the Brandhof, his estate in the Hochschwab region of Styria. He also provided the preliminary drawings for the stained glass windows of the Romantic Franzensburg castle in Laxenburg. Later, he worked as custodian of the Imperial Picture Gallery in the Upper Belvedere.

Schnorr concentrated mainly on religious, historical, and literary themes, as well as portraits. He earned great acclaim, for example, for his 1818 painting *Faust and Mephisto in the Study* (Belvedere, Vienna), one of the earliest oil paintings about Goethe's *Faust* (premiere 1808). From the 1830s, he focused increasingly on landscape painting, continuing the heroic-romantic style of Josef Anton Koch (1768–1839) until the mid-century. Schnorr was not in fact a Romantic as such, since his concept of nature was also influenced by the ideas of contemporary Realism. An excellent example of this is *The Large Pine next to the Brühl near Mödling*, which depicts one of the best-known natural monuments near Vienna at the time, a popular destination for day trips but also revered as a sacred site. Because of the tree's wide, spreading crown, the artist chose a wide picture format, unusual for the time. The central positioning of the tree in front of a wide-open sky emphasizes its grandeur and also highlights the artist's "poetically romantic view of the landscape," as Fritz Novotny wrote.[42] The figures are to be understood as *pars pro toto*, idealized portrayals representing the wide spectrum of social classes (bourgeois townsfolk, farm workers, itinerant craftsmen, and beggars) and behavior (charity, hard work, piety, humility).[43] The elevated location also offers a panoramic view of a real landscape, past the Anninger and Eichkogel toward the Vienna Basin and the distant horizon beyond. The picture is notable for its saturated colors, from the deep blue sky to the fresh green vegetation, and the low sun bathing the tree in a warm golden light.

The painting shows the region immediately after its reforestation by John I, Prince of Liechtenstein. The tree had to be cut down in 1997 for safety reasons, and its remains are kept today in the Niederösterreichisches Landesmuseum in St. Pölten.

Fritz Novotny, *Hundert Jahre österreichischer Landschaftsmalerei* (Vienna, 1948); Alexander Strasoldo-Graffemberg, *Ludwig Ferdinand Schnorr von Carolsfeld (1788–1853)*, unpublished diss., Freiburg i. Br., 1986; Martin Tanzwirt, *Der Strömungspluralismus im Werk von Ludwig Ferdinand Schnorr von Carolsfeld*, unpublished diss., Vienna, 1999; Gerbert Frodl, ed., *19. Jahrhundert* (= Geschichte der bildenden Kunst in Österreich 5) (Munich et al., 2002), pp. 347–48; Werner Telesko, "'Heimatbilder': Landschaftskunst und Identitätssuche in der österreichischen Malerei des 19. Jahrhunderts," in *Belvedere: Zeitschrift für bildende Kunst*, no. 2 (2004), pp. 4–17; Sabine Grabner, *Mehr als Biedermeier: Klassizismus, Romantik und Realismus in der Österreichischen Galerie Belvedere* (Munich, 2006), pp. 66–67.

SG

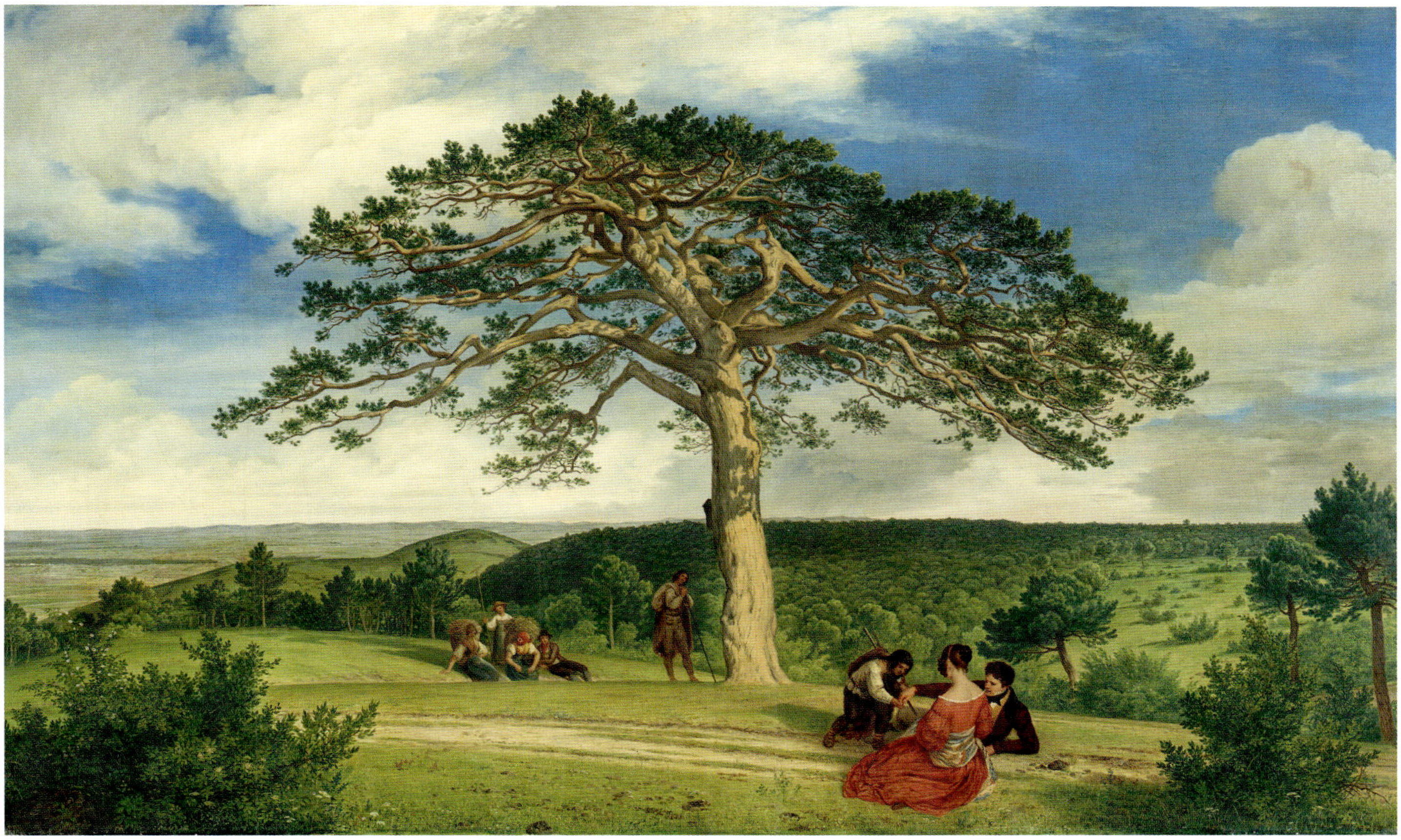

Ferdinand Georg Waldmüller
Josef Leopold Gierster, Captain of the Civil Guard, With His Wife Katharina, née Kandl, and Five Children, 1838
Oil on canvas, 174 x 143 cm
Signed (lower left): Waldmüller 1838
Roland Collection

Waldmüller rarely took on commissions for family portraits, possibly because he considered the arranging of several figures while retaining a portrait-like effect to be beyond his capabilities. The greatest challenge in this regard may well have been the portrait of *The Notary Dr. Josef August Eltz With His Wife Caroline (née Schaumburg) and His Eight Children in Ischl* (1835, Belvedere, Vienna). He painted this as a genre scene, making it one of the most unconventional family portraits in Austrian painting. By comparison, the painting of the Gierster family with seven figures, three fewer than the Eltz family, is conventional in composition and portrayal, the coherence within the group being achieved through the compact, block-like composition. The figures are connected by a structural framework of lines underpinning their gazes and hand movements, guiding the eye of the viewer through the picture. Each face is drawn individually and highlights the resemblance between parents and children. The arrangement also clearly shows the patriarchal structure, with Josef Leopold Gierster (c. 1800–1863) in the uniform of a captain of the Civil Guard as head of the family at the center. His correct posture is mirrored by his two daughters Elisabeth und Katharina by his side, while the older boy August (1828–1865) and his younger brother Josef (born 1834) stand respectfully in the foreground. Only Karoline (1836–1877), the small child in the center of the picture, is more relaxed, no doubt reflecting her childish innocence, as she attempts to grab the red rose held by her mother Katharina (1798 née Kandl). The flower, however, is intended for her father, as his wife's gesture suggests. Katharina is looking reverently toward her husband, who meets her gaze sternly, but also full of admiration. A greater show of affection would not have been proper for Josef Gierster, in particular as he wanted to be seen not only as head of the family but also, as indicated by his uniform and stance, as a public dignitary. When the picture was painted, Gierster was owner of a brewery and country inn, and was also school inspector for Gaudenzdorf, a village south of Vienna (now part of the 12th district); from 1850 to 1861 he was mayor of Gaudenzdorf. The Gold Cross of Merit with Crown and the Gold Civil Medal of Honor shown in the picture were awarded by Emperor Franz Joseph I after the painting had been completed and were added later by an unknown artist.

Bürgersinn und Aufbegehren: Biedermeier und Vormärz in Wien 1815–1848, exh. cat. Historisches Museum der Stadt Wien (Vienna, 1988), p. 194; Hans Bisanz, comp., *Ferdinand Georg Waldmüller zum 200. Geburtstag: Werke im Besitz des Historischen Museums der Stadt Wien*, exh. cat. Historisches Museum der Stadt Wien (Vienna, 1993), cat. no. 12; Rupert Feuchtmüller, *Ferdinand Georg Waldmüller, 1793–1865: Leben, Schriften, Werke* (Vienna/Munich, 1996), pp. 117–20, cat. rais. no. 558; *im Kinsky, 58. Kunstauktion*, auction cat., im Kinsky, Vienna (Vienna, 2006), cat. no. 543.

SG

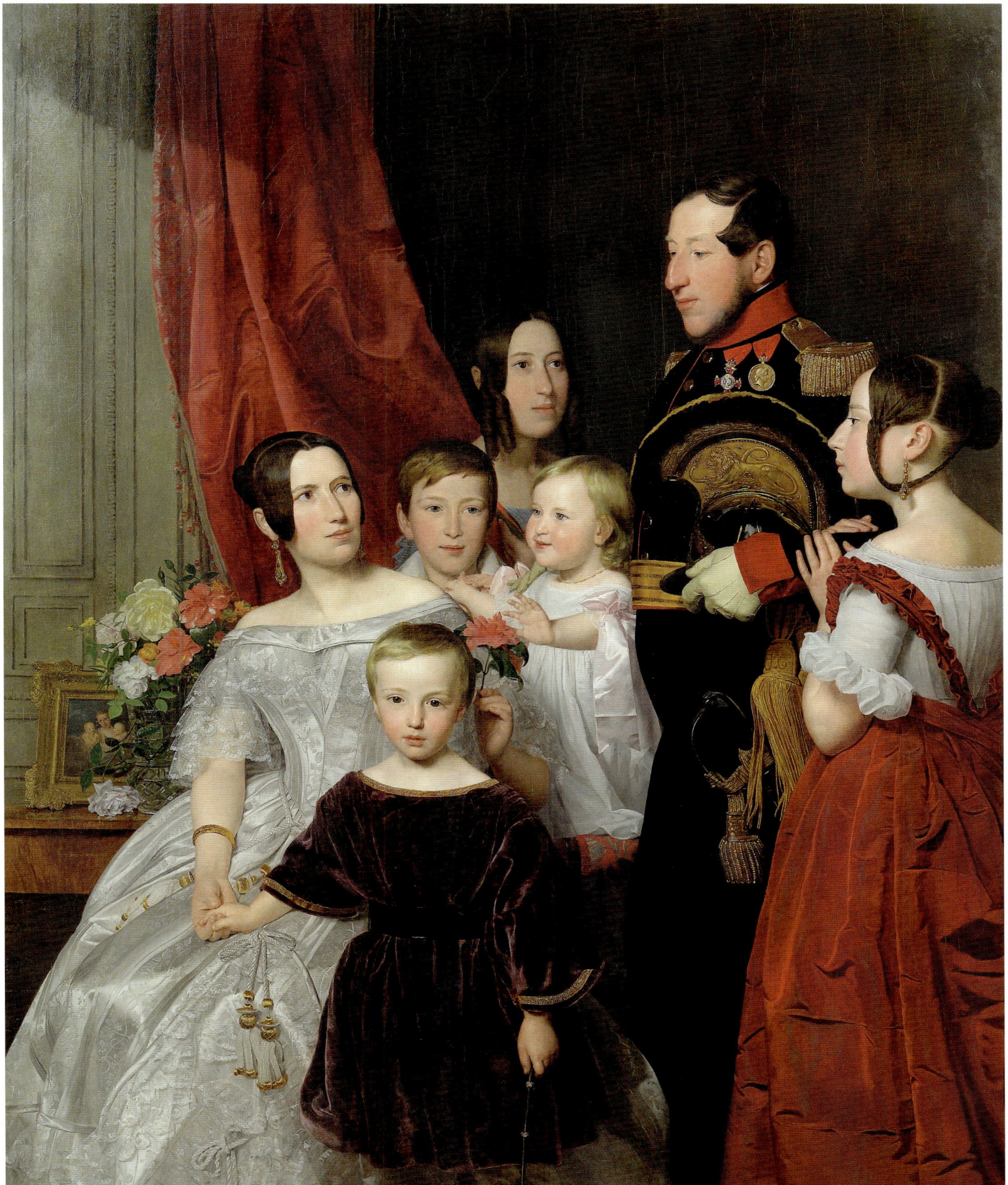

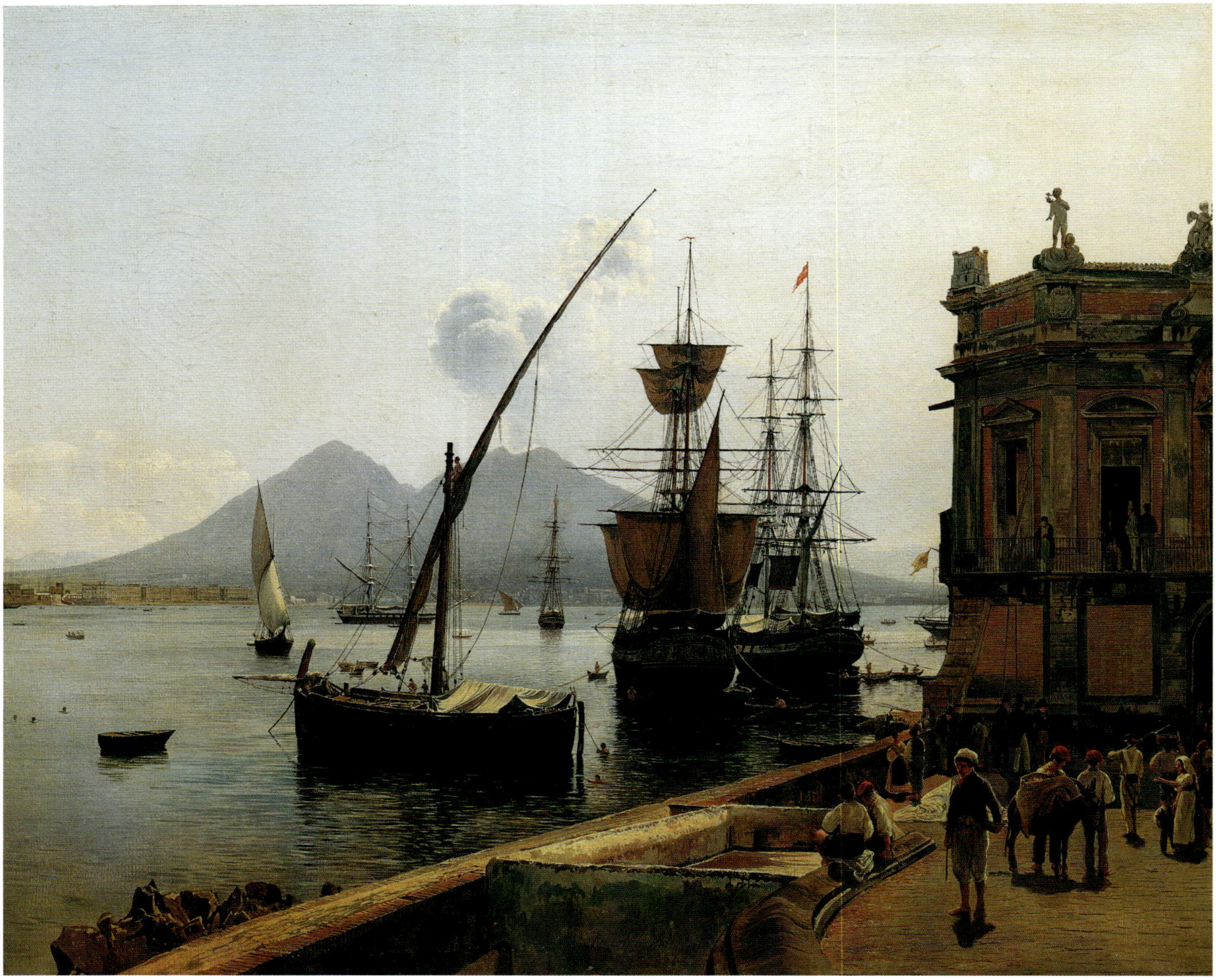

Rudolf von Alt
The Port of Naples with Vesuvius, 1836
Oil on canvas, 53 × 66.5 cm
Signed (lower center): Rudolph Alt / 1836
Belvedere, Vienna, inv. no. 4382

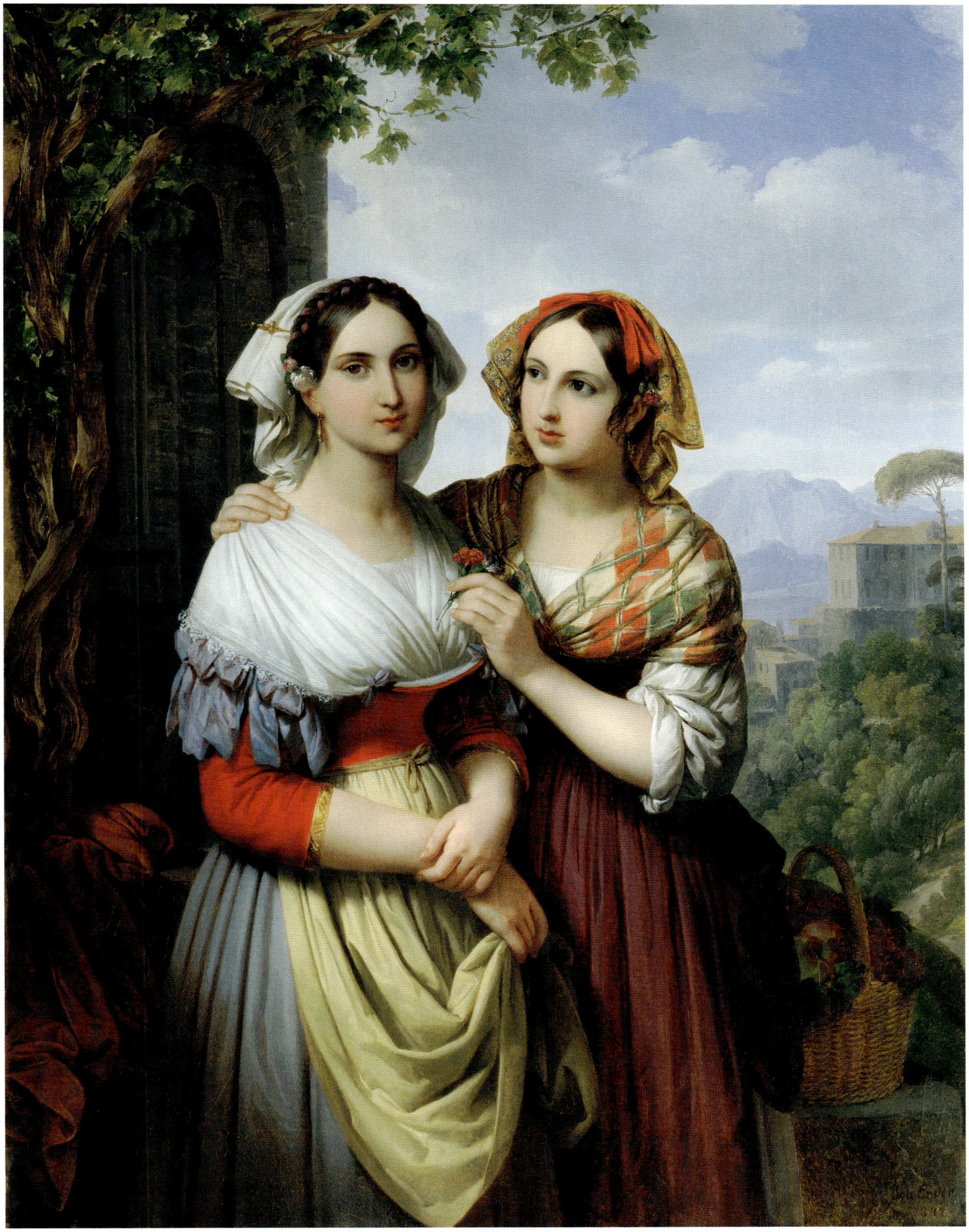

Johann Nepomuk Ender
Two Girls in a Landscape, 1842
Oil on canvas, 79 × 63 cm
Signed (lower right): Joh. Ender / 1842
Belvedere, Vienna, inv. no. 7826

Friedrich von Amerling
Girl with Doves, 1840
Oil on canvas, 97.5 × 119 cm
Unsigned
Private collection, Germany

It was during his Rome years, between 1840 and 1843, that Amerling turned his attention to the "beautiful Italian girl" as a motif. These were portrait-like depictions of peasant girls dressed in vibrant costumes. They had become well known through Friedrich Overbeck (1789–1869) and his painting *Vittoria Caldoni from Albano* (1821, Neue Pinakothek, Munich). Similar pictures had also been painted by the French artist Horace Vernet (1789–1863), a resident of Rome for several years, and the Franco-Swiss painter Léopold Robert (1794–1835). These "Italian girls" provided Amerling with a suitable equivalent to his subjects from Vienna in the 1830s (cf. plates pp. 117-119). He adapted them in his own way to secure a good income, especially from travelers to Italy who bought the pictures as souvenirs.

Girl with Doves, however, painted by Amerling during his longer sojourn in Rome, bears only a passing resemblance to this approach and cannot really be categorized in the group of Italian girls. Although it shows a girl dressed in traditional costume, the picture's content is not centered around the expressions and gestures of a young beauty, but around a narrative. The girl is sitting on the floor of a dovecote, gracefully playing with the birds. From her pose we can see that she is not focusing on feeding, but the young woman is pondering some memory and is oblivious to her surroundings. The picture's message stems from this reverie and gives free rein to its interpretation. Possibly the painter was alluding to the symbolism of a girl and dove, as in the poem *Die Unschuld* by Franz Grillparzer (1833, "Oh, you beautiful white dove, / Are you shaking like an aspen leaf? [...]").

Günther Probszt, *Friedrich von Amerling: Der Altmeister der Wiener Porträtmalerei* (Zurich/Leipzig/Vienna, 1927), cat. rais. no. 495; Sabine Grabner, ed., *Friedrich von Amerling: 1803–1887*, exh. cat. Österreichische Galerie Belvedere, Vienna (Leipzig, 2003), p. 33.

SG

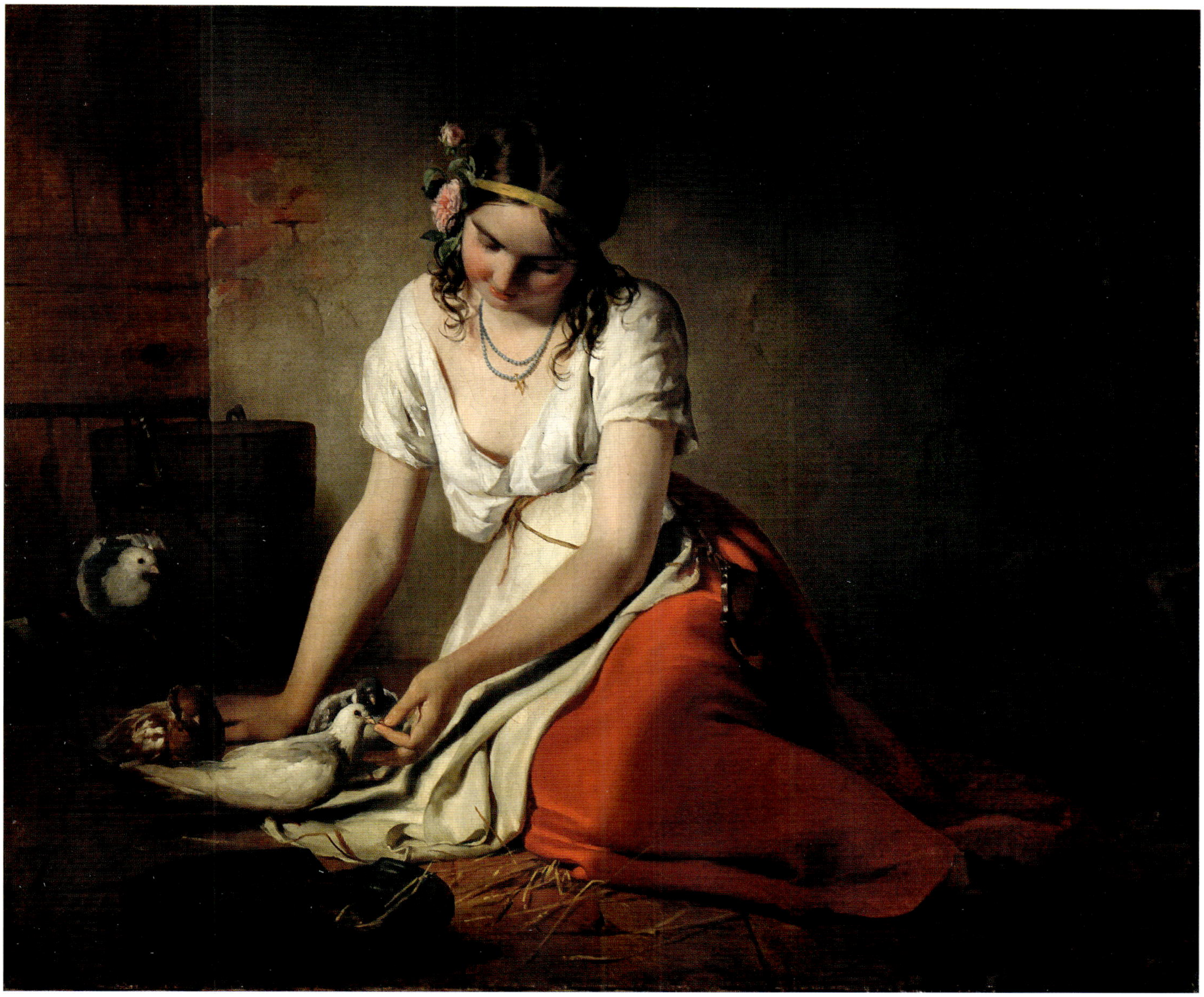

Károly Markó the Elder
Southern Landscape with Sunset, 1847
Oil on canvas, 155 × 244 cm
Signed (lower center): C. Markó / p. Flor. 1847
Belvedere, Vienna, inv. no. 9552

Markó's landscapes are permeated with the clash between Realism and an idealized image of nature. Few of his scenes can be traced to a specific location, although almost all seem to be set in Italy. The remarkable verisimilitude of the details goes back to the numerous outdoor sketches Markó completed while still a boy in northern Hungary, a practice he continued during his training at the Vienna Academy. The artist's profound knowledge of botany is clearly reflected in his precise depiction of plants. Equally, in his exact observation of mountain and rock formations, he put into practice the art-historical theories expounded in 1816 by his teacher at the Academy, the landscape painter Johann Nepomuk Schödlberger (1779–1853).[44]

In 1832, Markó finally moved to Italy, first settling in Rome and then in the region around Florence. Inspired by the southern light and, above all, influenced by the work of Claude Lorrain (1600–1682) and Nicolas Poussin (1594–1665), the artist developed his own, very personal approach to nature, harmoniously combining past and contemporary influences. The generalized interpretation of nature characteristic for his paintings resulted in nondescript titles such as *Southern Landscape with Sunset*. This depiction, acquired in 1847 for the Imperial Collection, was one of his major works. As was so often the case in Markó's pictures, the role of the figures in their classical costumes remains unclear, and the same applies to the architectural elements in this fantasy landscape. Only the warm Mediterranean light immersing this scene from a distant past fosters a sense of earthly reality. The many admirers Markó's pictures attracted in Vienna, Budapest, and Italy testify to the popularity of this subject and prove that Markó appealed to the tastes of his affluent contemporaries.

Id. Markó Károly (1791–1860), exh. cat. Hungarian National Gallery, Budapest/Landesgalerie im Schloss Esterházy, Eisenstadt (Budapest, 1991); Katalin Sinkó, "Italienfahrer aus Ungarn," in *Italienische Reisen. Landschaftsbilder österreichischer und ungarischer Maler. 1770 bis 1850*, eds. Sabine Grabner/Claudia Wöhrer, exh. cat. Österreichische Galerie Belvedere, Vienna (Vienna, 2001), pp. 68–79, especially p. 74; Gábor Bellák/Zoltán Dragon/Orsolya Hessky, comp., *Markó Károly és köre: Mítosztól a képig*, exh. cat. Hungarian National Gallery, Budapest (Budapest, 2011), with further literature; Sabine Grabner, "Károly Markó der Ältere und seine Beziehungen zu Wien," *Wiener Geschichtsblätter*, yr. 68, no. 3 (2013), pp. 201–18.

SG

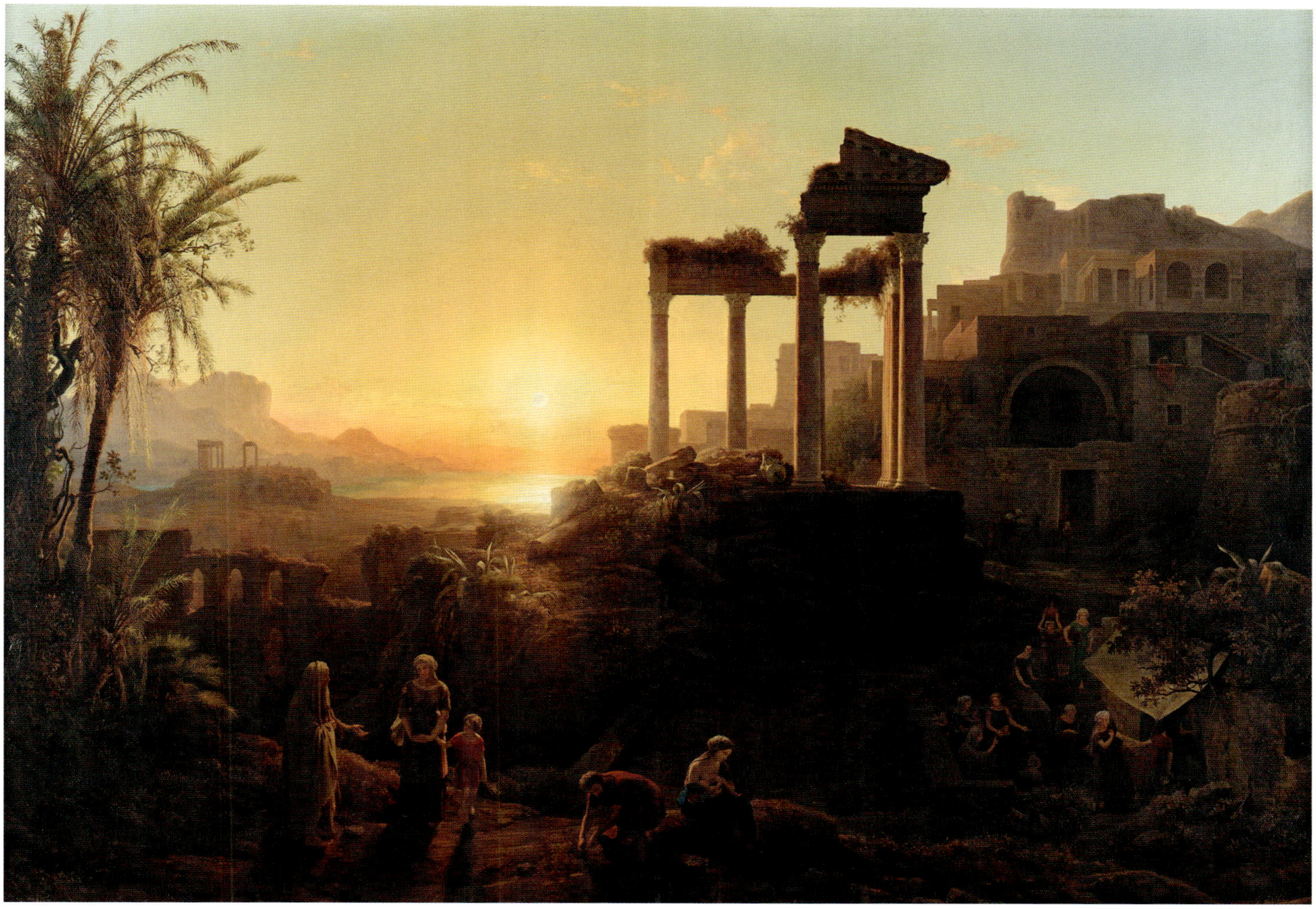

Francesco Hayez
Secret Accusation, c. 1847
Oil on canvas, 153 × 120 cm
Unsigned
Musei Civici di Pavia, Castello Visconteo, inv. no. P600

Around 1850, Francesco Hayez devoted three pictures to his home town of Venice. He was most probably inspired by his friend and patron, the writer Andrea Maffei (1798–1885), who had written a short story about defamation as a result of love betrayed, set in the lagoon city. The picture with the title *Secret Accusation* (*L'accusa segreta*) references the end of the story—the climax of events and point of no return. This will be triggered by the letter the young woman is clutching, addressed to: "A S. Eccelenza / I tre bai / del Consiglio di X." It is for the Consiglio dei Dieci, the Council of Ten, Venice's supreme judicial authority. In great agitation, she hurries across the loggia of the Doge's Palace. The lion's head, visible on the picture's left margin, suggests that the intentions of this letter are not entirely honest, as, in the Venice of the doges, the lion's mouth, the "Bocca di Leone" as it was known, was established by the supreme authorities as a collection point for all manner of denunciations.

Secret Accusation was the first picture Hayez painted from Maffei's story and is also the most successful work in this triptych as regards composition, color, and lighting. The painting with the title *Il consiglio alla vendetta* of 1851 is today in the collections of the Princes of Liechtenstein in Vienna. The whereabouts of the third painting, entitled *Vendetta di una rivale* (*Le Veneziane*) and painted in 1853, are unknown.

Marina Botteri/Barbara Cinelli/Fernando Mazzocca, *L'ottocento di Andrea Maffei*, exh. cat. Museo Civico, Comune di Riva del Garda (Trento, 1987); Fernando Mazzocca, ed., *Francesco Hayez* (Milan, 2015), pp. 264–65 (F. Mazzocca).

SG

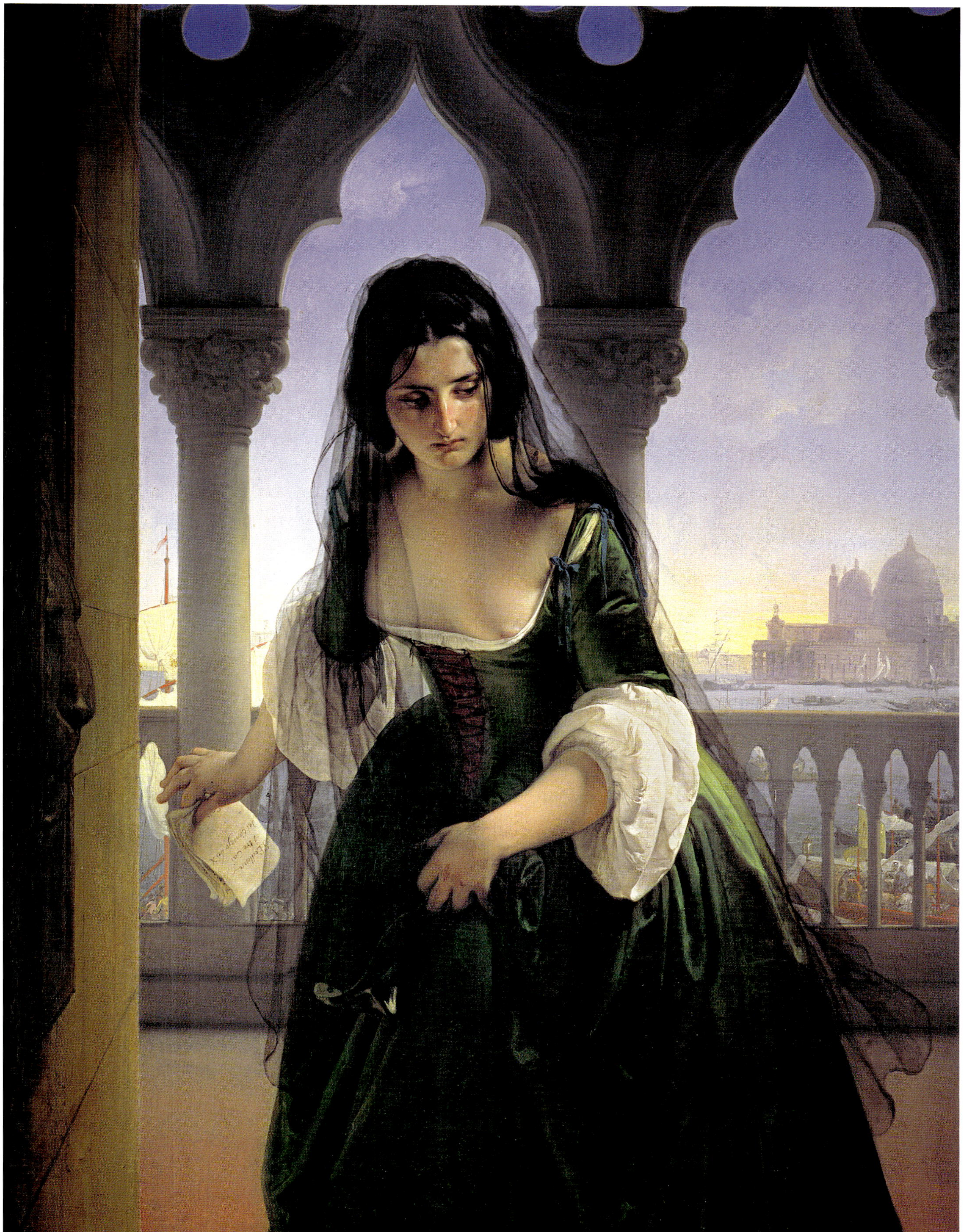

József Borsos
The Emir of Lebanon (*Portrait of Count Edmund Zichy*), 1843
Oil on canvas, 154 × 119 cm
Signed (lower left): Borsos József 1843
Museum of Fine Arts - Hungarian National Gallery, Budapest, inv. no. 2003. 3 T

"As a painter, Borsos found the philosopher's stone, as his ability to use shades of yellow truly transformed the rings and brocades into gold," the critic Hermann Meynert praised the artist behind the painting *The Emir of Lebanon*, on show at the Vienna Academy in 1843.[45] Other reviewers were equally enthusiastic about this, the most sought-after piece in the exhibition.[46] In addition to the outstanding quality of the painting technique and the balanced composition, people also enthused about the sitter's oriental attire, as Vienna had been enthralled by this subject matter since Amerling's *Young Eastern Woman* (fig. p. 22). The main source of delight here were the exotic garments and it did not matter whether these were worn by Amerling's girl or Borsos's depiction of a person from the Orient. In fact, the man shown here in a casual, cross-legged pose was not a high-ranking personality from the Lebanon but Count Edmund Zichy (1811–1894). He had recently returned from a journey to the Orient and wanted a portrait in the garments he had brought back with him. In Borsos he found the perfect man for the job and, in turn, Zichy's souvenir established the young painter's fame as a portraitist.

Borsos was from Hungary and had been taught for a brief period by Miklós Barabás in Budapest before moving to Vienna in 1840 to study history painting at the Imperial Academy. He learned the basics of composition and painting technique from Josef Danhauser who was a corrector there at the time. Borsos also took private lessons with Ferdinand Georg Waldmüller.[47] Thus equipped, the young artist went on to develop his own signature style, emulating his teachers in his choice of subject matter and honing his skills by studying the work of Friedrich von Amerling. He saw his ambition fulfilled when exhibition reviews in 1845 compared him to Amerling.[48] Borsos became a prolific painter of genre scenes and portraits, most of which are now in Hungary. In his later career he also turned his attention to photography. Although Borsos spent the majority of his time as a painter in Vienna, he is hardly known in Austria. In Hungary, on the other hand, he is regarded as one of the greatest artists of the nineteenth century.

Constant von Wurzbach, *Biographisches Lexikon des Kaisertums Österreich*, vol. 2 (Vienna, 1857), pp. 78–79; *Saur/De Gruyter Allgemeines Künstlerlexikon: Die bildenden Künstler aller Zeiten und Völker*, vol. 13 (Munich etc., 1996), p. 127 (Katalin Sz. Kürti); Jane Turner, ed., *The Dictionary of Art*, vol. 4 (London, 1996), p. 438 (Katalin Gellér); *Borsos József: Festő és fotográfus (1821–1883)/József Borsos: Painter and Photographer (1821–1883)*, exh. cat. Hungarian National Gallery, Budapest (Budapest, 2009), pp. 87–88, with further literature.

SG

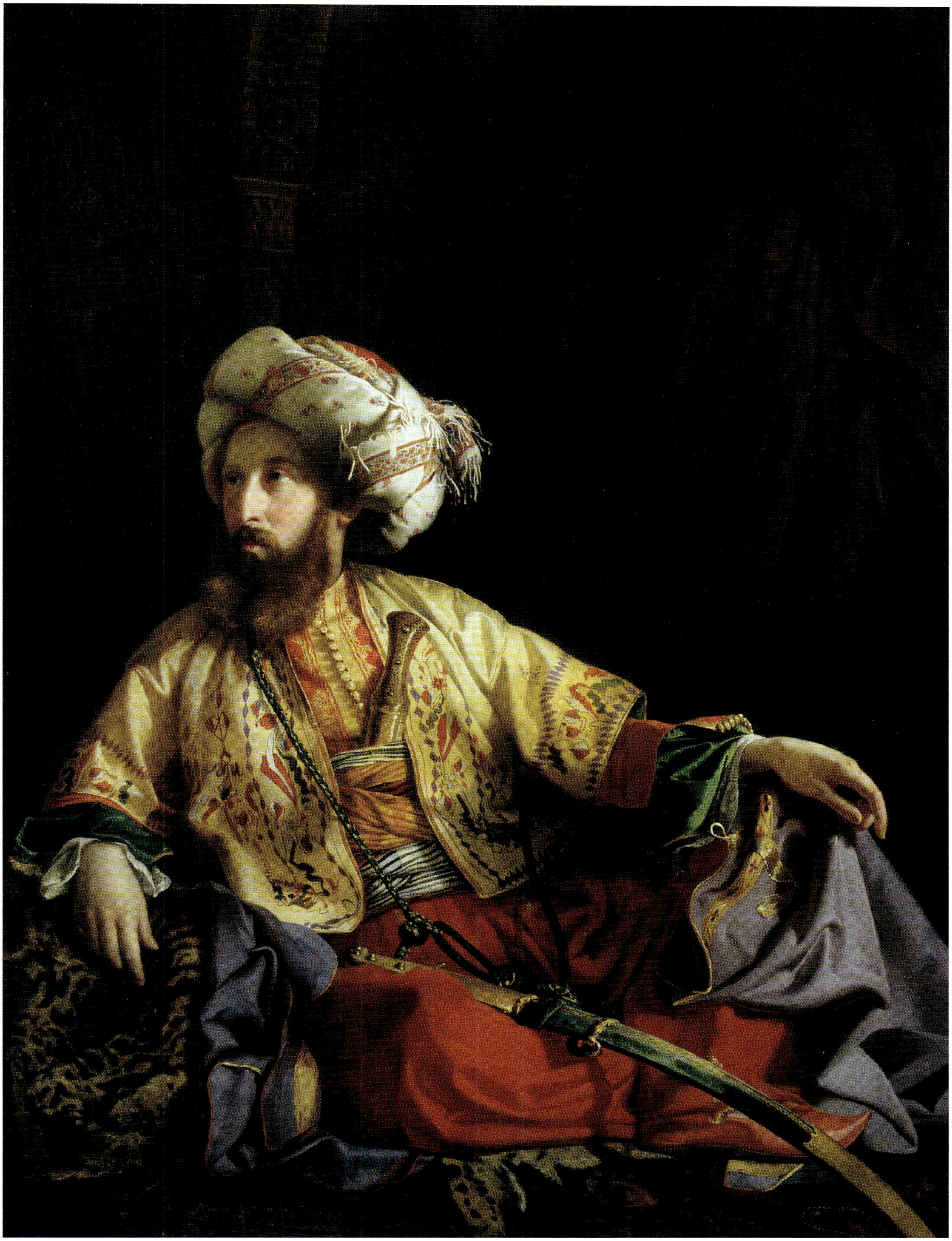

Eliseo Sala
Pia de' Tolomei, 1846
Oil on canvas, 120 × 90 cm
Signed (lower right): Sala Eliseo 1846
Civici Musei d'Arte e Storia, Brescia, inv. no. DI 343

"Ricorditi di me, che son la Pia:
Siena mi fé, disfecemi Maremma:
salsi colui che ´nnanellata pria

disposando m 'avea con la sua gemma."
Dante, Purgatorio, cant. V, 136

With these famous words from Canto V of the Purgatorio in Dante's *Divine Comedy*, the female protagonist expresses her desire to be remembered forever. It can be inferred that she came from Siena and it is generally assumed that she was a member of the house of Tolomei. In 1284, Pia married the Guelph Nello dei Pannocchieschi, who ruled over the territory of southern Tuscany and lived in Castel di Pietra in the Maremma region. It was here that she met her end, because when Nello tired of her, he hatched the murderous plan of simply throwing her out of the castle window to enable him to marry another woman. For all his attempts to cover up the murder afterwards, it was remembered in Dante's Canto, as Pia had wished.

This story, which to this day has inspired artists from a wide range of artistic genres (including, for example, several films and a recent song by Gianna Nannini), was particularly popular in the nineteenth century. Gaetano Donizetti wrote an opera (*Pia de' Tolomei*, premiere 1837), and in Britain it was commemorated particularly in a painting by the Pre-Raphaelite Dante Gabriel Rossetti (c. 1868, Spencer Museum of Art, Kansas).

The plaintive mood reflecting the disappointment at the loss of love was the underlying motif in Sala's painting. He depicts the woman standing deep in thought, leaning against a parapet overlooking the sea. Both the composition and the tasteful arrangement of colors in combination with the historical setting are indicative of Sala's training as a history painter. He had studied the subject with Luigi Sabatelli (1772–1850) at the Brera in Milan from 1832 to 1838 and refined his skill during study visits to Venice and Rome. Like most history painters, he also acquired skill in portrait painting. His realistic portrayals and sensitive depiction of the human face made him highly successful and popular. He also specialized in genre painting. One of his favorite themes was pictures of young girls, whom he showed, like his Upper Austrian contemporary Johann Baptist Reiter, in situations that were not really intended for public display (see fig. 8, p. 24; plate p. 175).[49] Even during his lifetime, *Pia de' Tolomei* was regarded as one of Sala's most important works. It was reproduced in 1847 in *Gemme d'arti italiane* and its outstanding painterly skill singled out in the accompanying essay by P. M.[50]

Sergio Rebora, *Eliseo Sala: Un ritrattista e la sua committenza nell'Italia romantica, 1813–1879* (Milan, 2001).

SG

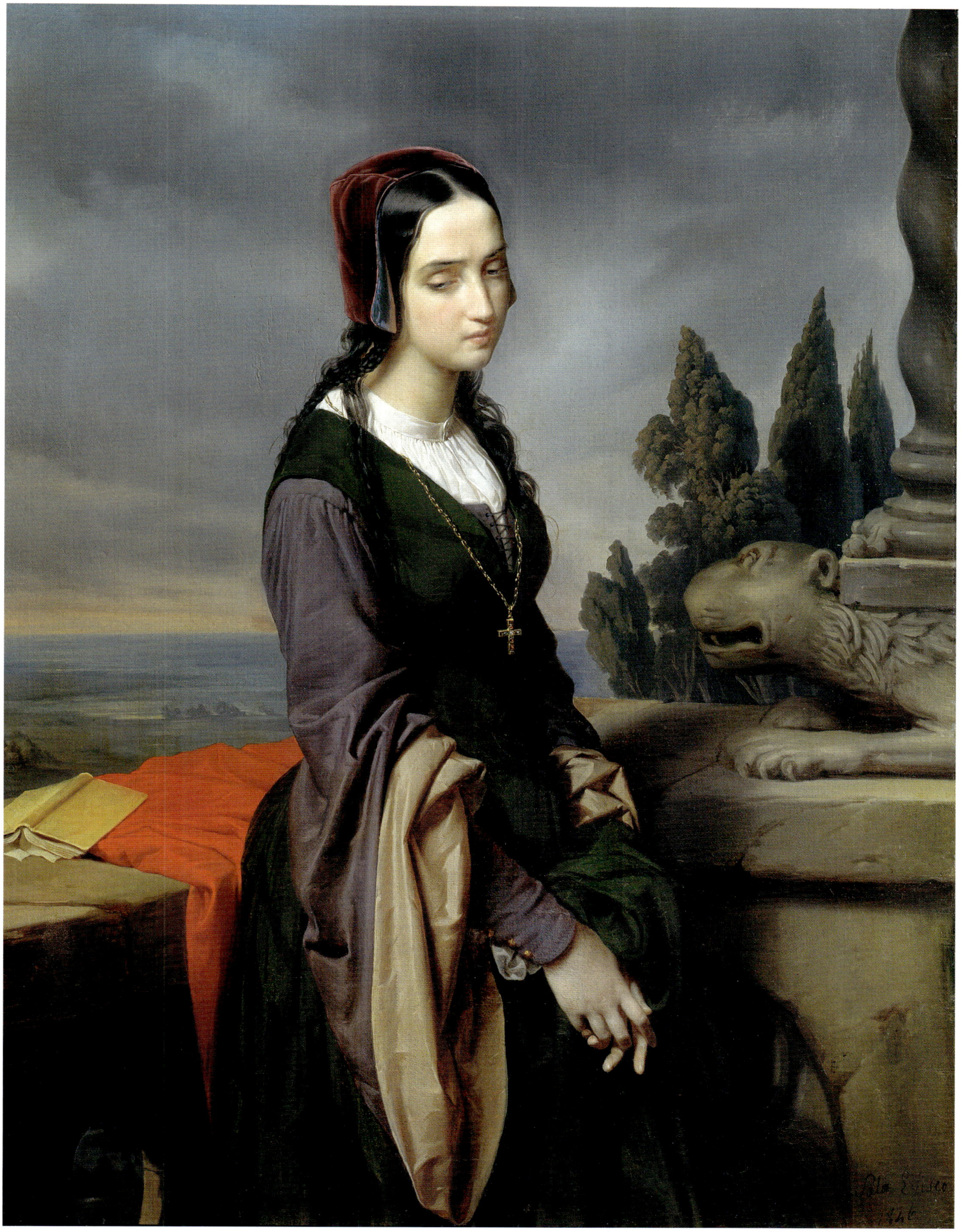

Natale Schiavone
Malinconia (*Melancholy*), 1841
Oil on canvas, 73 × 59 cm
Signed (lower right): N. Schiavoni / 1841
Belvedere, Vienna, inv. no. 8956

Schiavone forms an exception among the painters in this exhibition because he acquired his skill as a painter not through academic study but from various teachers willing to encourage his talent. He quickly earned a reputation as a successful portrait painter and obtained numerous commissions in both Trieste and Milan. Following the reorganization of Europe in the wake of the Congress of Vienna, he was summoned to Vienna in 1816 by Emperor Francis I. While he was there, he completed portraits, above all, of the imperial family and the nobility. After five years he moved with his family to Venice, where he remained for the rest of his life. He began to explore reproductive techniques and was also highly successful as an art restorer. He painted a number of portraits and depictions of the Virgin Mary, as well as pictures with historical and religious themes. The painting *Penitent Magdalene* to be seen on the easel in his *Self-Portrait* of 1831 (Galleria Nazionale d'Arte Moderna e Contemporanea, Rome), was acquired in 1832 for the Imperial Picture Gallery in Vienna (now Belvedere). In 1840, he was appointed professor at the Accademia di Belle Arti in Venice. Until 1846/47 he took part in practically every Academy exhibition in Vienna, Venice, and Milan. He also received numerous commissions, which he completed together with his sons Felice (1803–1868) and Giovanni (1805–1849) in his studio in Palazzo Giustinian, where he lived with his family. In the late 1830s, he began to paint allegories, i.e. pictorial interpretations of abstract concepts such as "temptation," "evil," "guile," "first love," or, as here, "melancholy." He liked to illustrate the meaning of these words using half-length female figures with suitable accessories—here a black veil and weeping willow—and adopting the appropriate pose. Although reviewers noted "a certain family resemblance in the facial features in all of the paintings,"[51] the pictures earned him the nickname "pittore delle grazie," or "painter of beauty."

The Museo Civico Revoltella in Trieste contains a painting of a woman in a similar pose but without the weeping willow, entitled *Mestizia* (*Sadness*) painted in 1840. Another version of the Vienna picture of the same size and painted the same year is at the Braunschweig Municipal Museum.

Lina Gasparini, "Natale Schiavoni a Trieste," in *La Porta Orientale*, 11th yr., October 1933, pp. 5–16; Agostino Mario Comanducci, *I Pittori Italiani dell'Ottocento* (Milan, 1934), p. 658; *Meister von Heiligenkreuz bis Elke Krystufek: Neuerwerbungen Österreichische Galerie Belvedere 1992–1999*, exh. cat. Österreichische Galerie Belvedere, Vienna (Vienna, 1999), pp. 40–41 (Sabine Grabner); Alessandra Tiddia, *La coscienza del vero: Capolavori dell'Ottocento da Courbet a Segantini* (Milan, 2015), p. 185.

SG

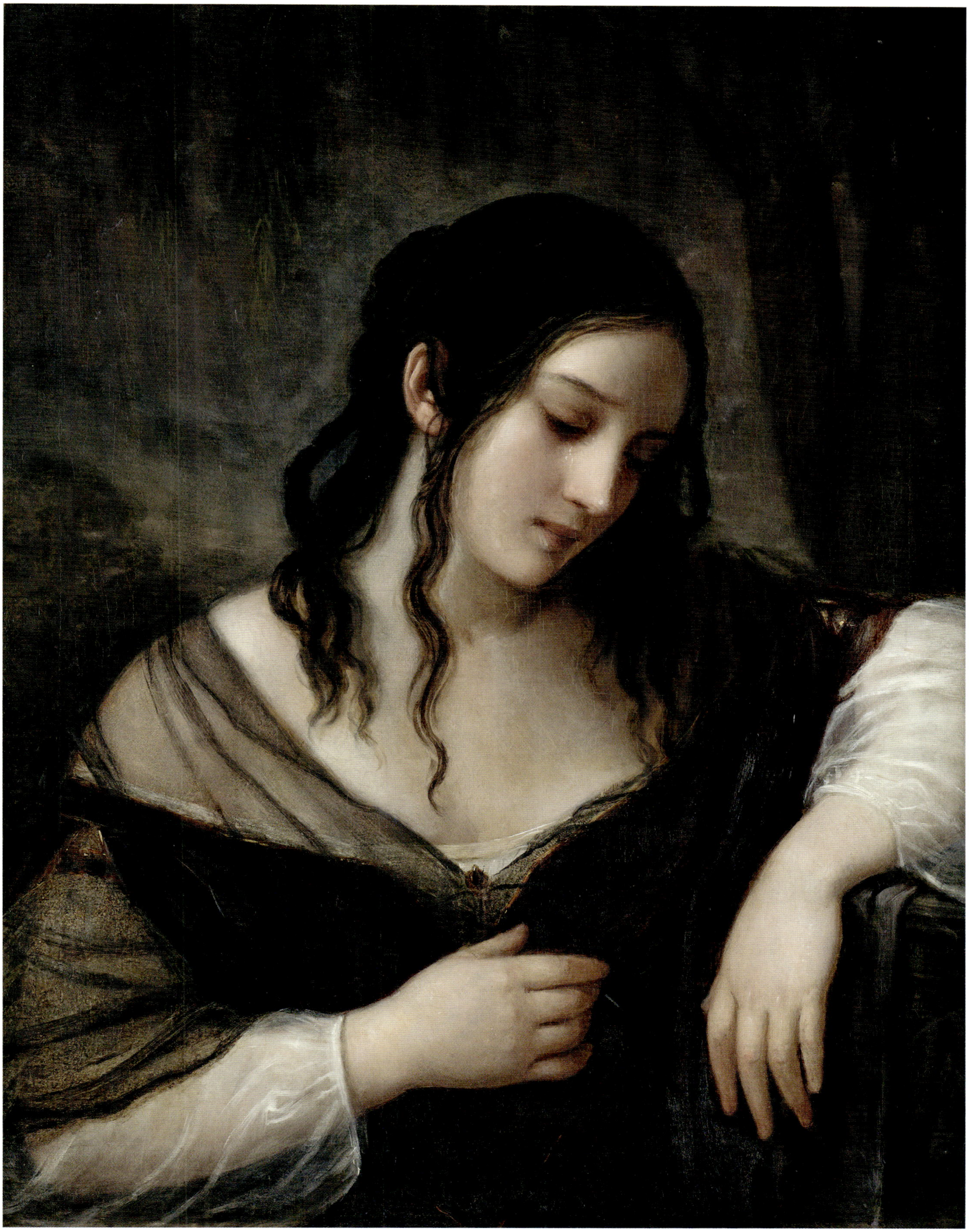

August Piepenhagen
Old Village Bridge
Oil on canvas, 35 × 46 cm
Signed (lower left): AP. (lig.)
Belvedere, Vienna, inv. no. 4470

August Piepenhagen
Moonlit Night
Oil on wood, 31.7 × 39.4 cm
Unsigned
Moravian Gallery in Brno, inv. no. A 1362

August Piepenhagen
Landscape with Pilgrim, 1850s
Oil on canvas, 40 × 31.5 cm
Signed (lower right): AP
Národní galerie v Praze/ National Gallery, Prague, inv. no. O 12398

August Piepenhagen, born in 1791 in Soldin near Frankfurt an der Oder as the son of a button maker, originally learned his father's trade. His journeyman years took him to Switzerland, where the impressive scenery encouraged him to try out his hand at painting. He moved to Prague in 1830/31 and married into a button-making business. He lived and worked in Prague until his death in 1868.

While Piepenhagen's early works are clearly influenced by Rococo composition, in his later work in the 1830s and 1840s he shows a freer interpretation of nature, achieving an idealized subjective perception of reality in this way. Inspired by a romantic view of nature, his favored motifs were ruined castles in the moonlight, or landscapes with solitary wanderers. *Landscape with Pilgrim* (plate p. 170), for example, shows a man in silent communion with nature. The theme recalls Caspar David Friedrich's Monk by the Sea (1808–1810, Alte Nationalgalerie, Berlin) with a small figure depicted in sublime natural surroundings, humbly suffering the earthly darkness while hoping for the bright light of divine grace.

Piepenhagen's landscapes were extremely popular in Prague. Adalbert Stifter also appreciated the artist highly: "Your paintings are incomparably atmospheric. They float before the eyes in the most delicate fragrance, disdaining intrusive and obvious effects, while faithfully reproducing every intimate nuance commanded by nature."[52] Stifter wrote these admiring words in his first letter to Piepenhagen in 1859. In his reviews for the Upper Austrian Cultural Association he consistently extolled the artist's landscapes and—being of a poetic disposition—was frequently inspired to poetic descriptions recalling the vivid landscape portrayals in his own stories. Stifter also owned some of Piepenhagen's paintings, including a moonlit landscape given to him by his publisher Gustav Heckenast. The correspondence also makes reference to sketches lent to him by his artist friend for study.

Fritz Novotny, "Stifter und Piepenhagen," in ibid., *Über das Elementare in der Kunstgeschichte und andere Aufsätze* (Vienna, 1968); ibid., "Adalbert Stifter als Maler," in *Kunstjahrbuch der Stadt Linz 1978* (Vienna, 1979), no. 39; Brigitte Hauptner, "'... unvergleichlich an Stimmung ...': Die künstlerischen Beziehungen zwischen Adalbert Stifter, August Piepenhagen und Carl Blumauer," in *Kunstjahrbuch der Stadt Linz 1997/98* (Vienna, 1998), pp. 54–86; Naděžda Blažíčková-Horová, ed., *Czech 19th Century Painting: Catalogue of the Permanent Exhibition. Convent of St. Agnes of Bohemia* (Prague, 1998), pp. 62–65.

BH

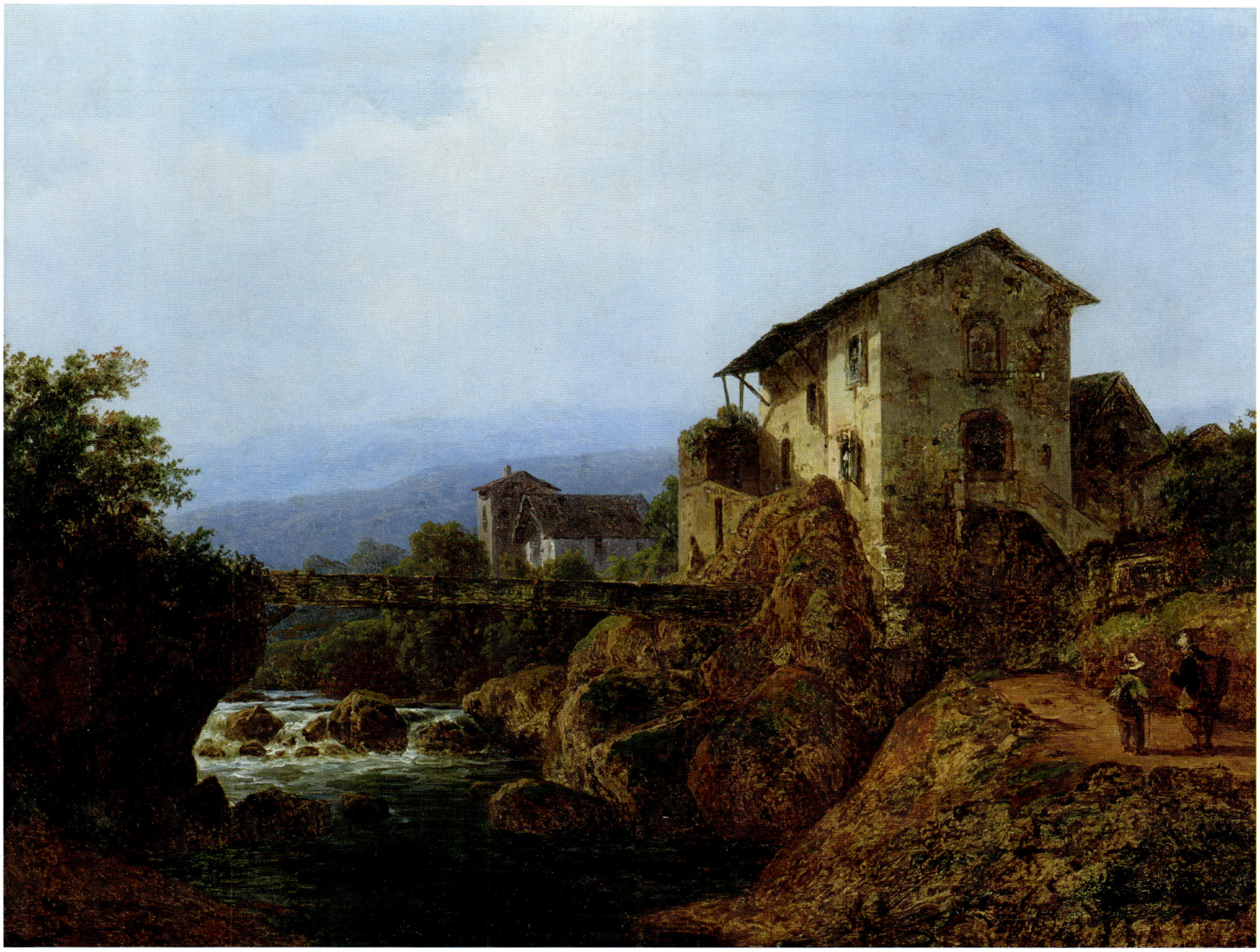

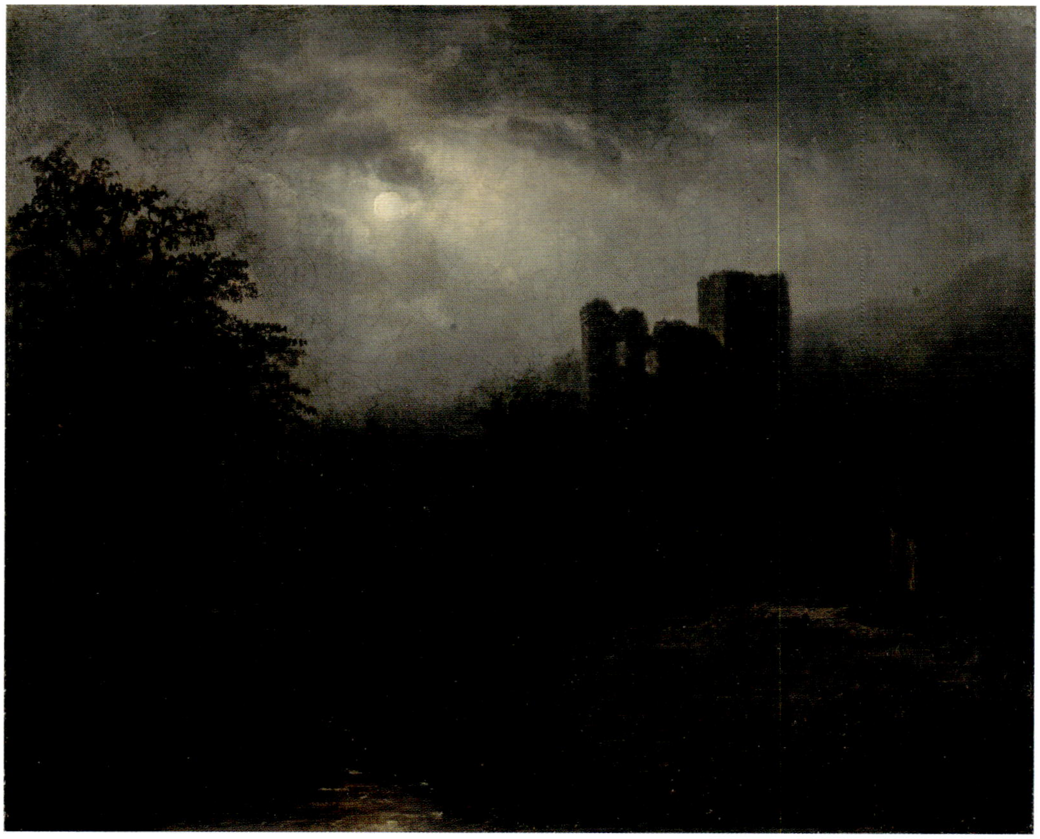

August Piepenhagen
Moonlit Night

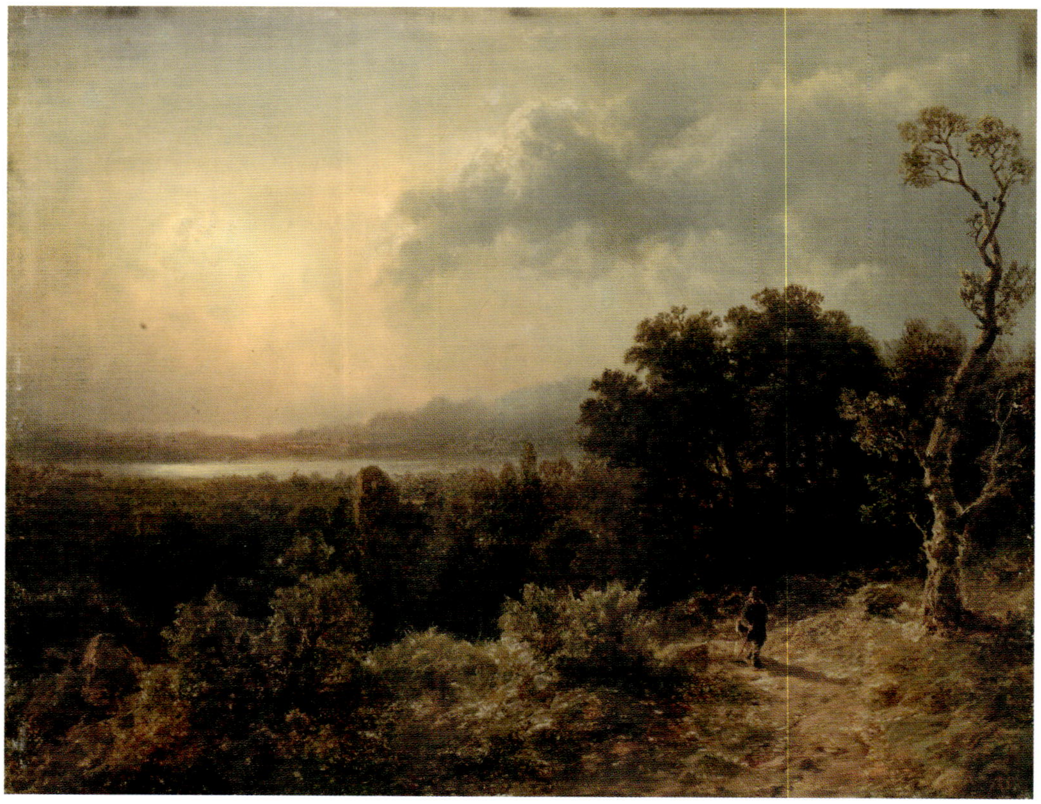

August Piepenhagen
Landscape with Pilgrim, 1850s

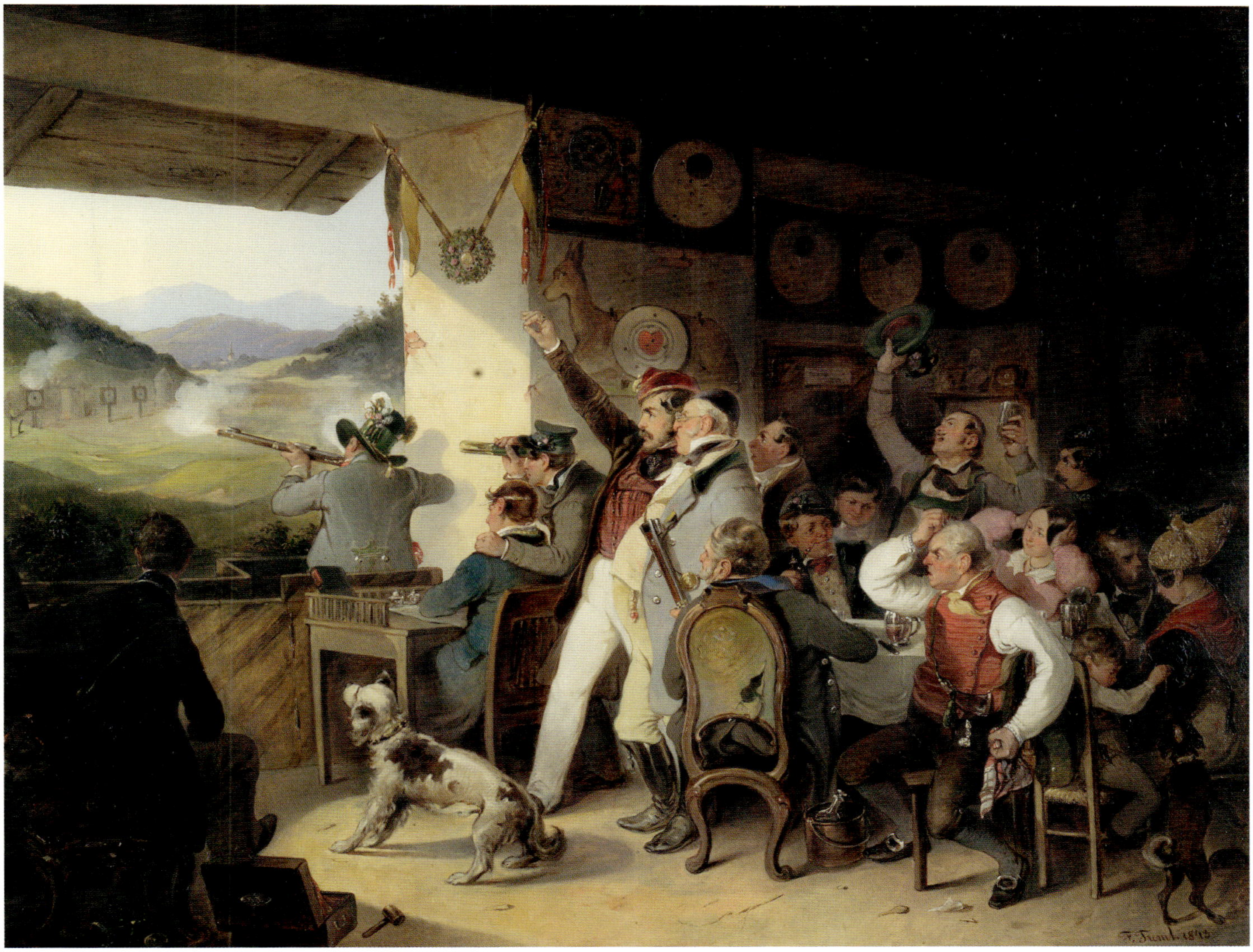

Friedrich Treml
Target Practice, 1843
Oil on canvas, 52 × 59 cm
Signed (lower right): F. Treml. 1843.
Wien Museum, inv. no. 61.004

Josef Navrátil
Fox Hunt, 1850–53
Oil on canvas, 45 x 55 cm
Unsigned
Národní galerie v Praze/National Gallery, Prague, inv. no. O 10219

Josef Navrátil was born in 1789 as the son of a craftsman in Slaný, Bohemia, to the north-west of Prague. He studied from 1819 to 1823 at the Prague Academy, specializing in murals and landscape painting. After completing his studies, he worked initially as a decorator and painter of murals for castles and manor houses. Among the Czech painters of the time, he was a close friend of August Piepenhagen, frequently visiting his summer residence at Jenerálka near Prague. A stroke at the age of sixty-two ended his artistic career, and he spent his last years until his death in 1865 in poverty and oblivion.

Navrátil's initial artistic inspiration came from the Alps, which he explored from 1832 onwards on walking tours in Switzerland, Germany, and France. His landscape and mountain studies served as the basis for his monumental wall paintings. In the 1850s he traversed the Giant Mountains and Bohemian Forest, where he found new subjects and developed a more realistic style. With its detailed and pastose brown and grey tones, *Fox Hunt* is one of a group of pictures of fox hunting scenes in the morning mist. Reflecting the Biedermeier predilection for narrative pictures, the artist repeatedly resorted to the theme of the cunning fox outwitting the hunters.

Naděžda Blažíčková-Horová, ed., *Czech 19th Century Painting: Catalogue of the Permanent Exhibition. Convent of St. Agnes of Bohemia* (Prague, 1998), pp. 66–75; Radim Vondráček, ed., *Biedermeier: Art and Culture in the Bohemian Lands 1814–1848*, exh. cat. Museum of Decorative Arts in Prague and Gallery (Prague, 2010), p. 440.

BH

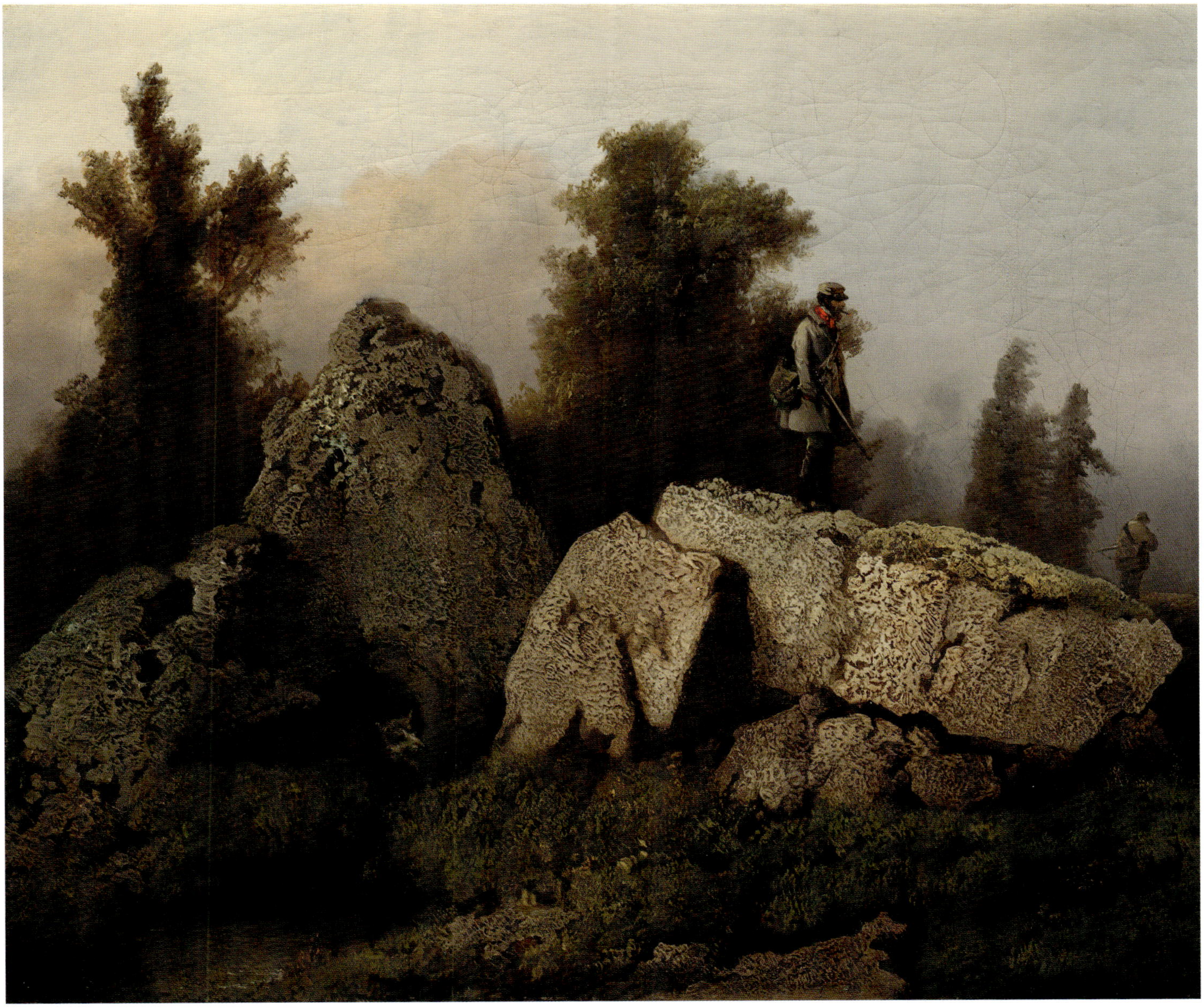

Johann Baptist Reiter
Slumbering Woman, 1849
Oil on canvas, 55 × 68 cm
Signed (lower right): J. B. Reiter Vienna / 849.
Belvedere, Vienna, inv. no. 5547

Several of Reiter's pictures after the 1840s were very private views of young women, depicting situations that were extremely intimate and not meant for public display (e.g. *Rising Woman*, 1850, *Woman at Her Toilet*, 1842, both in private collections, or *Lady in a Negligée*, 1847, Belvedere, Vienna. fig. 8, p. 24). As the subjects appear to feel unobserved, there is a suggestion of voyeurism, which makes the situation even more titillating. The familiarity and the impression of privacy are further enhanced by the skillful lighting. The most intimate work in this group is the *Slumbering Woman* lying unclothed on a bed. The artist avoids all coquetry, conveying the impression that the woman does not know she is being painted. In this context, he pays particular attention to the interplay of concealing and exposing, and uses the light falling from the right to sculpt the body and cloak it in a golden tonality. The warm coloring combines harmoniously with the cool shimmering sheets, giving this nude painting a sense of comfort and contentedness.

The work was never shown publicly during the artist's lifetime, and its significance and unique position were only recognized during the twentieth century.

Alice Strobl, *Johann Baptist Reiter* (Vienna/Munich, 1963), pp. 33–34, no. 123; Lothar Schultes, "Johann Baptist Reiter – Leben und Werk," in *Bilder des Lebens: Johann Baptist Reiter und der Realismus des 19. Jahrhunderts*, exh. cat. Museum Francisco-Carolinum, Linz/Schloss Grafenegg (Linz, 1990), p. 20, no. 123; ibid., *Johann Baptist Reiter*, exh. cat. Oberösterreichisches Landesmuseum, Linz (Linz, 2013), pp. 116–25 (with further reading).

SG

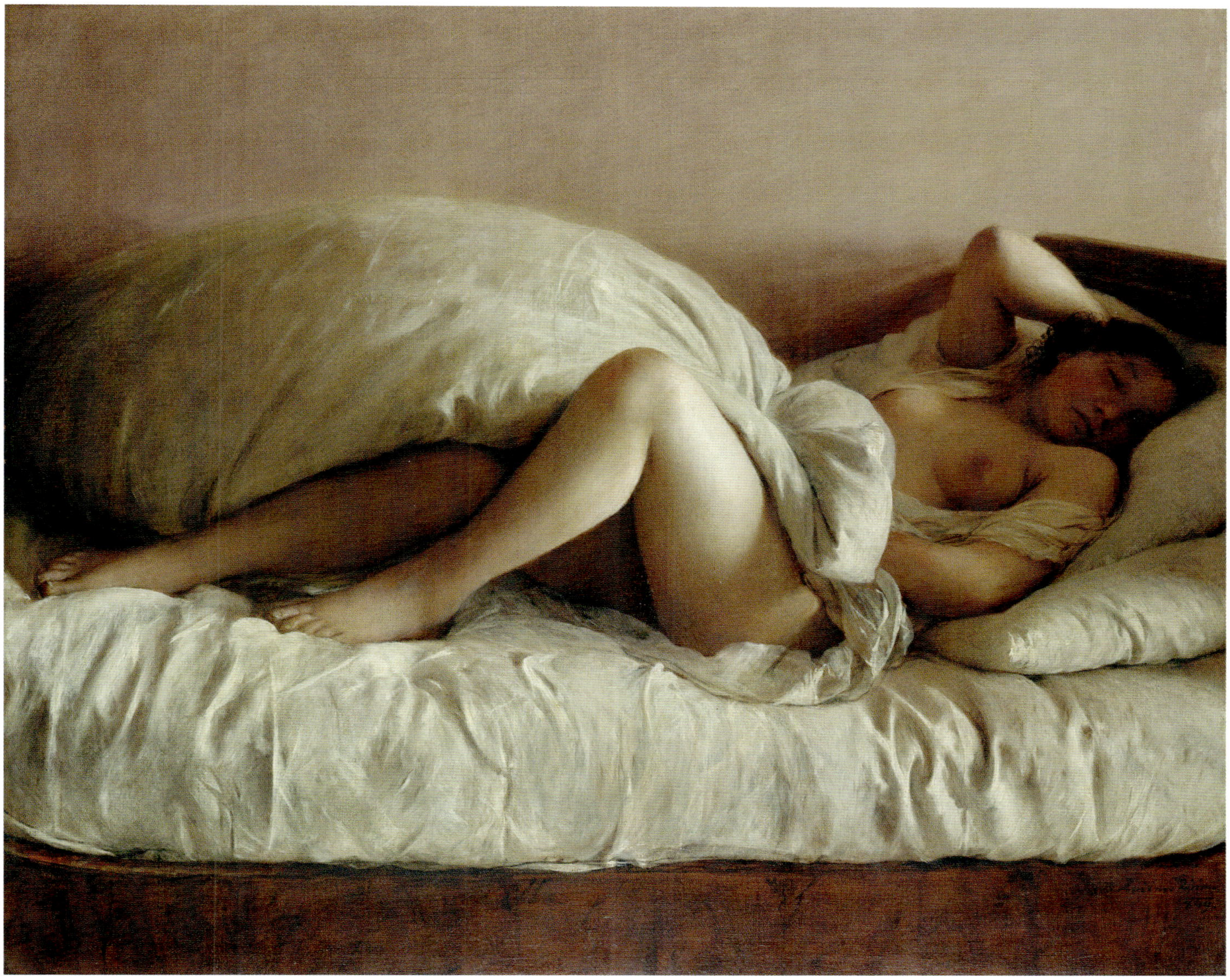

Michael Neder
Return of the Herd, 1844
Oil on wood, 41.5 x 52 cm
Signed (lower right): Neder / 1844
Belvedere, Vienna, inv. no. 3664

Neder's *Return of the Herd* is possibly the most idiosyncratic work of art created in Vienna in the first half of the nineteenth century. The artist discarded all academic traditions and developed a form of presentation that was not adopted generally by artists until many decades later.[53] The picture is reduced to the foreground and middle ground and ends with a plain wall. The impression of space is achieved solely through the animals, which are placed in parallel lines, with only a trivial attempt at perspective confined to the slope in the foreground. This formal limitation is also reflected in the restrained color palette of yellow, brown, and green tones.

Return of the Herd is without doubt the artist's most important work. Karl Hareiter, who wrote the first Neder monograph, also emphasized the modernity of the painting, pointing to the successful combination of Old Vienna subject matter and Dutch painting.[54] The simple form is an example of the artist's deliberate attempt to highlight the formulaic nature of everyday life as he experienced it throughout his life in the petit-bourgeois environment of the Viennese suburb where he lived. He emphasized the solitude of the individual and the monotony of daily life, which he liked to depict through stereotyped movements. Yet none of his pictures are monotonous or dull, thanks to the sophisticated painting technique, which he developed throughout the 1830s and 1840s.[55] His subjects, by contrast, are unusual, dating from a time when painters were able to succeed with refined composition and bright colors. Neder's work is nevertheless an important component of nineteenth-century Viennese art, because he was the only artist to create anything like an authentic picture of people who lived remote from the bourgeois world.

Michael Krapf, "Das moralisierende Element im Wiener Sittenbild," in *Bürgersinn und Aufbegehren: Biedermeier und Vormärz in Wien 1815–1848* (Vienna, 1988), pp. 148–56, especially p. 154; Gerbert Frodl/Klaus Albrecht Schröder, eds., *Wiener Biedermeier: Malerei zwischen Wiener Kongress und Revolution*, exh. cat. Kunstforum der Bank Austria, Vienna/Österreichische Galerie Belvedere, Vienna (Munich, 1992), cat. no. (Sabine Grabner); Gerbert Frodl, ed., *19. Jahrhundert* (= Geschichte der bildenden Kunst in Österreich 5) (Munich et al., 2002), pp. 348–49; Sabine Grabner, *Mehr als Biedermeier: Klassizismus, Romantik und Realismus in der Österreichischen Galerie Belvedere* (Munich, 2006), pp. 106–07; Agnes Husslein-Arco/Sabine Grabner, eds., *Michael Neder: Ohne Kompromisse*, exh. cat. Belvedere, Vienna (Munich, 2013).

SG

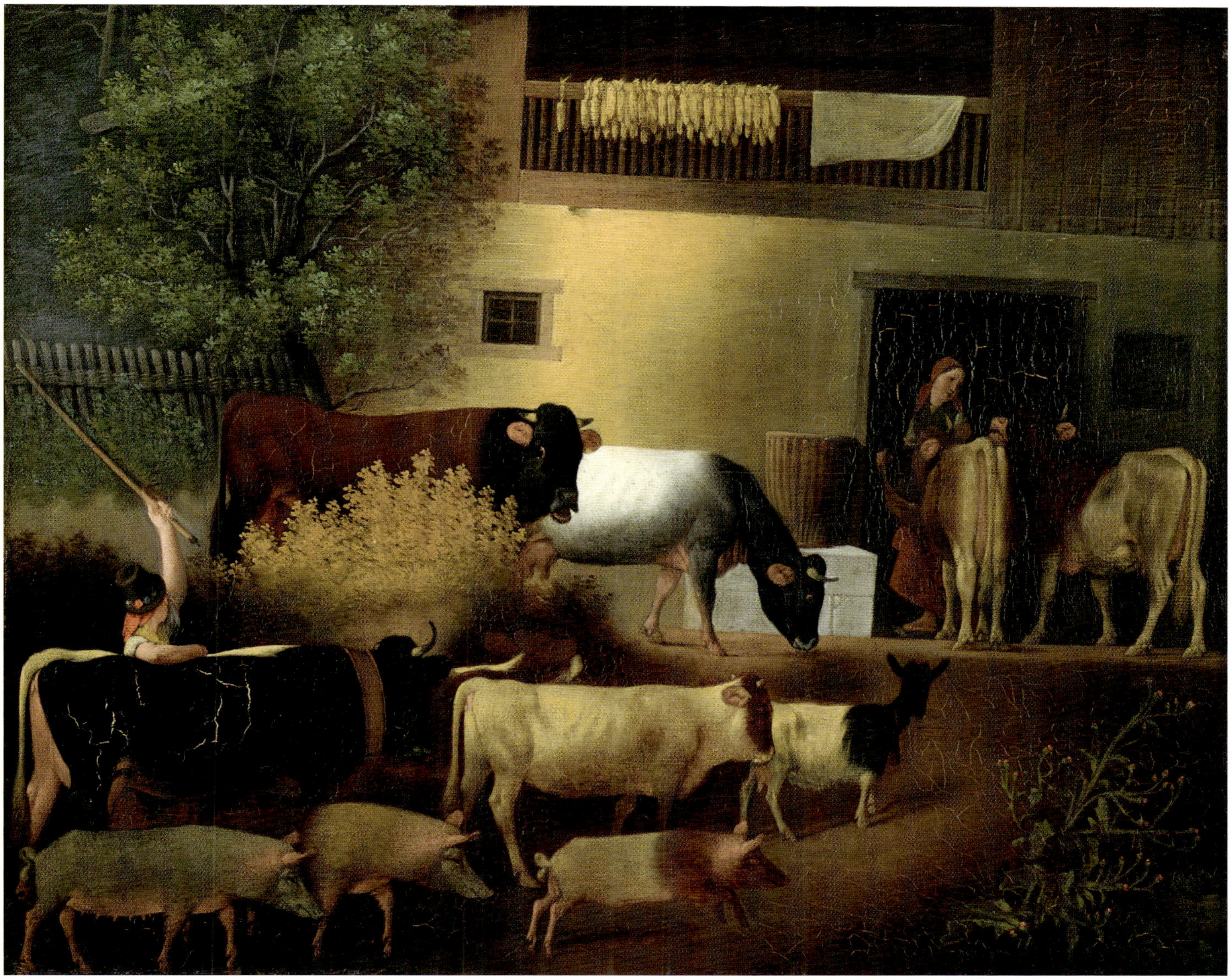

Giuseppe Molteni
Lamenting the Loss of a Loved One, 1850
Oil on canvas, 156 × 123 cm
Signed (lower left): G. Molteni
Castello Ducale, Agliè

Alongside Francesco Hayez, Molteni was one of the most important Milanese artists, renowned for his portraits and, above all, his genre paintings. One obituary even stated that he had played a "pioneering role in Italian painting by introducing and successfully cultivating genre painting in Italy."[56] Early works included depictions of children as chimney sweeps (*spazzacamini*), which were extremely popular in the 1830s. He concentrated his outstanding talent, however, on the depiction of young women, mostly in full figure. Molteni's immaculate brushwork is best revealed in his treatment of skin tones and fabrics, as here with the black dress and dark cashmere scarf. The quality of his work had already been recognized earlier in Vienna, and some of his paintings, such as *Shepherdess from Brianza*[57] in 1839 or *An Italian Spinner* in 1841, had been shown in exhibitions at the Academy.[58] *The Confession*, paintec in 1838, was even acquired by Emperor Ferdinand I for the imperial collection (today Fondazione Cariplo, Milan, fig. p. 56). In 1836 at the latest, Molteni met Friedrich von Amerling during a visit to Vienna. The works of these two painters have considerable similarities, and it may therefore be assumed that the artistic exchange continued during Amerling's visit to Milan in 1838. Apart from Molteni's painting achievement, mention should also be made of his work as a restorer, which greatly influenced his artistic oeuvre. He was appointed curator of the Brera Academy in 1855, where he conserved and restored several important works, including *The Marriage of the Virgin* by Raphael. The most spectacular commission in this regard was the restoration of *The Last Supper* by Leonardo da Vinci, which had been severely damaged by French soldiers during the Napoleonic rule. Molteni crowned his career in 1861 with his appointment as director of the Brera, a position he was to hold until 1866.

Constant von Wurzbach, *Biographisches Lexikon des Kaisertums Österreich*, vol. 19 (Vienna, 1868), pp. 29–31; *Giuseppe Molteni (1800–1867) e il ritratto nella Milano romantica: Pittura, collezionismo, restaurc, tutela*, exh. cat. Museo Poldi Pezzoli, Milan/Museo di Storia Contemporanea, Milan (Milan, 2000); *Saur/De Gruyter Allgemeines Künstlerlexikon: Die bildenden Künstler aller Zeiten und Völker*, vol. 90 (Munich et al., 2016), p. 256 (Heidrun Kurz).

SG

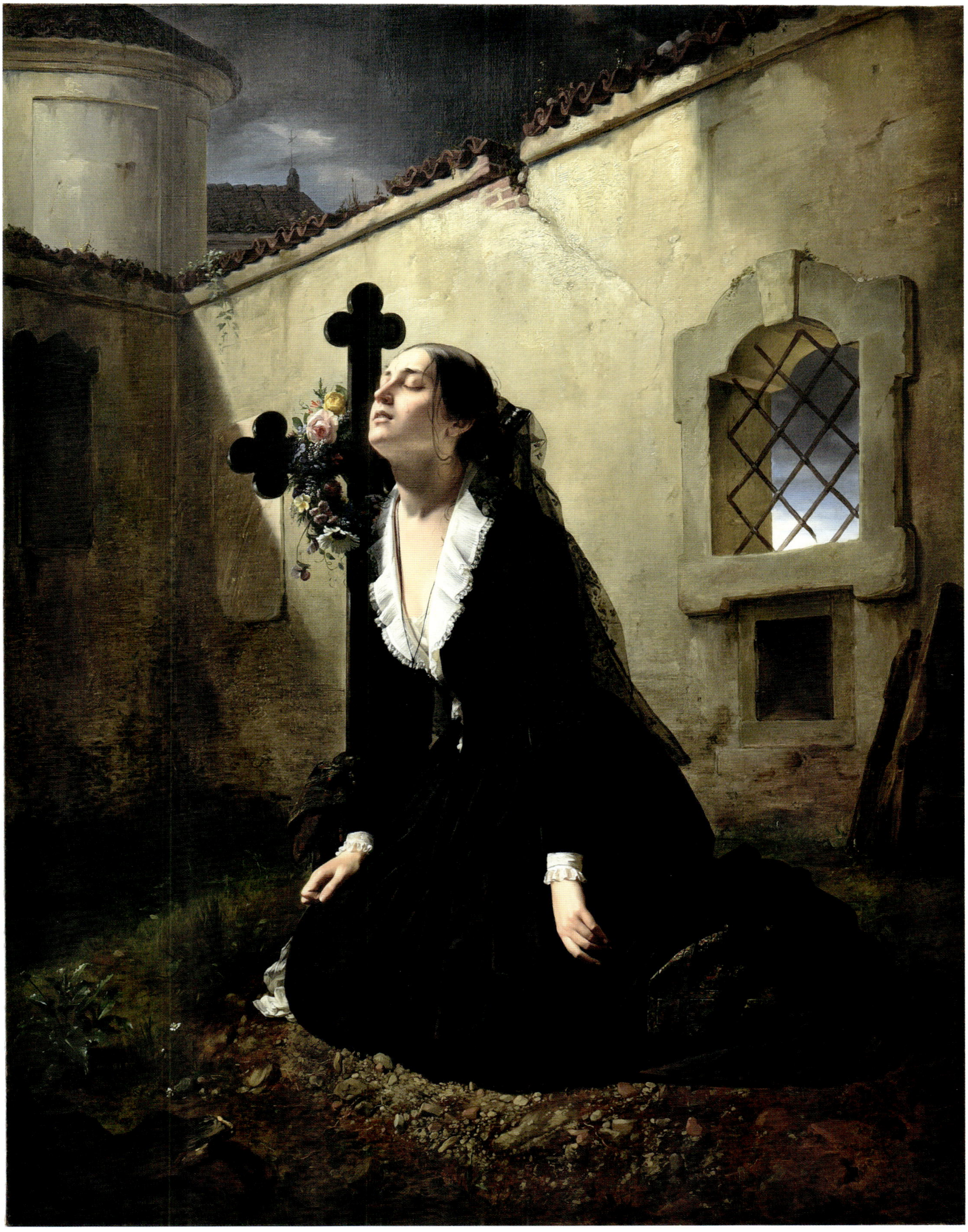

Pompeo Marino Molmenti
Vespasiano Muzzarelli, 1846
Oil on canvas, 64.5 × 46.5 cm
Signed (middle right, on the door): P. Molmenti
Musei Civici, Bassano del Grappa, inv. no. 434

The portrait of *Vespasiano Muzzarelli* is one of the most interesting paintings from the Veneto during the third quarter of the nineteenth century. Even his casual pose is perplexing. His crossed legs appear to trigger a twist in his body, which is restabilized by the *contrapposto* support of the right arm, causing the sitter to gaze straight out of the portrait. The perspective is also astonishing, combining vantage points both above and opposite the figure. This has the effect of exaggerating the proportions of the body and giving prominence to the bold patterns of the carpet, which seems to tilt upward to the middle of the picture. All details are represented very realistically, interwoven with a vivid intensity of color. These many optical stimuli enrich the painting and—interestingly—are pleasing to behold, rather than being taxing on the eye. Little is known of the sitter, only that he was a man of independent means living in Venice, at least this was how the *Wiener Zeitung* described him when noting his arrival in Vienna on November 21, 1862.[59] Due to his association with Bassano del Grappa, he bequeathed his portrayal, together with the landscape by Carlo Grubacs (1810–1870), also shown in the portrait, to the Musei Civici.

The painter Pompeo Molmenti was from Motta di Livenza, near Treviso, and in 1834, at the age of fifteen, started studying at the Accademia di Belle Arti in Venice. Here he became close to the history painter Ludovico Lipparini (1800–1856). The majority of his work consists of religious paintings that can be found in various churches in Veneto and Friuli. Molmenti also painted many portraits with pioneering, unconventional compositions. He preferred history painting, however. *Filippo Calendario, architect of the Doge's Palace, is forcefully taken from his family by order of the signoria and sentenced to death for joining the conspiracy of Marino Faliero* was a work he started in 1849 commissioned by Princess Giovanelli. It was highly praised by art critics[60] for its naturalism and superb light effects, and featured at the 1858 Vienna Academy exhibition.[61] After traveling to Greece and Syria in 1843, Molmenti became professor of history painting at the Academy of Fine Arts in Venice, where he taught his students a realistic style of representation that they would take forward into the following century.

Constant von Wurzbach, *Biographisches Lexikon des Kaisertums Österreich*, vol. 19 (Vienna, 1868), pp. 20–21; Sergio Marinelli/Giuseppe Mazzariol/Fernando Mazzocca, *Il Veneto e l'Austria: Vita e cultura artistica nelle città venete 1814–1866* (Milan, 1989), pp. 249–50.

SG

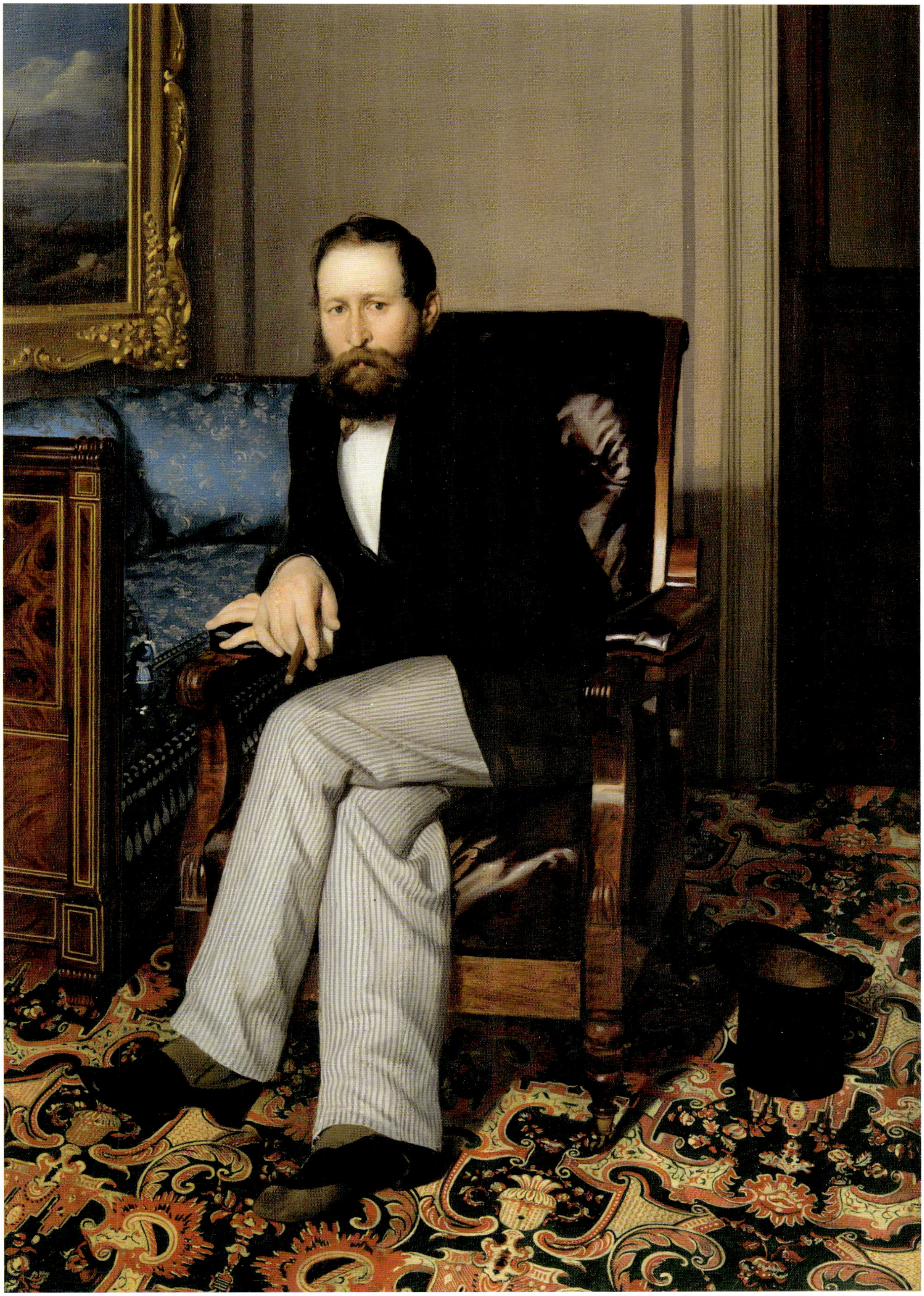

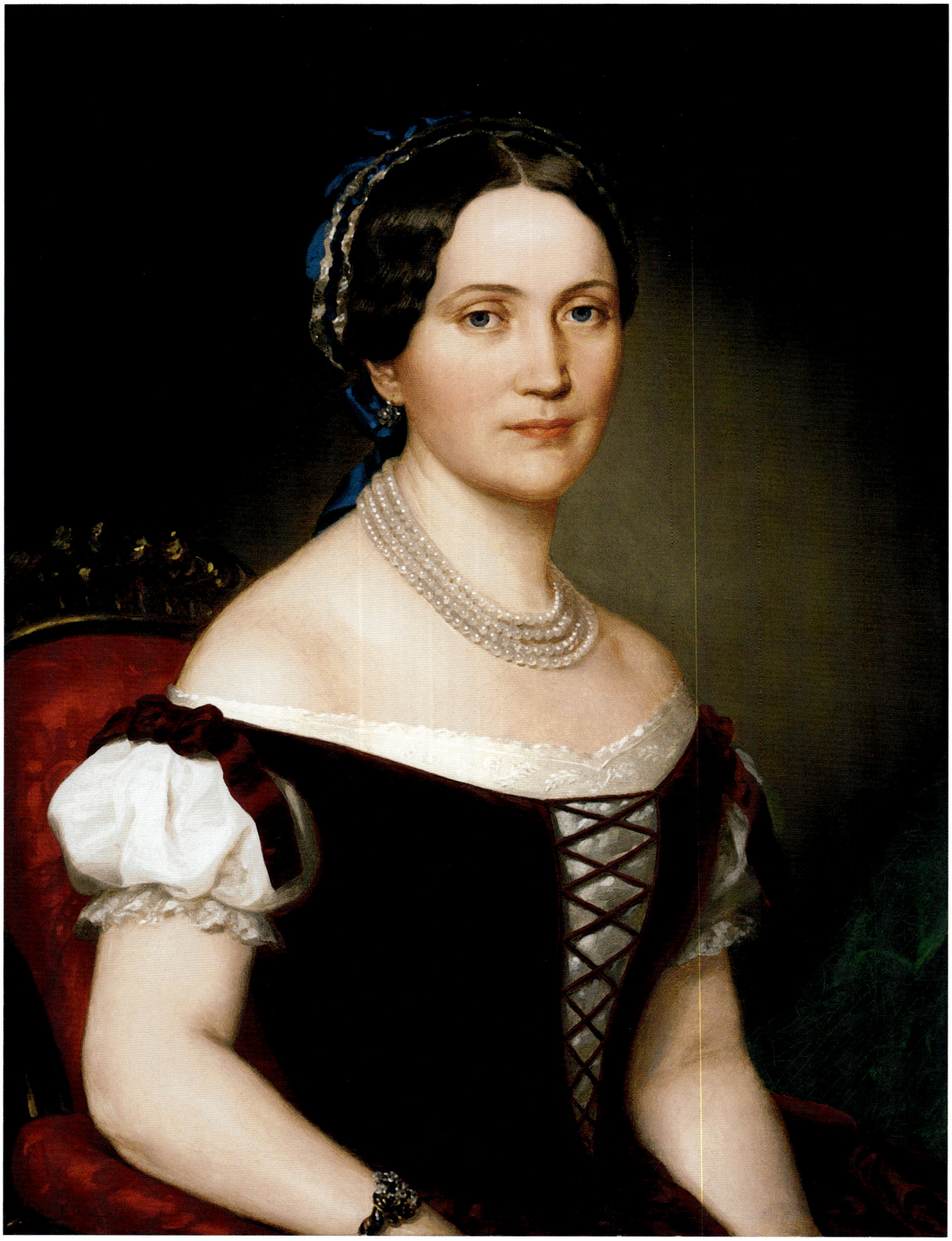

Miklós Barabás
Portrait of a Lady, 1853
Oil on canvas, 73.5 × 57.5 cm
Signed (Middle right): Barabás 853
Gábor Kovács Art Collection, Budapest

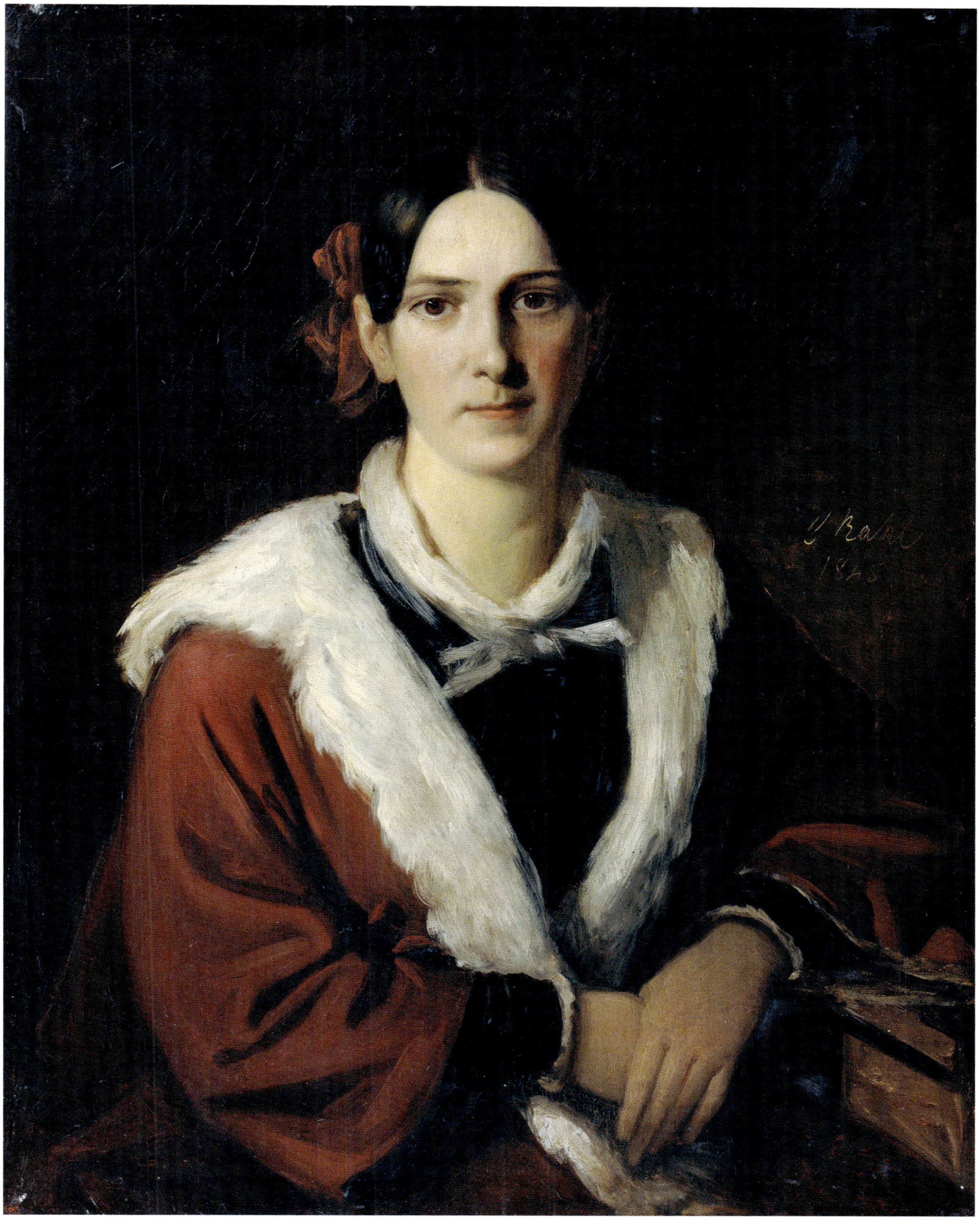

Carl Rahl
Luise von Schwind, Wife of the Painter Moritz von Schwind, 1845
Oil on canvas, 86.5 × 69.5 cm
Signed (center right): C Rahl / 1845
Belvedere, Vienna, inv. no. 2599

Domenico Induno
Malinconia (*Melancholy*), c. 1849
Oil on canvas, 55 × 42.5 cm
Signed (lower left): D. Induno
Museo Civico Revoltella - Galleria d'arte moderna, Trieste, inv. nr. 247

Induno studied history painting from 1831 to 1839 under Luigi Sabatelli (1772–1850) and Francesco Hayez at the Brera in Milan where he acquired his skills to tell stories in images. He first used these abilities to represent everyday events and his pictures became highly popular. During the course of his life, which became increasingly influenced by the idea of a unified Italy, he realized that he could use history painting to serve his political convictions, as demonstrated in *Return of the Wounded Soldier* (plate p. 189). Induno had already honed his individual style as a student and this blossomed during the 1840s, characterized by a rather unique combination of clear forms and agitated brushwork. As a result, his paintings appear extremely vibrant and modern, and the artist thus holds a special position among his contemporaries.

After Induno was involved in the anti-Austrian revolts in 1848, culminating in the Five Days of Milan, he thought it advisable to withdraw to Switzerland for a while. It was probably during this period of self-imposed exile in the mountains of Astano, between Lago Maggiore and Lago di Lugano, that the artist painted this sad image, with the poignant title *Malinconia* (*Melancholy*). The girl's pose, her clothing and disheveled hair betray her desperate, hopeless situation. There is a grave opposite her with a small wooden cross entwined with flowers in the colors of the Italian tricolore, a hidden reference to the painter's mood. Although the oval format is puzzling in this context, as this is usually found only in decorative pictures and does not feature in the rest of Induno's work, it harmonizes perfectly with the content of the image. It must have been a deliberate choice, as the never-ending form of the oval ultimately enhances the elegiac atmosphere that prevails in the painting.

Giuliano Matteucci, ed., *Domenico e Gerolamo Induno: La storia e la cronaca scritte con il pennello*, exh. cat. Palazzo Guidobono, Tortona (Turin etc., 2006), pp. 190–91 (Paul Nicholls).

SG

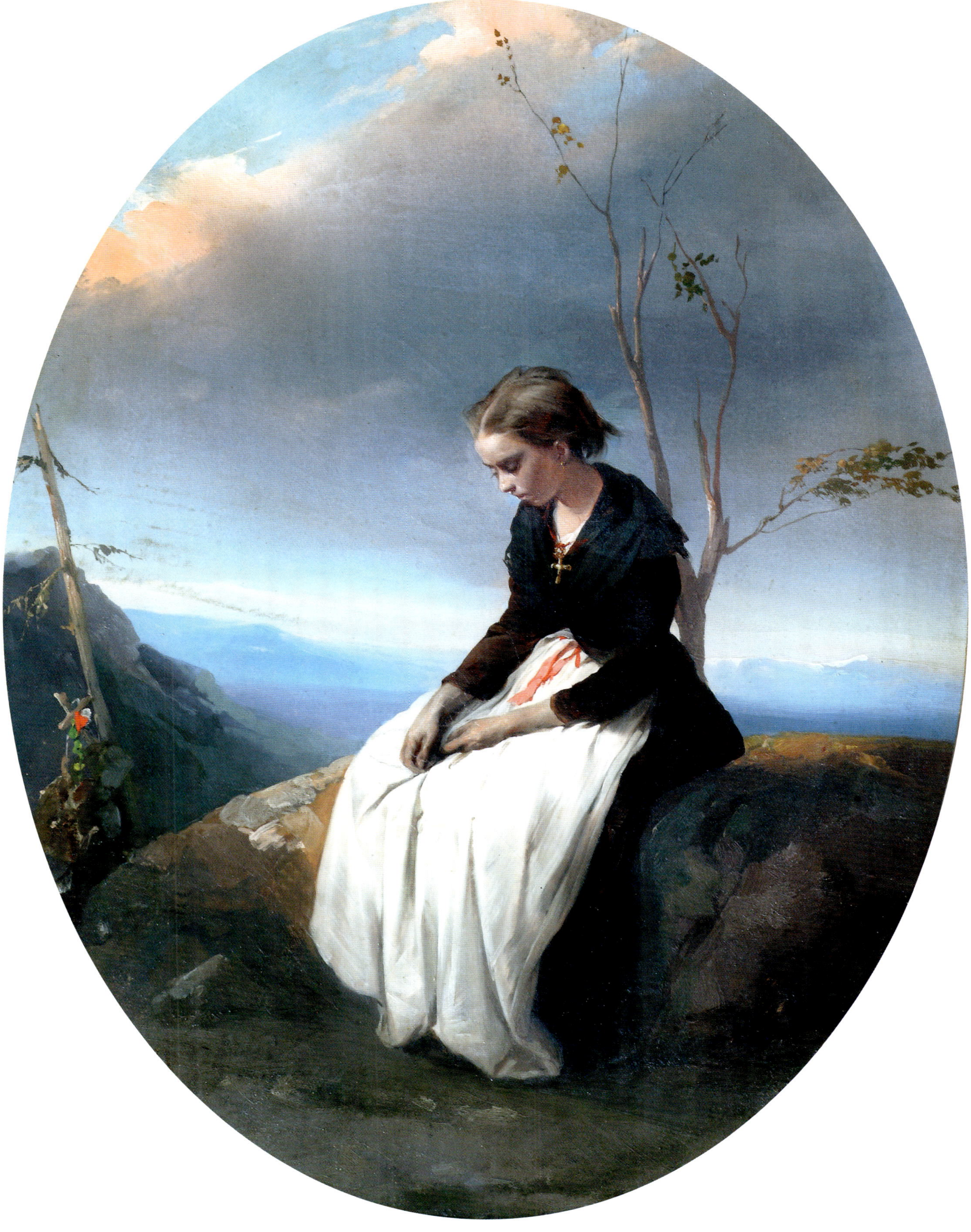

Franz Dobiaschofsky
Faust and Gretchen in the Nineteenth Century, 1848
Oil on canvas, 74 × 60 cm
Signed (lower left under the layers of paint): Dobiaschofsky pinx 1848
Belvedere, Vienna, inv. no. 2914

Dobiaschofsky, who belonged to the younger generation of Nazarenes, trained as a history painter at the Vienna Academy under Josef von Führich (1800–1876) and Leopold Kupelwieser (1796–1862). Throughout his life he mainly painted religious and historical subjects, but soon surpassed his teacher's approach by capturing his protagonists as if they were in a genre scene, thus adding verisimilitude. He had great technical skill as a painter and a predilection for lucid colors, delicately shaded to present a nuanced picture.

In 1849, Dobiaschofsky made a brief foray into genre painting, creating this, arguably his most popular work. It immediately caused an uproar because, when he came to present it at the Academy exhibition,[62] the police intervened. The cause of the commotion was the male figure's modern attire: Dobiaschofsky had depicted a modern Faust, a student of the Revolution of 1848, with a black, red, and gold sash across his chest, his sword strapped at his side, clutching a Calabrese hat. It was these props that unsettled the authorities. The events of the Revolution were still too fresh in their minds and they feared unpleasant reactions. The artist was told to remove all these provocative elements from the painting. What remains is an elegant young man in a black suit with a gray top hat, shown caressing his girl. Her attire has not been changed, but, in this new context, the red, white, and blue has lost its reference to the French Revolution and may be interpreted merely as a whim of fashion. Thus censored, the painting did not meet with critical acclaim and was deemed "a too modern, innocent approach to a profound idea," as the *Wiener Zeitung* put it.[63]

As the man's suit was changed immediately after the picture's completion, it is not possible to distinguish the original version from the overpaintings. With the naked eye, the red shade of the sash can only be detected in the craquelure, and even there in only a few places. An analysis using infrared reflectography, however, brought some interesting findings to light.[64] It revealed both the original form of the uniform and hat as well as the sword's hilt between the two bodies. Furthermore, it revealed the artist's signature on the lower left, invisible to the naked eye. The theory that the layer of paint covering this was added by the artist himself, possibly in response to his humiliation, is pure speculation.

"Nekrolog," *Neues Fremden-Blatt*, December 11, 1867, p. 6; Werner Kitlitschka, *Die Malerei der Wiener Ringstraße* (Wiesbaden, 1981), pp. 40–41.

SG

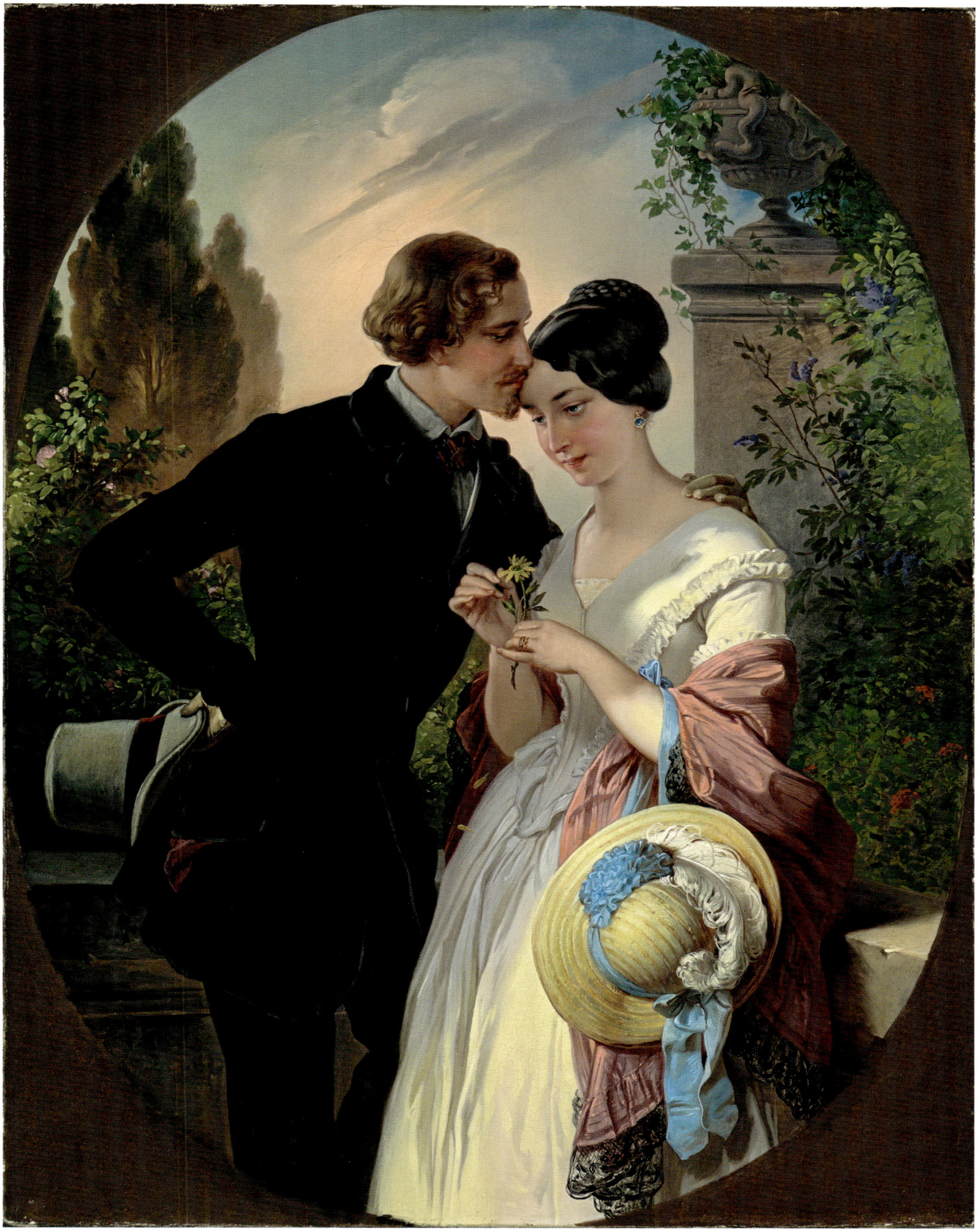

Domenico Induno
Return of the Wounded Soldier, 1854
Oil on canvas, 42.4 × 53 cm
Signed (lower left): D.o Induno
Fondazione Cariplo Iniziative Patrimoniali S.p.A., Milan, inv. no. FCIP 0039

Similar to his younger brother Gerolamo (1825–1890), Domenico Induno was a politically involved artist who felt compelled to express his personal views in his paintings. Consequently, soon after completing his studies at the Milan Academy, he opted to paint everyday life during the period of Risorgimento. The artist's oeuvre is characterized by his many depictions of the suffering population during this very difficult time in Italy, but his chef d'oeuvre was the large-scale painting *Bulletin of July 14, 1859 Announcing the Peace of Villafranca* (fig. p. 59). This painting was commissioned by King Viktor Emanuel II in 1860, and exists in two versions in Milan and in Rome. *Return of the Wounded Soldier* also addresses the subject of Italy's liberation. The artist chose an everyday scene, which he used as a snapshot to represent the wider political situation in his homeland. A soldier wearing the red shirt of Garibaldi has evidently been wounded fighting for his cause. He is visiting his sick, bedridden wife. His anger, causing his body to tense up, may arise from the fact that he knows full well that his help is needed at home and the letter in his right hand may be responsible for his predicament. Possible interpretations range from the soldier facing arrest to his impotence when confronted with Italy's hopeless situation under foreign rule.

The explosive force of the scene is heightened by the painting style with rapid brushwork that suggests rather than describes. Induno developed this characteristic style as a young painter in the 1830s and many artists would later imitate and adapt it.

Giuliano Matteucci, ed., *Domenico e Gerolamo Induno: La storia e la cronaca scritte con il pennello*, exh. cat. Palazzo Guidobono, Tortona (Turin etc., 2006), pp. 66–67 (Silvia Regonelli).

SG

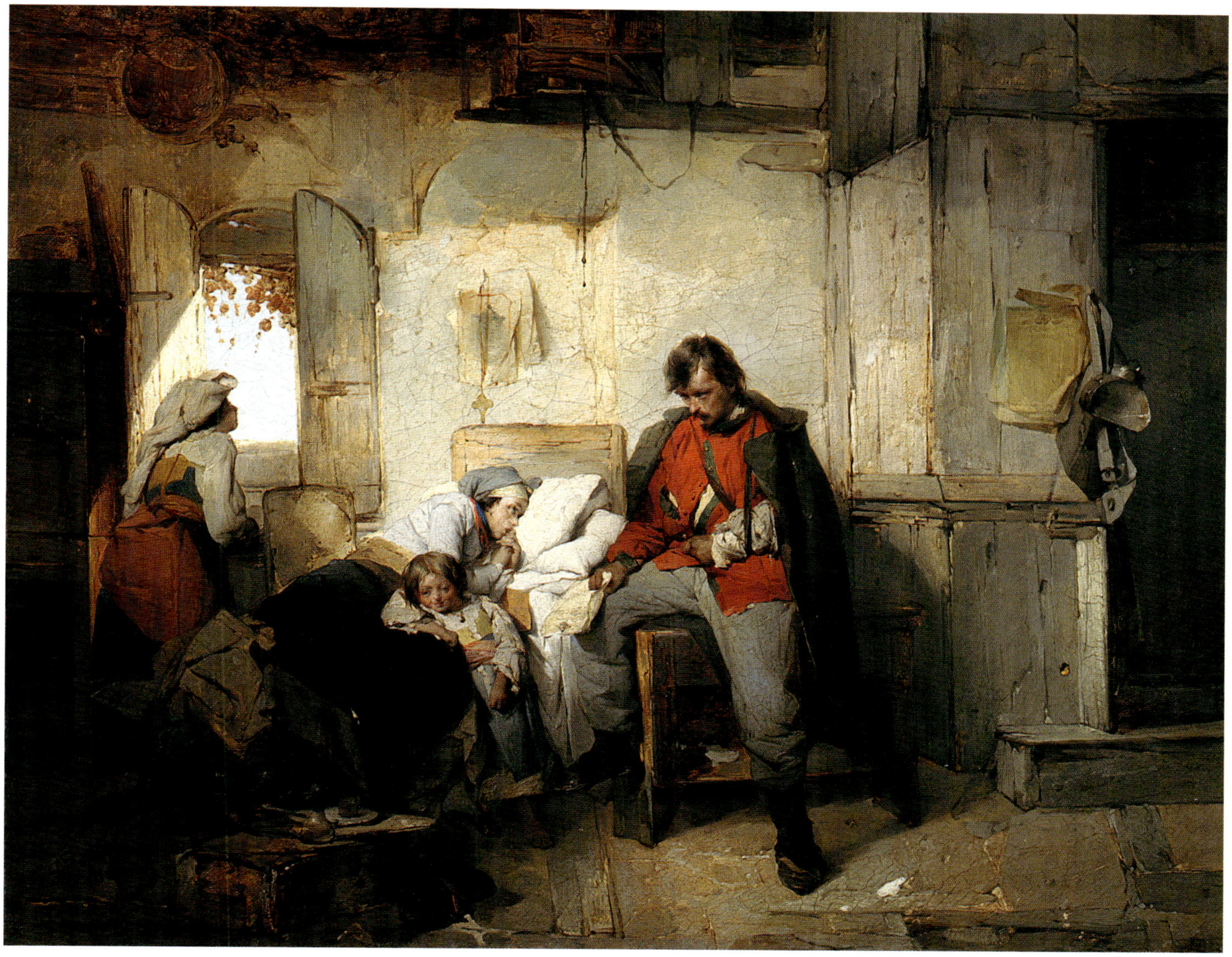

Bedřich Havránek
The Chiemsee at Sunset, 1844
Oil on canvas, 29 × 41.5 cm
Unsigned
Národní galerie v Praze/National Gallery, Prague

Bedřich Havránek
Street near Sázava (*Landscape with River*), 1843
Oil on paperboard, 27.5 × 37.5 cm
Signed (lower right): F. Hawrk
Národní galerie v Praze/National Gallery, Prague, inv. no. 5025

Bedřich Havránek
Near Rájec in Moravia, c. 1850
Oil on paperboard, 82 × 105 cm
Signed (lower right): FHawranek
Národní galerie v Praze/National Gallery, Prague, inv. no. O 15419

Bedřich Havránek, born in Prague in 1821, was one of the most important exponents of Bohemian landscape painting in the nineteenth century. His teachers at the Prague Academy of Fine Arts included the German landscapist Maximilian Haushofer (1811–1866), who introduced to Bohemia ideas from the Romantic landscape tradition of the Munich School. Havránek also worked for the researcher and chronicler of the Mediterranean Sea, Archduke Ludwig Salvator of Austria-Tuscany. Based on Salvator's drawings, the artist produced the illustrations for his books. From 1843 until his death in 1899, Havránek regularly contributed to the annual exhibitions in Prague.

Bohemian landscape painting experienced its heyday during the periods of Romanticism and subsequent Realism. It reached its pinnacle in the works of Maximilian Haushofer and his students. Haushofer acquainted his students not only with Alpine nature but also with the Czech landscape. From the 1840s, Havránek often traveled to the large lakes in the Bavarian Alps, following in his teacher's footsteps, as it was here, at the Chiemsee, that Haushofer had honed his own drawing skills from 1828. With its wide and peaceful landscape in the light of the setting sun, Havránek's *Chiemsee* scene (plate p. 191) echoes Haushofer's intention to represent the lake in different seasons and times of day.

From the 1850s, Havránek focused on Bohemian and Moravian landscapes. The painting *Near Rájec in Moravia* (plate 193) shows a view of the picturesque, rugged Punkva valley.[65] His depiction of the dry bed of the partly underground Punkva River in the Moravian Karst region stands out on account of his skilled composition of the rock formations and the atmospheric intensity. A similarly dominant expanse of scree and stones can be found in Ferdinand Georg Waldmüller's *Liechtenstein Ruin near Mödling* (plate 195). In this unspectacular scene, the painterly and sculptural effects of light and shadow are the landscape's main subject.

Naděžda Blažíčková-Horová, ed., *Czech 19th-Century Painting: Catalogue of the Permanent Exhibition. Convent of St. Agnes of Bohemia* (Prague, 1998), pp. 118–25; Radim Vondráček, ed., *Biedermeier: Art and Culture in the Bohemian Lands 1814–1848*, exh. cat. Museum of Decorative Arts in Prague and Gallery (Prague, 2010), p. 440.

BH

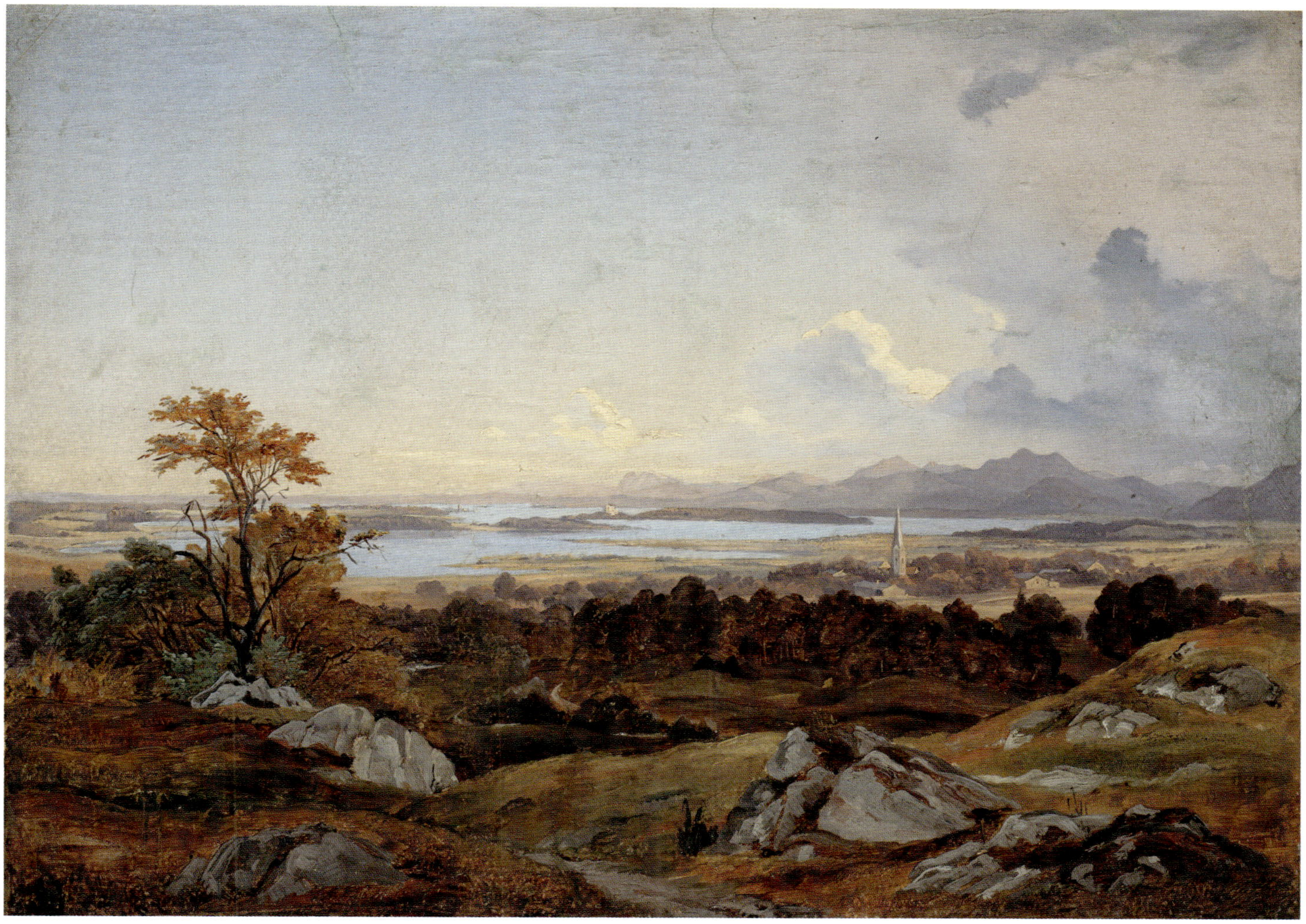

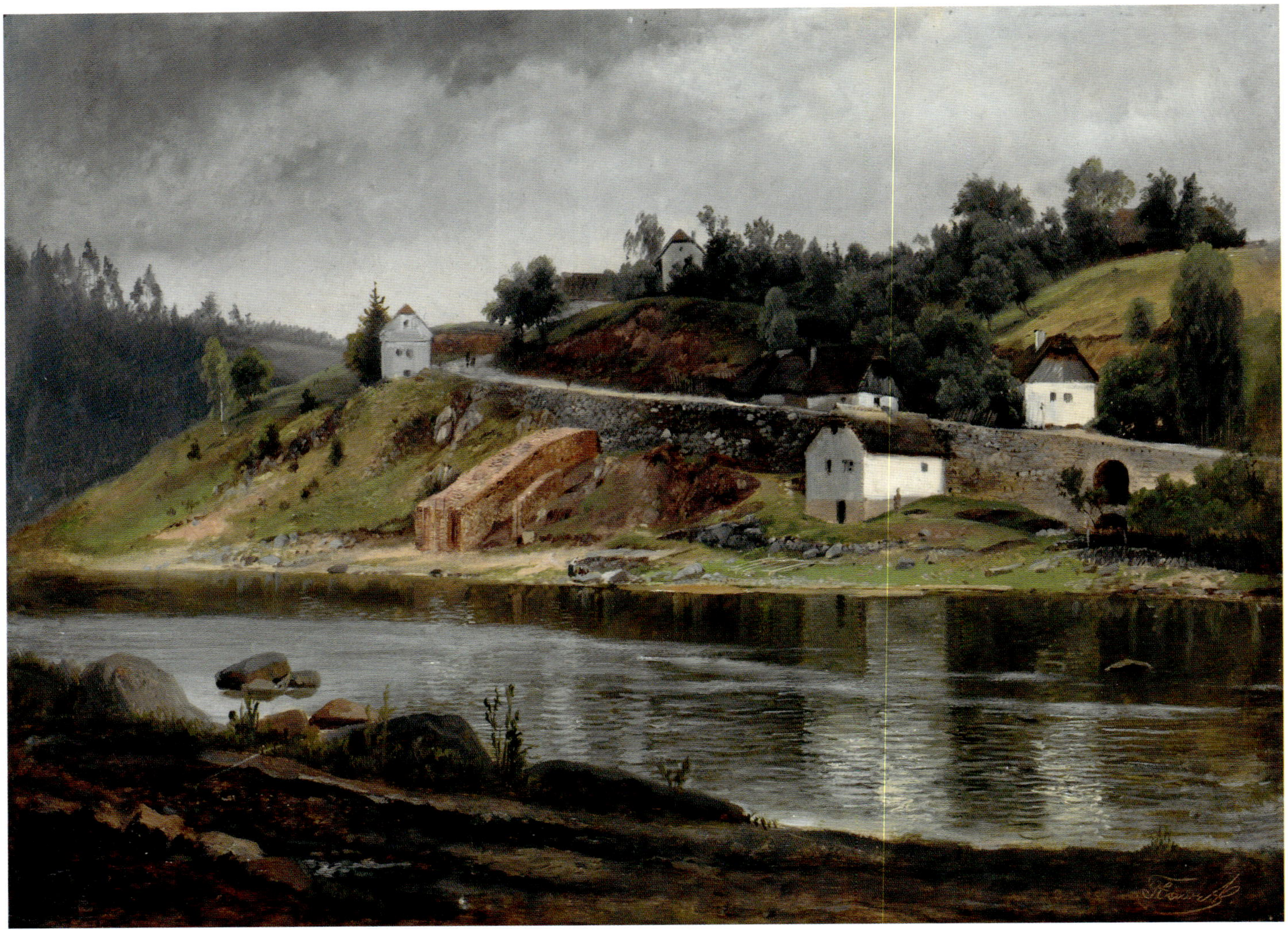

Bedřich Havránek
Street near Sázava (Landscape with River), 1843

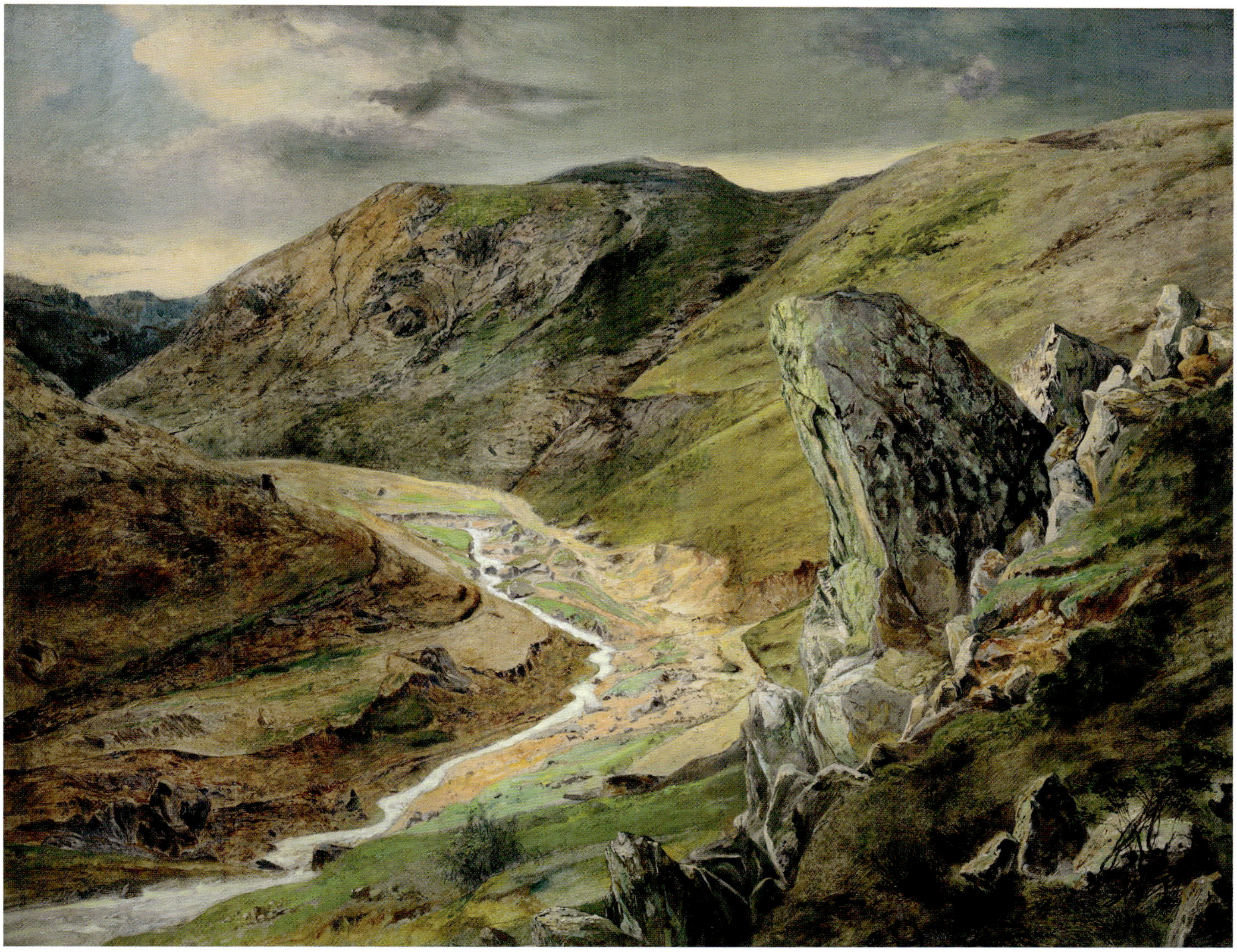

Bedřich Havránek
Near Rájec in Moravia, c. 1850

Ferdinand Georg Waldmüller
Ruin of Liechtenstein near Mödling, 1848
Oil on canvas, 55.5 × 68 cm
Signed (lower middle): Waldmüller 1848
Belvedere, Vienna, inv. no. 1375

"In his old age, Waldmüller finally realized that to achieve radiant colors you had to paint in sunlight," Carl von Lützow commented wryly in his obituary of the artist, describing "the strangely dazzling coloration in many of his later pictures."[66] Even during his lifetime, Waldmüller had already heard comments like this. Yet, although he must have known that he stood outside the mainstream, it did not prevent him from attempting to convince his contemporaries of his view of art. He promulgated his ideas in his written criticism of academic teaching. The humiliations he suffered as a result eventually prompted him to lash out by declaring that the academy as an institution was obsolete and should be closed down. He claimed that two years of training with a master were sufficient and that talent and the study of nature would do the rest. He also pointed out that the government could spend the money thus saved to purchase works of art and support young artists.[67]

But we are getting ahead of ourselves, as this conflict did not actually escalate until 1857. In 1848, when Waldmüller painted *Ruin of Liechtenstein near Mödling*, the discussion had only just begun. The unconventional depiction of nature nevertheless hints at the painter's difficult personality. First of all the composition is perplexing, in that at its center we see a path washed out by rain and gently curving upwards. The motif itself is also confusing, since the title promises the view of a ruin, which in fact is barely visible behind the crest of the hill and can only be seen at all because its walls are lit up by the sun. It is therefore clear that Waldmüller was not interested in painting a pleasing motif, but rather in solving compositional or painterly problems, in creating a credible rendering of foreground and distance, and in mastering the juxtaposition of light and shade. His contemporaries failed to appreciate these ambitions, and only the artists of the Secession recognized how much his nature depictions had anticipated their ideas. They rehabilitated him by declaring him the "original Secessionist." Since this time, he has been regarded incontestably as one of the most important Viennese painters of the nineteenth century.

Rupert Feuchtmüller, *Ferdinand Georg Waldmüller, 1793–1865: Leben, Schriften, Werke* (Vienna/Munich, 1996), cat. rais. no. 786; Claudia Wöhrer, "'Ein Märthyrthum für die Sache der Kunst': Ferdinand Georg Waldmüller in eigenen und fremden Darstellungen," in *Ferdinand Georg Waldmüller* (= Belvedere. Zeitschrift für bildende Kunst, Sonderheft 1) (Vienna, 1997), pp. 6–23; Sabine, *Mehr als Biedermeier: Klassizismus, Romantik und Realismus in der Österreichischen Galerie Belvedere* (Munich, 2006), pp. 116–17; ibid./Agnes Husslein-Arco, eds., *Ferdinand Georg Waldmüller 1793–1865*, exh. cat. Belvedere, Vienna/Musée du Louvre, Paris (Vienna, 2009).

SG

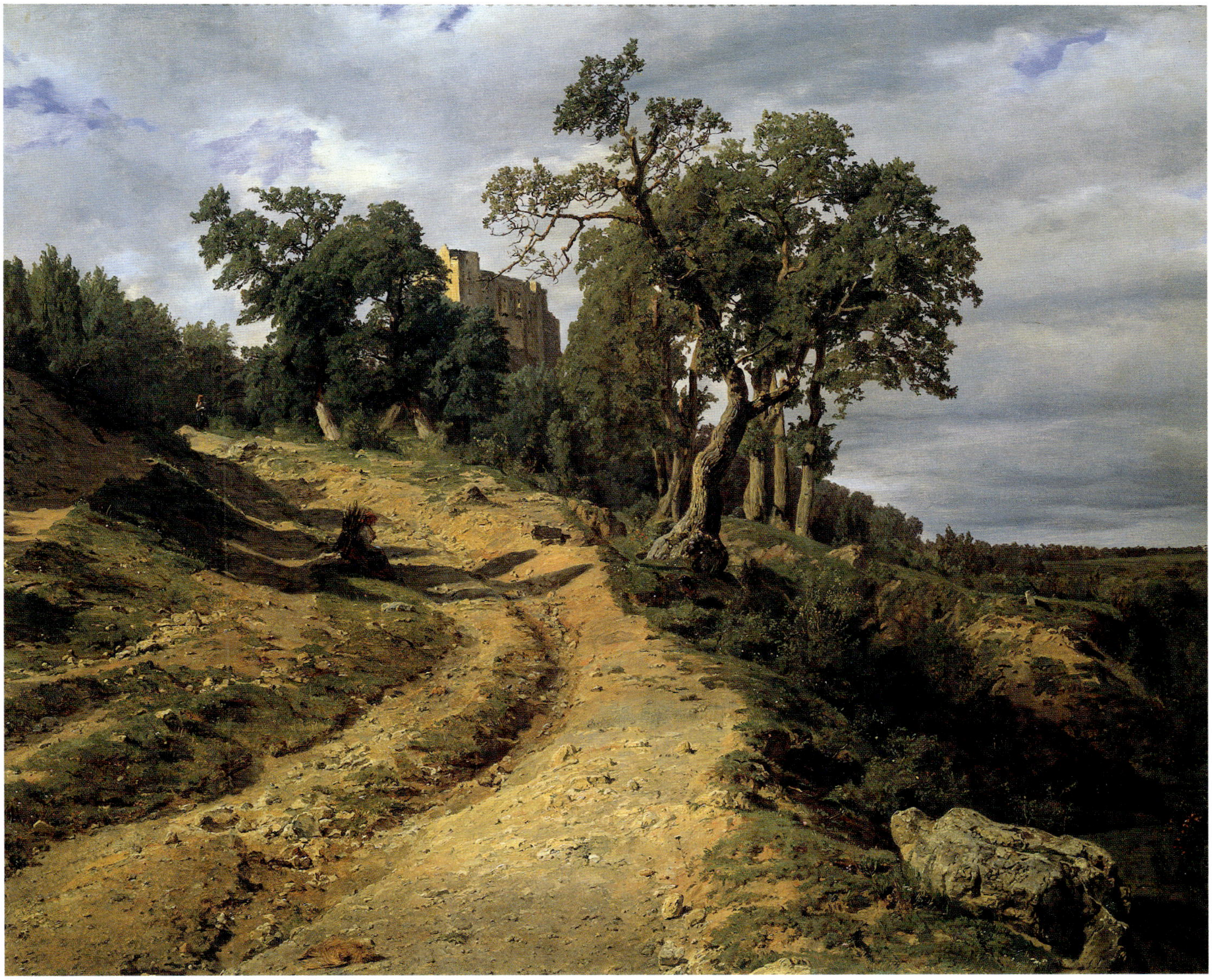

Ferdinand Georg Waldmüller
Large Prater Landscape, 1849
Oil on wood, 70 × 93 cm
Signed (lower left): Waldmüller 1849.
Belvedere, Vienna, inv. no. 1255

Views of the Prater date from Waldmüller's early attempts at landscape painting. Several pictures from the early 1830s show old, weathered, solitary trees without branches or crowns. They bear witness to the fact that Waldmüller liked to wander through the Prater meadows to practice his artistic skills on these motifs. It is impossible to guess what prompted him to do so. Although his trip to France in 1830 may have been a motivating factor, there is no indication in his travel journal that he undertook any nature studies while in France or studied the landscape paintings of his young French colleagues. On the contrary, Waldmüller seems to have spent most of his stay in Paris in the Palais du Luxembourg studying history pictures by his contemporaries, or looking at the Old Masters in the Louvre.[68] It is interesting to note, however, that he embarked on landscape painting shortly after his return to Vienna.

His nature depictions were influenced initially by the Dutch painters Jacob van Ruisdael (1628–1682), Meindert Hobbema (1638–1709), and Allart van Everdingen (1621–1675), whose works he would have seen both in the Louvre and in various Viennese collections. Apart from detailed and realistic portrayals of individual trees and tree stumps, he devoted much attention to conquering pictorial space. The various views of the Prater or the Salzkammergut show how he struggled to achieve a realistic distinction between foreground and distance and gradually moved away from foreground props. Although he soon achieved his aim in portrait format, which allowed a narrower view, in landscape format he continued to use the device of combining different perspectives. For example, the panoramic *View of the Dachstein with Lake Hallstatt from the Hütteneck Alp near Ischl* in 1838 (Wien Museum) benefits from the elevated vantage point, as does the impressive *View of Mödling* (Collections of the Princes of Liechtenstein, Vaduz–Vienna) painted ten years later. Staffage figures placed prominently in the foreground of *Evening Landscape with Herd of Goats* from 1847 (Neue Pinakothek, Munich) help to give the impression of an expansive plain extending far into the distance. In his *Large Prater Landscape* from 1849, by contrast, the artist shows himself liberated at last from all conventional artistic devices. Here he finally succeeded in ignoring the foreground and drawing the focus directly to the center of the picture, where he positioned a magnificent oak tree with spreading branches, guiding the viewer's gaze into the distance on the left and into the forest undergrowth on the right. Waldmüller, too, appears to have been pleased with the result and satisfied with his achievement, for *Large Prater Landscape* marks the end of his focus on inanimate nature. In subsequent landscape pictures like *Brushwood Gatherers in the Vienna Woods* (plate p. 227), *Time of Roses* (c. 1864, Wien Museum, fig. 9, p. 25), and *Country People Resting* (plate p. 228), the staffage figures were used differently and became inherent to the picture, resulting in large-scale and restful compositions showing man and nature in harmony.

Bruno Grimschitz, *Ferdinand Georg Waldmüller* (Salzburg, 1957), pp. 44–54; Rupert Feuchtmüller, *Ferdinand Georg Waldmüller, 1793–1865: Leben, Schriften, Werke* (Vienna/Munich, 1996), cat. rais. no. 793; Martina Haja, "'Nach der Natur gemahlt': Überlegungen zur Landschaftsmalerei Ferdinand Georg Waldmüllers," in *Ferdinand Georg Waldmüller* (= Belvedere. Zeitschrift für bildende Kunst, Sonderheft 1) (Vienna, 1997), pp. 116–31; Walter Krause, "Waldmüller und die Landschaftsmalerei," in Agnes Husslein-Arco/Sabine Grabner, eds., *Ferdinand Georg Waldmüller 1793–1865*, exh. cat. Belvedere, Vienna/Musée du Louvre, Paris (Vienna, 2009), pp. 79–85.

SG

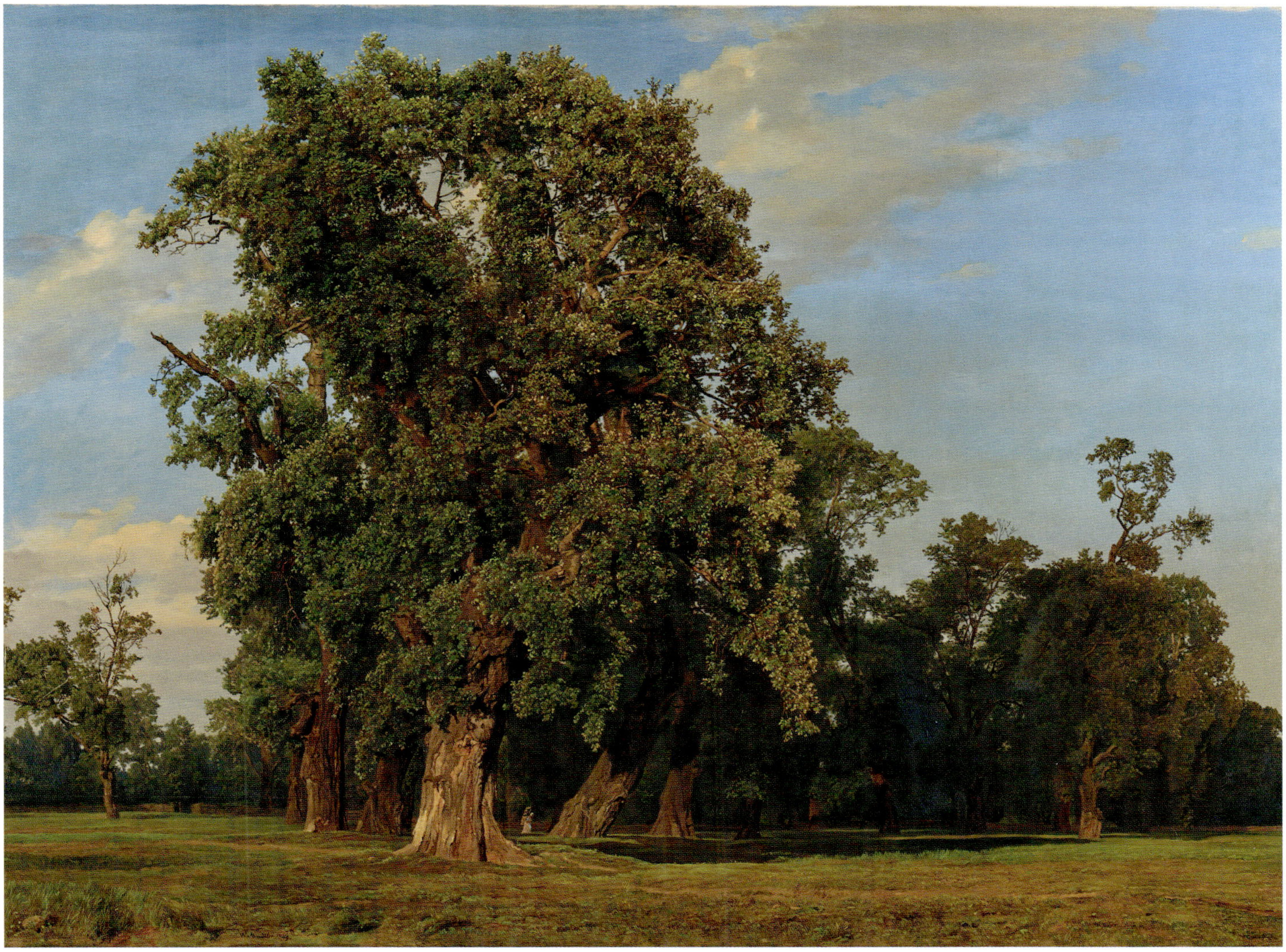

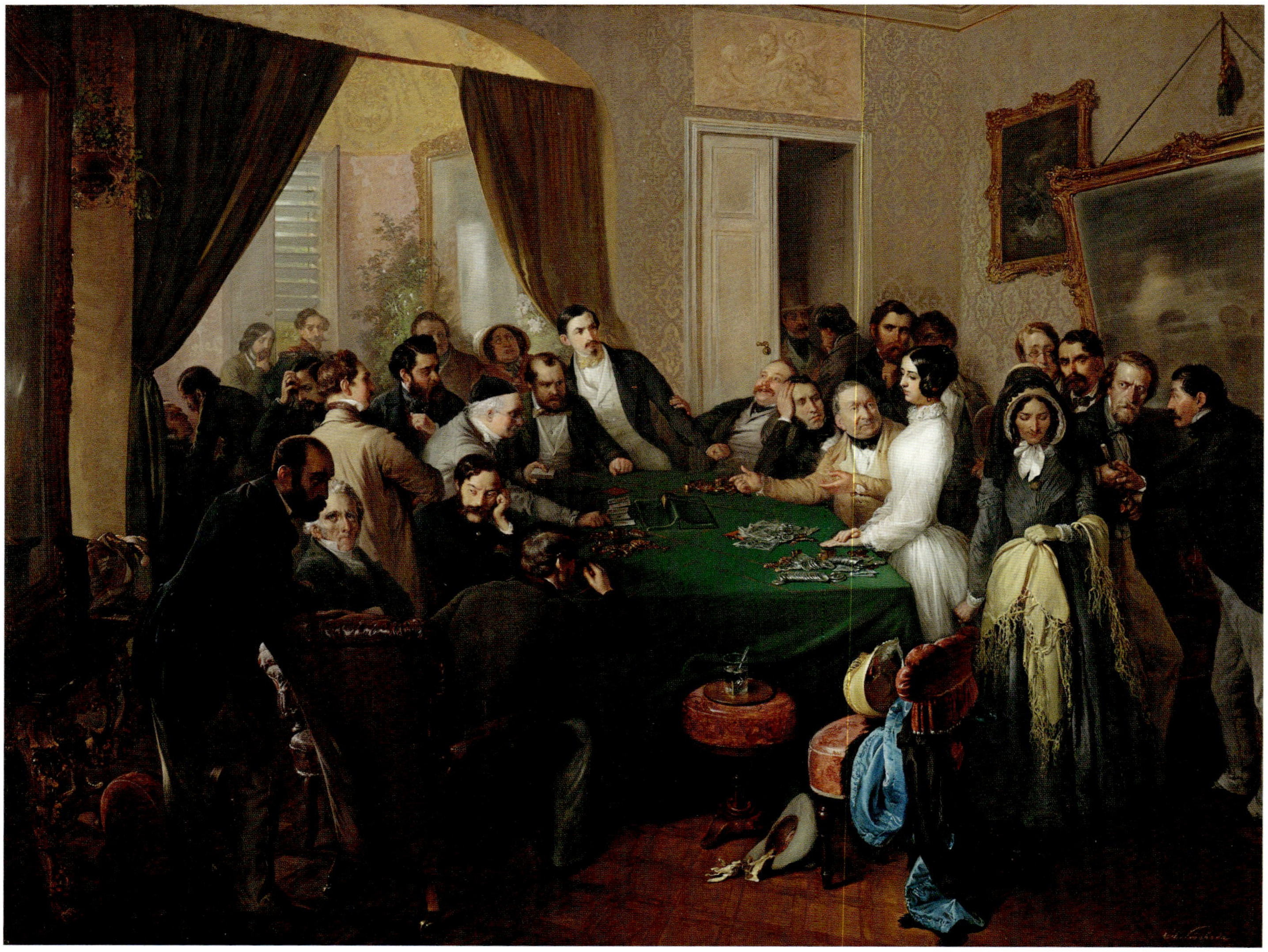

Eduard Swoboda
Va Banque (*Gambling*), 1849
Oil on canvas, 94.5 × 126.5 cm
Signed (lower right): Ed. Swoboda / 1849
Belvedere, Vienna, inv. no. 3742

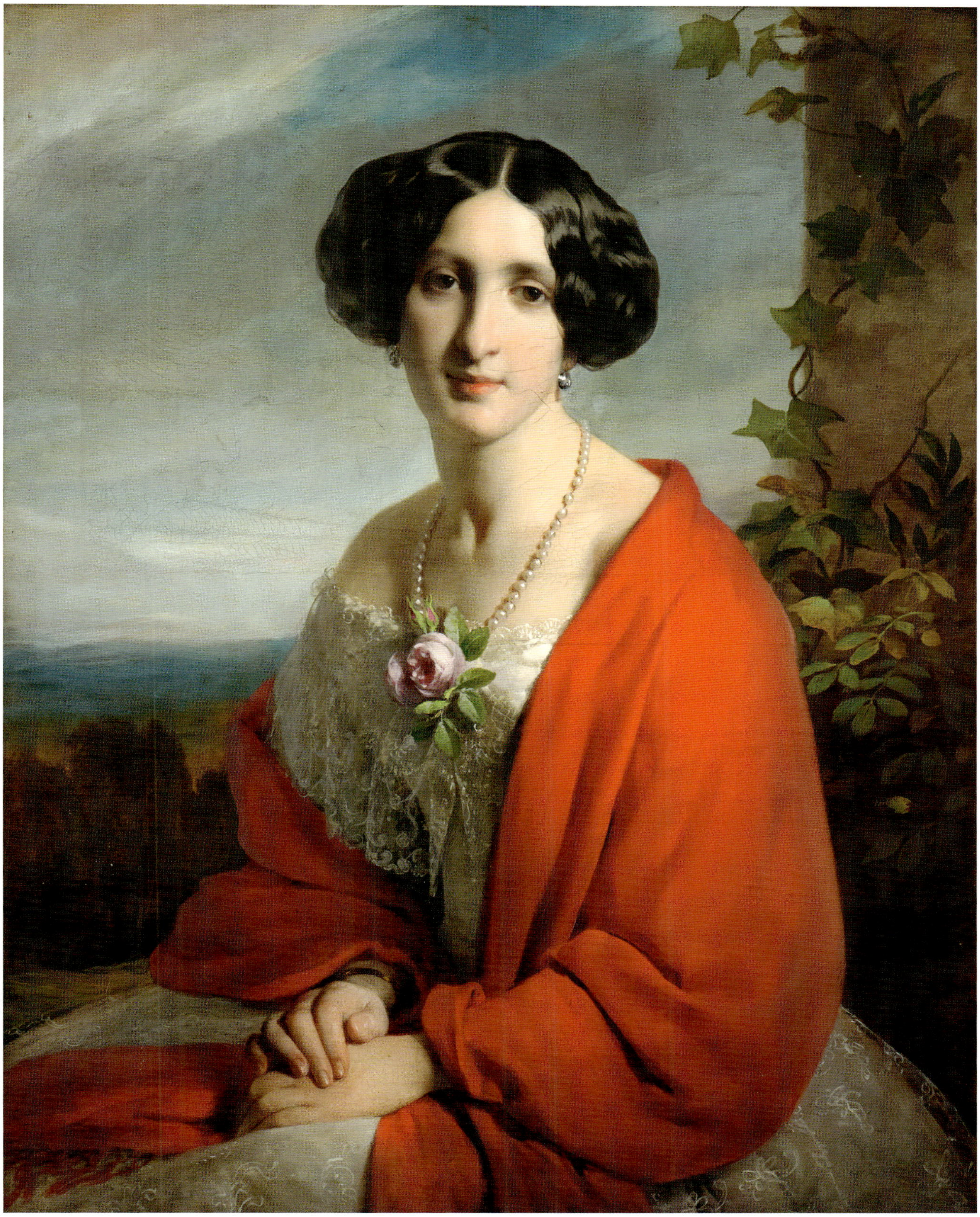

Friedrich von Amerling
Carolina Josepha Feldmüller, Wife of the Timber Merchant Matthias Feldmüller jun., 1851
Oil on canvas, 94.5 × 78 cm
Unsigned
Austrian private collection

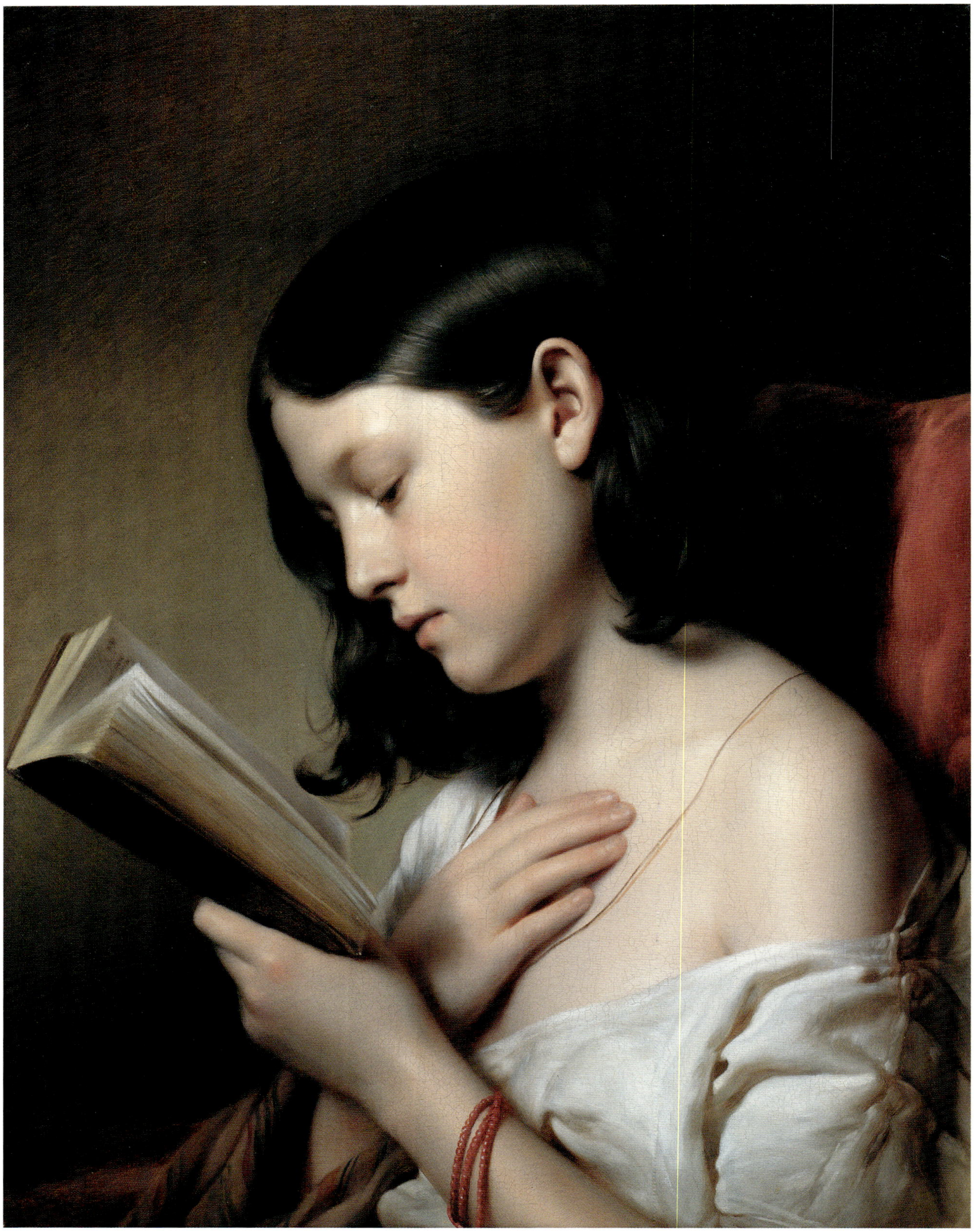

Franz Eybl
Girl Reading, 1850
Oil on canvas, 53 × 41 cm
Signed (lower left): F. EIBL. / 1850.
Belvedere, Vienna, inv. no. 7333

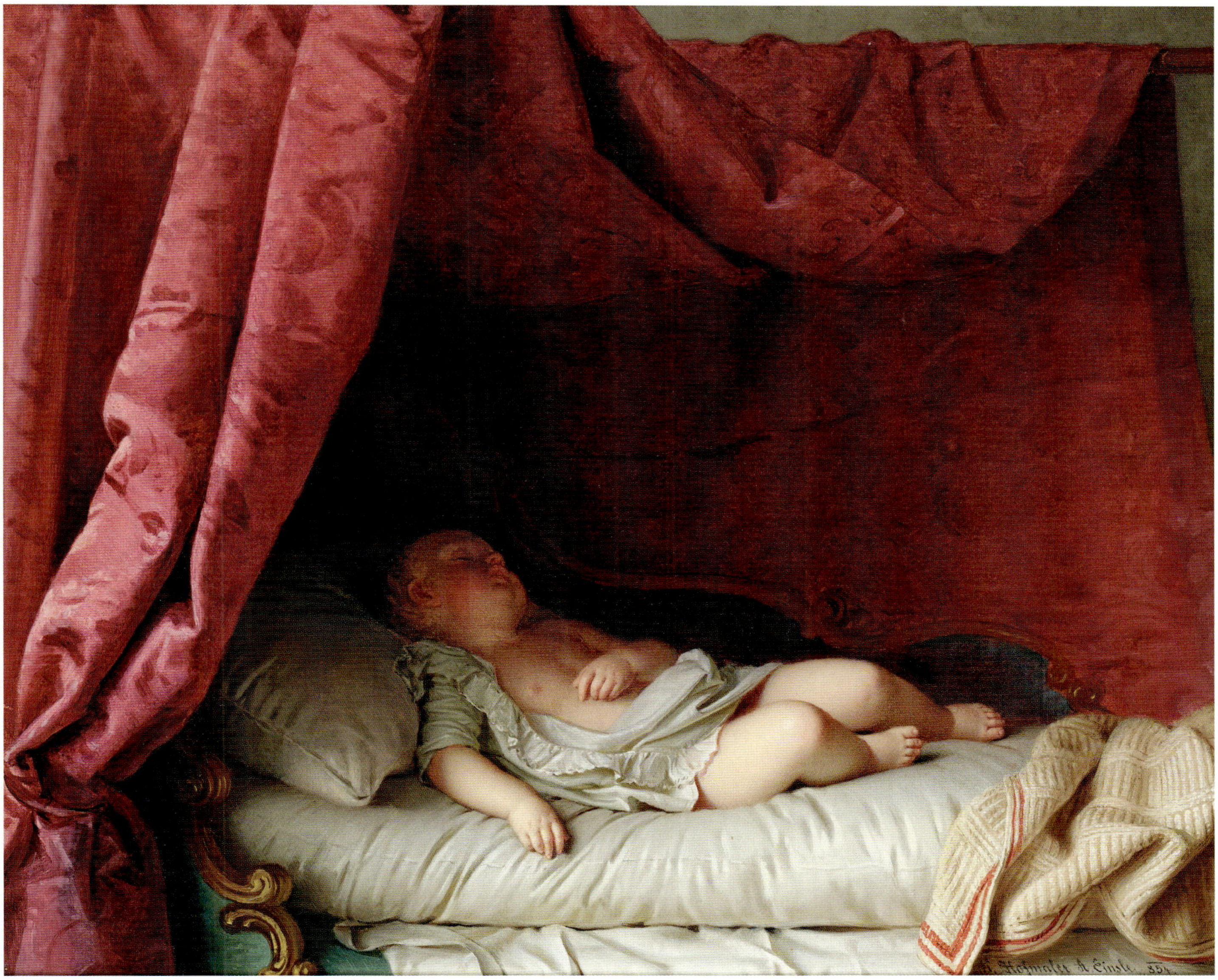

Anton Einsle
Sleeping Child, 1854
Oil on canvas, 43 × 53 cm
Signed (lower right): K. Hofmaler A. Einsle 854
Boris Wilnitsky Fine Arts Vienna

Sándor Kozina
The Pejacsevich Children (*Julian, Agneza, and Gabriel Pejacsevich*), 1848
Oil on canvas, 104 × 82 cm
Signed (lower left): AKozina 1848.
Gábor Kovács Art Collection, Budapest

The Hungarian artist Sándor Kozina studied history painting at the Imperial Academy in Vienna for two years, from 1827 to 1829, under Johann Peter Krafft (1780–1856), Anton Petter (1781–1858), and Leopold Kupelwieser (1796–1862). This was followed by a scholarship that funded a long period in Italy, predominantly in Venice, Florence, and Rome, where the artist copied the Old Masters and did studies from nature. Back in Hungary in 1835, he first concentrated on portraits, working in Budapest and Upper Hungary. In 1841 he was called to Russia, where he secured a vast number of commissions, especially in Odessa and St. Petersburg, returning to Hungary in 1844 a wealthy man. Word soon got round about his now polished skills in capturing and characterizing people's faces, leading to many further portrait commissions and opening the doors to some of the finest houses in the country. This portrait of the three children from the Pejacsevich family, a commission he was given at the end of the 1840s, shows the painter at the height of his career. In all likelihood the portrait was commissioned by the sitters' father, Count Ferdinand Pejacsevich de Verőcze (1800–1878), the head of the Našice branch of the family.[69] The painter has adeptly positioned the three figures so their heads meet at the center and, in direct juxtaposition, form a triangle. While the two boys Julian (1833–1906) and Gabriel (1839–1907) look out of the picture, Agneza (born 1838) is sitting in three-quarter profile on a garden bench made of bent branches, highly fashionable at the time. This unusual composition has an appealing effect on account of the artist's skilled drawing and fluid brushwork. The varied nuances of the pink and brown shades in the children's garments reflect great technical skill; their colors are tastefully attuned to the surrounding trees and shrubs and even permeate the clouds in the background.

Júlia Szabó, *Painting in Nineteenth Century Hungary* (Békécsaba, 1988), p. 162; *Saur/De Gruyter Allgemeines Künstler-lexikon: Die bildenden Künstler aller Zeiten und Völker*, vol. 81 (Munich etc., 2014), pp. 429–30 (Nóra Veszprémi).

SG

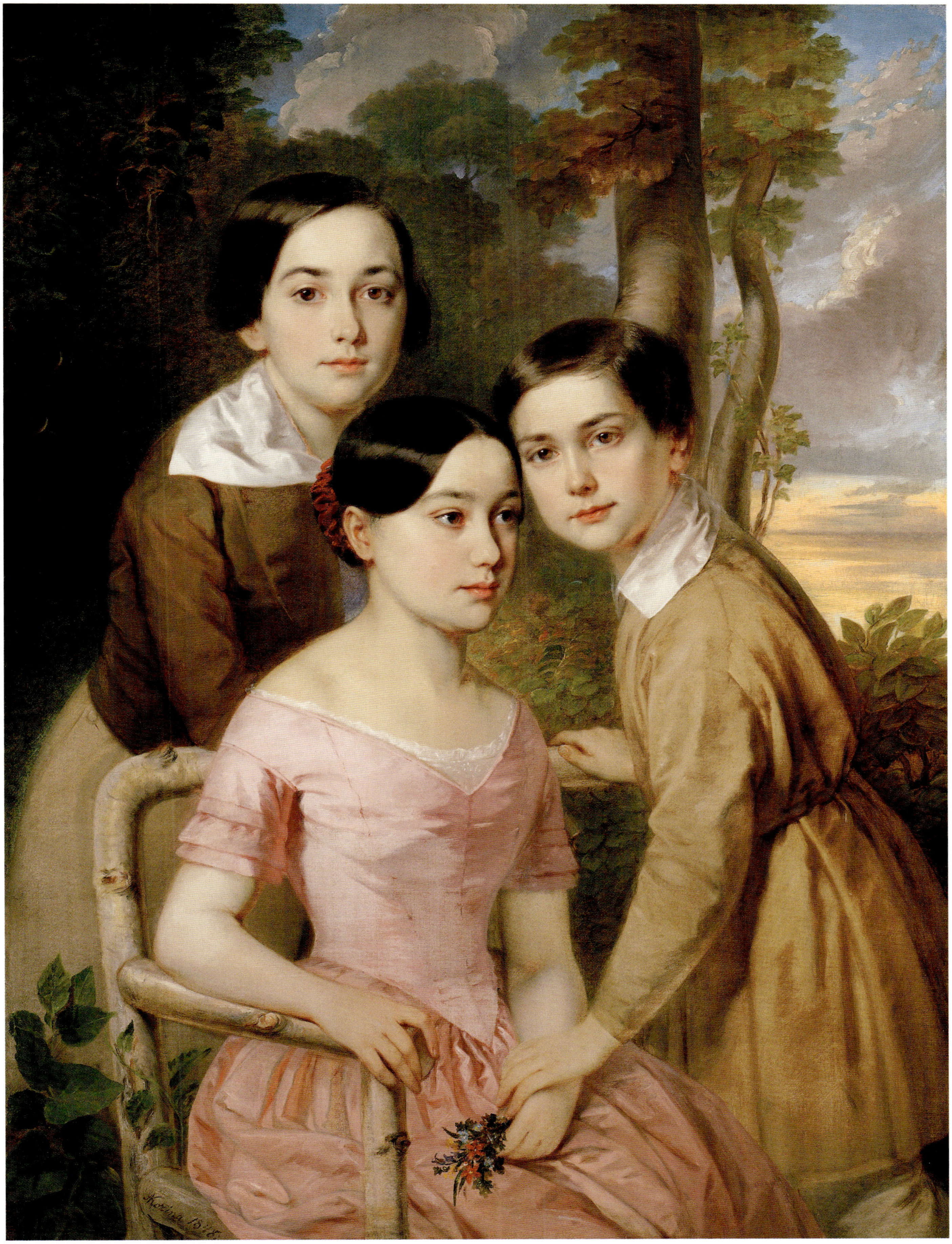

Johann Mathias Ranftl
The Kill, 1851
Oil on wood, 127 × 94 cm
Signed (lower right): Ranftl 1851
Belvedere, Vienna, inv. no. 3235

The depiction of the hunters, especially the one slumbering on the steps, inevitably recalls the novels of Sir Walter Scott (1771–1832), which enjoyed great popularity throughout Europe at the time. The precious accessories scattered throughout the picture also confirm this association and are further examples of the Viennese admiration for England, which came to the fore from the 1820s onwards and was reflected in the adoption of its technical achievements and an enthusiastic imitation of the British lifestyle. In Ranftl's case, this predilection was the result of a three-month stay in London in 1838 at the invitation of the Austrian ambassador Prince Paul Esterházy, during which he was able to discover British art. He also studied the work of his contemporaries John Constable (1776–1837), William Turner (1775–1851), and above all Edwin Landseer (1802–1873), whose pictures of dogs and hunting scenes were very popular in the British capital at the time. Like him, Ranftl had developed a fondness for dogs, which he liked to incorporate in genre scenes or make the main subject of his narrative pictures. He had already demonstrated his skill in this regard in the early 1830s, long before his visit to England, earning him the nickname "Dog Raphael" and spreading his fame. Over the years he perfected his portrayals of the appearance and behavior of various dog breeds. This was to serve him well in his work as an illustrator, in particular of Eduard von Bauernfeld's *Die Republik der Tiere* in 1848, a satire on the revolution of that year played out by animals.[70]

This picture here is also dominated by dogs, even if the main theme is the kill itself, which is artfully arranged in the foreground and decoratively supplemented by colorful accessories, including the demurely perched falcon. It is not known whether the painting was a commission for a hunting still life, although the large format suggests that this may well have been the case. At all events, the location is a product of the artist's imagination, and the sculptures are mere decorative props that are also to be found in other compositions.

L. A. Frankl, "Mathias Johann Ranftl: Biographische Skizze," in *Neue Freie Presse*, morning edition, no. 1758, July 21, 1869, n.p.; Leo Grünstein, "Johann Matthias Ranftl," in *Neue Freie Presse*, evening edition, no. 14547, February 21, 1905, pp. 3–4; Almut Krapf, "Johann Matthias Ranftl als Illustrator von Eduard v. Bauernfelds Revolutions-Satire, 'Die Republik der Thiere,'" in *Wissenschaftliche Zeitschrift der Ernst-Moritz-Arndt-Universität Greifswald*, vol. 34, no. 1–2 (1985), pp. 59–64.

SG

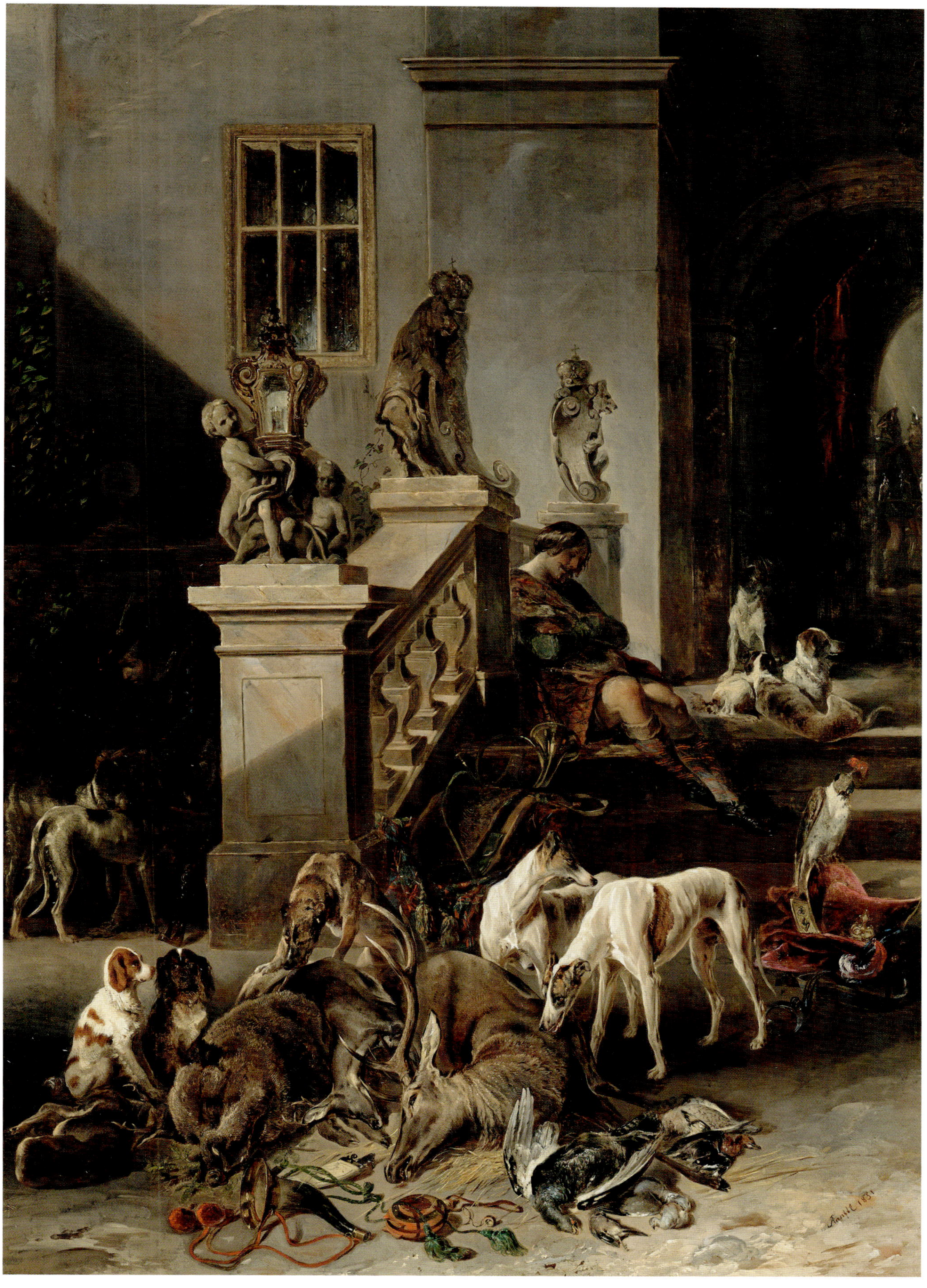

Franz Schrotzberg
Counts Zeno Vinzenz and Leopold von Goëss, 1852
Oil on canvas, 146.5 × 120 cm
Signed (lower left): Schrotzberg 1852.
Private collection, Ebenthal Castle

Schrotzberg, who studied history painting from 1825 at the Imperial Academy in Vienna under Johann Peter Krafft (1780–1856), soon realized that he had more interest and talent in portraiture than in narrative painting. On study trips to Italy (1837, 1843, 1847), Germany and Belgium (1842), Paris and London (1843) he perfected his artistic skills. His works reveal his knowledge not only of the great portraitists from the past, but also of his contemporaries. In his depiction of people he shows strong similarities with Friedrich von Amerling, Vienna's leading portraitist of the time, as well as with Josef Stieler (1781–1858), then working in Munich, and Franz Xaver Winterhalter (1805–1873), a leading portraitist in western Europe and England. Despite the fact that Schrotzberg's works reveal great technical and composition skill, they rarely attain the standards of the artists he so emulated.

One example is his portrait of the two young Goëss counts. In the artist's register of paintings we read: "Zwey Knaben der Gräfin Goess Welsersheim [sic]" ("Countess Goess Welsersheim's [sic] two boys"). The work was therefore commissioned by Countess Maria Johanna Goëss, née Countess von Welsersheimb and depicts her two sons, who would later become important politicians. The older boy, Count Zeno Vinzenz von Goëss (1846–1911), was governor of Carinthia from 1897 to 1909, while the younger, Count Leopold von Goëss (1848–1922), was governor of Trieste and the Austrian Littoral from 1897 to 1904. Schrotzberg placed both figures in the midst of nature and in the background he added Schloss Gradisch, an estate of the Goëss family near Feldkirchen in Carinthia.

The artist's register also reveals that he was paid the handsome sum of 1,200 guilders for this painting. This high price can be explained by the portrait's size and the full-figure depictions, a style of portraiture rarely encountered in Schrotzberg's art. The register also records that this picture was his 446th work. In this list of works, today in the manuscript collection of the Vienna City Library, the artist recorded every completed painting, from the start of his career until 1884, five years before he died. He noted the sum he was paid and occasionally the name of the patron as well. This list reveals that, from the mid-1840s at least, Schrotzberg earned a very good income from his portraits. It also shows that his portraiture was very much in vogue as, from that point on, his register reads like a "Who's Who" of Austrian high society. Starting at the top with the Imperial family, it features almost every important family name in the Habsburg Empire.

Franz Schrotzberg, "Verzeichnis der Einnahmen 1828–1846," Wienbibliothek im Rathaus, manuscript collection, inv. no. 58497/1; Gabriele Pröll, "Franz Schrotzberg: 1811–1889," unpublished PhD diss., Vienna, 1991.

SG

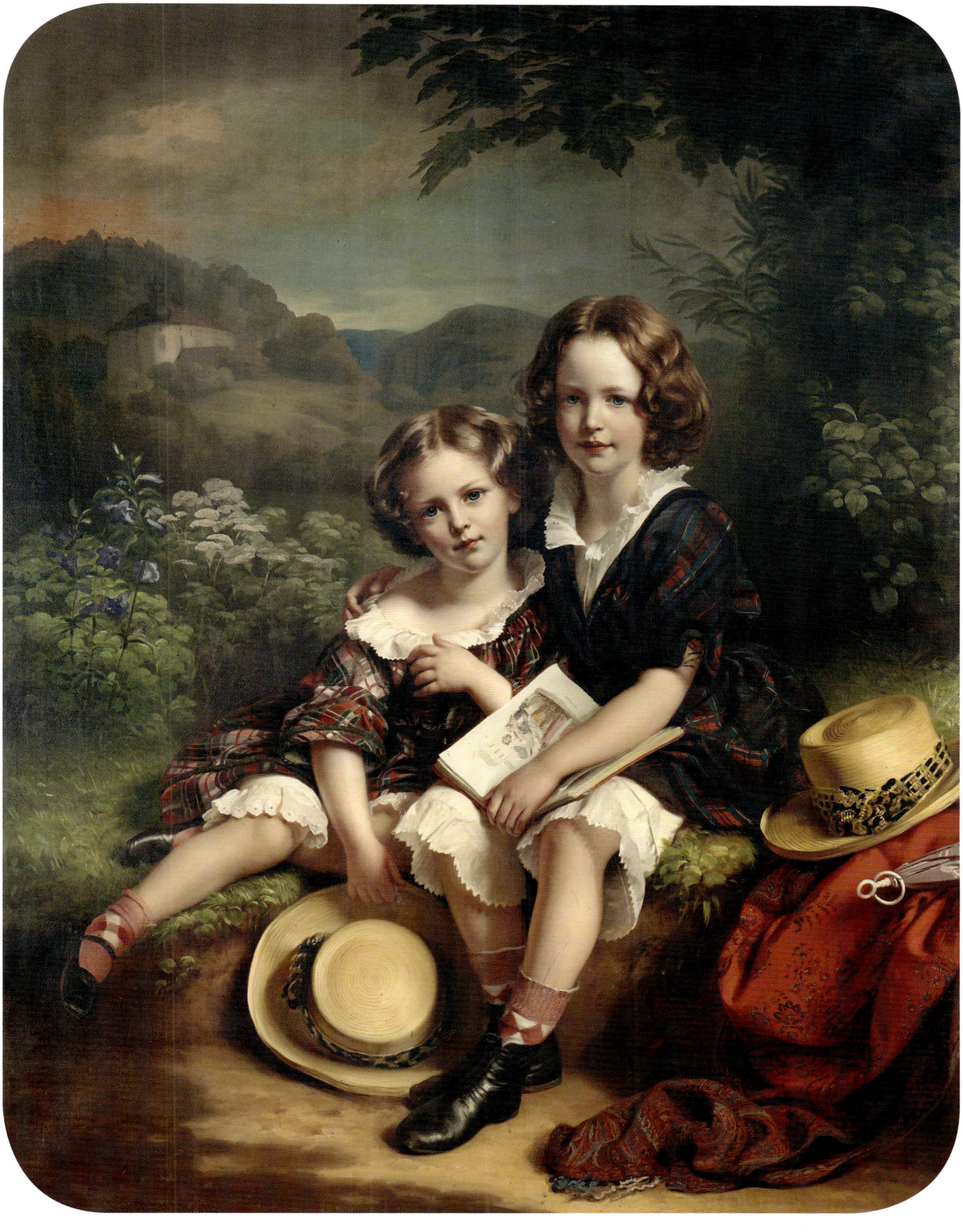

József Borsos
The Widow, 1853
Oil on canvas, 98.5 × 83 cm
Signed (lower right): Borsos József 1853
Museum of Fine Arts - Hungarian National Gallery, Budapest, inv. no. 4622

József Borsos
After the Battle, 1854
Oil on canvas, 131 × 106 cm
Signed (lower left): Borsos Jozsef / 854
Neue Galerie am Universalmuseum Joanneum, Graz, inv. no. I/339

These two pictures, painted one year apart, present the greatest mystery in Borsos's work, as neither image is self-explanatory, giving rise to a variety of interpretations. *The Widow* was obviously the wife of an officer, as the coat, hat, and sword of her deceased husband can be seen on the table behind her. The woman's resigned pose suggests that her husband did not die of natural causes but in the line of duty. For a long time, Hungarian art historians have proposed that the depiction concerns the Revolution of 1848/49 and that the soldier fell fighting for his Hungarian fatherland.[71] Eszter Békefi disproved this theory by noting that Borsos did not sympathize with any nationalist group and pointing out that the officer's uniform is from an Imperial regiment.[72] Furthermore, when he painted this, the artist was living in Vienna, where he moved in affluent bourgeois circles and his portraiture and genre scenes were much in demand among the Austrian nobility. The Neuer Österreichischer Kunstverein (New Austrian Art Association) was also interested in Borsos's work. It bought *The Widow* for four hundred guilders in the year it was painted. In the following year, for the same sum, it purchased the other painting featured here, *After the Battle*.[73]

The two soldiers in historical garb are even more mysterious than *The Widow*, as the significance of these two men standing next to each other and filling the picture is entirely unclear. There is also no indication as to why the background represents a battlefield after the fray with corpses strewn on the ground and riderless horses. Nóra Veszprémi suggests that the painting may have been inspired by the popular swashbuckler novels by authors such as Alexandre Dumas.[74] Nevertheless, the picture's message remains mysterious. It could be an allegory of war. Possibly the warriors' ages are symbolic, as the old soldier, looking dazed and with a frozen expression, is in complete contrast to the dreamy-looking youth, possibly envisioning fame as a war hero.

Constant von Wurzbach, *Biographisches Lexikon des Kaisertums Österreich*, vol. 2 (Vienna, 1857), pp. 78–79; *Saur/De Gruyter Allgemeines Künstlerlexikon: Die bildenden Künstler aller Zeiten und Völker*, vol. 13 (Munich etc., 1996), p. 127 (Katalin Sz. Kürti); Jane Turner, ed., *The Dictionary of Art*, vol. 4 (London, 1996), p. 438 (Katalin Gellér); *Borsos József: Festő és fotográfus (1821–1883)/József Borsos: Painter and Photographer (1821–1883)*, exh. cat. Hungarian National Gallery, Budapest (Budapest, 2009), pp. 146–50, with further literature.

SG

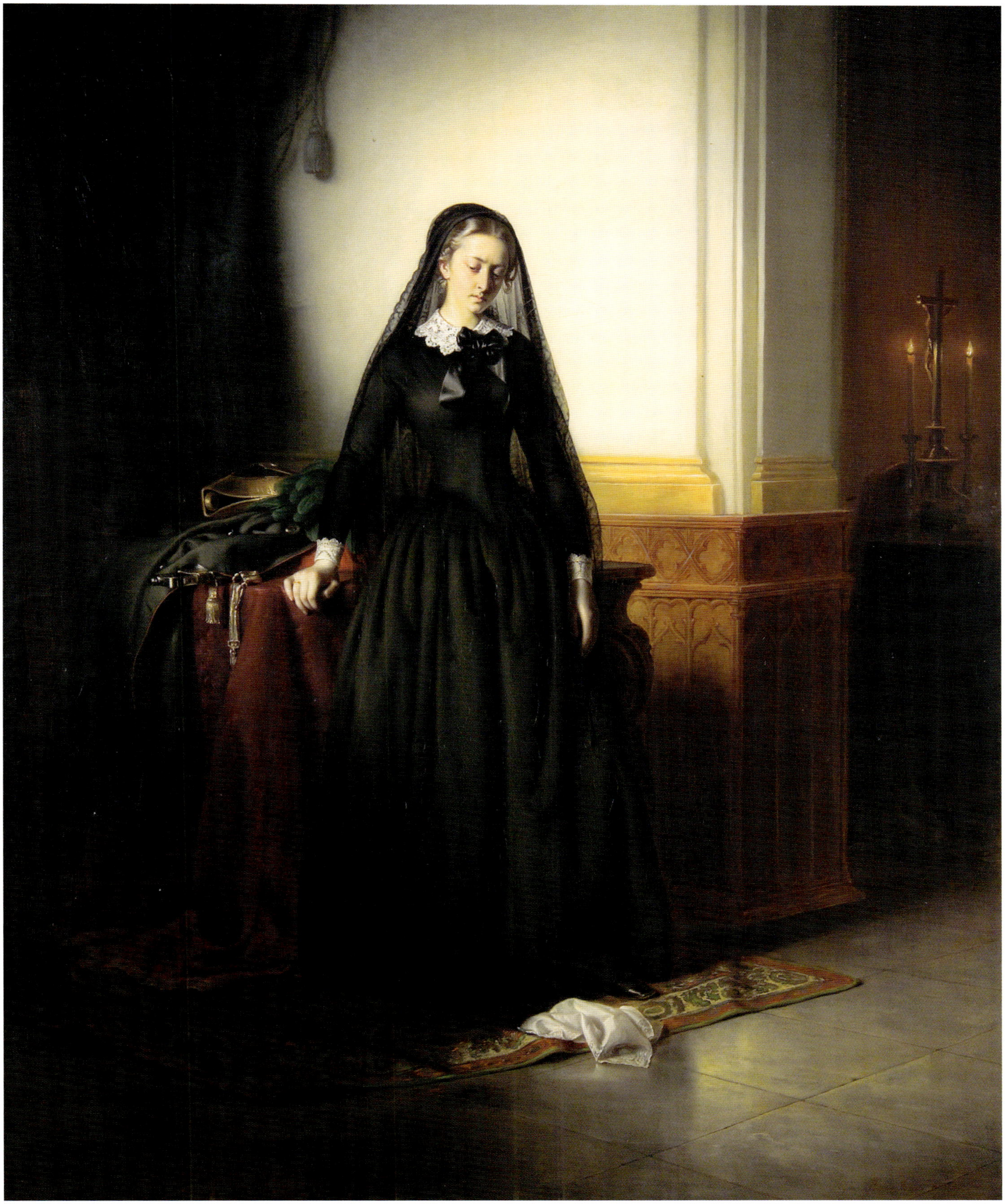

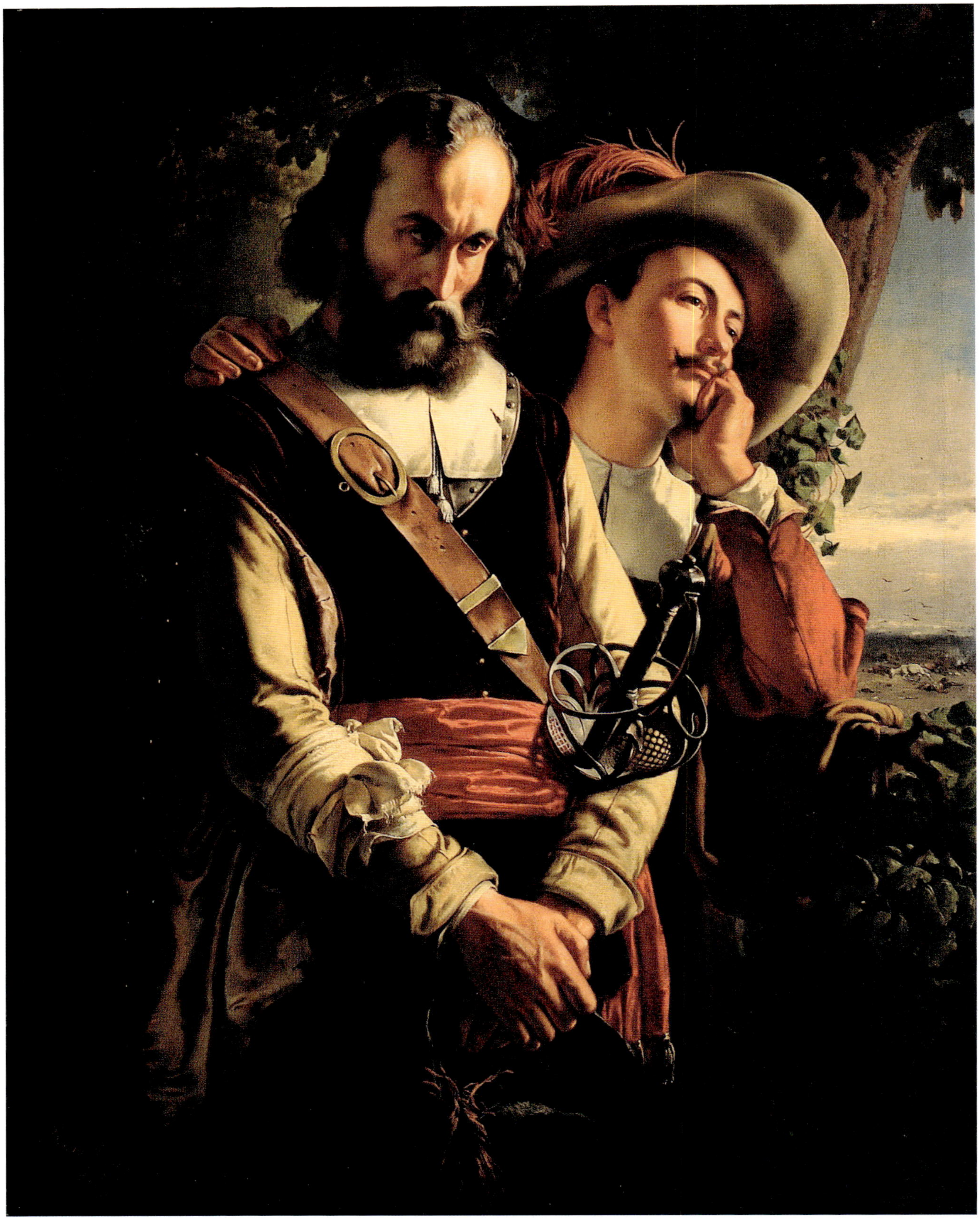

József Borsos
After the Battle, 1854

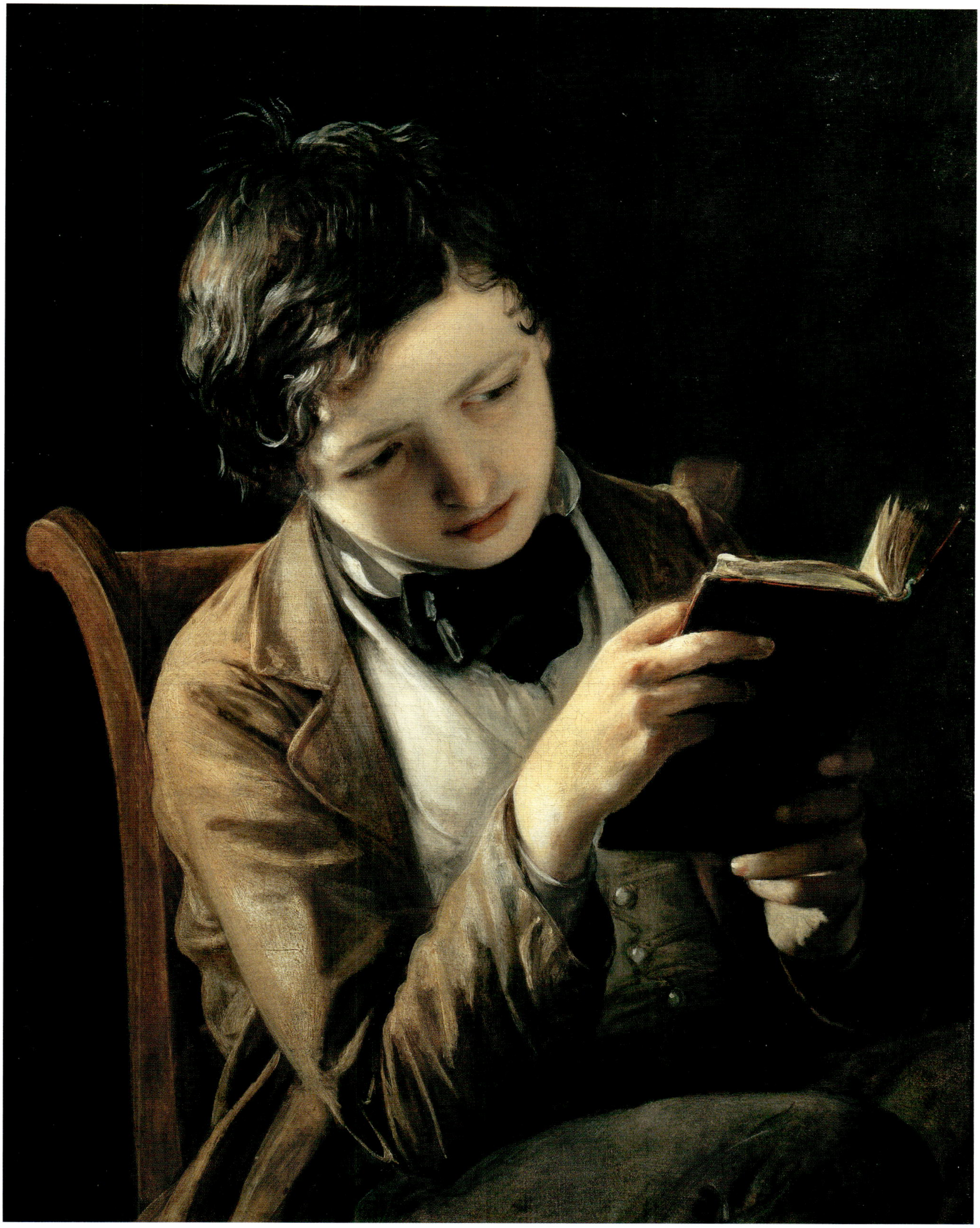

Johann Baptist Reiter
Boy Reading, c. 1860
Oil on canvas, 59.5 × 48 cm
Signed (on the left at the side): J. B. Reiter
Belvedere, Vienna, inv. no. 4029

Pavel Künl
Marija Giontini, 1847
Oil on canvas, 90 × 74 cm
Signed (lower left): P. KÜNL. / 1847
National Gallery of Slovenia, Ljubljana, inv. no. S 170

Pavel Künl
Portrait of a Child, 1857
Oil on canvas, 64 × 49 cm
Signed verso: PAUL KÜNL PINXIT / 1857
National Gallery of Slovenia, Ljubljana, inv. no. S 168

Künl was twenty-six years old when he started studying landscape and history painting at the Imperial Academy in Vienna under Franz Steinfeld (1787–1868), Josef von Führich (1800–1876), and Leopold Kupelwieser (1796–1862). Prior to this, he had attended the cadet-corps school in Ljubljana and taught himself to draw and paint. Although, in 1841, he found a position as a drawing teacher in his home town, he soon decided to devote himself entirely to art and to train as an artist. Despite spending only about a year and a half at the Vienna Academy, it seems that during this time the artist was able to thoroughly acquaint himself with the art world and study the work of his contemporaries in great detail.

In art literature he is often compared to Waldmüller[75] but, in fact, the depiction of *Marija Giontini* is highly unique and is quite unlike anything else in this period. This does not refer to the woman's posture, which, with her slightly stooped shoulders and hands in her lap, can be found throughout European painting in the nineteenth century, but the rendering of her face, its melancholy and introspective expression infusing the image with searing modernity. This impression is further emphasized by the dark background, which on the left seems to depict a dense forest. The structure of the tree trunks and the light shining from the left recall contemporary depictions by the Pre-Raphaelites in Britain.

Portrait of a Child is also interesting in that the position of the figure in relation to its background seems incongruous. The child's pose and face reflect an awareness of the honor of being portrayed. Yet he seems lost in the lofty space beside a large armchair with a wide backrest, reaching for the seat as if looking for support. Incidentally, Künl's landscapes were also highly individual, toning down or even negating foreshortened perspective, as seen in his views of Ljubljana. In addition to portraits and landscapes, Künl occasionally painted religious subjects and also worked as a restorer. Finally, the chairs in both paintings deserve a mention. The artist must have chosen them very carefully as, at the time when the pictures were painted, these forms were highly modern.

Barbara Jaki, *Meščanska slika: Slikarstvo prve polovice 19. stoletja iz zbirk Narodne galerije*, exh. cat. National Gallery of Slovenia, Ljubljana (Ljubljana, 2000), pp. 130–45; *Saur/De Gruyter Allgemeines Künstlerlexikon: Die bildenden Künstler aller Zeiten und Völker*, vol. 82 (Munich etc., 2014), pp. 200–01 (Gudrun Dauner).

SG

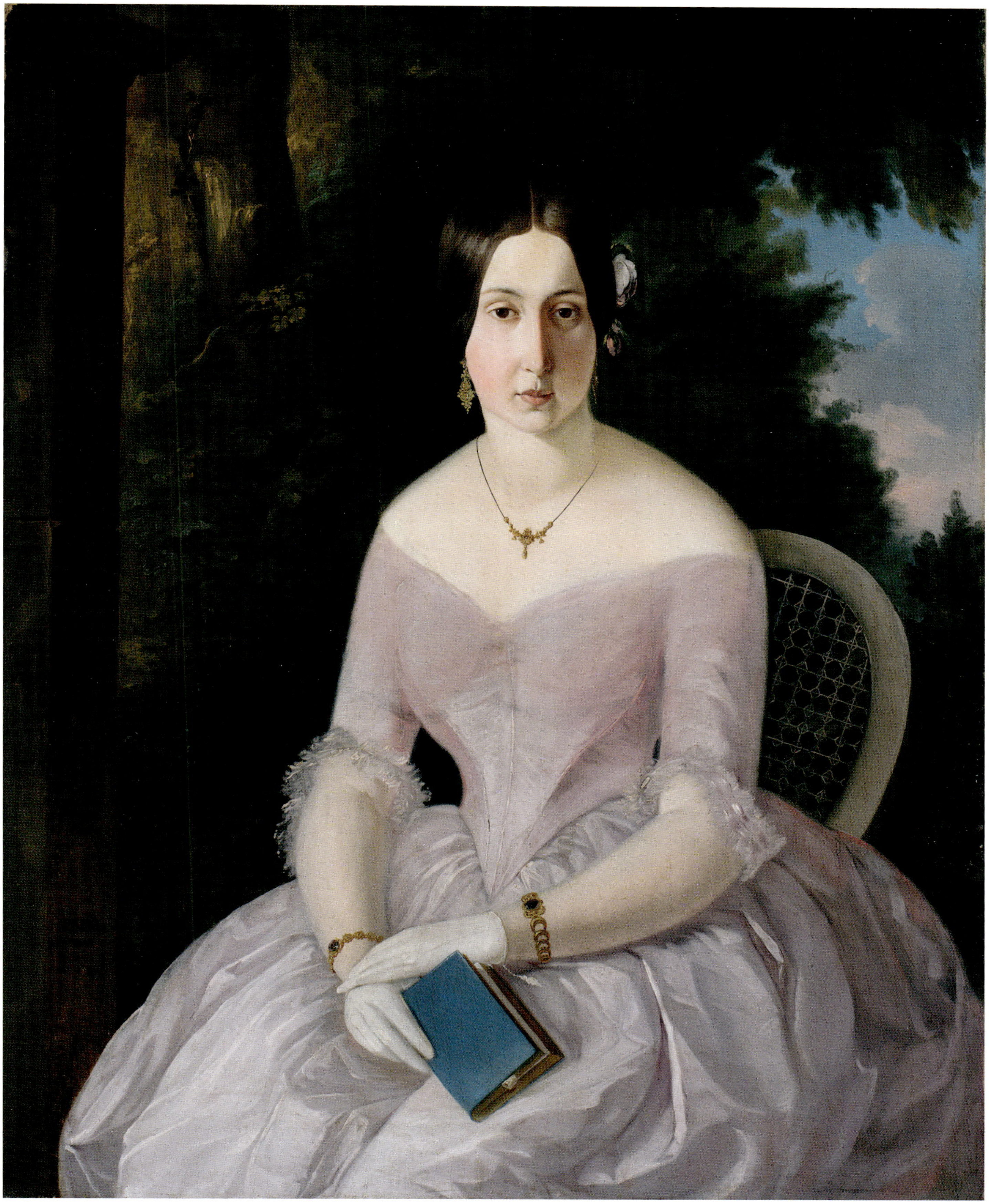

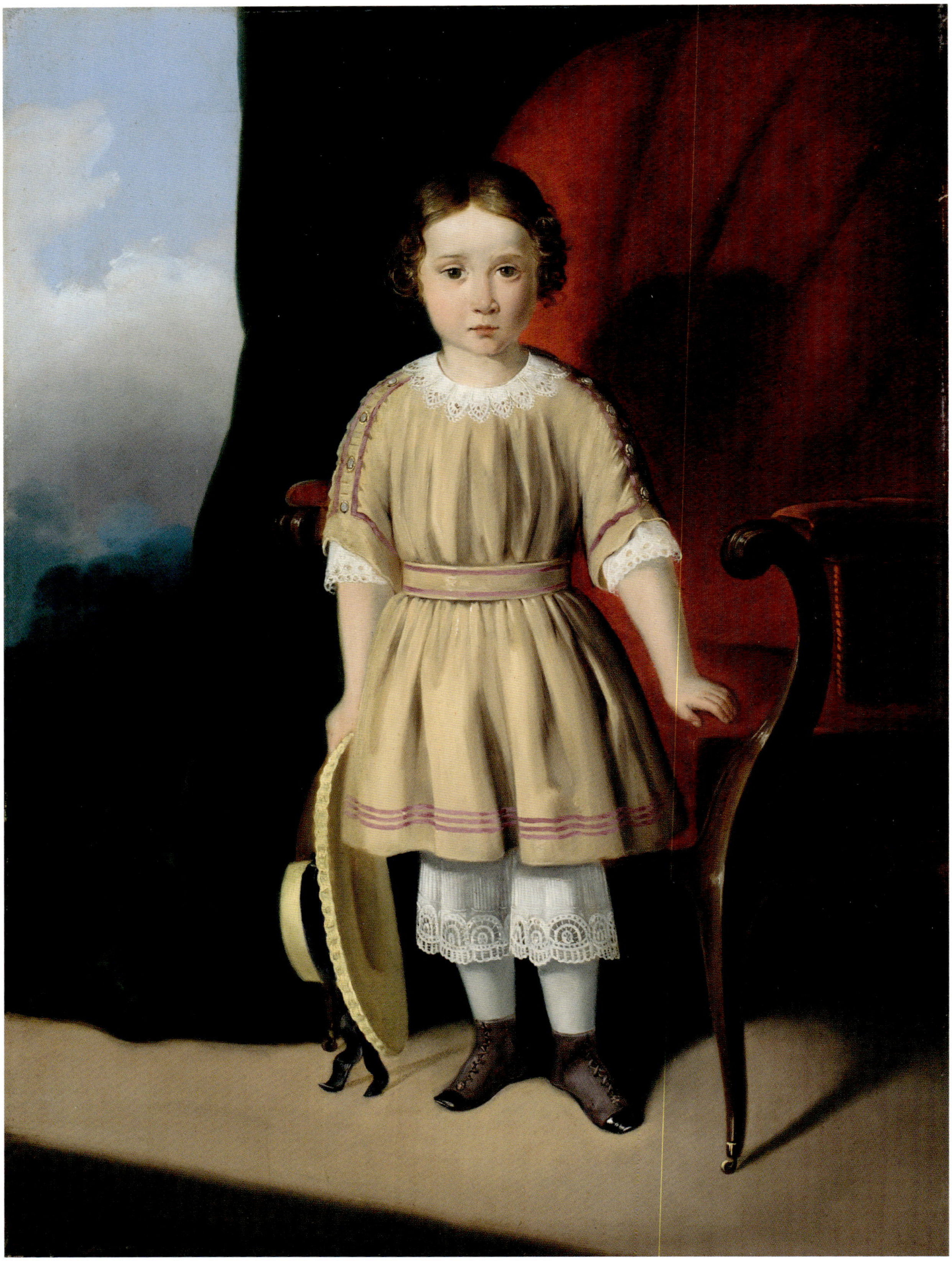

Pavel Künl
Portrait of a Child, 1857

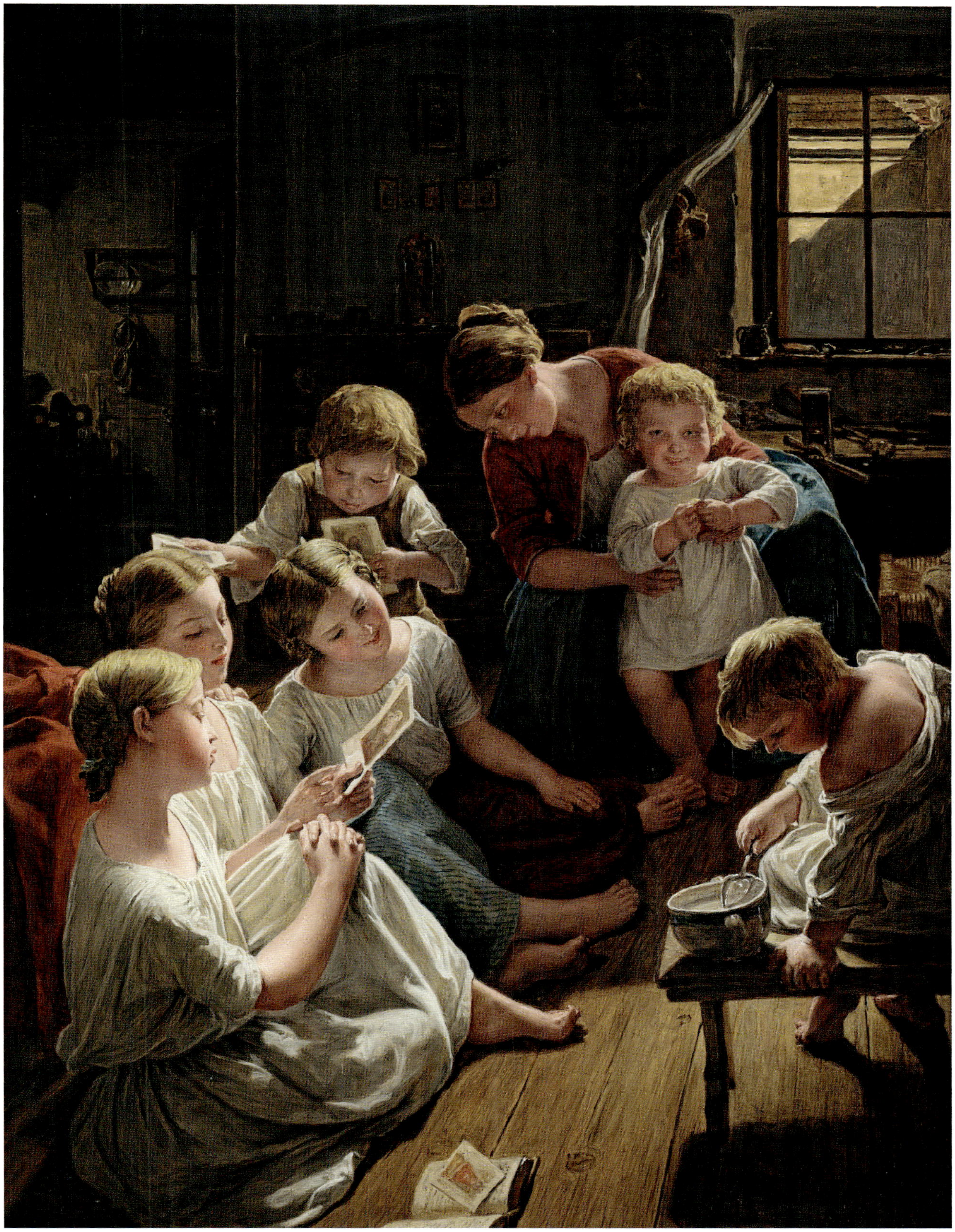

Ferdinand Georg Waldmüller
Children Looking at Pictures in the Morning, 1853
Oil on wood, 55 × 44 cm
Signed (lower right): Waldmüller 1853
KR Hubert Steinleitner

Josef Mánes
Children of the Lawyer Josef Haušild, 1851
Oil on canvas, 97.5 × 114 cm
Unsigned
Národní galerie v Praze/National Gallery, Prague, inv. no. O 9478

Josef Mánes was born into a family of artists. His father Antonín Mánes (1784–1843) was an important landscape painter, while his brother Quido (1828–1880) established genre painting in Bohemian art. Consequently, Josef Mánes's early tuition was from his family. From 1835 to 1844 he studied at the Prague Academy under František Tkadlík (1786–1840), Christian Ruben (1805–1875), and his uncle Vaclav Mánes (1793–1858). This was followed by four years at the Munich Academy. During this time and over the ensuing years he undertook numerous trips, for example to Rome, Hungary, and St. Petersburg. Although already working as an artist at the time, Josef Mánes took his time to decide on a specialism. In fact, this impression still continues into his later career, as his work encompasses landscapes, history paintings, and portraits, as well as illustrations of fairy tales and stories, decorative schemes, designs for monuments, and much more besides. All this made him an extremely interesting personality who was highly esteemed by his contemporaries.

Mánes met the patron of this picture, the legal scholar Josef Haušild, at the Kremsier Imperial Diet in 1848, where he was to portray the Bohemian delegates on behalf of Prague's association of artists (which Mánes had co-founded that same year). The lawyer was evidently very impressed by the artist's abilities and commissioned portraits both of himself and his wife shortly thereafter (both National Gallery, Prague). Šárka Brůhová notes that here the self-confidence of the emerging middle class is very much reflected in the setting and the sitters' attire.[76] Mánes's portrait of the three Haušild children, dating from the same year, reveals a similar approach, their courteous manner in keeping with the bourgeois Biedermeier values that continued to influence society far beyond the middle of the century.

Naděžda Blažíčková-Horová, ed., *Czech 19th-Century Painting: Catalogue of the Permanent Exhibition. Convent of St. Agnes of Bohemia* (Prague, 1998), pp. 90–103 (Šárka Brůhová); *Biedermeier: Art and Culture in Central Europe 1815–1848*, exh. cat. Palazzo della Ragione, Padua (Milan, 2001), p. 237 (Šárka Brůhová); *Saur/De Gruyter Allgemeines Künstlerlexikon: Die bildenden Künstler aller Zeiten und Völker*, vol. 87 (Munich etc., 2015), pp. 10–11 (Annette Wagner-Wilke).

SG

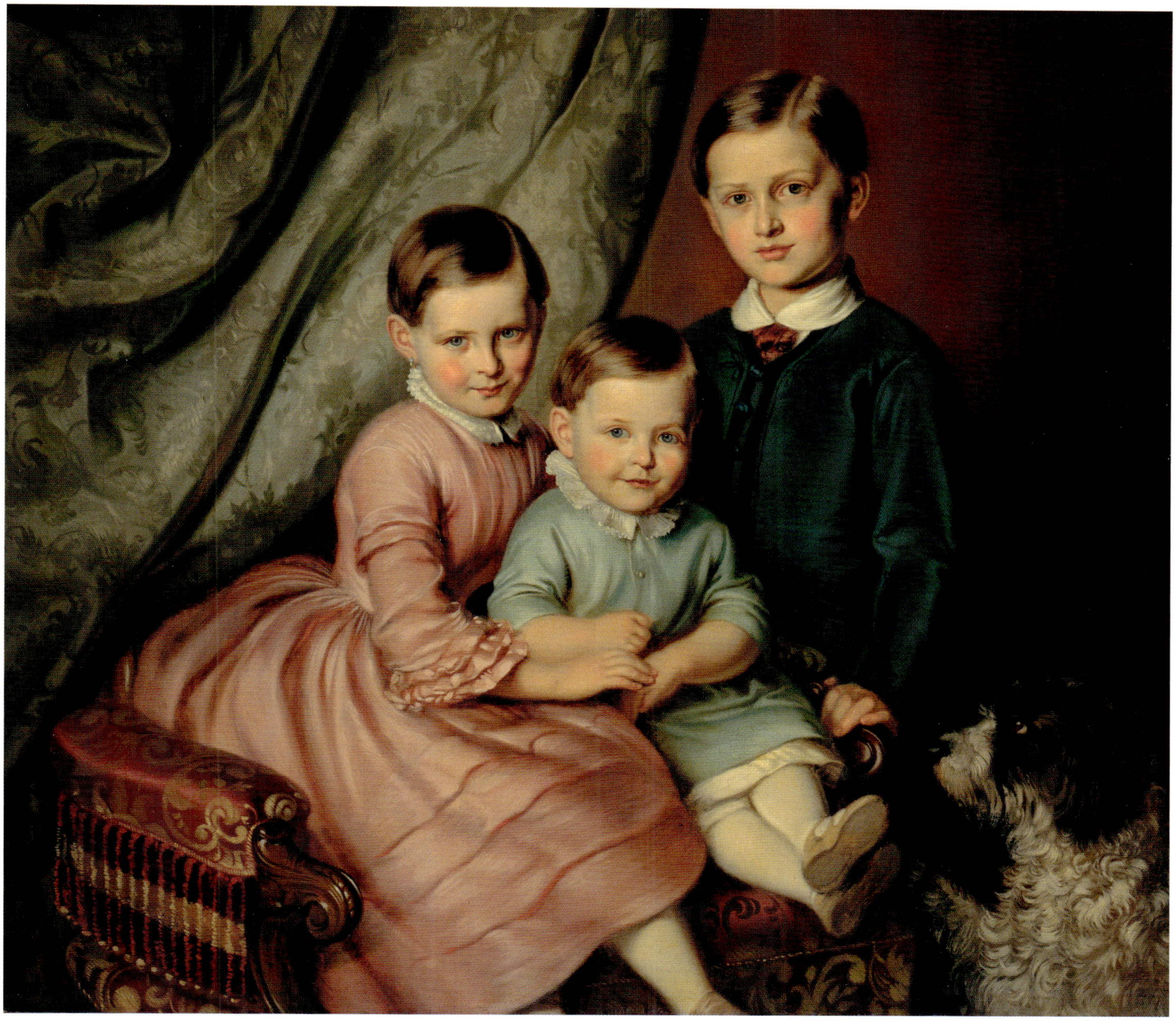

Karl von Blaas

Countess Leonie Lanckorońska, née Countess Potocka, with her Son Karl, 1852
Oil on canvas, 179 × 127 cm
Signed (right at the side): C Blaas 1852
Belvedere, Vienna, inv. no. 5983

Karl von Blaas, from Nauders in Tyrol, began his artistic career in 1832 when he enrolled at the Venice Academy to study history painting with Ludovico Lipparini (1802–1856). From there he successfully applied for a scholarship to Rome from the Vienna Academy, which made it possible for him to spend five years in Italy from 1837.[77] In Rome he associated with the Nazarene circle of artists centered around Friedrich Overbeck (1789–1869), but also befriended the Viennese artist Friedrich von Amerling, as well as Massimo d'Azeglio (1798–1866), who was still working mainly as a painter at the time. Blaas was already a popular portraitist, especially among British tourists, even then. He regarded himself as a history painter, however, as demonstrated by his long period spent working in Italy, particularly in Venice. It was not until 1851 that the artist finally emerged on the Vienna art scene. That year he was appointed director of the General School of Painting at the Imperial Academy. Five years later he returned to Venice to take up the professorship of history painting at the Accademia. Whilst in Italy, he was awarded the commission for the ceiling paintings in the Hall of Fame at the Vienna arsenal (1859–1872). This was to be his magnum opus and he traveled between Venice and Vienna to work on it. Although his absences from the Accademia were covered by "painter and Professor [Pompeo] Molmenti in a most excellent manner,"[78] to simplify life, in 1865 he applied for a professorship at the Vienna Academy. He was appointed to the post in the following year and was permanently resident in Vienna thereafter.

Soon after his first appearance in Vienna, he became one of the most famous portraitists in the imperial city: "My studio in Annagasse was packed with visiting gentlemen and ladies every Thursday from 1 till 4, the hours I had allocated for consultation, and each time I was given new commissions," he noted in his autobiography.[79] One of his most important patrons was Count Kasimir Lanckoroński, who wanted a portrait of his wife Leonie with their older son Karl. There is no evidence as to whether this was painted in the Lanckoroński's apartment on Schenkenstrasse (no. 10, then called Hintere Schenkenstrasse no. 51) or at the painter's studio. We can, however, assume that Blaas had the usual portraitist's paraphernalia to create an elegant and well-designed ambiance in his own studio, too. The monumental column in the background both contributes to the composition and emphasizes the importance of the sitters. The patron was of Polish descent and from one of the wealthiest families in the Habsburg Empire at the time. Interestingly, the boy in the portrait, then only just four, later became the art connoisseur Count Karl Lanckoroński (1848–1933), who, from 1894, amassed an important art collection with works from the Italian Renaissance and Dutch Baroque, which he housed at his Neobaroque palace near the Upper Belvedere.[80] He was also interested in contemporary art, associated with art historians like Max Dvořák, supported painters and sculptors, including Hans Makart, Arnold Böcklin, Auguste Rodin, and Ludwig Hans Fischer, inviting one or the other to accompany him on his long expeditions, and was active in the conservation of monuments and art.

Karl Blaas, *Selbstbiographie des Malers Karl Blaas: 1815–187* (Vienna, 1876); *Neue Freie Presse*, Morgenblatt, no. 10622, March 20, 1894, p. 5; Johannes Max, "Karl von Blaas: Sein Leben und seine Werke," *Allgemeine Kunst-Chronik: Illustrierte Zeitschrift für Kunst, Kunstgewerbe, Musik, Theater und Litteratur*, yr. 18, vol. 10/11 (1894), pp. 289–98; Barbara Wild, comp., *Carl von Blaas: 1815–1894*, exh. cat. Österreichische Galerie Belvedere, Vienna (Vienna, 1985).

SG

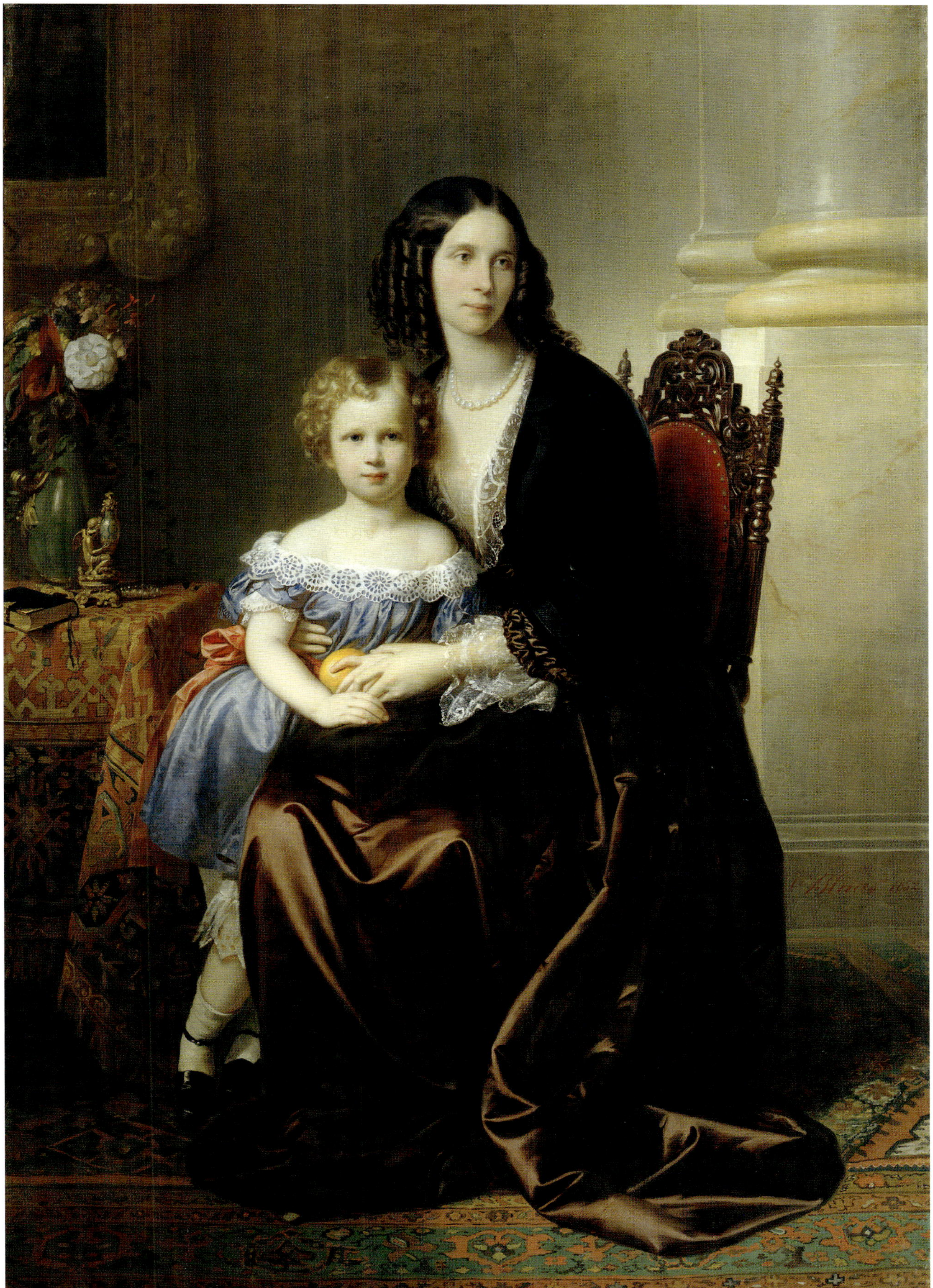

Ferdinand Georg Waldmüller
Exhausted Strength, 1854
Oil on canvas, 64 × 75 cm
Signed (lower right): Waldmüller / 1854
Belvedere, Vienna, inv. no. 3656

From the 1840s, Waldmüller concentrated increasingly on genre painting. His subjects were taken from the rural milieu, farmers and cottagers on the outskirts of Vienna, in the Vienna Woods, or the Salzkammergut. The content focuses less on the hard work and living conditions in the country and more on life itself, particularly contrasting the different generations. His favorite motifs were children, women, and old people. Most of these pictures show the happier side of life, but he also used genre painting to draw attention to the hardship of farm girls and builders or the wretched situation of families made destitute by the death of the head of the household. Titles like *The Bailout* (1859, Staatsgalerie, Stuttgart), *Evicted* (1859, Staatliche Kunstsammlungen, Dresden, Gemäldegalerie Neue Meister), *Repossession* (1847), or *Day Laborers Receiving Their Breakfast* (1859/60, both Wien Museum) may be mentioned in this context. He also depicted good deeds and charity, be it by individuals (*Compassion*, 1863, Von der Heydt-Museum, Wuppertal) or through a Christian welfare organization, as in *The Soup Kitchen* (1858) or *Children of Poor Parents Receiving Winter Clothes in Spittelberg on St. Michael's Day* (1857, both Belvedere, Vienna).

Exhausted Strength is possibly the most striking example from this group. It vividly portrays the despondency and misery, where every glimmer of hope seems to be immediately stifled. Waldmüller increases this impression through the confusing lighting: The glow of the lamp directs attention initially on the child sleeping innocently in his bed. It is only then that the meaning of the picture's title is explained, with the woman lying almost imperceptibly on the floor in the foreground, dead tired and motionless. Here the artist depicts the dire situation that single mothers would often find themselves in. None of his other pictures portray reality with such unmitigated directness. Its uncompromising statement also makes it unique, not only in Austrian painting.

Klaus Albrecht Schröder, *Ferdinand Georg Waldmüller*, exh. cat. Kunstforum Länderbank, Vienna (Munich, 1990), pp. 39–43; Rupert Feuchtmüller, *Ferdinand Georg Waldmüller, 1793–1865: Leben, Schriften, Werke* (Vienna/Munich, 1996), cat. rais. no. 884; Sabine Grabner, "Bilder aus dem Leben: Die Genremalerei bei Ferdinand Georg Waldmüller," in ibid./Agnes Husslein-Arco, eds., *Ferdinand Georg Waldmüller 1793–1865*, exh. cat. Belvedere, Vienna/Musée du Louvre, Paris (Vienna, 2009), pp. 133–46, especially pp. 138–39.

SG

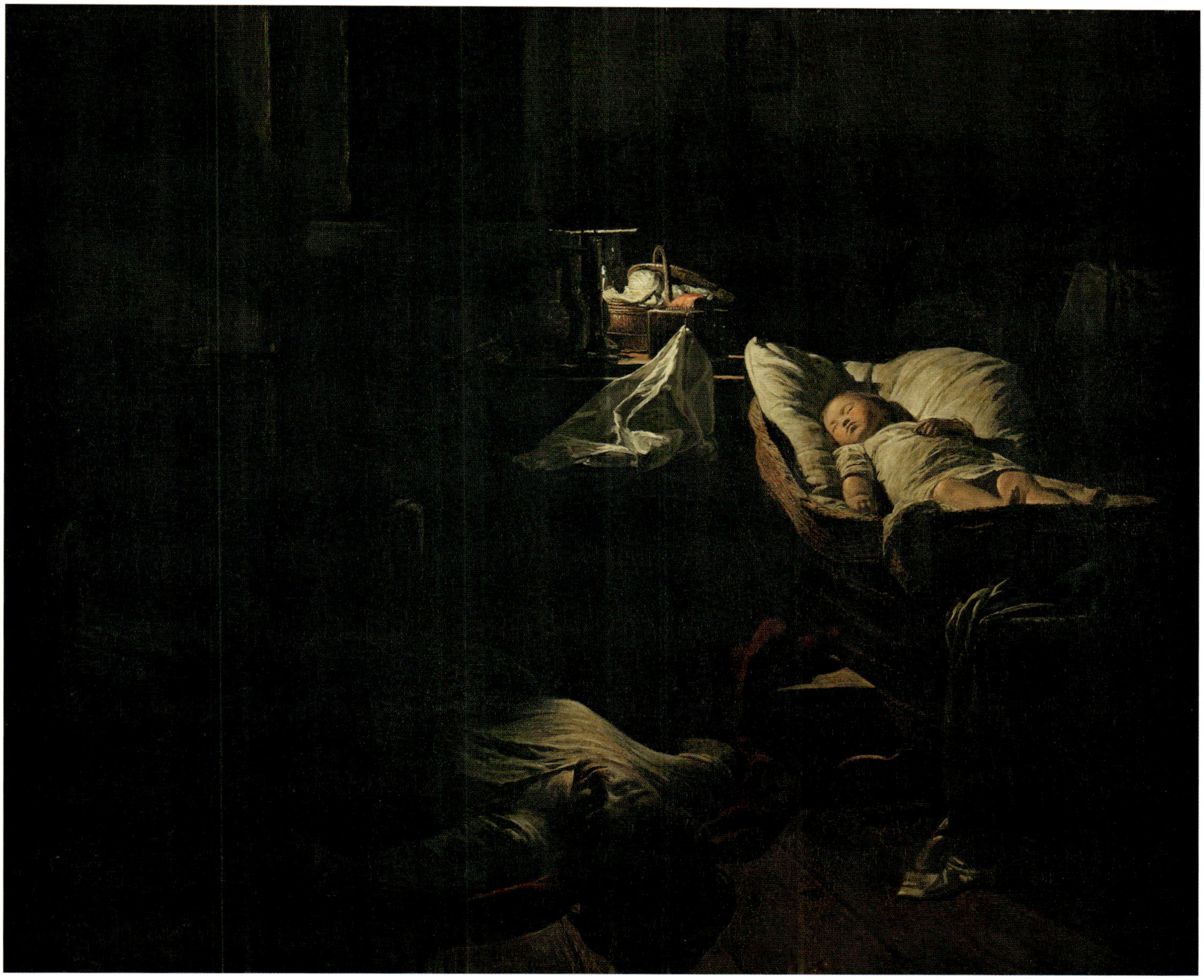

Ferdinand Mallitsch
The Foundling, c. 1851/52
Oil on canvas, 74 × 92.5 cm
Unsigned
Belvedere, Vienna, inv. no. 2186

Ferdinand Mallitsch's life was centered around Graz and the region of the Slovene Hills, where he managed the farm left to him by his mother. Before being obliged to take on this role he had wanted to pursue an artistic career. He even abandoned his studies in philosophy and law at the University of Graz in order to concentrate on drawing. Mallitsch's initial training in this field was at the drawing academy in Graz under Ernst Christian Moser and Joseph Tunner (1792–1877). Later, in 1842, he transferred to the Imperial Academy in Vienna, where the teachers included Anton Petter (1781–1858), Johann Nepomuk Ender, and Leopold Kupelwieser (1796–1862). However, he felt a greater affinity with Ferdinand Georg Waldmüller, who at the time was first custodian of the Academy Picture Gallery, while also offering private tuition to many students. Waldmüller had developed a special style of teaching whereby he only suggested improvements verbally, as he was convinced that a student's development could be guided only by his own insights, and any corrections undertaken by the master would lead his pupil down the wrong path and stymie his individuality.[81] Mallitsch was Waldmüller's student for many years. His training was interrupted by the Revolution of 1848, which occurred while Mallitsch was in Graz, and he did not return to his teacher until 1851. Immediately after his return, he painted this crowded scene entitled *The Foundling*. It shows the moment when the infant is welcomed into the family, as reflected by the loving attention of the farmer's wife and the amicable poses and gestures of the two men at the center. The picture's composition, design of the figures, and the cohesion of the group created through their gazes and hand movements clearly reflect Waldmüller's influence. Mallitsch, like Waldmüller, focused mainly on the lives of peasants in his genre pictures. It was only later that he started to explore landscape painting, possibly inspired by the months he spent in Paris in 1854. The majority of his works are in the collections of the Neue Galerie at the Universalmuseum Joanneum in Graz. This particular painting was exhibited in spring 1852 at the Österreichischer Kunstverein (Austrian Art Association) and acquired for the Imperial Picture Gallery.

Constant von Wurzbach, *Biographisches Lexikon des Kaisertums Österreich*, vol. 16 (Vienna, 1867), p. 335; Trude Aldrian, "Ferdinand Mallitsch," *Carinthia I: Mitteilungen des Geschichtsvereins für Kärnten*, yr. 146 (Klagenfurt 1956), pp. 712–44; Herta Farnberger, "Leben und Werk des steirischen Künstlers Ferdinand Mallitsch: 1820–1900," unpublished PhD diss., Graz 1995; Gudrun Danzer, "Ferdinand Mallitsch, Der Findling," in *Zur Natur des Menschen: Genremalerei des 19. und frühen 20. Jahrhunderts. Aus der Sammlung der neuen Galerie*, ed. Gudrun Danzer/Peter Peer/Christa Steinle (Weitra, 2006), pp. 66–67.

SG

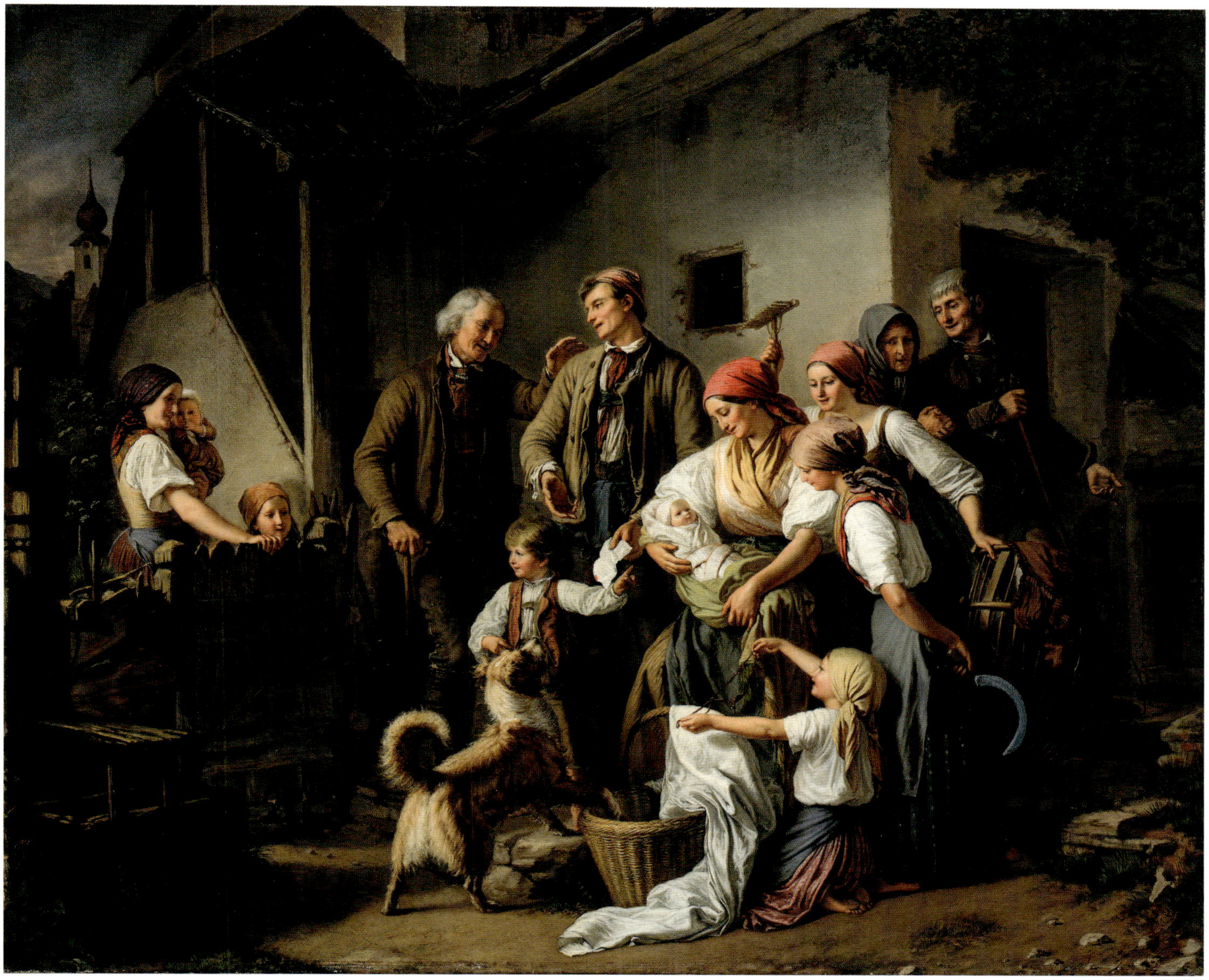

Ferdinand Georg Waldmüller
On Corpus Christi Morning, 1857
Oil on wood, 65 × 82 cm
Signed (left middle): Waldmüller 1857
Belvedere, Vienna, on loan from the Society of Friends of the Österreichische Galerie Belvedere, inv. no. Lg 63

Ferdinand Georg Waldmüller
After Confirmation (Departure of the Godmother), 1859
Oil on wood, 80,5 × 61 cm
Signed (lower right): Waldmüller 1859
Belvedere, Vienna, inv. no. 353

Ferdinand Georg Waldmüller
Brushwood Gatherers in the Vienna Woods, 1855
Oil on wood, 60 × 75.5 cm
Signed (lower middle): Waldmüller 1855
Belvedere, Vienna, inv. no. 2106

Ferdinand Georg Waldmüller
Country People Resting, 1859
Oil on wood, 61 × 75.5 cm
Signed (lower right): Waldmüller 1859
Private collection

Ferdinand Georg Waldmüller
Early Spring in the Vienna Woods (The Violet Pickers), 1861
Oil on wood, 52 × 66 cm
Signed (lower right) Waldmüller 186[1]
Belvedere, Vienna, inv. no. 1501

On Corpus Christi Morning (plate p. 225) has special significance in Waldmüller's oeuvre. It is his most famous work, demonstrating the painter's incomparable skill at using nothing more than the light to convey the joyous mood of the children and the pleasant warmth of the spring morning. The natural behavior of the protagonists makes it easy to overlook the fact that this is simply derived from the combination of their gestures and gazes. Waldmüller always constructed his groups using this device. It is also reported that for compositions containing many figures he sometimes used extra models, whom he "placed in groups as he needed them for the picture and just copied them with his brush," as Friedrich Kaiser, one of the painter's students, relates.[82] Probably the most sophisticated figural composition is *Departure of the Godmother* (plate p. 226). The group is arranged in the form of a rhombus standing on its end at the front, giving the composition an unstable appearance, while at the same time creating an impression of continuous rotation. This perception is reinforced by the two girls on the left kissing the woman's hand. Waldmüller regarded this unusual composition as a way of making the pictorial space more credible. The view of the figures slightly from below is also part of this device, a technique he used frequently from the 1850s onwards to reduce the foreground.

Waldmüller proceeded in a similar fashion with landscapes. Adjacent elements would be depicted in different sizes so as to increase the impression of space, as in the case of the tree stumps in *Brushwood Gatherers in the Vienna Woods* (plate p. 227). A more radical approach is achieved with the figures in *Country People Resting* (plate p. 228), whose bodies are cut off at the bottom of the picture, shortening the gap between the viewer and the picture. Waldmüller thus constantly sought new ways of making his depiction of space more credible, trying to overcome the limitations of two-dimensionality and to make the subject matter part of actual reality. It can be assumed that he had also encountered the works of the emerging group of young Pre-Raphaelites while visiting London in 1856 and found confirmation for his philosophy in some of their paintings. It is certain that their approach to art, so unlike the Viennese tradition, was sufficiently motivating for Waldmüller to continue in this direction. It is not therefore surprising that he went on working with picture elements of unequal proportions, creating one of his most interesting compositions in the final version of *Early Spring in the Vienna Woods* (plate p. 229).

Rupert Feuchtmüller, *Ferdinand Georg Waldmüller, 1793–1865: Leben, Schriften. Werke* (Vienna/Munich, 1996), cat. rais. nos. 948, 988, 905, 994, 1036; Elke Doppler-Wagner, *F. G. Waldmüller und die Präraffaeliten*, unpublished diss., Vienna, 2000; Sabine Grabner, *Mehr als Biedermeier: Klassizismus, Romantik und Realismus in der Österreichischen Galerie Belvedere* (Munich, 2006), pp. 120–21; Andrew Wilton, "Ferdinand Georg Waldmüller und England," in Agnes Husslein-Arco/Sabine Grabner, eds., *Ferdinand Georg Waldmüller 1793–1865*, exh. cat. Belvedere, Vienna/Musée du Louvre, Paris (Vienna, 2009), pp. 147–60.

SG

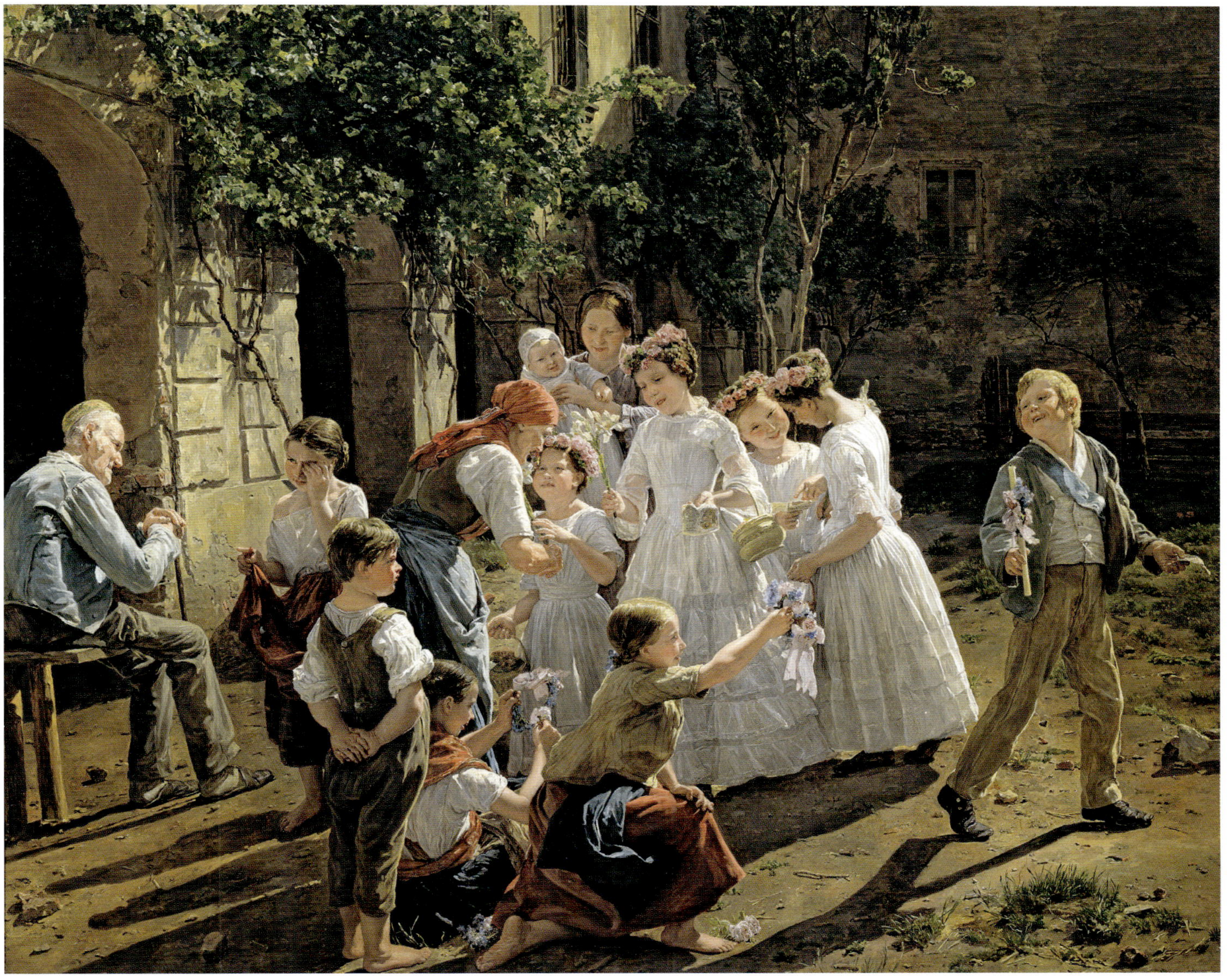

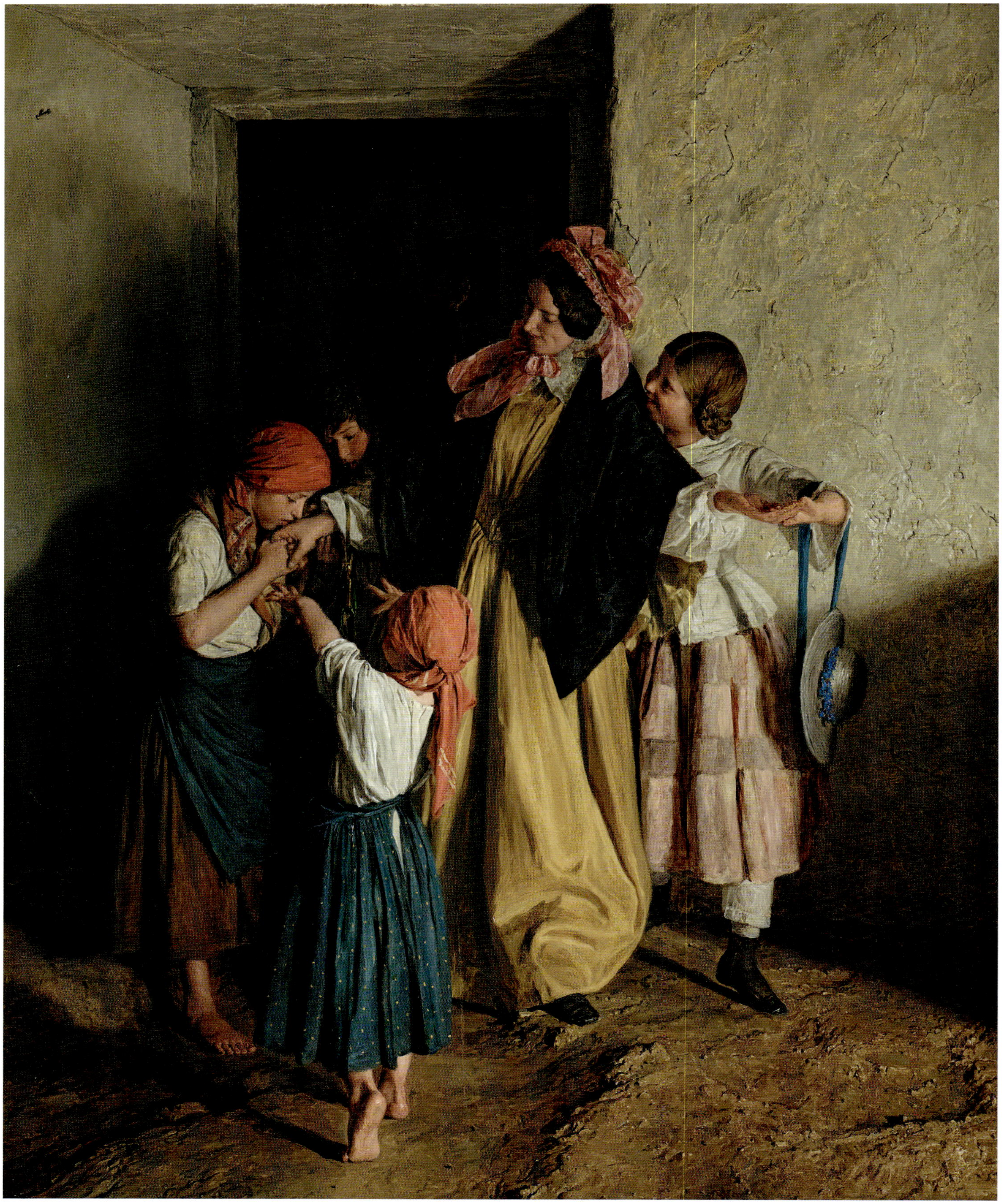

Ferdinand Georg Waldmüller
After Confirmation (Departure of the Godmother), 1859

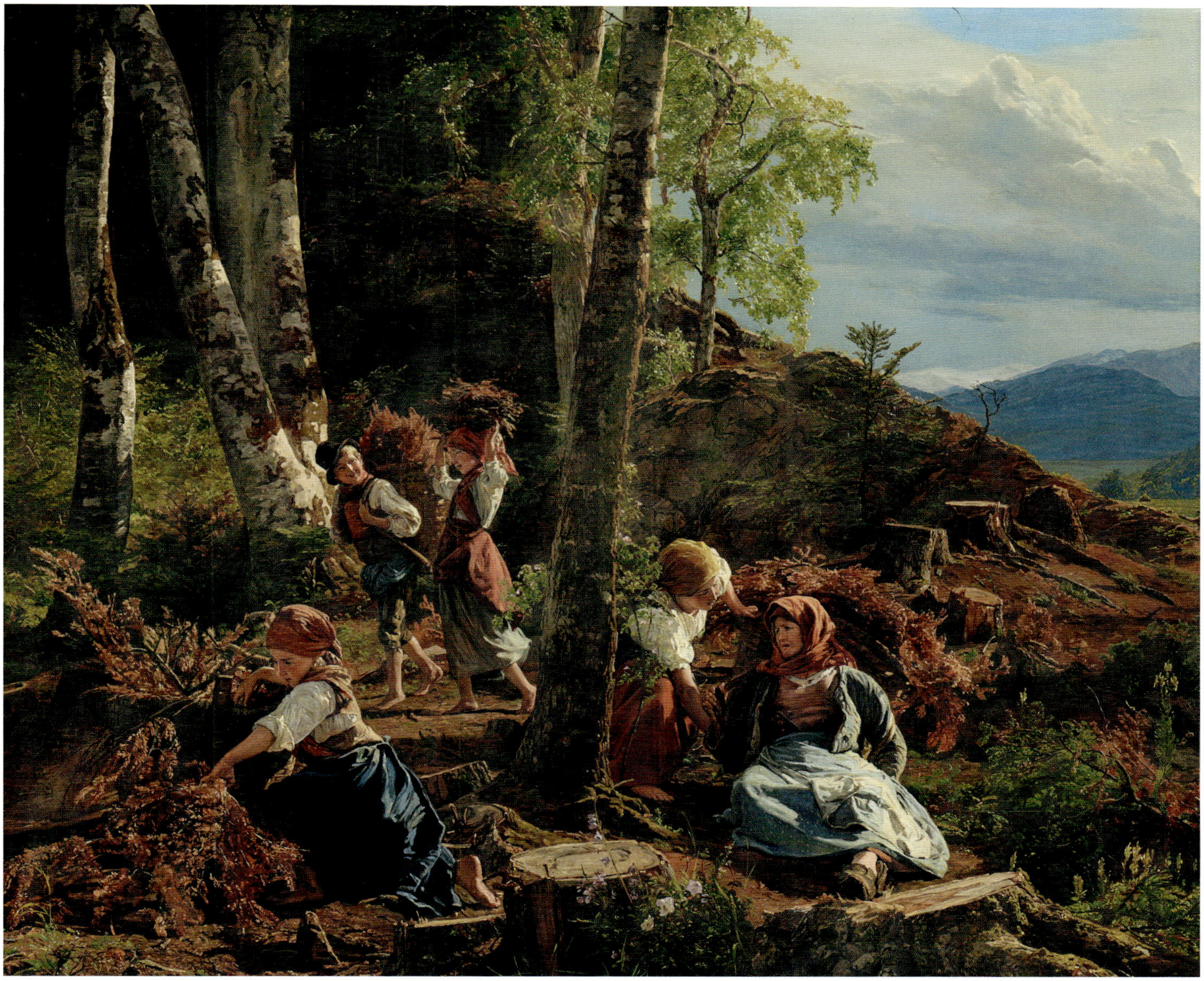

Ferdinand Georg Waldmüller
Brushwood Gatherers in the Vienna Woods, 1855

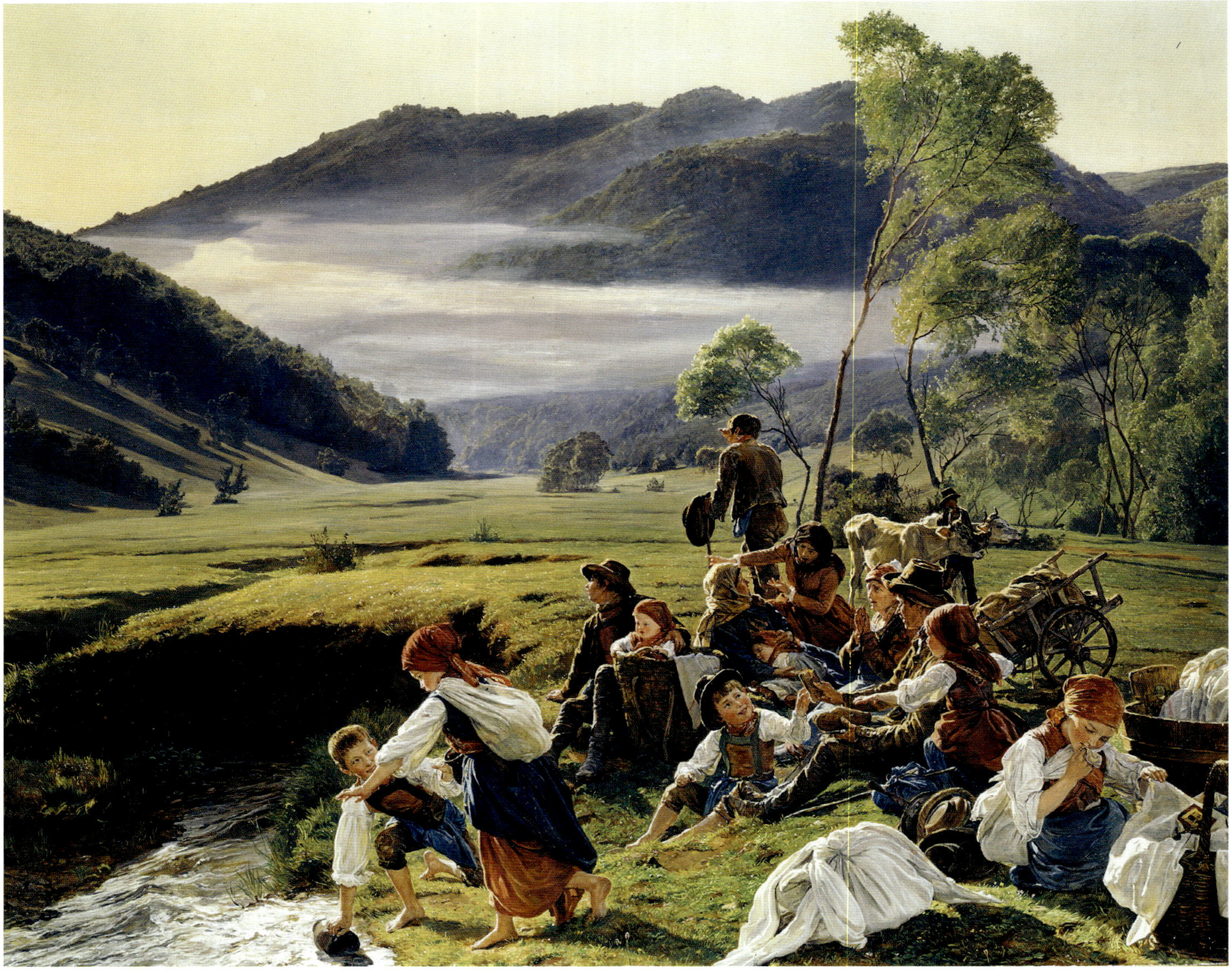

Ferdinand Georg Waldmüller
Country People Resting, 1859

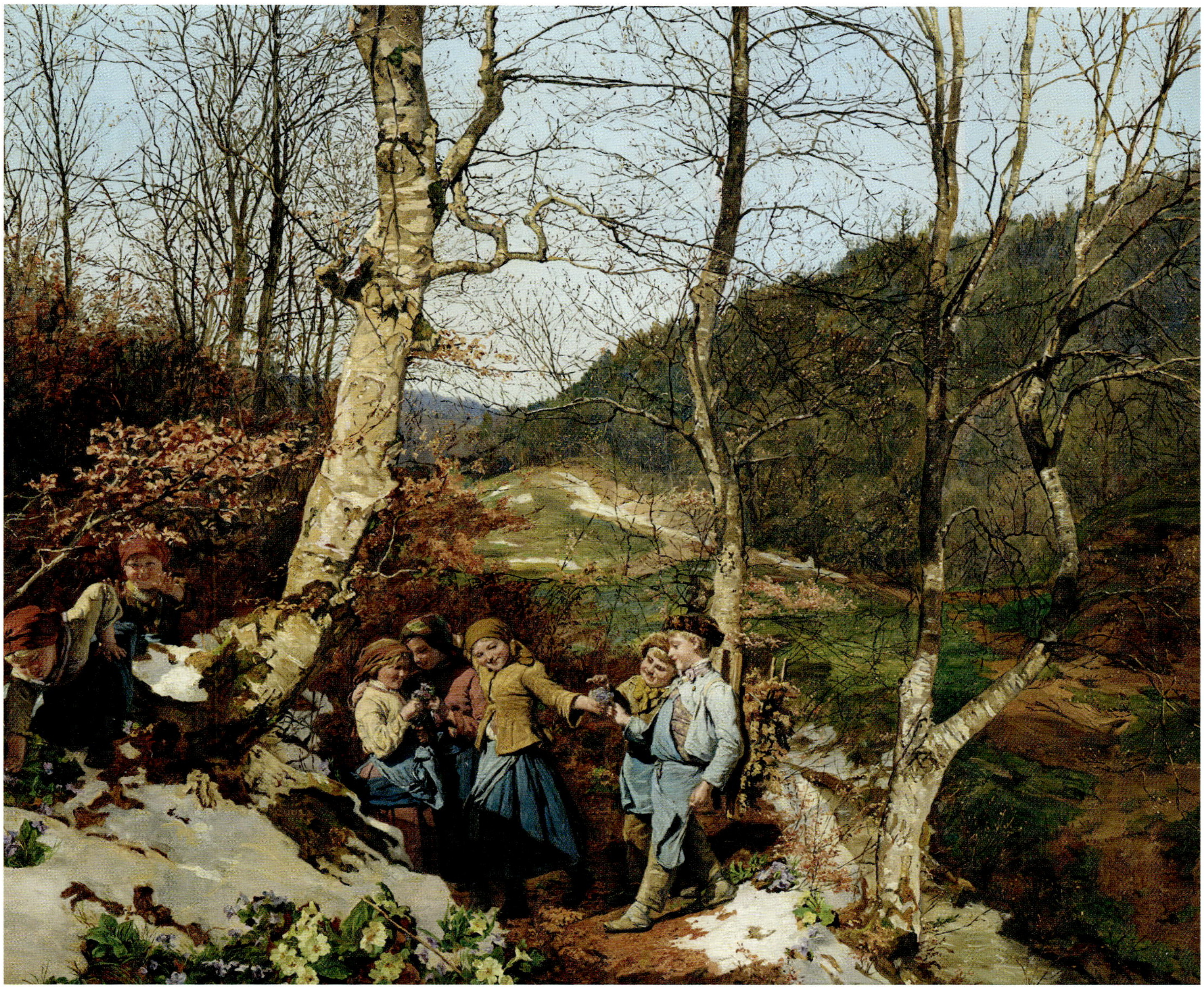

Ferdinand Georg Waldmüller
Early Spring in the Vienna Woods (The Violet Pickers), 1861

Anton Hansch
Palü Glacier, 1855
Oil on canvas, 63 × 52.5 cm
Signed (lower right): Hansch
Belvedere, Vienna, inv. no. 4716

Anton Hansch
The Wenger Alp in the Bernese Oberland (*Eiger, Mönch, and Jungfrau*), 1853
Oil on canvas, 140 × 190 cm
Signed (lower left): Hansch / 853
Belvedere, Vienna, inv. no. 3083

These two Alpine scenes are the product of long travels undertaken by Hansch in Switzerland in the early 1850s. The Viennese painter was following in the footsteps of the artists and intellectuals who, from the late eighteenth century, sought out and were inspired by the sublime. Possibly Hansch was also in search of the motifs painted by the much revered Genevan artist Alexandre Calame (1810–1864). Traveling for his art had always been important for Hansch, who even as a student at the Vienna Academy under Joseph Mössmer (1780–1845) had explored the regions around Vienna to sketch from nature, later basing his pictorial compositions on these studies. From the 1840s, he ventured further afield to the mountains of northern Styria, to the Salzkammergut and Berchtesgadener Land, North and South Tyrol, Vorarlberg and Switzerland.

The two paintings shown here are vivid examples of Hansch's preferred method of composition, as in both he has meticulously rendered the foreground. This is juxtaposed with nature in the background in all its awe-inspiring magnitude, without a middle distance to form a bridge between the two. In the case of the *Palü Glacier*, Hansch has captured an irrecoverable scene, as the icefield was at its highest level during this period; nowadays only vestiges of the glacier remain. For the view of the triple peaks of Eiger, Mönch, and Jungfrau, he chose the Wenger Alp as his vantage point, looking out toward the glaciated North Wall. The mountain range's proximity to this location had already fascinated generations of walkers, with Lord Byron among their number. It is even said that it was here that Byron found the inspiration for his poem *Manfred*. Hansch, too, shows its importance as a tourist destination, depicting a group of travelers at the center. When the artist presented this large painting at the January exhibition of the Österreichischer Kunstverein (Austrian Art Association) in 1854, it was not met with universal acclaim. The art critic for the newspaper *Die Presse*, for instance, stated that the size of the view detracted from the quality usually associated with this artist's work, as Hansch showed "great delicacy and charm only in the details, but lacks a feel for the magnificent."[83] Nevertheless, the painting was purchased that February by the Imperial Picture Gallery and immediately placed on display at the Upper Belvedere.[84]

"Nekrolog," *Neue Freie Presse*, Abendblatt, no. 4418, December 11, 1876, p. 2; August Schaeffer, *Die kaiserliche Gemälde-Galerie in Wien: Moderne Meister* (Vienna, 1903), pp. 132–33; Alexander Wied, "Österreich," *Die Alpen in der Malerei* (Rosenheim, 1981), pp. 189–90; Gerbert Frodl, *Malerei der Biedermeierzeit* (Rosenheim, 1987), p. 250.

SG

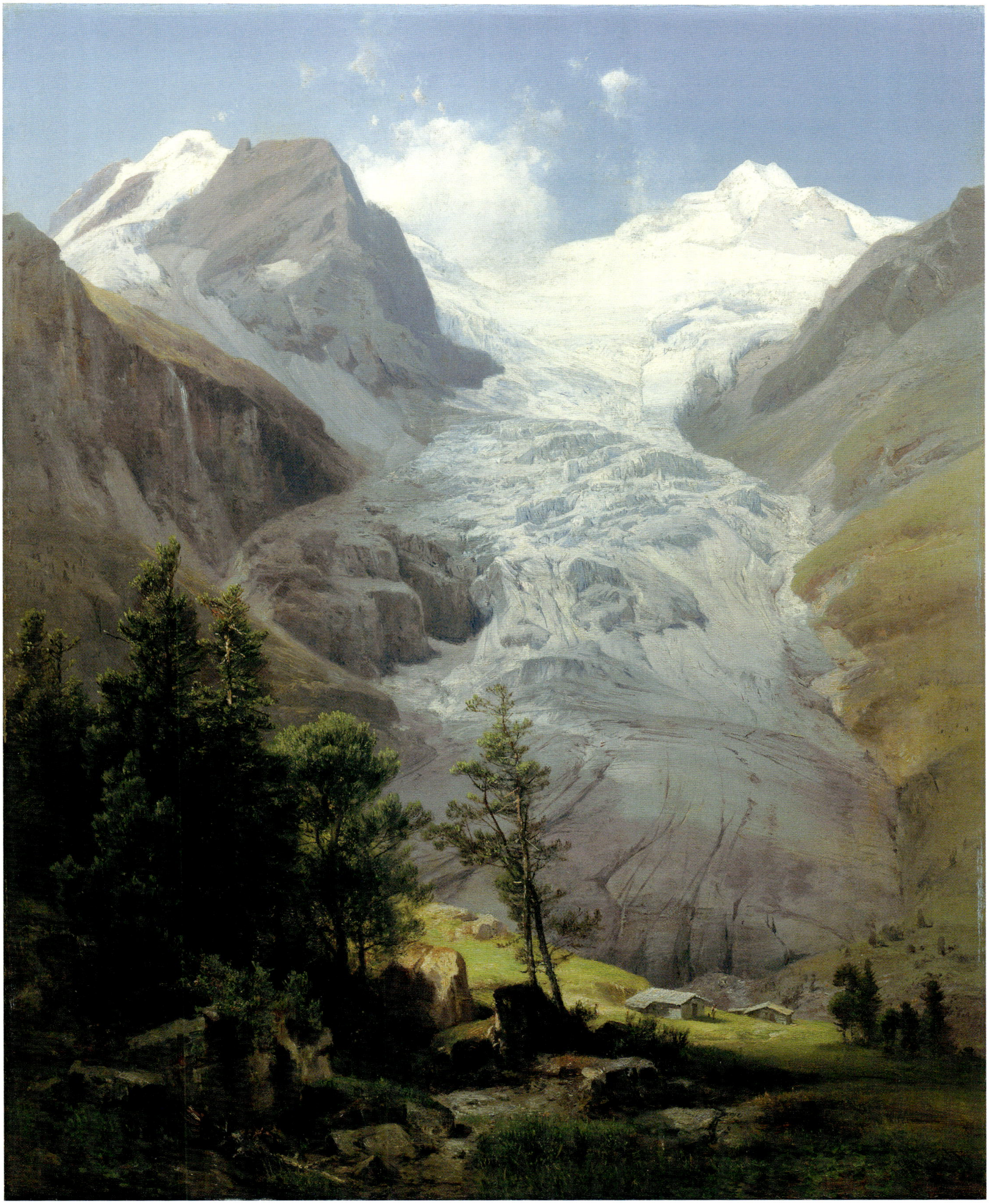

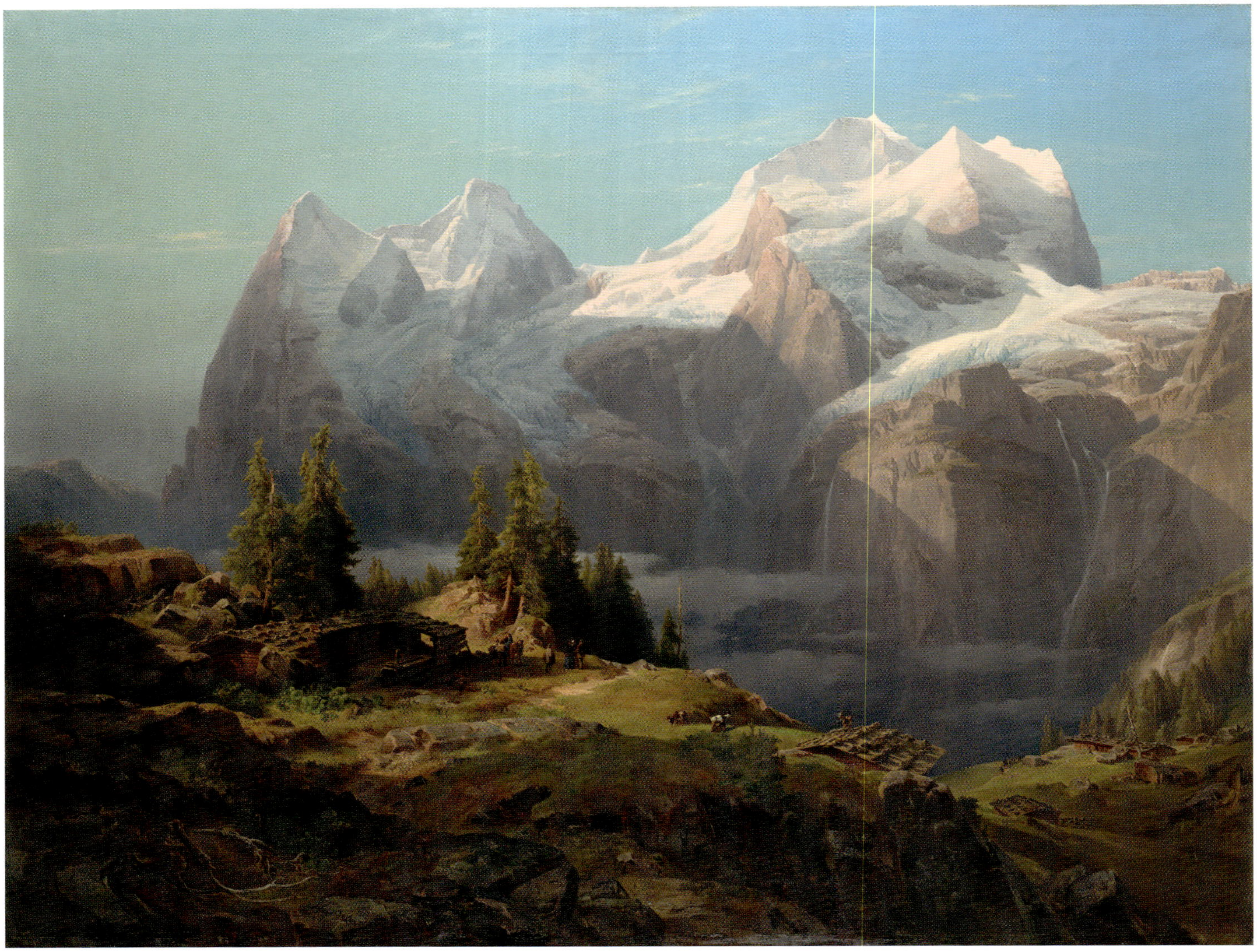

Anton Hansch
The Wenger Alp in the Bernese Oberland (Eiger, Mönch, and Jungfrau), 1853

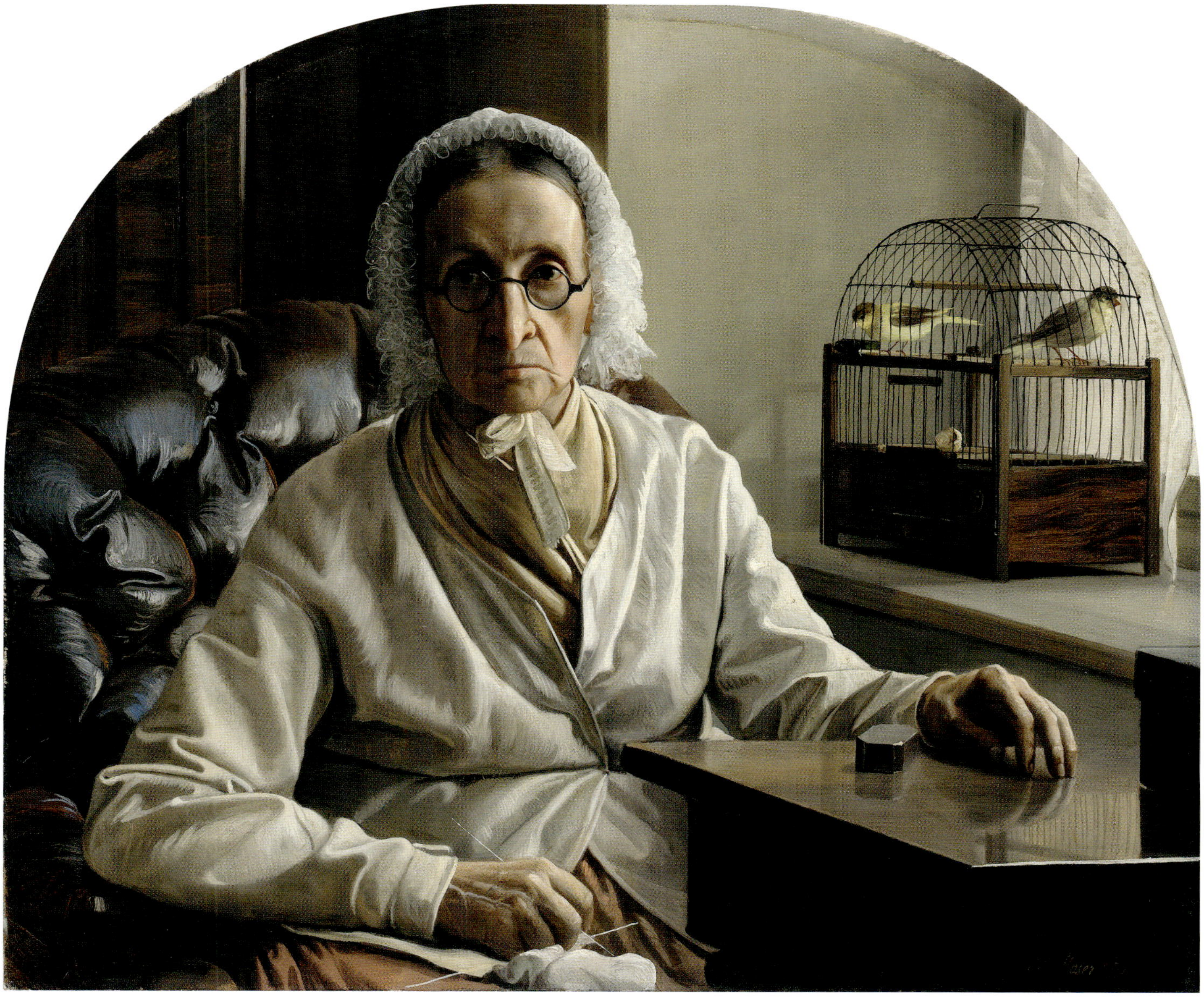

Ernst Christian Moser
Portrait of the Artist's Mother, 1859
Oil on canvas, 72 × 87 cm
Signed (lower right): Chr. E. Moser 859
Neue Galerie am Universalmuseum Joanneum, Graz, inv. no. I/381

Albert Zimmermann
Sunset on Lake Hintersee in Berchtesgaden, 1858
Oil on canvas, 211 × 268 cm
Signed (lower right): Albert Zimmermann
Belvedere, Vienna, inv. no. 13

Given the artist's place of birth and death, it might be asked why this work is included here. In his day, however, Zimmermann was one of the foremost landscape painters in the Habsburg territories and still enjoys a reputation today for his pioneering role, particularly as a teacher. His name is closely linked with the Viennese artists Eugen Jettel (1845–1901), Robert Russ (1847–1922), Julius Payer (1841–1915), Rudolf Ribarz (1848–1904), and Emil Jakob Schindler (1842–1892), all students at the Vienna Academy and representatives of the future generation of painters. In this context, Zimmermann's biography is interesting because he was essentially self-taught, having acquired his basic skills through landscape studies. He later met Caspar David Friedrich (1774–1840) at the Dresden Academy, but preferred the study of pictures by the Dutch landscape painter Jacob van Ruisdael (1628–1682) to Friedrich's teachings. It was not until he attended the Munich Academy that his work underwent a transformation. On his numerous walking tours he discovered the multifaceted motifs of the Bavarian and Tyrolean Alps, which were to occupy him henceforth. In 1854 he was appointed professor of landscape painting at the Milan Academy, transferring in 1859 on account of the changed political situation to the same position at the Imperial Academy in Vienna, where he remained until 1873. Zimmermann was able to communicate to the above-mentioned artists a new view of nature and in particular the awareness that the *pars pro toto* was more interesting than the so-called postcard motif. Most of his surviving work is in the form of cartoons with views of nature, mostly created en plein air in front of the subject. Paintings like *Sunset on Lake Hintersee in Berchtesgaden* are an exception in his oeuvre. Moreover, in this motif the painter appears to have been less interested in depicting the natural scenery than in the spectacle of light and the atmospheric colors of the setting sun immersing the surroundings in such exceptional hues. This also explains why the picture dramatically exaggerates the scenery to produce a kind of *Weltlandschaft* familiar to us from Albrecht Altdorfer's *The Battle of Alexander at Issus* (1529, Neue Pinakothek, Munich), but in this case based on a real scene from nature.

A. H., "Albert Zimmermann," in *Allgemeine Kunst-Chronik: Illustrirte Zeitschrift für Kunst, Kunstgewerbe, Musik, Theater und Litteratur*, 12th yr., vol. 43, October 27, 1888, pp. 1078–79; Constant von Wurzbach, *Biographisches Lexikon des Kaisertums Österreich*, vol. 60 (Vienna, 1891), pp. 111–14; Gerbert Frodl, "Landschaftsmalerei," in ibid., ed., *19. Jahrhundert* (= Geschichte der bildenden Kunst in Österreich 5) (Munich et al., 2002), pp. 309–16, especially p. 310.

SG

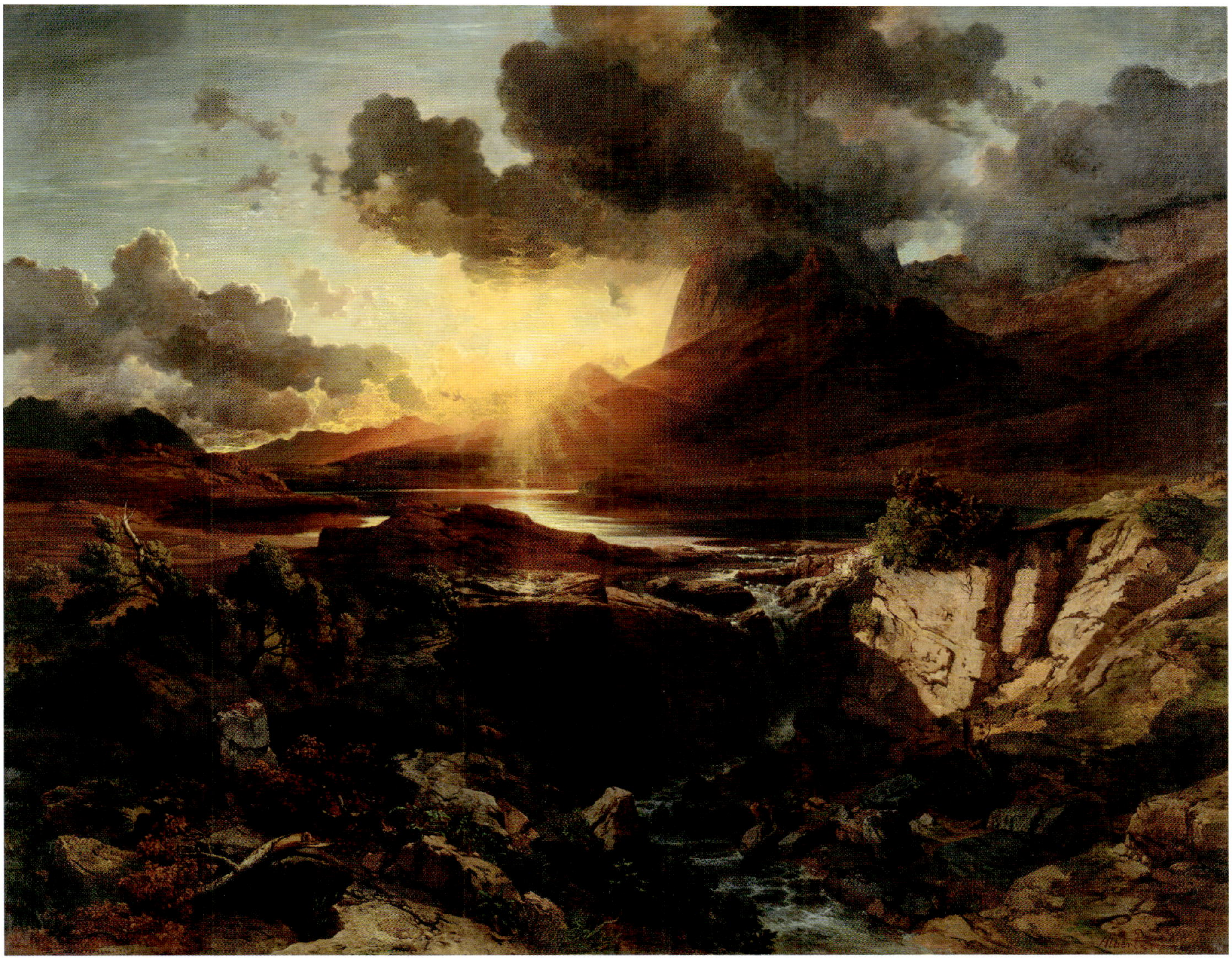

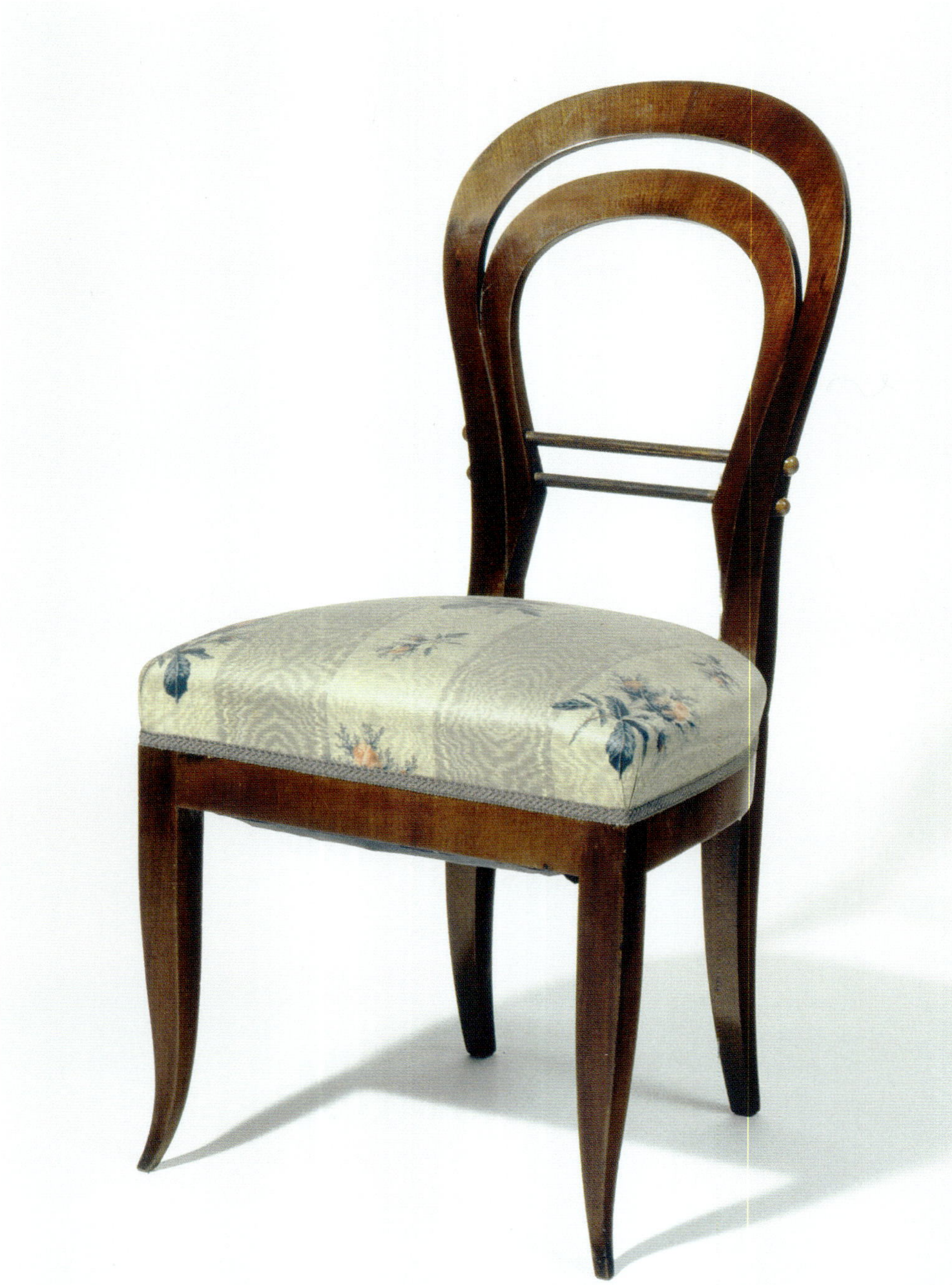

Chair from Laxenburg
Vienna, around 1825
Mahogany, polished veneer on base wood, padding and fabric cover renewed, 93.5 × 47.5 × 42.5 cm
Federal Furniture Administration/exhibited at Imperial Furniture Collection – Furniture Museum Vienna, inv. no. MD 45.873 (old Laxenburg number: L 6.138)

The chair belongs to a group of eight and bears an old inventory number from Laxenburg. It is thought to originate from the "Blauer Hof," where Archduke Franz Karl and Archduchess Sophie's summer apartment was refurbished by the court decorator Friedrich Stöger in 1824/25.

The form of this chair corresponds to the "chair no. 18" from the Danhauser furniture factory. The two curves on the backrest hint toward Michael Thonet's famous "No. 14" bentwood chair.

EO

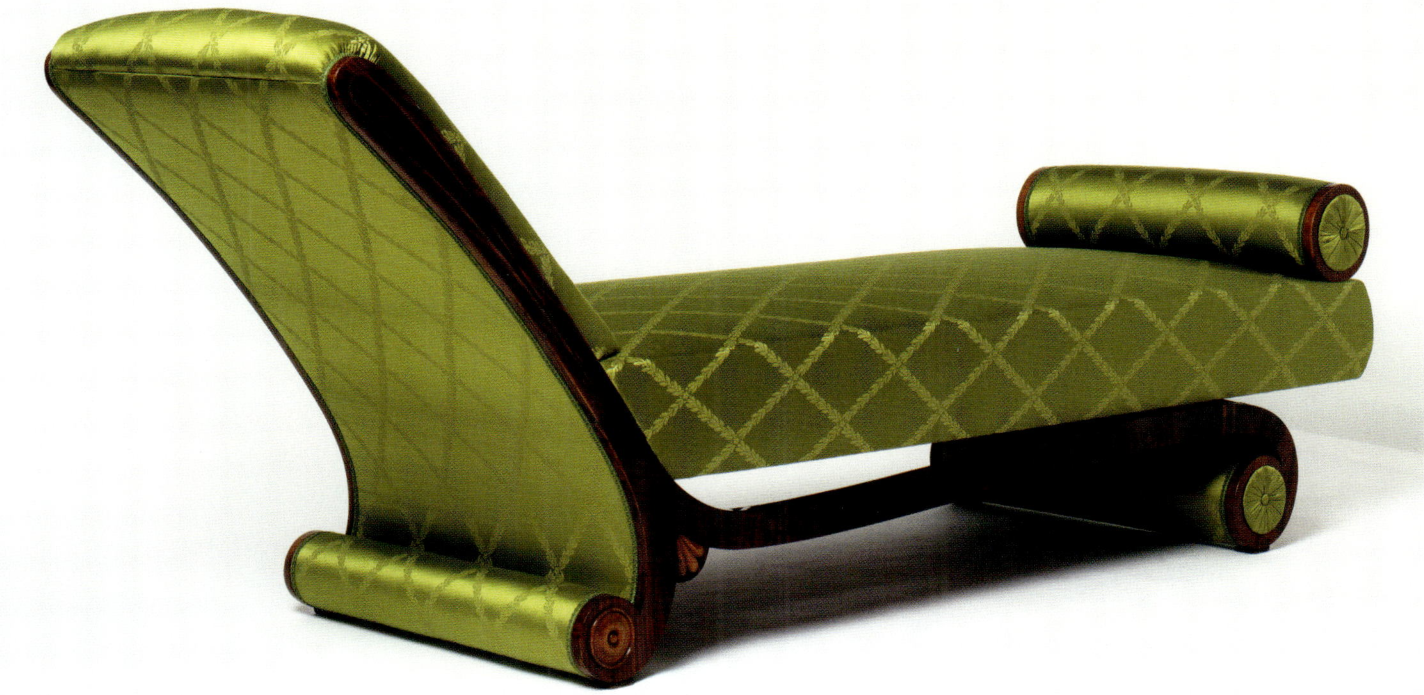

Ottoman from the apartment of Crown Prince Ferdinand in the Vienna Hofburg
Vienna, 1831
Walnut, polished veneer on base wood, maple inlays, padding and fabric cover renewed, 92 × 230 × 75 cm
Federal Furniture Administration/exhibited at Imperial Furniture Collection – Furniture Museum Vienna, inv. no. MD 53.296 (old Hofburg number: 16.198)

During the Biedermeier period, Viennese furniture was especially prized for its "serpentine" forms. The ottoman's curved wooden frame is a high-quality example of this.

The ottoman was originally in Crown Prince Ferdinand's apartment in the Amalienhof at the Hofburg in Vienna, which was newly furnished in 1831 on the occasion of the wedding of the subsequent Emperor Ferdinand I of Austria and Maria Anna of Sardinia.

The item of furniture is recorded in the Hofburg inventory as a "rest bed with three cushions of green merino." The fabric covering was reconstructed based on sources in the workshops of the Federal Furniture Administration.

EO

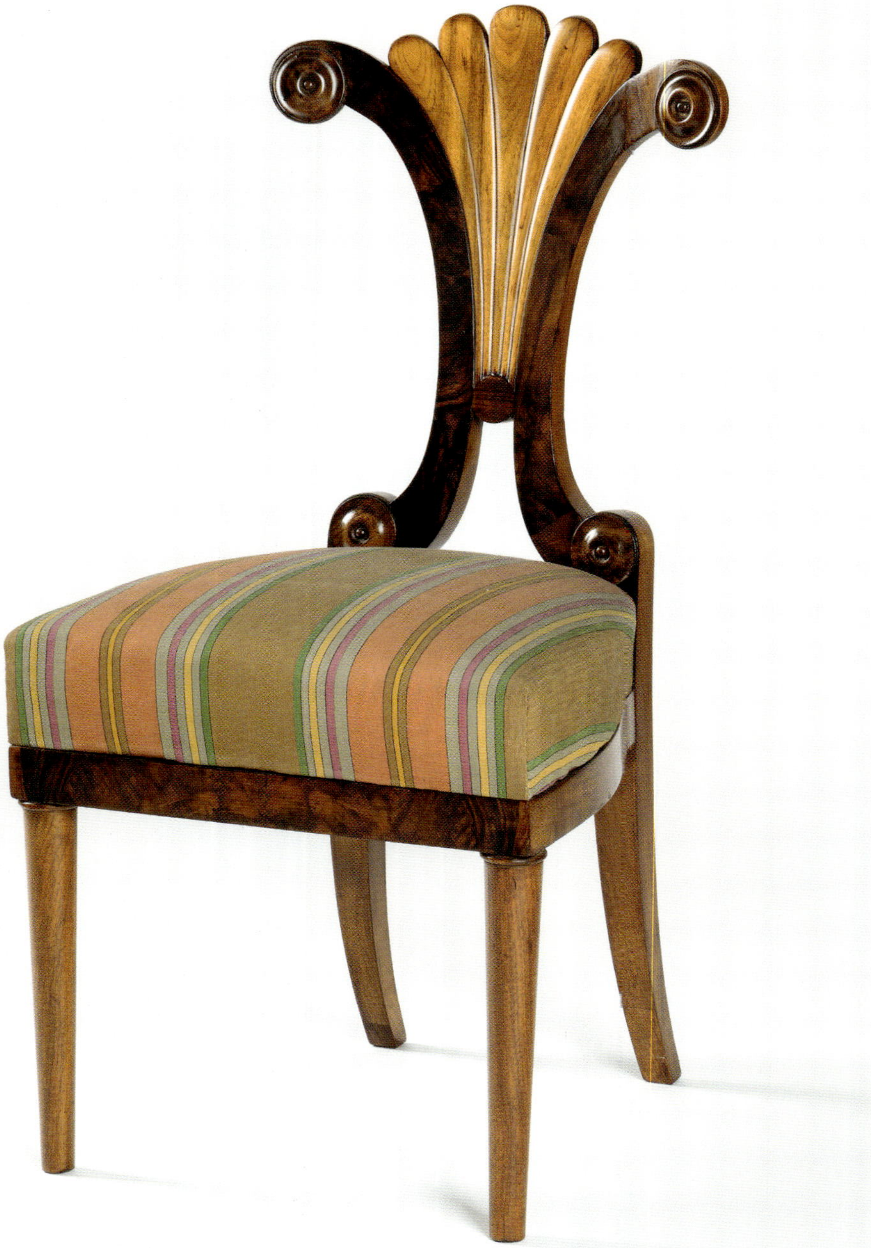

Chair
Vienna, around 1825–1830
Walnut, carved, veneered, polished, padding and fabric cover renewed, 92 × 47 × 43 cm
MAK – Austrian Museum of Applied Arts / Contemporary Art, Vienna, inv no. H 1779-2

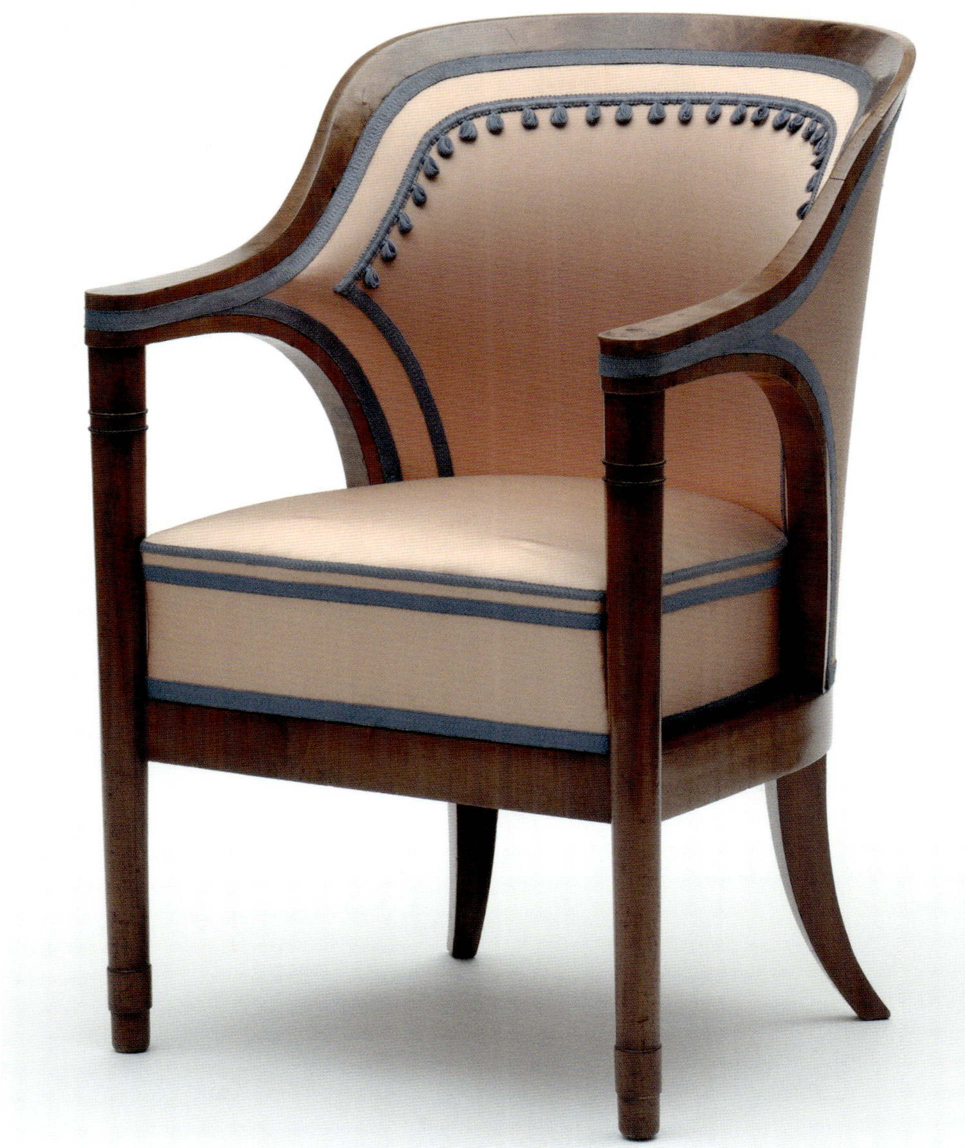

Josef Ulrich Danhauser sen., armchair
Made by: Danhauser Privileged Imperial and Royal Furniture Factory, Vienna, around 1825
Mahogany, veneer on softwood, padding and fabric cover renewed (reconstructed original upholstery), 92 × 57 × 52 cm
MAK – Austrian Museum of Applied Arts / Contemporary Art, Vienna, inv. no. H 1785-1

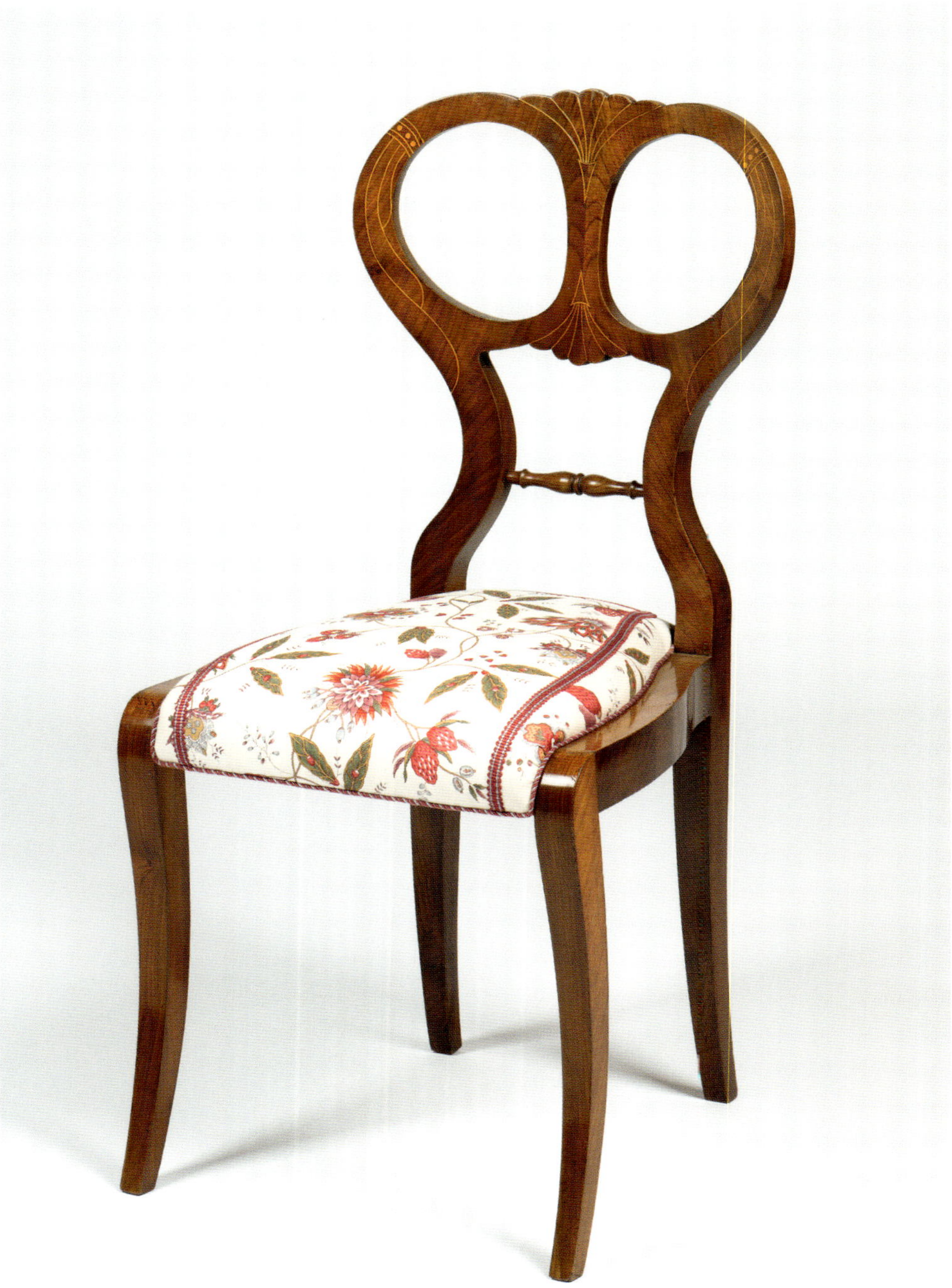

Chair
Made by: Johann Nepomuk Geyer, Innsbruck (?), 1835–1840
Mahogany, maple stripe inlays, padding and fabric cover renewed, 93 × 44 × 46 cm
MAK – Austrian Museum of Applied Arts / Contemporary Art, Vienna, inv. no. H 2070-2

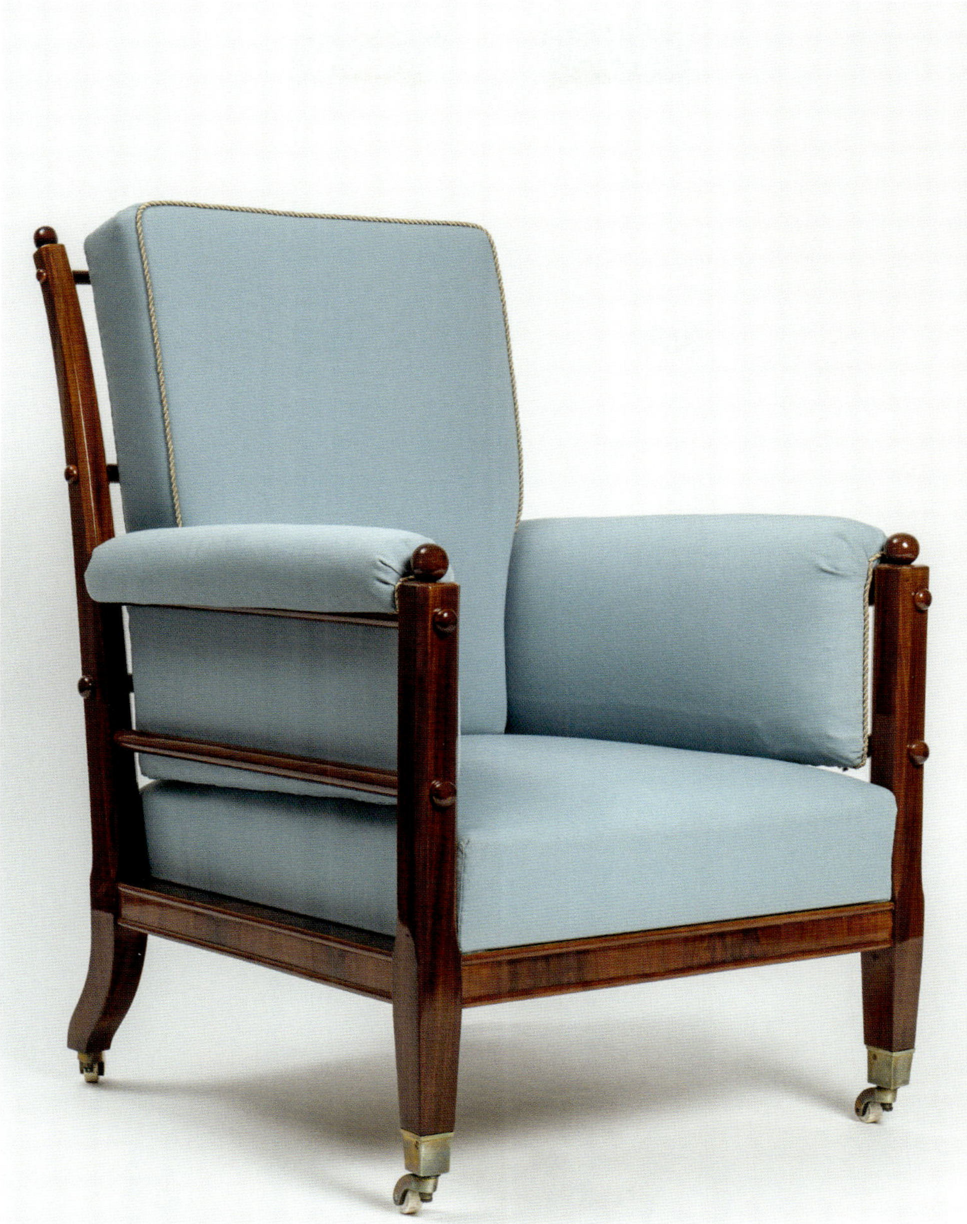

Armchair from the apartment of Mistress of the Robes Kinsky in the Vienna Hofburg
Vienna, after 1824,
Mahogany, polished veneer on base wood, padding and fabric cover renewed, 115 × 72 × 95 cm
Federal Furniture Administration/exhibited at Imperial Furniture Collection – Furniture Museum Vienna, inv. no. MD 42.874 (old Hofburg number: 16.233)

The armchair with removable cushions comes from the first floor apartment of the Imperial Chancellery Wing, residence of Princess Karoline Maria Kinsky, Mistress of the Robes to Archduchess Sophie. The piece of furniture is described in the Hofburg inventory as follows: "Cushioned mahogany armchair, with blue silk covering."

The form of the armchair corresponds to the "fauteuil no. 86" from the Danhauser furniture factory. The fabric covering was reconstructed based on sources in the workshops of the Federal Furniture Administration.

EO

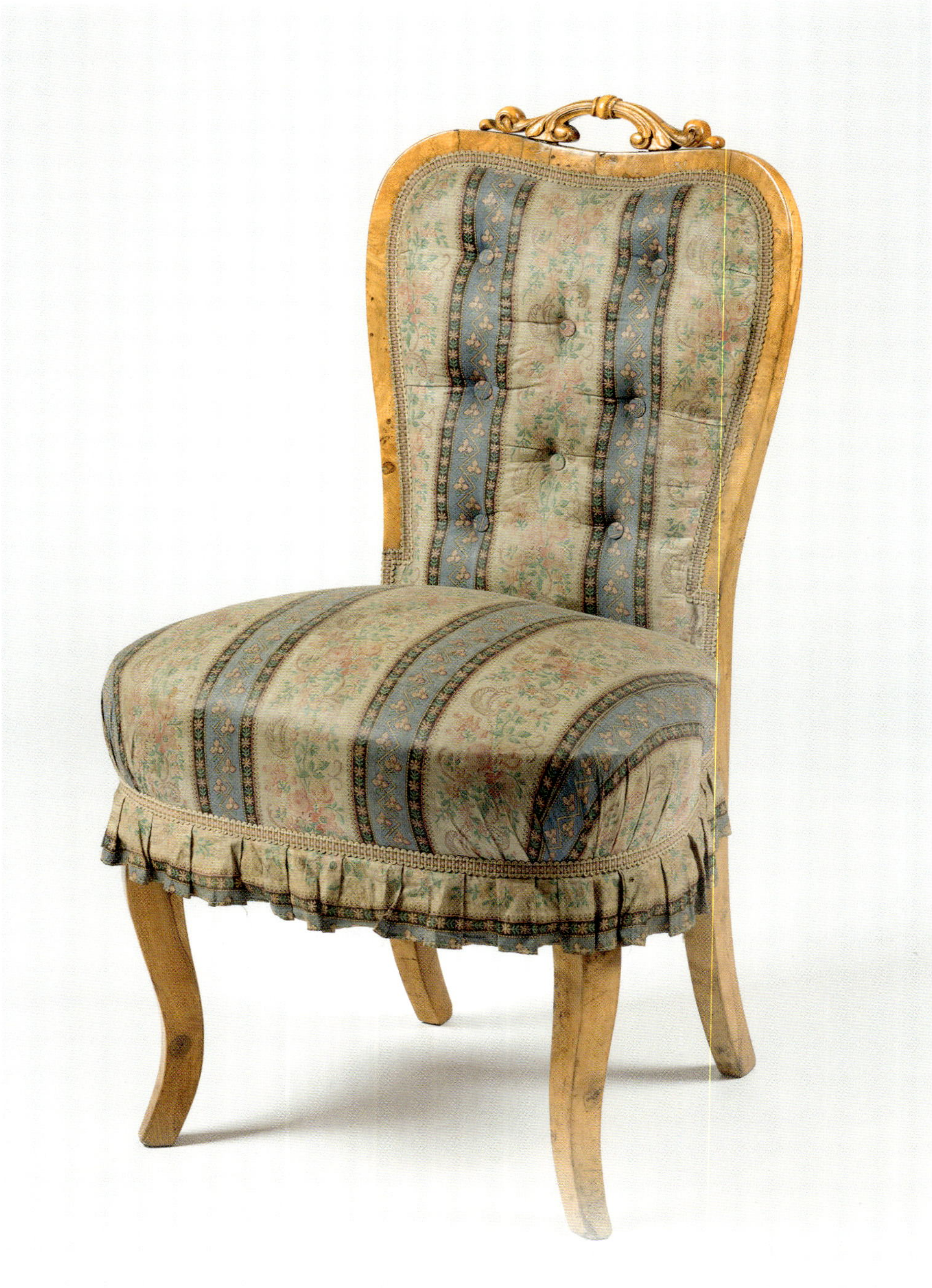

Upholstered Chair
Vienna, around 1840
Birch grain, maple, reconstructed original upholstery (chintz), 89 × 54 × 54.5 cm
MAK – Austrian Museum of Applied Arts / Contemporary Art, Vienna, inv. no. H 3863-2

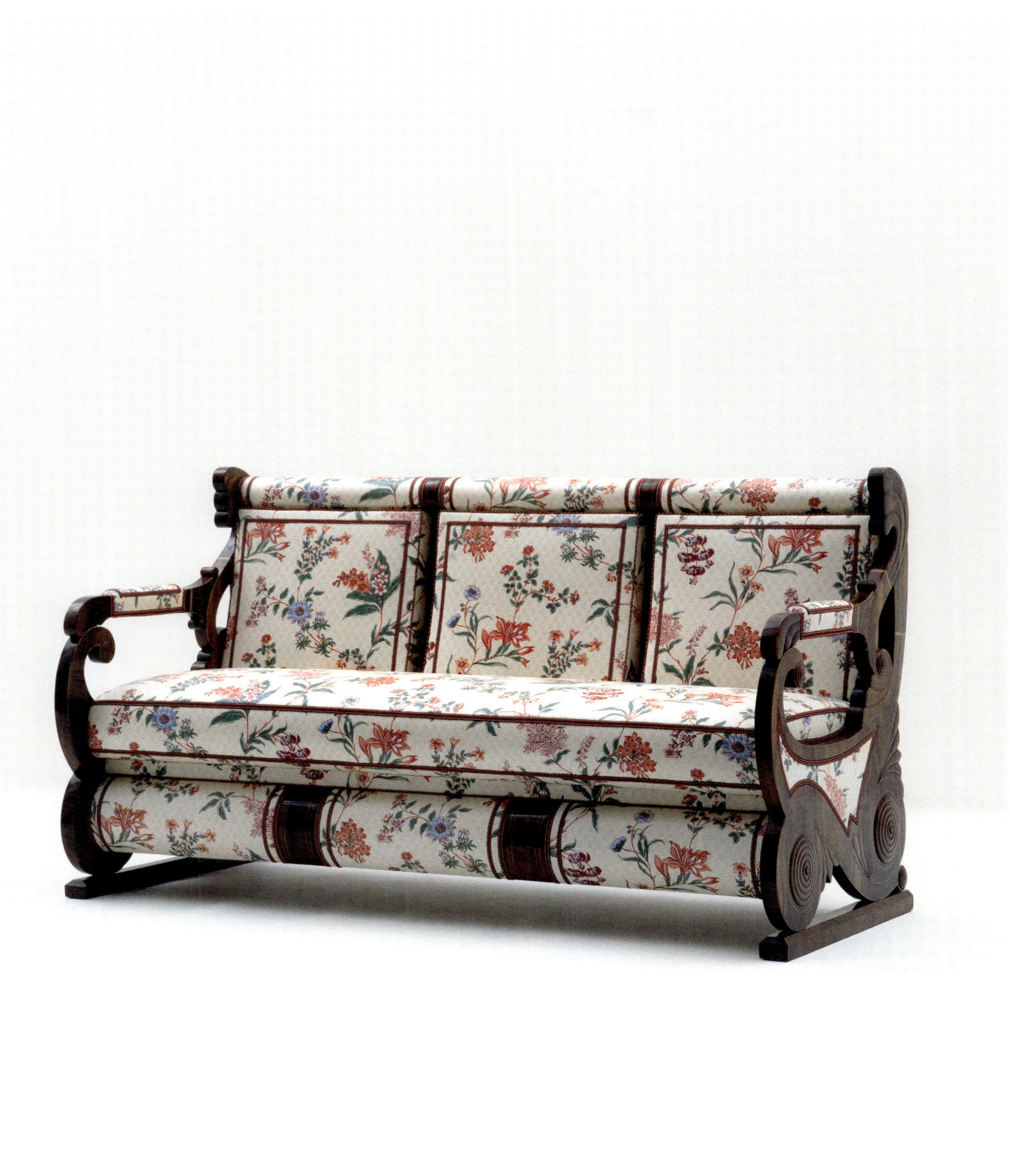

Sofa
Vienna, around 1835
Walnut, maple inlays, reconstructed original upholstery, 89 × 224 × 80 cm
MAK – Austrian Museum of Applied Arts / Contemporary Art, Vienna, inv. no. SOB 317-3

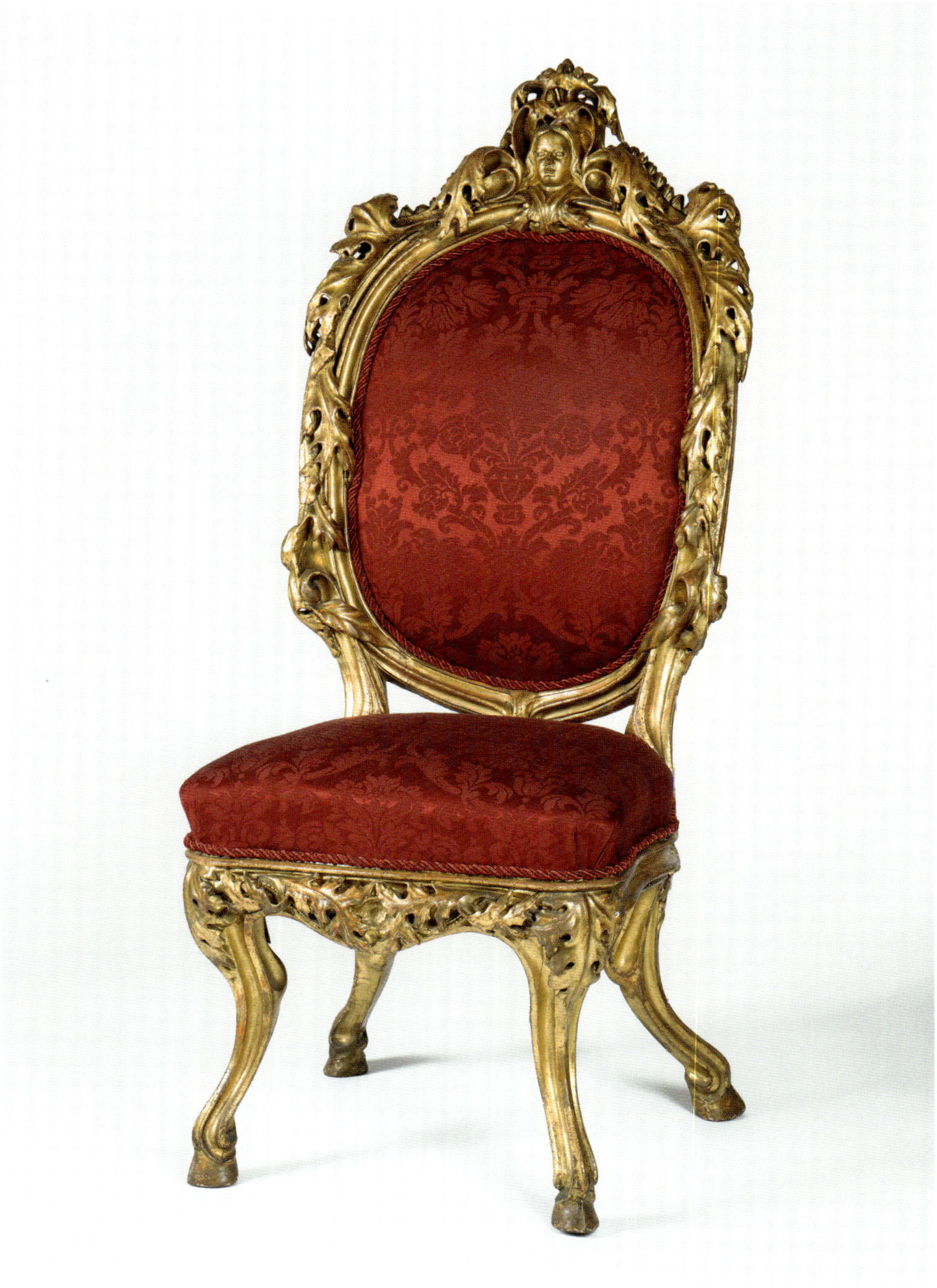

Chair
Vienna, around 1845
Wood, carved and gilded, fabric cover renewed, 125 × 53 × 53 cm
MAK – Austrian Museum of Applied Arts / Contemporary Art, Vienna, inv. no. H 3044

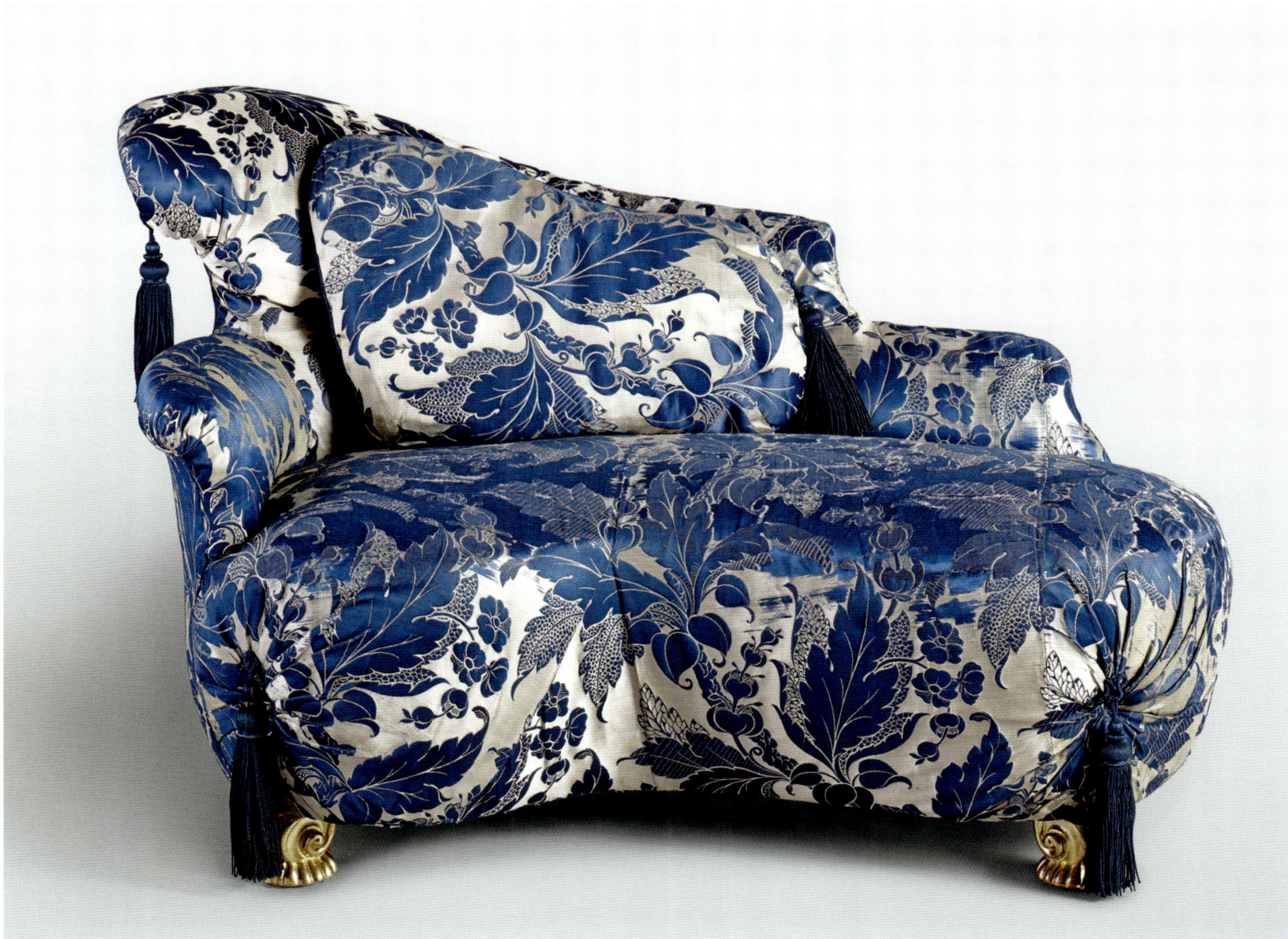

Peter Hubert Desvignes (?), sofa (ottoman) from the Vienna palace of the Princes of Liechtenstein
Vienna, around 1847
Softwood, carved and gilded, white silk damask with dark blue floral and foliate ornamentation, 96 × 140 × 84 cm
LIECHTENSTEIN. The Princely Collections, Vaduz–Vienna, inv. no. MO 862

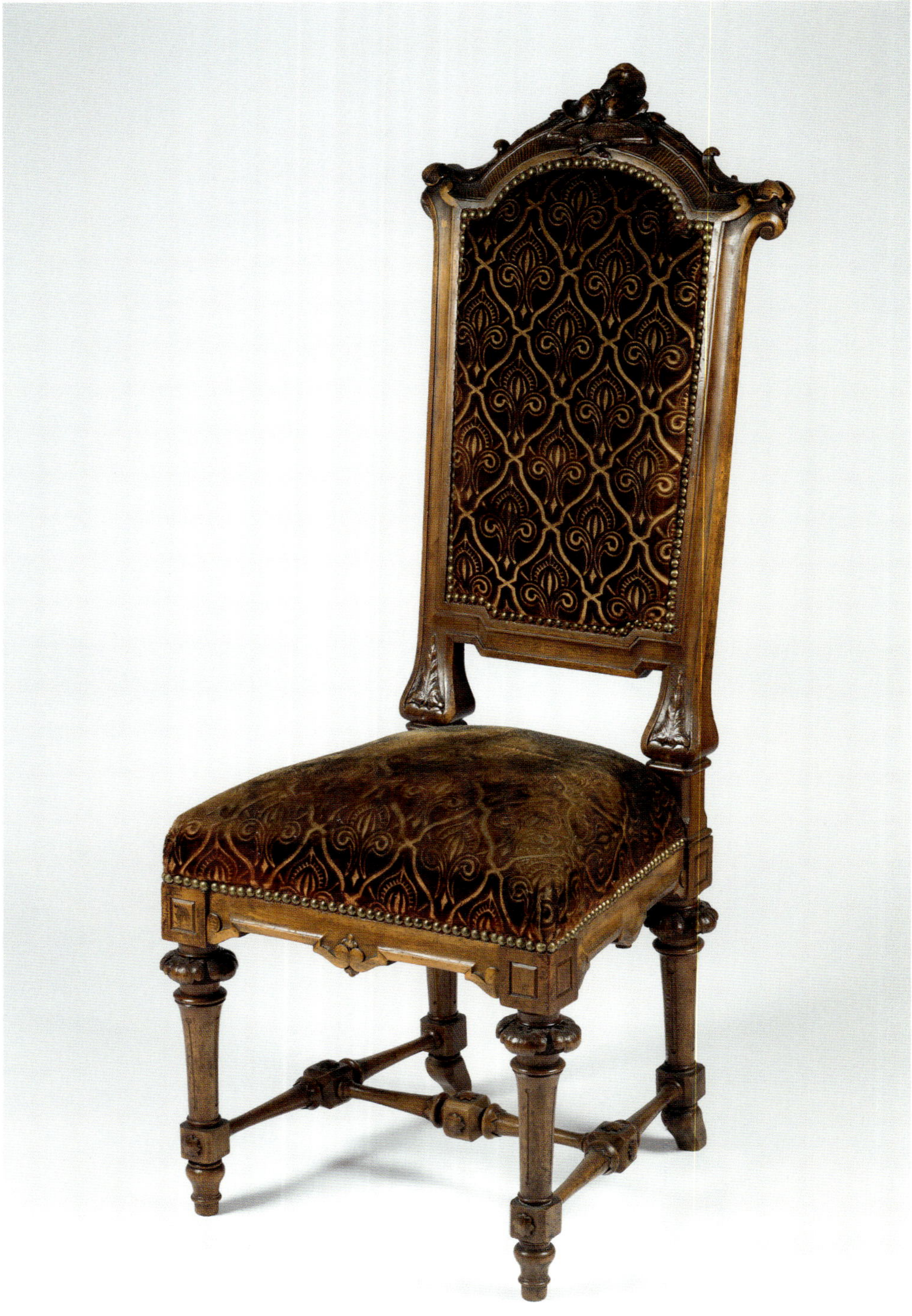

Chair from a dining room suite
Vienna, around 1855
Walnut, carved, veneer, beech, original upholstery (velvet), 123 × 50 × 51 cm
MAK – Austrian Museum of Applied Arts / Contemporary Art, Vienna, inv. no. H 2751-5

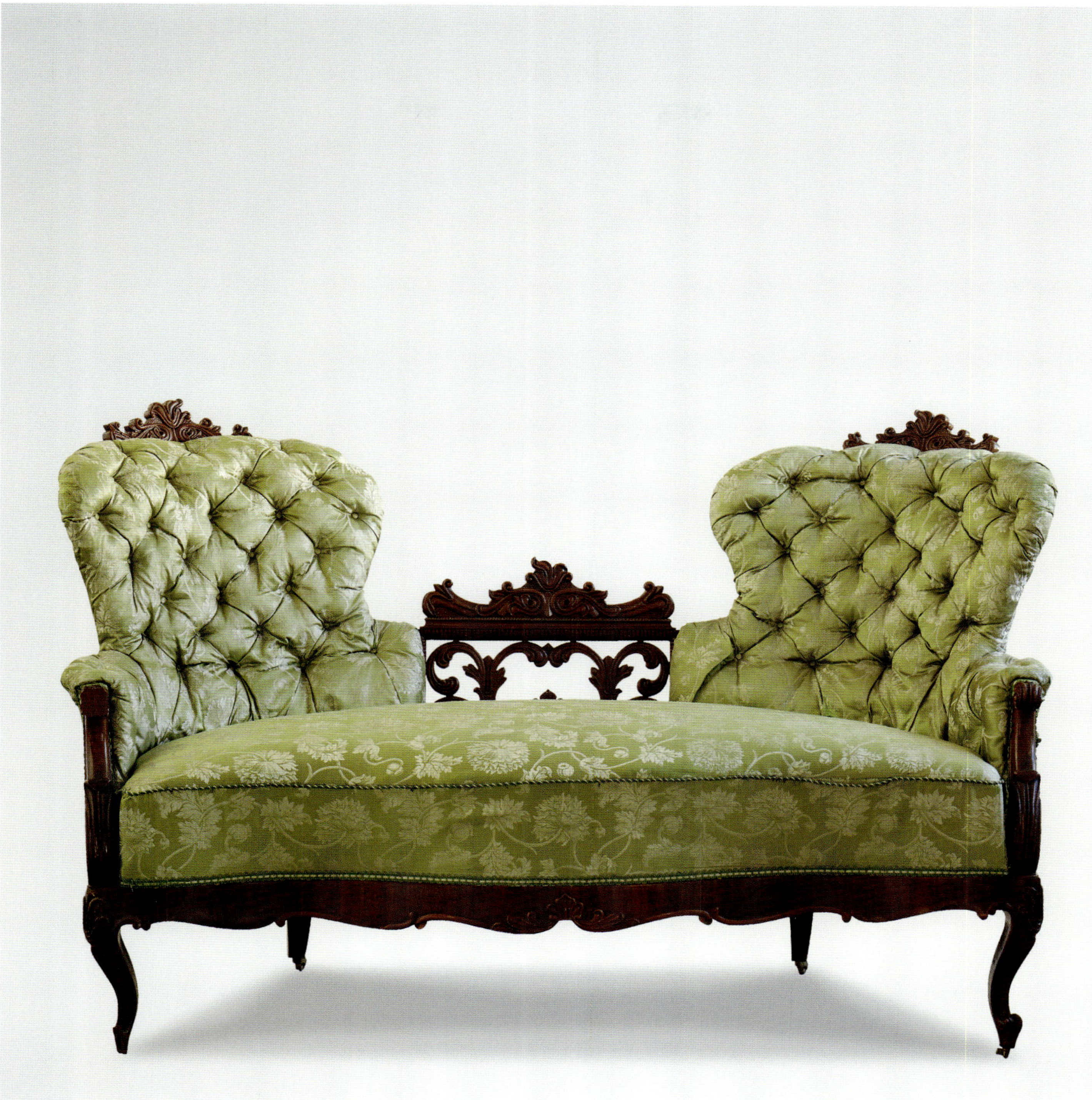

Sofa
Vienna, around 1840
Solid veneered mahogany, original cover (silk damask), 107 × 175 × 70 cm
Cistercian Abbey of Lilienfeld

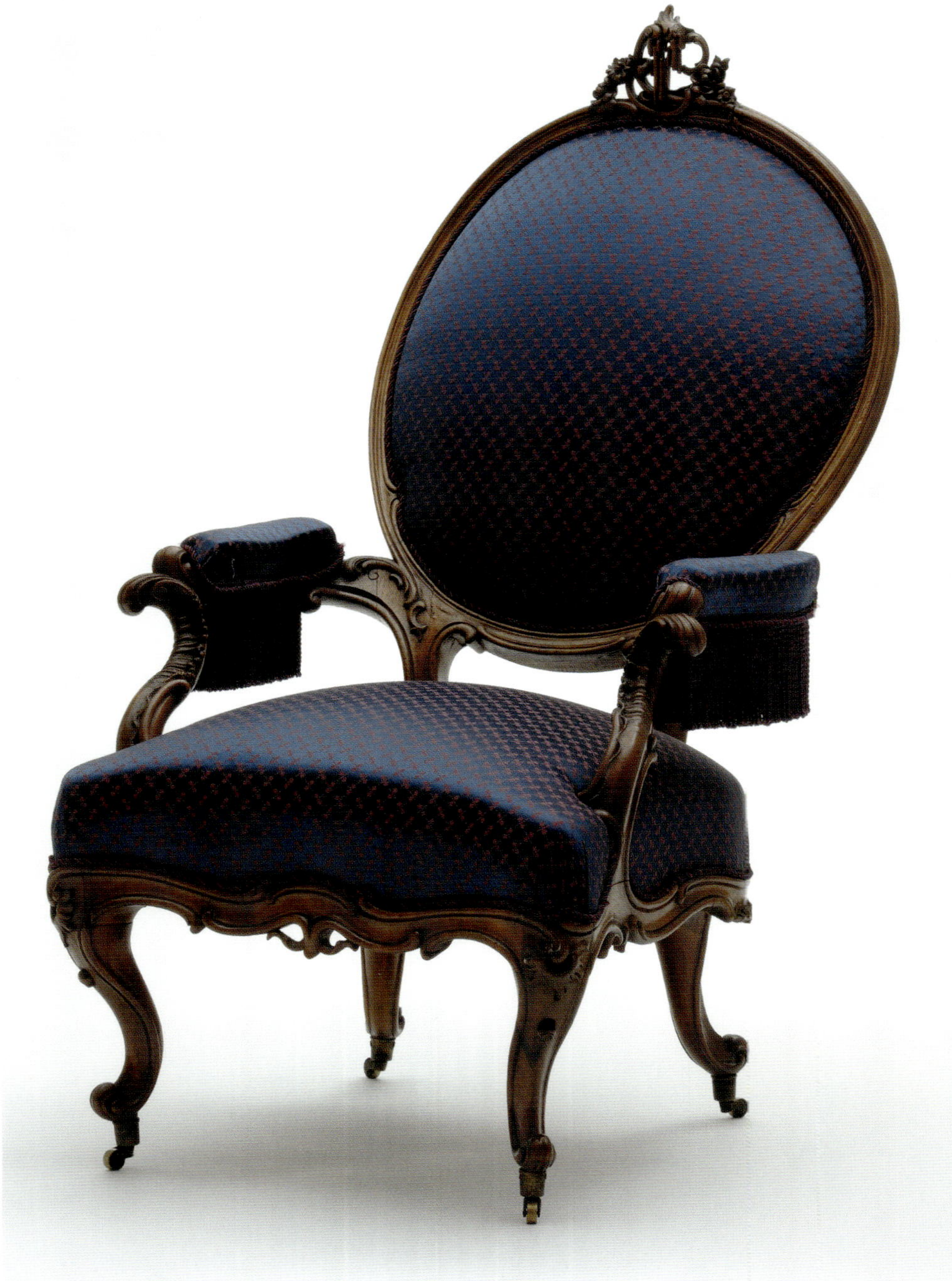

Fauteuil
Austria, around 1840
Walnut, carved, padding and fabric cover renewed, 102 × 51 × 52 cm
MAK – Austrian Museum of Applied Arts / Contemporary Art, Vienna, inv. no. H 1518

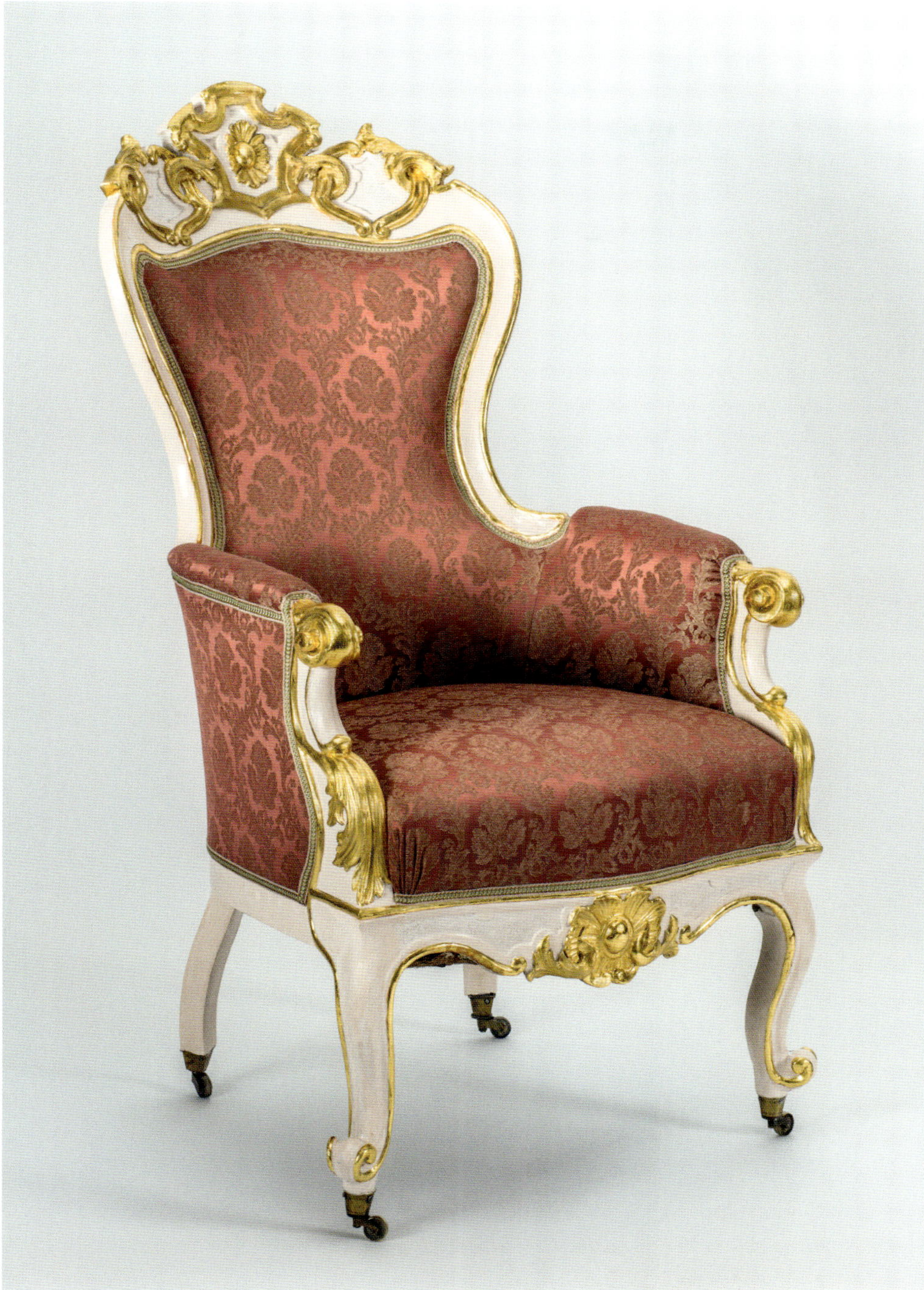

Armchair from the Salzburg Residence
Salzburg, around 1855/60
Wood, partially carved, painted trims, partially gilded, padding and fabric cover renewed,
116 × 66 × 83 cm
Federal Furniture Administration/exhibited at Imperial Furniture Collection – Furniture Museum Vienna,
inv. no. MD 45.610 (old Salzburg number: S. 6.371)

The ornately carved armchair with a polychrome frame in white, pink, and gold displays the opulent Neo-Rococo forms typical of the mid-nineteenth century. The chair originates from the Salzburg Residence, where the lodgings of Emperor Joseph I and Empress Elisabeth had been refurbished in the 1850s.

For this, silk fabrics and chandeliers were delivered by Viennese firms, while the new furniture was made by Salzburg craftsmen. Archive sources mention the names of the cabinet-maker Joseph Wessiken, the gilder Johann Ettl, and the upholsterer Johann Pfanzelter.

EO

1 Fernando Mazzocca, ed., *Hayez dal mito al bacio*, exh. cat. Palazzo Zabarella, Padua (Venice, 1998), pp. 142–43.
2 Mazzocca 1998 (see note 1), pp. 142–43.
3 Alessandro Quinzi refers to the watercolor *Naufragio del Brig.no Aristide del Cap.no Drago Poppovich* by François Geoffroy Roux, signed "Marseille 1832" and now in the Civici Musei di Storia e Arte di Trieste; see Alessandro Quinzi, *Giuseppe Tominz* (Collana d'Arte della Fondazione CRTrieste, vol. 13) (Trieste, 2011), cat. no. 64.
4 Quinzi 2011 (see note 3), pp. 65–66.
5 L. A. Frankl, "Mathias Johann Ranftl: Biographische Skizze," in *Neue Freie Presse*, morning edition, no. 1758, July 21, 1869, n.p.
6 For the biographies of the children, see Susanne Walter, "Die Familien Wisgrill, Lang und von Förster: Ein genealogischer und kulturhistorischer Streifzug durch das Wiener Patriziat," in *Wiener Geschichtsblätter*, 57th yr., no. 2 (2002), pp. 126–53, especially pp. 136–42.
7 See Giuseppe Pavanello, "Michelangelo Grigoletti (1801–1870): appunti per un profilo," in *Il Museo Civico d'Arte di Pordenone*, ed. Gilberto Ganzer (Vicenza, 2001), pp. 51–58.
8 Grigoletti was inspired by Lord Byron's play *The Two Foscari* (1821, act 3, scene 1), on which, in turn, Giuseppe Verdi's 1844 opera *I due Foscari* was based. See Gilberto Ganzer, ed., *Michelangelo Grigoletti*, exh. cat. Museo Civico d'Arte, Pordenone (Pordenone, 2002), pp. 150–51; Gilberto Ganzer/Vania Gransinigh, *Michelangelo Grigoletti* (Milan, 2007), pp. 46–47.
9 *Oesterreichischer Beobachter*, no. 134, May 14, 1843, p. 532; *Wiener Zuschauer*, no. 73, July 19, 1843, pp. 774–76.
10 Guglielmo Coronini, *Mostra di Giuseppe Tominz*, exh. cat. Palazzo Attems, Gorizia (Gorizia, 1966), p. 126.
11 Sabine Grabner, *Der Maler Josef Danhauser: Biedermeierzeit im Bild. Monografie und Werkverzeichnis* (= Belvedere catalogues raisonnés 1) (Vienna/Cologne/Weimar, 2011), cat. rais. nos. 131–58.
12 "Porträt Frau v. Hell, Kniestück, 15 : 6." (Arthur Roessler, *Josef Danhauser* [Vienna, 1946], p. 81).
13 Roessler 1946 (see note 12), p. 81; *Noli me Tangere*, 1833, see Grabner 2011 (see note 11), cat. rais. no. 123.
14 Auct. cat. Dorotheum Vienna, May 7, 1906, no. 14 (with figs.).
15 Dorotheum 1906 (see note 14), p. 3.
16 Adolph Lehmann, ed., *Allgemeines Adressbuch und Geschäfts-Handbuch für die k. k. Haupt- und Residenzstadt Wien und dessen Umgebung*, yr. 1 (Vienna, 1859), p. 252.
17 *Neuester verbesserter SCHEMA aller in der k. k. Haupt- und Residenzstadt Wien und in ihren Vorstädten befindlichen Häusern* (Vienna, 1833), p. 188. Under the heading "house sign or name," it says here: "H. Florian" (the 1906 name "Held-Haus" would surely have been "Hell-Haus"). I would like to thank Stefan Lehner from the Belvedere Archive for his help in finding the address and occupants.
18 Possibly, through another marriage, she is also Anna Gsiller, who is registered in 1859.
19 *Wiener Zeitung*, no. 52, March 5, 1830, p. 259
20 *Der Wanderer*, no. 64, March 5, 1830, p. 2.
21 In Giuseppe Bergamini, ed., *Tra Venezia e Vienna: Le arti a Udine nell'Ottocento* (Milan, 2004), p. 382.
22 For further details about Rudolf von Arthaber see Sabine Grabner, "Rudolf von Arthaber: Kaufmann und Mäzen," *Parnass: Das Kunstmagazin*, yr. 22, no. 4 (2002), pp. 86–93.
23 Villa Wertheimstein, today Döbling's Bezirksmuseum (district museum). The collection is listed in *Catalog der von Arthaber'schen Gemäldesammlung auf dem "Tullnerhofe" in Ober-Döbling bei Wien* (Vienna, 1856 and 1863).
24 The children are Johann Josef Rudolf (1828–1899), Emilie Caroline (1830–1842), and Gustav Michael (1832–1857).
25 This is an enlarged version of the now missing portrait that Moritz Michael Daffinger painted for Rudolf von Arthaber in 1833, see Emil Pirchan, *Moritz Michael Daffinger: Miniaturmaler des Vormärz* (Vienna/Leipzig, 1943), plate XX.
26 *Kunstwerke, öffentlich ausgestellt im Gebäude der Oesterreichisch-kaiserlichen Akademie der bildenden Künste bey St. Anna im Jahre 1826* (Vienna, 1826), nos. 104, 124.
27 Barbara Jaki, *Meščanska slika: Slikarstvo prve polovice 19. stoletja iz zbirk Narodne galerije*, exh. cat. National Gallery, Ljubljana (Ljubljana, 2000), p. 233.
28 Heinrich Schwarz, *Salzburg und das Salzkammergut*, 3rd ed. (Vienna/Munich, 1958), p. 36.
29 Andreas Andresen/Joseph Erhard Wessely, eds., *Die deutschen Maler-Radirer (Peintres-Graveurs) des neunzehnten Jahrhunderts nach ihren Leben und Werken*, vol. 2 (Leipzig, 1867), p. 201; Rolf H. Johannsen, "Friedrich Loos—der weite Blick: Ein Künstlerleben zwischen Wien, Rom und dem Norden," in *Friedrich Loos: Ein Künstlerleben zwischen Wien, Rom und dem Norden*, Rolf H. Johannsen/Agnes Husslein-Arco eds., exh. cat. Belvedere, Vienna (Vienna, 2015), pp. 20–23.
30 "Ideen über die Landschaftsmahlerei und Perspective: Öffentlich vorgetragen an der k. k. Akademie der bildenden Künste zu Wien vom Prof. Johann Nep. Schödelberger, Mitglied der k. k. Akad. der bild. Künste," unpublished manuscript, Vienna, 1816, p. 42.
31 For more details about the tour see Walter Koschatzky, *Thomas Ender. 1793–1875: Kammermaler Erzherzog Johanns* (Graz, 1982), p. 60.
32 Marianne Klemun, *... mit Madame Sonne konferieren: Die Großglockner-Expeditionen 1799 und 1800* (Klagenfurt, 2000), p. 252.
33 On the whereabouts of these studies see Koschatzky 1982 (see note 31), pp. 199–200.

34 Peter Pötschner, "Franz Steinfelds 'Hallstätter See' von 1834," in *Mitteilungen der Österreichischen Galerie*, 6th yr., no. 50 (1962), pp. 29–32, especially p. 30.
35 Adalbert Stifter, *Feldblumen* (1841), Zürich 1946, p. 42.
36 Ludwig von Hevesi, *Rudolf Alt: Sein Leben und sein Werk* (Vienna, 1911), p. 65.
37 *Der Stock am Eisen Platz*, from *Collections of Views from the Imperial City of Vienna* [...] (1779), Wien Museum; see *Schöne Aussichten: Die berühmten Wien-Bilder des Verlags Artaria*, exh. cat. Wien Museum (Vienna, 2007), pp. 18–20 and 58–61.
38 *Kunstwerke, öffentlich ausgestellt im Gebäude der österreichisch-kaiserlichen Akademie der bildenden Künste bey St. Anna im Jahre 1832* (Vienna, 1832), no. 165.
39 Quoted from Marc-Oliver Schuster, ed., *Eduard Ritter: Biographische Skizze meines Lebens*, publication pending, p. 9. Eduard Ritter's autobiography, edited and published by Marc-Oliver Schuster, will be available soon as a book. I thank the editor for permission to consult the manuscript.
40 *Wiener Zeitschrift*, no. 117, September 29, 1838, plate next to p. 936. The wall and ceiling decorations are the same as in the painting; the picture on the wall shows the chess player.
41 *Werke der Kunstausstellung, welche die Oesterreichisch-kaiserliche Akademie der vereinigten bildenden Künste im Gebäude zu St. Anna 1845 veranstaltet hat* (Vienna, 1845), no. 250.
42 Fritz Novotny, *Hundert Jahre österreichischer Landschaftsmalerei* (Vienna, 1948), p. 4.
43 For an interpretation of the figures, see Alexander Strasoldo-Graffemberg, *Ludwig Ferdinand Schnorr von Carolsfeld (1788–1853)*, unpublished diss., Freiburg i. Br., 1986, pp. 139–41; Martin Tanzwirt, *Der Strömungspluralismus im Werk von Ludwig Ferdinand Schnorr von Carolsfeld*, unpublished diss., Vienna, 1999, pp. 161–62; Werner Telesko, "'Heimatbilder': Landschaftskunst und Identitätssuche in der österreichischen Malerei des 19. Jahrhunderts," in *Belvedere. Zeitschrift für bildende Kunst*, no. 2 (2004), pp. 4–17, especially pp. 7–8.
44 "Ideen über die Landschaftsmahlerei und Perspective öffentlich vorgetragen an der k. k. Akademie der bildenden Künste zu Wien vom Prof. Johann Nep. Schödelberger, Mitglied der Akad. der bild. Künste," unpublished manuscript, Vienna, 1816. The manuscript from this lecture, one of the first pieces of evidence relating to studies of nature at the Vienna Academy, is at the archives of the Vienna Academy of Fine Arts. See Sabine Grabner, "Die Wiener Akademie und die Landschaftsmalerei," in *Italienische Reisen: Landschaftsbilder österreichischer und ungarischer Maler 1770 bis 1850*, Sabine Grabner/Claudia Wöhrer, eds., exh. cat. Österreichische Galerie Belvedere, Vienna (Vienna, 2001), pp. 97–108, especially p. 103.
45 *Theater-Zeitung*, yr. 36, no. 114, May 13, 1843, p. 511; *Werke der Kunstausstellung, welche die Oesterreichisch-kaiserliche Akademie der vereinigten bildenden Künste im Gebäude des k. k. polytechnischen Institutes im Jahre 1843 veranstaltet hat* (Vienna, 1843), no. 275 ("Costume of an Emir from Lebanon").
46 See also *Morgenblatt*, yr. 8, no. 63, May 27, 1843, p. 251.
47 On the subject of Borsos's training in Vienna see Sabine Grabner, "'Von bewundernswürdiger Wahrheit eines Amerling würdig.' Die Ausbildung zum Maler abseits der Akademie in Wien am Beispiel des ungarischen Malers József Borsos (1821–1883)," *Wiener Geschichtsblätter*, yr. 65, no. 4 (2010), pp. 243–53 (published in Hungarian: "'Csodálatraméltó, szinte olyan, mint Amerling.' Borsos József Bécsi tanulóévei," *Borsos József: Festő és fotográfus [1821–1883]/József Borsos: Painter and Photographer [1821–1883]*, exh. cat. Hungarian National Gallery, Budapest [Budapest, 2009], pp. 55–65).
48 *Beilage zu den Sonntagsblättern*, yr. 4, no. 23, June 8, 1845, p. 545 (Eduard Melly).
49 The painting *Il saluto del mattino* exists only in reproduction today. A further picture, *La toeletta del mattino* from 1846, is in a private collection in London; see Maria Vittoria Marini Clarelli/Fernando Mazzocca/Carlo Sisi, eds., *Ottocento. Da Canova al Quarto Stato*, exh. cat. Scuderie del Quirinale, Rome (Milan, 2008), pp. 178–79 (Giovanna Capitelli).
50 P. M., "La Pia de' Tolomei: Dipinto di Eliseo Sala," in *Gemme d'arti italiane*, 3rd yr. (1847), p. 131.
51 Anon., "Künstlerbiografien: Natale Schiavoni," in *Sonntags-Blätter*, 1st yr., no. 26, June 26, 1842, pp. 466–67, especially p. 467.
52 Letter no. 399, August 11, 1859, in *Prager Gesamtausgabe der Werke Stifters*, vol. 19 (Prague, 1901), p. 166.
53 For parallels between Neder's work and twentieth-century art, see Harald Krejci, "Zur Rezeption des Werks von Michael Neder im 20. Jahrhundert in Wien," in Agnes Husslein-Arco/Sabine Grabner, eds., *Michael Neder: Ohne Kompromisse*, exh. cat. Belvedere, Vienna (Munich, 2013), pp. 115–23.
54 Karl Hareiter, *Michael Neder* (Vienna, 1948), p. 47.
55 For the changes in painting technique and unsuccessful experiments in this context, see Elisabeth Foissner, "König des Frühschwundrisses: Überlegungen zur Maltechnik von Michael Neder," in Husslein-Arco/Grabner 2013 (see note 53), pp. 45–55.
56 *Fremden-Blatt*, 21st yr., no. 32, February 1, 1867, p. 6.
57 *Kunstwerke, öffentlich ausgestellt im Gebäude der Österreichisch-kaiserlichen Akademie der vereinigten bildenden Künste bei St. Anna im Jahre 1839* (Vienna, 1839), no. 436.
58 *Werke der Kunstausstellung, welche die Oesterreichisch-kaiserliche Akademie der vereinigten bildenden Künste im Gebäude des k. k. polytechnischen Institutes im Jahre 1841 veranstaltet hat* (Vienna, 1841), no. 284 ("Eigenthum des Herrn Prévot").
59 *Wiener Zeitung*, no. 268, November 21, 1862, p. 1596.

60 Federica Millozzi, in *La coscienza del vero. Capolavori dell'Ottocento da Courbet a Segantini*, ed. Alessandra Tiddia (Milan, 2015), p. 182.

61 *Verzeichniss der öffentlich ausgestellten Kunstwerke an der kaiserl. Königl. Akademie der bildenden Künste bei St. Anna im Jahre 1858* (Vienna, 1858), no. 17.

62 *Verzeichnis der Kunstwerke, welche in der von dem Wiener Kunst-Vereine veranstalteten Ausstellung in dem Gebäude der k. k. Akademie der bildenden Künste zu St. Anna öffentlich ausgestellt sind* (Vienna, 1849), no. 214.

63 *Beilage zum Morgenblatte der Wiener Zeitung*, October 6, 1849, n.p.

64 I would like to thank Stefanie Jahn and Bettina Urban from the Belvedere's Conservation Department for their analysis.

65 Naděžda Blažičková-Horová, ed., *Czech 19th-Century Painting: Catalogue of the Permanent Exhibition. Convent of St. Agnes of Bohemia* (Prague, 1998), p. 121, no. 84.

66 Quoted from Ludwig Hevesi, *Oesterreichische Kunst im 19. Jahrhundert. Erster Teil: 1800–1848* (= Geschichte der modernen Kunst II) (Leipzig, 1903), p. 83.

67 See Waldmüller's article in Rupert Feuchtmüller, *Ferdinand Georg Waldmüller, 1793–1865: Leben, Schriften, Werke* (Vienna/Munich, 1996), pp. 329–72; see also Sabine Grabner, "Ferdinand Georg Waldmüller – Künstler und Rebell," in Husslein-Arco/Grabner 2009 (see note 81), pp. 13–17; as well as the essay by Werner Busch in this volume (pp. 68–75).

68 Waldmüller's journal of his trip to Paris in 1839 is in the manuscript collection of the Vienna City Library; see Sabine Grabner, "Ferdinand Georg Waldmüllers Tagebuch der Reise nach Paris im Jahre 1830," in *Wiener Geschichtsblätter*, to be published in late 2016.

69 My heartfelt thanks to Christopher Wentworth-Stanley as well as Silvija Lučevnjak from the Našice Local History Museum for their help in identifying these names.

70 Almut Krapf, "Johann Matthias Ranftl als Illustrator von Eduard v. Bauernfelds Revolutions-Satire 'Die Republik der Thiere,'" in *Wissenschaftliche Zeitschrift der Ernst-Moritz-Arndt-Universität Greifswald*, vol. 34, no. 1–2 (1985), pp. 59–64.

71 Most recently in Zsuzsanna Bakó/Tayfun Belgin, eds., *Die ungarische Seele: Romantik und Realismus im Land der Magyaren*, exh. cat. Kunsthalle Krems (Heidenreichstein, 2006), pp. 80–81.

72 *Borsos József: Festő és fotográfus [1821–1883]/József Borsos: Painter and Photographer (1821–1883)*, exh. cat. Hungarian National Gallery, Budapest (Budapest, 2009), pp. 146–48 (Eszter Békef).

73 Constant von Wurzbach, *Biographisches Lexikon des Kaisertums Österreich*, vol. 2 (Vienna, 1857), p. 79.

74 *Borsos József* 2009 (see note 47), pp. 148–50 (Nóra Veszprémi).

75 See, for example, Barbara Jaki, *Meščanska slika: Slikarstvo prve polovice 19. stoletja iz zbirk Narodne galerije*, exh. cat. National Gallery of Slovenia, Ljubljana (Ljubljana, 2000), p. 139; *Saur/De Gruyter Allgemeines Künstlerlexikon: Die bildenden Künstler aller Zeiten und Völker*, vol. 82 (Munich etc., 2014), p. 200 (Gudrun Dauner).

76 In Naděžda Blažíčková-Horová, ed., *Czech 19th-Century Painting: Catalogue of the Permanent Exhibition. Convent of St. Agnes of Bohemia* (Prague, 1998), p. 95.

77 Karl Blaas, *Selbstbiographie des Malers Karl Blaas: 1815–1876* (Vienna, 1876), p. 101.

78 Blaas 1876 (see note 77), p. 247.

79 Blaas 1876 (see note 77), p. 227.

80 The Neobaroque palace, built in 1894/95 by the architects' practice Fellner & Helmer, was demolished soon after World War II. In its place is now a building erected between 1960 and 1962 by the architect Georg Lippert (1908–1992).

81 For a summary of Waldmüller's teaching methods, see Sabine Grabner, "Ferdinand Georg Waldmüller—Künstler und Rebell," in *Ferdinand Georg Waldmüller 1793–1865*, Sabine Grabner/Agnes Husslein-Arco eds., exh. cat. Belvedere, Vienna/Musée du Louvre, Paris (Vienna, 2009), pp. 13–17, especially pp. 14–15.

82 Quoted from Bruno Grimschitz, *Ferdinand Georg Waldmüller: Leben und Werk* (Vienna, 1943), p. 75.

83 Anon., *Die Presse*, January 28, 1854, n.p.

84 *Der Humorist*, February 21, 1854, p. 168; *Morgenpost*, February 21, 1854, n.p.

Louis Janmot, *Fleur des champs* (detail), 1845
Musée des Beaux-Arts, Lyon

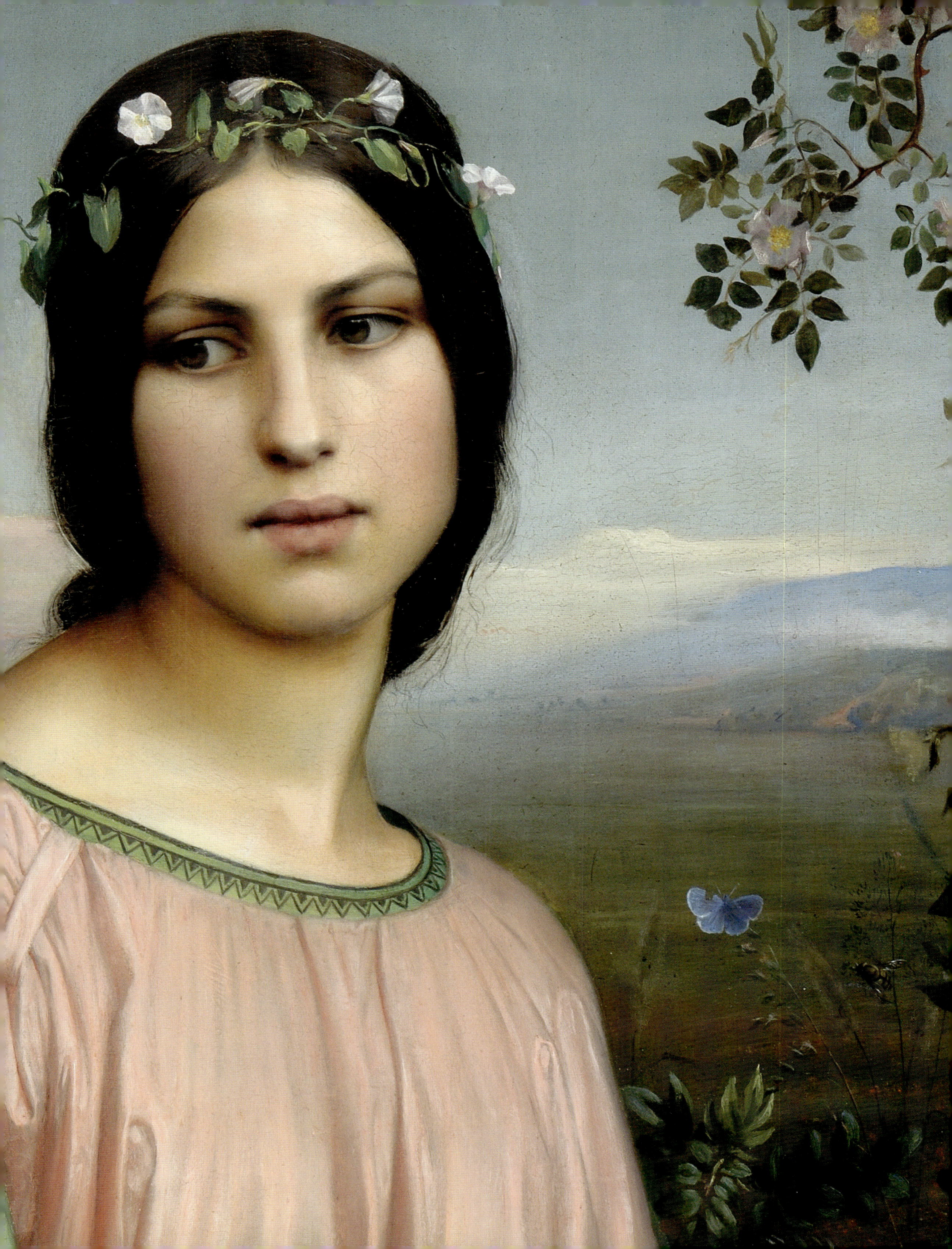

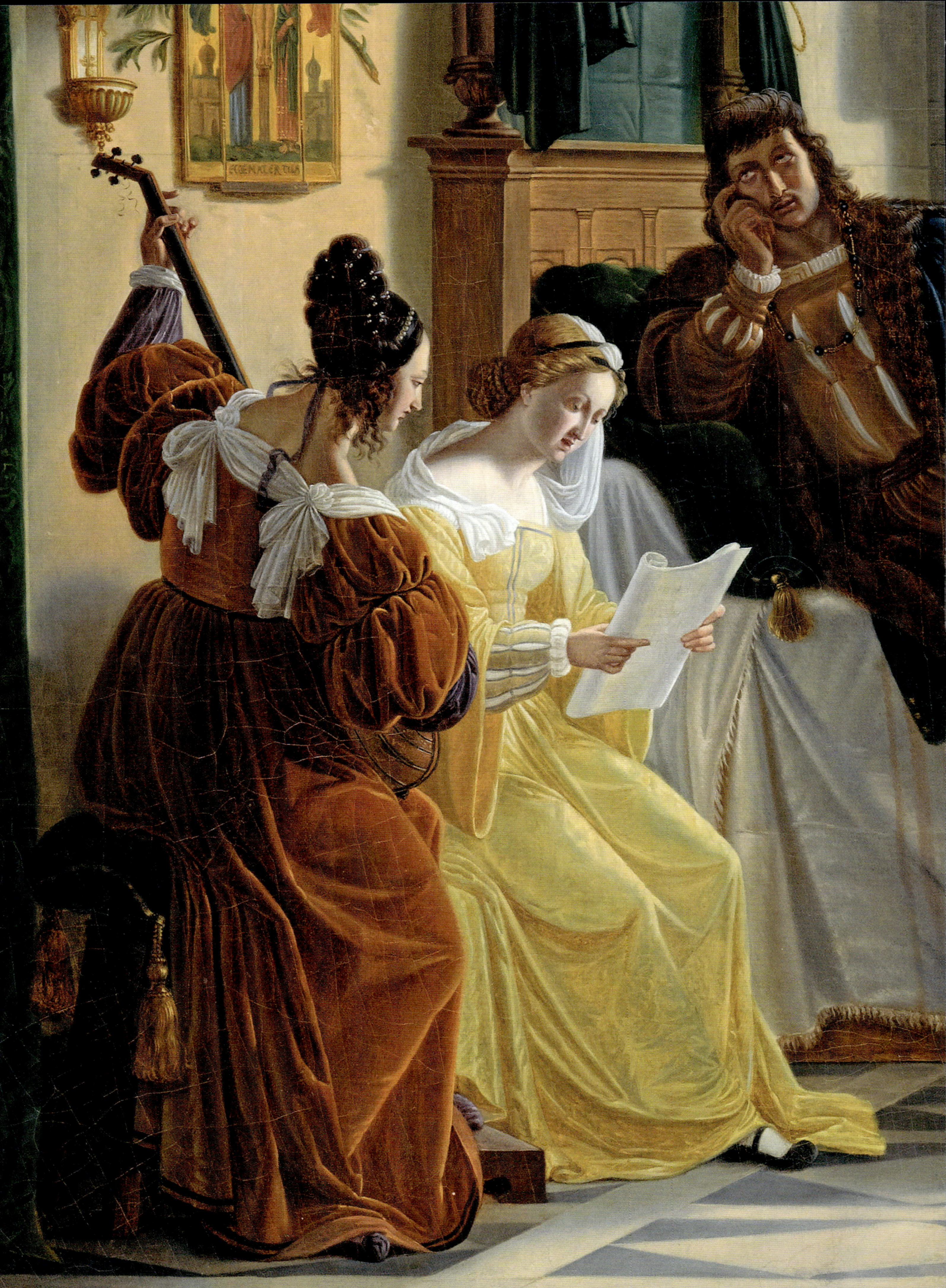

NEAR AND FAR
FRENCH PAINTING AND BIEDERMEIER

Stéphane Paccoud

Little attention has been paid to date to the artistic interactions between France and Austria during the first two thirds of the nineteenth century. Austrian artists are generally regarded as having played no part in the French art scene and as having been ignored by their fellow artists there. The first serious contact did not take place until the Exposition Universelle in Paris in 1855. For the first time, the exhibition devoted a section to fine arts and offered the participating nations the opportunity to compare their paintings, sculptures, drawings, and prints. The Austrian section was a poorly conceived, last-minute affair and therefore attracted little interest.[1] It featured works by artists from different provinces, including Karl von Blaas, Eduard von Engerth, Ferdinand Georg Waldmüller, Franz Eybl, Rudolf von Alt, Friedrich Gauermann, Joseph Führich from Bohemia, József Borsos from Hungary, and the Polish artist Zofia Fredro, among others. There was a strong contingent of northern Italian painters, including Carlo Arienti and Francesco Hayez, whom the reviewers presumed to treat separately.

There were various reasons for this cold reception. In the first place, practically all of these artists were exhibiting for the first time in Paris and were thus unknown to the local audience. In addition, in the French mind, all artistic creativity in the German-speaking world and in central Europe was associated with the Nazarenes. The discovery in particular of the works of Peter Cornelius (1783–1867) and Wilhelm Kaulbach (1805–1874) was therefore regarded in advance as one of the highpoints of the exhibition. In view of this predominance, further encouraged by the Catholic critics and reinforced through the admiration of many artists, especially those trained in Ingres's studio, there was no room for a style such as Biedermeier, despite the fact that it offered an alternative model. The 1855 exhibition may be regarded as a missed and unrepeatable opportunity that was to mark the start of the continued neglect of Austrian art of the time by both the French public and its art critics.

Looking beyond this episode, however, some interesting earlier points of contact can be discerned. It is highly likely that French works circulated in Austria in the same way as they did in Germany.[2] In 1865, for example, the art dealer Adolphe Goupil opened a branch in Vienna, in which he organized traveling exhibitions of works handled by him. No detailed study has yet been made of this phenomenon that could help establish a basis for determining its impact. Since the Paris Salon had proved to be the most important exhibition venue in previous decades, some Austrian artists had also tried their luck there by submitting genre scenes and portraits. Mention might be made, for example, of Carl Rahl in 1846 and Johann Nepomuk Ender and his son Eduard from 1847 to 1849. The most striking example is Heinrich Wilhelm Schlesinger (1814–1893). Born in Frankfurt, he had studied at the Academy of Fine Arts in Vienna before settling in Paris, where he exhibited his works almost every year between 1840 and 1849. The Goncourt brothers disdainfully described "this Schlesinger eighteenth century, which was now spreading to artists' studios after having conquered vaudeville theaters,"[3] such was the audience attracted by this artist. Schlesinger was made a member of the French Legion of Honor in 1866 and became a French citizen four years later.

A search for possible connections between the French and Austrian art scenes in the era of the July Monarchy and the start of the Second Empire takes us away from the long-prevailing focus by historians on two individuals, Eugène Delacroix (1798–1863) and Jean-Auguste-Dominique Ingres (1780–1867), as contrasting representatives of the new Romantic school and the Neoclassical tradition. A closer examination of the successive Salon catalogues shows how genre painting and portraits gradually came to the fore from the 1820s as the dominant categories of contemporary

Pierre Révoil, *La Convalescence de Bayard* (detail), 1817
Musée du Louvre, Paris

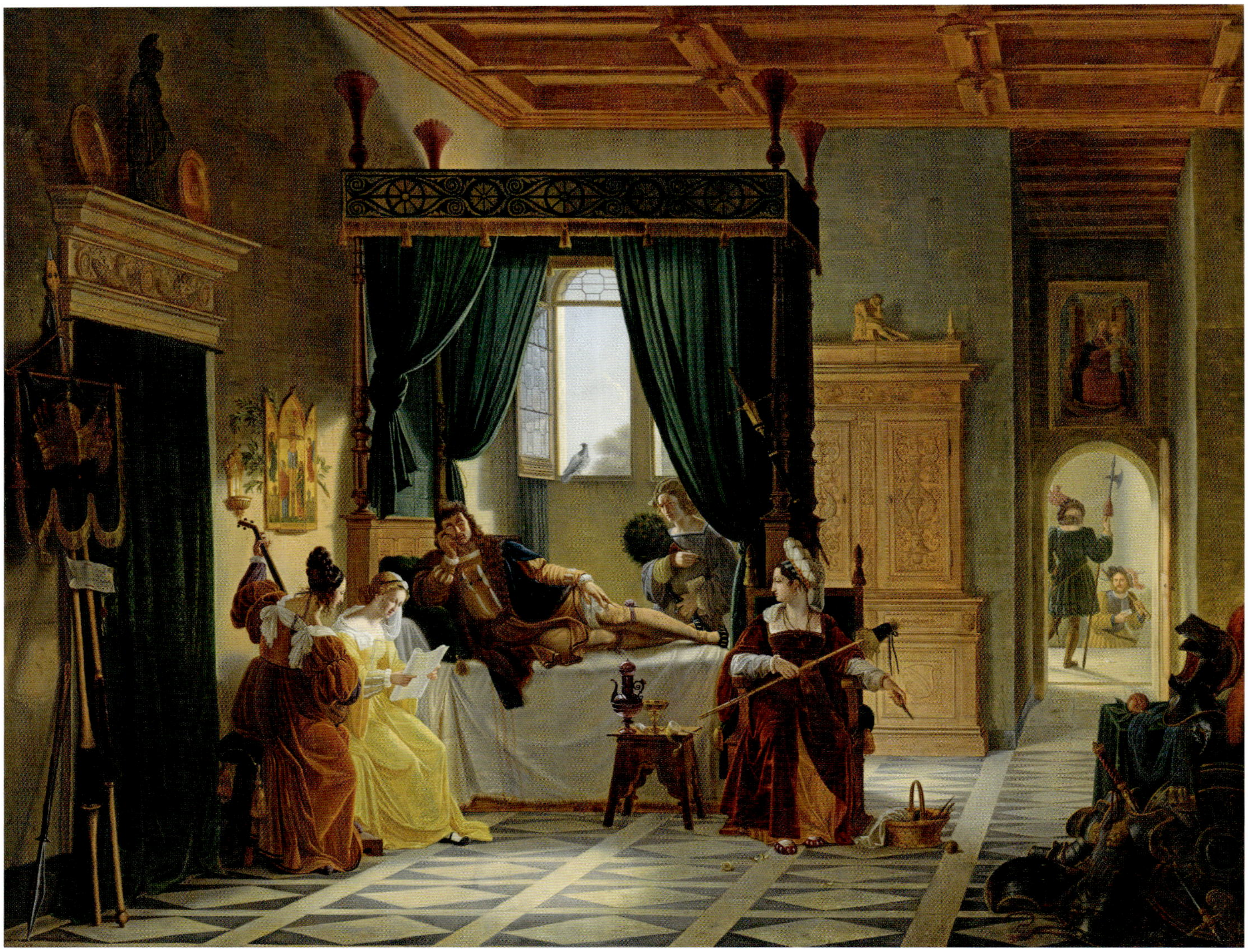

Fig. 1: **Pierre Révoil**, *La Convalescence de Bayard*, 1817
Musée du Louvre, Paris

production, while history painting lost its luster—so much so that these two categories, long regarded in the academic ranking as minor players, established themselves as new areas of research into a certain form of modernity. The critic Étienne Delécluze, a former student of Jacques-Louis David (1748–1825), noted bitterly in his review of the 1855 exhibition: "Anecdotal themes abound, and this genre is cultivated everywhere. [...] Switzerland, Belgium, Austria, England, Spain, and France are full of paintings like these. In general, whatever artists produce that is entertaining or pleasant to behold will also appeal today to the broader public."[4]

All commentators agree that this genre had its origins in the early years of the nineteenth century, when the predominance of the Neoclassical style advocated by David was questioned in the works of some of his own students. The result was a hybrid form of historical representation, moving away from mythological or classical subjects in favor of themes from the "national past," such as the rediscovered Middle Ages or the sixteenth and seventeenth centuries. The formats became smaller to attract more customers, the themes anecdotal and sentimental, but the execution was extremely meticulous with well-placed details and effects. The critics created the new category of *genre anecdotique* to describe works that are now subsumed in a category more commonly known as "troubadour." These pictures were admired by art lovers from all over Europe. A change took place, paving the way for the future success of genre painting. Probably the most symptomatic example was the painter Pierre Révoil (1776–1842) from

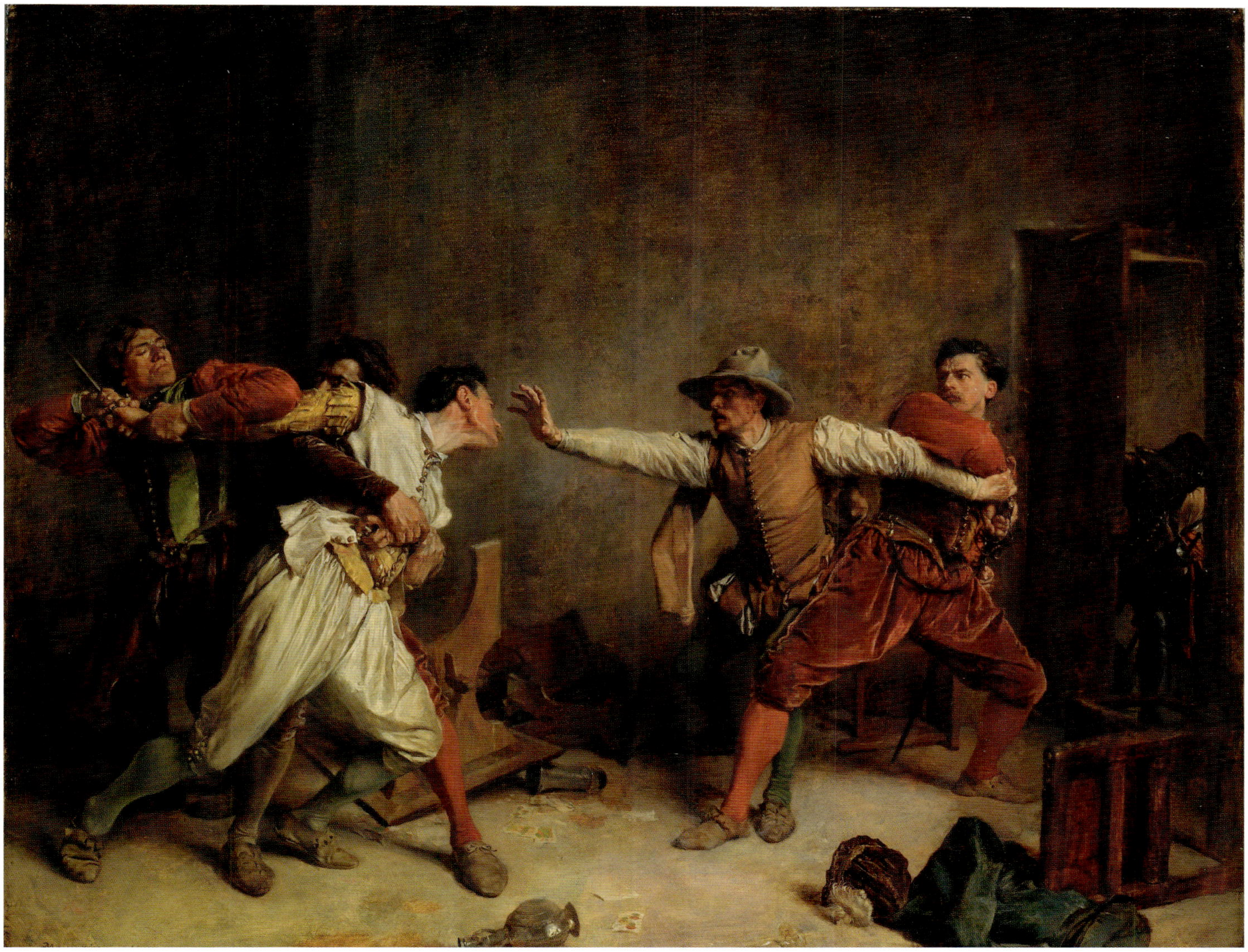

Fig. 2: **Ernest Meissonier**, *Une Rixe*, 1855
Royal Collection Trust / © HM Queen Elizabeth II

Lyon—one of the most striking characters in this trend—who had a predilection for historical details, which he made vast use of. In *La Convalescence de Bayard* (fig. 1), the subject is drowned in a plethora of objects, many from his extensive private collection. He was also criticized for this: "The figures are too subordinate, the accessories too numerous and dominant; this is because the arrangement, which is very good for a family scene, is not suitable for a history painting, however domestic it may be."[5]

This new approach to the past was more vibrant and colorful than before and ultimately produced a genuine taste for genre scenes in historical costumes, which was further developed in the Romantic era. This fashion persisted successfully until the end of the century and infused all of Europe.[6] It attained its highpoint with the work of Ernest Meissonier (1815–1891), whose small-format pictures showing figures in historical costumes in ordinary situations were fought over by collectors willing to pay high prices for them. For example, *Une Rixe* (fig. 2) in 1855 was hugely successful as a simple genre picture without a precise subject, showing the artist's admiration for the paintings of Adriaen Brouwer (c. 1605–1638) and David Teniers the Younger (1610–1690).

A penchant for Nordic themes appears to have been a common thread in many French genre scenes in the first half of the century, an interest shared by Biedermeier artists. The Dutch pictures of the Golden Age, which had been particularly popular with collectors for decades, were a point of reference for many artists.[7] This model, successfully applied from the 1790s and

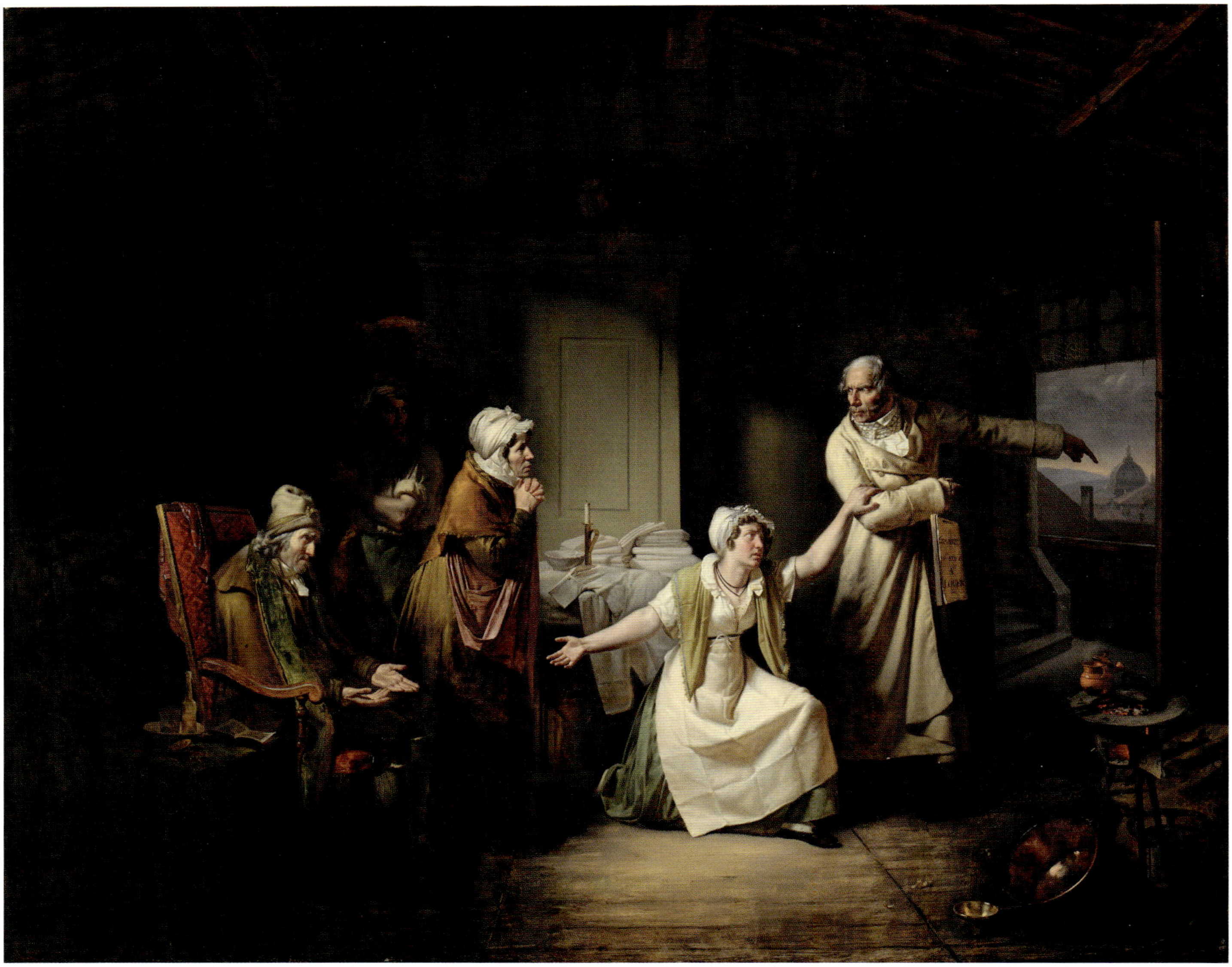

Fig. 3: **Claude Bonnefond**, *Le mauvais propriétaire*, 1824
Musée des Beaux-Arts, Lyon

1800s by Louis-Léopold Boilly (1761–1845), Martin Drolling (1752–1817), and Marguerite Gérard (1761–1837), continued to exert an influence. Lyon was to an extent the epicenter of this phenomenon in the 1820s, so much so that critics even spoke of a specific regional school. The students of Révoil, Claude Bonnefond (1796–1860), Michel Genod (1795–1862), Augustin Thierriat (1789–1870), and Anthelme Trimolet (1798–1866) preferred sentimental and anecdotal themes, which they executed with great attention to detail, precision, and finesse. Bonnefond, a successor to Jean-Baptiste Greuze (1725–1805), appealed to the viewer's emotions, showing the wretched living conditions of Savoyard children in Paris or the intransigence of an evil landlord as he unfeelingly evicts his impecunious tenants (fig. 3). The reproduction of these scenes in the form of lithographs made them more well-known and accessible to a wider audience. Many artists continued in this style until the 1840s, albeit with diminishing success.

Other artists, by contrast, attempted to step away from this Dutch model by adopting a more modern form of expression. One source of inspiration for this was literature. Joseph-Désiré Court (1797–1865), a traditional history and portrait painter, had great success in the Salon of 1844 with a scene from an extremely popular serial novel called *Les Mystères de Paris* by Eugène Süe (fig. 4). Rigolette, the heroine, has just learned of the arrest of her fiancé Germain, who is accused of theft. Sitting in front of her window with the banks of

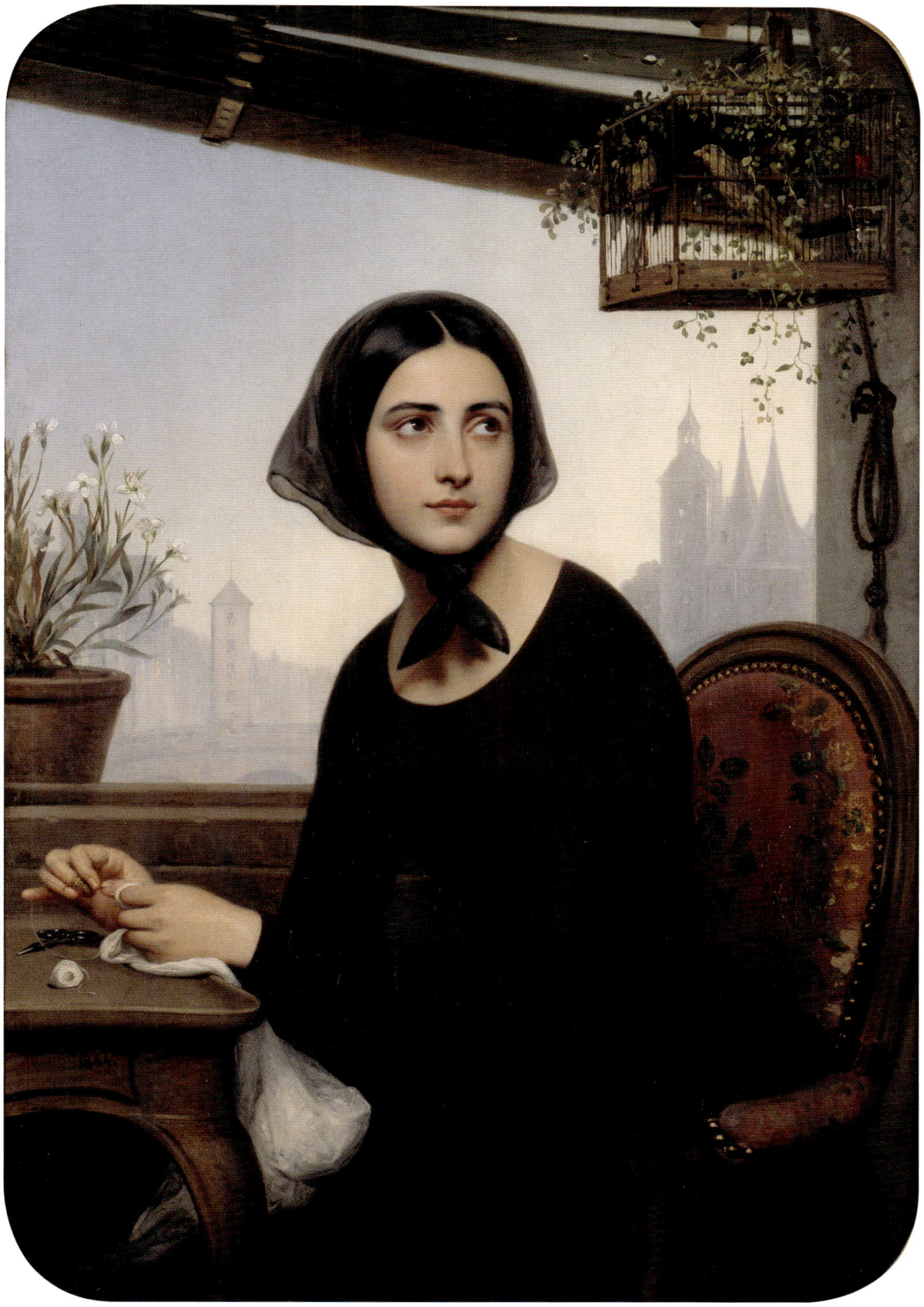

Fig. 4: **Joseph-Désiré Court**, *Rigolette cherchant à se dirstraire pendent l'absence de Germain*, 1844
Musée des Beaux-Arts, Rouen

the Seine in the background, she is trying to distract herself by sewing. The painting makes use of the symbolism of two birds locked in a cage, referring to the situation of the unfortunate young protagonists.

Italy was another source of inspiration that proved popular among artists and audiences even beyond France's borders. This trend was initiated by the Swiss painter Léopold Robert (1794–1835), who took as his model Italian folk figures—peasants, shepherds, fishermen, brigands, and musicians—depicting them in traditional costumes and placing them in magnificent settings reminiscent of classical models. After unsuccessfully trying his luck with history painting, he turned to this source of inspiration, which he sought to elevate to a new genre in its own right: "I wanted to choose an as yet unknown genre, and this one appealed. It is always an advantage to be the first."[8] He was looking for an alternative to history painting, which was in decline,

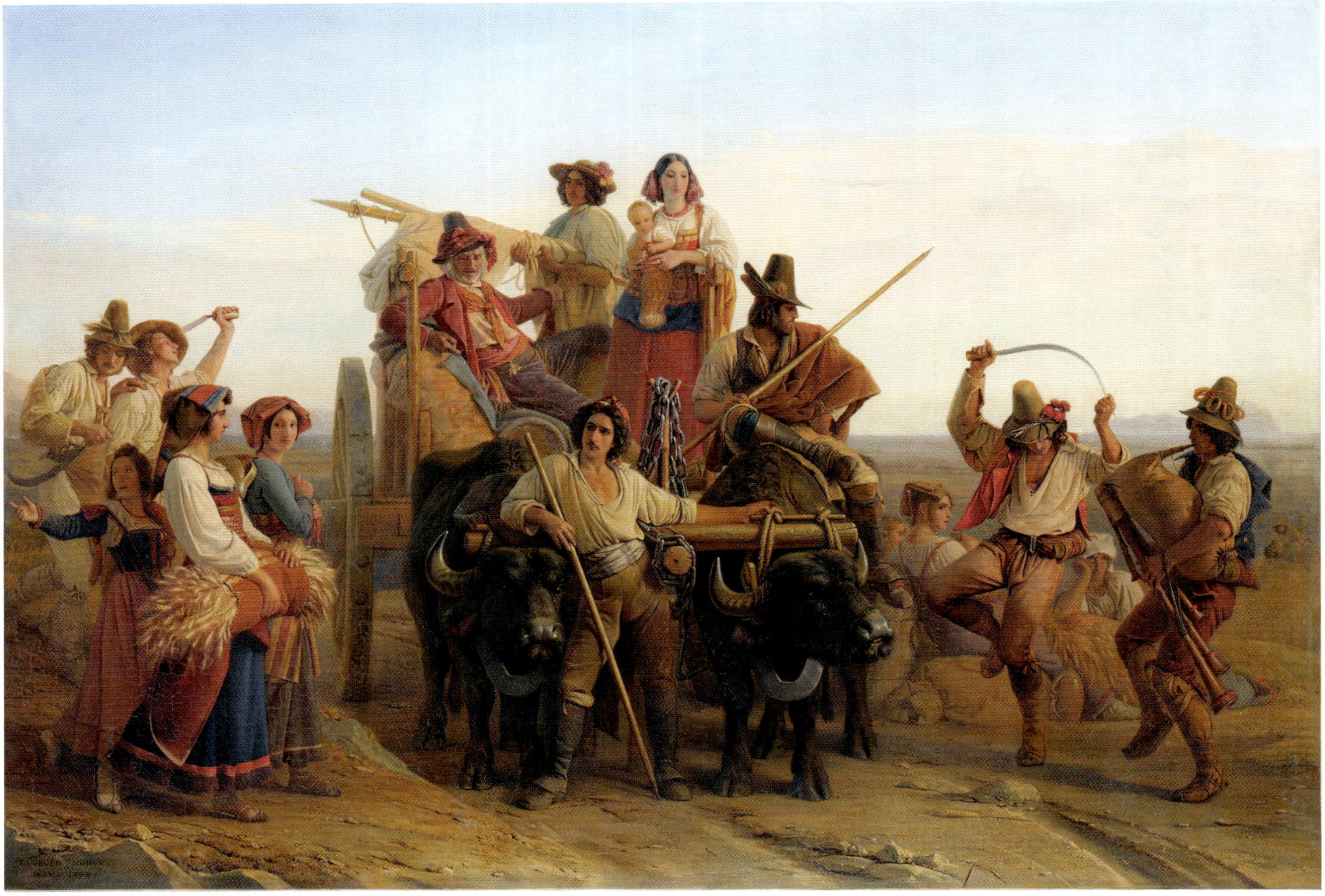

Fig. 5: **Léopold Robert**, *L'Arrivée des moissonneurs dans le marais Pontins*, 1831
Musée du Louvre, Paris

and to the anticipated triumph of genre painting by attempting to raise the latter through the nobility of the setting, a poetry at times of epic proportions, and an unyielding pursuit of an ideal, as if trying to revive classical antiquity with these folk figures. The art-loving public was tired of repetitive concepts and welcomed the picturesque nature of these new subjects. The critics also praised the painter's far-sightedness and his approach, which was the exact opposite of anecdotal genre painting. For Delécluze, the "style" was more interesting than the theme: "One doesn't become a history painter through the choice of subject, but through the way it is handled."[9] Count Atanazy Raczyński, a connoisseur of the European art scene, was of the same opinion: "His genre pictures always have something historical about them: Perhaps to console us for the fact that all too many history paintings are just genre paintings or, more often, mere showpieces."[10]

The success of *L'Arrivée des moissonneurs dans le marais Pontins* (fig. 5) at the 1831 Paris Salon was the highpoint of Robert's career. His suicide in 1835, at the zenith of his fame, raised his status to that of a genuine Romantic hero. Many artists followed in his footsteps, including Victor Schnetz (1787–1870), François-Joseph Navez (1787–1869), Guillaume Bodinier (1795–1872), and Claude Bonnefond, who abandoned his earlier representations of poverty. All nationalities came together in this great European studio by the name of Italy, and English, German, Belgian, Dutch, and Russians artists—Johann Nepomuk Ender (plate p. 155) was one of them—took up the same subjects. But the search for the picturesque soon led to stereotypes, while the social reality was neglected. In the face of the uncertainties of the time and the rapid social change, these pictures represented a paradise that was already lost. For Delécluze, "these were creatures who had fallen from the sky, like the snow on the mountains, untouched by

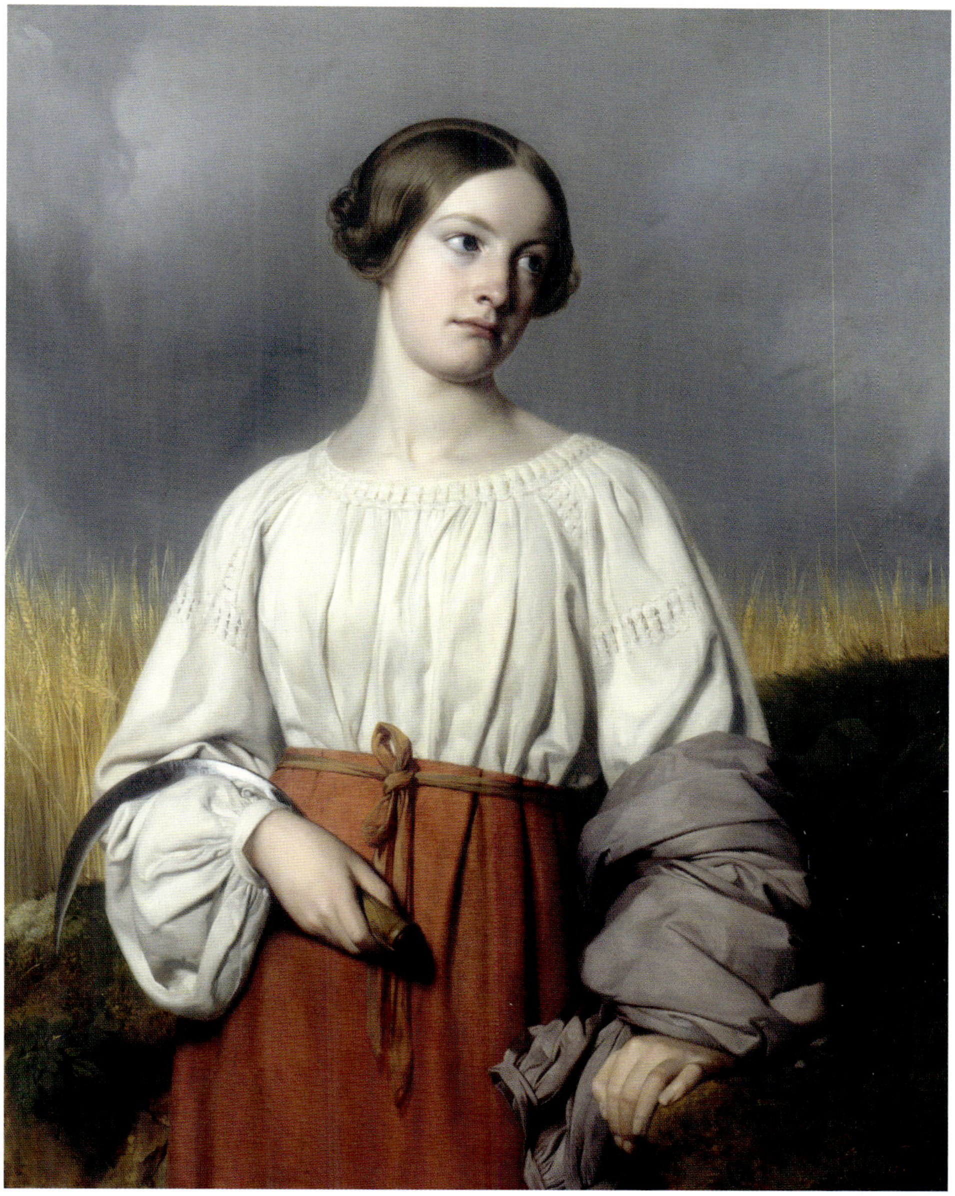

Fig. 6: **Alexandre Hesse**, *Moissonneuse tenant sa faucille*, 1837
Musée des Beaux-Arts, Nantes

our civilization. Although they exist, they cannot be part of or understand it."[11]

These pictures can also be interpreted as one of the precursors of the artistic current of Realism that emerged in the late 1840s and was to assert itself over the following two decades. In fact, peasants were popular subjects even before the work of Gustave Courbet (1819–1877) and Jean-François Millet (1814–1875). Even if the search for an ideal and a style was still dominant, Alexandre Hesse's (1806–1879) *Moissonneuse tenant sa faucille* (fig. 6), shown at the 1837 Salon, illustrated this new interest in the French countryside. At the same time, Adolphe Leleux (1812–1891) and Philippe-Auguste Jeanron (1809–1877) were traveling in Brittany and Limousin looking for subjects presenting a supposedly intact world. Hesse preserved a style influenced by the teachings of the grand masters and arranged his subject like a Madonna by Raphael. Leleux and Jeanron, on the other hand, preferred a less polished execution that was more in keeping with their subjects.

Apart from genre pictures, portraits were the major theme of the modernists in these decades. Never before had there been so many portraits at exhibitions, as the critic Auguste Jal pointed out in a withering commentary: "I counted up to 1,250 portraits and stopped there, horrified by this torrent of figures—aristocratic, bourgeois, large, small, ugly, beautiful, pretty, affected, silly, naïve, yellow, red, violet, grey, young, old, standing, busts, in oils, pastels, as miniatures, in pencil, plas-

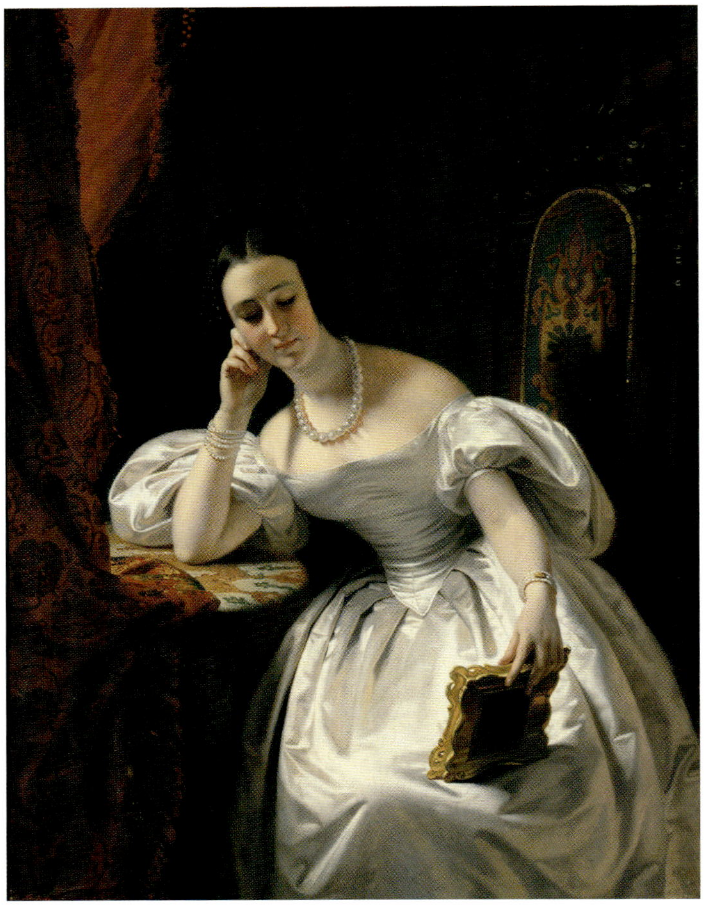

Fig. 7: **Claude-Marie Dubufe**, *Jeune fille au portrait*, 1840
Les Arts décoratifs, Paris

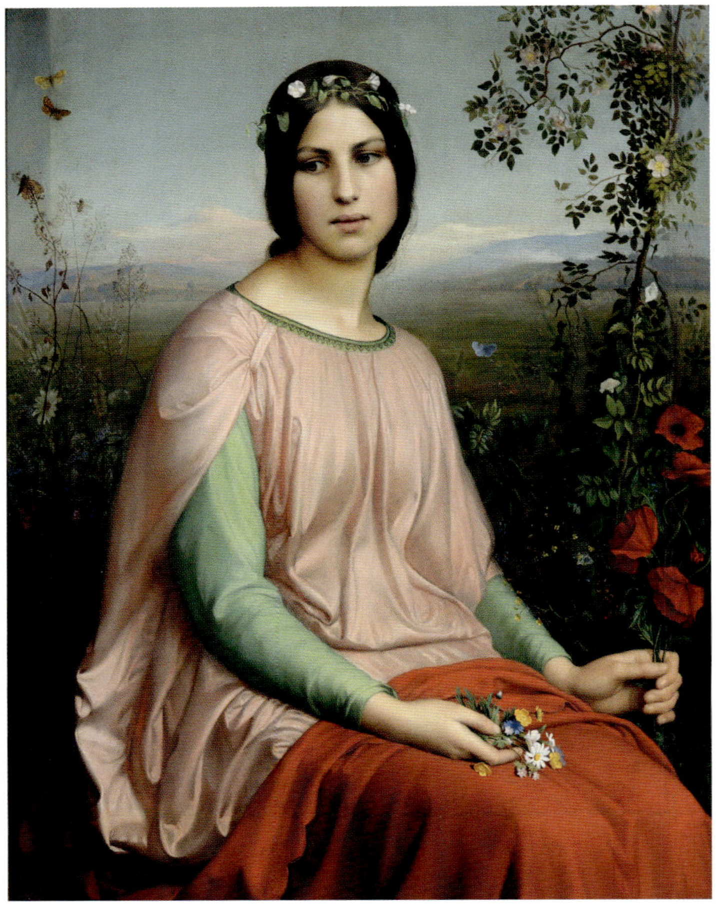

Fig. 8: **Louis Janmot**, *Fleur de champs*, 1845
Musée des Beaux-Arts, Lyon

ter, marble, and who knows what else."[12] Once again, the critics were in agreement on the increase in anecdotal and decorative elements to the detriment of simplicity and psychological characterization. The poses appeared to correspond to a conventional pattern derived from traditional sources, such as the works of van Dyck, supplemented by a certain sentimentality. Claude-Marie Dubufe (1790–1864) is a typical example of this trend towards stereotypes, piling on the effects (fig. 7). Gustave Planche spoke without hesitation about the "marketable beauty" of his models,[13] which some of the critics were so indignant about. Jal, too, complained about it: "I have seen all these vain families in their elegant settings, each one trying to outdo the other, trying to attract attention with the unreal luminosity of the colors, the exaggerated sumptuousness of the arrangement, and their affected poses."[14] In 1834, the arrival in Paris of the German painter Franz Xaver Winterhalter (1805–1873) gave a boost to this fashion for portraits and, through the numerous commissions he received, attracted many admirers of this genre throughout Europe.

The French portrait painting of this time was thus generally distinct from the aesthetic developed by the Biedermeier artists in this genre. While there may have been the same attention to décor and accessories, the realism and psychological characterization found among the Austrian artists was mostly absent in France. A certain poetic dimension and the search for a style appeared to be the main aim of most French artists. It is therefore interesting to note how much historical portraits were in vogue in the 1830s and 1840s. The arrangements in historical attire or in the style of the Old Masters were not intended to confirm reactionary patterns but rather to identify a new language. Although some writers, like Charles Baudelaire or Théophile Gautier, stressed the need for modern clothing,[15] many artists complained at the monotony of the uniform and omnipresent black. The return to historical models offered them a more poetic alternative. Their point of reference was no longer the seventeenth century, as had been the case with Friedrich von Amerling (plate p. 97), but the Italian Renaissance. *Flowers of the Field* by Louis Janmot (fig. 8), a modern rereading of the works of Raphael and Leonardo da Vinci, is a figure of fantasy that reflects this trend, combining references to old German art and the Nazarenes. This picture, symbolizing the rejection of everyday realism, is in some way an indication of this distance that was to remain between French and Biedermeier painters.

1 Sébastien Allard, "Waldmüller und Österreich auf der Weltausstellung 1855: ein verpasstes Rendezvous," in Agnes Husslein-Arco/Sabine Grabner, eds., *Ferdinand Georg Waldmüller (1793–1865)*, exh. cat., Musée du Louvre, Paris; Belvedere (Vienna/Paris, 2009), pp. 217–21.

2 France Nerlich, *La peinture française en Allemagne 1815–1870* (Paris, 2010).

3 Edmond de Goncourt/Jules de Goncourt, *Études d'art: le Salon de 1852 – la peinture à l'Exposition de 1855* (Paris, 1896), p. 55.

4 Étienne Delécluze, *Les Beaux-Arts dans les deux mondes en 1855* (Paris, 1856), p. 5.

5 François Miel, *Essai sur le Salon de 1817* (Paris, 1817), p. 97.

6 Michaël Vottero, *La peinture de genre en France après 1850* (Rennes, 2012), pp. 77–133.

7 Eveline Deneer, "Between Dou and David: The importance of Dutch seventeenth century art to troubadour painting in France 1790–1830," in *Simiolus: Netherlandish Quarterly for the History of Art*, vol. 35, no. 3 (2012), pp. 218–36.

8 Letter from Léopold Robert to Henri-François Brandt, October 3, 1822, quoted in Félix Sébastien Feuillet de Conches, *Léopold Robert, sa vie, ses œuvres et sa correspondance* (Paris, 1854), p. 58; see Pascal Griener, "'Un genre qu'on ne connaît pas encore': Léopold Robert et l'élévation du genre sous la monarchie de Juillet," in *Art et architecture en Suisse*, no. 4 (1994), pp. 346–53.

9 Étienne Delécluze, "Exposition du Louvre, 1824, no. XXII," in *Journal des débats*, December 12, 1824, p. 3.

10 Atanazy Raczyński, *Histoire de l'art moderne en Allemagne*, vol. 1 (Paris, 1836–41), p. 27.

11 Étienne Delécluze, *Carnet de route d'Italie (1823–1824), impressions romaines* (Paris, 1942), p. 177.

12 Auguste Jal, *Salon de 1831, ébauches critiques* (Paris, 1831), p. 222; see Sébastien Allard, "Entre le roman et l'histoire, le portrait français vers 1835," in ibid./Guilhem Scherf, eds., *Portraits publics, portraits privés 1770–1830*, exh. cat., Galeries nationales du Grand Palais, Paris/Royal Academy, London (Paris, 2006), p. 43–57.

13 Gustave Planche, *Salon de 1831* (Paris, 1831), p. 82.

14 Auguste Jal, *Salon de 1833, les causeries du Louvre* (Paris, 1833), p. 83.

15 Théophile Gautier, "Du costume moderne," in *La Presse*, January 3, 1837.

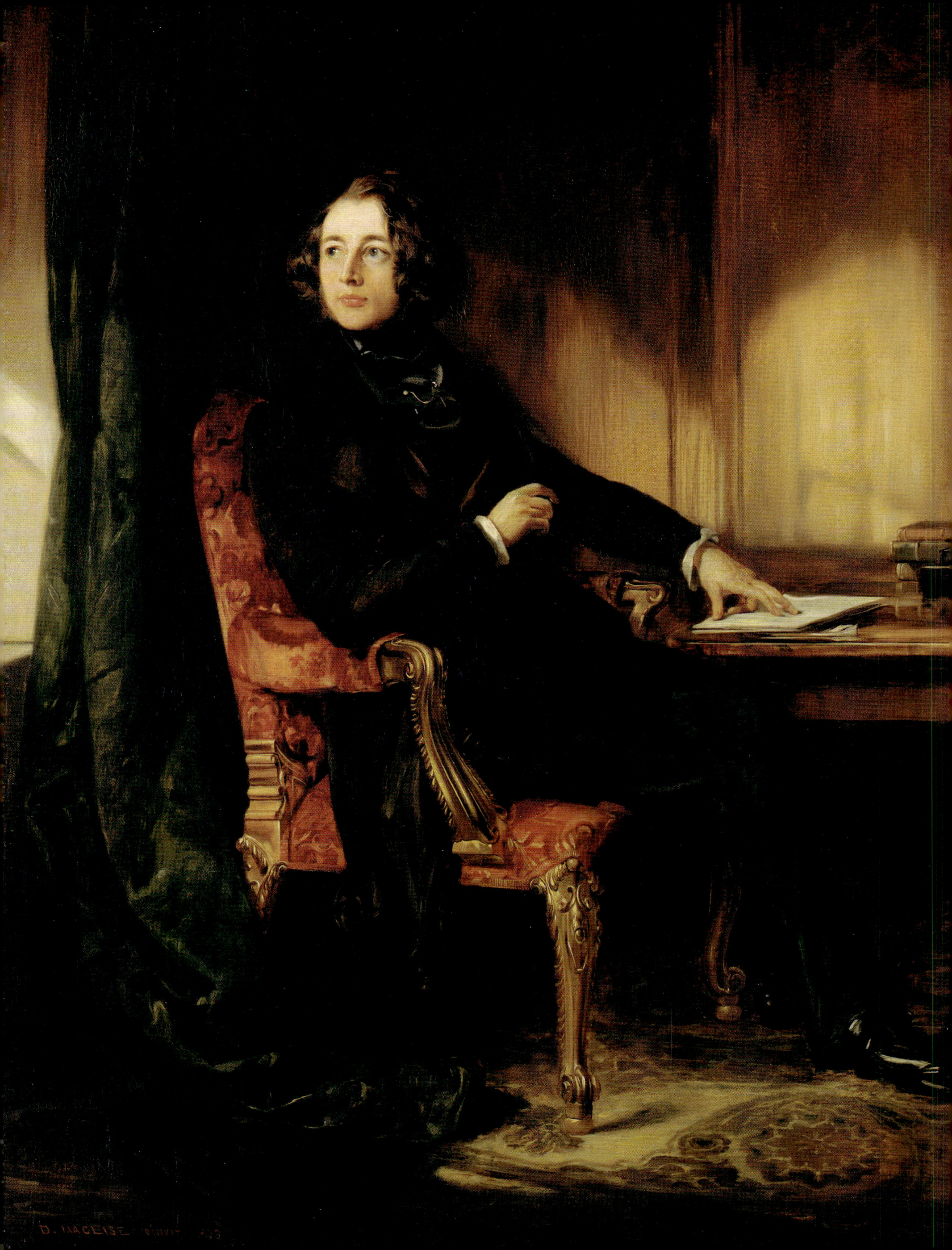
D. MACLISE

ART IN GREAT BRITAIN AT THE TIME OF THE BIEDERMEIER PARALLELS AND INFLUENCES

Arnika Schmidt

"Art in England, to all appearances, is heading toward a bright future."[1]

This favorable prediction for the development of British art was made by an Austrian critic in the *Wiener Zeitschrift für Kunst, Literatur, Theater und Mode* in his review of the Royal Academy Exhibition of 1839 in London. Before devoting himself to a discussion of the works exhibited, he informs his readers about the beginnings of British painting: "The actual English school, the school of portraiture, begins with Reynolds."[2] For a long time, Great Britain was overshadowed by other nations as far as artistic production was concerned, and British painters had set their bearings by the art of successful foreign colleagues. The call for high-quality national art grew in volume. Sir Joshua Reynolds (1723–1792) recognized the need to raise the status of the visual arts in his country by means of focused training and regular exhibitions based on the Parisian Salon model.[3] In 1768 Reynolds founded the Royal Academy of Arts under the patronage of King George III (1738–1820), remaining its president for the rest of his life. As in other countries, theory and drawing was taught at the Academy, while the aspiring artist had to acquire technique and the use of color in the studios of renowned artists and through copying the Old Masters. In 1824 the National Gallery was founded, which in 1838 moved into one half of the building on Trafalgar Square designed by William Wilkins (1778–1839). Its growing collection and proximity to the Royal Academy, which had resided in the other part of Wilkins' building since 1837, must have made it significantly easier for students to work from originals in their own country. A good twenty years before the founding of the National Gallery, aristocrats with an interest in art had established the British Institution, a kind of art association, with the mission "to encourage and reward the talents of the artists of the United Kingdom."[4] The focus was on history painting, already propagated by Reynolds as the highest art form, which brought forth excellent works on the Continent, yet had never resounded in the same way with the public and patrons in Great Britain. Portraiture, on the other hand, was—in Reynolds' time and subsequently—in constant demand. It was and remained the genre with which artists could earn their living. Reynolds himself was an outstanding example in this field. He was known for his impressive "Grand Manner" portraits, which showed his patrons in splendid attire, often adopting historic poses.[5] The portraits by his successor Sir Thomas Lawrence (1769–1830), meanwhile, were notable for the subtle depiction of the character and state of mind of the subject portrayed. An individualizing approach to the person depicted and the liberal application of paint became hallmarks of his portraits, bringing him international renown.

To commemorate the victorious Battle of Waterloo against Napoleon, King George IV commissioned Lawrence to paint portraits of the main protagonists in the war against the French ruler, which were to adorn the walls of his newly created Waterloo Chamber at Windsor Castle. By way of preparation, Lawrence traveled through Europe and came to Vienna in 1818–19 to portray Emperor Francis I. It is reported that Austrian artists were thrilled by the innovations his paintings introduced them to. The work of Moritz Michael Daffinger (1803–1887), who became known as a miniaturist, as well as paintings by Friedrich von Amerling (1803–1887), clearly show traces of the fascination Lawrence's work exerted.[6] In the late 1820s Amerling traveled to London, where he engaged in studying Lawrence's paintings. In the 1830s a trend can be detected in British portraiture toward depicting the subject within a private setting that expressed something about the person portrayed. Daniel Maclise (1806–1870) painted the young writer Charles Dickens (1812–1870; fig. 1) about one year after the publication of his serial novel *The Pickwick Papers*, which had made him famous over-

Fig. 1: **Daniel Maclise**, *Charles Dickens*, 1839
National Portrait Gallery, London, on permanent loan from the Tate Gallery, London

night. The elegant interior, books, and his fashionable attire show Dickens as a self-confident, self-made man, with no visible trace of the poor conditions that marked Dickens' childhood and youth.

Alongside their ongoing enthusiasm for portraiture, early to mid-nineteenth-century audiences increasingly developed a taste for works that took the native landscape as their theme, as well as contemporary, mundane-familiar, and moral topics. This trend reflects the impact that political events and the rapidly advancing industrialization had on society. The 1832 Reform Act altered the distribution of boroughs eligible to elect seats in the British parliament, which gave more political influence to the emerging middle class of industrialists and merchants. Thus the political weight shifted from the rural south, dominated by the aristocracy and gentry, to the industrial cities of the north.[7] Economically and politically strengthened, the middle classes emerged as the new purchasers of art, yet with very different needs from traditional patrons such as the church and landed gentry.

In 1870, the writer and art historian Lady Elizabeth Eastlake describes the changes that had taken place throughout the 1830s and 1840s: "The patronage, which had been almost exclusively the privilege of the nobility and higher gentry, was now shared (to be subsequently almost engrossed) by a wealthy and intelligent class, chiefly enriched by commerce and trade."[8] At the beginning of the nineteenth century this trend could already be felt. In order to create opportunities for artists and potential buyers to meet, artists' associations were set up in various parts of the country, for example in London in 1805. Norwich was the first city to do this, in 1803; Edinburgh and Bath followed in 1808. One year later the first exhibition of the Northern Society was opened.[9] With the help of William Roscoe (1753–1831), a lawyer, parliamentary deputy, banker, and art collector, the Art Academy in Liverpool was founded in 1810.[10] Due to the size and strategic location of its harbor, the city had become one of England's most important economic centers early on in the century. Some years later, in 1824, Edinburgh also set up its own academy. This development shows that, although London remained the undisputed center of British culture, other cities were also actively interested and involved in the education and promotion of British artists. Above all, art patrons from the ranks of the *nouveaux riches* effected a paradigm shift in the arts, as Lady Eastlake asserts: "To this gradual transfer of patronage another advantage very important to the painter was owing; namely that collections, entirely of modern, and sometimes only of living artists began to be formed. For one sign of the good sense of the *nouveau riche* collector consistec in a consciousness of his ignorance in matters of connoisseurship. This led him to seek an article fresh from the painter's loom, in preference at the discrimination of any older fabrics."[11] The new buyers wanted works that depicted themselves, their native land, their culture, and their society.

Besides portraiture, nature increasingly became the main focus in painting. Top rank in this genre belonged to Joseph Mallord William Turner (1775–1851) with his diverse interpretations of real and visionary landscapes. He studied the art of the Old Masters and was a great admirer of the classical landscape compositions by Claude Lorrain (1600–1682). Turner was concerned with lost empires, forces of nature, and the modern world, and found inspiration in his home country as well as on the Continent. The public, both at home and abroad, showed little understanding of the later works of this artist initially celebrated as a genius. His increasing concentration on the pictorial came at the expense of the representational, and the results contrasted markedly with the meticulous steel engravings based on his works, which had made him widely known on the Continent.[12] Alongside Turner, John Constable (1776–1837) is today synonymous with British landscape painting, although at the time he was ranked below the aforementioned and was also eclipsed by colleagues such as Sir Augustus Wall Callcott (1779–1844) and William Collins (1788–1847). Constable's work is marked by precise observation of nature and the neglect of the line in favor of the effect of color, and provided important stimuli for the development of landscape painting in Britain and on the Continent. His participation in the Paris Salon of 1824 caused a great stir. The works exhibited at the time are generally considered the initial spark that brought about a shift in landscape painting which later culminated in the Barbizon School.[13] In Paris, Constable's painting *The Hay Wain* (fig. 2) was awarded the Gold Medal by the French King Charles X. It shows a clearly identifiable stretch of land near Flatford in Suffolk, Constable's birthplace. The cart and small cottage have made the picture an icon of British rural life, its traditional working practices and slower pace representing an antipole to the industrialized city. At the same time, with its cumulus clouds in the sky and rich-green pastures and trees, Constable

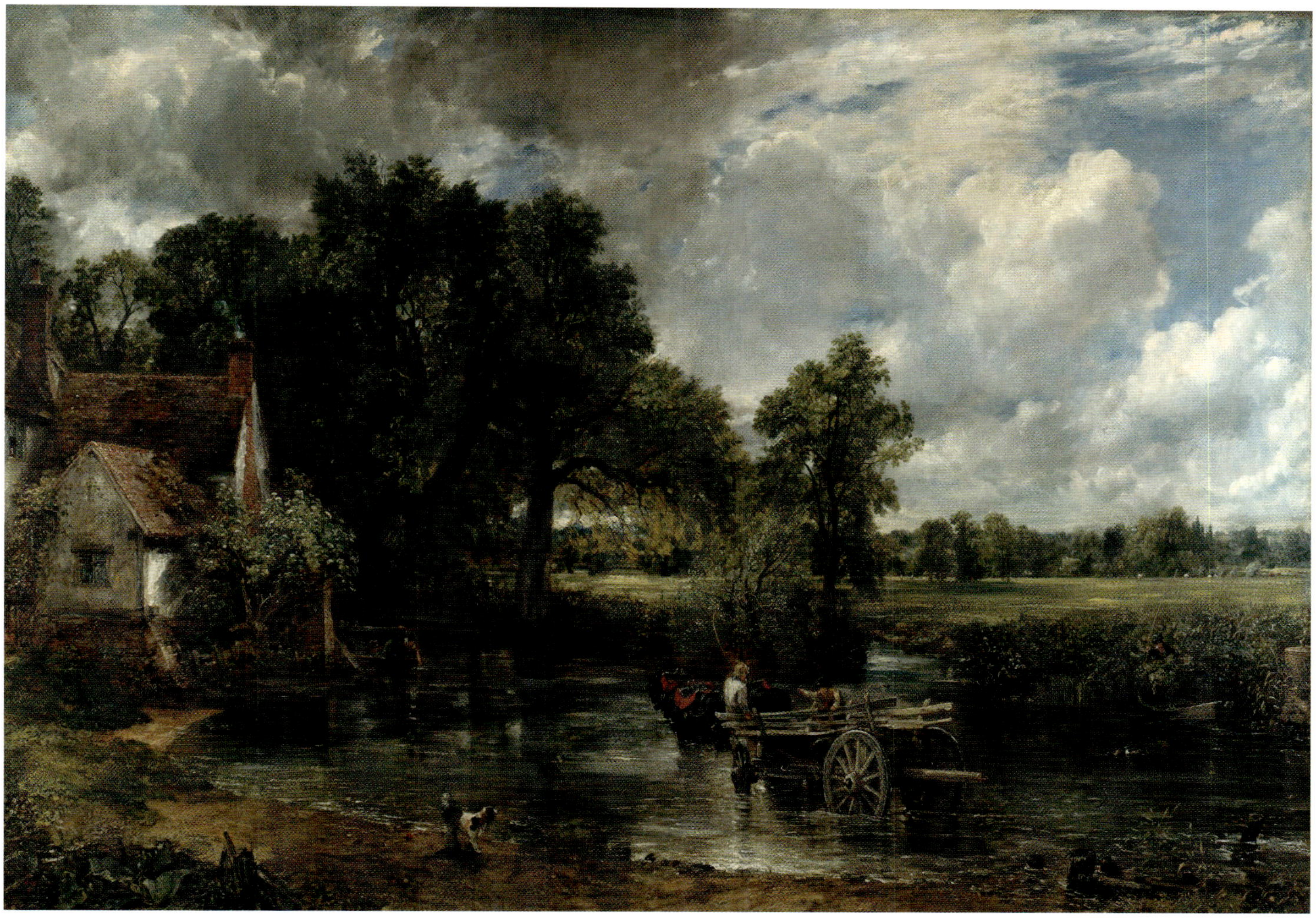

Fig. 2: **John Constable**, *The Hay Wain*, 1821
National Gallery, London

had captured the mood of the southern English landscape, which was seen as representative of Great Britain, not least thanks to Constable's compositions and their dissemination through engravings. To offset the industrialized reality and as an expression of national allegiance, the native countryside became a popular motif in British art. The long years of war with France, which lasted intermittently from the French Revolution until Napoleon's defeat at Waterloo (1815), greatly reduced opportunities for travel, consequently leading to a focus on the home country.[14] This prioritization, however, was above all motivated by a wish to express national identity, and the rural British landscape became a conveyor of meaning for a proud nation.

One popular destination within Great Britain was Scotland. The characteristic landscape of the Highlands and the Scots' traditional kilts and scarves in tartan patterns were linked unmistakably with the region, and painters liked to use them as a pictorial motif. The Londoner Sir Edwin Landseer (1802–1873) succumbed to the rough charm of the north on his very first visit in 1824, and many of his most impressive compositions were created here.[15] He achieved renown with his sensitive depictions of animals. Examples such as the proud stag in *Monarch of the Glen* (fig. 3) and the faithful dog in *The Old Shepherd's Chief Mourner* show his particular talent for soulful illustrations of animals in their natural or assumed habitat. The mixture of pathos and realism, paired with a sophisticated technique, spoke to all levels of society. In addition, Landseer carried out commissions for Queen Victoria and painted works that took life in the Scottish Highlands as their theme. With *The Illicit Highland Whisky Still* (fig. 4) he created a successful hybrid of animal picture, landscape, and genre painting. The bleak setting and the poacher's roguish features stand in clear contrast to the innocent chil-

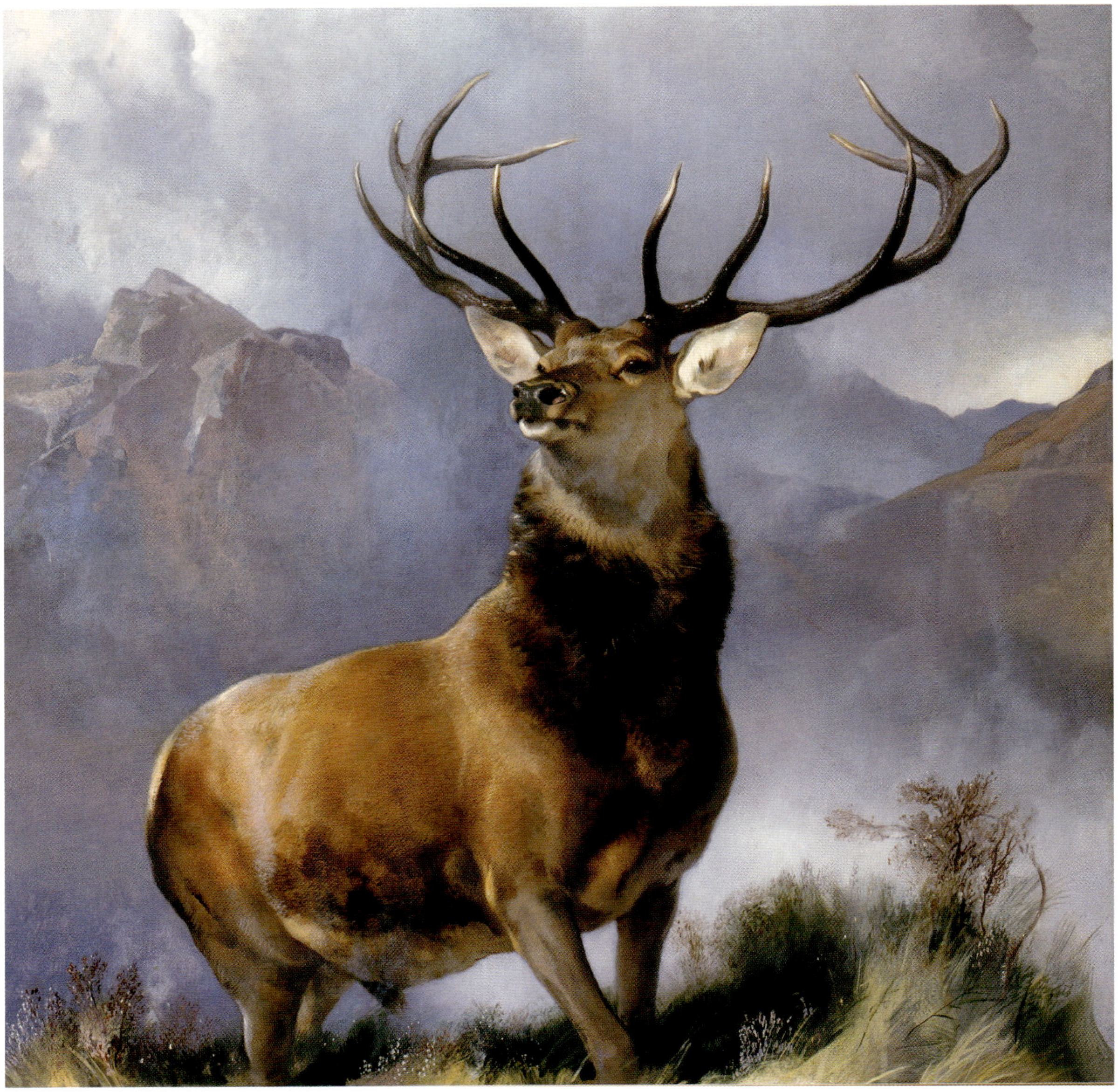

Fig. 3: **Sir Edwin Landseer**, *Monarch of the Glen*, 1851 National Museum of Scotland, Edinburgh (on loan from Diageo Scotland Ltd)

Fig. 4: **Sir Edwin Landseer**, *The Illicit Highland Whisky Still*, 1826–1829 English Heritage, The Wellington Museum, Apsley House, London

dren. Landseer's skill in conveying moral values through the characterization of the human and animal protagonists and in producing a sentimental mood was greatly praised beyond the borders of Great Britain.[16]

Genre painting became the most popular artistic category in the first half of the nineteenth century as it represented everything the public wanted to see: trueness to nature, emotion, and contemporary motifs. Sources of inspiration were everyday life and contemporary society, Dutch and Flemish genre pictures from the seventeenth century, paintings and prints by William Hogarth (1697–1764), as well as popular literature. The stories written by the British poets and writers William Shakespeare (1564–1616), Oliver Goldsmith (1728–1774), Laurence Sterne (1713–1768), Sir Walter Scott (1771–1832), Lord Byron (1788–1824), Robert Burns (1759–1796), and, later, Charles Dickens offered rich and varied material for paintings with moral overtones, acceptable humor, and, in part, social criticism.[17] *The Vicar of Wakefield* (1766) and *She Stoops to Conquer* (1773), as well as other novels and plays by the Irishman Oliver Goldsmith were used as themes for pictures so frequently that the novelist and critic William Makepeace Thackeray made it known that he would refuse to write about any further work inspired by these sources. He made an exception, however, in the case of William Mulready's *Choosing the Wedding Gown* (fig. 5), which was based on one of the first sentences in Goldsmith's novel *The Vicar of Wakefield*.[18] Thackeray praised the painting in *The Morning Chronicle* in glowing terms: "For colour and finish it may rank by any cabinet picture of any master. It does not create pleasure merely, but astonishment [...] a blaze of fireworks is not more intensely brilliant."[19]

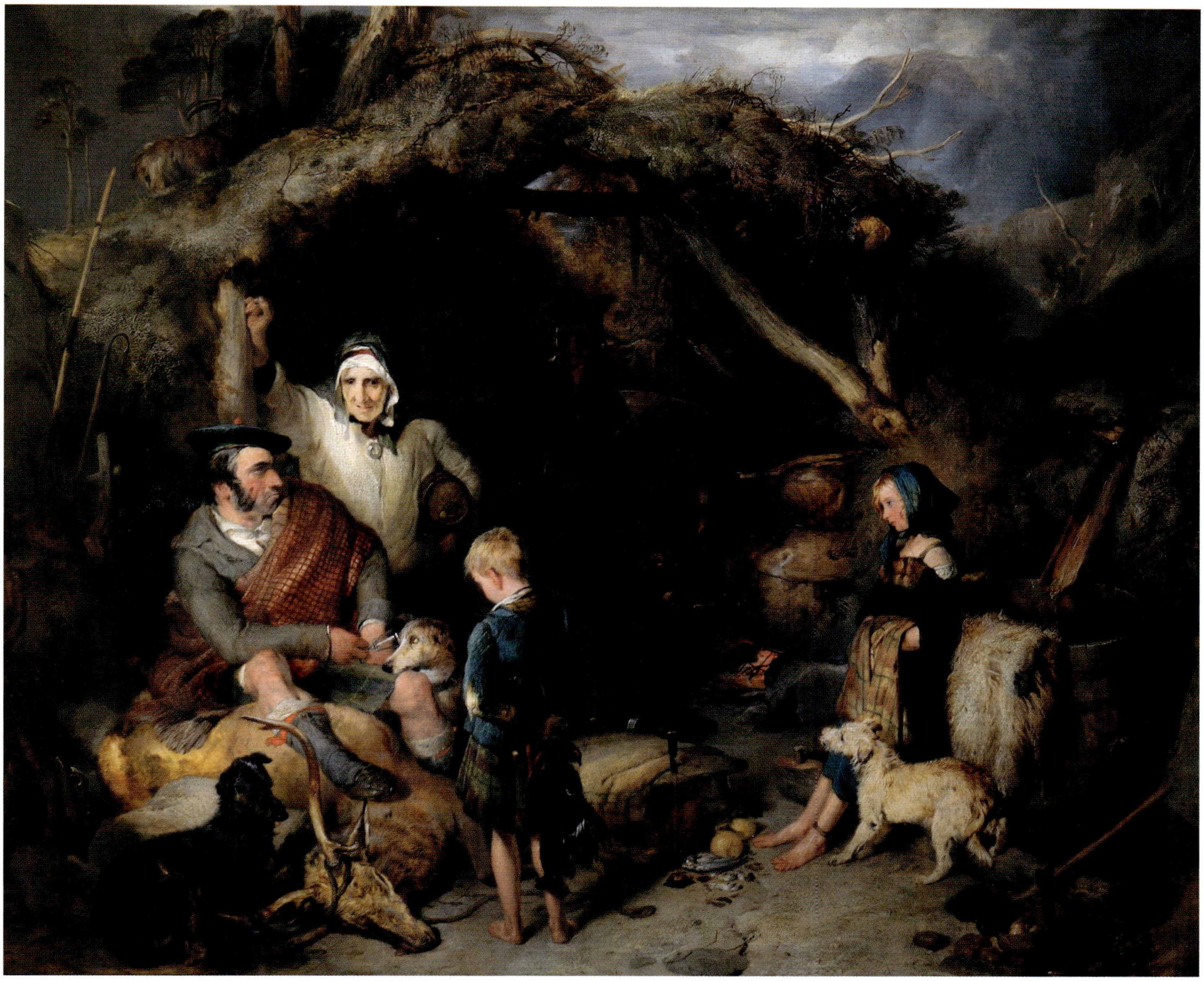

The close connection between literature and painting is also evident in the increasingly important practice of book illustration. For example, Mulready, Landseer, and many other British artists delivered templates for the engravings of the Waverley Novels series, which Sir Walter Scott wrote and published over the course of several decades. Various templates also came from the Scotsman Sir David Wilkie (1785–1841). When the edition with his illustrations was first published in 1829, Wilkie was already the best-known British genre painter of his time.[20] *Village Politicians* (fig. 6) was his first significant painting with a rural motif. It was presented with great success at the Royal Academy Annual Exhibition of 1806. His models were William Hogarth, David Teniers (1610–1690), and Adriaen van Ostade (1610–1685), among others. Although these artists enjoyed great popularity in Wilkie's day, their works were in fact a little too satirical, vulgar, and exaggerated for the contemporary public. Wilkie approached the genre with more subtlety and trueness to nature. In response to the criticism that Wilkie drew too heavily on his models, William Hazlitt outlined the decisive difference between Wilkie's works and those of the aforementioned artists: "Mr. Wilkie's pictures, generally speaking, derive almost their whole value from their reality, or the truth of the representation, [...] his pictures may be considered diaries, or minutes of what is passing constantly about us."[21] Wilkie's work corresponded to the desire of contemporary audiences to see themselves, their environment, and emotions reflected in genre pictures. This empathy and technical skill made Wilkie's art popular in all strata of society. Rich aristocrats and industrialists bought his paintings for high prices, while less affluent art enthusiasts decorated the walls of their homes with

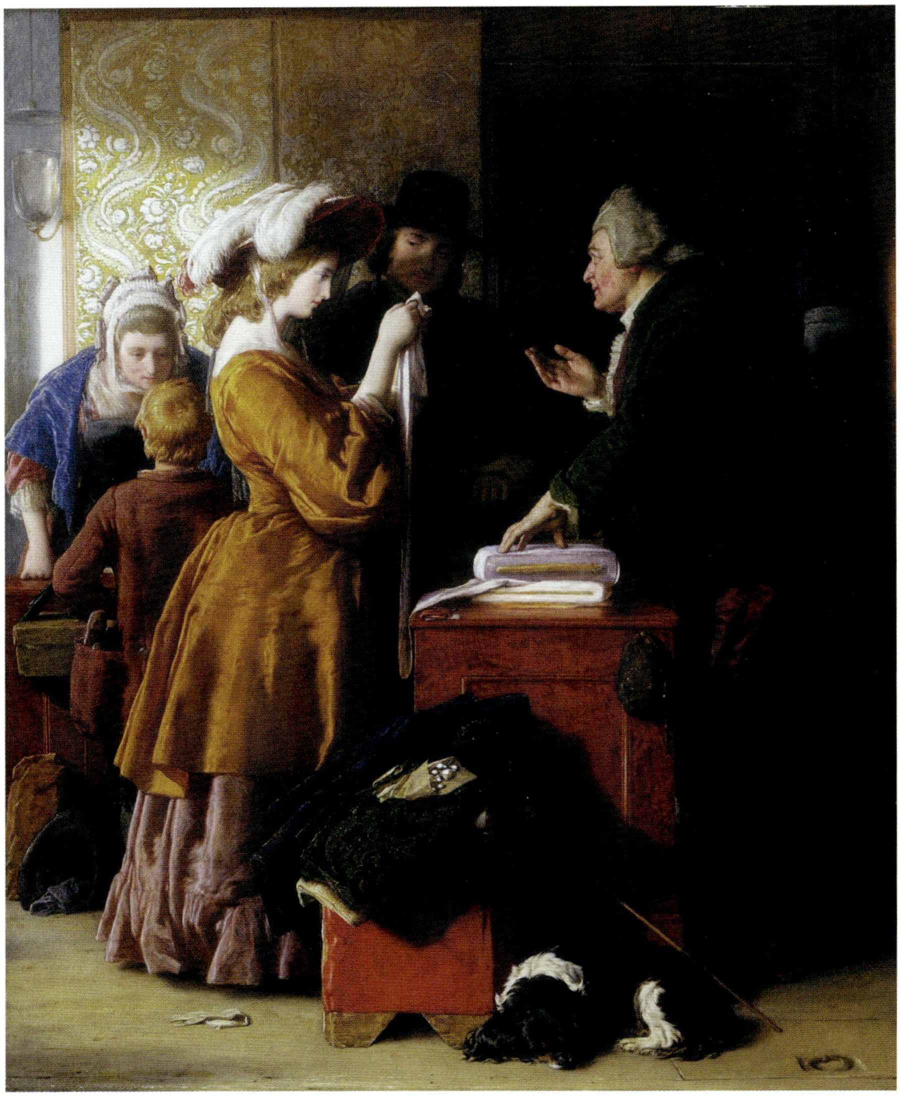

Fig. 5: **William Mulready**, *Choosing the Wedding Gown*, 1845
Victoria and Albert Museum, London

Fig. 6: **Sir David Wilkie**, *Village Politicians*, 1806
The Earls of Mansfield, Scone Palace, Perth, Scotland

engravings of his works.[22] Through the medium of copper engraving, his work also spread far beyond the borders of his home nation, influencing the developments of the genre in other countries.

In collections in German-speaking countries, only few paintings by British artists were to be found.[23] One of the rare exceptions was *Reading the Will* (fig. 7), which Maximilian I Joseph King of Bavaria had commissioned from Wilkie. The painting was hung in the Munich residence in 1820, amid seventeenth century Dutch paintings, and could be viewed upon request.[24] When the regent's collection was auctioned following his death in 1825, the *Prager Zeitung* reported: "The famous painting by Wilkie, *Reading the Will,* of which a beautiful copper engraving exists, is preserved here, for the great enjoyment of all friends of the arts, and has been purchased for the Royal Painting Gallery for 12,000 florins."[25] It was the only painting within the extensive collection to be mentioned by name in this short note, which denotes the prominence of this work and its creator in German-speaking parts of central Europe.

On account of the lively artistic exchange between Munich and Vienna, we can assume that some Austrian artists saw the painting in the Bavarian capital. This and other compositions became famous, however, due to the dissemination of engravings. An episode in Allan Cunningham's biography *The Life of Sir David Wilkie; with His Journals, Tours and Critical Remarks on Works of Art; and a Selection of His Correspondence*, published in 1843, offers further evidence of the efficiency of this medium. On his way to Italy, Wilkie had been invited to dine *en famille* with Klemens von Metternich and reports: "He [Metternich] told me my works were familiar to him through the engravings, and that he had seen the picture I had painted for the late King of Bavaria, about which he complimented me very highly."[26] The fact that prints were appreciated beyond aristo-

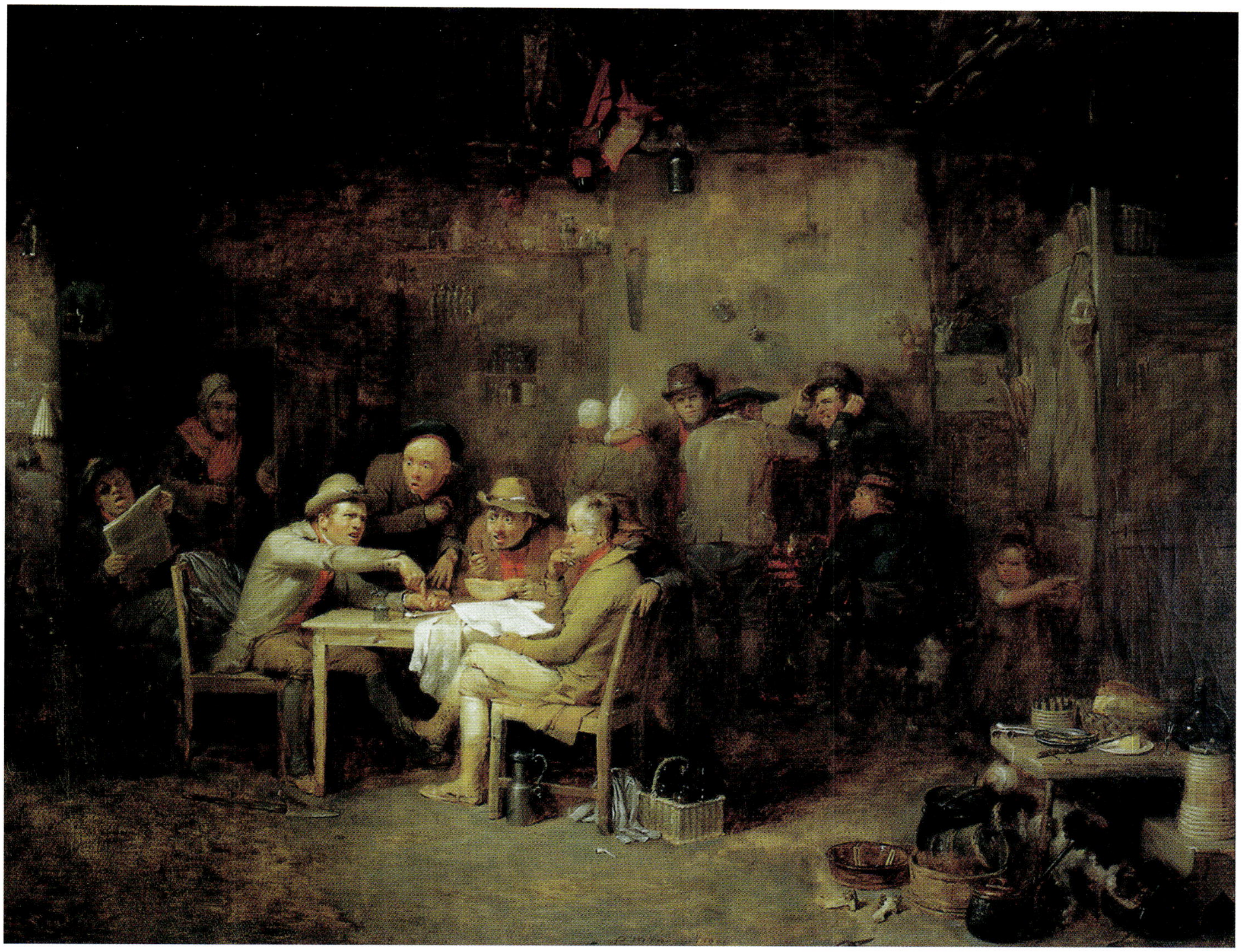

cratic circles is also revealed by the casual comment made by a critic in the *Wiener Zeitschrift für Kunst, Literatur, Theater und Mode* about Wilkie's *Gazette of the Battle of Waterloo*, "the copper engraving of which has surely come to your notice."[27] The assumption that the engraving based on the painting under discussion was known to the reader clearly indicates the importance of graphic prints for the international reputation of British artists. The extent to which Wilkie's compositions became known was so wide-reaching that in 1845 an Austrian theater critic referred to them in his praise of the performance of an actor at Vienna's Theater in der Josefstadt: "Beckmann's Mengler is one of those masterly genre pictures, harmonious in every way and true to nature down to the smallest detail, as only the brush of Hogarth or Wilkie can evoke."[28]

Austrian print media such as the *Wiener Zeitschrift für Kunst, Literatur, Theater und Mode*, *Der* Österreichische *Zuschauer* and *Wiener Zuschauer* informed the Austrian Biedermeier public about British art, culture, and lifestyle, reflecting a special interest in Great Britain among the educated public. Critics pointed out time and again the parallels in the art of the two countries, and revealed specific stimuli that Austrian artists had received from their British colleagues. With regard to painting in both countries, John Steegman notes the similar expectations of the new acquisitive classes: "Whether a picture were genre or straight narrative, to be successful it must have either humour or pathos, but neither vulgarity nor tragedy; it must be accurate and minute in detail; its paint must be easily perceived and quickly comprehended."[29] The most successful protagonists of the Biedermeier period, such as Ferdinand Georg Waldmüller (1793–1865), Friedrich von Amerling, and Josef Danhauser (1805–1845) combined these aspects in their work. Achievements such as the establishment of the new hierarchy of genres, with history being replaced by landscape, portrait, and genre, the

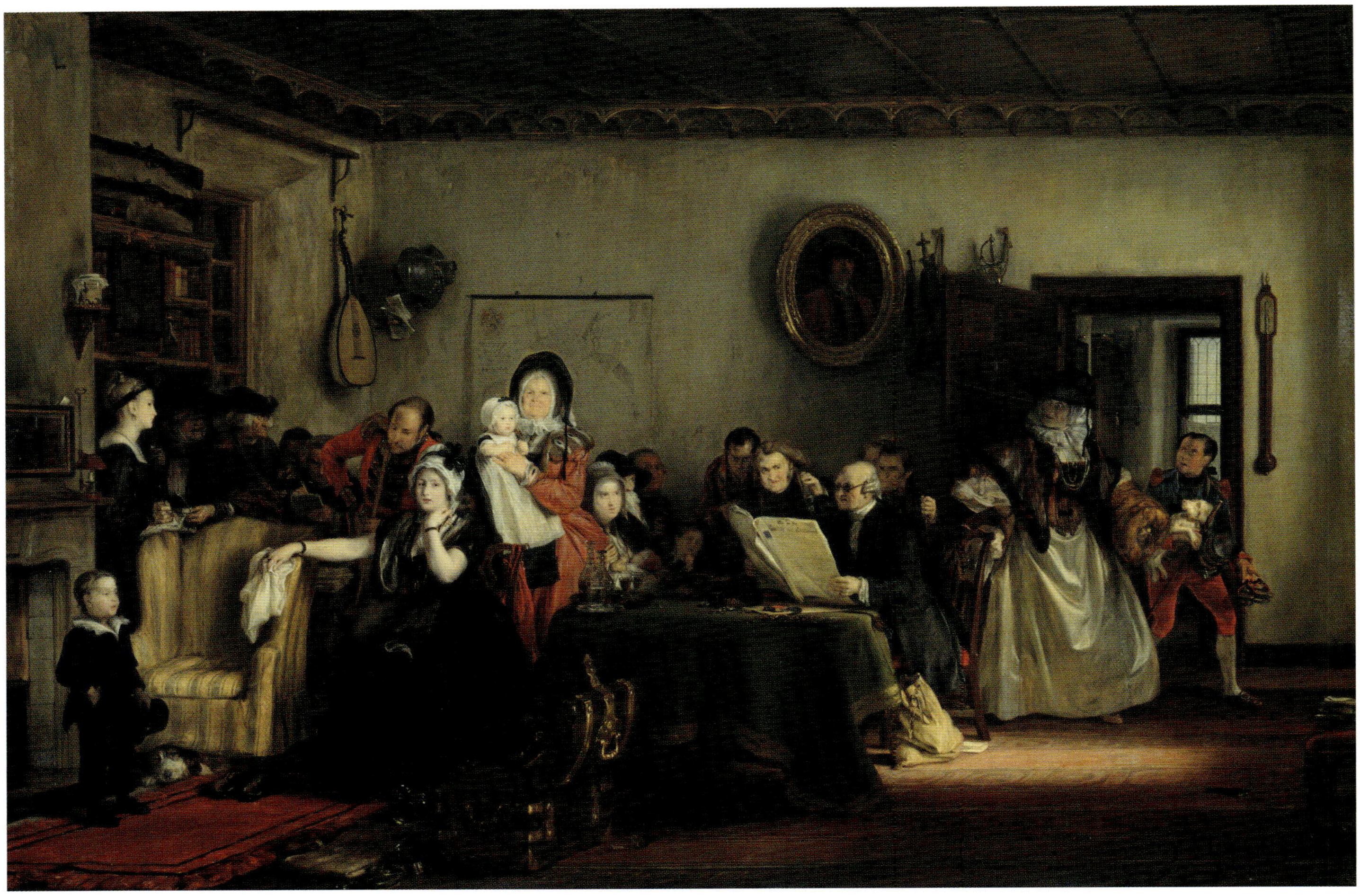

Fig. 7: **Sir David Wilkie**, *Reading the Will*, 1820
Bayerische Staatsgemäldesammlungen Munich, Neue Pinakothek

development of genre art with a focus on the narrative and, later on, the expression of emotions, as well as the themes and compositions in Austrian painting that reflect an interest in British art, all show the island nation as an important direct and indirect source of inspiration for Biedermeier art.

1 Anon., "Kunstausstellung in London 1839", in *Wiener Zeitschrift für Kunst, Literatur, Theater und Mode*, no. 100, August 20, 1839, p. 799.
2 Anon., "Kunstausstellung in London 1839", in *Wiener Zeitschrift für Kunst, Literatur, Theater und Mode*, no. 98, August 15, 1839, p. 784.
3 Lionel Lambourne, *Victorian Painting* (London, 1999), p. 9.
4 Founders of the British Institution quoted from Michael Rosenthal, "The Fine Arts," in Boris Ford, ed., *Romantics to Early Victorians* (The Cambridge Guide to the Arts in Britain, vol. 6) (Cambridge, 1990), p. 125.
5 Lambourne 1999 (see note 3), p. 11.
6 William Vaughn, "Die Aufnahme der britischen Kunst in Deutschland und Frankreich im 19. Jahrhundert," in Allen Brian/John Gage, eds., *Zwei Jahrhunderte englische Malerei. Britische Kunst und Europa 1680 bis 1880*, exh. cat., Haus der Kunst, Munich (Munich, 1979), p. 498.
7 Lambourne 1999 (see note 3), p. 23.
8 Quoted from Lambourne 1999 (see note 3), pp. 28–29.
9 Rosenthal 1990 (see note 4), p. 125.
10 Anna Sophie Frasca-Rath, *John Gibson. Die Canova-Rezeption in Großbritannien*, dissertation, University of Vienna, 2015, p. 29.
11 Quoted from Lambourne 1999 (see note 3), pp. 28–29.
12 Vaughn 1979 (see note 6), p. 500.
13 John Steegman, *Victorian Taste: A Study of the Arts and Architecture from 1830 to 1870*, with a foreword by Nikolaus Pevsner (Cambridge [Mass.], 1970), p. 40.

14 Vaughn 1979 (see note 6), p. 426.
15 E.g. *The Hunting of Chevy Chase*, 1826, oil on canvas, 143 × 171 cm, Birmingham Museum and Art Gallery; *Rent Day in the Wilderness*, 1868, oil on canvas, 122 × 265 cm, Scottish National Gallery.
16 Here an example from the Austrian press: "Painting the soul in England's fine arts extends, if the expression is permitted, to the animal kingdom, it has found a representative in Landseer, whom no nation can rival." Anon., "Briefe über die moderne Kunst Frankreichs VIII", in *Österreichische Blätter für Literatur und Kunst*, no. 39, September 24, 1855, p. 287.
17 Among non-British authors, Miguel de Cervantes (1547–1616), Molière (1622–1673), and Alain-René Lesage (1668–1747) were especially popular. Lambourne 1999 (see note 3), p. 129.
18 "I had scarce taken orders a year before I began to think seriously of matrimony, and chose my wife, as she did her wedding gown, not for a fine glossy surface, but for such qualities as would wear well." Quoted from Ronald Parkinson, *Catalogue of British Oil Paintings 1820–1860*, coll. cat., Victoria and Albert Museum, London (London, 1990), pp. 205–206.
19 William Makepeace Thackeray, "The Exhibition at the Royal Academy", in *The Morning Chronicle*, May 5, 1846.
20 Sir Walter Scott, *Waverley Novels* (Magnum Opus edition), 48 vols. (Edinburgh, 1829).
21 Quoted from Lindsay Errington, "The Genre Paintings of Wilkie," in H. A. D. Miles/David Blayney Brown, eds., *Sir David Wilkie of Scotland*, exh. cat., North Carolina Museum of Art, Raleigh (Raleigh, 1987), p. 3.
22 Contemporary reports provide information on the furnishing of British homes. Here, for example, an article on "Die Comforts der Engländer," which Dr. Franz Kottenkamp published in *Der Österreichische Zuschauer: Zeitschrift für Kunst, Wissenschaft und geistiges Leben* (January 27, 1827, p. 114) in 1837: "The rich man decorates the walls of his rooms with works of art, which as a rule are as well-chosen as they are expensive, and for this reason alone contradict the hitherto common assertion that the English have no taste or feeling for fine art, an assertion that has been proven false since Hogarth, Lawrence, Wilkie, Chantrey. The poor man is content with copper engravings, with copies of Wilkie, Hogarth, or with portraits after Lawrence etc."
23 In Vienna, a painting by Wilkie was held in Rudolf von Arthaber's collection. The industrialist and co-founder of the Vienna Kunstverein had purchased the artist's work *The Bride at her Toilet on the Day of her Wedding* in 1838.
24 Sophie Kruijssen, "The Middle Classes and Contemporaries as *dramatis personae*: David Wilkie and the Emancipation of Genre Scenes in Europe," in *Simiolus*, 37th yr., no. 3/4 (2013/14), pp. 254–55.
25 Anon., "Deutschland," in *Prager Zeitung*, no. 203, December 26, 1826, p. 1.
26 Allan Cunningham, *The Life of Sir David Wilkie; with His Journals, Tours and Critical Remarks on Works of Art; and a Selection of His Correspondence*, 3 vols. (London, 1843), vol. 2, p. 363.
27 Anon., "Correspondenz-Nachrichten, London, im Mai 1832," in *Wiener Zeitschrift für Kunst, Literatur, Theater und Mode*, no. 94, August 7, 1832, p. 759.
28 "Mittwoch den 19. Februar zum ersten Mal: 'Endlich hat er es doch gut gemacht' Lustspiel in 3 Akten, nach einer englischen Idee (?) für die deutsche Bühne bearbeitet von Albini. Herr Beckmann: Mengler und Mlle. Tondorussi, Jettchen als Gäste." "K. K. priv. Theater in der Josephstadt," in *Wiener Zeitschrift für Kunst, Literatur, Theater und Mode*, no. 37, February 21, 1845, p. 147.
29 Steegman 1970 (see note 13), p. 38.

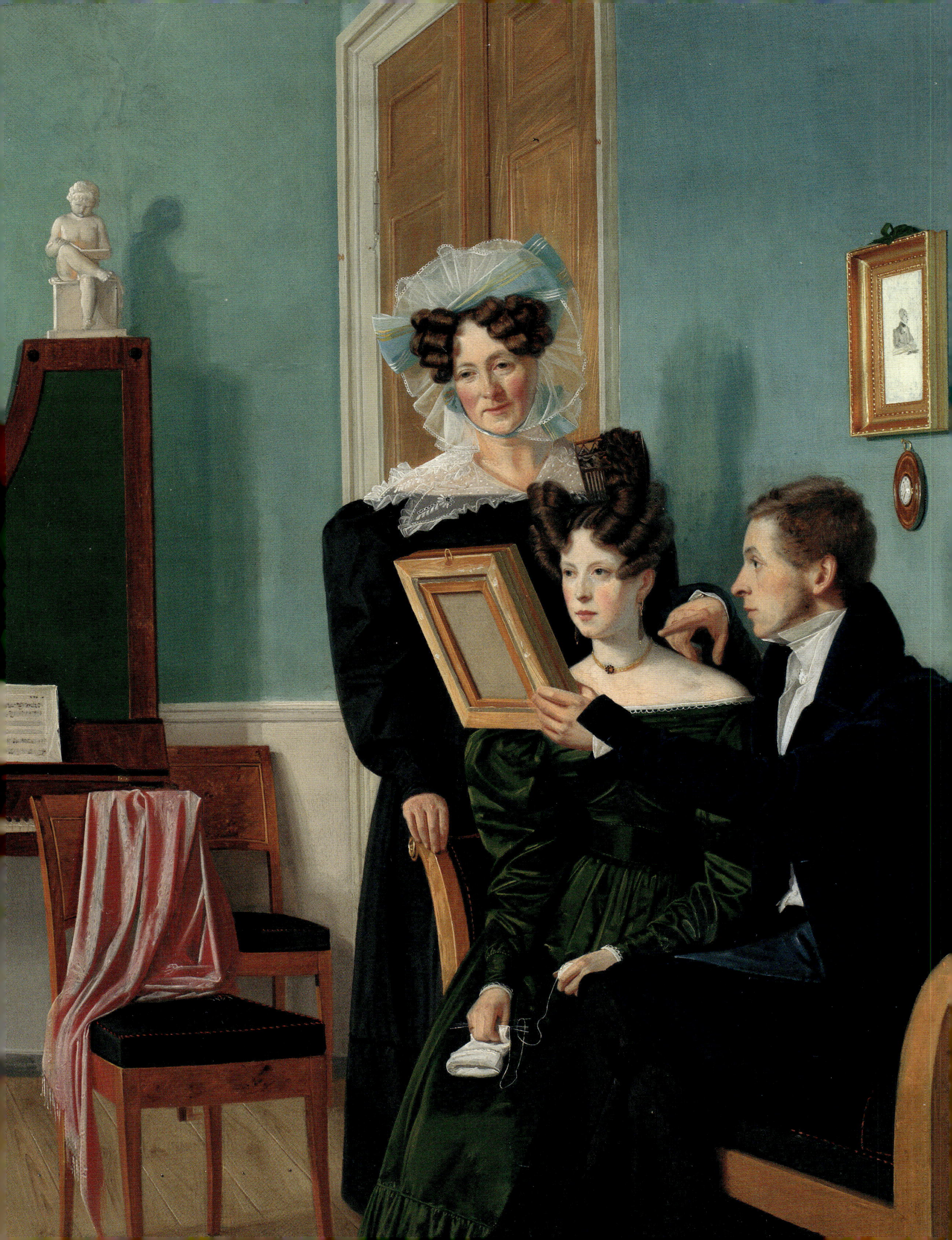

THE COPENHAGEN SCHOOL OF PAINTERS 1830–1860

Kasper Monrad

In 1830, the Danish painter Wilhelm Bendz (1804–32) painted a group portrait of *The Raffenberg Family* (fig. 1).[1] The customs officer Michael Raffenberg is sitting on a sofa with his fiancée, his mother standing behind them, all three of them absorbed in looking at a painting. As is characteristic of Bendz, he does not show us the front of the canvas, so we can only guess at the motif. Judging from the mother's gaze, it is likely to be a portrait of her deceased husband, and Bendz's painting may depict Michael Raffenberg's introduction of his fiancée to his mother, in which case it would be appropriate for him to show her a portrait of his late father.

Raffenberg played an active role in the art scene in Copenhagen in the 1830s, but the painting does not deal primarily with his great interest in art, but rather with his sense of family. The family was the foundation stone of Danish society in the first half of the nineteenth century, and the painting thus reflects fundamental Danish values of the period. At the same time, the painter gives an exhaustive impression of the interior of a Danish middle class home. Simplicity and modesty characterized the home of the Raffenberg family—and of most other Danish bourgeois homes at the time.

The profound financial crises in Denmark after the Napoleonic Wars had not yet been overcome and the Danes had been forced to adjust their way of life to the limited opportunities for individual achievement. The restricted room for maneuver—and the narrow horizon that was thus imposed upon them—had a deep impact, not only on the subjects that Danish painters chose for their paintings, but also on the taste of collectors.[2] Artists focused on motifs that had a close affinity to contemporary life in Denmark. They painted portraits, domestic scenes, everyday scenes from the streets of Copenhagen, and landscape motifs from the sparsely built-up areas outside of the old ramparts of the city.

Fig. 1: **Wilhelm Bendz**, *The Raffenberg Family*, 1830
Statens Museum for Kunst, Copenhagen

On the other hand, history painting, which was still officially regarded as the most important category of painting, lost ground and soon played a secondary role, apart from official commissions from the Royal Castle of Christiansborg.

The development of Danish painting in the 1830s and 1840s was to a great extent determined by the achievements of the painter Christoffer Wilhelm Eckersberg (1783–1853). During his sojourn in Rome in 1813–16 he had redefined Danish painting. In introducing open-air painting, he made keen personal observation and a wealth of detail crucial aspects of an artist's work, and in his paintings he combined a realistic rendering of motifs with an idealistic endeavor to present the subjects from an ideal viewpoint, always in tight and clearly structured compositions. Eckersberg's new mode of expression turned out to be very well suited for the new artistic climate in Denmark. As a professor at the Royal Academy of Art in Copenhagen from 1818 to 1853, he exerted an enormous influence on almost all young Danish painters for more than three decades. During this period, there was an immense growth in artistic activity in Denmark, with an unprecedented number of practicing artists, and the period has been named the Golden Age of Danish Painting.

Bendz was one of Eckersberg's many talented pupils, and with his portraits he set the standard for several of his slightly younger fellow students. Many Northern German artists also went to Copenhagen to study and, around 1830, almost as much German as Danish was spoken at the Royal Academy.[3] A similarly broad movement cannot be found in any of the other Scandinavian countries at the time. In both Sweden and Norway, artistic achievements were to a large extent created by solitary artists. Johan Christian Dahl (1788–1857) had a great impact on other Norwegian landscape painters, but not in other fields of painting, as Eckersberg did.

In the 1830s, theories on perspective in art came to absorb Eckersberg to an ever-growing extent, and much of his teaching focused on this aspect.[4] He even-

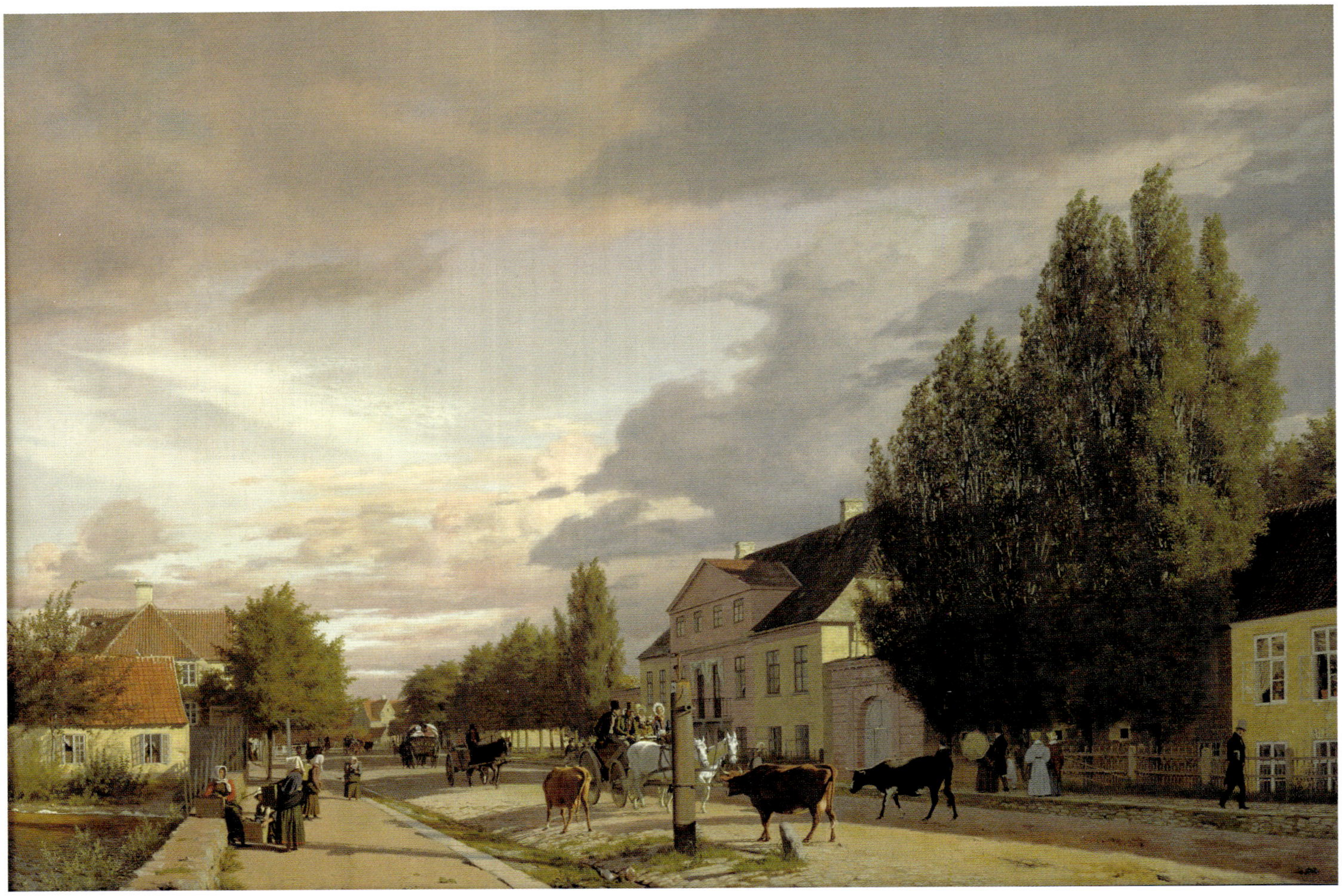

tually developed his theories to the point of summing them up in two treatises. His interest in the subject also had a strong effect on many of his students.

In 1836, Christen Købke (1810–48) painted a view of a street in the suburban area Østerbro, outside the old ramparts of Copenhagen (fig. 2).[5] In the painting, he gave a number of everyday scenes a monumental form. On an early summer morning, some fishermen's wives are resting on the embankment on their way to the market with the night's catch, peasants are on their way to town in their carriages, cows are plodding on their own from their stables in the city to the common, and bourgeois citizens are walking along in the shade of the buildings. All this takes place while the first rays of the sun fall on the houses, the poplars, the street and, notably, the water pump in the middle of the street. Everything is recorded in a matter-of-fact way that leaves little room for romantic sentiment or mood—which is very typical of Danish painting of the period. The scene is presented by the painter in a tightly constructed composition that seems to be based on Eckersberg's perspective theories, with diagonals defining the pictorial space. The sky takes up the greater part of the canvas, with a variety of clouds that may be seen as an attempt at describing weather typical of Copenhagen.

In the 1830s, Eckersberg was probably influenced by his pupils when he turned to genre painting again after an interruption of almost two decades. In these paintings he also employed his principles of construction, most strikingly in *Long Bridge, Copenhagen, in the Moonlight with Running Figures* from 1836 (fig. 3).[6] The painting clearly reflects his interest in the construction of light and shadow as well as his concern with perspective, formed here by the railings and the shadows falling on the bridge. But what is most remarkable in this picture is the inscrutable motif. A number of people come running across the bridge, but Eckersberg has not revealed what is going on. Perhaps a fire has broken out; perhaps someone is drowning in the harbor. No other artist in Denmark—and arguably in all of Europe—used this kind of mystification as the dominant feature in their genre paintings at the time.

Eckersberg never executed hastily painted oil studies. Even though he himself described his views of Rome as

Fig. 2: **Christen Købke**, *A View of a Street in Østerbro outside Copenhagen. Morning Light*, 1836
Statens Museum for Kunst, Copenhagen

Fig. 3: **Christoffer Wilhelm Eckersberg**, *Long Bridge, Copenhagen, in the Moonlight with Running Figures*, 1836
Statens Museum for Kunst, Copenhagen

"sketches," they were in fact carefully crafted paintings.[7] He maintained this practice all throughout his life. But in the 1830s many of his pupils started painting sketches in the proper sense of the term, which might serve as the basis for a larger, more carefully finished depiction. This allowed them to rapidly capture their chosen subject. In many cases, the sketches were an end in itself, and this allowed the painters to employ a much freer approach to the subjects, with looser brushstrokes and often applying completely unorthodox viewpoints. Most radical was Købke when he painted *The Garden Steps Leading to the Artist's Studio on Blegdammen, Copenhagen* (fig. 4).[8] He did not try to give a representative impression of his home, but looked at the building from an oblique angle. The façade towards the street is extremely foreshortened, and he even cropped the image so that the left part of the end wall and the stairs has been cut off. Thus the main focus is not on the building, but on the vigorous and unruly tree growing next to the stairs as well as on the sunlight that

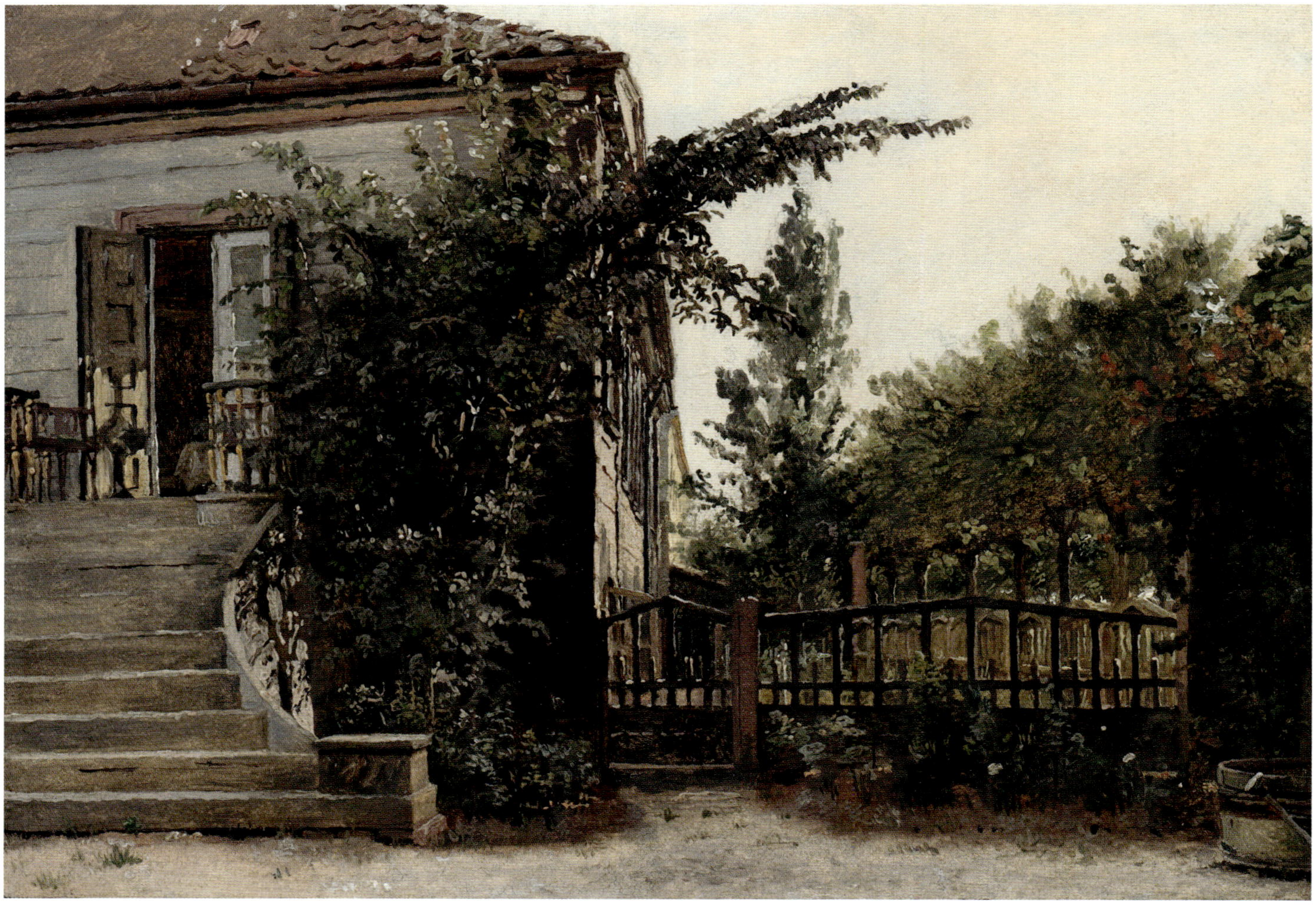

catches the façade, the open door and the tree.

Female artists were not admitted to the Royal Academy in Copenhagen in the nineteenth century.[9] Their only possibility of getting a regular artistic education was to seek private tuition from one of the academy professors, and Eckersberg had several female students. But, since women were not allowed to take part in the life classes with nude models, most of them limited their subject matter to flower painting. Only one female artist stood out among the rest and, characteristically, she did not have a Danish background. This was Elisabeth Jerichau Baumann (1819–1881) who was born in Warsaw to German parents and was educated in Düsseldorf from 1838 to 1845, before meeting the Danish sculptor Jens Adolf Jerichau, whom she married in Rome in 1846. Three years later the couple settled in Copenhagen, which became the basis of her many future travels (fig. 5).

In 1846, before moving to Copenhagen, she painted a large portrait of her husband. He is seen sitting with a lump of clay in one hand and a tool in the other, gazing into the distance, apparently deep in thought about his work. In the background is the clay model of his sculpture *Hercules and Hebe*, which had given him his artistic breakthrough the year before. The painter has given the sculptor an almost dreamy appearance, lit up by a strong light before a hazy background. She thus broke with a strong tradition of showing the sitter in a bright, even light, and added new, romantic aspects to Danish portraiture. However, Elisabeth Jerichau Baumann was a lone figure on the Danish art scene and did not have any followers. Her later paintings of mermaids and odalisques in Arabic harems had no parallels in Copenhagen.

The year 1838 marked a decisive change in Danish art. A long dormant controversy about the affiliation of the two duchies Schleswig and Holstein to the Danish crown had become more and more pronounced during the 1830s and now turned into an open conflict.[10] In 1830, a local movement had started in Kiel, campaigning for a change from absolute rule to local democracy, but it had been turned down by the king, and then

Fig. 4: **Christen Købke**, *The Garden Steps Leading to the Artist's Studio on Blegdammen, Copenhagen*, c. 1845
Statens Museum for Kunst, Copenhagen

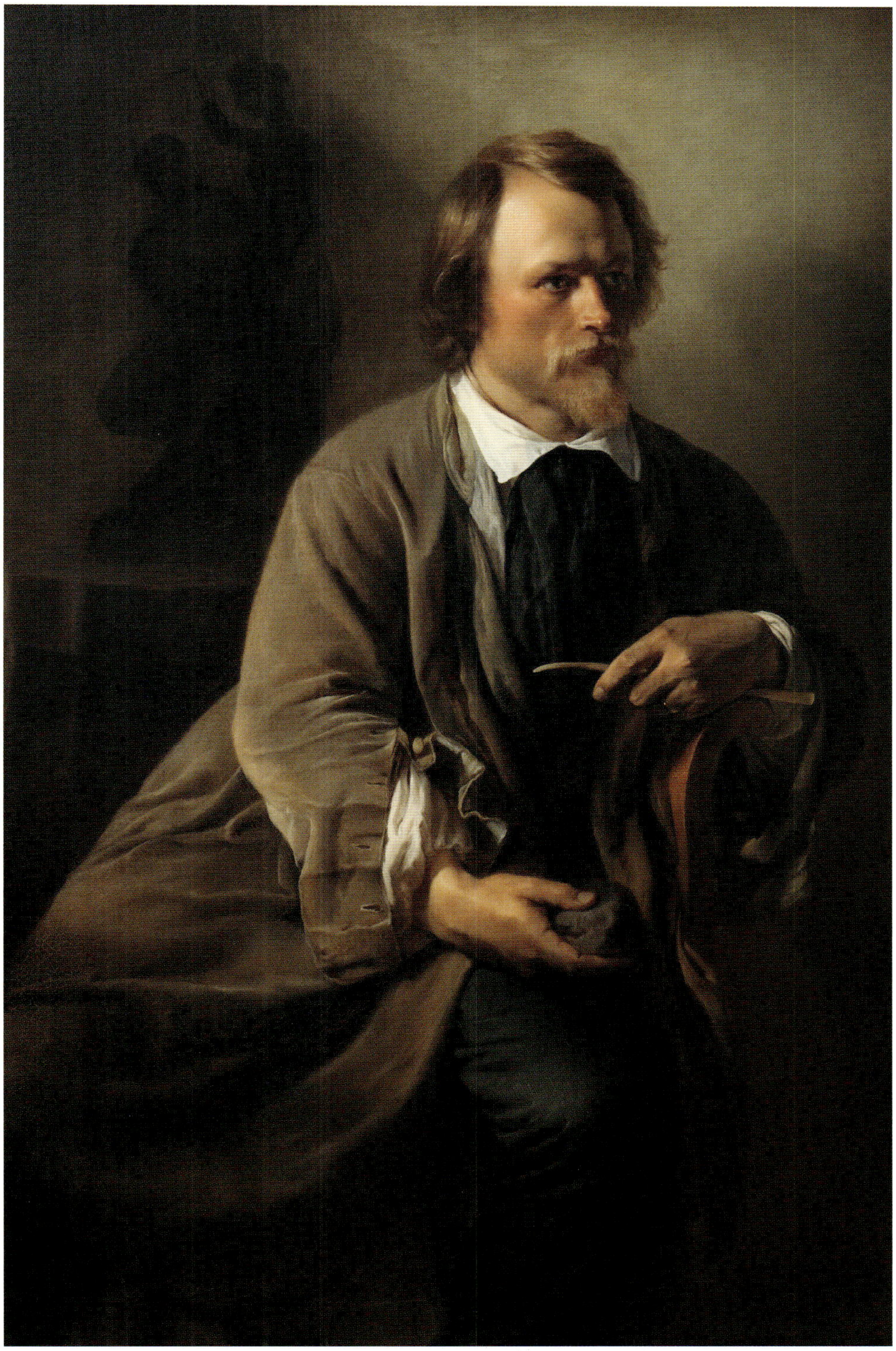

Fig. 5: **Elisabeth Jerichau-Baumann**, *The Sculptor Jens Adolph Jerichau, the Artist's Husband*, 1846
Statens Museum for Kunst, Copenhagen

changed into a demand for independence. With a view to the Danish-speaking part of the population in Schleswig, leading circles in Copenhagen began to work persistently to promote Danish nationalism, not only in the duchies, but also in Denmark itself. Several Danish artists joined this new national movement, especially many landscape painters, as the general belief was that there was connection between a country's natural landscape and the national character of the people living in that country. The conflict resulted in two wars, the first in 1848–50, in which the Danish gained the upper hand once Prussia withdrew its support for the rebels in the duchies. However, the second war, in 1864, ended with Prussia's quick victory over Denmark and the loss of Schleswig and Holstein as the result.

During the 1840s, conflicts also gradually arose between previously collegial Danish and German artists in Copenhagen, and around the time the first of the two

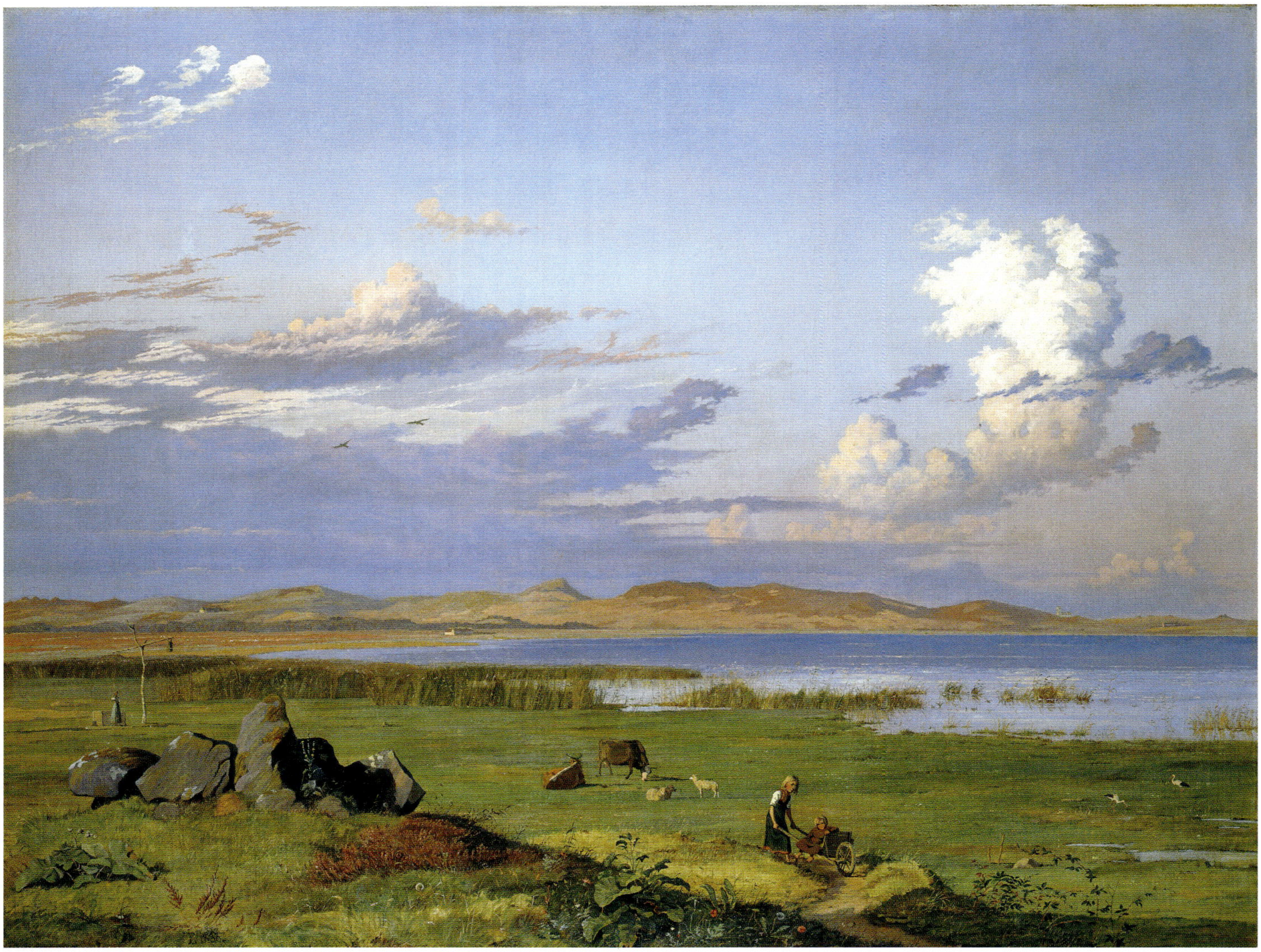

Fig. 6: **Johan Thomas Lundbye**, *Landscape at Lake Arre with a View of the Shifting Sand Dunes at Tisvilde*, 1838
Thorvaldsens Museum, Copenhagen

wars broke out, many German-speaking painters left the country.

One painting more than any other marks the shift in Danish painting: Johan Thomas Lundbye's (1818–1848) *Landscape at Lake Arre with a View of the Shifting Sand Dunes at Tisvilde* from 1838 (fig. 6).[11] Although the starting point is a specific locality in North Zealand, the painter aimed to give the landscape a typically Danish character. He painted a panoramic view of the relatively flat landscape, which he made more impressive by depicting the sandy hills in the background like stately mountains. The monumental cloud formations contribute further to this effect. In order to add a historical dimension to the landscape, he painted a burial mound in the foreground – on a low, swampy ground where the prehistoric Danes would never have placed it! Lundbye's nationalistic aspirations were immediately appreciated when he exhibited the painting at the Royal Academy. A critic declared that the painting had "a genuinely Danish patriotic character,"[12] and it was promptly acquired by the Copenhagen Fine Arts Society (Kunstforening). Later, the famous sculptor Bertel Thorvaldsen won it in a lottery.

The 1840s became the heyday of Danish landscape painting and Lundbye was joined by a number of other young painters who all responded to Eckersberg's objectivity and adopted a more romantic style.

In the middle of the decade, the nationalistic debate took a new turn, however. Based on the assertion that Danish nature had more parallels with German nature

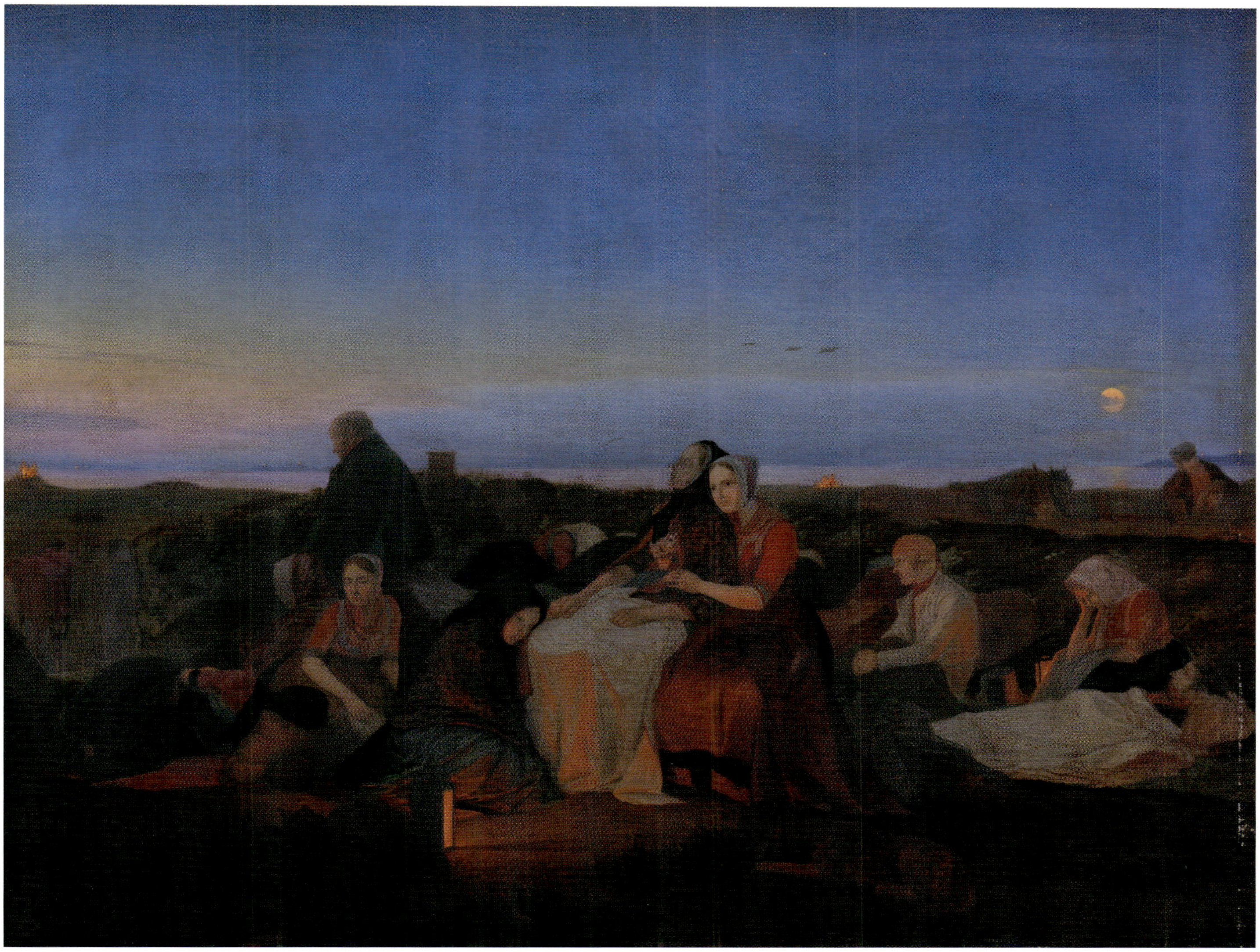

Fig. 7: **Jørgen Sonne**, *Midsummer's Eve. Sick People Asleep on the Grave of St. Helena at Tisvilde, North Zealand*, 1847
Statens Museum for Kunst, Copenhagen

than with that of the rest of Scandinavia, some nationalistic protagonists began arguing that it was the nation's history and the people's language, rather than its scenery, that determined the national character of the people. The art historian and critic Niels Laurits Høyen, who had close contact with the artists, gave a now famous lecture in 1844, in which he urged painters to aim to revive a national history painting. By way of preparation he encouraged them to seek out and study farmers and fishermen in outlying regions where old customs and traditions were still being upheld. As a consequence, many painters engaged in a new, romantic folk painting in Denmark. Until then, almost all painters had focused on the lives of townspeople. The first artist to embark on the new project was Jørgen Sonne (1801–90), who had already taken up this subject matter while Høyen was still preparing his lecture.

In 1847, Sonne painted *Midsummer's Eve. Sick People Asleep on the Grave of St. Helena at Tisvilde, North Zealand* (fig. 7).[13] Here he focused on an old popular belief that the sick would gain strength and be healed from their illnesses if they spent this special night on the grave of the saint. He got his inspiration for the painting from Lundbye, who had witnessed the scene a few years earlier. Despite their supposedly weak condition, most of the sick shown in the painting have a surprisingly strong appearance. Sonne maintained much of the idealization he had shown in his many Italian folk scenes from the previous decade. He did not attempt any kind of social realism. As the very first painter he

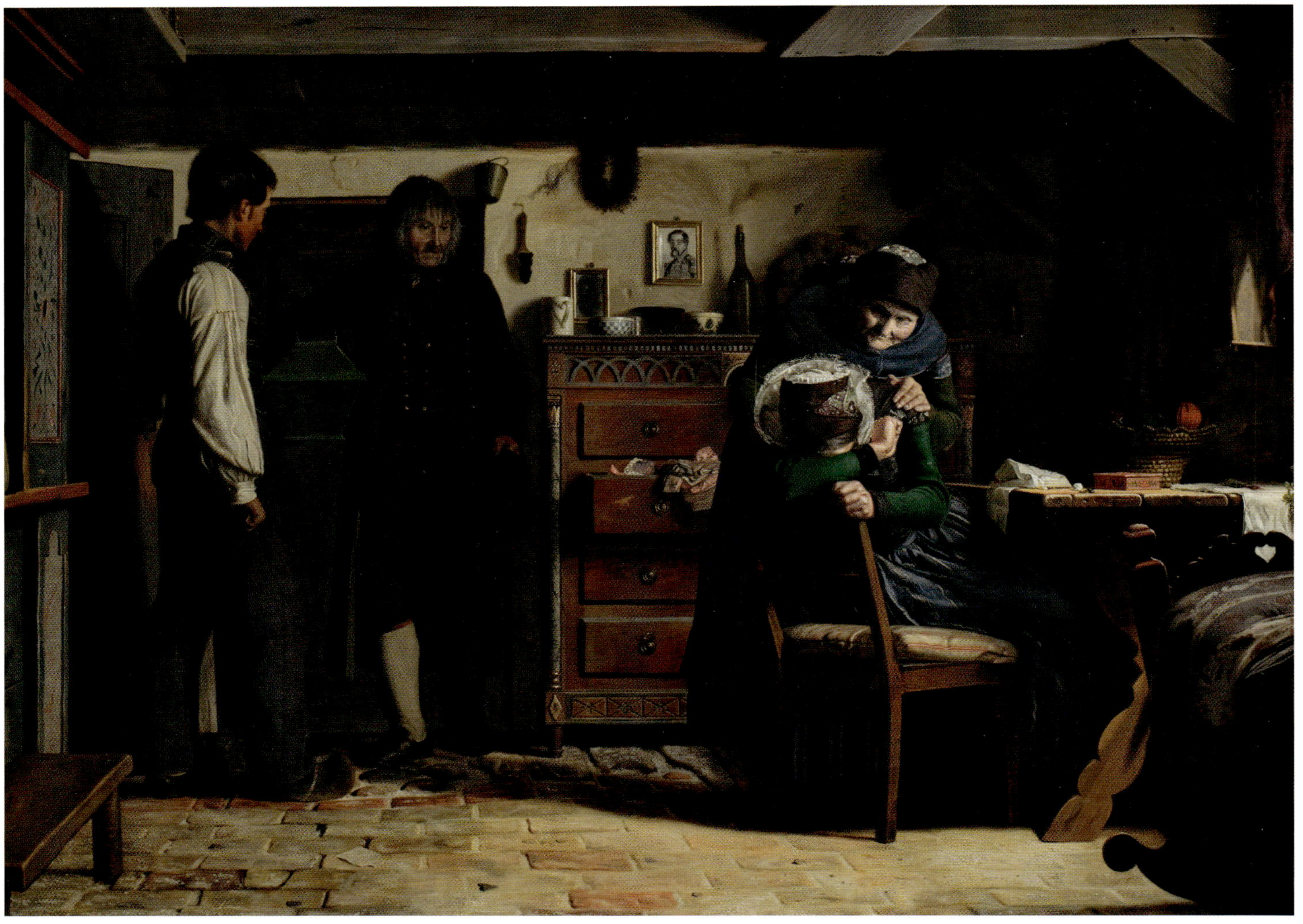

Fig. 8: **Christen Dalsgaard**, *The Village Carpenter Bringing a Coffin for a Dead Child*, 1857
Statens Museum for Kunst, Copenhagen

tried to capture the characteristic quality of the light Nordic summer night.

A few years after Sonne, several young painters took up the same challenge and made Danish folk painting their specialist field. But a new history painting did not emerge. In the hands of a new generation of painters the genre scenes developed a decidedly ethnographic character. In preparation of their large exhibition pictures, they made numerous studies of country folk and fishermen in remote parts of the country as well as of the interiors of their homes. They took great care in ensuring that all details were in keeping with the local traditions.[14] The large paintings always have a clear narrative with a story that is easy to comprehend, whether the painting depicts an amusing incident or a tragic event.

Christen Dalsgaard (1824–1907) made a point of focusing on psychological drama in his genre paintings, often with people in contrasting personal situations, as is the case in *The Village Carpenter Bringing a Coffin for a Dead Child* from 1857 (fig. 8).[15] The studies for the painting reveal that the artist's starting point was probably a drawing of the central character, the mother lost in grief, and the next step would be a detailed oil study of a room in a farm and finally drawn studies for each figure.[16] In the final painting several details were added or changed in order to make the scene characteristic of a Danish country home.

The dominance of genre painting with national folkloristic subjects was not exceptional for Denmark. In Norway and Sweden the same tendencies were prevailing, but, unlike the Danish painters, many of the Norwegians and Swedes went to Düsseldorf to study. For political reasons the Danes had broken the previously close ties with the German art scene. The result was an artistic isolation of Danish art from the rest of Europe, which lasted for more than two decades and led to provincialism and artistic decay.

1 Cf. Marianne Saabye, ed., *Wilhelm Bendz 1804–1832: A Young Painter of the Danish Golden Age*, exh. cat., The Hirschsprung Collection, Copenhagen (Copenhagen, 1996), p. 109–11, cat. 45; Kasper Monrad, *Dansk guldalder: Lyset, landskabet og hverdagslivet* (Copenhagen, 2013), pp. 154–55.

2 For a general survey of Danish painting of the early nineteenth century, see Kasper Monrad, "The Copenhagen School of Painting," in Philip Conisbee, ed., *The Golden Age of Danish Painting*, exh.cat., Los Angeles County Museum of Art, Los Angeles and Metropolitan Museum of Art, New York (New York, 1993), pp. 11–19; Patricia G. Berman, *In Another Light: Danish Painting of the Nineteenth Century* (London, 2007); Monrad 2013 (see note 1).

3 Cf. Kasper Monrad, "Blick durch drei Bogen: Deutsch-dänische Künstlerbegegnungen in Dänemark, Deutschland und Italien," in Helmut R. Leppien, ed., *Im Lichte Caspar David Friedrichs: Frühe Freilichtmalerei in Dänemark und Norddeutschland*, exh. cat., Hamburger Kunsthalle (Hamburg, 2000), pp. 4–5.

4 Cf. Kasper Monrad, "Eckersberg on the European Stage," in Kasper Monrad, ed., *Christoffer Wilhelm Eckerersberg*, exh. cat., Statens Museum for Kunst, Copenhagen (Copenhagen, 2015), pp. 50–51; German version: "Eckersberg auf der europäischen Bühne," in Markus Bertsch/Hubertus Gaßner/Neela Struck, eds., *Eckersberg. Faszination Wirklichkeit*, exh.cat., Hamburger Kunsthalle (Hamburg, 2016), pp. 30–31.

5 Hans Edvard Nørregård-Nielsen in Hans Edvard Nørregård-Nielsen/Kasper Monrad, eds., *Christen Købke 1810–1848*, exh. cat., Statens Museum for Kunst, Copenhagen (Copenhagen, 1996), pp. 229–35 (also English, German and French editions); David Jackson, *Christen Købke: Danish Master of Light*, exh. cat., The National Gallery, London and The National Galleries of Scotland, Edinburgh (Edinburgh, 2010), pp. 78–79.

6 Monrad 2013 (see note 1), pp. 214–16; Monrad in Bertsch/Gaßner/Struck 2016 (see note 4), pp. 31, 288, cat. 84.

7 Monrad 2015 (see note 4), pp. 24–34; Monrad in Bertsch/Gaßner/Struck 2016 (see note 4), pp. 15–21.

8 Conisbee 1993 (see note 2), cat. 77 (Kasper Monrad); Jackson 2010 (see note 5), p. 97.

9 Peter Nørgaard Larsen, "Med ryggen mod fremtiden," in Anneli Fuchs/Emma Salling, eds., *Kunstakademiet 1754–2004*, vol. 1 (Copenhagen, 2004), pp. 174–77.

10 See Kasper Monrad, "Die dänische Landschaftsmalerei des sogenannten Goldenen Zeitalters," in Götz Czymmek, ed., *Aus Dänemarks goldener Zeit: Landschaftsmalerei des früheren 19. Jahrhunderts aus dem Statens Museum for Kunst, Kopenhagen*, exh. cat., Wallraf-Richartz-Museum, Cologne (Cologne, 1995), pp. 37–38.

11 Conisbee 1993 (note 2), pp. 178–79, cat. 80 (Kasper Monrad).

12 Quoted ibid., p. 178.

13 Dyveke Helsted/Eva Henschen/Bjarne Jørnæs, eds., *Jørgen Sonne 1801–1890*, exh.cat. Thorvaldsens Museum, Copenhagen/Aarhus Kunstmuseum, Aarhus (Copenhagen, 1988), p. 73, cat. 34 (Eva Henschen).

14 Marianne Zenius, *Genremaleri og virkelighed* (Copenhagen, 1976).

15 Peter Nørgaard Larsen, "Mellem vaudeviller og homeriske helteepos – Om Christen Dalsgaards livsbilleder," in Charlotte Sabroe/Christine Buhl Andersen/Inge Bucka, eds., *Christen Dalsgaard 1824–1907*, exh.cat., Vestsjællands Kunstmuseum, Sorø/Skive Kunstmuseum, Skive/Hirschsprungs Samling, Copenhagen (Sorø, 2001), pp. 18–35.

16 Zenius 1976 (see note 14), pp. 182–88.

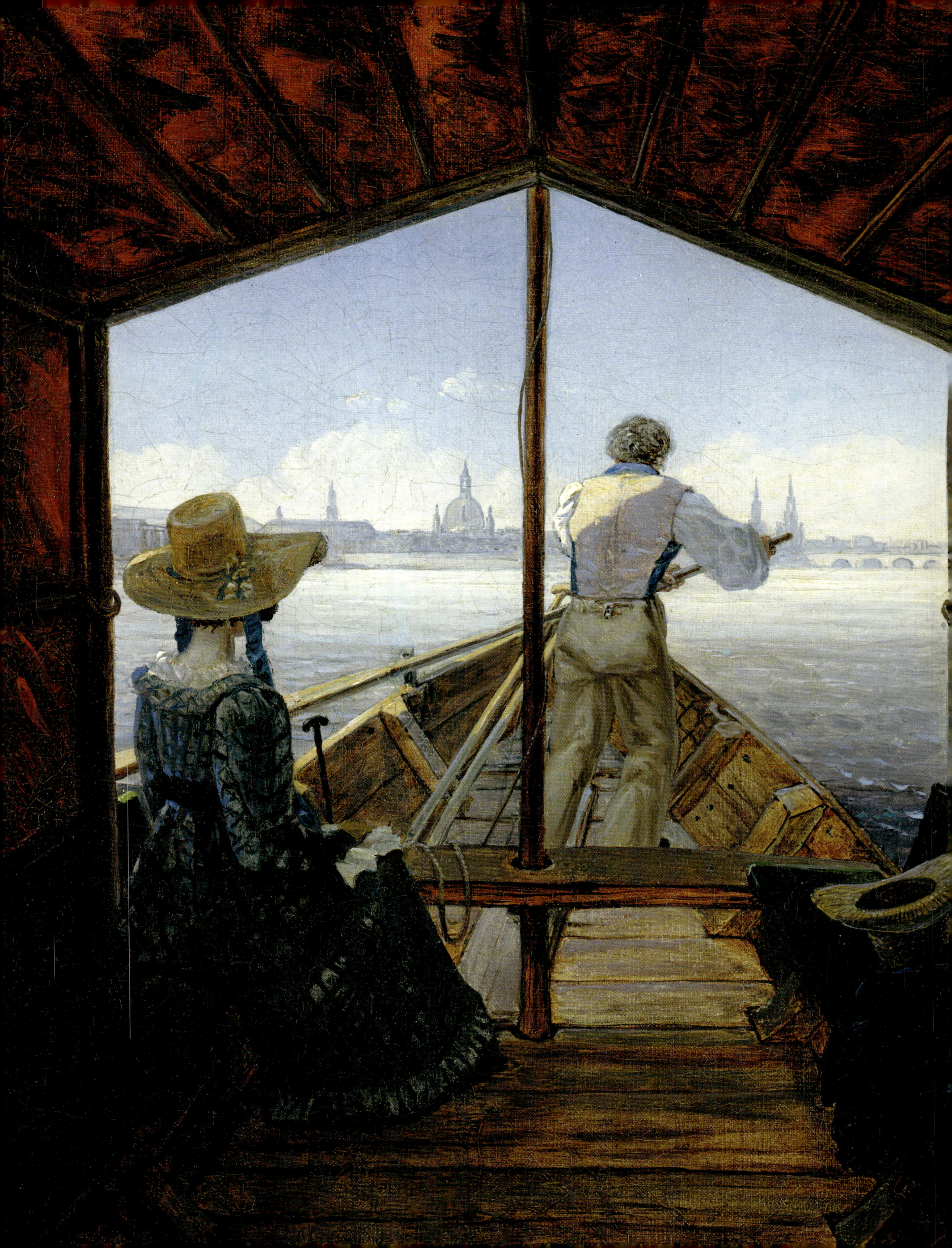

"AND IN FEELING ART COMPLETES ITSELF"[1] PAINTING IN GERMANY 1820–1860

Udo Felbinger

Painting in Germany at the time of the German Confederation (1815–1866) was highly varied as there was no political or artistic center like in other European countries. Besides the academies of Berlin, Munich, Dresden, and Düsseldorf, many artistic sub-centers existed in trading cities and at small royal courts.[2] Moreover, the key dates of political history frequently found in specialist literature correspond in no way to those in the development of art. What is more, the terminology used in art history to this day often appears contradictory: terms such as Neoclassicism, Romanticism, Biedermeier, and Realism are not differentiated from one another. This imprecision in stylistic terminology reflects the variety of painting of this era. Using a selection of works, the development of German painting between 1820 and 1860 is briefly outlined in the following. Beginning with Caspar David Friedrich, the founder of Romantic landscape painting, the development in style and motifs of this genre will be explained by means of landscapes featuring couples. The portrait genre, less innovative at the time, is represented with a Nazarene-influenced, courtly family portrait and a portrait of an artist based on Baroque models. Due to its popularity at the time, the genre is considered the second emerging pictorial genre of the century alongside landscape painting. It points toward the arising trend of outdoor painting as well as the pathos-filled social critique that surfaced in history painting.

Landscape painting

Of all the genres of painting, landscape developed the most from 1800 onwards. In Dresden, Caspar David Friedrich (1774–1840) created a new, subjective pictorial language, which, although working with symbols, left their interpretation largely to the viewer. Friedrich's elitist claim that only intellectually and emotionally advanced people could truly understand his art makes his work accessible to a variety of interpretations. The few extant statements made by Friedrich about his art suggest, however, that he concealed specific content in his works.[3] While this radical innovation was recognized by his contemporaries, its purpose was frequently not. One exception to this was a newspaper article written by Heinrich von Kleist, Clemens Brentano, and Achim von Arnim. In this report on the Berlin Academy exhibition, published in the *Berliner Abendblätter* on October 13, 1810, fascination is expressed at Friedrich's paradigmatic companion paintings *The Monk by the Sea* and *The Abbey in the Oakwood*.[4] That especially writers were able to relate to Friedrich's work is also evident in two poems about *The Abbey in the Oakwood* entitled *Friedrichs Totenlandschaft*, written by Theodor Körner. At the end of the second poem, Körner gives an instruction on how to conceive of the subject seen: "Here I can boldly trust my heart; / Cold admiration I shall not have – no, I feel, / And in feeling art completes itself."[5] Created around 1819/20, the painting *Riesengebirge Landscape with Rising Fog* (fig. 2) is the earliest in a series of similar pictures and shows the unique qualities of Friedrich's art at the beginning of a new creative period: The viewer is positioned at the top of a hill, looking toward three scraggy trees flanking a precariously balanced rock formation. The rising mountain ranges in the background form a transcendentally heightened world that contrasts with the rationally discernible area in the foreground. The mountain edges are accentuated by means of gradually lighter coloring, combined with the rising mist, which further enhances the sense of depth. The writer and translator Karl Foerster (1784–1841) visited Friedrich's studio on April 18, 1820. He was shown several paintings, including probably the one discussed here: "Then he shows me one more beautiful picture, a section of the Giant Mountains, or rather painted in the character of the same, at an altitude where vegetation no longer grows, apart from a few meagre dwarf pines; higher up everything is barren."[6] In Foerster's brief description of the picture's special features his use of "in the character

Fig. 1: **Carl Gustav Carus**
Boat Ride on the Elbe near Dresden, 1829
Stiftung Kunstpalast, Düsseldorf

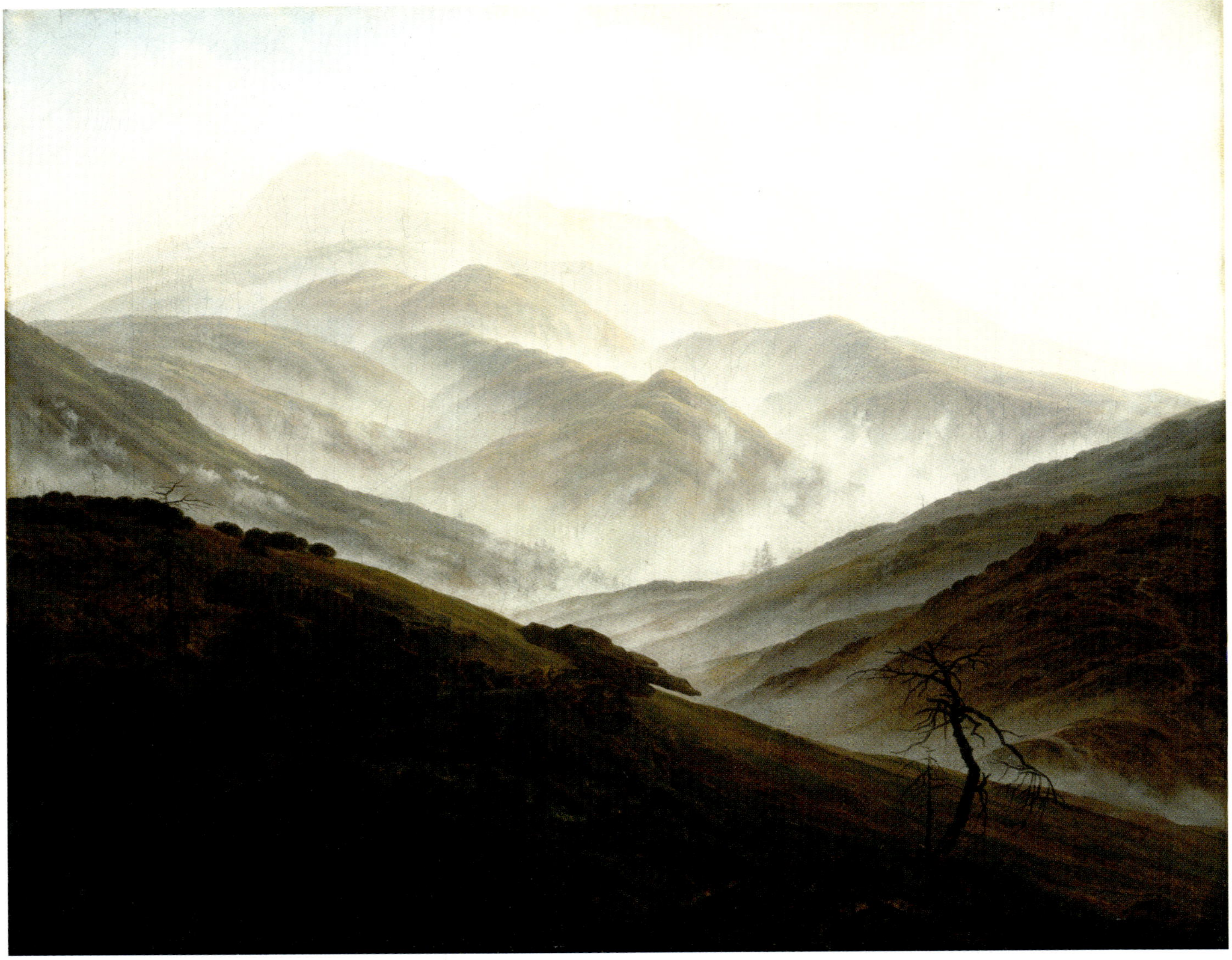

Fig. 2: **Caspar David Friedrich**, *Riesengebirge Landscape with Rising Fog*, 1819/20
Bayerische Staatsgemäldesammlungen Munich, Neue Pinakothek

of the same" is notable in that it makes clear that Friedrich's concern is not with the reproduction of reality, but rather with the heightened reality of an artistic composition. The lack of vegetation, unaccustomed for viewers at the time, is one of the particular features of the picture. The artist had painted over both of the human figures originally intended,[7] obviously in order to intensify the picture's impact. He had already done the same in *The Monk by the Sea*, where he painted over three ships, thereby significantly enhancing the painting's effect. The elimination of any form of narrative emphasizes the static character of the landscape shown, drawing our attention to the bare trees and precarious rock formation. Their contradictory qualities—the hard rock threatening to topple over, yet the trees, misshapen by the harsh climate, will bud again in spring—point to two prevailing themes in Friedrich's work: the eternal cycle of growth and decay, and a symbolism relating to faith and death.

In his painting *Afternoon on Capri* (fig. 3), Carl Blechen (1798–1840) testifies to the fondness for Italian themes among German artists. Building on Friedrich's achievements—such as the extreme scaling of man and landscape—he brings an unprecedented synthesis of nature depiction, light effects, and Mediterranean exoticism to the canvas. Like few other landscape painters before him, Blechen succeeds in addressing all the senses through the medium of seeing. In contrast to Friedrich's picture, a narrative element is integrated into the landscape in the depiction of two lovers: a man sitting on a wall with his legs crossed, apparently performing a song on a stringed instrument for the woman lying beside him. His red fisherman's cap adds a touch of color to the surrounding nature, thereby placing man at the center of the idyll that unfolds—pervaded by traces of civilization—before the backdrop of the mountains. Yet this picture, unusually cheerful for Blechen, still contains a menacing undertone: The dark shadow that falls on the parched earth, almost reaching the couple, could be a hint that this moment of happiness may be of short duration. During an enforced stay on Capri due to a storm, Blechen used the time to study the particulars of the island's landscape. What interested him about Italy was mainly the yet unseen, the rough and authentic. The *Spener'sche Zeitung* wrote on the occasion of the picture's display at the Berlin Academy Exhibition in 1832: "It is not so easy to accommodate oneself to Professor Blechen's unusual perception. Yet if successful in this, one can quite readily perceive nature in the same way the artist has seen it, finding in it the bold lighting in the sunshine and hard shadows effective and faithful, indeed faithful in an outstanding way, if one follows this—admittedly always quite oddly spiritual—conception of nature, such as, for example, in the woods that rise up toward the town of Capri."[8] These new artistic achievements make Blechen one of the first representatives of Realism in the painting of his time.

Johann Wilhelm Schirmer (1807–1863) provides an example for trends in landscape painting after 1840: *The Geroldsau Valley near Baden-Baden*[9] (fig. 4) shows a view combining two perspectives from different vantage points. In the interplay of light and shadow our gaze is directed south along the valley toward the horizon. Notable is a penchant for the detailed and anecdotal, which lends plausibility to the subject depicted. Without any trace of pathos, man and his dwellings are perceived as foreign bodies within the tranquil, serene beauty of nature. Dressed in city clothes and equipped with parasol and gloves, the couple is no longer a part of nature, as was still the case in Blechen's painting. These are spa guests, perhaps a mother and son, exploring the countryside. The smoke rising from the chimneys dulls the clear light of the late summer's day, heralding the industrial age in which nature as a "cultural landscape" is made to serve man for production and recreation. The glorifying perspective of Romanticism now irrevocably makes way for the immediacy of experience. In nascent Realism, allegorical content and romanticizing harmony gradually become less significant. Schirmer's art, here unusually close to the reality of nature, nevertheless found no successor. The next generation of artists was more than ever interested in spontaneously capturing

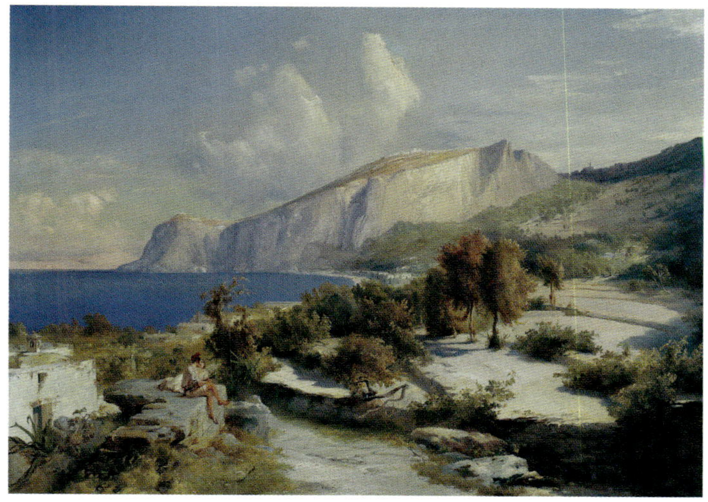

Fig. 3: **Carl Blechen**, *Afternoon on Capri*, around 1832
Belvedere, Vienna

their immediate impressions as experienced on the spot, and no longer necessarily completed their paintings in the studio. Outdoor painting, which was increasingly practiced, opened up new freedoms in landscape art.

Portraiture

Portraiture experienced a renaissance thanks to a new generation of well-trained artists. The Berlin artist Wilhelm von Schadow (1788–1862) looked toward Italy—like Friedrich Overbeck (1789–1869), disappointed by the Vienna Academy, had done before him—to study the art of the Quattrocento. He joined the group of artists now known as the Nazarenes, and found so much recognition in Berlin that the art-loving Prince Wilhelm of Prussia commissioned him in 1821 to produce the life-sized portrait *Princess Marianne of Prussia with her Children*[10] (fig. 5). Following the death of Queen Louise in 1810, the princess had become the first lady at the Prussian court. She enjoyed high regard as educator of the royal children and for her charity work. Her strictly anti-Napoleon stance made her a key figure of resistance during the Wars of Liberation from 1813 to 1815: In a spectacular appeal to the women of Prussia she asked them to donate their jewelry to help finance the campaign against Napoleon Bonaparte. In recompense for their donation they received an iron ring with the inscription: "I gave gold for iron." The royal insignia, such as the crown and the ermine cloak, single her out as a member of the royal family. At the same time, the close contact with her children shows her in her role as loving mother. The painting is characterized by an innovative, suggestive materiality and brilliance in color. Its combi-

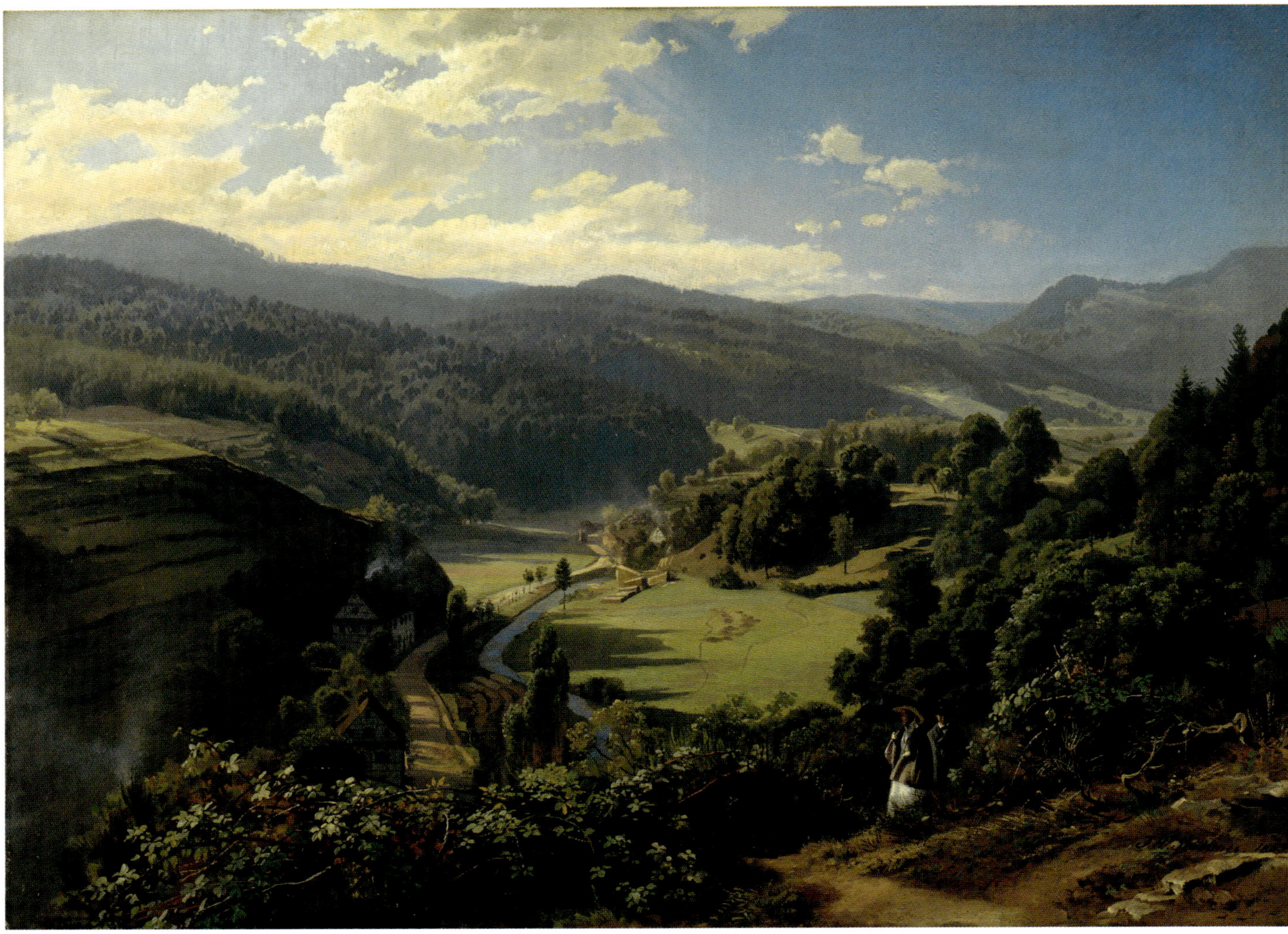

Fig. 4: **Johann Wilhelm Schirmer**, *The Geroldsau Valley near Baden-Baden*, 1855
Staatliche Kunsthalle Karlsruhe

nation of the clear lines and local color of the Italian Renaissance and the varnishing technique of Neoclassicism makes this picture one of the major works of portraiture of this period. Typical of Berlin painting of this epoch is also the topographical veduta—here Bad Homburg Castle, where the princess grew up—which establishes a personal connection to the subjects depicted. Although Schadow has idealized their physiognomies, this was not at the expense of similarity and vividness.[11] As Director of the Düsseldorf Art Academy from 1826, Schadow was to become a decisive player in shaping German art of the nineteenth century.

From the 1830s, a new generation of artists attempted to breathe new life into the increasingly sclerotic painting style through the reception of Baroque portraiture. The painter of the Berlin high society, Eduard von Magnus (1799–1872),[12] shows *Felix Mendelssohn-Bartholdy* (fig. 6) before a dark background, slightly rotated from the central axis. The composer's head alone is accentuated by light, whereby an allusion is made to the musical compositions as creations of his genius. The curly black hair and black necktie, which looks particularly sculptural, frame his face. The dark-red jacket, on the other hand, is barely visible; only the shirt buttons with connecting small gold chain form a decorative element.[13] Surprisingly, the brilliant pianist and conductor's hands remain largely concealed. Mendelssohn's eyes are slightly narrowed, his gaze focused in the distance. Tense and concentrated, he seems to be listening to some far-off melody. The realistically reproduced physiognomy and pale-green skin tone make him appear strained and unwell, a fact that is confirmed in reports by his contemporaries. Magnus has dispensed with the beautification of his model, usually found in portraiture. The departure from treating all elements of the picture equally—still evident in Schadow's painting—and the use of dynamic,

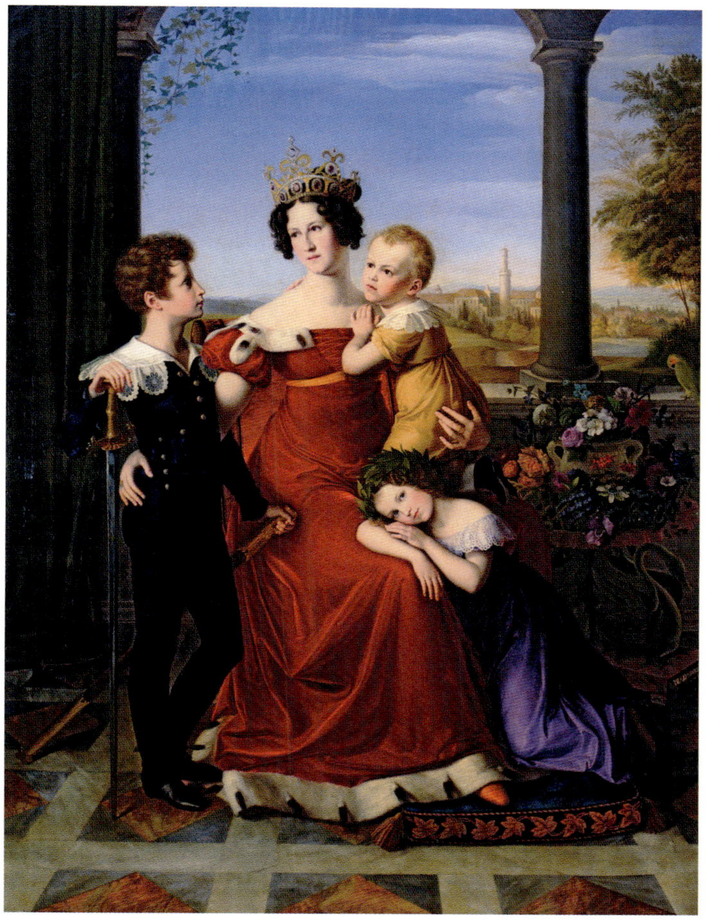

Fig. 5: **Wilhelm von Schadow**, *Princess Marianne of Prussia with her Children*, 1822
Hessische Hausstiftung, Schlossmuseum Darmstadt

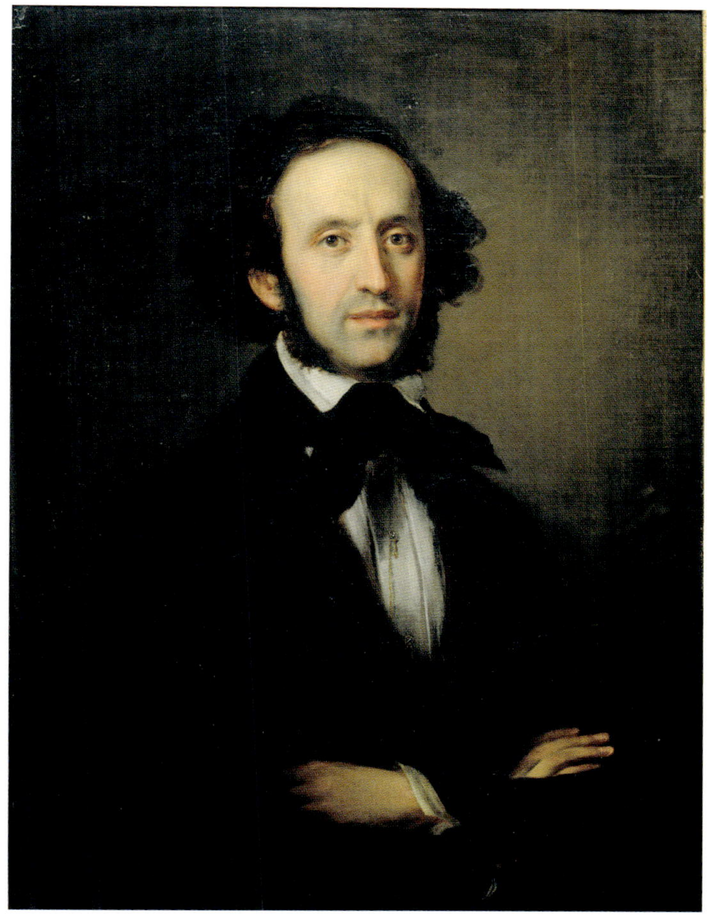

Fig. 6: **Eduard von Magnus**, *Felix Mendelssohn-Bartholdy*, 1845/46
Staatsbibliothek Preußischer Kulturbesitz, Berlin

pictorial values anticipate Realism. Clothing and accessories merge into the background; instead there is a concentration on the essence of the person depicted. In the emerging Realism, the portrait was to become an important medium for artists, not as a commissioned work, but as a creation of one's own volition. The individual became an object of study for the artist, akin to landscape.

Genre painting

Genre painting was devoted to the depiction of everyday scenes, mostly contemporary, but also in historical costume. With his *Boat Ride on the Elbe near Dresden* (fig. 1), the doctor and painter Carl Gustav Carus (1789–1869) took up a subject of his teacher Caspar David Friedrich, who, with his works *On the Sailing Boat* and *Boat Skipper on the Elbe near Dresden*,[14] had taken as his theme the commonality of man and woman, as well as the motif of the home-coming. In Carus's version this became the boat outing of a fashionable young couple. Although he trivialized Friedrich's pictorial aesthetic, Carus created something new here, a hybrid of interior painting, still shaped by Neoclassicism, Romanticism's window motif and rear-view figure (*Rückenfigur)*, and a new kind of outdoor painting. The sun on the wood and on the couple's clothing, the hazy silhouette of Dresden in the distance, are all evidence of the contemporary interest in optical effects. The shimmer of the water in the morning mist seems to anticipate the atmospheric effects of later decades.

The extent to which, years later, social reality was adopted in painting is demonstrated by the 1844 work *The Silesian Weavers*[15] (fig. 7) by Carl Wilhelm Hübner (1814–1879). Here, the artist takes a stance against the plight of the cottage weavers and their dependency on intermediary merchants, which in the same year was to lead to hunger revolts and political turmoil. The work was a manifesto with highly charged political content, closely

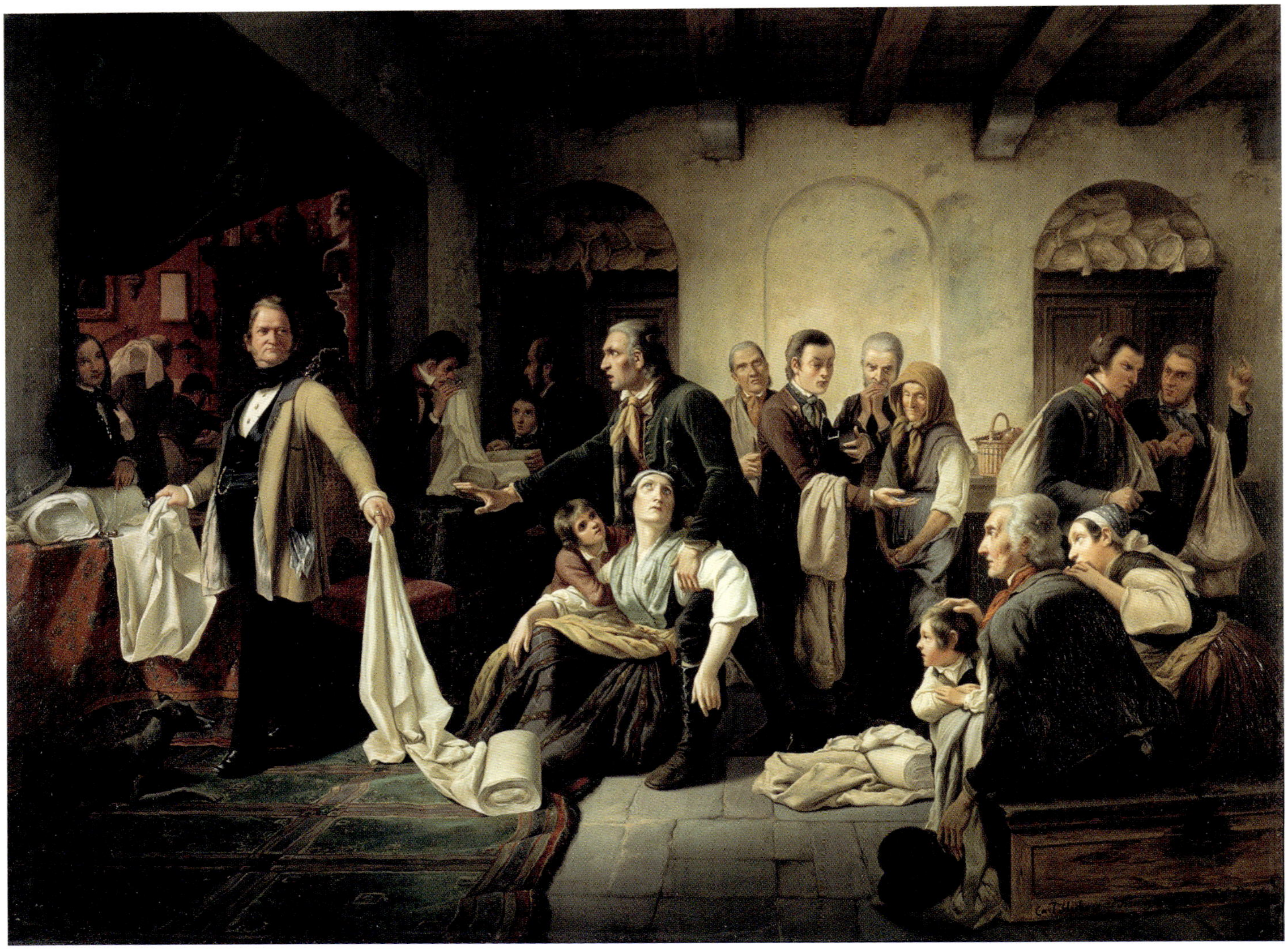

Fig. 7: **Carl Wilhelm Hübner**, *The Silesian Weavers*, 1844
Rheinisches Landesmuseum Bonn

linking genre painting with history painting. By cleverly quoting Baroque artworks, such as Hyacinthe Rigaud's portrait of Louis XIV and other examples, Hübner enriches the genre scene with emotional formulae that strengthen the picture's message. The hard-hearted merchant standing in self-important pose in front of a throne-like chair within a luxurious interior is set in contrast to the despondent weavers, shown in a greenish light, forced to offer their products at rock-bottom prices. One woman, collapsed in a martyr-like pose, gazing up toward heaven in despair, serves as a figure of identification for the viewer. Newspaper reports in the *Düsseldorfer Zeitung* about the dire situation of the Silesian weavers had inspired Hübner to create this remarkable work in February and March of 1844. Following its presentation in Düsseldorf,[16] the painting was sent on a tour of Germany to collect donations in support of the starving people, and was also shown in Vienna, probably even before 1850.[17] The liberal middle classes found in it a striking depiction of the period's social injustices, and flocked to see the painting. The *Kölnische Zeitung* described it as "socialist and, as such, contemporary, because it allegorizes the efforts made in our time to eliminate such crass class distinctions."[18] In the view of the art world, too, the painting was very successful. Johann Gottfried Schadow described it as one of "the most excellent character paintings" of the Berlin Academy Exhibition of 1844.[19] In this example, the topical relevance of the *Silesian Weavers* proved superior to history painting, which had hitherto been the more prestigious genre.

This short summary of the developments in German painting over four decades gives an impression of the pictorial worlds of an era subjected to a multitude of social and political upheavals following the Wars of Liberation. Caspar David Friedrich taking viewers off to locations that confront them with existential questions; Blechen discovering in Italy a world of light beyond any artistic convention, which he transfers to the canvas with little modification and an unaccustomed directness. In contrast to this, Schirmer's late Black Forest landscape is stripped of all romantic longing; under the influence of the Nazarenes, the courtly portrait is transformed into a hybrid painting style with bourgeois elements, while the Baroque-inspired chiaroscuro produces a new, realistic depiction of man. Genre painting proves to be the real beneficiary of this period, in which bourgeois art associations propagate the popularization of painting. Accessible and easily digestible without any special knowledge, the narrative depiction of figures becomes a commercial success among middle-class art buyers, even as social injustice is openly decried. Yet Hübner's composition remains an exception, for the gradual slide of genre painting into the trivial, the playful, and anecdotal was to continue right up to the end of the century.

1 Theodor Körner, "Abtei im Eichwald," quoted from Caspar David Friedrich, *Bekenntnisse*, ed. Kurt Karl Eberlein (Leipzig, 1924), p. 261. Translation from Joseph Leo Körner, *Caspar David Friedrich and the Subject of Landscape*, 2nd ed. (London, 2009), p. 132.

2 See Helmut Börsch-Supan, *Die deutsche Malerei von Anton Graff bis Hans von Marées 1780–1870* (Munich, 1988).

3 Thomas Noll, *Die Landschaftsmalerei von Caspar David Friedrich* (Munich, 2006), pp. 71–89.

4 1808–1810, Staatliche Museen zu Berlin, Nationalgalerie. The article was mainly written by Brentano with Arnim's help, but significantly expanded by Kleist shortly before publication. Cf. Friedrich 1924 (see note 1), pp. 250–259. The second (not printed) part of the article consists of quotes from visitors to the Berlin Art Exhibition compiled to parade their ignorance in parody form. For this, cf. Lothar Jordan/Hartwig Schultz, ed., *Empfindungen vor Friedrichs Seelandschaft. Caspar David Friedrichs Gemälde "Der Mönch am Meer" betrachtet von Clemens Brentano, Achim von Arnim und Heinrich von Kleist*, exh.-cat., Kleist-Museum Frankfurt (Oder) (Frankfurt [Oder], 2006).

5 Quoted from Friedrich 1924 (see note 1), p. 261.

6 Quoted from Friedrich 1924 (see note 1), p. 248.

7 The overpainted figures were originally placed between the two trees to the right and the rock formation. It is likely that Friedrich concealed a symbolic message in the proportion of the rock that points precisely toward the tip of the smaller tree, which is "sheltered" by the larger one.

8 *Spener'sche Zeitung*, no. 251, October, 25, 1832, quoted from Paul Ortwin Rave, *Carl Blechen* (Berlin, 1940), p. 27.

9 The picture belongs to a four-part cycle of the times of day; cf. Roman Theilmann, *Großherzogliche Lieblingspromenaden: Johann Wilhelm Schirmers fünf Ansichten aus der Umgebung von Baden-Baden* (Karlsruhe, 1999).

10 On the variations of this picture, see Cordula Grewe, *Wilhelm Schadow (1788–1862)*, dissertation Freiburg (Breisgau), 1998 (microfiche), pp. 175–178.

11 Cf. the numerous portraits of the princess and her family by Wilhelm von Schadow, Wilhelm Wach, Karl Begas, Caroline Bardua, and others.

12 On Magnus's work cf. Ludwig Gläser, *Eduard von Magnus* (Berlin, 1963).

13 Presumably the painting has darkened later on because of the use of bitumen paint.

14 1818/19, Hermitage, St. Petersburg, as well as around 1818, only passed on as a watercolor. Cf. Rolf Andree, *Kunstmuseum Düsseldorf. Die Gemälde des 19. Jahrhunderts* (Mainz, 1981), pp. 60–62.

15 The first version of 1844 (111 × 158 cm) at the Rheinisches Landesmuseum Bonn, the second version of 1844 (77.5 × 105.5 cm) at the Stiftung Kunstpalast, Düsseldorf, and a third version of 1846 (39.2 × 52 cm) at the Deutsches Historisches Museum, Berlin.

16 Lilian Landes, *Carl Wilhelm Hübner (1814–1879): Genre und Zeitgeschichte im deutschen Vormärz* (Munich, 2008), p. 72, note 68, lists as the exhibition venues Cologne, Stuttgart, Vienna, Leipzig, Dresden, Berlin, Halberstadt, and Bremen, without specifying dates.

17 Cf. the reports in *Verzeichnis sämmtlicher vom dem oesterreichischen Kunst-Vereine in Wien in seinem ersten Vereinsjahre 1850–1851 ausgestellten Kunst-Werke*, p. 2; *Humorist*, no. 247, November 16, 1850, p. 1 (oil sketch of the picture); *Sonntagsblätter*, no. 48, December 1, 1844, p. 1142 (on the exhibition of the picture in Berlin); *Wiener Zeitschrift für Kunst, Literatur und Mode*, no. 124, June 23, 1845, p. 496 (on the exhibition of the picture, or a print of it, in Leipzig).

18 On the history of the picture's reception see Landes 2008 (see note 19), pp. 62–87.

19 Johann Gottfried Schadow, *Kunstwerke und Kunstansichten* [1849], 3 vols., commented and re-published by Götz Eckardt (Berlin, 1987), vol. 1, p. 241.

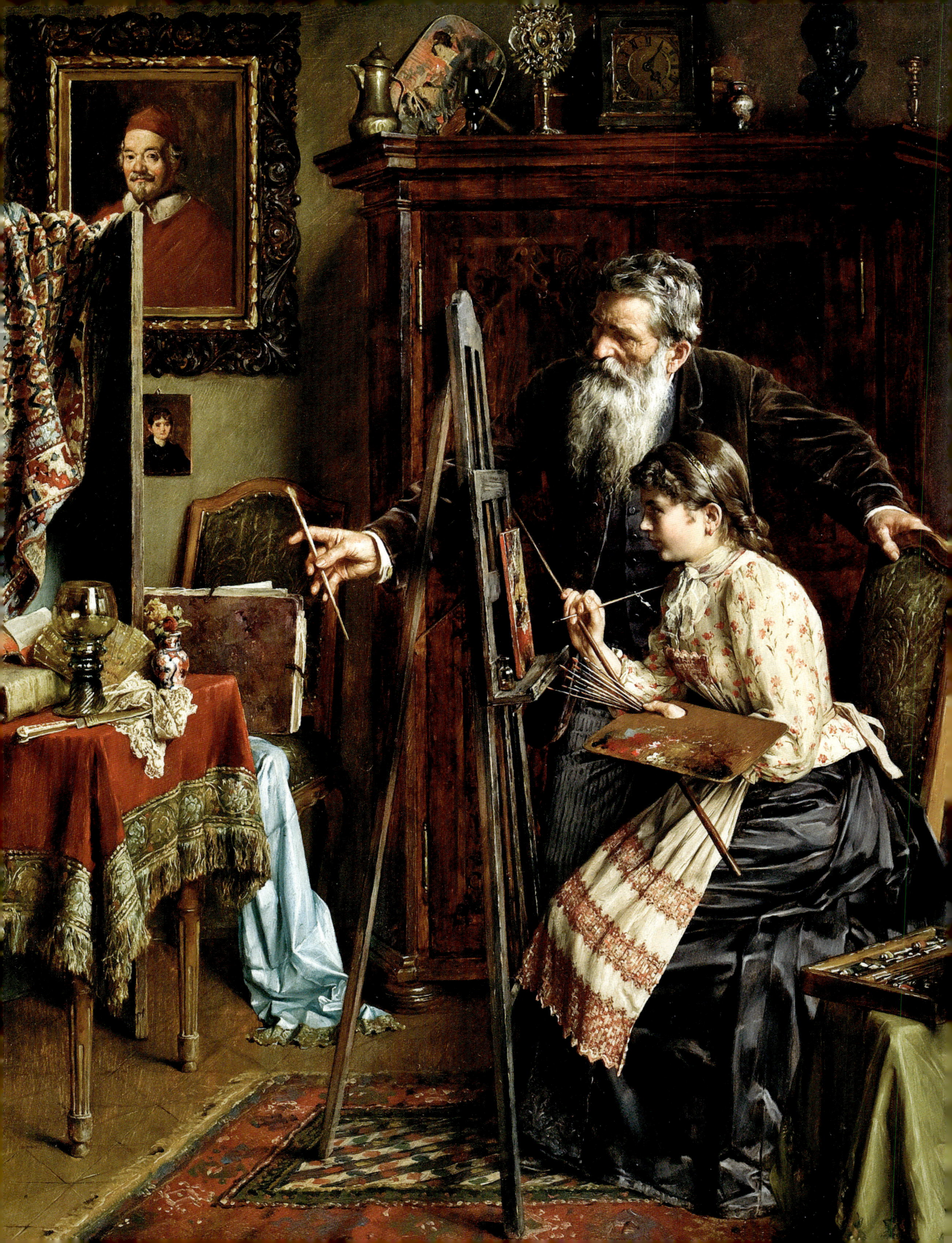

THE "SCHWARZ ARTISTS" OBSERVATIONS ON THE REVIVAL OF "OLD VIENNESE" GENRE PAINTING

Elke Doppler

Genre painting from the Biedermeier era was by no means cast aside after 1850. On the contrary: "The cheerful wave of pre-1848 Viennese painting continued to roll on well into the reign of the emperor [...]," as Ludwig Hevesi commented in 1903.[1] Today we may consider this afterlife as being on a modest scale and of little artistic interest.[2] Yet from the 1870s and especially in the 1880s, there was an obvious revival of genre painting that, at least on the surface, borrowed formally and thematically from "Alt-Wiener Malerei" (Old Viennese painting),[3] and was interpreted by art critics as being from this tradition. It included works by Friedrich Friedländer (1825–1901), a student of Ferdinand Georg Waldmüller, who Hevesi claimed was "actually the last 'Old Viennese' genre painter."[4] Many of the typical exponents, such as Josef Gisela (1851–1899), Johann Hamza (1850–1927), Isidor Kaufmann (1853–1921), Anton Müller (1853–1897), Carl Zewy (1855–1929), Emil Strecker (1841–1925), and Ernst Nowak (1851–1919), were represented by an art dealer called Friedrich Schwarz and have therefore come to be known as "the Schwarz artists."[5] He commissioned them to capture small-scale, meticulously painted anecdotes from the life of the "common" Viennese people. Hevesi referred to a "small popular genre," that had "worked its way back to a type of pre-1848 style."[6]

This essay aspires to a closer characterization of late-nineteenth-century genre painting in the Biedermeier tradition. Which subjects were particularly popular? To what extent was it traditional or even "outmoded"? What was the response in contemporary newspaper reviews? A further aim is to demonstrate some of the conditions behind the particular success of this art on the contemporary art market.

Fig. 1: **Anton Müller**, *The Painting Lesson*
Auktionshaus im Kinsky GmbH

The inflation of cheerful banalities

Late-nineteenth-century genre painting almost consistently presented a cheerful, humorous, and mainly conflict-free image of everyday events. The underlying moral tone and the educational message that had characterized genre painting in the first half of the century were now given a humorous slant. Social problems and modern ways of life were largely ignored; paintings were essentially apolitical. Although there was not much of a narrative behind the images, a great deal was told, an abundance of painted details compensating for the lack of storyline (fig. 1). The strikingly poetic titles, often adding commentary, also have a narrative role.[7] Known as "Feinmaler" (literally "fine painters"), these artists revived small and miniature formats and the Biedermeier era's meticulous style of painting in glazes. Many placed great emphasis on a detailed, heightened realism in their rendering of materials. They were influenced not only by pre-1848 Austrian art but also seventeenth-century Dutch painting—as the tonal interiors by Emil Strecker and Friedrich Friedländer demonstrate—as well as the painstakingly detailed work of the French artist Ernest Meissonier (1815–1891), emulated in the popular Rococo scenes.

Men were depicted playing chess, reading the newspaper or sitting in the tavern talking; women would be gathered over their handicrafts or having a coffee break in a domestic environment, gazing dreamily out of the window or chatting in the market square (fig. 2). Groups of people were often divided by gender, their activities reflecting gender stereotypes. Mixed-gender groups or couples, unless depicting a family, were almost always shown flirting (figs. 3, 4). Although ostensibly playing music or working, the attraction between protagonists was usually, at the very least, a subtext of the "plot." And, even if they were playing, chatting, celebrating, making music, and flirting, the figures were rarely boisterous in their activities. Subtle emotions and restrained gestures predominated. As in pre-1848 painting, children were particularly popular. They were generally shown playing with a cat or dog, helping at home, as

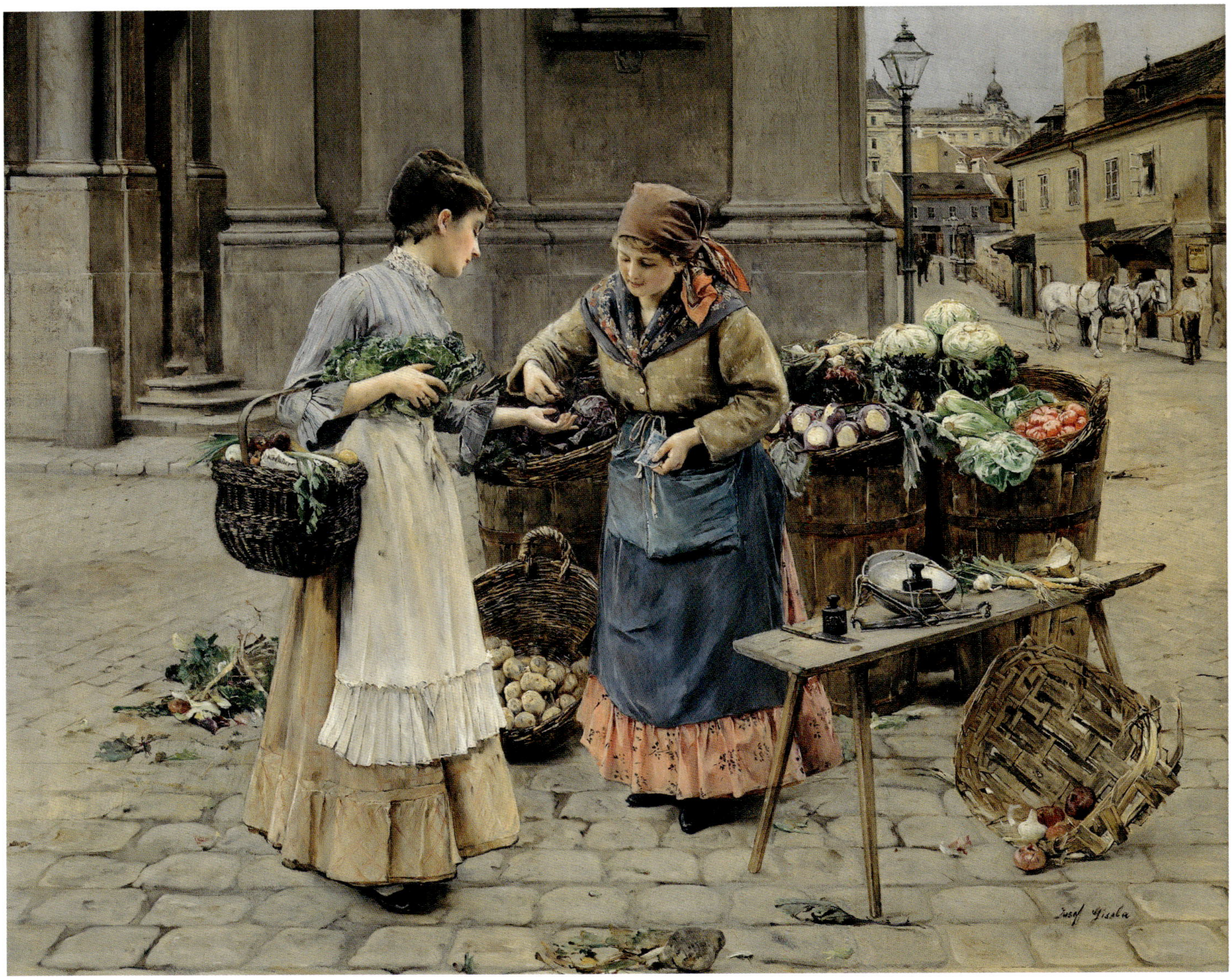

Fig. 2: **Josef Gisela**, *Scene by the Vegetable Stall*, c. 1894
Wien Museum

well-wishers, or being caught out in the midst of some harmless prank or misadventure (fig. 5).

The scenes often played out in the countryside. However, in contrast to Waldmüller, for example, the subjects were not derived from rural life or countryside settings. Rustic interiors served more as a stage or backdrop. Johann Hamza, for instance, transferred the erotically charged tavern scene to a farmhouse parlor peopled with boozing hunters and blushing Alpine landladies (fig. 6). The hunter, in the guise of either strapping daredevil or caring animal lover, was particularly popular and competed with the peasant, the key genre subject in the Biedermeier era. However, artists most liked to show the urban lives of the "common" people. An exception was Johann Hamza, who depicted the contemporary bourgeoisie, with a particular penchant for crowded middle-class family celebrations in flamboyant costumes. On the whole, wealth and decadence were rejected and "outsourced" to the past. In addition to everyday contemporary scenes, many of the "fine painters" also captured historical, nostalgically romanticized genre scenes from the Thirty Years War, the Rococo era, or the Napoleonic occupation (fig. 7). "They all flirted with the illusion of the 'good old days,' by setting their often uninspired, but brilliantly painted episodes in yesterday or the day before yesterday and thus removing them from current social and societal problems."[8]

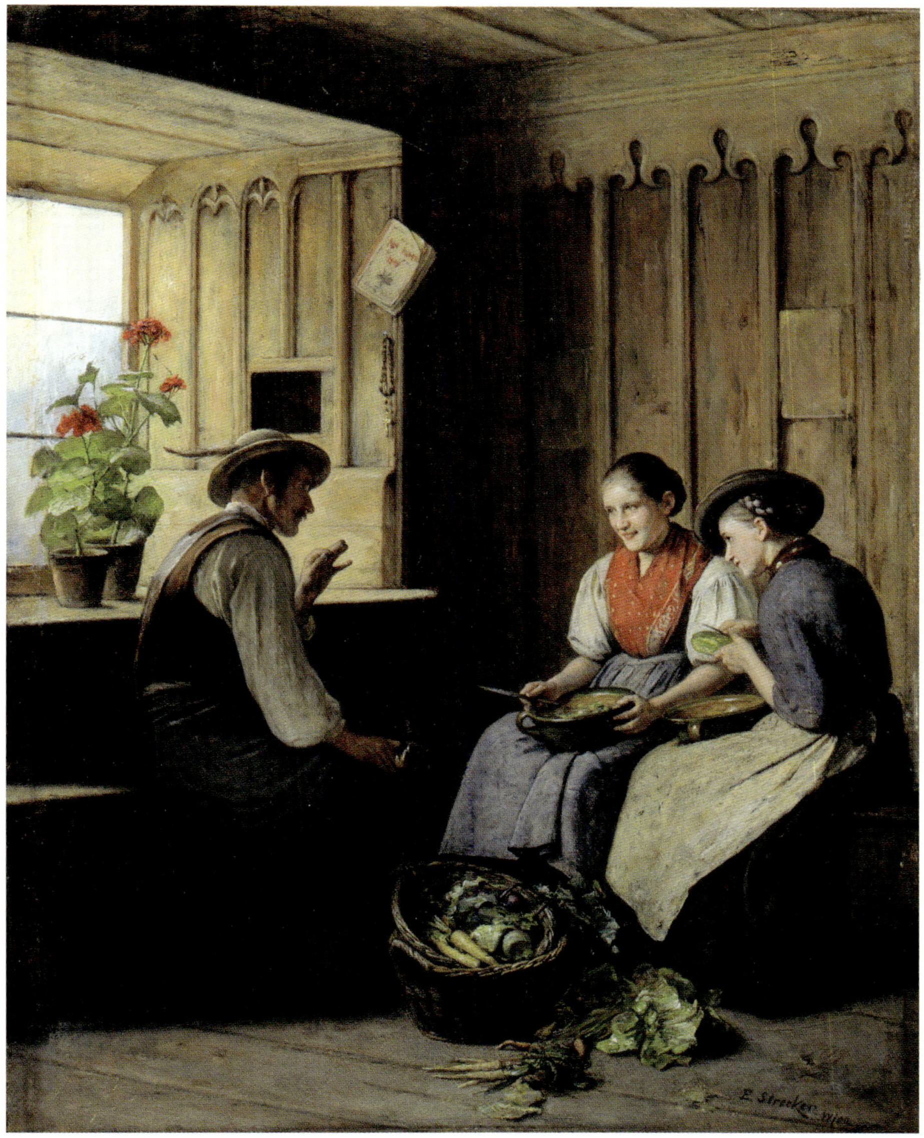

Fig. 3: **Emil Strecker**, *Jolly Gossip*, 1889
Wien Museum

A certain cast of "character types" stands out among the male protagonists in genre scenes. Besides hunters, war invalids and monks were particularly popular and were the specialisms of certain artists. For decades, Friedrich Friedländer painted his trademark cheerful scenes of soldiers, romanticizing the unquestionably precarious fate of the many war invalids in cozy, tranquil images (fig. 8). Ernst Nowak, meanwhile, focused on the life of monks, usually characterized as a little tipsy, a genre also practiced successfully by Eduard von Grützner (1846–1925) in Munich. Genre painting therefore concentrated on male characters who, on account of their profession or inability to work, were not part of the patriarchal, performance-oriented urban society. Isidor Kaufmann also found his own niche specializing in scenes of Jewish life.[9] Female protagonists were usually young, beautiful girls and women. A development of female "character types" as the sole pictorial subject by and large did not occur, however. One exception was Eugen von Blaas (1843–1931), who was from a Viennese family of painters but worked in Venice. His work can be classified as genre in the exotic rather than the Biedermeier style. He specialized in Venetian beauties, painting them posed seductively in front of picturesque brick walls, rather like pin-ups. Eroticism thus found its way into the domestic salons under this exotic guise. Blaas's paintings still enjoy great popularity today and command top prices on the international art market (fig. 9).[10]

"Old Vienna" and "New Vienna"

Today's art-historical literature does not ascribe much artistic importance to the affable genre painting of the late nineteenth century. It is thought to have been

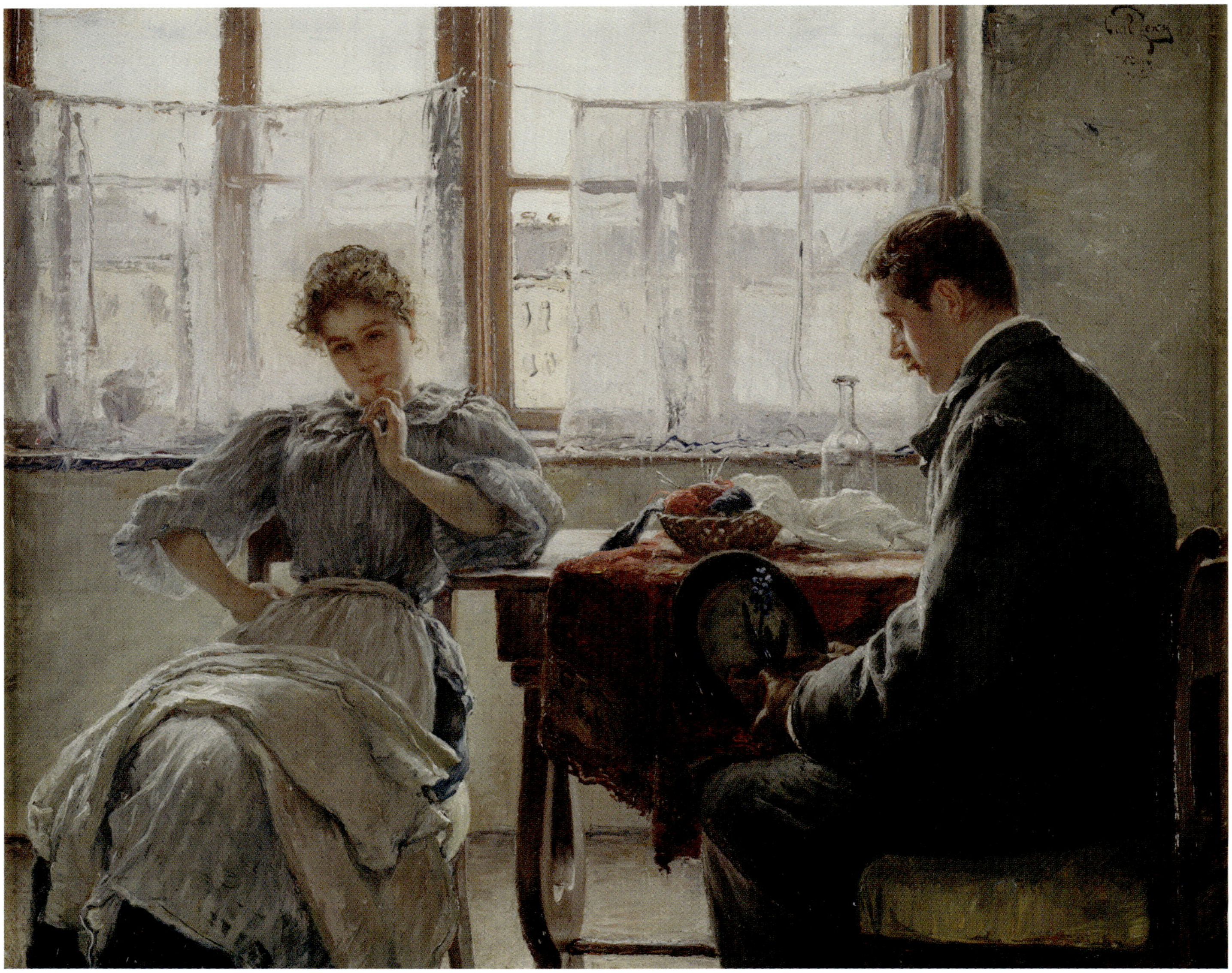

Fig. 4: **Karl Zewy**, *Courtship*, 1896
Wien Museum

stripped of its original function and significance by its arbitrary content and the loss of its once prevailing moral tenor. "Genre in painting had lost its artistic purpose and moral authority in this new environment. It became superficial entertainment."[11] It was, however, also noted that this was the final outcome of a late Biedermeier development that placed too much emphasis on taste, as seen in the work of Johann Matthias Ranftl or Franz Eybl.[12]

Contemporary art criticism presents a far more nuanced impression. Although genre painting was often "slated," it also met with a great deal of positive response and some reviews pinned their hopes precisely on those "Old Viennese"-style pictures from the 1880s and 1890s as representing a "New Viennese" painting. Some of the critiques also shed light on the success and popularity of the pictures. For example, there were positive comments about the fact that the paintings captured easily understandable situations without complex layers of meaning, running no risk of confusing or overtaxing their audience. In his obituary, Josef Gisela was praised for having "always narrated and depicted in the character demanded by the situation, serious or light-hearted, but, above all, with clarity, so that none of his pictures caused the beholder to think at all."[13] The newspaper reviews criticized what they described as an arbitrary choice of subject matter in genre painting. This was ascribed to artists shortsightedly gearing their work to the changeable tastes of the market and the public. In the words of Joseph Bayer in 1887: "This is the situation with art that only delivers for

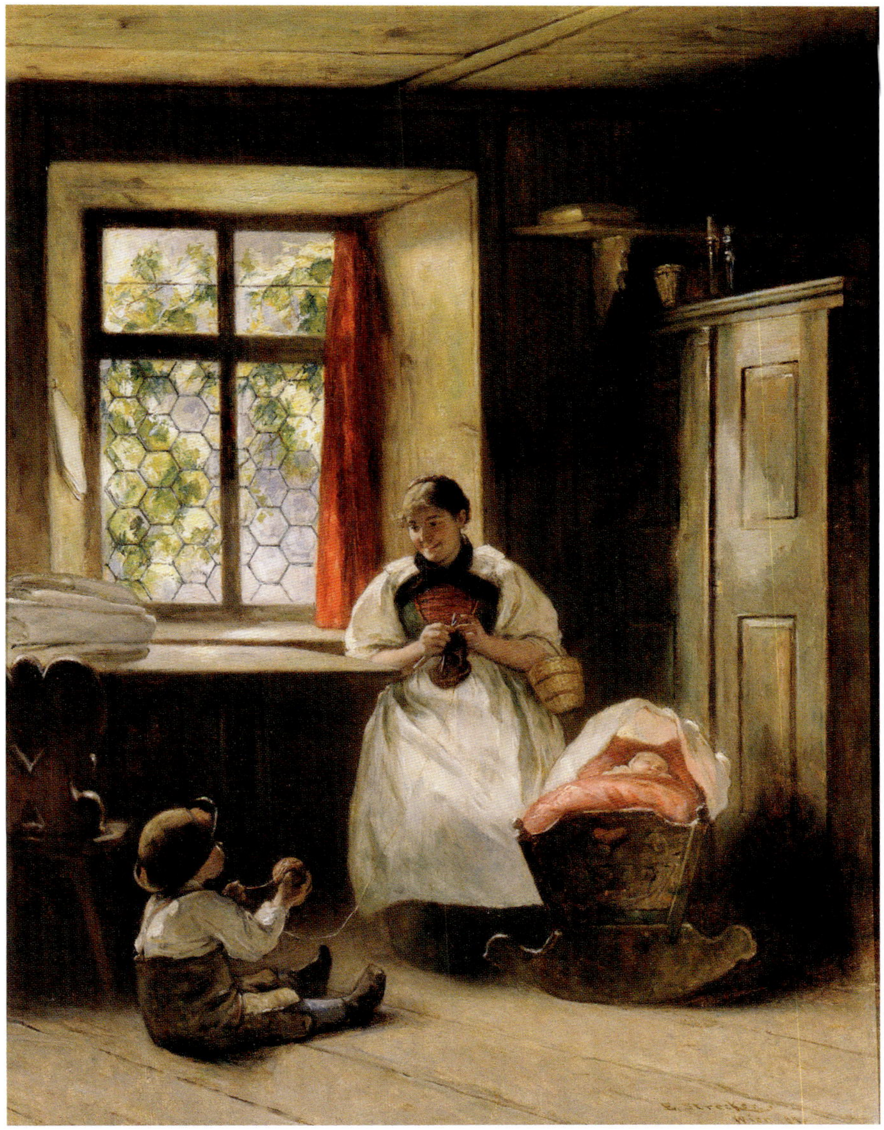

Fig. 5: **Emil Strecker**, *The Little Helper (Farmhouse Parlor)*, 1884
Belvedere, Vienna

today and wants to make money immediately. But to return to the choice of subject matter by our painters who bend to fashion and the market: What a muddled mix of painting! It is as if they all held their brushes aloft in order to absorb every fleeting impression, atmosphere, and temporary mood that buzzes through the air. And their material is simply what is caught as a result."[14] The reproach about old-fashioned subject matter overlapped with the discussion about what current "modern" genre painting should achieve. What was seen as particularly old-fashioned was the depiction of traditional, established situations instead of stories from life, and a lack of drama and originality. As Albert Ilg put it in 1887: "There is rarely a trace of drama and storyline. As a rule, under the aegis of a well-chosen title, painters tend only to present several typical, posed mannequins, whom we are all too familiar with: The worthy priest, the boastful forester, the gaunt school assistant, the anemic seamstress, the plump landlady, the saucy chambermaid etc." What contemporary genre painting lacked in order to be truly modern was "an honest reflection of the important circumstances that rule and move the present." The author therefore proposed a renewal of genre painting in the spirit of the English artist William Hogarth. In his work he saw a "purely objective scrutiny of contemporary life." It was pointless asking whether enough material à la Hogarth existed for the modern artist, for it did in abundance: "the genuine genre picture must have local color, like Hogarth's creations that are practically a portrait of Old England, otherwise it is vacuous, run-of-the-mill painting without any core or truth."[15]

It seems almost paradoxical that it was precisely the "Schwarz artists," which today seem so unmodern and

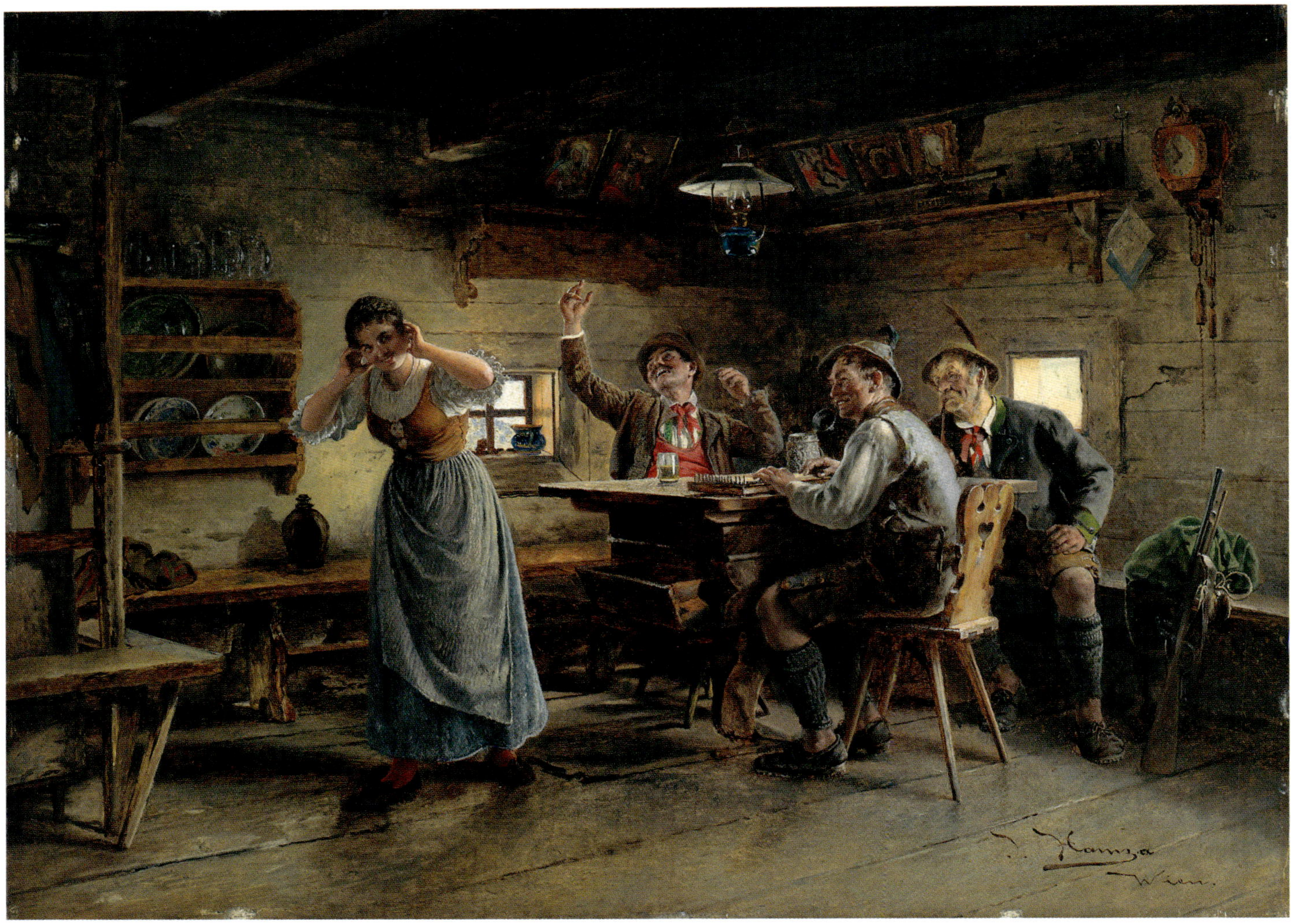

Fig. 6: **Johann Hamza**, *Musical Entertainment at the Alm*
Dorotheum Wien, auction catalogue, April 17, 2012

outmoded, on whom some contemporaries pinned their hopes for a revived, up-to-date style of genre painting. In 1888, Carl von Vincenti wrote: "And are we not witnessing at this moment how the young 'Schwarz artists,' kept in bread and nourished with affection by the art dealer Schwarz, are providing hope for a New Vienna genre painting drawing on the work of Old Viennese genre artists?"[16] Also in 1888, Albert Ilg, who the previous year had poked fun at the foresters and chambermaids, went into raptures about the "Schwarz artists": "Their work should be extremely welcome. I salute these exceptional artists as those whose works I pause in front of with true delight, whose creations and the entire thrust of their ideas I can at last recognize as something truly healthy on our genuine home soil. [...] Their inclination is right, because every true art draws from the homeland, their abilities are extraordinary and their sentiment is noble and moderate. They represent our people honestly, truly, and genuinely, as honestly as Fendi, Waldmüller, Danhauser etc. did decades ago [...] These young people are masters—all due respect! Their exemplary pictures, their drawing as well as colors are exactly perfected and are on a par with the best Dutch artists of the seventeenth century. It is all made, carefully, correctly, and with technical brilliance; this is not about effects, about a swift dashing impact, but is based on solid ability and complete honesty."[17] These small-scale genre pictures with scenes from Viennese life were perfectly suited to Albert Ilg's commitment, guided by a rekindled national pride and patriotism, to raising the image of local art trends in the first half of the nineteenth century and to a local art that was self-regenerating and drew inspiration from Austrian artists.[18] The success of a traditional style and the revival of Old Viennese painting also had a political dimension, as this trend was understood as genuinely "Austrian" and thus commended as being patriotic.

Interestingly, these traits of late-nineteenth-century genre pictures—cheerful, merry, inoffensive—correspond with the characterization around 1900 of "genuine" Old Viennese painting as the expression of an essentially cheerful and life-affirming "Viennese spirit."[19] As Hevesi wrote in 1903 about pre-1848 genre painting: "It reflects a cheerful, honest, benevolent, live-and-let-live world, a life best taken lightly; everywhere a merry spirit, bright sunshine, stimulation without too much excitement, delight in the small things, and an unobjectionable abstention from greater endeavours that are more difficult to achieve."[20] Contemporaries may therefore have found it easier than we do today to connect the late-nineteenth-century pictures to those from the early part of the same century. It was certainly no coincidence that Prince Johann II von und zu Liechtenstein, who, contributing to the bourgeois quest for identity, not only donated an outstanding collection of Old Viennese masters to the recently founded Historical Museum of the City of Vienna in 1894, but later also added works by Josef Gisela, Emil Strecker, and Isidor Kaufmann.[21] Incidentally, prominent clients such as Prince Liechtenstein demonstrate that, despite the fact that the small scale and the choice of subject matter were tailored to the bourgeois living room, their popularity was not confined to the bourgeoisie.[22] Prominent clients even included members of the Imperial family (fig. 10).[23]

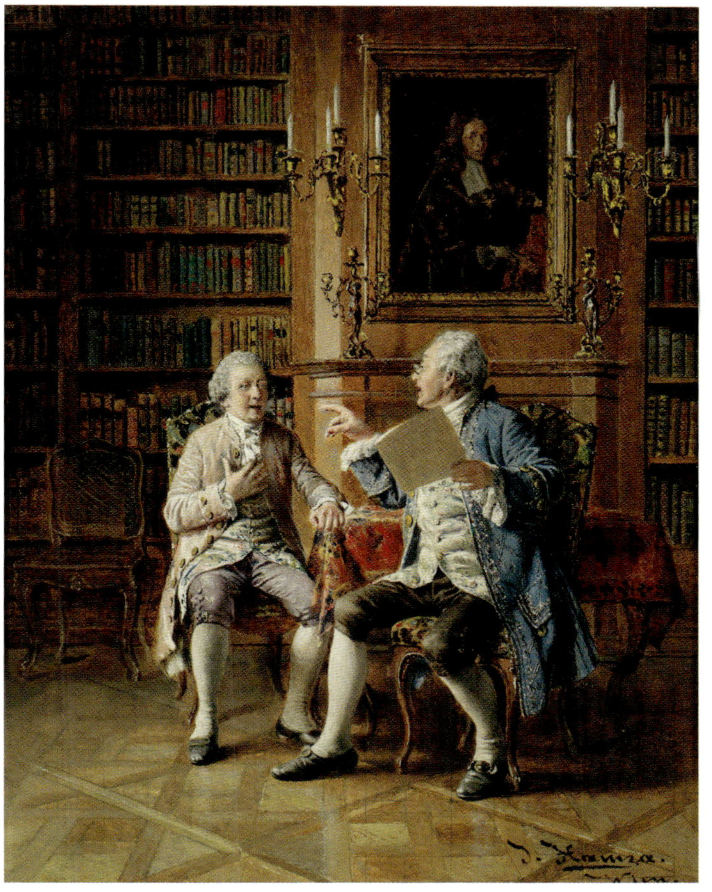

Fig. 7: **Johann Hamza**, *Argument in the Library*
Dorotheum Wien, auction catalogue, October 23, 2014

Art market and marketing

A thorough investigation of the social and cultural-political background underpinning the popularity of these genre pictures would certainly be worthwhile. In any event, two factors behind their success were their good positioning in the market and effective marketing. In this respect, it is no contradiction that these paintings, which drew on tradition and nostalgia, made use of modern sales and business models. Friedrich Friedländer, the master of the homely soldier scene, was one of the main founders of Vienna's artists' association, the Genossenschaft der bildenden Künstler Wiens. In this way, at the end of the 1860s, he helped Viennese artists to finally acquire the exhibiting and sales opportunities they so urgently needed: "Until then, Viennese artists had been through a miserable enough time. The 1850s in particular represented pure desperation. [...] The actions of Friedlaender and his group put an end to these conditions."[24] As previously discussed, the art dealer Friedrich Schwarz's business model provided important impetus in the 1880s. Schwarz commissioned young artists to paint small-scale anecdotes from the life of the Viennese "common" people. He took care of the marketing and sales and it is quite likely that he also suggested subjects.[25] Enterprising art dealers or gallerists exclusively marketing artists, even effectively "leasing" them,[26] was a modern phenomenon on the art market in the late nineteenth century. Clearly this model gave priority to art that enjoyed good prospects of being sold. "The business is risky and as such there must be the prospect of a rich haul, otherwise the deal will not be made in the first place."[27] Another advantage from a business point of view was that tastes in genre painting had become sufficiently uniform—at least throughout the German-speaking world—that many of these pictures could be presented in German cities as well as in Vienna.[28] Finally, the role of the emerging periodicals market deserves a mention, as mass-distributed illustrated magazines made an important contribution to advertising and disseminating these cheerfully trivial genre paintings.[29]

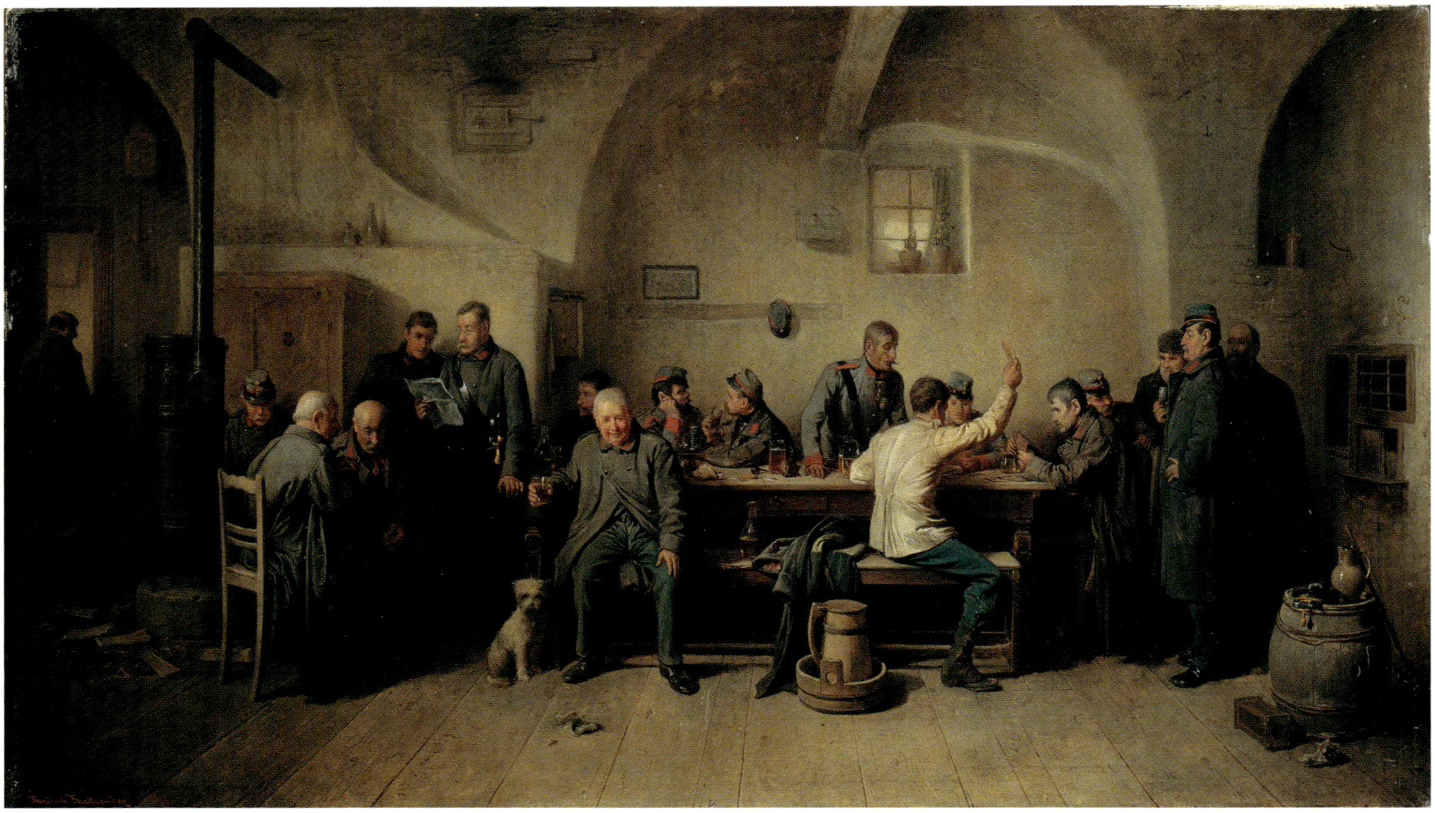

Fig. 8: **Friedrich Friedländer**, *Soldiers in the Mess Hall, 1875*
Belvedere, Vienna

The usually rapid specialization in a particular subject repertoire helped artists provide a bespoke service for the market and also push demand for "new" motifs. While several painters, such as Friedrich Friedländer or Isidor Kaufmann, concentrated primarily on one pictorial type, the majority had mastered several contradictory modes in both subject and style. Johann Hamza, for instance, painted Rococo scenes à la Meissonier in delicate pastel shades, coarse and rustic tavern scenes, and imposing bourgeois family celebrations. Similarly, Carl Zewy painted his way through styles and periods to such an extent that it is difficult to distinguish his own signature manner today. Alongside this "fashionable painting," some artists created works that reflected current trends in French art, at least in the choice of subject matter.[30] At the same time, however, the oeuvre of Karl Karger (1848–1913), one of the few genre painters who dared tackle large-scale depictions of modern city life and its transportation, also includes appealing historicist images. Evidently, few artists could afford to abandon this source of income entirely.

To sum up, the revival of pre-1848 genre painting later in the nineteenth century was far more than merely an attempt to reinstate genre as a subject. Rather it was a fashionable, commercial, and nostalgic phenomenon. Paintings in the style of Old Vienna, produced on a mass scale, were extremely successful at catering for a large, appreciative market. The "outmoded nature" of this type of painting had various facets. It was traditional as it revived the tried and tested; nostalgic, as it escaped to bygone days, and unmodern as it did not result in, or indeed aspire to, any artistic innovation. And it was also a bearer of hope for a patriotic mindset critical of modernism. It seems as if here, once again, modernism was accompanied by a revival of nostalgia and tradition.

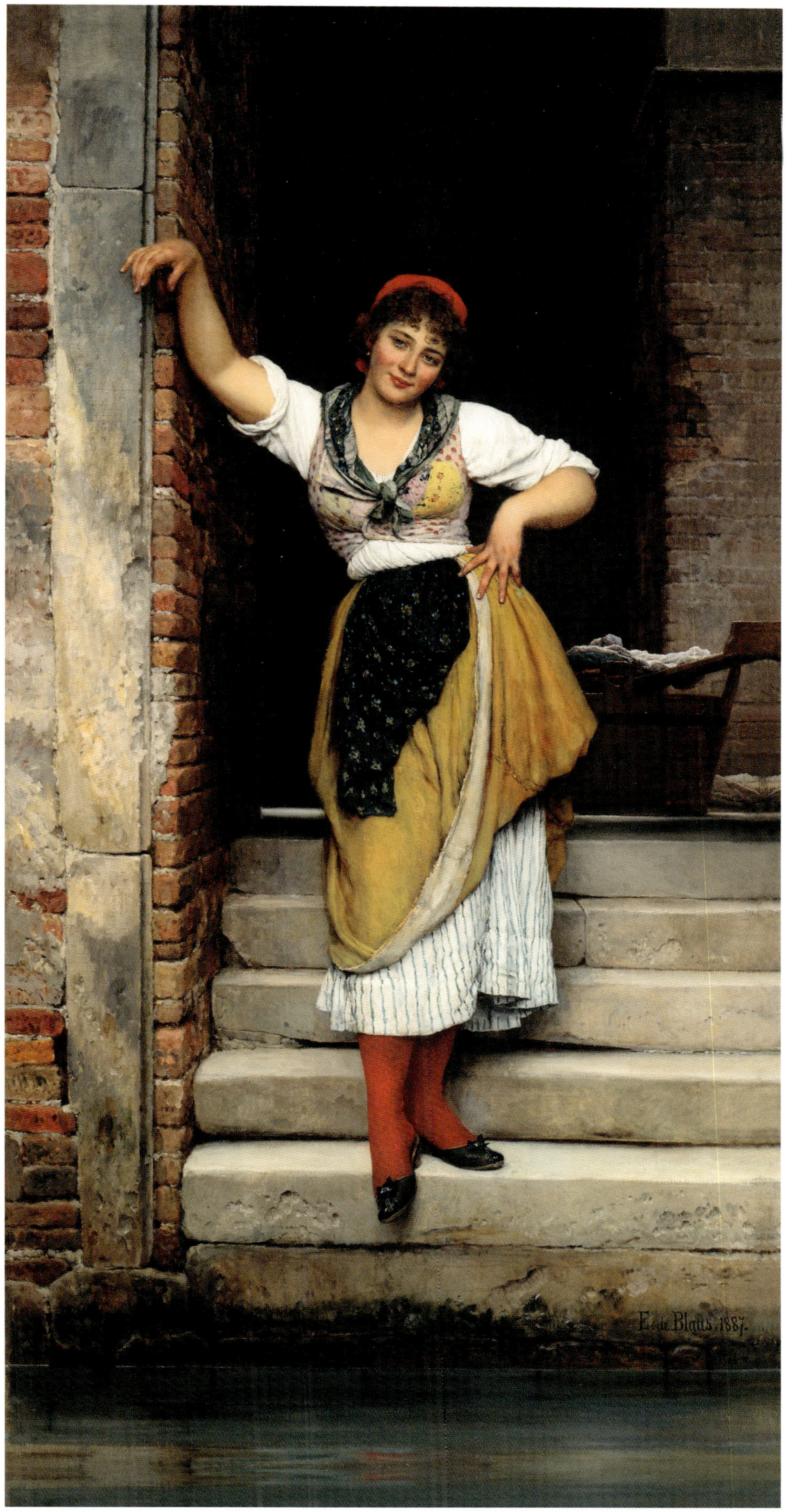

Fig. 9: **Eugen von Blaas**, *Ninetta*, 1887
Private collection, United States

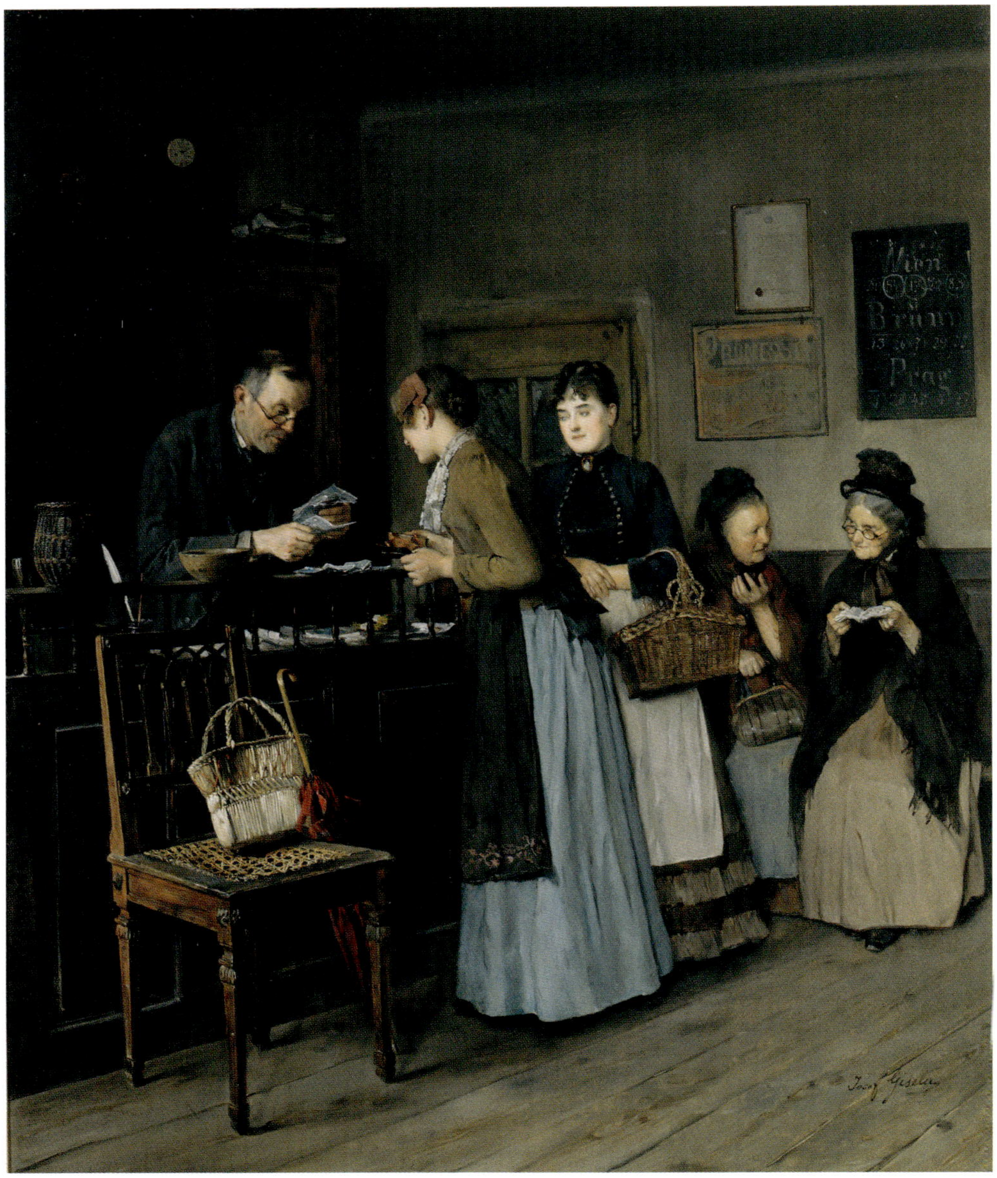

Fig. 10: **Josef Gisela**,
"Lottery Sisters," c. 1888
Belvedere, Vienna

1 Ludwig Hevesi, *Oesterreichische Kunst im 19. Jahrhundert. Erster Teil: 1800-1848 (= Geschichte der modernen Kunst II)* (Leipzig, 1903), p. 185.
2 Gerbert Frodl, "Malerei Biedermeier," *19. Jahrhundert* (= *Geschichte der bildenden Kunst in Österreich V)* (Munich/Berlin/London/New York, 2002), p. 280.
3 For a discussion of the term and characterization of "Alt-Wiener Malerei" (Old Viennese painting) in the late nineteenth century see Werner Telesko, "Auf der Suche nach dem 'Wiener Wesen': 'Alt-Wiener Malerei' als Begriff in der Kunstgeschichte," in *Alt-Wien: Die Stadt, die niemals war*, ed. Wolfgang Kos/Christian Rapp, exh. cat. Wien Museum (Vienna, 2004), pp. 243–49.
4 Hevesi 1903 (see note 1), p. 198.
5 G. Tobias Natter, "'Geschreibsel und Zuckerwasser'?—Verklärung und Standpunkte bei Isidor Kaufmann," *Rabbiner. Bocher. Talmudschüler: Bilder des Wiener Malers Isidor Kaufmann 1853–1921*, exh. cat. Jüdisches Museum der Stadt Wien (Vienna, 1995), pp. 10–41, here p. 16. Tobias Natter states that the term "Schwarzkünstler" (Schwarz artists) was coined by Adalbert Franz Seligmann.
6 Hevesi 1903 (see note 1), p. 241.
7 A selection of Emil Strecker's picture titles are cited here by way of example: *Also a Nursemaid, The First Step, Maternal Bliss, Cozy, Delighted, Hidden Cordiality, Little Envious One, Harmless Pleasures, After Difficult Days, Jolly Gossip, He is Coming, Every Bird has its Nest, Empty Insights, Good Mood, Important Secret, Teasing, Agreeable, Sweet Tooth, Grandfather's Delight, Entertainment* (Friedrich Boetticher, *Malerwerke des neunzehnten Jahrhunderts*, vol. 2.2 [Dresden, 1901], pp. 851–52).
8 Hannes Etzlstorfer, "Das Nachleben der Genremalerei: Vom Spätbiedermeier zum Naturalismus," in *Wiener Biedermeier: Malerei zwischen Wiener Kongreß und Revolution*, eds. Gerbert Frodl/Klaus Abrecht Schröder, exh. cat. Kunstforum der Bank Austria, Vienna (Munich, 1992), pp. 60–70, here p. 67.
9 Natter 1995 (see note 5).
10 For example, on April 25, 2016 the work *Gossip* was sold at auction for USD 461,000; http://www.christies.com/lotfinder/paintings/eugen-von-blaas-gossip-5989865-details.aspx (accessed on August 3, 2016).
11 Frodl 2002 (see note 2), p. 280.
12 Etzlstorfer 1992 (see note 8), pp. 61–62.
13 K. K. Versteigerungsamt Wien, *Gemälde-Auction: Künstlerischer Nachlass des Malers Josef Gisela* [...], (Vienna, 1902), p. 4, quoted

from Marcella Stern, "Der Wiener Genremaler Josef Gisela," *Wiener Geschichtsblätter*, yr. 40, no. 1 (1988), pp. 17–20, here p. 20.

14 Joseph Bayer, "Von Bildern und Ausstellungen," *Neue Freie Presse*, Morgenblatt, July 15, 1887, p. 2.

15 I. (= Albert Ilg), "Hogarth?," *Die Presse*, December 4, 1887, p. 2.

16 Carl von Vincenti, "Vierzig Jahre Wiener Kunst: Zur Eröffnung der Internationalen Jubiläums-Kunst-Ausstellung," *Allgemeine Kunst-Chronik*, yr. 12, no. 9 (March 3, 1888), p. 233.

17 I. (= Albert Ilg), "Internationale Kunstausstellung. VI. Oesterreich," *Die Presse*, May 8, 1888, p. 1.

18 On Albert Ilg's role see Roswitha Feger, "Fürst Johann II. von Liechtenstein (1858–1929) und seine Sammlung der Wiener Biedermeiermalerei," *Jahrbuch des Historischen Vereins für das Fürstentum Liechtenstein*, vol. 102 (2003), pp. 2–87, here pp. 61–63.

19 Telesko 2004 (see note 3), pp. 243–45.

20 Ludwig Hevesi, *Österreichische Kunst im 19. Jahrhundert. Erster Teil: 1800–1848* (Leipzig, 1903), p. 71.

21 These included Emil Strecker, *Jolly Gossip*, Wien Museum, inv. no. 10.306; Josef Gisela, *Scene by the Vegetable Stall*, Wien Museum, inv. no. 13.280; Isidor Kaufmann, *Chess Problem*, Wien Museum, inv. no. 17.182; Carl Zewy, *Courtship*, Wien Museum, inv. no. 27.313. Concerning the Liechtenstein gift see Renata Kassal-Mikula, "Die Schenkung des Fürsten Liechtenstein: Ein Beitrag zur Museumsgeschichte," *Johann II. von und zu Liechtenstein: Ein Fürst beschenkt Wien 1894–1916*, exh. cat. Historisches Museum der Stadt Wien (Vienna, n.d. [2003]), pp. 23–31.

22 The works were certainly not cheap. Josef Gisela's *Soothsayer* was offered in 1886 at the Künstlerhaus for 6,000 marks, *Fortune-Teller* for 4,000 marks. (Künstlerhaus Archiv, Vienna, Einlaufbuch 1886, nos. 1557 and 1559).

23 Paintings acquired by Emperor Franz Joseph I include: Josef Gisela, *"Lottery Sisters,"* c. 1888, Belvedere, Vienna, inv. no. 7924; Emil Strecker, *The Little Helper*, 1884, Belvedere, Vienna, inv. no. 7921; Emil Strecker, *Departure*, Belvedere, Vienna, inv. no. 6567.

24 Hevesi 1903 (see note 1), p. 200.

25 Natter 1995 (see note 5), p. 20, conjectures that Isidor Kaufmann could have been encouraged by his gallerist Schwarz to expand his repertoire of subjects to include Jewish characters in order to fill a gap in the market.

26 B. G. "'Genie, à la Hausse.' Künstler in Pacht," *Neues Wiener Journal*, April 18, 1897, p. 11.

27 B. G. 1897 (see note 26). On the subject of the modern type of gallerist and his growing influence on the art market see Christian Huemer, "Charles Sedelmeyer (1837–1925): Kunst und Spekulation am Kunstmarkt in Paris," *Belvedere: Zeitschrift für bildende Kunst*, yr. 2 (1999), pp. 4–19.

28 Anton Müller's *The Bird Lover* (*An Old Peasant and his Grandson Enjoy their Cage Birds*) was shown in 1886 at the Berlin jubilee exhibition, 1887 at the Viennese annual exhibition, and 1891 at Stuttgart's international paintings exhibition (Friedrich Boetticher, *Malerwerke des neunzehnten Jahrhunderts*, vol. 2.1 [Dresden, 1898], p. 94), Carl Zewy's *Poor Poet* 1887 in Berlin, 1888 in Munich and Vienna (Boetticher 1901 [see note 7], p. 1047).

29 Etzlstorfer 1992 (see note 8), p. 63.

30 Josef Gisela's *Young Ladies' Gathering on the Balcony* (*Gemälde und Orientmalerei des 19. Jahrhunderts*, auct. cat. Dorotheum, Vienna [Vienna, 2007], p. 219) recalls the subject of Édouard Manet's *The Balcony* (Musée d'Orsay, Paris), his *Women Working in the Fields* (*Meisterzeichnungen 15.–19. Jahrhundert, 20. Jahrhundert, Bilder des 19. und 20. Jahrhunderts, Kunst nach 1945, Antiquitäten*, auct. cat. Wiener Kunstauktionen GmbH [Vienna, 1995], p. 133) is reminiscent of works by the Barbizon School.

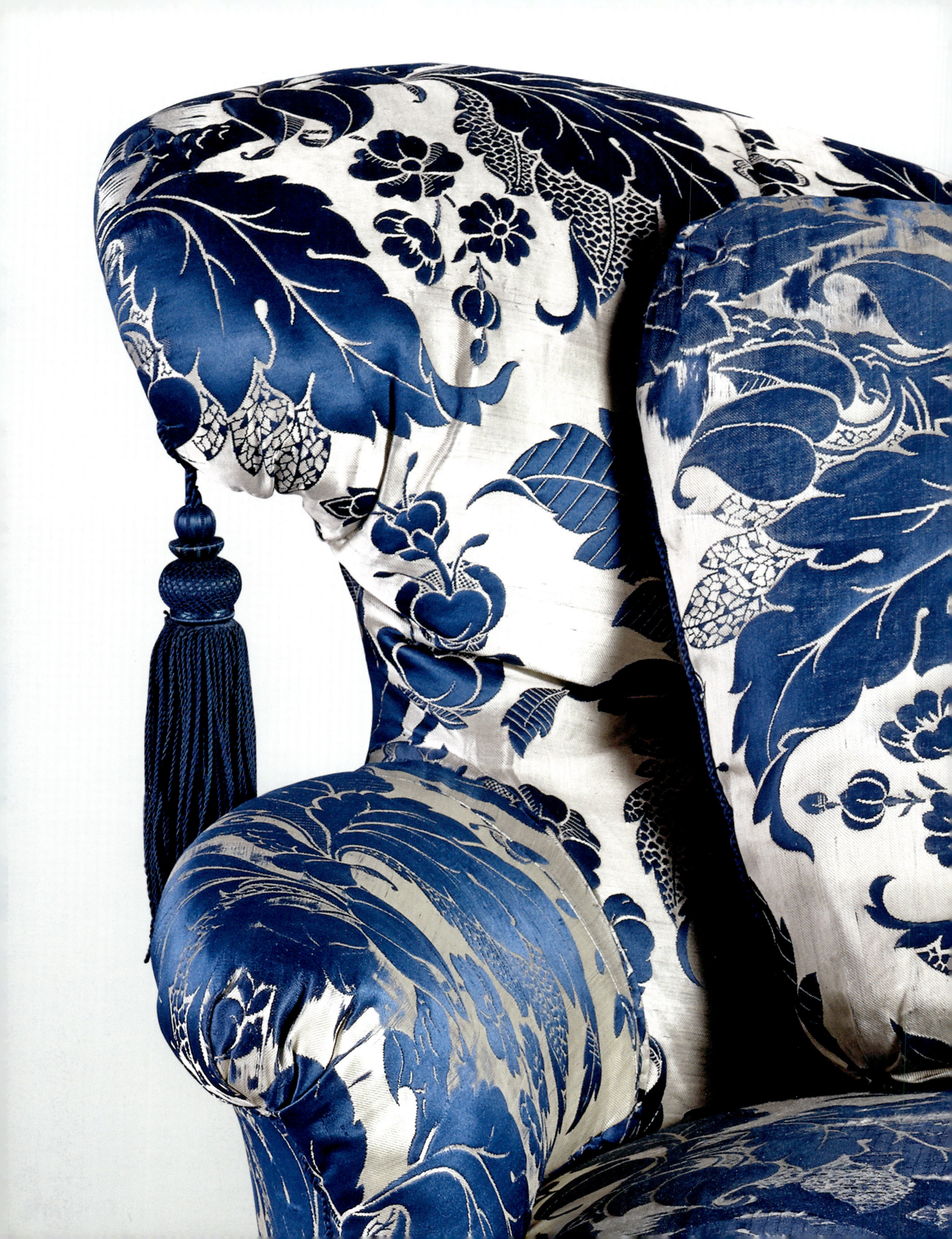

Appendix

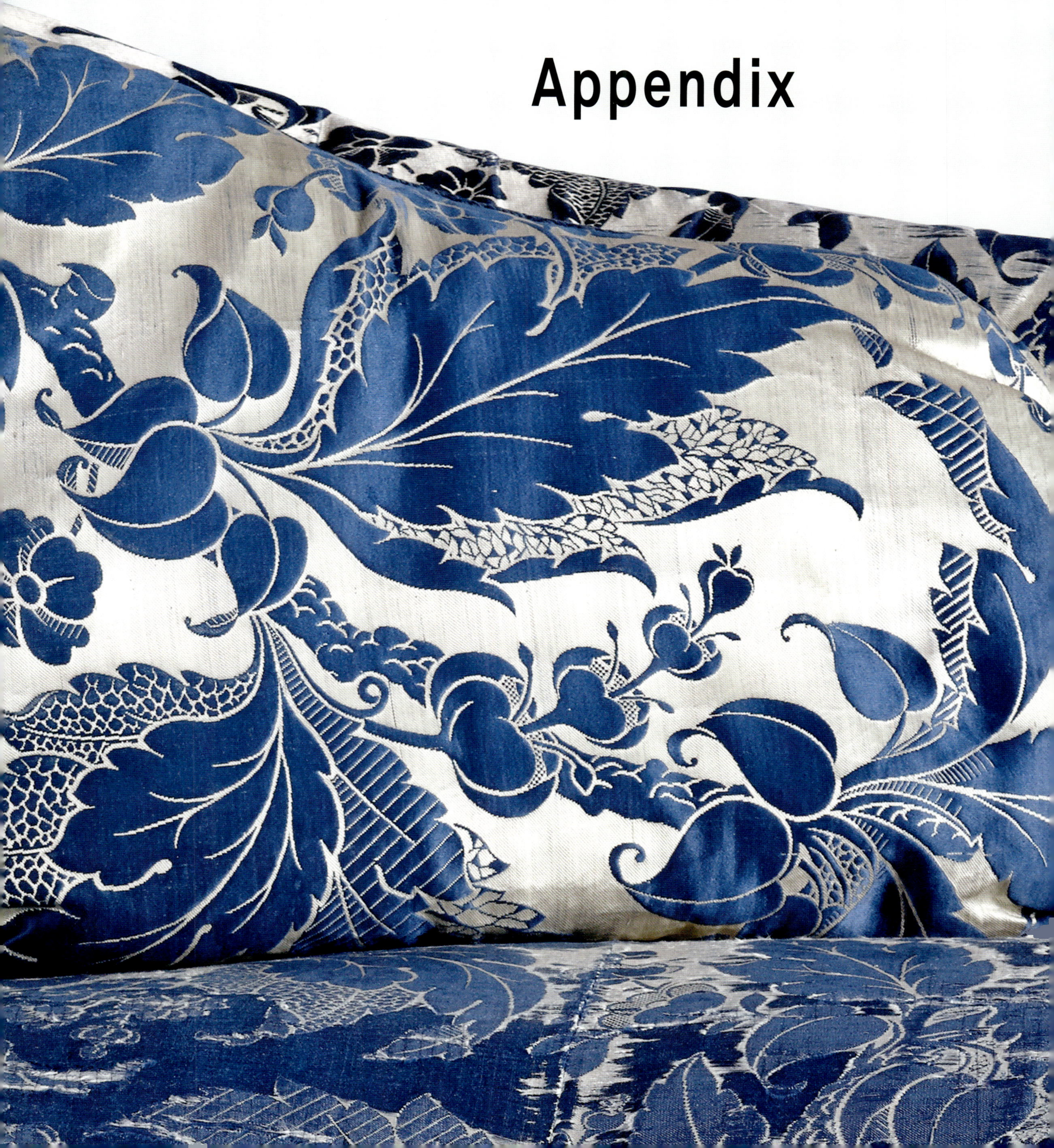

THE ARTISTS

Franz Alt 132
Jakob Alt 132
Rudolf von Alt (Vienna 1812 – 1905 Vienna) 56, 132f., 154, 255
Albrecht Altdorfer 234
Friedrich von Amerling (Vienna 1803 – 1887 Vienna) 6f., 17f., 21–23, 55, 84, 96f., 108f., 110, 116–119, 156f., 162, 178, 199, 206, 218, 262, 265, 271
Andrea Appiani 49, 56
Carlo Arienti 55, 56, 255
Massimo d'Azeglio (Turin 1798 – 1866 Turin) 53, 98f., 218
Miklós Barabás (Kézdimárkosfalva 1810 – 1898 Budapest) 38–41, 43, 162, 182
Luigi Basiletti 53
Jacopo Bassano 49
Giovanni Bellini 49
Wilhelm Bendz 274f.
Joseph Bergler 28–30
Giuseppe Bertini 56
Joseph Beuys 74
Luigi Bisi 52, 54, 56
Michele Bisi 56
Eugen von Blaas 295, 301
Karl von Blaas (Nauders, Tyrol 1815 – 1894 Vienna) 218f., 255
Carl Blechen 286f., 291
Arnold Böcklin 218
Guillaume Bodinier 260
Louis-Léopold Boilly 257
Claude Bonnefond 258, 260
Giuseppe Borsato 50
József Borsos (Vészprém 1821 – 1883 Budapest) 18, 36–39, 42f., 45, 162f., 208–210, 255
Giuseppe Bossi 49
Karl Pavlovich Bryullov 55
Károly Brocky 38, 45f.
Adriaen Brouwer 257
Georges-Louis Leclerc de Buffon 72
Joseph Karl Burde 29
Ippolito Caffi 55f.
Alexandre Calame 230
Sir Augustus Wall Callcott 266
Giuseppe Canella 53f.
Antonio Canova 50, 106
Giovanni Carnovali ("Il Piccio") 51f.
Vittore Carpaccio 49
Asmus Jakob Carstens 70f., 74
Carl Gustav Carus 284, 289
Franz Caucig 110
Francis Legatt Chantrey 273 (note 22)
William Collins 266
John Constable 204, 266f.
Peter von Cornelius 72, 255
Cherubino Cornienti 55f.
Gustave Courbet 261
Joseph-Désiré Court 258f.
Lucas Cranach the Elder 72
Moritz Michael Daffinger 16, 265
Johan Christian Dahl 275
Christen Dalsgaard 282
Josef Danhauser (Vienna 1805 – 1845 Vienna) 8f., 16, 20–22, 94f., 134–136, 140–143, 162, 271, 298
Josef Ulrich Danhauser sen. (Vienna 1780 – 1829 Vienna) 239
Jacques-Louis David 72, 74, 256
Eugène Delacroix 255
Étienne-Jean Delécluze 256, 260
Peter Hubert Desvignes 245
Christoph Albert Dies 126
Franz Dobiaschofsky (Vienna 1818 – 1867 Vienna) 186f.
Johann Donat 38
Martin Drölling 258
Claude-Marie Dubufe 262
Albrecht Dürer 72f.
Anton van Dyck 262
Christoffer Wilhelm Eckersberg 275–278, 280
Anton Einsle (Vienna 1801 – 1871 Vienna) 201
Eduard Ender 255
Johann Nepomuk Ender (Vienna 1793 – 1854 Vienna) 22, 37, 155, 222, 255, 260
Thomas Ender (Vienna 1793 – 1875 Vienna) 37, 126f.
Eduard von Engerth 255
Johann Christoph Erhard 124
Allart van Everdingen 18, 196
Franz Eybl (Vienna 1806 – 1880 Vienna) 18, 83, 123, 147, 200, 255, 296
Placido Fabris 51
Federico Faruffini 55
Josef Feid 18
Peter Fendi (Vienna 1796 – 1842 Vienna) 21f., 43, 104f., 298
Carl Ludwig Fernow 70
Ludwig Hans Fischer 218
Zofia Fredro 255
Friedrich Friedländer 293, 295, 299f.
Caspar David Friedrich 168, 234, 285f., 289, 291
Friedrich Heinrich Füger 15, 150
Josef Führich 22, 56, 186, 212, 255

Friedrich Gauermann (Miesenbach near Wiener Neustadt 1807 – 1862 Vienna) 18, 98, 100–103, 128, 255
Jacob Gauermann 100
Hans Christian Genelli 71, 74
Michel Genod 258
François Gérard 78
Marguerite Gérard 258
Johann Nepomuk Geyer 240
Alajos Györgyi Giergl 38
Giorgione (acc. Giorgio del Castelfranco) 49
Josef Gisela 293f., 296, 299, 302, 303 (note 30)
Marco Gozzi 53
Jean-Baptiste Greuze 258
Michelangelo Grigoletti (Rorai Grande near Pordenone 1801 – 1870 Venice) 51, 88f., 106
Carlo Grubacs 180
Eduard von Grützner 295
Karl Gsellhofer 132
Remy van Haanen 56
Johann Hamza 293f., 298–300
Anton Hansch (Vienna 1813 – 1876 Salzburg) 230–232
Maximilian Haushofer 32, 190
Bedřich Havránek (Prague 1821 – 1899 Prague) 32f., 190–193
Francesco Hayez (Venice 1791 – 1882 Milan) 22, 48–51, 54–57, 78f., 93, 106, 160f., 178, 184, 255
Alexandre Hesse 261
Aloys Ludwig Hirt 71–73
Meindert Hobbema 18, 196
William Hogarth 72, 134, 268f., 271, 273 (note 22), 297
Josef Höger (Vienna 1801 – 1877 Vienna) 121
Hans Holbein the Younger 72
Carl Wilhelm Hübner 289–291
Domenico Induno (Milan 1815 – 1878 Milan) 54, 56, 184f., 188f.
Gerolamo Induno 54, 56–57, 59
Angelo Inganni 52–54, 56
Jean-Auguste-Dominique Ingres 78, 106, 255
Louis Janmot 252f., 262f.
Laurenz Janscha 126
Philippe-Auguste Jeanron 261
Jens Adolf Jerichau 279
Elisabeth Jerichau-Baumann 278f
Eugen Jettel 19, 234
Friedrich Kaiser 224
Karl Karger 300
Isidor Kaufmann 293, 295, 299f.
Wilhelm Kaulbach 72, 255
Christen Købke 276-279
Josef Anton Koch 150
Josef Koruna 34
Sándor Kozina (Felsőság 1808 – 1873 Felsőpulya) 43, 202f.
Johann Peter Krafft 18f., 21f., 37, 86, 110, 136, 144, 202, 206
Josef Kreutzinger 37
Leopold Krones 29
Pavel Künl (Mladá Boleslav, Czech Republic 1817 – Ljubljana 1871) 212–214
Leopold Kupelwieser 22, 56, 186, 202, 212, 222
Johann Baptist Lampi the Elder 15, 18
Sir Edwin Landseer 204, 267–269
Josef Lanzedelli the Elder 20
Sir Thomas Lawrence 265, 273 (note 22)
Adolphe Leleux 261
Friedrich Lieder 37
Lodovico Lipparini 54f., 106, 180, 218
Friedrich Loos (Graz 1797 – 1890 Kiel) 18, 124f., 128
Claude Lorrain (acc. Gelée) 158, 266
Lorenzo Lotto 49
Johan Thomas Lundbye 280f.
Antonín Machek (Podlažice near Chrast 1775 – 1844 Prague) 28–31, 35 (note 4), 148f.
Daniel Maclise 264f.
Viktor Madarász 41
Eduard von Magnus 288f
Hans Makart 218
Ferdinand Mallitsch (Graz 1820 – 1900 St. Leonhard, Styria) 222f.
Antonín Mánes 26, 29, 31–32, 34, 216
Josef Mánes (Prague 1820 – 1871 Prague) 34, 216f.
Quido Mánes 33f., 216
Vaclav Mánes 216
Jacopo Marastoni 38
Károly Markó the Elder (Levoča 1793 – 1860 Villa Appeggi near Florence) 38, 40, 43, 158f.
Pasquale Massacra 55
Teodoro Matteini 88, 106
Ernest Meissonier 257, 293, 300
Adolph Menzel 68f., 71–73
Giovanni Migliara 52f.
Jean-François Millet 261
Josef Mössmer 132, 230
Federico Moja 52
Pompeo Marino Molmenti (Villanova di Motta di Livenza 1819 – 1894 Venice) 55, 180f., 218
Giuseppe Molteni (Affori 1800 – 1867 Milan) 16, 22, 51, 54–56, 178f.
Christian Ernst Bernhard Morgenstern 32
Karl Philipp Moritz 70
Ernst Christian Moser (Graz 1815 – 1867 Graz) 144–146, 222, 233
Anton Müller 292f., 303 (note 28)
William Mulready 268–270
Mihály Munkácsy 37
Bartolomé Esteban Murillo 116
François-Joseph Navez 260
Josef Navrátil (Slaný 1798 – Prague 1865) 30, 32–34, 172f.
Michael Neder (Vienna 1807 – 1882 Vienna) 176f.
Eugen Napoleon Neureuther 71
Pietro Nobile 106
Ernst Nowak 293, 295
Ferdinand Olivier 128
Friedrich Olivier 128
Adriaen van Ostade 269
Friedrich Overbeck 150, 156, 218, 287
Eleuterio Pagliano 56
Pelagio Palagi 51

Julius Payer 234
Anton Petter 110, 202, 222
August Piepenhagen (Soldin, Brandenburg 1791 – 1868 Prague) 30, 34, 168–170, 172
Jean Baptiste Pigalle 72
Odorico Politi (Udine 1785 – 1846 Venice) 88, 106f.
Karel Postl 29
Paulus Potter 100
Nicolas Poussin 158
August Prinzhofer 10
Anton Pucherna 29
Raphael 261
Carl Rahl (Vienna 1812 – 1865 Vienna) 183, 255
Johann Mathias Ranftl (Vienna 1804 – 1854 Vienna) 86f., 204f., 296
Josef Rebell 18, 22, 100, 132
Johann Baptist Reiter (Urfahr near Linz 1813 – 1890 Vienna) 18, 22, 24, 84, 120, 164, 174f., 211
Rembrandt Harmensz. van Rijn 69f.
Pierre Révoil 254–256, 258
Sir Joshua Reynolds 265
Rudolf Ribarz 234
Eduard Ritter (Vienna 1808 – 1853 Vienna) 21, 92, 114, 136–138
Léopold Robert 156, 259f.
Auguste Rodin 218
Pietro Ronzoni 53
Dante Gabriel Rossetti 164
Carl Rottmann 32
Christian Ruben 216
Jacob van Ruisdael 18, 34, 98, 196, 234
Philipp Otto Runge 71, 86
Robert Russ 234
Luigi Sabatelli 164, 184
Eliseo Sala (Milan 1813 – 1879 Truggio) 51, 56, 164f.
Johann Michael Sattler 124
Johann Gottfried Schadow 290
Wilhelm von Schadow 287–289
Felice Schiavone 166
Giovanni Schiavone 166
Natale Schiavone (Chioggia 1777 – 1858 Venice) 22, 166f.
Friedrich Schilcher (Vienna 1811 – 1881 Vienna) 139
Emil Jakob Schindler 19, 234
Johann Wilhelm Schirmer 287f., 291
Heinrich Wilhelm Schlesinger 255
Victor Schnetz 260
Ludwig Ferdinand Schnorr von Carolsfeld (Königsberg/Kaliningrad 1788 – 1853 Vienna) 150f.
Johann Nepomuk Schödlberger 124, 158
August Theodor Schoefft 38
Franz Schrotzberg (Vienna 1811 – 1889 Graz) 18, 206f.
Carl Schütz 132
Luigi Scrosati 56
Giuseppe Sogni 56
Jørgen Sonne 281f.
Franz Steinfeld (Vienna 1787 – 1868 Pisek) 18f., 128f., 212
Károly Sterio 38f.
Josef Stieler 206
Adalbert Stifter (Oberplan in the Bohemian Forest 1805 – 1868 Linz) 27, 33f., 130f., 168
Heinrich Stohl 56
Emil Strecker 293, 295, 297, 299, 302 (note 7), 303 (note 21)
Johann Nepomuk Strixner 72
Mihael Stroj (Ljubno 1803 – 1871 Ljubljana) 18, 110–113
Eduard Swoboda (Vienna 1814 – 1902 Hallstatt) 198
Bertalan Székely 41
David Teniers 257, 269
Gerard Ter Borch 46
Augustin Thierriat 258
Tiziano Vecellio 22, 49f., 69f., 116
Michael Thonet 236
František Tkadlík 30f, 35 (note 4), 216
Giuseppe Tominz (Gorizia 1790 – 1866 Gradisca) 51, 80–82, 90f.
Friedrich Treml (Vienna 1816 – 1852 Vienna) 171
Anthelme Trimolet 258
Joseph Tunner 222
Joseph Mallord William Turner 204, 266
Horace Vernet 156
Peter Vischer 72
Ferdinand Georg Waldmüller (Vienna 1793 – 1865 Hinterbrühl near Vienna) 7, 9, 12–14, 18f., 21–23, 25, 43, 56, 69–74, 84f., 100, 115, 122, 128, 152f., 162, 190, 194–197, 212, 215, 220–222, 224–229, 255, 271, 293f., 298
Henrik Weber 38
Sir David Wilkie 142, 269–272, 273 (note 22 and 23)
William Wilkins 265
Franz Xaver Winterhalter 206, 262
Philips Wouwerman 98
Karl Zewy 293, 296, 300, 303 (note 28)
Mihaly Zichy 41, 43–45
Albert Zimmermann (Zittau 1808 – 1888 Munich) 9, 18, 234f.

AUTHORS

Agnes Husslein-Arco became director of the Belvedere in Vienna in 2007. Since taking office, she has promoted wide-ranging infrastructure measures and repositioned the museum both nationally and internationally. Among the projects for which Husslein-Arco has been responsible are the restructuring, growth, and digitization of the collection, the foundation of a research center, and the successful architectural and institutional expansion of the Belvedere. Agnes Husslein-Arco studied art history and archeology at the University of Vienna, the Sorbonne, and the École du Louvre in Paris before receiving her doctorate in Vienna in 1979. In 1981 she opened the Vienna branch of Sotheby's, whose business she managed until 2000. Since 2001 Husslein-Arco has worked as a museum director. In this role she has been responsible for large-scale projects such as running the Rupertinum in Salzburg, founding the Museum der Moderne Salzburg, and establishing the MMKK – Carinthian Museum of Modern Art in Klagenfurt. Agnes Husslein-Arco has curated numerous exhibitions and is the editor of over two hundred exhibition catalogues and scientific publications.

Eszter Békefi graduated in 1995 with an art history degree from Eötvös Loránd University in Budapest. She is presently working on her Ph.D., specializing in Hungarian Biedermeier painting. Since 1995 she has been working at the Hungarian National Museum. She was a member and later became leader of the Hungarian Research Group for Restitution, which researches the art objects taken during the Second World War. She then became a monographer of József Borsos and has written several publications on the subject. In 2009 she was one of the curators of the exhibition *József Borsos. Painter and Photographer* (2009). She now works in the Archive Department of the Budapest Museum of Fine Arts – Hungarian National Gallery, which contains the largest collection of documents related to artists and the art scene of Hungary in the nineteenth and twentieth centuries.

Werner Busch studied art history in Tübingen, Freiburg, Vienna, and London and completed his doctorate in 1973 with a dissertation on William Hogarth. From 1974 to 1981 he was an academic assistant in Bonn, where he earned his qualification as a professor in 1980. From 1981 to 1988 he held a professorship in Bochum. From 1983 to 1985 he was director at the Funkkolleg Kunst. In the years from 1988 to 2010 he was professor of art history at the FU Berlin. Busch is a member of the Berlin-Brandenburg Academy of Sciences and Humanities. From 2003 to 2009 he directed the Special Research Area (SFB) 626 "Aesthetic Experience and the Dissolution of Artistic Limits." His most recent publications include: *Das unklassische Bild: Von Tizian bis Constable und Turner* (Munich, 2009), *Englishness: Beiträge zur englischen Kunst des 18. Jahrhunderts von Hogarth bis Romney* (Berlin/Munich, 2010), *Great wits jump: Laurence Sterne und die bildende Kunst* (Munich, 2011), *Verwandlung der Welt: Die romantische Arabeske* (exh. cat. Freies Deutsches Hochstift/Frankfurter Goethe-Museum/Hamburger Kunsthalle [Petersberg, 2013], together with Petra Maisak), *Adolph Menzel: Auf der Suche nach der Wirklichkeit* (Munich, 2015).

Elke Doppler studied art history and journalism in Vienna and Berlin. Since 1993 she has been a member of the academic staff and a curator at the Arts Department of the Wien Museum. Her research and publications focus on Austrian art history of the eighteenth and nineteenth centuries, history and theory of portraiture and artists' portraits, veduta painting, and urban images, as well as the history of the Wien Museum and its collections.

Udo Felbinger studied art history, classical archaeology, and romance studies in Bonn and Berlin. In 1999 he completed his doctoral dissertation on François Gérard and the French portrait from 1795–1815. An internship at the Staatsgalerie Stuttgart followed. In 2002 he curated the exhibition *Drawings and Watercolors of the Romantic Era* (Budapest/Warsaw/Stuttgart). Numerous publications, mainly on German, Austrian, and French painting of the nineteenth century, including in *Enlightened Bourgeoisie* (Munich, 2006), *Ferdinand Georg Waldmüller* (Vienna, 2009), and *Europe in Vienna. The Congress of Vienna 1814/15* (Vienna, 2015). Since 2008 he has worked as research associate at the Werkbundarchiv—Museum der Dinge in Berlin, where he is responsible for the digitization of the objects collection for the Deutsche Digitale Bibliothek.

Sabine Grabner studied art history at the University of Graz. She wrote her dissertation on the painter Josef Danhauser (1805–1845). Since 1991 she has been curator of nineteenth-century collections at the Belvedere, focusing on Neoclassicism, Romanticism, and Biedermeier. She has written numerous publications on the art of the nineteenth century and curated the exhibitions *Italian Journeys: Landscape Pictures by Austrian and Hungarian Painters from 1770 to 1850* (2001);

Friedrich von Amerling 1803–87 (2003); *Enlightened Bourgeoisie: Portraits from Gainsborough to Waldmüller 1750–1840* (2006); *Waldmüller* (2009); *Josef Danhauser: Pictorial Narratives* (2011); *Orient & Occident: Travelling 19th Century Austrian Painters* (2012); *Michael Neder: Ohne Kompromisse*, (Vienna, 2013) and *Europe in Vienna. The Congress of Vienna 1814/15* (2015).

Brigitte Hauptner studied art history in Vienna and Graz. Since 1996 she has been working at the Belvedere in Vienna, supporting the department of art education as well as taking part in the realization of numerous exhibitions. She has been curator of exhibitions on Moritz von Schwind and has written several books and catalogue essays on Austrian painting, focusing on the first half of the nineteenth century, especially Adalbert Stifter. Brigitte Hauptner currently works as an art educator at the Belvedere and as a freelance art therapist.

Fernando Mazzocca studied art history at the Scuola Normale Superiore in Pisa, where he also carried out research for ten years. He teaches at the Università Ca' Foscari in Venice and the University of Milan. His research focus is on the nineteenth and early twentieth centuries, especially the art of Neoclassicism. Mazzocca has published numerous books and, since 1978, has organized major exhibitions on the themes of Neoclassicism, the nineteenth century, Canova, Lampi, Hayez, and others at the Pinacoteca di Brera/Museum Poldi Pezzoli and the Palazzo Reale in Milan, the Castello del Buonconsiglio in Trento, the Galleria Borghese in Rome, the Gallerie d'Italia a Milano, and the Musée d'Orsay in Paris. His extensive academic production is concerned with the history of collecting, artistic literature, and the relationship between art, literature, and music. Mazzocca is a member of the Comitato Nazionale per l'Edizione delle Opere di Antonio Canova and of the Istituto di ricerca per gli studi su Canova e il Neoclassicismo.

Kasper Monrad is a Danish art historian and curator. From 1971 to 1981 he studied art history at the University of Copenhagen and was an assistant at the SMK Statens Museum for Kunst from 1977 to 1981. In 1985 he became a curator there and has been Senior Research Curator since 1995. His research areas are Danish and international art from 1780 to 1900; publications include *Dansk guldalder. Lyset, landskabet og hverdagslivet* (Copenhagen, 2013) and *C. W. Eckersberg – dansk malerkunsts fader* (Copenhagen, 2005, together with Peter Michael Hornung). Monrad has curated exhibitions on Christen Købke, Henri Matisse, The Golden Age of Danish Painting, and William Turner.

Stéphane Paccoud is Chief Curator, in charge of nineteenth-century paintings and sculptures, at the Musée des Beaux-Arts, Lyon, France. He has organized several exhibitions, including *Juliette Récamier, muse et mécène* (2009), *Un Siècle de paysages, les choix d'un amateur* (2010), *L'Invention du Passé. Histoires de cœur et d'épée en Europe 1802–1850*, with Prof. Stephen Bann (2014), and *Autoportraits, de Rembrandt au selfie*, in partnership with the Staatliche Kunsthalle Karlsruhe and the National Galleries of Scotland (2016). His field of research is nineteenth-century art, especially history painting, as well as artistic transfers between France and Poland.

Arnika Schmidt has been assistant curator at the Belvedere since 2015. Prior to that she worked at the National Gallery in London. She studied art history in Freiburg i. Br. and completed her Ph.D. in Dresden. Her research focuses on nineteenth- and twentieth-century art, the development of landscape painting, and transnational exchange among artists and their peers.

Radim Vondráček studied history, philosophy, and art history in Prague and Vienna. Since 1991 he has worked as curator for the print collection of the Museum of Decorative Arts in Prague and became chief curator of the museum in 2008. Since 2005 he has been lecturer of design theory and art history at the Academy of Arts, Architecture and Design in Prague. His research focuses on nineteenth-century art and culture, in particular of the Biedermeier period, on Czech design history (Art Nouveau, Cubism), and its theoretical reflection. He is author, co-author, and editor of numerous books and exhibition catalogues, including *Biedermeier. Art and Culture in the Bohemian Lands 1814–1848* (Prague, 2010).

Christian Witt-Dörring studied art history and archeology in Vienna. From 1979 to 2004 he was head of the furniture collection at the MAK – Austrian Museum of Applied Arts in Vienna. He currently works as a freelance art historian in Vienna and as curator at the Neue Galerie New York. His specialism is the history of furniture and interior space with a focus on the nineteenth and twentieth centuries. In addition to his extensive activities as a lecturer and teacher on art and art-historical subjects, he has also curated a number of major exhibitions, such as *Dagobert Peche and the Wiener Werkstätte* (1998), *Yearning for Beauty: For the 100th Anniversary of the Wiener Werkstätte* (2003/04), *Viennese Silver: Modern Design 1780–1918* (2003–2005), *Josef Hoffmann: Interiors 1902–1913* (2006/07), *Koloman Moser: Designing Modern Vienna* (2013/14), and *Ways to Modernism: Josef Hoffmann, Adolf Loos and their Impact* (2014/15).

PICTURE CREDITS

Accademia Carrara – Museo, Bergamo: p. 51 – Apsley House, The Wellington Museum, London / © Historic England / Bridge-man Images: p. 269 – © Auktionshaus im Kinsky GmbH: p. 292 – © Archivio Fotografico e Mediateca Mart: p. 79 – Archivio fotografico Musei di Brescia – Photo Studio Rapuzzi: p. 165 – Associazione Villa Vigoni – Centro Italo-Tedesco: p. 93 – © Bayerisches Nationalmuseum München: p. 62 left – Belvedere, Vienna: pp. 2-3; 6, 8, 17, 20, 24, 76-77, 85, 96–97, 101, 109, 114–115, 118–122, 125–135, 138, 141–143, 147, 151, 154–155, 159, 167–169, 175–177, 183, 187, 195–198, 200, 205, 211, 219–227, 229–232, 235, 287, 297, 300, 302 – bpk: pp. 68 (Kupferstichkabinett, SMB / Jörg P. Anders); 272, 286 (Bayerische Staatsgemäldesammlungen); 288 (Staatliche Kunsthalle Karlsruhe/Annette Fischer/Heike Kohler); 289 right (Staatsbibliothek zu Berlin); 290 (Rheinisches Landesmuseum, Bonn) – Bridgeman Images: pp. 22 (Cleveland Museum of Art, OH, USA / Mr. and Mrs. William H. Marlatt Fund); 23 (Galleria degli Uffizi, Florence); 48 (Pinacoteca di Brera, Milan); 59 (Galleria Nazionale d'Arte Moderna, Rome / Mondadori Portfolio/Archivio Alessandro Vasari/Alessandro Vasari); 99 (Accademia di Belle Arti di Brera Quadreria, Milan, Italy / Mondadori Portfolio/Electa/Bruno Balestrini); 107 (De Agostini Picture Library / A. Dagli Orti) –Family Buchler: p. 91 (Carlo Boldrin, Padua) – © Bundesmobilienverwaltung: Photo: Edgar Knaack: pp. 237, 241, 249; Photo: Fritz Simak: 236 – Castello Ducale, Agliè: p. 179 (© 2016. DeAgostini Picture Library/Scala, Florence) – The City of Prague Museum: p. 149 – Civica Galleria d'Arte Moderna, Verona: p. 58 (Photo: © 2016. DeAgostini Picture Library/Scala, Florence) – Civico Museo Sartorio, Trieste: p. 55 – Dorotheum Wien, auction catalog 17.4.2012: p. 298 – Dorotheum Wien, auction catalog 23.10.2014: p. 299 – © The Earls of Mansfield, Scone Palace, Perth, Scotland: p. 271 – Fondazione Cariplo, Gallerie d'Italia – Piazza Scala, Milan: pp. 52, 54, 56–57, 189 – Gábor Kovács Art Collection, Budapest: pp. 182, 203 – © Hessische Hausstiftung, Schlossmuseum Darmstadt: p. 289 left – Kunsthandel Boris Wilnitsky: p. 201 (Photo: Belvedere, Vienna) – © Land Niederösterreich, Landessammlungen Niederösterreich: p. 19 – Les Arts Décoratifs, Paris: p. 262 left – LIECHTENSTEIN. The Princely Collections, Vaduz–Vienna: p. 245, 304–305 – © Lyon MBA – Photo Alain Basset: pp. 252, 258, 262 right – © MAK: p. 63 left; Nathan Murrell: pp. 60, 238, 240, 242, 244, 246; Georg Mayer: pp. 62 right, 63 right, 64–65, 239, 243, 248 – Moravian Gallery in Brno: p. 170 above – MBA Musei Biblioteca Archivio di Bassano del Grappa: pp. 161, 181 – © Museum Kunstpalast – ARTOTHEK: p. 284 – © The National Gallery, London: p. 267 – © National Gallery in Prague 2016: pp. 26, 28, 30–33, 170 below, 173, 191–193, 217 – National Gallery of Slovenia, Photo: Janko Dermastja, Bojan Salaj: pp. 111–113, 213–214 – National Museum of Scotland, Edinburgh: p. 268 – Neue Galerie Graz am Universalmuseum Joanneum, Photo: N. Lackner, UMJ: pp. 21, 146, 210, 233 – Austrian Private Collection: p. 199 (Photo: Belvedere, Vienna) – Österreichische Nationalbibliothek: p. 10 – 2016 © Photo Archive – Fondazione Musei Civici di Venezia: p. 50 – Pinacoteca dell'Accademia Carrara, Bergamo: p. 51 – Polo museale del Friuli Venezia Giulia – Galleria Nazionale d'Arte Antica Archivio Fotografico della Soprintendenza Archeologia Belle Arti e Paesaggio: p. 82 – Pordenone, Pinacoteca. © 2016. Photo Scala, Florence: p. 89 – Private Collection: pp. 29; 53 (© 2016. DeAgostini Picture Library/Scala, Florence); 102–103 (Photo: Ulrich Ghezzi); Photo: Belvedere, Vienna: pp. 14, 95, 117, 139, 145, 228, 304-305 – Private Collection, Germany: p. 157 – Private Collection Schloss Ebenthal: p. 207 (Photo: Belvedere, Vienna) – Revoltella Museum, Gallery of Modern Art – Trieste: pp. 81, 185 – © RMN-Grand Palais: 255–256 (Musée du Louvre / Franck Raux); 259 (Philipp Bernard); 260 (Musée du Louvre / Martine Beck-Coppola); 261 (Gérard Blot) – Sammlung Roland: p. 153 – Royal Collection Trust / © Her Majesty Queen Elisabeth II 2016: p. 257 – Dr. Rudolf Schuster, Photo: Belvedere, Vienna: pp. 92, 137 – © SMK Photo: pp. 274–279, 281–282 – Sotheby's New York, 19th Century European Art, Auktionskatalog 9.5.2013: p. 301 – KR Hubert Steinleitner: p. 145, 215 (Photo: Belvedere, Vienna) – Stiftsarchiv Lilienfeld © Harald Schmid: p. 247 – Szépművészeti Múzeum / Museum of Fine Arts, Budapest, 2016: pp. 36–45, 209; 38 (Photo Archive); 163 (Tibor Mester) – © Tate, London 2016: p. 264 – Thorvaldsens Museum: p. 280 (Photo: Pernille Klemp) – © Victoria and Albert Museum, London: p. 270 – Wien Museum: pp. 25, 83, 87, 105, 123, 171, 294, 295–296.

If in spite of our thorough research any individual illustrations have not been correctly attributed or acknowledged, we offer our apologies and would appreciate any information that will allow us to rectify the matter in future editions.

COLOPHON

This catalogue has been published in conjunction
with the exhibition
Is that Biedermeier? Amerling, Waldmüller, and More,
held at the Belvedere, Vienna,
from October 21, 2016 to February 12, 2017.

Exhibition
Director: Agnes Husslein-Arco
Curator: Sabine Grabner

Belvedere
Prinz Eugen-Straße 27
1030 Vienna
www.belvedere.at

Publication
Editors: Agnes Husslein-Arco, Sabine Grabner
Graphic Design: Peter Baldinger
Translation German to English: Andrew Horsfield,
Rebecca Law, Lisa Rosenblatt, Nick Somers
Editing & proofreading English: Betti Moser
Picture editing: Theresa Neureiter
Lithography: Pixelstorm, Vienna
Printing and Binding: Printer Trento S.r.l.

Published by:
Hirmer Verlag GmbH
Nymphenburger Straße 84
D – 80636 Munich
www.hirmerpublishers.com

Bibliographic information published by the Deutsche
Nationalbibliothek
The Deutsche Nationalbibliothek lists this publication in the
Deutsche Nationalbibliografie; detailed bibliographic data
are available on the internet at http://dnb.de.

Printed and bound in Italy

ISBN 978-3-903114-12-8 (Museum edition)
ISBN 978-3-7774-2779-9 (Retail edition)

Cover illustration: József Borsos, *The Emir of Lebanon (Portrait of Count Edmund Zichy)*, 1843 (detail)
Museum of Fine Arts – Hungarian National Gallery,
Budapest, inv. no. 2003. 3 T

Authors Abbreviations
SG: Sabine Grabner
BH: Brigitte Hauptner
EO: Eva B. Ottillinger